ESSAY
Second Edition

edited by

Hans P. Guth
SAN JOSE STATE COLLEGE

Wadsworth Publishing Company, Inc.
Belmont, California

L.C. Cat. Card No.: 66–13323

Printed in the United States of America

Preface to the Second Edition

In this second edition of *Essay*, the guiding principles and the basic format of the first edition remain unchanged. A few essays have been omitted to make room for more substantial or more recent ones; the total number of essays has been raised to forty-eight. There has been some regrouping of selections and extensive rewriting of editorial materials in order to make the treatment of rhetorical principles more explicit and more continuous. There are many new theme topics and questions for analysis, as well as many suggestions for longer papers. As in the first edition, there has been a special effort to avoid any artificial separation of content from form, of substance from structure, of purpose from style. The intention of the book continues to be to give the student a better understanding of the process of writing as an organic whole. Through the kind of study and practice here encouraged, the student should be able to increase his respect for, and his control over, the power of the written word.

Preface to the First Edition

The authors in this book write with conviction and force about matters of general interest to educated men and women. There is no anonymous written-to-formula prose, no hackneyed "writing up" of the topical and soon forgotten. Each selection can teach the student something about articulate, purposeful writing as the expression of forceful personality, about style as a clue to the quality of an author's mind.

The authors represented in this volume are writers first and travelers, critics, linguists, or philosophers second. The selections reflect the editor's belief that it is not the composition teacher's task to provide a kind of freshmen's digest of other academic disciplines. There is no attempt here to "introduce" the student to psychoanalysis and nuclear fission, to sociology and aesthetics, to cybernetics and anthropology. It *is* the composition teacher's task to have his students study and practice effective and responsible writing—considered not as a vehicle for specialized technical knowledge but as the mark of the liberally educated man. Teachers of writing concern themselves not with "subject matter" but with subject matter as organized, interpreted, evaluated by the first-rate writer. They deal not with "issues" but with issues as reflected in the personal commitments of a perceptive and responsible observer. They study not "ideas" but ideas developed in forceful, cogent, significant prose.

The readings found in this book, then, represent the "generalist" rather than the specialist, or, if the specialist, the kind of specialist who can see his specialty in context, who can estimate its humane significance. Thus, this volume includes Eiseley and Krutch rather than a lecture in biology, Priestley and Orwell rather than sociological studies, Stegner and Mumford rather than an analysis of Civil War strategy. Above all, this volume includes writers—from Henry Thoreau to James Baldwin—who address the reader not as a student of special disciplines but as a responsible human being.

Many of the selections in this book will broaden the student's understanding of language and literature. In addition to the sections on "The Writer's Tools" and "The Experience of Literature," many essays in other sections have been chosen because of an author's thoughtful awareness of problems of language and writing. Again, however, the emphasis is not on the technical study of language—on language about language, on writing about writing. The emphasis is on making the student see language at work, on promoting that study of the humane uses of language that provides the central subject matter of college English.

Essay aims to achieve a balance of the fresh and contemporary with the historically significant. Though each selection is self-contained, the thematic organization and the correlations between essays suggested in the questions for discussion and writing make possible an organically developed course. Within each section, and in the book as a whole, an attempt has been made to lead the students from the simple and familiar to the difficult and new. An alternative analytic table of contents suggests ways of organizing the selections according to rhetorical principles or types of writing. The suggestions for further reading are designed to lead the student beyond the concerns of a particular course and to make the book a genuine and lasting introduction to serious reading.

H. Guth

Table of Contents

(*Essays new to this edition)

Alternative Table of Contents

Introduction to
Expository Prose

*No one can write intelligibly unless he lets his own mind do
the writing.* VALBORG ANDERSON

As the vehicle of information and persuasion, expository prose is
with us much of every working day. Business increasingly means consultation, reporting, evaluation, advertising, public relations. Politics more and
more consists in the production and exchange of words. Formal education is
largely verbal. In articles, books, and speeches men formulate their purposes,
promote their goals, and record their achievements.

Considering the ever present role of expository prose, our dealings with it
are often surprisingly uncritical. Apart from passing anxiety over grammatical correctness, the layman seldom concerns himself with the difference
between good and bad writing. As a result, failure to understand, or failure
to be understood, leaves him angry but baffled. Exceptional articulateness
leaves him envious rather than appreciative. Irresponsible attacks or appeals
may leave him resentful but largely helpless. A systematic study of expository
writing can make him more competent as a writer and more perceptive as a
reader.

It is true that each piece of successful prose in some way reflects the personality of the author. Part of the secret of writing is doubtless the author's
ability to be himself—rather than an echo of his teacher or fashionable
literary models. However, it is just as true that successful prose has recurrent traits that the learner can cultivate. Alistair Cooke once developed a
definition of good and bad journalism that can be easily adapted as a general
definition of good and bad expository writing: Good writing is vivid, informed, and judicious; bad writing is "tritely observed, crudely felt, and
foggily communicated." The writer who "keeps his eye on the object" can
give us the "sharp sense of a part of contemporary life, focused and arrested"

and remaining memorable after passages in our own lives are faded and forgotten.[1]

THE RELEVANCE OF DETAIL

In the hands of a good writer, even a factual account is more than a flat, summary statement. It includes the graphic, revealing **detail** that creates an illusion of reality. It makes the reader share the experience rather than merely note the fact. The role of such detail is most noticeable in fiction; there is a world of difference between "The dog sat at the bedside" and Charles Dickens's writing, in *Oliver Twist,*

> The dog sat at the bedside: now eyeing his master with a wistful look, and now pricking his ears, and uttering a low growl as some noise in the street, or in the lower part of the house, attracted his attention.

The beginning writer is likely to put in the dog and leave out the growl.

The observant eye and the quick ear, though perhaps the most basic equipment of the writer, will take him only part of the way. Unedited experience is like a changing landscape seen from a moving train. Like the view from a train window, unedited writing may leave the reader tired and dizzy. Among the countless details he observes, the writer has to select what is significant: detail that suggests the prevailing mood, illuminates someone's character, or becomes a link in an argument. In the competent expository paragraph, relevant detail is used to illustrate a point, to support a generalization, to round out a picture. As an eminently successful historian said about the writing of history:

> When I come across a generalization or a general statement in history unsupported by illustration I am instantly on guard; my reaction is, "Show me." If a historian writes that it was raining heavily on the day war was declared, that is a detail corroborating a statement, let us say, that the day was gloomy. But if he writes merely that it was a gloomy day without mentioning the rain, I want to know what is his evidence; what made it gloomy. Or if he writes, "The population was in a belligerent mood," or, "It was a period of great anxiety," he is indulging in general statements which carry no conviction to me if they are not illustrated by some evidence. I write for example that fashionable French society in the 1890s imitated the English in manners and habits. Imagining myself to be my own reader—a complicated fugue that goes on all the time at my desk— my reaction is of course, "Show me." The next sentence does. I write *"Le Grand Steeple* was held at Auteuil, *le Derby* at Longchamps, unwanted

---

[1] "Journalists Who Make History," *The Atlantic Monthly,* November 1959, pp. 155–156.

members were *blackboulé* at the Jockey Club, Charles Swann had 'Mr' engraved on his calling cards."[2]

Part of every writer's task is to arrest the changing spectacle. He must establish perspective, bring things into **focus**. The process of selection may be relatively spontaneous, or it may take the form of deliberate planning, outlining, and revising. What is essential is that the reader will be carried along by a feeling of purpose, a conviction that the author is in control of his material and will arrive at his destination in his own good time. When the writer's account of a process or a problem is complete, or when an argument has been carried to its conclusion, the reader will feel the satisfaction to be derived from an ordered whole. He will escape the frustration that accompanies what is aimless, fragmentary, and confused.

PATTERNS OF ORGANIZATION

There are many ways of organizing a piece of expository prose. The most elementary is to follow the **chronological order** of a simple report of events. Much biographical and historical writing naturally falls into this pattern. Frederick Lewis Allen, in "The Ballyhoo Years," follows significant developments in American journalism over several years.

Among the other essays in this volume, several examples of autobiographical reminiscence follow a chronological order. For instance, Lois Phillips Hudson's "Children of the Harvest" follows her experiences as a child from midsummer into early August, into September, and into October. Many paragraphs begin with a reference to time: "On a suffocating summer day..."; "...one day early in August"; "Then one day in the second week..."; "By that time it was September...." However, being a thoughtful account of significant events, the essay does not follow the more miscellaneous, unsorted sequence of a diary. Crucial episodes are selected and treated in detail; earlier periods in the child's life are brought in for comparison and contrast. Similarly, Mr. Allen, in "The Ballyhoo Years," has selected a number of outstanding incidents that together tell a coherent story.

When chronological order is followed too mechanically, it obscures rather than clarifies important relationships. Irrelevant events intervene between cause and effect; side issues distract from a key point. Thus, the biographer or historian is often forced to abandon mere sequence in time in order to discuss events and their causes or to trace important motives. He then organizes his material to support a major point. The most flexible kind of organization in expository prose is development of a **thesis**, or key statement, by **explanation and example**.

---

[2] Barbara W. Tuchman, "History by the Ounce," *Harper's*, July 1965, p. 67.

In the following opening portion of an essay by the American naturalist John Burroughs, the central point summed up in the title is systematically developed. The thesis is variously restated, with repetition serving for support rather than padding. In the following excerpt, some of the phrases echoing the theme of fear have been italicized:

A LIFE OF FEAR

thesis

As I sat looking from my window the other morning upon a red squirrel gathering hickory nuts from a small hickory, and storing them up in his den in the bank, *I was forcibly reminded of the state of constant fear and apprehension in which the wild creatures live,* and I tried to picture to myself what life would be to me, or to any of us, *hedged about by so many dangers,* real or imaginary.

first extended example

The squirrel would shoot up the tree, making only a brown streak from the bottom to the top; would seize his nut and rush down again in the most precipitate manner. Half way to his den, which was not over three rods distant, he would rush up the trunk of another tree for a few yards to make an observation. *No danger being near,* he would dive into his den and reappear again in a twinkling.

Returning for another nut, he would mount the second tree again for another observation. *Satisfied that the coast was clear,* he would spin along the top of the ground to the tree that bore the nuts, shoot up it as before, seize the fruit, and then back again to his retreat.

Never did he fail during the half hour or more that I watched him to take an observation on his way both to and from his nest. It was "snatch and run" with him. Something seemed to say to him all the time: *"Look out! look out!"* "The cat!" "The hawk!" "The owl!" "The boy with the gun!"

It was a bleak December morning; the first fine flakes of a cold, driving snowstorm were just beginning to sift down, and the squirrel was eager to finish harvesting his nuts in time. It was quite touching to see how *hurried and anxious and nervous* he was. I felt like going out and lending a hand. The nuts were small, poor pig-nuts, and I thought of all the gnawing he would have to do to get at the scanty meat they held. My little boy once took pity on a squirrel that lived on the wall near the gate and cracked the nuts for him and put them upon a small board shelf in the tree where he could sit and eat them at his ease.

The red squirrel is not as provident as the chipmunk. He lays up stores irregularly, by fits and starts; he never has enough put up to carry him over the winter; hence he is more or less active all the season. Long before the December snow the chipmunk has for days been making hourly trips to his den with full pockets of nuts or corn or buckwheat, till his bin holds enough to carry him through to April. He need not, and I believe does not, set foot out of doors during the whole winter. But the red squirrel trusts more to luck.

As alert and watchful as the red squirrel is, he is *frequently caught* by the cat. My Nig, as black as ebony, knows well the taste of his flesh. I have known him to be caught by the black snake and successfully swallowed. The snake, no doubt, *lay in ambush* for him.

first restatement of thesis

first parallel

second parallel

This fear, this ever present source of danger of the wild creatures, we know little about.... The early settlers in this country must have experienced something of this *dread of apprehension* from the Indians.... Our ancestors, back in prehistoric times, or back of that in geologic times, must have known *fear as a constant feeling.* Hence the *prominence of fear* in infants and children when compared with the youth or the grown person. Babies are *nearly always afraid* of strangers.

In the domestic animals also, *fear* is much more active in the young than in the old. Nearly every farm boy has seen a calf but a day or two old, which its mother has secreted in the woods or in a remote field, charge upon him furiously with a wild bleat, when first discovered. After this *first ebullition of fear,* it usually settles down into the tame humdrum of its bovine elders.

second restatement of thesis

further example

Eternal vigilance is the price of life with most of the wild creatures. There is only one among them whose wildness I cannot understand, and that is the common water turtle. Why is this creature *so fearful?* What are its enemies? I know of nothing that preys upon it. Yet see *how watchful and suspicious* these turtles are as they sun themselves upon a log or a rock. Before you are fairly in gunshot of them, they slide down into the water and are gone....

This selection illustrates a number of points about the effective development of a key idea: (1) The unity of a piece of prose is often reflected in the recurrence of **key terms** and phrases ("fear," "anxiety," "danger," "vigilance"). (2) The examples that support a generalization will be convincing if they are both detailed and clearly relevant. (3) A striking and detailed example used at the beginning is likely to fix the topic firmly in the reader's mind. (4) A powerful aid to explanation is the use of parallels or **analogies**, such as those taken from human life in this essay. If well chosen, they help the reader relate what he reads to the familiar or to his own experience. (5) Above all, the ease with which we follow a competent writer—far from being the result of a casual, rambling style—is the result of his moving purposefully in a given direction.

The support of generalization by example is one of the most routine tasks the beginning writer must master. Another basic procedure is the working out of distinctions between things or ideas that are closely related. Serious discussion can seldom proceed without **definition** of terms. In practice, definition often means carefully distinguishing one kind of freedom or conformity or Americanism from another. In many of the essays in this volume, the chief goal of the writer is to pin down a key term. Thus, Robert

Hutchins defines liberal education; Walter Lippmann, free speech; William James, religion; T. H. Huxley, science; Matthew Arnold, culture. Setting out to define democracy, Bernard Shaw observed that "we should never accept anything reverently until we have asked it a great many very searching questions, the first two being What are you? and Where do you live?" In answer to the first question, for instance, a writer would have to decide whether he is treating democracy as a political system or more generally as a way of life. In answer to the second question, he would have to distinguish between democracy as envisaged by the Founding Fathers, as the current system of politics in the United States, as a system found in varying forms in the United States and elsewhere, and so on. In organizing his discussion, he would arrange the alternatives in the most plausible order. He could, for instance, eliminate inadequate possibilities in order of importance and arrive at a satisfactory definition at the end.

Familiarity dulls our perception; contrast illuminates. Aldous Huxley once said that strange things are easier to understand "than those we know too well." We take for granted the things that are around us every day, and we are inarticulate in pointing out their characteristic features. This is why a foreign observer of the American scene, like Dan Jacobson or J. B. Priestley, sometimes notices important facts about American life that we have missed. The native gains the same advantage of a fresh perspective when he relies on **comparison and contrast** to bring out the salient features of familiar things. Thus, Santha Rama Rau, in "Return to India," shows how her travels in the Soviet Union illuminated for her some of the things precious to her in Indian life. Several other essays in this volume make more or less extended use of comparison and contrast: Jacques Barzun, in "Innocents at Home," contrasts American and European sights, institutions, and mentalities. Aldous Huxley, in "Tragedy and the Whole Truth," contrasts two basic ways in which literature may deal with reality.

The study of significant differences provides the basic pattern for many essays devoted to the **analysis** of a complicated situation. The writer may start by identifying something familiar or easily grasped. He may then relate it to other relevant elements or modify it by adding qualifications, conditions, implications. Thus, T. H. Huxley, in "On the Advisableness of Improving Natural Knowledge," starts from the familiar view of science as a magician's wand. He then proceeds to discuss its spiritual appeal and its moral implications. Lewis Mumford, in "The Romanticism of the Pioneer," starts from the view of nature held by European Romanticism and shows how it was modified by the realities of the pioneer's life.

The simplest kind of analysis merely sorts out things observed into several major groups. Through such **classification**, a writer uses distinctive differences as the basis for assigning things to the most appropriate of several pigeonholes. In "Is Kindness Killing the Arts?" Russell Lynes thus distinguishes the several major audiences for the modern artist. Even in such apparently simple classification, the author is likely to have made important decisions about how many major classes to recognize and in what order to present them.

Organized writing is thoughtful writing. The more systematic the writer's thought, the more likely an essay is to follow the pattern of a logical argument. The essay that states a thesis and then develops it has the advantage of clarity. The essay that takes the reader step by step through an argument to a final conclusion is more difficult to follow but can leave the reader more firmly convinced. One basic logical pattern is that of **induction,** or **inductive thinking.** The writer surveys a number of related instances and extracts what they have in common. He proceeds from detailed observation to a general conclusion. Thus, in "What's American about America?" John A. Kouwenhoven starts with an apparently miscellaneous list of things typically American. Examining them in detail, he arrives at a significant common quality.

Deduction, or **deductive thinking,** on the other hand, starts from general assumptions, or **premises.** It then applies them to specific situations. In Plato's "Educating the Guardians," the speakers deduce conclusions from general principles they have previously accepted. Few essays follow this pattern systematically and at great lengths. Nevertheless, the internal logic of an essay often consists in the writer's applying basic assumptions (which may be merely implied) to concrete cases. Thus, Henry David Thoreau, in "On the Duty of Civil Disobedience," works with a number of widely accepted premises concerning the consent of the governed and the authority of the individual conscience. From these he deduces a number of concrete applications concerning the citizen's relations with his government. Similarly, André Gide, in "Return from the Soviet Union," starts with certain assumptions concerning an ideal society. He applies these to Soviet reality and finds it wanting.

THE WRITER'S PURPOSE

As these examples imply, a writer does not choose a pattern of organization arbitrarily. Among the possibilities, he chooses the one that best fits his topic and his purpose. The over-all aim of the writer has much to do with his choice of means. The most elementary purpose of writing is to report, to record, to describe. For instance, Dan Jacobson, in "Cars, Cars, Cars, Roads, Roads, Roads," is first of all interested in recording his impressions of what he has seen. **Description** puts a premium on accurate observation. However, it also requires the writer to keep detail sorted out, to arrange material to advantage. It thus shades over into writing designed to clarify, to explain.

Writing becomes instructive when the writer has a knack for leading from the simple to the difficult, or for taking apart a complicated whole into simple parts. Journalists like Walter Lippmann owe their influence to their gift for **interpretation**; they give meaning to bewildering events. A critic of art or literature often practices interpretation in the most literal sense, translating the obscure into the meaningful. In the following passage, John Ciardi interprets a difficult passage from modern poetry, lines from Wallace Stevens's "Bantam in Pine Woods": "Chieftain Iffucan of Azcan in caftan/ Of tan with henna hackles, halt!"

> Note the title. A bantam may certainly be taken as a pretentious and pompous bird strutting around in his half-pint ego as if he owned the world, and refusing to be dwarfed even by the pine woods . . .
>
> . . . the Azcan business is a fact from the world . . . Have you ever looked into a pedigree book? I assume this to be a pure-bred bantam and that he is registered as Chieftain Iffucan of Azcan. Stevens begins by reporting the fact, obviously relishing its pretentiousness. "Caftan" is his first "poetic" addition. But note this: a caftan is a garment that hangs down just about the way the leg-feathers of a bantam do. The detail is physically right. And the sound of the word itself is exactly right for the sound-sequence Stevens builds. That's always a sign of the poet—the ability to do more than one thing at once and to have his choices come out equally right on all levels.[3]

Again, only a thin line separates interpretation from **evaluation**. Once we understand something, we are in a position to judge its worth. Thus, Ciardi's explanation of the difficulties of modern poetry is at the same time a plea for recognition of its value. Reporting, interpreting, and evaluating are not mutually exclusive, even though in a given piece of writing one of these is often clearly the main purpose. In this volume, the essays by Eiseley and Krutch illustrate the way in which observation inspires reflection, and reflection is in turn tested by further observation.

A writer presumably expects his readers to consider his reporting factual, his interpretations valid, and his judgments just. A statement is an implied plea for assent. However, when to convince is the writer's main goal, his methods are likely to reflect his motive. Persuasive writing and objective, factual exposition coincide to a large extent when readers insist on evidence and sound logic. However, **persuasion** can employ a wide variety of techniques that either supplement rational argument or take its place.

The persuasive writer is likely to have a masterful command of the possibilities of **emphasis**, of selection, of slanting. He will know what to play up and what to play down, what to repeat and what to omit. Whereas objectivity requires fair representation of the other side, the persuasive writer will be tempted to give his own position unqualified support and keep

---

3 "Dialogue with the Audience," *Saturday Review*, November 22, 1958, p. 12.

second thoughts to himself. Much persuasive writing relies on **overstatement**, on exaggerated claims. Here, as elsewhere, the writer must be well aware of the limits of the reader's patience and credulity. If exaggeration becomes too obvious, the reader will lose confidence in the author.

Persuasion addresses itself more directly than informative prose to the reader's motives. Thomas Paine's *The American Crisis* and Edmund Burke's *Reflections on the Revolution in France* illustrate the **emotional appeals** that can stir passionate assent. Love of country, fear of danger, hatred for enemies, pity for the unfortunate, admiration for greatness, fear of ridicule: all these are emotions that the persuasive writer can bring into play—and that the demagogue can exploit.

In the hands of the persuasive writer, ridicule becomes a powerful weapon. **Satire** employs the resources of humor for the aims of persuasion. Pretentiousness and all kinds of insincerity are especially vulnerable to derisive laughter. Thus, Marya Mannes, in "The Conquest of Trigger Mortis," demolishes some of the rationalizations advanced in support of television violence. H. L. Mencken, in "The Anglo-Saxon," deals a body blow to the myth of racial superiority. James Thurber, in "The Bat That Got the Hell Out," performs the same service for popularized, hard-sell religion. The satirist's methods include **parody**, which mimics objectionable features, making them ridiculous by exaggeration. The satirist relies heavily on **irony**, which exploits the comic contrast between naïve statement and malicious intention, or between pious pretense and hard fact. **Sarcasm** is a bitter kind of irony, illustrated in Mark Twain's acid comments on human weaknesses in "The Pudd'nhead Wilson Maxims."

Not every essay, of course, has a serious purpose. Not every essay is designed to inform or persuade. Much prose is written first of all for the entertainment of writer and reader. The **informal essay**, whatever its serious overtones, reflects above all a tradition of elegant leisure, or well-mannered ease. Joseph Addison's "Advertisements" and Robert Louis Stevenson's "An Apology for Idlers" in varying degrees combine charm and substance. Among more recent writers in this volume, Stephen Leacock and Ben Hecht illustrate the kind of humor that is not mere clowning. Even the most serious essays in this volume are included in part because they are a pleasure to read.

THE RESOURCES OF STYLE

Thinking is inseparable from the ability to put one's thoughts into words. Prose soon becomes lumpy if the writer does not have an ear for language. The first-rate writer is pleased by the happy phrase and annoyed by the opaque mumble. He has a feeling for words as words. This does not mean that he collects decorative words the way a child collects marbles. The striking word, the telling phrase, is the one that seems exactly right for the job to be done. A good writer can achieve a lasting effect with the simplest means, as did the reporter who wrote the following newspaper item:

DEATH LEAP
BY CONVICT
AT QUENTIN

Richard G. Heckman, a 49-year-old chiropractor, serving a six-month to 2½-year sentence for attempted abortion, jumped to his death from a fourth-floor landing at San Quentin Prison yesterday afternoon.

Heckman, found dead on a brick-paved alley after several witnesses saw him jump, had this terse note in his pocket: " 'Man's inhumanity to man.' Going home. . . . Doc Heckman."

Heckman, from Riverside county, had entered San Quentin only six days ago. He is survived by a son and daughter.

As a good craftsman prefers the efficient tool to the improvised one, so a good writer appreciates **economy** of expression. He will share the pleasure of the English teacher who saw an expert label designer cut down to its essentials a lengthy paragraph like the following:

When stored at normal refrigerator temperature this food will retain its taste, lightness, color, and value as a food product; but when exposed to air or kept at freezing temperature will suffer a chemical change which may render it unfit for human consumption. It is therefore recommended that it be kept at refrigerated temperature when not being used. However, it may be stored at room temperature safely if the lid has never been removed.

When printed on a jar lid, these instructions, greatly improved, would appear like this:

AFTER OPENING, KEEP IN REFRIGERATOR
DO NOT FREEZE[4]

By the same token, the competent writer will be impatient with the various affectations that keep the writer from looking steadily at his subject. He will sympathize with the editor who objected to the pretentious pseudo-technical **jargon** of a passage by two fishing experts.

Of the many things which influence angling success, the size of population of the species sought must be a prime factor. In order to gain information on the relationship between population and yield to fishermen

---

[4] Ken Macrorie, "World's Best Direction Writer," *College English*, XIII (February 1952), 276. Reprinted by permission.

> in a fishery based mainly on large mouth bass, *Micropterus salmoides* (Lacépède), we have experimented . . .

As the editor observed,

> The trouble with this is not *Micropterus salmoides*. Technical Latin words are precise and useful. The trouble lies in *influence, population, factor, information, relationship, population,* and the ambiguous *yield to*—all slushing along together through the weedy connectives. Does your subject seem mundane or trivial? Then give it a Latin diploma and it will graduate into elegant dullness. . . . If we traded our Latin words for Anglo-Saxon ones wherever we could make a bargain, and long words for short ones; if we wrote *find* for *determine, see* for *inquire, watch* for *observe, book* for *volume;* if we banished all words containing *tion,* and then let not more than three sneak back into any one paragraph, our writing would be clearer.[5]

Jargon annoys because of its false air of importance. However, excessive formality and technicality is not the only obstacle to profitable reading. At the opposite extreme, a strained folksiness can be equally distracting. Much advertising uses the "jargon of chumminess," a breezy style that has little in common with the natural speech of the shrewd experts who run advertising agencies. When such a "Hi, folks!" approach is transferred to expository prose, it is bound to antagonize the reader. This does not mean that all simple, folksy language, all **colloquial** phrasing, is taboo in serious writing. Arthur Miller's "The American Theater" illustrates the kind of **informal style** that gains in freshness and ease from the skillful use of occasional colloquial expressions.

The chief aim of the expository writer is to say clearly and directly what he has to say. To keep his style from becoming a barrier between himself and his readers, he must cultivate those resources of style that give freshness and vigor to language. Language owes its vitality to features that enable us to go beyond what is strictly literal-minded and predictable. Many a memorable sentence has the happy touch missing in what is ploddingly functional:

> The settlement of America had its origin in the unsettlement of Europe. (Lewis Mumford)
>
> An institution is the lengthened shadow of one man. (Ralph Waldo Emerson)
>
> A man is rich in proportion to the number of things which he can afford to let alone. (Henry David Thoreau)

[5] Sheridan Baker, "Scholarly Style, or the Lack Thereof," *AAUP Bulletin,* XLII (Autumn 1956), 468. Reprinted by permission.

> Truth is a naked and open daylight that does not show the masques and mummeries and triumphs of the world half so stately and daintily as candlelights. (Sir Francis Bacon)
>
> Man is the only animal that blushes. Or needs to. (Samuel Clemens)

The writer who uses language well is sensitive to verbal echoes and nuances. He emphasizes relationships between ideas by exploiting relationships between words. He responds to the imaginative appeal of figurative language, to subtle twists of irony and humor. He responds to the power of **metaphor** to translate an abstract idea into a striking image. He thus takes pleasure in the pregnant phrase, the provocative formula, such as Leslie Fiedler's description of television as "the electronic keyhole from which it is impossible to remove one's eye." He is sensitive to **word play**, to nuances of verbal humor, such as Gertrude Stein's saying about a city without profile "There's no there there" or Irwin Edman's reference to the welfare or "the illfare of the state."

Going beyond the individual word or phrase, a good writer exploits the resources of **rhythm and balance.** He uses repetition and parallelism to pull things together that belong together, or to line up ideas for comparison and contrast:

> Read not to contradict and confute, nor to believe and take for granted, nor to find talk and discourse, but to weigh and consider. (Sir Francis Bacon)
>
> No man is an island, entire to itself; every man is a piece of the continent, a part of the main. (John Donne)

Patterns of repetition and variation help give good writing its grace, its elegance, its verve. A sensitive reader is likely to share the sense of loss of the reviewer who compared the King James Version of the Bible with a recently published "Revised Standard Version":

> The most damaging effect of modernizing the usage is the alteration of rhythm, which is all-important in a book so often read aloud; quite aside from literary grace, the ceremonial effect of the Bible is enhanced by the interesting, varied, and suitable rhythms of K.J.V. But to (partially) avoid inversion, the Revisers render "Male and female created He them" (Genesis 1:27) "Male and female He created them," breaking the rhythm's back simply by changing the position of two words. In K.J.V., Ecclesiastes moves to a slow, mourning music:
>
>> What profit hath a man of all his labor which he taketh under the sun? One generation passeth and another generation cometh, but the earth abideth forever. . . . For there is no remembrance of the wise more than of the fool forever, seeing that which now is in the days to come shall all be forgotten. And how dieth the wise man? As the fool.

This now steps along to a brisker, less complex, and also less authoritative measure:

> What does a man gain by all the toil at which he toils under the sun? A generation goes and a generation comes, but the earth remains forever. . . . For of the wise man as of the fool there is no enduring remembrance, seeing that in the days to come all will have been long forgotten. How the wise man dies just like the fool![6]

In this volume, Jeremy Taylor's "The Vanity and Shortness of Man's Life" illustrates the solemn rhythms of a prose richer and more complex than most contemporary writing. Thomas Paine's *The American Crisis* shows the way highly emotional prose echoes the rhythms of passionate oratory. Jean-Jacques Rousseau's *On Education* echoes the brisk, energetic rhythm of argument by an animated talker. Part of the pleasure in reading prose lies in our responding to the characteristic movement of the author's style.

WRITING TO BE READ

Writers differ greatly in the way they respond to and profit from **criticism.** No matter how self-critical a writer becomes, he can never be truly objective about his own work. Doubtless criticism, like writing generally, can be ill-natured and wrong-headed—or simply irrelevant, a vehicle for grudges that have little to do with the work being criticized. But assuming that the critic's interest is genuine, writers must be thankful for his recording in some detail the reactions of a reasonably sensitive reader. The silencing—or the ignoring—of criticism is a mere illusion. In the reader's mind, criticism continues—the more rigorous because unedited and uninhibited, the less constructive because unheard and unheeded.

Critics and teachers may at times seem so preoccupied with the style of writing as to neglect the ideas it conveys. We must remember, however, that the writer's thoughts are revealed through language. Not what the writer thought and felt but what he wrote is our primary evidence; what he actually said rather than what he might have said if he had been more articulate or more candid or more resourceful. A competent writer has to reach a degree of skill that will enable him to feel adequately represented by the written word. He must take care of possible afterthoughts in time or else be prepared to hold his peace.

Successful communication depends on some degree of harmony between what the writer has to give and what the reader is willing to accept. The writer who writes because he must, with consideration for no one except a remote posterity, must be prepared to find himself surrounded by a kind of silence that few ordinary men can take. At the opposite extreme, the writer

---

[6] Dwight Macdonald, "The Bible in Modern Undress," *The New Yorker,* November 14, 1953, pp. 197–198.

who too eagerly adapts himself to the expectations of his audience loses his own identity. Fortunate is the writer who can combine integrity of thought and feeling with due consideration for an audience that he can respect.

Ultimately, a writer commands our attention because he has something to tell us. "Effectiveness of assertion," as Bernard Shaw observed, is the final test of style. It is true that writers have different purposes: the author of a travel book may want to re-create places and events; a textbook author may want to explain a technical process; the author of a political pamphlet may want to influence our attitudes. But in much significant and effective prose these purposes merge or supplement one another: the author may describe people and places to make his writing concrete; he may trace relationships to enable us to understand his subject; he may develop a logical argument to make us follow his thought; he may appeal to our emotions to make us give his argument more than cold assent. In fact, writing may lose its vitality as it approaches one of the extremes of rigorous exposition, relentless argument, or shrilly irrational persuasion. Prose that makes rewarding reading is likely to be complex and alive. Graphic detail, clarity of thought, and sincerity of emotion are likely to go hand in hand.

Since serious writing tends to involve the author's full personality, it has an obvious ethical dimension. Every writer needs constant self-discipline; he must make a constant effort to do without the heated reply or the snide remark. He must overcome ingrained mental habits: his refusal to re-examine what he considers self-evident, the temptation to overstate the evidence for a conclusion which he is certain of anyway, his natural reluctance to concede error. Expository prose, the vehicle for much that is trivial and short-lived, is also the medium in which we formulate basic attitudes and convictions. A free society is based on the principle that people of different interests and convictions can work together through tolerance and compromise. We must therefore make our interests and convictions intelligible and, at least to some extent, acceptable to others. To do so, we try to show that our beliefs are not arbitrary or wrong-headed but the result of careful consideration.

Curiosity, sensitivity, and open-mindedness are incompatible with the kind of indoctrination that produces one-track minds. Traditional liberal education acquaints the student with outstanding contributions from different periods and schools of thought. In such a system of education, the study and practice of expository prose plays an important part.

1

Sights and Sounds

The morning wind forever blows, the poem of creation is uninterrupted; but few are the ears that hear it. HENRY DAVID THOREAU

A competent writer must be first of all a receptive observer. All of the writers in the section that follows are distinguished by their vivid response to the texture of experience and by their ability to grasp and communicate what they have seen and heard and felt. At the same time, however, they have the ability to seize on what is significant—to focus on the revealing detail, to work observations at first random into a meaningful pattern. Their writing is the writing of the *thoughtful* observer—who is not a mere recorder but an interpreter of scenes and events. The first two essays contain the reflections of writers looking at our natural environment, from which many of us are becoming isolated by successive layers of urbanized, mechanized civilization. Loren Eiseley, in "The Slit," shows how the casual exploration of an outing to the prairie can lead from specific sights and sounds to basic questions about man's role on this planet. Joseph Wood Krutch, in "April ... The Day of the Peepers," writes about natural phenomena—not in the spirit of analytical dissection but in the spirit of sympathy with "things seen, and heard, and felt." Dan Jacobson, in "Cars, Cars, Cars, Roads, Roads, Roads," looks at the American scene with the fresh interest of a traveler from another continent, if not from another planet. V. S. Pritchett, in "Striverstown," writes about Harlem with the candor of a visitor detached enough to see clearly, involved enough to care, and honest enough to tell the truth.

LOREN EISELEY

The student interested in the world of nature often has to choose between two sharply divergent roads: that of the scientist and that of the poet, the road of scientific measurement and experiment and the road of imaginative response. Loren C. Eiseley (born 1907) is an American anthropologist who has escaped the narrowing of outlook that specialization in either scientific or literary pursuits can produce. With a more thorough scientific grounding then some of his literary fellow-naturalists, with a more lively sense of wonder than some of his fellow-scientists, he helps his readers to recover a thoughtful awareness of their natural environment. Mr. Eiseley has taught at universities and colleges including Columbia University, University of California at Berkeley, Harvard University, and University of Pennsylvania. The present selection is the introductory chapter from his *The Immense Journey* (1957). It shows the author's exceptional ability to make his readers share concretely in his own observations and reflections.

The Slit

Some lands are flat and grass-covered, and smile so evenly up at the sun that they seem forever youthful, untouched by man or time. Some are torn, ravaged and convulsed like the features of profane old age. Rocks are wrenched up and exposed to view; black pits receive the sun but give back no light.

It was to such a land I rode, but I rode to it across a sunlit, timeless prairie over which nothing passed but antelope or a wandering bird. On the verge where that prairie halted before a great wall of naked sandstone and clay, I came upon the Slit. A narrow crack worn by some descending torrent had begun secretly, far back in the prairie grass, and worked itself deeper and deeper into the fine sandstone that led by devious channels into the broken waste beyond. I rode back along the crack to a spot where I could descend into it, dismounted, and left my horse to graze.

The crack was only about body-width and, as I worked my way downward, the light turned dark and green from the overhanging grass. Above me the sky became a narrow slit of distant blue, and the sandstone was cool to my hands on either side. The Slit was a little sinister—like an open grave, assuming the dead were enabled to take one last look—for over me the sky seemed already as far off as some future century I would never see.

I ignored the sky, then, and began to concentrate on the sandstone walls that had led me into this place. It was tight and tricky work, but that cut was a perfect cross section through perhaps ten million years of time. I hoped to find at least a bone, but I was not quite prepared for the sight I finally came upon. Staring straight out at me, as I slid farther and deeper into the green twilight, was a skull embedded in the solid sandstone. I had come at just the proper moment when it was fully to be seen, the white bone gleaming there in a kind of ashen splendor, water worn, and about to be ground away in the next long torrent.

It was not, of course, human. I was deep, deep below the time of man in a remote age near the beginning of the reign of mammals. I squatted on my heels in the narrow ravine, and we stared a little blankly at each other, the skull and I. There were marks of generalized primitiveness in that low, pinched brain case and grinning jaw that marked it as lying far back along those converging roads where cat and man and weasel must leap into a single shape.

It was the face of a creature who had spent his days following his nose, who was led by instinct rather than memory, and whose power of choice was very small. Though he was not a man, nor a direct human ancestor, there was yet about him, even in the bone, some trace of that low, snuffling world out of which our forebears had so recently emerged. The skull lay tilted in such a manner that it stared, sightless, up at me as though I, too, were already caught a few feet above him in the strata and, in my turn, were staring upward at that strip of sky which the ages were carrying farther away from me beneath the tumbling debris of falling mountains. The creature had never lived to see a man, and I, what was it I was never going to see?

I restrained a panicky impulse to hurry upward after that receding sky that was outlined above the Slit. Probably, I thought, as I patiently began the task of chiseling into the stone around the skull, I would never again excavate a fossil under conditions which led to so vivid an impression that I was already one myself. The truth is that we are all potential fossils still carrying within our bodies the crudities of former existences, the marks of a world in which living creatures flow with little more consistency than clouds from age to age.

As I tapped and chiseled there in the foundations of the world, I had ample time to consider the cunning manipulability of the human fingers. Experimentally I crooked one of the long slender bones. It might have been silica, I thought, or aluminum, or iron—the cells would have made it possible. But no, it is calcium, carbonate of lime. Why? Only because of its history. Elements more numerous than calcium in the earth's crust could have been used to build the skeleton. Our history is the reason—we came from the water. It was there the cells took the lime habit, and they kept it after we came ashore.

It is not a bad symbol of that long wandering, I thought again—the human hand that has been fin and scaly reptile foot and furry paw. If a stone should fall (I cocked an eye at the leaning shelf above my head and waited, fatalistically) let the bones lie here with their message, for those who might decipher it, if they come down late among us from the stars.

Above me the great crack seemed to lengthen.

Perhaps there is no meaning in it at all, the thought went on inside me, save that of journey itself, so far as men can see. It has altered with the chances of life, and the chances brought us here; but it was a good journey—long, perhaps—but a good journey under a pleasant sun. Do not look for the purpose. Think of the way we came and be a little proud. Think of this hand—the utter pain of its first venture on the pebbly shore.

Or consider its later wanderings.

I ceased my tappings around the sand-filled sockets of the skull and wedged myself into a crevice for a smoke. As I tamped a load of tobacco into my pipe, I thought of a town across the valley that I used sometimes to visit, a town whose little inhabitants never welcomed me. No sign points to it and I rarely go there any more. Few people know about it and fewer still know that in a sense we, or rather some of the creatures to whom we are related, were driven out of it once, long ago. I used to park my car on a hill and sit silently observant, listening to the talk ringing out from neighbor to neighbor, seeing the inhabitants drowsing in their doorways, taking it all in with nostalgia—the sage smell on the wind, the sunlight without time, the village without destiny. We can look, but we can never go back. It is prairie-dog town.

"Whirl is king," said Aristophanes, and never since life began was Whirl more truly king than eighty million years ago in the dawn of the Age of Mammals. It would come as a shock to those who believe firmly that the scroll of the future is fixed and the roads determined in advance, to observe the teetering balance of earth's history through the age of the Paleocene. The passing of the reptiles had left a hundred uninhabited life zones and a scrambling variety of newly radiating forms. Unheard-of species of giant ground birds threatened for a moment to dominate the earthly scene. Two separate orders of life contended at slightly different intervals for the pleasant grasslands—for the seeds and the sleepy burrows in the sun.

Sometimes, sitting there in the mountain sunshine above prairie-dog town, I could imagine the attraction of that open world after the fern forest damp or the croaking gloom of carboniferous swamps. There by a tree root I could almost make him out, that shabby little Paleocene rat, eternal tramp and world wanderer, father of all mankind. He ruffed his coat in the sun and hopped forward for a seed. It was to be a long time before he would be seen on the grass again, but he was trying to make up his mind. For good or ill there was to be one more chance, but that chance was fifty million years away.

Here in the Paleocene occurred the first great radiation of the placental mammals, and among them were the earliest primates—the zoological order to which man himself belongs. Today, with a few unimportant exceptions, the primates are all arboreal in habit except man. For this reason we have tended to visualize all of our remote relatives as tree dwellers. Recent discoveries, however, have begun to alter this one-sided picture. Before the rise of the true rodents, the highly successful order to which present-day prairie dogs and chipmunks belong, the environment which they occupy had remained peculiarly open to exploitation. Into this zone crowded a varied assemblage of our early relatives.

"In habitat," comments one scholar, "many of these early primates may be thought of as the rats of the Paleocene. With the later appearance of true rodents, the primate habitat was markedly restricted." The bone hunters, in other words, have succeeded in demonstrating that numerous primates reveal a remarkable development of rodent-like characteristics in the teeth and skull during this early period of mammalian evolution. The movement is progressive and distributed in several different groups. One form, although that of a true primate, shows similarities to the modern kangaroo rat, which is, of course, a rodent. There is little doubt that it was a burrower.

It is this evidence of a lost chapter in the history of our kind that I used to remember on the sunny slope above prairie-dog town, and that enables me to say in a somewhat figurative fashion that we were driven out of it once ages ago. We are not, except very remotely as mammals, related to prairie dogs. Nevertheless, through several million years of Paleocene time, the primate order, instead of being confined to trees, was experimenting to some extent with the same grassland burrowing life that the rodents later perfected. The success of these burrowers crowded the primates out of this environment and forced them back into the domain of the branches. As a result, many primates, by that time highly specialized for a ground life, became extinct.

In the restricted world of the trees, a "refuge area," as the zoologist would say, the others lingered on in diminished numbers. Our ancient relatives, it appeared, were beaten in their attempt to expand upon the ground; they were dying out in the temperate zone, and their significance as a widespread and diversified group was fading. The shabby pseudo-rat I had seen ruffling his coat to dry after the night damps of the reptile age, had ascended again into the green twilight of the rain forest. The chatterers with the ever-growing teeth were his masters. The sunlight and the grass belonged to them.

It is conceivable that except for the invasion of the rodents, the primate line might even have abandoned the trees. We might be there on the grass, you and I, barking in the high-plains sunlight. It is true we came back in fifty million years with the cunning hands and the eyes that the tree world gave us, but was it victory? Once more in memory I saw the high blue evening fall sleepily upon that village, and once more swung the car to leave, lifting, as I always did, a figurative lantern to some ambiguous crossroads sign within my brain. The pointing arms were nameless and nameless were the distances to which they pointed. One took one's choice.

I ceased my daydreaming then, squeezed myself out of the crevice; shook out my pipe, and started chipping once more, the taps sounding along the inward-leaning walls of the Slit like the echo of many footsteps ascending and descending. I had come a long way down since morning; I had projected myself across a dimension I was not fitted to traverse in the flesh. In the end I collected my tools and climbed painfully up through the colossal debris of ages. When I put my hands on the surface of the crack I looked all about carefully in a sudden anxiety that it might not be a grazing horse that I would see.

He had not visibly changed, however, and I mounted in some slight trepidation and rode off, having a memory for a camp—if I had gotten a foot in the right era—which should lie somewhere over to the west. I did not, however, escape totally from that brief imprisonment.

Perhaps the Slit, with its exposed bones and its far-off vanishing sky, has come to stand symbolically in my mind for a dimension denied to man, the dimension of time. Like the wistaria on the garden wall he is rooted in his particular century. Out of it—forward or backward—he cannot run. As he stands on his circumscribed pinpoint of time, his sight for the past is growing longer, and even the shadowy outlines of the galactic future are growing clearer, though his own fate he cannot yet see. Along the dimension of time, man, like the rooted vine in space, may never pass in person. Considering the innumerable devices by which the mindless root has evaded the limitations of its own stability, however, it may well be that man himself is slowly achieving powers over a new dimension—a dimension capable of presenting him with a wisdom he has barely begun to discern.

Through how many dimensions and how many media will life have to pass? Down how many roads among the stars must man propel himself in search of the final secret? The journey is difficult, immense, at times impossible, yet that will not deter some of us from attempting it. We cannot know all that has happened in the past, or the reason for all of these events, any more than we can with surety discern what lies ahead. We have joined the caravan, you might say, at a certain point; we will travel as far as we can, but we cannot in one lifetime see all that we would like to see or learn all that we hunger to know.

DISCUSSION AND WRITING

1. Define or explain: *ravaged, profane, torrent, devious, sinister, ravine, forebears, strata, receding, fatalistic, decipher, radiate, arboreal, nostalgia, domain, ambiguous, habitat, propel, discern, caravan.* How much knowledge of geology and biology does the author expect from his readers? Study his use of technical terminology (prepare a brief list). What is the proportion of scientific words ("carboniferous") and the familiar or colloquial ("bone hunters")?

2. Show how the author helps us imagine ourselves in his place—through a specific accounting of his movements and position ("squatted on my heels in the narrow ravine"); through sensory detail ("the sandstone was cool to my hands"); through movement, drama, and emotion introduced into what could be static description.

3. Mr. Eiseley characteristically translates abstract scientific knowledge ("was led by instinct") into graphic, concrete terms ("spent his days following his nose"). Cite further examples, paying special attention to external objects that the author explicitly identifies as symbolic of abstract ideas.

4. Examine the author's use of figurative language—language that departs from the literal and prosaic to bring in imaginative comparison and association. Cite examples of metaphor ("grinning jaw"), simile ("like an open grave"), and personification (lands "smile" and seem "youthful"). Cite examples of the author's use of unusual perspective to arouse interest ("we are all potential fossils").

5. Examine the pattern of repetition, parallelism, and variation that in the first three paragraphs determines sentence structure and sentence style.

6. The essay proceeds from the concrete facts of the excursion to general reflections on man's biological history. Examine the relationship between the chronological order of the trip and the logical progression of the author's ideas. Identify the paragraphs that come closest to summing up the author's general outlook or central theme. Write a paragraph restating it in your own words. What makes the Slit especially appropriate as a unifying symbol for the essay?

7. Write a one-paragraph theme on each of the following: (a) a relatively limited but complex and unified object of observation—for instance, a human hand or face, or the head of an animal; (b) the interior of a building—for instance, a church, a court building, an auditorium; (c) a natural scene—for instance, a meadow, a cornfield, the ocean during a storm, a mountain valley. Limit each paragraph to concrete descriptive detail but make the object of description emerge as a unified whole. Make your use of language as graphic as you can.

8. Describe a building, tree, street, square, or the like, that for you has strong emotional associations or symbolic significance. Use concrete descriptive details but at the same time convey the larger significance of your subject.

9. What opportunities have you had to explore the natural world on your own? Write an account of a relevant excursion or experience. Use concrete detail.

10. Would you agree that man's biological history "was a good journey," even if "Perhaps there is no meaning in it at all"? Would you be prepared to say, with Mr. Eiseley, "Do not look for the purpose"?

FURTHER READING

Some scientists who have written on scientific subjects with a vivid awareness of their imaginative and human dimensions are Julian Huxley (*Essays of a Biologist* and many later books), J. B. S. Haldane (*Possible Worlds*), Hans Zinsser (*Rats, Lice and History*), Rachel Carson (*The Sea around Us, The Edge of the Sea*), Arthur C. Clarke (*The Exploration of Space*). Read an article, or chapter from a book, by one of these writers and compare his treatment of scientific subject matter with Mr. Eiseley's.

JOSEPH WOOD KRUTCH

Whereas Loren Eiseley is a scientist with a strong imaginative bent, Joseph Wood Krutch (born 1893) is an imaginative writer who shares the scientific naturalist's patience with factual detail. As writer, teacher, and critic, Mr. Krutch has broad interests in English and American literature and drama. The most influential of his books is *The Modern Temper* (1929). Readers of *The American Scholar* are familiar with his column "If You Don't Mind My Saying So." He has published several volumes of nature writing; the present selection is the opening essay of one of these, *The Twelve Seasons* (1949). One of the recurrent themes of Mr. Krutch's writing has been that nature supplies "the inescapable context of man's life, physically and spiritually" and that he cannot, "without unhappiness and ultimate disaster, cut himself off completely from either her sights and sounds" or from the sense that he and she are "part of a large enterprise together." The following essay shows the author's uncommon ability to revive our interest in the natural world, to make us take a fresh look at familiar natural phenomena.

April . . . The Day of the Peepers

Hyla crucifer is what the biologists call him, but to most of us he is simply the Spring Peeper. The popularizers of natural history have by no means neglected him but even without their aid he has made himself known to many whose only wild flower is the daisy and whose only bird is the robin. Everyone who has ever visited the country in the spring has heard him trilling from the marsh at twilight, and though few have ever caught sight of him most know that he is a little inch-long frog who has just awaked from his winter sleep. In southern Connecticut he usually begins to pipe on some day between the middle of March and the middle of April, and I, like most country dwellers, listen for the first of his shrill, cold notes.

Throughout the winter, neighbors who met in the village street have been greeting one another with the conventional question: "Is it cold enough for you?" Or, perhaps, if they are of the type which watches a bit more carefully than most the phenomenon of the seasons, they have been comparing thermometers in the hope that someone will admit to a minimum at least one degree higher than what was recorded "over my way." Now, however, one announces triumphantly: "Heard the peepers last night," and the other goes home to tell his wife. Few are High Church enough to risk a "Christ is risen" on Easter morning, but the peepers are mentioned without undue self-consciousness.

Even this, however, is not enough for me and I have often wondered that a world which pretends to mark so many days and to celebrate so many occasions should accept quite so casually the day when *Hyla crucifer* announces that winter is over. One swallow does not make a spring, and the robin arrives with all the philistine unconcern of a worldling back from his Winter at Aiken or Palm Beach. But the peeper seems to realize, rather better than we, the significance of his resurrection, and I wonder if there is any other phenomenon in the heavens above or in the earth beneath which so simply and so definitely announces that life is resurgent again.

We who have kept artificially warm and active through the winter act as though we were really independent of the seasons, but we forget how brief our immunity is and are less anxious than we might be if habit had not dulled our awareness. One summer which failed to arrive and we should realize well enough before we perished of hunger that we are only a little less at the mercy of the seasons than the weed that dies in October. One winter which lasted not six months but twelve and we should recognize our affinity

From *The Twelve Seasons* by Joseph Wood Krutch. Copyright 1949 by Joseph Wood Krutch. By permission of William Sloane Associates.

with the insects who give up the ghost after laying the eggs that would never hatch if they did not lie chill and dead through the cold of a winter as necessary to them as warmth was to the males who fertilized and the females who laid them. We waited through the long period during which our accumulated supplies of food grew smaller and we waited calmly in a blind assurance that warmth would return and that nature would reawaken. Now, the voice of the peeper from the marsh announces the tremendous fact that our faith has been justified. A sigh of relief should go up and men should look at one another with a wild surprise. "It" has happened again, though there was nothing during the long months that passed to support our conviction that it could and would.

We had, to be sure, the waiting pages of our calendars marked "June," "July," and even, of all things, "August." The sun, so the astronomers had assured us, had turned northward on a certain date and theoretically had been growing stronger day by day. But there was, often enough, little in the mercury of our thermometers or the feel of our fingers to confirm the fact. Many a March day had felt colder than the milder days of February. And merely astronomical seasons have, after all, very little relation to any actual human experience either as visible phenomena or as events bringing with them concomitant earthly effects.

Not one man out of a hundred thousand would be aware of the solstices or the equinoxes if he did not see their dates set down in the almanac or did not read them in the newspaper. They cannot be determined without accurate instruments and they correspond to no phenomena he is aware of. But the year as we live it does have its procession of recurring events, and it is a curious commentary on the extent to which we live by mere symbols that ten men know that the spring equinox occurs near the twenty-first of March to one who would give you even the approximate date when the peepers begin in his community; and that remains true even if he happens to be a countryman and even if he usually remarks, year after year, when they do begin.

It is true that the Day of the Peepers is a movable feast. But so is Easter, which—as a matter of fact—can come earlier or later by just about the same number of days that, on the calendar I have kept, separates the earliest from the latest date upon which *Hyla crucifer* begins to call. Moreover, the earliness or the lateness of the peepers means something, as the earliness or the lateness of Easter does not.

Whatever the stars may say or whatever the sun's altitude may be, spring has not begun until the ice has melted and life begun to stir again. Your peeper makes a calculation which would baffle a meteorologost. He takes into consideration the maximum to which the temperature has risen, the minimum to which it has fallen during the night, the relative length of the warmer and the colder periods, besides, no doubt, other factors hard to get down in tables or charts. But at last he knows that the moment has come. It has been just warm enough just long enough, and without too much cold in between. He inflates the little bubble in his throat and sends out the clear note audible for half a mile. On that day something older than any Christian God has risen. The earth is alive again.

The human tendency to prefer abstractions to phenomena is, I know, a very ancient one. Some anthropologists, noting that abstract design seems usually to come before the pictorial representation of anything in primitive man's environment, have said that the first picture drawn by any beginning culture is a picture of God. Certainly in the European world astronomy was the first of the sciences, and it is curious to remember that men knew a great deal about the intricate dance of the heavenly bodies before they had so much as noticed the phenomena of life about them. The constellations were named before any except the most obvious animals or plants and were studied before a science of botany or physiology had begun. The Greeks, who thought that bees were generated in the carcasses of dead animals and that swallows hibernated under the water, could predict eclipses, and the very Druids were concerned to mark the day on which the sun turned northward again. But the earliest of the sciences is also the most remote and the most abstract. The objects with which it deals are not living things and its crucial events do not correspond directly or immediately to any phenomena which are crucial in the procession of events as they affect animal or vegetable life.

Easter is an anniversary, and the conception of an anniversary is not only abstract but so difficult to define that the attempt to fix Easter used up an appalling proportion of the mental energy of learned men for many hundreds of years—ultimately to result in nothing except a cumbersome complexity that is absolutely meaningless in the end. Why should we celebrate the first Sunday after the first full moon on or after the twenty-first of March? What possible meaning can the result of such a calculation have? Yet even that meaningless definition of Easter is not really accurate. For the purpose of determining the festival, the date of the full moon is assumed to be, not that of the actual full moon, but that on which the full moon would have fallen if the table worked out by Pope Gregory's learned men had been— as it is not—really accurate. Even the relatively few men who remember the commonly given formula will occasionally find that they have missed their attempt to determine when Easter will be because they consulted a lay calendar to find the full moon instead of concerning themselves with the Epact and considering the theoretical ecclesiastical full moon rather than the actual one. How much easier it is to celebrate the Day of the Peepers instead, and how much more meaningful too! On that day something miraculous and full of promise has actually happened, and that something announces itself in no uncertain terms.

Over any astronomically determined festival, the Day of the Peepers has, moreover, another advantage even greater than the simplicity with which it defines itself or the actuality of its relation to the season it announces, for *Hyla crucifer* is a sentient creature who shares with us the drama and the exultation; who, indeed, sings our hosannahs for us. The music of the spheres is a myth; to say that the heavens rejoice is a pathetic fallacy; but there is no missing the rejoicings from the marsh and no denying that they are something shared. Under the stars we feel alone but by the pond side we have company.

To most, to be sure, Hyla is a *vox et praeterea nihil*.[1] Out of a thousand who have heard him, hardly one has ever seen him at the time of his singing or recognized him if perchance he has happened by pure accident to see squatting on the branch of some shrub the tiny inch-long creature, gray or green according to his mood, and with a dark cross over his back. But it was this tiny creature who, some months before, had congregated with his fellows in the cold winter to sing and make love. No one could possibly humanize him as one humanizes a pet and so come to feel that he belongs to us rather than—what is infinitely more important—that we both, equally, belong to something more inclusive than ourselves.

Like all the reptiles and the amphibians he has an aspect which is inscrutable and antediluvian. His thoughts must be inconceivably different' from ours and his joy hardly less so. But the fact is comforting rather than the reverse, for if we are nevertheless somehow united with him in that vast category of living things which is so sharply cut off from everything that does not live at all, then we realize how broad the base of the category is, how much besides ourselves is, as it were, on our side. Over against the atoms and the stars are set both men and frogs. Life is not something entrenched in man alone, in a creature who has not been here so very long and may not continue to be here so very much longer. We are not its sole guardians, not alone in enjoying or enduring it. It is not something that will fail if we should.

Strangely enough, however, man's development takes him farther and farther away from association with his fellows, seems to condemn him more and more to live with what is dead rather than with what is alive. It is not merely that he dwells in cities and associates with machines rather than with plants and with animals. That, indeed, is but a small and a relatively unimportant part of his growing isolation. Far more important is the fact that more and more he thinks in terms of abstractions, generalizations, and laws; less and less participates in the experience of living in a world of sights, and sounds, and natural urges.

Electricity, the most powerful of his servants, flows silently and invisibly. It isn't really there except in its effects. We plan our greatest works on paper

[1] ["A voice and nothing but a voice."]

and in adding machines. Push the button, turn the switch! Things happen. But they are things we know about only in terms of symbols and formulae. Do we inevitably, in the process, come ourselves to be more and more like the inanimate forces with which we deal, less and less like the animals among whom we arose? Yet it is of protoplasm that we are made. We cannot possibly become like atoms or like suns. Do we dare to forget as completely as we threaten to forget that we belong rejoicing by the marsh more anciently and more fundamentally than we belong by the machine or over the drawing board?

No doubt astronomy especially fascinated the first men who began to think because the world in which they lived was predominantly so immediate and so confused a thing, was composed so largely of phenomena which they could see and hear but could not understand or predict and to which they so easily fell victim. The night sky spread out above them defined itself clearly and exhibited a relatively simple pattern of surely recurring events. They could perceive an order and impose a scheme, thus satisfying an intellectual need to which the natural phenomena close about them refused to cater.

But the situation of modern man is exactly the reverse. He "understands" more and more as he sees and hears less and less. By the time he has reached high-school age he has been introduced to the paradox that the chair on which he sits is not the hard object it seems to be but a collection of dancing molecules. He learns to deal, not with objects but with statistics, and before long he is introduced to the idea that God is a mathematician, not the creator of things seen, and heard, and felt. As he is taught to trust less and less the evidence of the five senses with which he was born, he lives less and less in the world which they seem to reveal, more and more with the concepts of physics and biology. Even his body is no longer most importantly the organs and muscles of which he is aware but the hormones of which he is told.

The very works of art that he looks at when he seeks delight through the senses are no longer representations of what the eye has seen but constructions and designs—or, in other words, another order of abstractions. It is no wonder that for such a one spring should come, not when the peepers begin, but when the sun crosses the equator or rather—since that is only a human interpretation of the phenomenon—when the inclined axis of the earth is for an instant pointed neither toward nor away from the sun but out into space in such a way that it permits the sun's rays to fall upon all parts of the earth's surface for an equal length of time. For him astronomy does not, as it did for primitive man, represent the one successful attempt to intellectualize and render abstract a series of natural phenomena. It is, instead, merely one more of the many systems by which understanding is substituted for experience.

Surely one day a year might be set aside on which to celebrate our ancient loyalties and to remember our ancient origins. And I know of none more suitable for that purpose than the Day of the Peepers. "Spring is come!" I say when I hear them, and: "The most ancient of Christs has risen!" but I also add something which, for me at least, is even more important. "Don't forget," I whisper to the peepers; "we are all in this together."

DISCUSSION AND WRITING

1. Define or explain: *phenomenon, High Church, philistine, resurgent, affinity, concomitant, anthropologist, pictorial, Druids, ecclesiastical, sentient, exultation, hosannah, myth, perchance, inscrutable, antediluvian, inanimate, paradox, concept.* What is a "movable feast," the "music of the spheres," the "pathetic fallacy"?

2. To what extent does the author rely on technical terms from the natural sciences? (Make a brief list.) What other fields does he draw on for technical terms? What sort of relationship does he want to establish with his audience—is he addressing himself as an expert to a lay public, for instance? (Cite relevant evidence.)

3. Discuss examples of vivid or startling phrases that make the reader take a fresh look at familiar natural phenomena. What makes these phrases effective?

4. Trace in detail the organization of Mr. Krutch's essay. Pay attention to introduction and conclusion, to transition from paragraph to paragraph. How does he proceed from the identification of a zoological species to comprehensive judgments on contemporary civilization?

5. In a well-developed paragraph, explain in your own words what the author means when he says, "Over against the atoms and the stars are set both men and frogs."

6. Compare and contrast the attitude toward nature of Krutch, as a literary man, with that of Eiseley, as a scientist. Cite detailed evidence to substantiate parallels or differences in their outlook.

7. Have you ever raised, trained, or closely studied an animal other than the kittens or puppies that most of us remember as childhood pets? Write a detailed account of the experience.

8. How successful are national or state parks in giving city dwellers an authentic feeling for unspoiled nature? Or, can you defend sports like hunting or fishing against the charge that they show man's tendency to exploit and destroy his fellow creatures in the natural world? Use detailed reference to first-hand experience.

9. Is it true that man "less and less participates in the experience of living in a world of sights, and sounds, and natural urges"? Use detailed examples from your own experience or observation.

10. What holiday or festival has for you a truly personal meaning? Try to go beyond familiar sentimental or commercial associations.

FURTHER READING

Of earlier American books concerned with man's relationship to "the world which Nature gave him," the most famous is Henry David Thoreau's *Walden* (1854). In the chapter entitled "Where I Lived, and What I Lived For," Thoreau explains the meaning of his experiment in living in close contact with the natural world. Compare Thoreau's relationship to nature with that of Krutch, one of his modern champions and admirers.

DAN JACOBSON

The traveler visiting a foreign country has an important advantage over native observers. He sees a new environment for the first time; his curiosity has not yet been dulled by habit; he is ready to marvel at things that the native simply takes for granted. However, while the traveler's impressions are likely to be fresh and provocative, they may also be superficial and one-sided. Lacking the balanced over-all view that comes from long acquaintance, he may seize upon the striking, the different, the absurd. Worse, he may arrive with preconceptions that have come to him through sensational newspapers, biased history books, or second-rate movies. Thus, we are likely to regard the foreign traveler with mixed emotions: hope for understanding, fear of misrepresentation. Dan Jacobson (born 1929) is a South African writer whose short stories and novels have been published in America and England. In his account of a visit to this country, he avoids the extremes of propagandistic anti-Americanism and of insincere praise. The following article was first published in *The Reporter* in February 1957. It demonstrates an experienced writer's ability to seize on revealing details, to conjure up for the reader the authentic sights and sounds of an actual experience.

Cars, Cars, Cars,
Roads, Roads, Roads

At nightfall after thirty hours in the plane, we found ourselves level with the country we had been flying over during the day. We came out of the terminal building, and before us more parked motor cars than I had ever seen in a single place stretched in an expanse toward some kind of bridge in the distance. Cars were passing over the bridge and to the right and the left of the terrain of parked cars, and from the night sky broken by the

From *The Reporter*, February 21, 1957. Copyright © 1957 by The Reporter Magazine Company. Reprinted by permission of Dan Jacobson.

chasing headlights there came a continuous rustle, a fall of sound—a whisper out of the throat of the night. The cars moved all about us; they moved above us, until where we stood seemed to be the center of a circle of country that gleamed and whirred, and wheeled entirely around us.

Then we were taken to a car, and we too were moving around the plain of parked cars, and the road we were on suddenly fell away in an arc and then went up again, and around us other roads were rising and falling in arcs. Which road we were on I no longer knew. A broad, black width of tar, tilted down and curving to the right, rushed toward our headlights, and by their light we saw that none of the other roads were lying on the earth, but all were moving up from it or stepping down to it on great concrete stilts. And they were all wide, wide, and ran as fast as the headlights of our car, which rushed down to another road, wider than any we had yet seen, and flat before us, at an angle to our arc.

Suddenly we were no longer tilted, but on a level with the big road. Then, though neither we nor any other cars slowed down to let us onto it, we were moving on this new road, and cars came past with a curiously close and confidential rustle at their rear wheels, for in comparison with them, it seemed, we weren't traveling so very fast after all.

The cars were swollen and shining; their colors were different above and below; they bulged in front and they bulged at the back. Never had I seen, never could I have imagined so many of them moving so fast all at one time. It is the movement, I suppose, that paralyzes the mind: One could imagine cars, just cars, stretched out indefinitely, but set them moving, set them moving at sixty or seventy miles an hour, set them moving three or four abreast, set them moving in two directions, and the imagination simply retreats and despairs; the mind is numbed.

In two directions, I have said, but there were more than two directions. As we had joined the road by hurling ourselves at an angle into it, so other cars were doing along other roads that came into ours from the right; and so too roads suddenly sheered off to the right, some running level but others climbing onto structures that swung each road around in mid-air so that it crossed overhead, though the cars on it had a moment before been racing pell-mell in front of our own. Now they passed across in mid-air, their headlights still flinging light on the tar and the concrete. On the other side of the road, as in a mirror where everything was reversed, cars that had been coming with their lights toward us now crossed from left to right above our heads. The sensation was that not the cars but the roads themselves were moving, like giant escalators, ferrying hundreds of cars at a time, fast, fast, fast.

We have been some two months in California now; but the biggest single impression is still of that road.

I have been up and down it now a few times, and have seen the shabbiness that the thousand neon signs hid from us the first time we drove down it.

Then it was as if every motel or drive-in we passed was a place of light, bloated and palatial under the signs that stared and glared and gave each one of them a different name in letters three feet high. By daylight some of these places were not much better than shabby wooden lean-tos, or shabby brick-fronted buildings, or else cheap, jerry-built places vaguely Spanish in intention, with their plaster and arches and red-tiled roofs. None looks like its neighbors; they share no style, no size, they have no relation to one another but that imposed on them by the single thing they do share: a frontage on the road, a view of the traffic, a gaze across to the other side of the road where there are other motels, drive-ins, used-car lots, gas stations, other giant billboards, and other names—The Crown, Crazy Jack's, Ole Olsen's, Top-T Service, and a supermarket spaciously spelling out its name by a single letter in each of its stucco arches.

Even the shabbiest of them by daylight is resplendent with its colored lights by night. They sprawl wide, wide, drunkenly down the road, because each has to have sufficient parking space for the cars that it hopes will swing off the road, attracted for some reason to this drive-in rather than the fifty others in the last few miles, this supermarket rather than the last. Perhaps because in front of this one someone has advertised in huge black plastic letters on a white illuminated background "Celery 10 cents a stick." How can anyone go to so much trouble to sell even twenty or two hundred sticks of celery, one wonders, but one can wonder about nothing very long on this road, for in front of one a car is mounted on a platform twenty feet high, and slowly the whole platform turns around, bearing the car on its palm.

Below it and stretching away from it are other cars, acres of cars glittering in the open used-car lots; and then there is a service station, a motel, with all its little gabled, little Swiss chalets in a row, a second-hand furniture mart, a liquor store, more used-car lots. How to tell which of all the cars in ranks on the sand belongs to one lot and not to another I don't know, for there are no spaces between them; but there are names on poles, names on billboards, names as high as the little offices that bear them, and each name is different.

Beyond the lots rises the grandeur of a new shopping center. This looks something like the Palais de Chaillot in Paris. It is white; it gleams; it flings its arms open as if about to embrace not a terraced garden but a plain of parked cars as great as that first one we saw in front of the airport. These shopping centers are things we have never seen before—places that under a single sprawling roof house enough shops to supply the wants of a town. This one looks like the Palais de Chaillot; the next one is quaint, rural, timbered, with flagged walks, low buildings with overhanging eaves, at every corner a loudspeaker playing soft music.

And so the road goes away, all the signs and buildings, and the other roads that leap over it—giant-sized, like the cars that rush along it at all hours. To the one side it goes for all I know to Los Angeles, hundreds of miles to the south; on the other side the road comes to San Francisco, where the six and eight lanes of traffic are flung into swathes of tar and concrete that fill the sky in loops and curves dwarfing even the city beneath them as one approaches it. There the roofs of the cars, curved like the wing cases of beetles, flash above the concrete parapets in a hundred different colors; there are no shops there, no billboards; there are no people, and nowhere for people to walk but a kind of narrow catwalk along the side of the parapet where a man can clamber to the emergency telephones if his car breaks down. There, where there is no place for a man outside his moving car, the road reaches its purest, most abstracted state—it can be used for nothing but to carry cars from one end of its giant structures to the other. Its colors are black and gray; from afar it is desolate and beautiful, but unlike a natural desert it has no peace.

I am writing this some thirty miles away from those structures, outside San Francisco in a town attached to the road. In this case, the town seems to be the no man's land, not the road. Except for a house to live in, that road along its length is able to provide you with any material thing you might ever need. There are banks, travel agencies, money-lenders; real-estate agents who will sell you a house and furniture stores that will sell you the furniture to fill it with; there are bookstores and shops selling the latest selection of records; there are elegant little establishments that offer you tropical fish in bowls; there are at least three or four hospitals for dogs. But the curious, the frightening thing is that no one lives on the road; all these shops and facilities belong only to the road, and to no city. Nowhere along its length does the road contract, confine itself, center itself for a community around it. There are no parks, no statues, no plaques commemorating notable events; there are no vistas, no views, no streets that radiate from this point or that; no steps leading to public buildings. The road runs with all its businesses from San Francisco to here and beyond, and it is as if some kind of vital tendon has been severed, so that it can grasp nothing to itself, can enclose nothing in itself, can make no order of itself, but can only lie sprawling, incoherent, centerless, viewless, shapeless, faceless—offering all the products a community can need and yet making the establishment of a community impossible.

It is by that road and from that road that this town lives. Every morning half of its male inhabitants seem to get into their cars and go thundering to San Francisco along it, and every evening they come thundering back again; the women drive along it to do their shopping; the very air of the town is filled day and night with the whisper of the traffic along the road, and there has never been anything else. The road doesn't seem to have superseded something older and perhaps pleasanter, something that would in any case have forced the road to deviate, to have some respect for what had been there before it came. Or if the highway did supersede something else, it did it so completely that now the highway seems coterminous with the towns set back from it and the townsfolk who do their shopping along it. They weren't here before the road, waiting for it; they came with the road as it ran from San Francisco, and built their indistinguishable, dependent, flat little towns. The highway being what it is, these towns seem nothing but appendages to it—equal parts of a brand-new nameless sprawl.

We hadn't been here for more than two days before it became obvious that we simply couldn't manage without a car. It wasn't a luxury here but a necessity; we had lived for three years in England without a car, but California was clearly different. When everyone has a car, everything is built on the supposition that everyone has a car. For the pedestrian the distances are defeating, and the public transport is bad. Because everyone has a car, the busses run rarely, and because the busses run rarely, everyone buys a car. The man without a car is caught in the middle of this circle, from which point he is able to watch what busses there are going at infrequent and indeterminate intervals along routes that only the bus drivers seem to know about. These busses never have more than three or four passengers, and the driver's air of boredom and disbelief in his own occupation can be seen from a distance of many yards.

Clearly we had to have a car. Everyone said so too. "You can't manage without a car here," they said. "You can pick one up cheaply, you know." They made it sound so easy I was ashamed to admit that I didn't know how one actually went about buying a car. People always underestimate the helplessness of the bewildered newcomer, who finds it difficult enough to walk to his temporary lodgings from three blocks away, let alone do anything as hazardous as driving the distance. And I wanted a cheap car, a really cheap car. I had thought of something in the neighborhood of a hundred dollars, but when I said this they frowned; they said that you had to be careful if you went down that low (there was all the more reason to be careful if you went any higher, I couldn't help thinking); they said—and here my heart sank into my boots—that at that price it was purely a matter of luck. Luck, I have a feeling—that sort of luck, the luck purely of the draw—has never been mine. I felt this acutely when my requests for the name of a reasonably honest used-car dealer were met with such humorous remarks as "Now you're asking for something!"

What I was secretly asking for was someone who "knew about cars" to lead me to one particular car among the several thousand cars on display in the open nearby. There was no way I could distinguish one lot from another, and they all looked like circuses to me.

Suspended over the rows of cars in every lot there were rows of multi-colored plastic whirligigs that spin around when the wind blows. There were strings of streamers as if royalty were soon to pass by. There were neon signs, banners, chalked-up signs, and painted signs promising the prospective buyer easy credit or a radio in every car. There were also the cars themselves. They were all the circus anyone could want. They were swollen, puffed-up monsters of cars, shining in all colors; inside they were like rooms, with their lounge seats and their radios and their heaters and their color schemes; their steering wheels looked as though they had been made out of ivory and whalebone and jade and pewter and other semi-precious substances: their dashboards looked like the things that jazz bands play in front of on the films. And they all looked factory-new to me. It had been nearly four years since I was in a country where American cars were in free supply, so the styles of the last four years were all equally new to me; and there were so many of them—so many styles, so many colors, so many cars, thousands upon thousands of them parked bumper to bumper in great rows, platoons, phalanxes, armies of gleaming and curved metal and glass. "Clean!" the signs shouted. Clean? These cars positively shone, they glittered; why tell me that they were clean?

This was no way to buy a car, but things moved as they always did, and the fifth morning after our arrival in California I went with a friend who knew no more about cars than I did to inspect a two-hundred-dollar car that it had been arranged I was to see. Mr. Dickson, we had been told, was expecting us, and we drove down the highway to him.

We found him in a wooden shack behind a phalanx of cars, under the usual bits of bunting and rows of whirligigs. Mr. Dickson was dressed in a lightweight suit that shone like some kind of metal; he had a tall, thin frame, the anxious, lined face of a victim of dyspepsia, and the tanned skin of an outdoor man. He was eager to please. He shook hands, and "It sure is hot," and guffawed suddenly, a surprisingly deep sound that matched neither his frame, his restless eyes, nor the smile through which the sound was uttered. He took us across the sand between the cars to the purple one we had come to see. "She doesn't *look* so good," he admitted, "but that poke on the door doesn't mean a thing. Look, it opens, it closes." He guffawed again. "If it wasn't for that poke in the ribs there we'd be asking three hundred for her. But that doesn't mean she can't run. Get in, try her, look around, take your time, make up your mind." His patter was exhausted; he attempted to revive himself with the deepest and most sepulchral guffaw we had yet heard from him. He failed, and withdrew with a kind of listless tact to one side, leaving us to look around.

Tact was called for, for neither of us had much idea of what we should look for. I opened the hood and we both stared inside, and then I closed the hood. We opened and closed all the doors. We switched on the lights and switched them off again. We started the car and drove it around the lot; we revved the engine; we brought it back to where Mr. Dickson stood listlessly on the sand, his lean figure casting a lean shadow in front of him, and I saw at least how he got his tan.

We were back later that afternoon—my feeling about that highway was such that I was almost surprised we had managed to find the place again, that it was still there, that Mr. Dickson was still there, that Mr. Dickson recognized us, and that we recognized him. When I had signed the bill of sale, Mr. Dickson took it from me and looked carefully at the signature. "You won't regret it," he said. "You've bought a good car, Don."

Friends in England had written asking, "What's it *like* in California?" Until a used-car salesman in a lot somewhere along that highway has called you by what he imagines is your first name, you have no idea *what* California is like.

What the newcomer catches glimpses of here is a country of unimaginable size, to all appearances related only nominally to what past it has, peopled by millions of immigrants or the near descendants of immigrants, held together and apart by sprawling highways of frightening dimensions. Sooner or later he asks, "How does it keep together? Why doesn't it fall apart?" If the asking of such a question is one of the privileges of a newcomer, so too perhaps is having a guess at some small part of the answer.

I think anyone who comes to both England and America as a visitor cannot but be immediately struck by how much less he seems to have learned of contemporary America from the classic American novelists than he has learned about contemporary England from the English authors. Half the fun of living in England, one sometimes feels, is just that delighted confirmation of the expectations one has derived from literature. Dickens and George Eliot and even Jane Austen still seem to have far more to do with the England of today than, say, Hawthorne with anything in this particular part of America. Indeed, Hawthorne, or Melville, or James has so little to do with anything one can immediately see that the expectation that any one of them might do so begins to look naïve in the extreme.

California, after all, is almost as far from New England as England itself is; and Melville wrote mostly about the sea or the Marquesas, anyway—these are the things one begins to tell oneself in tones of reproof. But while it is true that California is a long way from New England, they are both, surely, American; and if they are both American, why shouldn't one expect Hawthorne to tell one something about California? There is after all a continuity of a particular kind that even the mountainous facts of geography and history have not broken—and the suspicion that one has learned nothing about modern California by reading the classic American authors is un- founded. There is a persistence, though unlike the English persistence it has little physical about it, and is not to be found directly in matters of appear- ance, ways of speech, or overt social relationships. This continuity or persistence, it seems to me, may most simply be described as the self-consciousness of Americans about being Americans.

It is obviously not a simple matter, no matter how simply a two months' residence encourages one to describe it. And an outsider is probably more aware of this self-consciousness than he should be, and tempted to read more into it than he should, for people always explain themselves to an outsider much more than they do among themselves. Yet I am continually being surprised by how very much the Americans do it—and not only to outsiders but to each other. The English, one might say exaggeratedly, have the air of always being faintly surprised and amused that there are any people in the world who are not English; the Americans, on the other hand, seem always a little surprised that they are Americans. Or if not surprised, at least they believe that there is something so special in being Americans as to demand exhortations to each other on the subject. In fact, there seems to be a positive campaign about America that actively and continually engages the institutions of government, the schools, assorted public bodies, and all the media of communication; this is the simplest and most popular expression of what operates as busily on many other levels of sophistication.

The self-consciousness that in the books of James and Hawthorne and Cooper takes the form of a debate between a postulated "America" and a postulated "Europe" is hardly the same thing as that which at election time sends out the Boy Scouts with placards shaped like the Liberty Bell urging people to vote because it is the American thing to do, or that which prompts the marshaling of six-year-olds to salute the American flag at school every morning; but there is a connection between them, and it is not a tenuous one.

To put it no higher, this American self-consciousness has important work to do. The Americans are talking themselves into a relationship with one another and with what is around them; they are continually giving themselves a common name; they are continually, determinedly becoming Americans. They take neither themselves nor their country for granted, and it is precisely in this tension that they seem to know their identity as Americans.

Intimately related to this—and indeed a part of it—is another feature of American life which is easily noted and which has been remarked on often before: friendliness. To one who drives down the highway for the first time, it seems that here in California there are no neighborhoods, no communities, no possibility of the development of a sense of mere distinctive localness—let alone the associated virtues of neighborliness, parochial interest, and local pride. Yet never have I been in a country where so high a value was put on sheer friendliness. In exactly the same measure that conditions seem to make it impossible, the Americans *are* good neighbors, *are* community-minded, *do* busy themselves with good works locally, *do* hail by their first names their neighbors of a few weeks' standing, *are* friendly to one another and to strangers.

It almost seems that America is a vast, deliberate exercise of the will. There is something frightening in the thought, for we have the belief that the will never acts but against its own counterimage, and that the more forcefully it is exerted the less secure is the equilibrium it has imposed.

One begins to suspect that if these people weren't so deliberately exerting themselves to be "good" and friendly Americans, there'd be nothing to stop California from declaring war on Oregon, people ramming their cars into one another all over the highways, the radio announcers screaming obscenities over the air, and the whole thing going up in a smash of asphalt, concrete, shining metal, toppling TV aerials, and broken packages of frozen foods.

Yet the fact that the fantasy presents itself in this form shows exactly how much of a fantasy it is. Not that American society is without its own tensions, which could become critical, like those of any other society; but rather that the use of the word "will" in this connection—despite its attractions—is misleading. Perhaps one should confine oneself to saying that the American need to be explicit about social aims and relationships seems at this time, here in California, an attempt to deal with the central problem of community in a mass society. There have been worse attempts to solve that problem.

DISCUSSION AND WRITING

1. Define or explain: *terrain, palatial, resplendent, chalet, swathe, parapet, commemorate, vista, supersede, coterminous, appendage, indeterminate, phalanx, sepulchral, reproof, exhortation, tenuous, parochial, equilibrium, explicit.*

2. Cite examples of graphic, closely observed detail. Study the role of specific, accurate words and of figurative language. Point out features that give life and movement to the author's account, that make the description dynamic rather than static.

3. In one paragraph each, summarize the author's account of three essential qualities that he ascribes to the American scene or the American national character.

4. Examine the full implications of the concluding sentence of the article. Show why it can be taken as an example of understatement—the deliberate avoidance of the sensational or the overdramatized. Examine the tone of the article as a whole, looking for understatement, irony, humor. What picture of the author's personality does the tone of this article convey to the reader?

5. Outline the essay. Show in detail how the author uses his first impression to unify the article.

6. Do you consider Mr. Jacobson's article objective or subjective, fair or unfair, friendly or unfriendly toward things American? Concentrate on one major aspect of his account, and cite detailed evidence in support of your answer.

7. Describe your impressions on first coming to a new town, a new state, or a new country. Concentrate on observation of specific, concrete detail. Work toward a unified over-all impression.

8. Using Jacobson's portrait of the car dealer as a model, describe the external appearance and behavior of some unusual person whom you have observed closely.

9. As used by some people, the very word *foreigner* carries overtones of suspicion and hostility. To judge from the attitudes and behavior of people you know well, how hostile or receptive are present-day Americans to people from foreign countries? Make use of statements, incidents, and the like from your own experience.

10. How often are we expected to do something "because it is the American thing to do"? How do you respond to such expectations—automatically, reluctantly, enthusiastically, not at all? Limit yourself to one major area and use detailed illustrations.

FURTHER READING

Have you ever had a chance to compare your impression of a region or of a way of life with the picture someone would have of it who knew it only through books? For instance, would you have any real-life experience to compare with the picture of the Pacific Northwest in the tales of Jack London; the world of industrial labor in the books of Upton Sinclair; the portrait of the American Indian in the books of James Fenimore Cooper; the American funeral industry as satirized by Evelyn Waugh in *The Loved One;* life in a big-city slum as depicted by James Farrell in books like *Studs Lonigan?* Discuss a book whose setting, characters, or atmosphere you can compare and contrast with relevant first-hand experience.

V. S. PRITCHETT

The following selection was first printed in the *New Statesman*, which is—along with the *Economist*, the *Spectator*, and the *Manchester Guardian* —a leading British weekly magazine of comment and opinion. The article illustrates the kind of impression the educated European reader might get of the United States—if he is lucky enough to rely on observers as thoughtful and experienced as the author of this essay. V. S. Pritchett, director of the *New Statesman*, has had a distinguished career as a journalist and a critic of literature. He is a seasoned traveler who served for many years as a special correspondent from various countries of Europe. He has taught at Princeton and at the University of California. His impressions are those not of a casual visitor but of someone who has lived and worked in the country he describes. His style is that of a writer not merely collecting random notes but working many details into a purposeful pattern. This article was first published in August 1963.

Striverstown

East of Fifth Avenue at 96th Street is New York's Berlin Wall. In one block one steps north from the moneyed quiet of the Upper East Side, the Belgravia and Mayfair of the city, and from the crest of the small hill at Park Avenue or Madison one looks down on the vale of Harlem, jumping in the pure flame of the August heat or sunk like a mud flat in the intolerable damp days of hot cloud. For the first time in New York one sees expanses of sky; no skyscrapers slice it into strips; for the first time the city looks spacious. Even the phalanxes of newish, high red-brick apartment blocks that stand for a mile or more between the littered streets and proletarian playgrounds along Madison, rising like fortifications and model prisons, have broad sky between them. At the Park Avenue hill the railway tracks shoot out from under the flower-beds of the respectable quarters, and the miles of blatant steel blind the eye, as they cut their way through the rusting fire-escapes of the tenements. Forbidden country. Most of my American friends said:"Don't go there now. There is too much tension. And it is worse in the heat." Just as they tell you not to go in Central Park at night. My European friends, not having the built-in American instinct for drama, said "All nonsense".

The European who crosses 96th Street at once feels at home. The foreignness does it—we are all foreigners in Europe—and also the liveliness of the streets. Activity is the principle of white New York; living is the business of Harlem. Strictly one is not immediately in Harlem but in Puerto Rico. The coffee faces at the crowded slum windows, the huge family groups sitting thin-legged and tattered on doorsteps, the men playing dominoes on the pavements, the barber who looks like a large fly in his grubby shop, shout Spanish. The ads on the walls are Spanish; South American music prances out of doorways. And no one can keep his fingers still. Half-asleep at the door the old man or the young drums on a tin or on his knee. The empty hours of life are filled with drum taps on imaginary drums. In the corner of a playground where youths are playing baseball, four others are huddled secretively in a corner over a man who actually has a real drum and deftly palms and knuckles it. They are so close to one another that their faces nearly touch, their eyes glance at one another recording exquisite recognitions as they listen. Nearby someone fields the ball in the game and as he does so two or three of those drum notes catch his ear. He throws the ball in and then turns and buckles his knees into a grotesque dance that seizes him

From the *New Statesman* for August 16, 1963. Reprinted by permission of the *New Statesman*.

like some unavoidable locomotor ataxia. Under the arches at Park Avenue one arrives in the middle of the raucous Puerto Rican market. A madman goes screaming through the crowd of women who are tearing at cotton dresses on the stalls: *"Cristo vivo; muerto No!"* he shouts. No one notices him.

There are Italian, even Spanish and Jewish Harlems—the big shops on 125th Street are Jewish and there is anti-semitism among the Negroes— "They take their money out of the community"—speaking as if Harlem were a nation; but so do many rich negroes. The place is money-minded and has its class system. 125th Street is the Main Street of Negro Harlem. Few white faces, but every kind of Negro face; no one stares. Suddenly blackness becomes your norm; you begin to feel the furnace heat has burned your face off and that you too are black. In a quarter of an hour you do not notice colour at all. You notice individuals, whereas in the rest of the city people look the same. You notice gait and stance, for some Negroes walk superbly and stand in a manner that suggests standing is an art in itself. They are people in their pride, not going anywhere, but hanging about, forever restless on their feet, skipping along, circling, idle. Children play round your legs. An audience on every fire-escape is part of the show in the street below. Every other shop is blaring out radio tunes; in every doorway, arguments, small dramas. Transistors everywhere. A Cadillac full of men and girls crawls by; they are all laughing. In a way the adults seem to be at play, like the children racing round the playgrounds. A white taxi-driver who dropped me at 135th Street one day said angrily "I haven't got anything against them but they're not regular people" and said he wanted to head for the East Side Highway and "get out of it." One sees his point; he had seen not colour but poverty, unemployment, low wages, the poorly fed; he was afraid and he had cringed before gaiety.

The unpleasant sight is the white cops. They stand in pairs, flexing their arms, twirling their batons as if getting ready for a crack, talking to each other but to no one else—and, by Harlem standards, overfed. The well-fed are policing those who do not feed so well. One recognises them too, not by colour, but by the innate stillness of bullies. James Baldwin, who has said something like this, does not exaggerate. The cops know how they are hated. They have their troubles. For there *is* that mysterious thing called tension. One night when the heat sat on one's chest like an elephant, I went up to 125th Street and, at various places, someone had turned on the fire-hydrants which were spouting water onto the cars and buses. At one corner several hundred Negroes were sitting on doorsteps, looking out of windows, grinning with happiness at a lonely cop who was trying to turn the water off. He failed. Three hours later buses were still being soaked. At the terminal when I got on the bus a Negro girl got on too, but got off at once when she saw the driver closing the windows and mopping his seat. One saw a moment of fear which the Negro easily conveys by his quick eyes, quickly covered by politeness. She got off. She smelt trouble. She said nervously:"I'll wait for my husband."

There is a group of Negro writers called the Harlem Writers Workshop. The organiser, John H. Clarke, edits a monthly review called *Freedomways,* which had just produced an interesting Harlem number. He invited me to a writers' meeting in one of the huge apartment forts for middle-income people. They are modern; and once you are out of the lift into the long corridors where people are slotted, the noise of television is violent. The walls are thin and there is no air-conditioning. About 16 of us sat sweating in a pretty book-lined room, talking about Rhodesia, Kenya, South Africa and Notting Hill Gate. One or two of the writers had been published in England and asked whether the English boom in the Negro novel was over. They suspected it was. They knew the race question was an economic one: lower wages than white people, higher rents, poor schools kept poor—the Negro is the permanent, sweated immigrant. But the mood of the group was dangerously elated."This year everything will be settled," they insisted (except the judicious Mr. Clarke who comes from Alabama and does not think things are going to be as simple as that: *Freedomways* is warning them that their struggle will be long)."Or else," shouted one laughing young man who hopped to his feet and danced about shooting an imaginary gun like a child playing cops and robbers. Everyone laughed at him but no one approved. Black Muslim racism, the notion of the Negro state and the return to Africa are rejected—otherwise their diagnosis is considered acceptable. They are the best-organised Negro group.

The Workshop included John O'Killens whose novels *Young Blood* and *And Then We Heard the Thunder* have been published in this country, a dramatist and an established Jamaican writer; and the tendency is broadly one of commitment to the Negroes' social struggle. They are not by any means the only Harlem writers. Ralph Ellison is aloof from them—he lives just outside Harlem in an apartment looking down on the Hudson and he believes a writer needs a discipline more exacting than loyalty to a racial group and that there is more to Negro humanity than can be seen by limiting it to its political and social situation. In the present excitement the view is unfashionable, but Ellison is the most impressive Negro writer I have met.

Harlem is a city in itself and contains all that a city has. It has a third of New York's million Negroes; it is the capital of the race. It has its rich, its middling people, its sedate streets where the well-off professional people live, its fantastic property speculators, its money-making churches run like businesses—like a good many church organizations in white New York. The churches bought real estate to house their congregations. Differences between white and black do not touch the fundamental American traits: there is chiefly the grim difference of status. And then, the Negro has escaped standardisation by living below the surface of American life. The Negro is proud to have moved into what, 60 years ago, was a comfortable white suburb, against all the opposition and chicanery of the established. Grave, academically inclined Mr. Clarke took me to see the vast Schomberg collection of books on Africa and the African Negro in the public library where students were working late. It has a fine bust of the first Negro actor to play Othello. There are a couple of blocks on Seventh Avenue which are historic for the Harlem Negro. They are the first property bought by a group who slaved to pay off the high-rate mortgages. These heroes of the ethnic property war—which has been basic in New York life in every generation, as one national group pushes another out, in pursuit of the thoroughly American desire for self-improvement—were known by the formidable moral name of The Strivers. The street is called Strivers' Row and is one of the most sedate in the whole city and has some of the best brownstones—the top status symbol of all.

The small bookshops of Harlem, stacked in disorderly fashion from floor to ceiling with new and second-hand books, are centres of local agitation. They have a natural connection with the street-corner meeting outside where the speakers range from the cranks and peculiars to the serious politicians. Go into a shop and in two minutes you are asked for your views on Rhodesia and Kenya; all the sensational and serious literature of the Negro revolt in the whole world is there. The Negro loves talk. There is always a group, perhaps behind a curtain or a door, talking politics. One might be among pre-revolutionary Russian exiles, but without Marx. "A white communist is a liar," someone said, "and a black one is a fool." In one shop you see the painted banners that are carried in protest meetings—lurid pictures of police dogs jumping at the throats of children in Birmingham or comic drawings of Southern Gentlemen.

The word is everything in Harlem. The long word or the book word beautifully uttered by the man driving his cab or talking in his shop; the rambling or the inciting word of the street meeting; the Biblical or inflaming word of the unctuous ranting preacher. These people have the gift of tongues which is scarcer among American whites; indeed conversation is commoner there than in white New York. On Sunday mornings in Harlem the word rules. Roars as of murder come from upper rooms over the cleaner's or the grocer's: it is a preacher in a one-room chapel screaming the name of Jesus, in paroxysms about Emmanuel. I found myself one wet Sunday at the notorious Abyssinian Baptist church which has a sweet-machine and a Credit Funeral Office in its entrance, swinging hand in hand with my two neighbours, singing "Down by the Riverside." Their hats were like gardens. They put the Communion crumb neatly on a little handkerchief on their knees. They drank the cocktail glass of red liquid which tasted of vaseline and red currant. And several women in the congregation screamed "Emmanuel" and "Oh, Jesus" and fell into convulsions. Groans came from the men. Sobs and sighs from the quieter women. And when we came to sing "Nobody Knows the Trouble I've Seen," chorus after chorus, the emotion did not seem too much and expressed something fundamental about the race, its loneliness and suffering. I don't know how many men and women I shook hands with at the end; no one *seemed* to notice that I was the only white person in the church. But I bet they did.

DISCUSSION AND WRITING

1. Define or explain the following terms, paying attention not only to their meanings but also to their history and typical uses. Point out their implications as used in this essay: *phalanx, proletarian, blatant, exquisite, grotesque, raucous, innate, judicious, sedate, chicanery, ethnic, lurid, unctuous, rant, paroxysm.*

2. Examine the author's use of specific, graphic words. For instance, the man with the drum does not simply beat it; he "deftly *palms* and *knuckles* it." Cite other examples and examine their effect.

3. Examine the author's use of figurative language, paying special attention to how it helps create mood or convey attitude. For instance, what impression is created, and how, by the sentence "South American music *prances* out of doorways"? Select and discuss other examples.

4. This essay is exceptionally rich in detail that enables the reader to see, hear, and feel with the author. Examine closely the kind of detail that the author selects to help him establish key characteristics of what he describes.

5. State in your own words the major parallels and contrasts that the author traces between life in Harlem and in "white" New York.

6. Describe in detail the structure of a paragraph that illustrates the author's ability to unify a paragraph around a key idea, developed by detailed examples. Does the essay as a whole have a key idea or dominant theme that would help tie together its wealth of detail?

7. Our observations are often channeled, or even distorted, by prior expectations and established attitudes. What interests, sympathies, or biases does Mr. Pritchett reveal? How do these steer his observations and reactions into channels different from those of some other observer—for instance, the taxi driver mentioned in the essay? Use detailed evidence.

8. Select *one* of the author's generalizations that you are in a position to challenge, modify, or support. Test it against your own experience and observation, comparing and contrasting your own point of view with that of the author.

9. The "white liberal" is often accused by conservatives of being uncritically favorable to Negroes; he is often accused by militant Negroes of being a fair-weather friend who lacks a true understanding of and commitment to the Negro's cause. Can you define a responsible position that would not be open to such charges?

10. Using this essay as a model, record your observations of a living area inhabited predominantly by an ethnic or racial group different from your own. Focus on a few major points, relating them insofar as possible to a dominant over-all impression.

FURTHER READING

Go through several issues of one of the following: the *New Statesman*, the *Economist*, the *Spectator*, the *Manchester Guardian*, the English-language edition of the French weekly *Réalités*. Find accounts by foreign observers of travel or study in the United States. As a group, how objective or how biased are they? Would you call them "anti-American," or "pro-American," or neither?

2

The Search for Identity

*One writes out of one thing only—one's own experience.
Everything depends on how relentlessly one forces from this
experience the last drop, sweet or bitter, it can possibly
give.* JAMES BALDWIN

Autobiography tests a writer's ability to come to terms with his
own experience. To some writers, autobiography merely provides
an excuse for meandering, self-indulgent personal reminiscence.
Other writers, however, seriously confront the question of who
they are and how they have become what they seem to be. The
essays in this group deal with personal experience; at the same
time, they have general social or historical significance. Lois
Phillips Hudson, in "Children of the Harvest," writes about
herself as a child, growing up in times of hardship and depriva-
tion yet eagerly open to new experience, catching her first
glimpse of the tensions and divisions of the adult world. James
Baldwin, in "Notes of a Native Son," traces his progress from
adolescent rebellion to adult understanding and acceptance, made
the more difficult by the American Negro's constant temptation
to let bitterness turn into mere destructive hatred. Benjamin
Franklin—like other early Americans, a figure familiar to all and
known by few—makes us see in accounts of childhood and
adolescence the early clues to characteristic traits of the adult's
personality. Sir Winston Churchill, in a selection from an early
autobiographical volume, takes us beyond schoolbook stereotypes
of the great man by looking at his student days with disarming
frankness and an engaging sense of humor.

LOIS PHILLIPS HUDSON

The formative years of many American authors now well known were those of the Great Depression. In the early thirties parents saw relentless economic pressure deprive them of the fruits of their work. College graduates received their diplomas and joined the queues of unemployed. The oratory of boosters sounded hollow, and people began to look for drastic remedies. Lois Phillips Hudson (born 1927) has published a number of autobiographical sketches about her childhood in the Middle West, where the economic depression compounded the ills of farming areas that years of drought were turning into a dust bowl. Her novel of the Midwest in the thirties, *The Bones of Plenty,* was published in 1962. The following article, first published in *The Reporter,* is an outstanding example of an author's honest stock-taking of her own experience, with an uncanny command of graphic detail and authentic incident.

Children of the Harvest

On a suffocating summer day in 1937, the thirteenth year of drought and the seventh year of depression, with our mouths, nostrils, and eyes full of the dust blowing from our bare fields, my family sold to our neighbors at auction most of the accoutrements of our existence. Then we loaded what was left into a trailer my father had made and drove West to find water and survival on the Washington coast.

During the auction the two classmates with whom I had just finished the fourth grade hung about the desultory bidders giving me looks of respect and undisguised envy. They envied me not so much for the things they could imagine as for the things they couldn't—the unimaginable distance I was going and the unimaginable things along it and at the end of it.

How could any of us have imagined an end to the prairie's limitless sky and the giddy encroachments rising higher and higher against that sky that were the Rocky Mountains? How could we have imagined how in burning summer the forested profiles of the Cascades could echo everywhere the shouts of white falls above us and green rivers below? Who could have

From *The Reporter,* October 16, 1958. Copyright © 1958 by the Reporter Magazine Company. Reprinted by permission of the publisher and the author.

imagined, once confronted with their gray expanse, that the waters of Puget Sound were not actually the Pacific, but only a minute stray squiggle of it? Who, finally, could have imagined that there were so many people in the world or that the world could offer them so hospitable a habitation?

There were so many things I could scarcely believe even when I was doing them or looking at them or eating them. We lived in a cabin on an island for a few weeks after we arrived, and it always seemed impossible to me that we could be surrounded by so much water. I spent every moment of the hour-long ferry trip from the mainland hanging over the rail gazing down at the exhilarating wake of my first boat ride. The island was exactly what any island should be—lavish green acres covered with woods and orchards and fields of berries, ringed by glistening sandy beaches richly stocked with driftwood. Once in North Dakota my aunt had brought a very small basket of black cherries to my grandfather's house, and I had made the four or five that were my share last all afternoon. I would take tiny bites of each cherry, then suck the pit and roll it around with my tongue to get the faint remaining taste, till it came out as clean and smooth as a brook-bottom pebble. But on the island I would climb into the trees with my five-year-old sister and have contests with her, seeing which of us could get the most cherries in our mouths at once. Then we would shoot the wet pits, no longer hungrily scoured of their slipperiness, at each other and at the robins who perched above us. Sometimes I would go into the fields with my mother and father and spend an hour helping pick raspberries or blackberries or loganberries or any of the other things they worked in, but there were really only two important things to do—play on the beaches and eat fruit.

It didn't occur to me that things would ever be different again, but one day early in August the last berry was picked and we took the ferry into Seattle, where we bought a big brown tent and a gas stove. We added them to our trailer load and drove back over the green-and-white Cascades, beneath the glacial sunrise face of Mount Rainier, and down into the sweaty outdoor factory that is the Yakima Valley. There the Yakima River is bled for transfusions to the millions of rows of roots, its depleted currents finally dragging themselves muddily to their relieved merger with the undiminishable Columbia. One can follow the Yakima for miles and miles and see nothing but irrigated fields and orchards—and the gaunt camps of transient laborers.

The workers come like a horde of salvaging locusts, stripping a field, moving to the next, filling their boxes or crates or sacks, weighing in, collecting the bonuses offered to entice them to stay till the end of the season, and disappearing again. They spend their repetitive days in rows of things to be picked and their sweltering nights in rows of tents and trailers. We pitched our tent beside the others, far from our pleasant island where the owners of the fields were neighbors who invited my sister and me among their cherry trees. Here the sauntering owners and their bristling foremen never smiled at those children who ran through the fields playing games and only occasionally at those who worked beside their parents.

In North Dakota I had worked on our farm—trampling hay, driving a team of horses, fetching cows, feeding calves and chickens—but of course that had all been only my duty as a member of the family, not a way to earn money. Now I was surrounded by grown-ups who wanted to pay me for working, and by children my own age who were stepping up to the pay window every night with weighing tags in their hands and collecting money. I saw that the time had come for me to assume a place of adult independence in the world.

I made up my mind I was going to earn a dollar all in one day. We were picking hops then, and of all the rows I have toiled my way up and down, I remember hop rows the most vividly. Trained up on their wires fifteen feet overhead, the giant vines resemble monster grape arbors hung with bunches of weird unripe fruit. A man who does not pick things for a living comes and cuts them down with a knife tied to a ten-foot pole so the people below can strip them off into sacks. Hops don't really look like any other growing thing but instead like something artificially constructed—pine cones, perhaps, with segments cleverly cut from the soft, limp, clinging leaves that lie next to the kernels of an ear of corn. A hop in your hand is like a feather, and it will almost float on a puff of air. Hops are good only for making yeast, so you can't even get healthily sick of them by eating them all day long, the way you can berries or peas.

Pickers are paid by the pound, and picking is a messy business. Sometimes you run into a whole cluster that is gummy with the honeydew of hop aphids, and gray and musty with the mildew growing on the sticky stuff. Tiny red spiders rush from the green petals and flow up your arms, like more of the spots the heat makes you see.

The professionals could earn up to six dollars a day. One toothless grandmother discouraged us all by making as much as anybody in the row and at the same time never getting out of her rocking chair except to drag it behind her from vine to vine. My father and mother each made over three dollars a day, but though I tried to work almost as long hours as they did, my pay at the end of the day would usually be somewhere between eighty and ninety cents.

Then one day in the second week of picking, when the hops were good and I stayed grimly sweating over my long gray sack hung on a child-sized frame, I knew that this was going to be the day. As the afternoon waned and I added the figures on my weight tags over and over again in my head, I could feel the excitement begin making spasms in my stomach. That night the man at the pay window handed me a silver dollar and three pennies. He must have seen that this was a day not for paper but for silver. The big coin, so neatly and brightly stamped, was coolly distant from the blurred mélange of piled vines and melting heat that had put it into my hand. Only its solid heaviness connected it in a businesslike way with the work it represented. For the first time in my life I truly comprehended the relationship between toil and media of exchange, and I saw how exacting and yet how satisfying were the terms of the world. Perhaps because of this insight, I did not want the significance of my dollar dimmed by the common touch of copper pettiness. I gave the vulgar pennies to my little sister, who was amazed but grateful. Then I felt even more grown-up than before, because not everybody my age was in a position to give pennies to kids.

That night I hardly slept, lying uncovered beside my sister on our mattress on the ground, sticking my hand out under the bottom of the tent to lay it on the cooling earth between the clumps of dry grass. Tired as I was, I had written post cards to three people in North Dakota before going to bed. I had told my grandmother, my aunt, and my friend Doris that I had earned a dollar in one day. Then, because I did not want to sound impolitely proud of myself, and to fill up the card, I added on each one, "I'm fine and I plan to pick again tomorrow. How are you?"

I couldn't wait to get to the field the next day and earn another dollar. Back home none of my friends would have dreamed of being able to earn so much in one day. The only thing to do back there for money was to trap gophers for the bounty; and even the big kids, who ran a fairly long trap line and had the nerve to cut the longest tails in half, couldn't make more than twenty cents on a good day, with tails at two cents apiece. I earned a dollar and forty cents the next day and the day after that, and at least a dollar every day for another week until we moved to another place of picking—a pear orchard.

By that time it was September, and most of us children from the rows of tents stood out at the gateway of the camp and waited each day for the long yellow school bus. I had never seen a school bus before, and my sister and I were shy about how to act in such a grand vehicle. We sat together, holding our lunch buckets on our knees, looking out at the trees beside the roads, trying to catch a glimpse of our mother and father on the ladders.

The school had about three times as many pupils in it as there were people in the town back in North Dakota where we used to buy coal and groceries. The pupils who were planning to attend this school all year were separated from those who, like me, did not know how many days or weeks we would be in that one spot. In our special classes we did a great deal of drawing and saw a number of movies. School was so luxurious in comparison with the hard work I had done in North Dakota the previous year that I wrote another post card to Doris, telling her that we never had to do fractions and that we got colored construction paper to play with almost every day. I copied a picture of a donkey with such accuracy that my teacher thought I had traced it until she held the two to the window and saw that the lines were indisputably my own. After that I got extra drawing periods and became very good at copying, which always elicited more praise than my few original compositions.

I was understandably sad when we left that school after two weeks and went to Wenatchee. For the first time, we were not in a regular camp. The previous year my father, recognizing that the crops had not brought in enough to get us through the winter, had taken the train to Wenatchee after the sparse harvest was in and picked apples for a man named Jim Baumann. Baumann wanted him back, so he let us pitch our tent on his land not far from his house. We made camp, and after supper Baumann came down to talk about the next day's arrangements. The school was not so large as the other one, and there was no school bus for us because we were only a half mile away from it. Baumann was shorthanded in the packing shed and needed my mother early in the morning. Besides, there was no reason why she should have to take us to school, because he had a daughter who was in my grade who could walk with us and take us to our respective rooms.

"Why, isn't that lovely!" my mother exclaimed with unwonted enthusiasm. "Now you'll have a nice little girl to play with right here and to be your friend at school."

Her excitement was rather remarkable, considering the dubious reaction she had to everybody else I had played with since we started camping. It hadn't seemed to me that she had liked even the boy who made me a pair of stilts and taught me to walk them. Now here she was favorably predisposed toward somebody I didn't even know. I agreed that it would be nice to have a nice little girl to play with.

The next morning my sister and I sat on the steps of the Baumanns' front porch, where Barbara's mother had told us to make ourselves at home, waiting for her to finish her breakfast. We had already been up so long that it seemed to me we must surely be late for school; I began picturing the humiliating tardy entrance into a roomful of strange faces.

Two of Barbara's friends came down the driveway to wait for her. They both wore the kind of plaid skirts I had been wondering if I could ask my mother about buying—after all, she *had* said all my dresses were too short this fall because of all the inches I'd grown in the summer. The two girls looked at us for a moment, then uncoiled shiny-handled jump ropes and commenced loudly shouting two different rhymes to accompany their jumping.

Barbara came out on the porch, greeted her friends with a disconcerting assurance, jumped down the steps past us, insinuated herself between them, and clasped their hands. "I have to show these kids where the school is," she told them. Turning her head slightly she called, "Well, come if you're coming. We're going to be late." Swinging their arms together, they began to skip down the driveway.

A couple of times on the way to school they stopped and waited until we got near them; I yanked irritably on my little sister's arm and thought about how her shorter legs had been holding me back ever since she was born. I always seemed to be the one who had to drag a little kid along.

The teacher kept me standing at her desk while she called the roll and started the class on a reading assignment. When she looked up at me, I got the irrational impression that I had already managed to do something wrong. She asked where I had come from and I said "North Dakota," thinking it would be simpler than trying to tell all the places I had been in the last three months. She gave me the last seat in a row behind a boy in dirty clothes. As she passed by him she made the faintest sound of exhalation, as though she was ridding her nostrils of a disagreeable smell.

At recess a boy in a bright shirt and new cream-colored corduroy pants yelled "North Dakota, North Dakota!" in a funny way as he ran past me to the ball field. The boy who sat ahead of me came up and said confidentially, "We been out all around here for two years. We come from Oklahoma. We're Okies. That's what you are too, even if you didn't come from Oklahoma." I knew I could never be anything that sounded so crummy as "Okie," and I said so. "Oh, yeah!" he rejoined stiffly. I walked away before he could argue any more and went to find my sister, but the primary grades had recess at a different time, so I went and stood by the door until the period was over. That afternoon I stayed in my seat reading a history book, but the teacher, who seemed to want to go outdoors herself, said "It's better for the room if everybody goes outside for recess." So I went out and stood around the fringes of two or three games and wondered what was funny about North Dakota. Somehow I had the feeling that it would hurt my mother if I asked her.

The last part of the day was given to a discussion period, when each of us who wanted to was given a chance to tell about an important day in his life. The important days of my classmates, all about having a part in a play or learning to ride a bike, seemed so pathetically juvenile that I was impelled to speak. I stood at my seat and told about how I had earned a dollar all in one day in the hop fields.

From two sides of the room Barbara's friends turned to send her looks which I intercepted but found inscrutable. I had been looking at her too, watching for her reaction. A boy near me poked another and whispered in mocking awe, "A whole dollar!"

The boy ahead of me jumped suddenly to his feet, banging his leg against the desk so hard that the entire row shook. "Heck," he cried, "we just come from there, too, and I made more'n a buck and a half *every* day." He gave me a triumphant smile and sat down. Then I knew I hated that boy. That night I told my mother about how there was a mean boy just like those other mean boys at the camps and how the teacher *would* have to put me right behind him. "Well," she sighed, "just try not to pay any attention to him."

By the time I had found my sister after school, Barbara and her friends had gone. The next morning when we went up to the big house she was gone, too.

After that, my sister and I walked together. Sometimes we would be close enough to hear Barbara's friends who were always with her laugh and call her "Bobby." I had never known any Barbaras before, and the name seemed full of unapproachable prestige and sophistication—the name that only a girl with as many dresses as Barbara Baumann would have. "Bobby" was yet more awesome, as if she were as consequential as a boy. At school, if I recited in class, she acted queerly self-conscious, as though she were responsible for me—the way I often felt around my sister when she said something stupid to kids my age.

For various reasons I had that same embarrassed feeling of an enforced distasteful relationship with the boy who sat ahead of me. Once in a while somebody in the class would tease me about him or would say something about "the hop pickers." I was bitterly determined to dissociate myself from the boy, and whenever he turned around to talk to me I would pretend he was trying to copy my paper. I would put my hand over it while I kept my eyes glued to the desk and felt my face grow hot.

There were some things about the school I liked very much. We were allowed to use the library a great deal, and for the first time in my life I had access to numbers of books I hadn't already read. By reading at noon and recess I could finish a book at school every two days. I would also have a book at home that I would read in a couple of nights. One of the nice things about living in a tent was that there were hardly any household chores to do and I could read as much as I wanted.

Frosty mornings came with October, and my sister and I would try to dress under the quilts before we got up to eat our oatmeal. Leaves began to blow across the road, apples grew redder with each cold night, pickers hurried from tree to tree, filling the orchards with the soft thunder of hard round fruit rolling out of picking sacks into boxes, and packers worked faster and faster, trying to get the apples twisted up in fancy tissue and into boxes before they jammed up too thickly on the perpetually moving belts. After school my sister and I would go to the box shed behind the big house where Harry, Barbara's big brother, would be nailing boxes together for a nickel apiece. He was always glad to have company, and would let us stand at a respectful distance and watch him pound in nail after nail with two strokes, a tap to set it, then a mighty clout to send it in, three to an end, six to a side.

One afternoon, with the chill blue sky brilliant behind the orange and black Halloween cutouts on the windows, I was sitting at my desk dreamily drawing a witch in a moon when the teacher called my name. She told me that she wanted me to take all my books out of my desk and take them to the front of the room. Then she told everybody in my row to pack up his books and move one seat back. My heart banged alarmingly up in my throat and I nearly gagged from the sudden acute sensations in my viscera. In North Dakota such drastic action was taken only when an offender, after repeated warnings, had proved too incorrigible to sit anywhere except right in front of the teacher's desk. The fact that I had no idea of why I was now classified as such an incorrigible only augmented my anguish. While books banged and papers and pencils fell to the floor and boys jostled each other in the aisle, I managed to sidle numbly up to the front. I sat down in my new seat, trying not to notice how shamefully close it was to the big desk facing it, and I was careful not to raise my eyes higher than the vase of zinnias standing on the corner nearest me.

When school was out I hurried to find my sister and get out of the schoolyard before seeing anybody in my class. But Barbara and her friends had beaten us to the playground entrance and they seemed to be waiting for us. We started to walk around them but they fell into step with us. Barbara said, "So now you're in the 'A' class. You went straight from the 'C' class to the 'A' class." She sounded impressed.

"What's the 'A' class?" I asked.

Everybody made superior yet faintly envious giggling sounds. "Well, why did you think the teacher moved you to the front of the room, dopey? Didn't you know you were in the 'C' class before, 'way in the back of the room?"

Of course I hadn't known. The Wenatchee fifth grade was bigger than my whole school had been in North Dakota, and the idea of subdivisions within a grade had never occurred to me. The subdividing for the first marking period had been done before I came to the school, and I had never, in the six weeks I'd been there, talked to anyone long enough to find out about the "A," "B," and "C" classes.

I still could not understand why that had made such a difference to Barbara and her friends. I didn't yet know that it was disgraceful and dirty to be a transient laborer and ridiculous to be from North Dakota. I thought living in a tent was more fun than living in a house. I didn't know that we were gypsies, really (how that thought would have thrilled me then!), and that we were regarded with the suspicion felt by those who plant toward those who do not plant. It didn't occur to me that we were all looked upon as one more of the untrustworthy natural phenomena, drifting here and there like mists or winds, that farmers of certain crops are resentfully forced to rely on. I didn't know that I was the only child who had camped on the Baumanns' land ever to get out of the "C" class. I did not know that school administrators and civic leaders held conferences to talk about how to handle the problem of transient laborers.

I only knew that for two happy days I walked to school with Barbara and her friends, played hopscotch and jump rope with them at recess, and was even invited into the house for some ginger ale—an exotic drink I had never tasted before.

Then we took down our tent and packed it in the trailer with our mattresses and stove and drove on, because the last apples were picked and sorted and boxed and shipped to the people all over the world, whoever they were, who could afford to buy them in 1937. My teacher wrote a letter for me to take to my next school. In it, she told me, she had informed my next teacher that I should be put in the "A" class immediately. But there wasn't any "A" class in my room, the new teacher explained.

By then I was traveled enough to realize that it was another special class for transients. The teacher showed us movies almost every day.

DISCUSSION AND WRITING

1. Define or explain: *accoutrements, desultory, encroachments, expanse, minute* (adj.), *gaunt, entice, saunter, wane, mélange, bounty, elicit, sparse, unwonted, dubious, predisposed, disconcert, insinuate, exhalation, rejoin, inscrutable, consequential, dissociate, incorrigible, augment.*

2. How formal or informal is the author's language? Is her vocabulary difficult, scholarly, folksy, slangy? (Cite examples.) Examine sentence structure and grammatical usage. Is the author's language and sentence style appropriate to her subject matter?

3. Examine the role of specific detail and apt or expressive language in Mrs. Hudson's description of scenes and events. Cite specific examples and explain their role, their implications, their effect. Examine figurative expressions for the moods, feelings, or associations they suggest.

4. How authentic or convincing is the author's re-creation of a world of childhood feelings and attitudes? Describe the children that play a major role in her account. In what ways do they appear familiar or strange, usual or unusual? Would you call them "normal" children?

5. The attitude of the underprivileged toward the more fortunate can easily become embittered, sarcastic, or rebellious. What is the author's attitude toward the economic system and its representatives, toward teachers and schools, toward Barbara and her classmates? How do you explain the author's treatment of the boy from Oklahoma? What attitude does the author adopt toward herself—condescension, irony, self-pity?

6. Demonstrate the economy with which the introductory paragraph provides essential information and establishes a general perspective. Explore the full implications of

the concluding sentence of the essay and its relationship to the essay as a whole. Examine the title. Does it provide clues to the author's attitude, emotions, intentions?

7. Does the account have coherence beyond that derived from chronological sequence? Point out passages, devices, or details of organization that help unify the essay.

8. Write a study of a child you have known well. Concentrate on a few significant character traits. Or, prepare a character portrait of the author of this article as you imagine her after she grew up. Use evidence from the essay to support your account.

9. Discuss the treatment—by teachers, classmates, yourself—of underprivileged children at a school you have attended.

10. Discuss in detail a childhood experience (or a number of closely related experiences) that taught you something important about the adult world: the value of money; the role of love, hate, or resentment; the importance of family background.

FURTHER READING

Many American novelists have described the American villages and towns of the depression era. The world of the poor, semiliterate Southern farmer and sharecropper is re-created in Erskine Caldwell's *God's Little Acre* (1933). Memories of an earlier rural America and the grim economic struggle of the thirties are reflected in Ellen Glasgow's *Vein of Iron* (1935). The classic treatment of the theme of the "Okie" is John Steinbeck's *The Grapes of Wrath* (1939).

JAMES BALDWIN

Some men grow into their adopted roles in life naturally and without much reflection. Others experience violent upheavals in trying to come to terms with the conditions of their existence and with their own passions and resentments. James Baldwin (born 1924) has eloquently expressed the special problems of adjustment faced by the American Negro. Cut off by and large from a history and culture of his own, the Negro lives in a white world that regards him with attitudes ranging from childish wonder at the Negro as an "exotic rarity" to "intent, paranoiac malevolence." Like other Negro writers and artists, Mr. Baldwin tried to find independence and peace of mind by living abroad. In the face of often formidable discouragement and opposition, he has pursued his ambition "to be an honest man and a good writer." The following essay was first published in *Harper's Magazine* in 1955. It became the title essay of a collection dealing with the Negro's struggle to be recognized "as a human being." Alfred Kazin has called this book "one of the two or three best books ever written about the Negro in America." A second collection of Mr. Baldwin's essays, *Nobody Knows My Name,* appeared in 1961. His novels, essays, and public lectures have won him much critical attention and a large audience.

Notes of a Native Son

On the 29th of July, in 1943, my father died. On the same day, a few hours later, his last child was born. Over a month before this, while all our energies were concentrated in waiting for these events, there had been, in Detroit, one of the bloodiest race riots of the century. A few hours after my father's funeral, while he lay in state in the undertaker's chapel, a race riot broke out in Harlem. On the morning of the 3rd of August, we drove my father to the graveyard through a wilderness of smashed plate glass.

The day of my father's funeral had also been my nineteenth birthday. As we drove him to the graveyard, the spoils of injustice, anarchy, discontent, and hatred were all around us. It seemed to me that God himself had devised, to mark my father's end, the most sustained and brutally dissonant of codas. And it seemed to me, too, that the violence which rose all about us as my father left the world had been devised as a corrective for the pride of his eldest son. I had declined to believe in that apocalypse which had been central to my father's vision; very well, life seemed to be saying, here is something that will certainly pass for an apocalypse until the real thing comes along. I had inclined to be contemptuous of my father for the conditions of his life, for the conditions of our lives. When his life had ended I began to wonder about that life and also, in a new way, to be apprehensive about my own.

I had not known my father very well. We had got on badly, partly because we shared, in our different fashions, the vice of stubborn pride. When he was dead I realized that I had hardly ever spoken to him. When he had been dead a long time I began to wish I had. It seems to be typical of life in America, where opportunities, real and fancied, are thicker than anywhere else on the globe, that the second generation has no time to talk to the first. No one, including my father, seems to have known exactly how old he was, but his mother had been born during slavery. He was of the first generation of free men. He, along with thousands of other Negroes, came North after 1919 and I was part of that generation which had never seen the landscape of what Negroes sometimes call the Old Country.

He had been born in New Orleans and had been a quite young man there during the time that Louis Armstrong, a boy, was running errands for the dives and honky-tonks of what was always presented to me as one of the most wicked of cities—to this day, whenever I think of New Orleans, I also helplessly think of Sodom and Gomorrah. My father never mentioned Louis Armstrong, except to forbid us to play his records; but there was a picture of him on our wall for a long time. One of my father's strong-willed female relatives had placed it there and forbade my father to take it down. He never did, but he eventually maneuvered her out of the house and when, some years later, she was in trouble and near death, he refused to do anything to help her.

He was, I think, very handsome. I gather this from photographs and from my own memories of him, dressed in his Sunday best and on his way to preach a sermon somewhere, when I was little. Handsome, proud, and ingrown, "like a toe-nail," somebody said. But he looked to me, as I grew older, like pictures I had seen of African tribal chieftains: he really should have been naked, with war-paint on and barbaric mementos, standing among spears. He could be chilling in the pulpit and indescribably cruel in his personal life and he was certainly the most bitter man I have ever met; yet it must be said that there was something else in him, buried in him, which lent him his tremendous power and, even, a rather crushing charm. It had something to do with his blackness, I think—he was very black—with his blackness and his beauty, and with the fact that he knew that he was black but did not know that he was beautiful. He claimed to be proud of his blackness but it had also been the cause of much humiliation and it had fixed bleak boundaries to his life. He was not a young man when we were growing up and he had already suffered many kinds of ruin; in his outrageously demanding and protective way he loved his children, who were black like him and menaced, like him; and all these things sometimes showed in his face when he tried, never to my knowledge with any success, to establish contact with any of us. When he took one of his children on his knee to play, the child always became fretful and began to cry; when he tried to help one of us with our homework the absolutely unabating tension which emanated from him caused our minds and our tongues to become paralyzed, so that he, scarcely knowing why, flew into a rage and the child, not knowing why, was punished. If it ever entered his head to bring a surprise home for his children, it was, almost unfailingly, the wrong surprise and even the big watermelons he often brought home on his back in the summertime led to the most appalling scenes. I do not remember, in all those years, that one of his children was ever glad to see him come home. From what I was able to gather of his early life, it seemed that this inability to establish contact with other people had always marked him and had been one of the things which had driven him out of New Orleans. There was something in him, therefore, groping and tentative, which was never expressed and which was buried with him. One saw it most clearly when he was facing new people and hoping to impress them. But he never did, not for long. We went from church to smaller and more improbable church, he found himself in less and less demand as a minister, and by the time he died none of his friends had come to see him for a long time. He had lived and died in an intolerable bitterness of spirit and it frightened me, as we drove him to the graveyard through those unquiet, ruined streets, to see how powerful and overflowing this bitterness could be and to realize that this bitterness now was mine.

When he died I had been away from home for a little over a year. In that year I had had time to become aware of the meaning of all my father's bitter warnings, had discovered the secret of his proudly pursed lips and rigid carriage: I had discovered the weight of white people in the world. I saw that this had been for my ancestors and now would be for me an awful thing to live with and that the bitterness which had helped to kill my father could also kill me.

He had been ill a long time—in the mind, as we now realized, reliving instances of his fantastic intransigence in the new light of his affliction and endeavoring to feel a sorrow for him which never, quite, came true. We had not known that he was being eaten up by paranoia, and the discovery that his cruelty, to our bodies and our minds, had been one of the symptoms of his illness was not, then, enough to enable us to forgive him. The younger children felt, quite simply, relief that he would not be coming home anymore. My mother's observation that it was he, after all, who had kept them alive all these years meant nothing because the problems of keeping children alive are not real for children. The older children felt, with my father gone, that they could invite their friends to the house without fear that their friends would be insulted or, as had sometimes happened with me, being told that their friends were in league with the devil and intended to rob our family of everything we owned. (I didn't fail to wonder, and it made me hate him, what on earth we owned that anybody else would want.)

His illness was beyond all hope of healing before anyone realized that he was ill. He had always been so strange and had lived, like a prophet, in such unimaginably close communion with the Lord that his long silences which were punctuated by moans and hallelujahs and snatches of old songs while he sat at the living-room window never seemed odd to us. It was not until he refused to eat because, he said, his family was trying to poison him that my mother was forced to accept as a fact what had, until then, been only an unwilling suspicion. When he was committed, it was discovered that he had tuberculosis and, as it turned out, the disease of his mind allowed the disease of his body to destroy him. For the doctors could not force him to eat, either, and, though he was fed intravenously, it was clear from the beginning that there was no hope for him.

In my mind's eye I could see him, sitting at the window, locked up in his terrors; hating and fearing every living soul including his children who had betrayed him, too, by reaching towards the world which had despised him. There were nine of us. I began to wonder what it could have felt like for such a man to have had nine children whom he could barely feed. He used to make little jokes about our poverty, which never, of course, seemed very funny to us; they could not have seemed very funny to him, either, or else our all too feeble response to them would never have caused such rages. He spent great energy and achieved, to our chagrin, no small amount of success in keeping us away from the people who surrounded us, people who had all-night rent parties to which we listened when we should have been sleeping, people who cursed and drank and flashed razor blades on Lenox Avenue. He could not understand why, if they had so much energy to spare, they could not use it to make their lives better. He treated almost everybody on our block with a most uncharitable asperity and neither they, nor, of course, their children were slow to reciprocate.

The only white people who came to our house were welfare workers and bill collectors. It was almost always my mother who dealt with them, for my father's temper, which was at the mercy of his pride, was never to be trusted. It was clear that he felt their very presence in his home to be a violation: this was conveyed by his carriage, almost ludicrously stiff, and by his voice, harsh and vindictively polite. When I was around nine or ten I wrote a play which was directed by a young, white schoolteacher, a woman, who then took an interest in me, and gave me books to read and, in order to corroborate my theatrical bent, decided to take me to see what she somewhat tactlessly referred to as "real" plays. Theater-going was forbidden in our house, but, with the really cruel intuitiveness of a child, I suspected that the color of this woman's skin would carry the day for me. When, at school, she suggested taking me to the theater, I did not, as I might have done if she had been a Negro, find a way of discouraging her, but agreed that she should pick me up at my house one evening. I then, very cleverly, left all the rest to my mother, who suggested to my father, as I knew she would, that it would not be very nice to let such a kind woman make the trip for nothing. Also, since it was a schoolteacher, I imagine that my mother countered the idea of sin with the idea of "education," which word, even with my father, carried a kind of bitter weight.

Before the teacher came my father took me aside to ask *why* she was coming, what *interest* she could possibly have in our house, in a boy like me. I said I didn't know but I, too, suggested that it had something to do with education. And I understood that my father was waiting for me to say something—I didn't quite know what; perhaps that I wanted his protection against this teacher and her "education." I said none of these things and the teacher came and we went out. It was clear, during the brief interview in our living room, that my father was agreeing very much against his will and that he would have refused permission if he had dared. The fact that he did not dare caused me to despise him: I had no way of knowing that he was facing in that living room a wholly unprecedented and frightening situation.

Later, when my father had been laid off from his job, this woman became very important to us. She was really a very sweet and generous woman and went to a great deal of trouble to be of help to us, particularly during one awful winter. My mother called her by the highest name she knew: she said she was a "christian." My father could scarcely disagree but during the four or five years of our relatively close association he never trusted her and was always trying to surprise in her open, Midwestern face the genuine, cunningly hidden, and hideous motivation. In later years, particularly when it began to be clear that this "education" of mine was going to lead me to perdition, he became more explicit and warned me that my white friends in high school were not really my friends and that I would see, when I was older, how white people would do anything to keep a Negro down. Some of them could be nice, he admitted, but none of them were to be trusted and most of them were not even nice. The best thing was to have as little to do with them as possible. I did not feel this way and I was certain, in my innocence, that I never would.

But the year which preceded my father's death had made a great change in my life. I had been living in New Jersey, working in defense plants, working and living among southerners, white and black. I knew about the south, of course, and about how southerners treated Negroes and how they expected them to behave, but it had never entered my mind that anyone would look at me and expect *me* to behave that way. I learned in New Jersey that to be a Negro meant, precisely, that one was never looked at but was simply at the mercy of the reflexes the color of one's skin caused in other people. I acted in New Jersey as I had always acted, that is as though I thought a great deal of myself—I had to *act* that way—with results that were, simply, unbelievable. I had scarcely arrived before I had earned the enmity, which was extraordinarily ingenious, of all my superiors and nearly all my co-workers. In the beginning, to make matters worse, I simply did not know what was happening. I did not know what I had done, and I shortly began to wonder what *anyone* could possibly do, to bring about such unanimous, active, and unbearably vocal hostility. I knew about jim-crow but I had never experienced it. I went to the same self-service restaurant three times and stood with all the Princeton boys before the counter, waiting for a hamburger and coffee; it was always an extraordinarily long time before anything was set before me; but it was not until the fourth visit that I learned that, in fact, nothing had ever been set before me: I had simply picked something up. Negroes were not served there, I was told, and they had been waiting for me to realize that I was always the only Negro present. Once I was told this, I determined to go there all the time. But now they were ready for me and, though some dreadful scenes were subsequently enacted in that restaurant, I never ate there again.

It was the same story all over New Jersey, in bars, bowling alleys, diners, places to live. I was always being forced to leave, silently, or with mutual imprecations. I very shortly became notorious and children giggled behind me when I passed and their elders whispered or shouted—they really believed that I was mad. And it did begin to work on my mind, of course; I began to be afraid to go anywhere and to compensate for this I went places to which I really should not have gone and where, God knows, I had no desire to be. My reputation in town naturally enhanced my reputation at work and my working day became one long series of acrobatics designed to keep me out of trouble. I cannot say that these acrobatics succeeded. It began to seem that the machinery of the organization I worked for was turning over, day and night, with but one aim: to eject me. I was fired once, and contrived, with the aid of a friend from New York, to get back on the payroll; was fired again, and bounced back again. It took a while to fire me for the third time, but the third time took. There were no loopholes anywhere. There was not even any way of getting back inside the gates.

That year in New Jersey lives in my mind as though it were the year during which, having an unsuspected predilection for it, I first contracted some dread, chronic disease, the unfailing symptom of which is a kind of blind fever, a pounding in the skull and fire in the bowels. Once this disease is contracted, one can never be really carefree again, for the fever, without an instant's warning, can recur at any moment. It can wreck more important things than race relations. There is not a Negro alive who does not have this rage in his blood—one has the choice, merely, of living with it consciously or surrendering to it. As for me, this fever has recurred in me, and does, and will until the day I die.

My last night in New Jersey, a white friend from New York took me to the nearest big town, Trenton, to go to the movies and have a few drinks. As it turned out, he also saved me from, at the very least, a violent whipping. Almost every detail of that night stands out very clearly in my memory. I even remember the name of the movie we saw because its title impressed me as being so patly ironical. It was a movie about the German occupation of France, starring Maureen O'Hara and Charles Laughton and called *This Land Is Mine*. I remember the name of the diner we walked into when the movie ended: it was the "American Diner." When we walked in the counterman asked what we wanted and I remember answering with the casual sharpness which had become my habit: "We want a hamburger and a cup of coffee, what do you thing we want?" I do not know why, after a year of such rebuffs, I so completely failed to anticipate his answer, which was, of course, "We don't serve Negroes here." This reply failed to discompose me, at least for the moment. I made some sardonic comment about the name of the diner and we walked out into the streets.

This was the time of what was called the "brown-out," when the lights in all American cities were very dim. When we re-entered the streets something happened to me which had the force of an optical illusion, or a nightmare. The streets were very crowded and I was facing north. People were moving in every direction but it seemed to me, in that instant, that all of the people I could see, and many more than that, were moving toward me, against me, and that everyone was white. I remember how their faces gleamed. And I felt, like a physical sensation, a *click* at the nape of my neck as though some interior string connecting my head to my body had been cut. I began to walk. I heard my friend call after me, but I ignored him. Heaven only knows what was going on in his mind, but he had the good sense not to touch me—I don't know what would have happened if he had—and to keep me in sight. I don't know what was going on in my mind, either; I certainly had no conscious plan. I wanted to do something to crush these white faces, which were crushing me. I walked for perhaps a block or two until I came to an enormous, glittering, and fashionable restaurant in which I knew not even the intercession of the Virgin would cause me to be served. I pushed through the doors and took the first vacant seat I saw, at a table for two, and waited.

I do not know how long I waited and I rather wonder, until today, what I could possibly have looked like. Whatever I looked like, I frightened the waitress who shortly appeared, and the moment she appeared all of my fury flowed towards her. I hated her for her white face, and for her great, astounded, frightened eyes. I felt that if she found a black man so frightening I would make her fright worth-while.

She did not ask me what I wanted, but repeated, as though she had learned it somewhere, "We don't serve Negroes here." She did not say it with the blunt, derisive hostility to which I had grown so accustomed, but, rather, with a note of apology in her voice, and fear. This made me colder and more murderous than ever. I felt I had to do something with my hands. I wanted her to come close enough for me to get her neck between my hands.

So I pretended not to have understood her, hoping to draw her closer. And she did step a very short step closer, with her pencil poised incongruously over her pad, and repeated the formula: ". . . don't serve Negroes here."

Somehow, with the repetition of that phrase, which was already ringing in my head like a thousand bells of a nightmare, I realized that she would never come any closer and that I would have to strike from a distance. There was nothing on the table but an ordinary water-mug half full of water, and I picked this up and hurled it with all my strength at her. She ducked and it missed her and shattered against the mirror behind the bar. And, with that sound, my frozen blood abruptly thawed, I returned from wherever I had been, I *saw*, for the first time, the restaurant, the people with their mouths open already, as it seemed to me, rising as one man, and I realized what I had done, and where I was, and I was frightened. I rose and began running for the door. A round, potbellied man grabbed me by the nape of the neck just as I reached the doors and began to beat me about the face. I kicked him and got loose and ran into the streets. My friend whispered, *"Run!"* and I ran.

My friend stayed outside the restaurant long enough to misdirect my pursuers and the police, who arrived, he told me, at once. I do not know what I said to him when he came to my room that night. I could not have said much. I felt, in the oddest, most awful way, that I had somehow betrayed him. I lived it over and over and over again, the way one relives an automobile accident after it has happened and one finds oneself alone and safe. I could not get over two facts, both equally difficult for the imagination to grasp, and one was that I could have been murdered. But the other was that I had been ready to commit murder. I saw nothing very clearly but I did see this: that my life, my *real* life, was in danger, and not from anything other people might do but from the hatred I carried in my own heart.

II

I had returned home around the second week in June—in great haste because it seemed that my father's death and my mother's confinement were both but a matter of hours. In the case of my mother, it soon became clear that she had simply made a miscalculation. This had always been her tendency and I don't believe that a single one of us arrived in the world, or has since arrived anywhere else, on time. But none of us dawdled so intolerably about the business of being born as did my baby sister. We sometimes amused ourselves, during those endless, stifling weeks, by picturing the baby sitting within in the safe, warm dark, bitterly regretting the necessity of becoming a part of our chaos and stubbornly putting it off as long as possible. I understood her perfectly and congratulated her on showing such good sense so soon. Death, however, sat as purposefully at my father's bedside as life stirred within my mother's womb and it was harder to understand why he so lingered in that long shadow. It seemed that he had bent, and for a long time, too, all of his energies towards dying. Now death was ready for him but my father held back.

All of Harlem, indeed, seemed to be infected by waiting. I had never before known it to be so violently still. Racial tensions throughout this country were exacerbated during the early years of the war, partly because the labor market brought together hundreds of thousands of ill-prepared people and partly because Negro soldiers, regardless of where they were born, received their military training in the south. What happened in defense plants and army camps had repercussions, naturally, in every Negro ghetto. The situation in Harlem had grown bad enough for clergymen, policemen, educators, politicians, and social workers to assert in one breath that there was no "crime wave" and to offer, in the very next breath, suggestions as to how to combat it. These suggestions always seemed to involve playgrounds, despite the fact that racial skirmishes were occurring in the playgrounds, too. Playground or not, crime wave or not, the Harlem police force had been augmented in March, and the unrest grew—perhaps, in fact, partly as a result of the ghetto's instinctive hatred of policemen. Perhaps the most revealing news item, out of the steady parade of reports of muggings, stabbings, shootings, assaults, gang wars, and accusations of police brutality, is the item concerning six Negro girls who set upon a white girl in the subway because, as they all too accurately put it, she was stepping on their toes. Indeed she was, all over the nation.

I had never before been so aware of policemen, on foot, or horseback, on corners, everywhere, always two by two. Nor had I ever been so aware of small knots of people. They were on stoops and on corners and in doorways, and what was striking about them, I think, was that they did not seem to be talking. Never, when I passed these groups, did the usual sound of a curse or a laugh ring out and neither did there seem to be any hum of gossip. There was certainly, on the other hand, occurring between them communication extraordinarily intense. Another thing that was striking was the unexpected diversity of the people who made up these groups. Usually, for example, one would see a group of sharpies standing on the street corner, jiving the passing chicks; or a group of older men, usually, for some reason, in the vicinity of a barber shop, discussing baseball scores, or the numbers, or making rather chilling observations about women they had known. Women, in a general way, tended to be seen less often together—unless they were church women, or very young girls, or prostitutes met together for an unprofessional instant. But that summer I saw the strangest combinations: large, respectable, churchly matrons standing on the stoops or the corners with their hair tied up, together with a girl in sleazy satin whose face bore the marks of gin and the razor, or heavy-set, abrupt, no-nonsense older men, in company with the most disreputable and fanatical "race" men, or these same "race" men with the sharpies, or these sharpies with the churchly women. Seventh Day Adventists and Methodists and Spiritualists seemed to be hobnobbing with Holyrollers and they were all, alike, entangled with the most flagrant disbelievers; something heavy in their stance seemed to indicate that they had all, incredibly, seen a common vision, and on each face there seemed to be the same strange, bitter shadow.

The churchly women and the matter-of-fact no-nonsense men had children in the Army. The sleazy girls they talked to had lovers there, the sharpies and the "race" men had friends and brothers there. It would have demanded an unquestioning patriotism, happily as uncommon in this country as it is undesirable, for these people not to have been disturbed by the bitter letters they received, by the newspaper stories they read, not to have been enraged by the posters, then to be found all over New York, which described the Japanese as "yellow-bellied Japs." It was only the "race" men, to be sure, who spoke ceaselessly of being revenged—how this vengeance was to be exacted was not clear—for the indignities and dangers suffered by Negro boys in uniform; but everybody felt a directionless, hopeless bitterness, as well as that panic which can scarcely be suppressed when one knows that a human being one loves is beyond one's reach, and in danger. This helplessness and this gnawing uneasiness does something, at length, to even the toughest mind. Perhaps the best way to sum all this up is to say that the people I knew felt, mainly, a peculiar kind of relief when they knew that their boys were being shipped out of the south, to do battle overseas. It was, perhaps, like feeling that the most dangerous part of a dangerous journey had been passed and that now, even if death should come, it would come with honor and without the complicity of their countrymen. Such a death would be, in short, a fact with which one could hope to live.

It was on the 28th of July, which I believe was a Wednesday, that I visited my father for the first time during his illness and for the last time in his life. The moment I saw him I knew why I had put off this visit so long. I had told my mother that I did not want to see him because I hated him. But this was not true. It was only that I *had* hated him and I wanted to hold on to this hatred. I did not want to look on him as a ruin: it was not a ruin I had hated. I imagine that one of the reasons people cling to their hates so stubbornly is because they sense, once hate is gone, that they will be forced to deal with pain.

We traveled out to him, his older sister and myself, to what seemed to be the very end of a very Long Island. It was hot and dusty and we wrangled, my aunt and I, all the way out, over the fact that I had recently begun to smoke and, as she said, to give myself airs. But I knew that she wrangled with me because she could not bear to face the fact of her brother's dying. Neither could I endure the reality of her despair, her unstated bafflement as to what had happened to her brother's life, and her own. So we wrangled and I smoked and from time to time she fell into a heavy reverie. Covertly, I watched her face, which was the face of an old woman; it had fallen in, the eyes were sunken and lightless; soon she would be dying, too.

In my childhood—it had not been so long ago—I had thought her beautiful. She had been quick-witted and quick-moving and very generous with all the children and each of her visits had been an event. At one time one of my brothers and myself had thought of running away to live with her. Now she could no longer produce out of her handbag some unexpected and yet familiar delight. She made me feel pity and revulsion and fear. It was awful to realize that she no longer caused me to feel affection. The closer we came to the hospital the more querulous she became and at the same time, naturally, grew more dependent on me. Between pity and guilt and fear I began to feel that there was another me trapped in my skull like a jack-in-the-box who might escape my control at any moment and fill the air with screaming.

She began to cry the moment we entered the room and she saw him lying there, all shriveled and still, like a little black monkey. The great, gleaming apparatus which fed him and would have compelled him to be still even if he had been able to move brought to mind, not beneficence, but torture; the tubes entering his arm made me think of pictures I had seen when a child, of Gulliver, tied down by the pygmies on that island. My aunt wept and wept, there was a whistling sound in my father's throat; nothing was said; he could not speak. I wanted to take his hand, to say something. But I do not know what I could have said, even if he could have heard me. He was not really in that room with us, he had at last really embarked on his journey; and though my aunt told me that he said he was going to meet Jesus, I did not hear anything except that whistling in his throat. The doctor came back and we left, into that unbearable train again, and home. In the morning came the telegram saying that he was dead. Then the house was suddenly full of relatives, friends, hysteria, and confusion and I quickly left my mother and the children to the care of those impressive women, who, in Negro communities at least, automatically appear at times of bereavement armed with lotions, proverbs, and patience, and an ability to cook. I went downtown. By the time I returned, later the same day, my mother had been carried to the hospital and the baby had been born.

III

For my father's funeral I had nothing black to wear and this posed a nagging problem all day long. It was one of those problems, simple, or impossible of solution, to which the mind insanely clings in order to avoid the mind's real trouble. I spent most of that day at the downtown apartment of a girl I knew, celebrating my birthday with whiskey and wondering what to wear that night. When planning a birthday celebration one naturally does not expect that it will be up against competition from a funeral and this girl had anticipated taking me out that night, for a big dinner and a night club afterwards. Sometime during the course of that long day we decided that we would go out anyway, when my father's funeral service was over. I imagine *I* decided it, since, as the funeral hour approached, it became clearer and clearer to me that I would not know what to do with myself when it was over. The girl, stifling her very lively concern as to the possible effects of the whiskey on one of my father's chief mourners, concentrated on being conciliatory and practically helpful. She found a black shirt for me somewhere and ironed it and, dressed in the darkest pants and jacket I owned, and slightly drunk, I made my way to my father's funeral.

The chapel was full, but not packed, and very quiet. There were, mainly, my father's relatives, and his children, and here and there I saw faces I had not seen since childhood, the faces of my father's one-time friends. They were very dark and solemn now, seeming somehow to suggest that they had known all along that something like this would happen. Chief among the mourners was my aunt, who had quarreled with my father all his life; by which I do not mean to suggest that her mourning was insincere or that she had not loved him. I suppose that she was one of the few people in the world who had, and their incessant quarreling proved precisely the strength of the tie that bound them. The only other person in the world, as far as I knew, whose relationship to my father rivaled my aunt's in depth was my mother, who was not there.

It seemed to me, of course, that it was a very long funeral. But it was, if anything, a rather shorter funeral than most, nor, since there were no overwhelming, uncontrollable expressions of grief, could it be called—if I dare to use the word—successful. The minister who preached my father's funeral sermon was one of the few my father had still been seeing as he neared his end. He presented to us in his sermon a man whom none of us had ever seen—a man thoughtful, patient, and forbearing, a Christian inspiration to all who knew him, and a model for his children. And no doubt the children, in their disturbed and guilty state, were almost ready to believe this; he had been remote enough to be anything and, anyway, the shock of the incontrovertible, that it was really our father lying up there in that casket, prepared the mind for anything. His sister moaned and this grief-stricken moaning was taken as corroboration. The other faces held a dark, non-committal thoughtfulness. This was not the man they had known, but they had scarcely expected to be confronted with *him;* this was, in a sense deeper than questions of fact, the man they had not known, and the man they had not known may have been the real one. The real man, whoever he had been, had suffered and now he was dead: this was all that was sure and all that mattered now. Every man in the chapel hoped that when his hour came he, too, would be eulogized, which is to say forgiven, and that all of his lapses, greeds, errors, and strayings from the truth would be invested with coherence and looked upon with charity. This was perhaps the last thing human beings could give each other and it was what they demanded, after all, of the Lord. Only the Lord saw the midnight tears, only He was present when one of His children, moaning and wringing hands, paced up and down the room. When one slapped one's child in anger the recoil in the heart reverberated through heaven and became part of the pain of the universe.

And when the children were hungry and sullen and distrustful and one watched them, daily, growing wilder, and further away, and running headlong into danger, it was the Lord who knew what the charged heart endured as the strap was laid to the backside; the Lord alone who knew what one *would* have said if one had had, like the Lord, the gift of the living word. It was the Lord who knew of the impossibility every parent in that room faced: how to prepare the child for the day when the child would be despised and how to *create* in the child—by what means?—a stronger antidote to this poison than one had found for oneself. The avenues, side streets, bars, billiard halls, hospitals, police stations, and even the playgrounds of Harlem—not to mention the houses of correction, the jails, and the morgue—testified to the potency of the poison while remaining silent as to the efficacy of whatever antidote, irresistibly raising the question of whether or not such an antidote existed; raising, which was worse, the question of whether or not an antidote was desirable; perhaps poison should be fought with poison. With these several schisms in the mind and with more terrors in the heart than could be named, it was better not to judge the man who had gone down under an impossible burden. It was better to remember: *Thou knowest this man's fall; but thou knowest not his wrassling.*

While the preacher talked and I watched the children—years of changing their diapers, scrubbing them, slapping them, taking them to school, and scolding them had had the perhaps inevitable result of making me love them, though I am not sure I knew this then—my mind was busily breaking out with a rash of disconnected impressions. Snatches of popular songs, indecent jokes, bits of books I had read, movie sequences, faces, voices, political issues—I thought I was going mad; all these impressions suspended, as it were, in the solution of the faint nausea produced in me by the heat and liquor. For a moment I had the impression that my alcoholic breath, inefficiently disguised with chewing gum, filled the entire chapel. Then someone began singing one of my father's favorite songs and, abruptly, I was with him, sitting on his knee, in the hot, enormous, crowded church which was the first church we attended. It was the Abyssinia Baptist Church on 138th Street. We had not gone there long. With this image, a host of others came. I had forgotten, in the rage of my growing up, how proud my father had been of me when I was little. Apparently, I had had a voice and my father had liked to show me off before the members of the church. I had forgotten what he had looked like when he was pleased but now I remembered that he had always been grinning with pleasure when my solos ended. I even remembered certain expressions on his face when he teased my mother—had he loved her? I would never know. And when had it all begun to change? For now it seemed that he had not always been cruel. I remembered being taken for a haircut and scraping my knee on the footrest of the barber's chair and I remembered my father's face as he soothed my crying and applied the stinging iodine. Then I remembered our fights, fights which had been of the worst possible kind because my technique had been silence.

I remembered the one time in all our life together when we had really spoken to each other.

It was on a Sunday and it must have been shortly before I left home. We were walking, just the two of us, in our usual silence, to or from church. I was in high school and had been doing a lot of writing and I was, at about this time, the editor of the high school magazine. But I had also been a Young Minister and had been preaching from the pulpit. Lately, I had been taking fewer engagements and preached as rarely as possible. It was said in the church, quite truthfully, that I was "cooling off."

My father asked me abruptly, "You'd rather write than preach, wouldn't you?"

I was astonished at his question—because it was a real question. I answered, "Yes."

That was all we said. It was awful to remember that that was all we had *ever* said.

The casket now was opened and the mourners were being led up the aisle to look for the last time on the deceased. The assumption was that the family was too overcome with grief to be allowed to make this journey alone and I watched while my aunt was led to the casket and, muffled in black, and shaking, led back to her seat. I disapproved of forcing the children to look on their dead father, considering that the shock of his death, or, more truthfully, the shock of death as a reality, was already a little more than a child could bear, but my judgment in this matter had been overruled and there they were, bewildered and frightened and very small, being led, one by one, to the casket. But there is also something very gallant about children at such moments. It has something to do with their silence and gravity and with the fact that one cannot help them. Their legs, somehow, seem *exposed,* so that it is at once incredible and terribly clear that their legs are all they have to hold them up.

I had not wanted to go to the casket myself and I certainly had not wished to be led there, but there was no way of avoiding either of these forms. One of the deacons led me up and I looked on my father's face. I cannot say that it looked like him at all. His blackness had been equivocated by powder and there was no suggestion in that casket of what his power had or could have been. He was simply an old man dead, and it was hard to believe that he had ever given anyone either joy or pain. Yet, his life filled that room. Further up the avenue his wife was holding his newborn child. Life and death so close together, and love and hatred, and right and wrong, said something to me which I did not want to hear concerning man, concerning the life of man.

After the funeral, while I was downtown desperately celebrating my birthday, a Negro soldier, in the lobby of the Hotel Braddock, got into a

fight with a white policeman over a Negro girl. Negro girls, white policemen, in or out of uniform, and Negro males—in or out of uniform—were
part of the furniture of the lobby of the Hotel Braddock and this was
certainly not the first time such an incident had occurred. It was destined,
however, to receive an unprecedented publicity, for the fight between the
policemen and the soldier ended with the shooting of the soldier. Rumor,
flowing immediately to the streets outside, stated that the soldier had been
shot in the back, an instantaneous and revealing invention, and that the
soldier had died protecting a Negro woman. The facts were somewhat
different—for example, the soldier had not been shot in the back, and was
not dead, and the girl seems to have been as dubious a symbol of woman-
hood as her white counterpart in Georgia usually is, but no one was interested in the facts. They preferred the invention because this invention
expressed and corroborated their hates and fears so perfectly. It is just as well
to remember that people are always doing this. Perhaps many of those
legends, including Christianity, to which the world clings began their
conquest of the world with just some such concerted surrender to distortion.
The effect, in Harlem, of this particular legend was like the effect of a lit
match in a tin of gasoline. The mob gathered before the doors of the Hotel
Braddock simply began to swell and to spread in every direction, and
Harlem exploded.

The mob did not cross the ghetto lines. It would have been easy, for
example, to have gone over Morningside Park on the west side or to have
crossed the Grand Central railroad tracks at 125th Street on the east side, to
wreak havoc in white neighborhoods. The mob seems to have been mainly
interested in something more potent and real than the white face, that is, in
white power, and the principal damage done during the riot of the summer
of 1943 was to white business establishments in Harlem. It might have been
a far bloodier story, of course, if, at the hour the riot began, these establishments had still been open. From the Hotel Braddock the mob fanned out,
east and west along 125th Street, and for the entire length of Lenox, Seventh,
and Eighth avenues. Along each of these avenues, and along each major side
street—116th, 125th, 135th, and so on—bars, stores, pawnshops, restaurants,
even little luncheonettes had been smashed open and entered and looted—
looted, it might be added, with more haste than efficiency. The shelves really
looked as though a bomb had struck them. Cans of beans and soup and dog
food, along with toilet paper, corn flakes, sardines, and milk tumbled every
which way, and abandoned cash registers and cases of beer leaned crazily out
of the splintered windows and were strewn along the avenues. Sheets,
blankets, and clothing of every description formed a kind of path, as though
people had dropped them while running. I truly had not realized that
Harlem *had* so many stores until I saw them all smashed open; the first time
the word *wealth* ever entered my mind in relation to Harlem was when I

saw it scattered in the streets. But one's first, incongruous impression of plenty was countered immediately by an impression of waste. None of this was doing anybody any good. It would have been better to have left the plate glass as it had been and the goods lying in the stores.

It would have been better, but it would also have been intolerable, for Harlem had needed something to smash. To smash something is the ghetto's chronic need. Most of the time it is the members of the ghetto who smash each other, and themselves. But as long as the ghetto walls are standing there will always come a moment when these outlets do not work. That summer, for example, it was not enough to get into a fight on Lenox Avenue, or curse out one's cronies in the barber shops. If ever, indeed, the violence which fills Harlem's churches, pool halls, and bars erupts outward in a more direct fashion, Harlem and its citizens are likely to vanish in an apocalyptic flood. That this is not likely to happen is due to a great many reasons, most hidden and powerful among them the Negro's real relation to the white American. This relation prohibits, simply, anything as uncomplicated and satisfactory as pure hatred. In order really to hate white people, one has to blot so much out of the mind—and the heart—that this hatred itself becomes an exhausting and self-destructive pose. But this does not mean, on the other hand, that love comes easily: the white world is too powerful, too complacent, too ready with gratuitous humiliation, and, above all, too ignorant and too innocent for that. One is absolutely forced to make perpetual qualifications and one's own reactions are always canceling each other out. It is this, really, which has driven so many people mad, both white and black. One is always in the position of having to decide between amputation and gangrene. Amputation is swift but time may prove that the amputation was not necessary—or one may delay the amputation too long. Gangrene is slow, but it is impossible to be sure that one is reading one's symptoms right. The idea of going through life as a cripple is more than one can bear, and equally unbearable is the risk of swelling up slowly, in agony, with poison. And the trouble, finally, is that the risks are real even if the choices do not exist.

"But as for me and my house," my father had said, "we will serve the Lord." I wondered, as we drove him to his resting place, what this line had meant for him. I had heard him preach it many times. I had preached it once myself, proudly giving it an interpretation different from my father's. Now the whole thing came back to me, as though my father and I were on our way to Sunday school and I were memorizing the golden text: *And if it seem evil unto you to serve the Lord, choose you this day whom you will serve; whether the gods which your fathers served that were on the other side of the flood, or the gods of the Amorites, in whose land ye dwell: but as for me and my house, we will serve the Lord.* I suspected in these familiar lines a meaning which had never been there for me before. All of my father's texts and songs, which I had decided were meaningless, were arranged before me at his death like empty bottles, waiting to hold the meaning which life would give them for me. This was his legacy: nothing is ever escaped. That bleakly memorable morning I hated the unbelievable streets and the Negroes and whites who had, equally, made them that way. But I knew that it was folly, as my father would have said, this bitterness was folly. It was necessary to hold on to the things that mattered. The dead man mattered, the new life mattered; blackness and whiteness did not matter; to believe that they did was to acquiesce in one's own destruction. Hatred, which could destroy so much, never failed to destroy the man who hated and this was an immutable law.

It began to seem that one would have to hold in the mind forever two ideas which seemed to be in opposition. The first idea was acceptance, the acceptance, totally without rancor, of life as it is, and men as they are: in the light of this idea, it goes without saying that injustice is a commonplace. But this did not mean that one could be complacent, for the second idea was of equal power: that one must never, in one's own life, accept these injustices as commonplace but must fight them with all one's strength. This fight begins, however, in the heart and it now had been laid to my charge to keep my own heart free of hatred and despair. This intimation made my heart heavy and, now that my father was irrecoverable, I wished that he had been beside me so that I could have searched his face for the answers which only the future would give me now.

DISCUSSION AND WRITING

1. Define or explain: *anarchy, dissonant, coda, apocalypse, barbaric, memento, unabating, emanate, intransigence, paranoia, communion, chagrin, asperity, ludicrous, vindictive, corroborate, intuitiveness, hideous, perdition, explicit, enmity, vocal, imprecation, predilection, sardonic, intercession, derisive, incongruous, exacerbate, hobnob, reverie, covert, querulous, incontrovertible, eulogize, reverberate, schism, gratuitous, rancor, intimation.* In context, what is the meaning of "rigid *carriage*," "*invested* with coherence," "*equivocated* by powder," "*concerted* surrender"?

2. Look up *ghetto*. What are the implications, associations, and overtones of the word? Do you consider the author's use of the term justified? Discuss other examples of words, figures of speech, and analogies that reveal the author's attitudes.

3. Baldwin comments on the irony in the film title *This Land Is Mine*. Examine the essay for other examples of irony. What generally is the tone of the essay—for instance, is it sarcastic, balanced, searching, extremist? (Cite detailed evidence.)

4. In your own words, describe Baldwin's father. What is the major point (or points) that the author is trying to bring out about his father or about their relationship to each other? What is the theme or general intention of the essay?

5. Study the way the author describes the thoughts, attitudes, and motives of other people (such as his aunt, his father's former friends at the funeral, the people participating in the Harlem riots). Are the attitudes and motives he discusses plausible or far-

fetched, conventional or different, complex or simple? How much insight does the author show into the way people think or feel?

6. Much autobiographical writing takes the form of more or less miscellaneous reminiscence, held together by a loose chronological sequence. Does this essay have a more definite structure? Examine the role of the opening and the concluding paragraphs, the sequence and relevance of the various incidents.

7. Compare and contrast Mrs. Hudson's and James Baldwin's treatment of the underprivileged. How do they differ in tone, attitude, emotion, effect on the reader? Or, compare and contrast V. S. Pritchett's treatment of Harlem as an outside observer with that of Baldwin as a personally involved participant.

8. What first-hand experience have you had with racial tension? Does segregation exist in your own community, or in your home state?

9. Words are cheap but real communication is difficult. To judge from your experience, what is the major obstacle to understanding and genuine human contact between different racial groups?

10. Satirists have often treated the ironic contrast between ideal and reality, between men's preaching and their practice. What has been the most striking illustration of this contrast in your own experience?

FURTHER READING

Among the most gripping documents of the rage and anguish that Baldwin describes as characteristic of the Negro's experience are Richard Wright's autobiography, *Black Boy* (1945), and Ralph Ellison's novel *Invisible Man* (1952). The South African writer Alan Paton has dealt with the race problem in South Africa in two powerful novels: *Cry, the Beloved Country* (1948) and *Too Late the Phalarope* (1953). The play *The Respectful Prostitute* (1946), by the French philosopher, novelist, and playwright Jean-Paul Sartre, is a sobering reflection of the way racial discrimination affects the American image abroad.

BENJAMIN FRANKLIN

Benjamin Franklin (1706–1790) has long been a national institution. His personality and achievements have weathered well the influence of forces that turn national heroes into distant and stereotyped figures. His shrewd competence as printer, publisher, and author assured him of business success and financial independence. In his adopted city of Philadelphia, he promoted pioneering civic, educational, and charitable projects. He gained recognition for scientific experiment and invention. He participated in the affairs of local colonial self-government and represented first the colonies and then the newly independent states in England and France. Biographers and critics have credited him with having helped to shape the American national character. In the following selection from his *Autobiography,* the man behind the legend speaks articulately and engagingly for himself.

Autobiography

I disliked the trade, and had a strong inclination for the sea, but my father declared against it; however, living near the water, I was much in and about it, learned early to swim well, and to manage boats; and when in a boat or canoe with other boys, I was commonly allowed to govern, especially in any case of difficulty; and upon other occasions I was generally a leader among the boys, and sometimes led them into scrapes, of which I will mention one instance, as it shows an early projecting public spirit, tho' not then justly conducted.

There was a salt-marsh that bounded part of the millpond, on the edge of which, at high water, we used to stand to fish for minnows. By much tramping, we had made it a mere quagmire. My proposal was to build a wharf there fit for us to stand upon, and I showed my comrades a large heap of stones, which were intended for a new house near the marsh, and which would very well suit our purpose. Accordingly, in the evening, when the workmen were gone, I assembled a number of my playfellows, and working with them diligently like so many emmets, sometimes two or three to a stone, we brought them all away and built our little wharf. The next morning the workmen were surprised at missing the stones, which were found in our wharf. Inquiry was made after the removers; we were discovered and complained of; several of us were corrected by our fathers; and, though I pleaded the usefulness of the work, mine convinced me that nothing was useful which was not honest.

I think you may like to know something of his person and character. He had an excellent constitution of body, was of middle stature, but well set, and very strong; he was ingenious, could draw prettily, was skilled a little in music, and had a clear pleasing voice, so that when he played psalm tunes on his violin and sung withal, as he sometimes did in an evening after the business of the day was over, it was extremely agreeable to hear. He had a mechanical genius too, and, on occasion, was very handy in the use of other tradesmen's tools; but his great excellence lay in a sound understanding and solid judgment in prudential matters, both in private and public affairs. In the latter, indeed, he was never employed, the numerous family he had to educate and the straitness of his circumstances keeping him close to his trade; but I remember well his being frequently visited by leading people, who consulted him for his opinion in affairs of the town or of the church he belonged to, and showed a good deal of respect for his judgment and advice: he was also much consulted by private persons about their affairs when any difficulty occurred, and frequently chosen an arbitrator between contending parties. At his table he liked to have, as often as he could, some sensible friend or neighbor to converse with, and always took care to start some ingenious or useful topic for discourse, which might tend to improve the minds of his children. By this means he turned our attention to what was good, just, and prudent in the conduct of life; and little or no notice was ever taken of what related to the victuals on the table, whether it was well or ill dressed, in or out of season, of good or bad flavor, preferable or inferior to this or that other thing of the kind, so that I was brought up in such a perfect inattention to those matters as to be quite indifferent what kind of food was set before me, and so unobservant of it that to this day if I am asked I can scarce tell a few hours after dinner what I dined upon. This has been a convenience to me in travelling, where my companions have been sometimes very unhappy for want of a suitable gratification of their more delicate, because better instructed, tastes and appetites.

My mother had likewise an excellent constitution: she suckled all her ten children. I never knew either my father or mother to have any sickness but that of which they died, he at 89, and she at 85 years of age. They lie buried together at Boston, where I some years since placed a marble over their grave, with this inscription:

JOSIAH FRANKLIN,
and
ABIAH his wife,
lie here interred.
They lived lovingly together in wedlock
fifty-five years,
Without an estate, or any gainful employment,
By constant labor and industry,
with God's blessing,
They maintained a large family
comfortably,
and brought up thirteen children
and seven grandchildren
reputably.
From this instance, reader,
Be encouraged to diligence in thy calling,
And distrust not Providence.
He was a pious and prudent man;
She, a discreet and virtuous woman.

Their youngest son,
In filial regard to their memory,
Places this stone.
J. F. born 1655, died 1744, Ætat 89.
A. F. born 1667, died 1752,——85.

By my rambling digressions I perceive myself to be grown old. I used to write more methodically. But one does not dress for private company as for a public ball. 'Tis perhaps only negligence.

To return: I continued thus employed in my father's business for two years, that is, till I was twelve years old; and my brother John, who was bred to that business, having left my father, married, and set up for himself at Rhode Island, there was all appearance that I was destined to supply his place, and become a tallow-chandler. But my dislike to the trade continuing, my father was under apprehensions that if he did not find one for me more agreeable, I should break away and get to sea, as his son Josiah had done, to his great vexation. He therefore sometimes took me to walk with him, and see joiners, bricklayers, turners, braziers, etc., at their work, that he might observe my inclination, and endeavor to fix it on some trade or other on land. It has ever since been a pleasure to me to see good workmen handle their tools; and it has been useful to me, having learned so much by it as to be able to do little jobs myself in my house when a workman could not readily be got, and to construct little machines for my experiments, while the intention of making the experiment was fresh and warm in my mind. My father at last fixed upon the cutler's trade, and my uncle Benjamin's son Samuel, who was bred to that business in London, being about that time established in Boston, I was sent to be with him some time on liking. But his expectations of a fee with me displeasing my father, I was taken home again.

From a child I was fond of reading, and all the little money that came into my hands was ever laid out in books. Pleased with the *Pilgrim's Progress*, my first collection was of John Bunyan's works in separate little volumes. I afterward sold them to enable me to buy R. Burton's Historical Collections; they were small chapmen's books, and cheap, 40 or 50 in all. My father's little library consisted chiefly of books in polemic divinity, most of which I read, and have since often regretted that, at a time when I had such a thirst for knowledge, more proper books had not fallen in my way, since it was now resolved I should not be a clergyman. *Plutarch's Lives* there was in which I read abundantly, and I still think that time spent to great advantage. There was also a book of Defoe's, called an *Essay on Projects*, and another of Dr. Mather's, called *Essays to do Good,* which perhaps gave me a turn of thinking that had an influence on some of the principal future events of my life.

This bookish inclination at length determined my father to make me a printer, though he had already one son (James) of that profession. In 1717 my brother James returned from England with a press and letters to set up his business in Boston. I liked it much better than that of my father, but still had a hankering for the sea. To prevent the apprehended effect of such an inclination, my father was impatient to have me bound to my brother. I stood out some time, but at last was persuaded, and signed the indentures when I was yet but twelve years old. I was to serve as an apprentice till I was twenty-one years of age, only I was to be allowed journeyman's wages during the last year. In a little time I made great proficiency in the business, and became a useful hand to my brother. I now had access to better books. An acquaintance with the apprentices of booksellers enabled me sometimes to borrow a small one, which I was careful to return soon and clean. Often I sat up in my room reading the greatest part of the night, when the book was borrowed in the evening and to be returned early in the morning, lest it should be missed or wanted.

And after some time an ingenious tradesman, Mr. Matthew Adams, who had a pretty collection of books, and who frequented our printing-house, took notice of me, invited me to his library, and very kindly lent me such books as I chose to read. I now took a fancy to poetry, and made some little pieces; my brother, thinking it might turn to account, encouraged me, and put me on composing occasional ballads. One was called *The Lighthouse Tragedy*, and contained an account of the drowning of Captain Worthilake, with his two daughters: the other was a sailor's song, on the taking of *Teach* (or Blackbeard) the pirate. They were wretched stuff, in the Grub Street ballad style; and when they were printed he sent me about the town to sell them. The first sold wonderfully, the event being recent, having made a great noise. This flattered my vanity; but my father discouraged me by ridiculing my performances, and telling me verse-makers were generally beggars. So I escaped being a poet, most probably a very bad one; but as prose writing has been of great use to me in the course of my life, and was a principal means of my advancement, I shall tell you how, in such a situation, I acquired what little ability I have in that way.

There was another bookish lad in the town, John Collins by name, with whom I was intimately acquainted. We sometimes disputed, and very fond we were of argument, and very desirous of confuting one another, which disputatious turn, by the way, is apt to become a very bad habit, making people often extremely disagreeable in company by the contradiction that is necessary to bring it into practice; and thence, besides souring and spoiling the conversation, is productive of disgusts and, perhaps, enmities where you may have occasion for friendship. I had caught it by reading my father's books of dispute about religion. Persons of good sense, I have since observed, seldom fall into it, except lawyers, university men, and men of all sorts that have been bred at Edinborough.

A question was once, somehow or other, started between Collins and me, of the propriety of educating the female sex in learning, and their abilities for study. He was of opinion that it was improper, and that they were naturally unequal to it. I took the contrary side, perhaps a little for dispute's sake. He was naturally more eloquent, had a ready plenty of words; and sometimes, as I thought, bore me down more by his fluency than by the strength of his reasons. As we parted without settling the point, and were not to see one another again for some time, I sat down to put my arguments in writing, which I copied fair and sent to him. He answered, and I replied. Three or four letters of a side had passed, when my father happened to find my papers and read them. Without entering into the discussion, he took occasion to talk to me about the manner of my writing; observed that, though I had the advantage of my antagonist in correct spelling and pointing (which I owed to the printing-house), I fell far short in elegance of expression, in method and in perspicuity, of which he convinced me by several instances. I saw the justice of his remarks, and thence grew more attentive to the manner in writing, and determined to endeavor at improvement.

About this time I met with an odd volume of the *Spectator*. It was the third. I had never before seen any of them. I bought it, read it over and over, and was much delighted with it. I thought the writing excellent, and wished, if possible, to imitate it. With this view I took some of the papers, and, making short hints of the sentiment in each sentence, laid them by a few days, and then, without looking at the book, tried to complete the papers again, by expressing each hinted sentiment at length, and as fully as it had been expressed before, in any suitable words that should come to hand. Then I compared my *Spectator* with the original, discovered some of my faults, and corrected them. But I found I wanted a stock of words, or a readiness in recollecting and using them, which I thought I should have acquired before that time if I had gone on making verses; since the continual occasion for words of the same import, but of different length, to suit the measure, or of different sound for the rhyme, would have laid me under a constant necessity of searching for variety, and also have tended to fix that variety in my mind, and make me master of it. Therefore I took some of the tales and turned them into verse; and, after a time, when I had pretty well forgotten the prose, turned them back again. I also sometimes jumbled my collections of hints into confusion, and after some weeks endeavored to reduce them into the best order, before I began to form the full sentences and complete the paper. This was to teach me method in the arrangement of thoughts. By comparing my work afterwards with the original, I discovered many faults and amended them; but I sometimes had the pleasure of fancying that, in certain particulars of small import, I had been lucky enough to improve the method or the language, and this encouraged me to think I might possibly in time come to be a tolerable English writer, of which I was extremely ambitious. My time for these exercises and for reading was at night, after work or before it began in the morning, or on Sundays, when I contrived to be in the printing-house alone, evading as much as I could the common attendance on public worship which my father used to exact on me when I was under his care, which indeed I still thought a duty, though I could not, as it seemed to me, afford time to practice it.

When about 16 years of age I happened to meet with a book, written by one Tryon, recommending a vegetable diet. I determined to go into it. My brother, being yet unmarried, did not keep house, but boarded himself and his apprentices in another family. My refusing to eat flesh occasioned an inconveniency, and I was frequently chid for my singularity. I made myself acquainted with Tryon's manner of preparing some of his dishes, such as boiling potatoes or rice, making hasty pudding, and a few others, and then proposed to my brother, that if he would give me, weekly, half the money he paid for my board, I would board myself. He instantly agreed to it, and I presently found that I could save half what he paid me. This was an additional fund for buying books. But I had another advantage in it. My brother and the rest going from the printing-house to their meals, I remained there alone, and, despatching presently my light repast, which often was no more than a biscuit or a slice of bread, a handful of raisins or a tart from the pastry-cook's, and a glass of water, had the rest of the time till their return for study, in which I made the greater progress, from that greater clearness of head and quicker apprehension which usually attend temperance in eating and drinking.

And now it was that, being on some occasion made ashamed of my ignorance in figures, which I had twice failed in learning when at school, I took Cocker's book of Arithmetic, and went through the whole by myself with great ease. I also read Seller's and Shermy's books of Navigation, and became acquainted with the little geometry they contain; but never proceeded far in that science. And I read about this time Locke *On Human Understanding,* and the *Art of Thinking,* by Messrs. du Port Royal.

While I was intent on improving my language, I met with an English grammar (I think it was Greenwood's), at the end of which there were two little sketches of the arts of rhetoric and logic, the latter finishing with a specimen of a dispute in the Socratic method; and soon after I procured Xenophon's *Memorable Things of Socrates,* wherein there are many instances of the same method. I was charmed with it, adopted it, dropped my abrupt contradiction and positive argumentation, and put on the humble inquirer and doubter. And being then, from reading Shaftesbury and Collins, become a real doubter in many points of our religious doctrine, I found this method safest for myself and very embarrassing to those against whom I used it; therefore I took a delight in it, practiced it continually, and grew very artful and expert in drawing people, even of superior knowledge, into concessions, the consequences of which they did not foresee, entangling them in difficulties out of which they could not extricate themselves, and so obtaining victories that neither myself nor my cause always deserved. I continued this method some few years, but gradually left it, retaining only the habit of expressing myself in terms of modest diffidence; never using, when I advanced anything that may possibly be disputed, the words *certainly, undoubtedly,* or any others that give the air of positiveness to an opinion; but rather say, *I conceive or apprehend a thing to be so and so; it appears to me;* or *I should think it so or so, for such and such reason;* or *I imagine it to be so*; or *it is so, if I am not mistaken.* This habit, I believe, has been of great advantage to me when I have had occasion to inculcate my opinions, and persuade men into measures that I have been from time to time engaged in promoting; and, as the chief ends of conversation are to *inform* or to *be informed*, to *please* or to *persuade*, I wish well-meaning, sensible men would not lessen their power of doing good by a positive, assuming manner, that seldom fails to disgust, tends to create opposition, and to defeat every one of those purposes for which speech was given to us, to wit, giving or receiving information or pleasure. For, if you would inform, a positive and dogmatical manner in advancing your sentiments may provoke contradiction and prevent a candid attention. If you wish information and improvement from the knowledge of others, and yet at the same time express yourself as firmly fixed in your present opinions, modest, sensible men, who do not love disputation, will probably leave you undisturbed in the possession of your error. And by such a manner, you can seldom hope to recommend yourself in *pleasing* your hearers, or to persuade those whose concurrence you desire. Pope says, judiciously:

> *"Men should be taught as if you taught them not,*
> *And things unknown proposed as things forgot;"*

farther recommending to us

> "To speak, tho' sure, with seeming diffidence."

And he might have coupled with this line that which he has coupled with another, I think, less properly,

> "For want of modesty is want of sense."

If you ask, Why less properly? I must repeat the lines,

> "Immodest words admit of no defense,
>   For want of modesty is want of sense."

Now, is not *want of sense* (where a man is so unfortunate as to want it) some apology for his *want of modesty?* and would not the lines stand more justly thus?

"Immodest words admit *but* this defense,
That want of modesty is want of sense."

This, however, I should submit to better judgments.

My brother had, in 1720 or 1721, begun to print a newspaper. It was the second that appeared in America, and was called the New England Courant. The only one before it was the Boston News-Letter. I remember his being dissuaded by some of his friends from the undertaking, as not likely to succeed, one newspaper being, in their judgment, enough for America. At this time (1771) there are not less than five-and-twenty. He went on, however, with the undertaking, and after having worked in composing the types and printing off the sheets, I was employed to carry the papers through the streets to the customers.

He had some ingenious men among his friends, who amused themselves by writing little pieces for this paper, which gained it credit and made it more in demand, and these gentlemen often visited us. Hearing their conversations, and their accounts of the approbation their papers were received with, I was excited to try my hand among them; but, being still a boy, and suspecting that my brother would object to printing anything of mine in his paper if he knew it to be mine, I contrived to disguise my hand, and, writing an anonymous paper, I put it in at night under the door of the printing-house. It was found in the morning, and communicated to his writing friends when they called in as usual. They read it, commented on it in my hearing, and I had the exquisite pleasure of finding it met with their approbation, and that, in their different guesses at the author, none were named but men of some character among us for learning and ingenuity. I suppose now that I was rather lucky in my judges, and that perhaps they were not really so very good ones as I then esteemed them.

Encouraged, however, by this, I wrote and conveyed in the same way to the press several more papers which were equally approved; and I kept my secret till my small fund of sense for such performances was pretty well exhausted, and then I discovered it, when I began to be considered a little more by my brother's acquaintance, and in a manner that did not quite please him, as he thought, probably with reason, that it tended to make me too vain. And, perhaps, this might be one occasion of the differences that we began to have about this time. Though a brother, he considered himself as my master, and me as his apprentice, and, accordingly, expected the same services from me as he would from another, while I thought he demeaned me too much in some he required of me, who from a brother expected more indulgence. Our disputes were often brought before our father, and I fancy I was either generally in the right, or else a better pleader, because the judgment was generally in my favor. But my brother was passionate, and had often beaten me, which I took extremely amiss; and, thinking my apprenticeship very tedious, I was continually wishing for some opportunity of shortening it, which at length offered in a manner unexpected.[1]

One of the pieces in our newspaper on some political point, which I have now forgotten, gave offense to the Assembly. He was taken up, censured, and imprisoned for a month, by the speaker's warrant, I suppose, because he would not discover his author. I too was taken up and examined before the council; but, though I did not give them any satisfaction, they contented themselves with admonishing me, and dismissed me, considering me, perhaps, as an apprentice, who was bound to keep his master's secrets.

During my brother's confinement, which I resented a good deal, notwithstanding our private differences, I had the management of the paper; and I made bold to give our rulers some rubs in it, which my brother took very kindly, while others began to consider me in an unfavorable light, as a young genius that had a turn for libelling and satire. My brother's discharge was accompanied with an order of the House (a very odd one), that "James Franklin should no longer print the paper called the New England Courant."

There was a consultation held in our printing-house among his friends, what he should do in this case. Some proposed to evade the order by changing the name of the paper; but my brother seeing inconveniences in that, it was finally concluded on as a better way, to let it be printed for the future under the name of BENJAMIN FRANKLIN; and to avoid the censure of the Assembly, that might fall on him as still printing it by his apprentice, the contrivance was that my old indenture should be returned to me, with a full discharge on the back of it, to be shown on occasion, but to secure to him the benefit of my service, I was to sign new indentures for the remainder of the term, which were to be kept private. A very flimsy scheme it was; however, it was immediately executed, and the paper went on accordingly, under my name, for several months.

At length, a fresh difference arising between my brother and me, I took upon me to assert my freedom, presuming that he would not venture to produce the new indentures. It was not fair in me to take this advantage, and this I therefore reckon one of the first errata of my life; but the unfairness of it weighed little with me, when under the impressions of resentment for the blows his passion too often urged him to bestow upon me, though he was otherwise not an ill-natured man: perhaps I was too saucy and provoking.

When he found I would leave him, he took care to prevent my getting employment in any other printing-house of the town, by going round and speaking to every master, who accordingly refused to give me work. I then thought of going to New York, as the nearest place where there was a

---

[1] I fancy this harsh and tyrannical treatment of me might be a means of impressing me with that aversion to arbitrary power that has stuck to me through my whole life.

printer; and I was rather inclined to leave Boston when I reflected that I had already made myself a little obnoxious to the governing party, and, from the arbitrary proceedings of the Assembly in my brother's case, it was likely I might, if I stayed, soon bring myself into scrapes; and farther, that my indiscreet disputations about religion began to make me pointed at with horror by good people as an infidel or atheist. I determined on the point, but my father now siding with my brother, I was sensible that, if I attempted to go openly, means would be used to prevent me. My friend Collins, therefore, undertook to manage a little for me. He agreed with the captain of a New York sloop for my passage, under the notion of my being a young acquaintance of his, that had got a naughty girl with child, whose friends would compel me to marry her, and therefore I could not appear or come away publicly. So I sold some of my books to raise a little money, was taken on board privately, and as we had a fair wind, in three days I found myself in New York, near 300 miles from home, a boy of but 17, without the least recommendation to, or knowledge of any person in the place, and with very little money in my pocket.

My inclinations for the sea were by this time worn out, or I might now have gratified them. But, having a trade, and supposing myself a pretty good workman, I offered my service to the printer in the place, old Mr. William Bradford, who had been the first printer in Pennsylvania, but removed from thence upon the quarrel of George Keith. He could give me no employment, having little to do, and help enough already; but says he, "My son at Philadelphia has lately lost his principal hand, Aquila Rose, by death; if you go thither, I believe he may employ you." Philadelphia was a hundred miles further; I set out, however, in a boat for Amboy, leaving my chest and things to follow me round by sea.

DISCUSSION AND WRITING

1. In context, what is the meaning of "polemic *divinity*," "*bound* to my brother," "correct spelling and *pointing*," "words of the same *import*," "men of some *character* among us for learning and ingenuity"? List and explain words or expressions that are no longer a part of everyday American English. What generalizations do they suggest concerning changes in the language since Franklin's time?

2. Though Franklin apologizes for the "rambling" quality of his writing, what unifies this selection? What is the pervading theme or most characteristic note? Point out as many illustrations or applications of it as you can.

3. Franklin's *Poor Richard's Almanac* is known for its collection of moral maxims, little gems of proverbial wisdom. Formulate half a dozen maxims stated or implied in this section of his *Autobiography*.

4. Write a one-paragraph theme stating your position on a current campus grievance or controversy. Prepare two versions, one in a "positive and dogmatical manner," the other expressed "in terms of modest diffidence."

5. Benjamin Franklin is often said to show typically American traits or attitudes. Does this selection support this view? Which of the traits or attitudes here illustrated have you encountered in your own life? Use detailed evidence.

6. Franklin says that in his youth he "was generally a leader among the boys." What qualities in Franklin's character would tend to make him a leader among men?

7. Some modern readers have vigorously attacked Franklin's attitude toward life as too narrow, too limited, too one-sided. To judge from this selection, how valid or justified is this charge?

8. Compare and contrast Franklin's and Baldwin's relation to their respective families.

9. Write an essay on one of the following topics: What has most influenced your own future plans or choice of a career? What topic that you have read or argued about in recent years has stirred up your feelings most? What was your most instructive attempt to gain recognition or success? Which book has influenced your thinking or your attitudes more than any other book you have read?

10. Franklin discusses some of the factors that make for friendship or enmity. Discuss in concrete detail an experience or association that taught you something important about the difficulties involved in "getting along" with other people.

FURTHER READING

Autobiographical novels that trace developments in the hero's life or personality in thoroughly documented detail are Charles Dickens, *David Copperfield* (1850); Samuel Butler, *The Way of All Flesh* (1903); Somerset Maugham, *Of Human Bondage* (1915); and Thomas Wolfe, *Look Homeward, Angel* (1929).

WINSTON CHURCHILL

Sir Winston Churchill (1874–1965) was British Prime Minister from 1940 to 1945 and played a decisive role in the conduct of World War II. His previous career had included service as war correspondent in the Boer War, as Member of Parliament, and as minister of munitions in World War I. His speeches and historical writings gave him a reputation as a master of English prose. The speech he made to the House of Commons upon the evacuation of the British Expeditionary Force from Dunkirk in 1940 is one of the great documents of political oratory. His *The Second World War* won the Nobel Prize for Literature in 1953. The following excerpts on his education are taken from an account he published in 1930. They illustrate a kind of candor that is absent from autobiographies written for self-glorification or self-justification.

My Early Life

The school my parents had selected for my education was one of the most fashionable and expensive in the country. It modelled itself upon Eton and aimed at being preparatory for that Public School above all others. It was supposed to be the very last thing in schools. Only ten boys in a class; electric light (then a wonder); a swimming pond; spacious football and cricket grounds; two or three school treats, or "expeditions" as they were called, every term; the masters all M.A.'s in gowns and mortarboards; a chapel of its own; no hampers allowed; everything provided by the authorities. It was a dark November afternoon when we arrived at this establishment. We had tea with the Headmaster, with whom my mother conversed in the most easy manner. I was preoccupied with the fear of spilling my cup and so making "a bad start." I was also miserable at the idea of being left alone among all these strangers in this great, fierce, formidable place. After all I was only seven, and I had been so happy in my nursery with all my toys. I had such wonderful toys: a real steam engine, a magic lantern, and a collection of soldiers already nearly a thousand strong. Now it was to be all lessons. Seven or eight hours of lessons every day except half-holidays, and football or cricket in addition.

When the last sound of my mother's departing wheels had died away, the Headmaster invited me to hand over any money I had in my possession. I produced my three half-crowns which were duly entered in a book, and I was told that from time to time there would be a "shop" at the school with all sorts of things which one would like to have, and that I could choose what I liked up to the limit of the seven and sixpence. Then we quitted the Headmaster's parlor and the comfortable private side of the house, and entered the more bleak apartments reserved for the instruction and accommodation of the pupils. I was taken into a Form Room and told to sit at a desk. All the other boys were out of doors, and I was alone with the Form Master. He produced a thin greeny-brown-covered book filled with words in different types of print.

"You have never done any Latin before, have you?" he said.

"No, sir."

"This is a Latin grammar." He opened it at a well-thumbed page. "You must learn this," he said, pointing to a number of words in a frame of lines. "I will come back in half an hour and see what you know."

Reprinted with the permission of Charles Scribner's Sons from *A Roving Commission*, pp. 9–13, 15–19, 20–21, by Winston S. Churchill. Copyright 1930 Charles Scribner's Sons; renewal copyright © 1958 Winston Churchill.

Behold me then on a gloomy evening, with an aching heart, seated in front of the First Declension.

Mensa	a table
Mensa	O table
Mensam	a table
Mensae	of a table
Mensae	to or for a table
Mensa	by, with or from a table

What on earth did it mean? Where was the sense of it? It seemed absolute rigmarole to me. However, there was one thing I could always do: I could learn by heart. And I thereupon proceeded, as far as my private sorrows would allow, to memorize the acrostic-looking task which had been set me.

In due course the Master returned.

"Have you learnt it?" he asked.

"I think I can *say* it, sir," I replied; and I gabbled it off.

He seemed so satisfied with this that I was emboldened to ask a question. "What does it mean, sir?"

"It means what it says. Mensa, a table. Mensa is a noun of the First Declension. There are five declensions. You have learnt the singular of the First Declension."

"But," I repeated, "what does it mean?"

"Mensa means a table," he answered.

"Then why does mensa also mean O table," I enquired, "and what does O table mean?"

"Mensa, O table, is the vocative case," he replied.

"But why O table?" I persisted in genuine curiosity.

"O table,—you would use that in addressing a table, in invoking a table." And then seeing he was not carrying me with him, "You would use it in speaking to a table."

"But I never do," I blurted out in honest amazement.

"If you are impertinent, you will be punished, and punished, let me tell you, very severely," was his conclusive rejoinder.

Such was my first introduction to the classics from which, I have been told, many of our cleverest men have derived so much solace and profit.

The Form Master's observations about punishment were by no means without their warrant at St. James's School. Flogging with the birch in accordance with the Eton fashion was a great feature in its curriculum. But I am sure no Eton boy, and certainly no Harrow boy of my day, ever received such a cruel flogging as this Headmaster was accustomed to inflict upon the little boys who were in his care and power. They exceeded in severity anything that would be tolerated in any of the Reformatories under the Home Office. My reading in later life has supplied me with some possible explanations of his temperament. Two or three times a month the whole school was marshalled in the Library, and one or more delinquents were haled off to an adjoining apartment by the two head boys, and there flogged until they bled freely, while the rest sat quaking, listening to their screams....

How I hated this school, and what a life of anxiety I lived there for more than two years. I made very little progress at my lessons, and none at all at games. I counted the days and the hours to the end of every term, when I should return home from this hateful servitude and range my soldiers in line of battle on the nursery floor. The greatest pleasure I had in those days was reading. When I was nine and a half my father gave me *Treasure Island*, and I remember the delight with which I devoured it. My teachers saw me at once backward and precocious, reading books beyond my years and yet at the bottom of the Form. They were offended. They had large resources of compulsion at their disposal, but I was stubborn. Where my reason, imagination or interest were not engaged, I would not or I could not learn. In all the twelve years I was at school no one ever succeeded in making me write a Latin verse or learn any Greek except the alphabet. I do not at all excuse myself for this foolish neglect of opportunities procured at so much expense by my parents and brought so forcibly to my attention by my Preceptors. Perhaps if I had been introduced to the ancients through their history and customs, instead of through their grammar and syntax, I might have had a better record.

I fell into a low state of health at St. James's School, and finally after a serious illness my parents took me away. Our family doctor, the celebrated Robson Roose, then practiced at Brighton; and as I was now supposed to be very delicate it was thought desirable that I should be under his constant care. I was accordingly, in 1883, transferred to a school at Brighton kept by two ladies. This was a smaller school than the one I had left. It was also cheaper and less pretentious. But there was an element of kindness and of sympathy which I had found conspicuously lacking in my first experiences. Here I remained for three years; and though I very nearly died from an attack of double pneumonia, I got gradually much stronger in that bracing air and gentle surroundings. At this school I was allowed to learn things which interested me: French, History, lots of Poetry by heart, and above all Riding and Swimming. The impression of those years makes a pleasant picture in my mind, in strong contrast to my earlier schoolday memories....

I had scarcely passed my twelfth birthday when I entered the inhospitable regions of examinations, through which for the next seven years I was destined to journey. These examinations were a great trial to me. The subjects which were dearest to the examiners were almost invariably those I fancied least. I would have liked to have been examined in history, poetry and writing essays. The examiners, on the other hand, were partial to Latin and mathematics. And their will prevailed. Moreover, the questions which they asked on both these subjects were almost invariably those to which I was unable to suggest a satisfactory answer. I should have liked to be asked to say what I knew. They always tried to ask what I did not know. When I would have willingly displayed my knowledge, they sought to expose my ignorance. This sort of treatment had only one result: I did not do well in examinations.

This was especially true of my Entrance Examination to Harrow. The Headmaster, Dr. Welldon, however, took a broad-minded view of my Latin prose: he showed discernment in judging my general ability. This was the more remarkable, because I was found unable to answer a single question in the Latin paper. I wrote my name at the top of the page. I wrote down the number of the question "I." After much reflection I put a bracket round it thus "(I)." But thereafter I could not think of anything connected with it that was either relevant or true. Incidentally there arrived from nowhere in particular a blot and several smudges. I gazed for two whole hours at this sad spectacle: and then merciful ushers collected my piece of foolscap with all the others and carried it up to the Headmaster's table. It was from these slender indications of scholarship that Dr. Welldon drew the conclusion that I was worthy to pass into Harrow. It is very much to his credit. It showed that he was a man capable of looking beneath the surface of things: a man not dependent upon paper manifestations. I have always had the greatest regard for him.

In consequence of his decision, I was in due course placed in the third, or lowest, division of the Fourth, or bottom, Form. The names of the new boys were printed in the School List in alphabetical order; and as my correct name, Spencer-Churchill, began with an "S," I gained no more advantage from the alphabet than from the wider sphere of letters. I was in fact only two from the bottom of the whole school; and these two, I regret to say, disappeared almost immediately through illness or some other cause.

The Harrow custom of calling the roll is different from that of Eton. At Eton the boys stand in a cluster and lift their hats when their names are called. At Harrow they file past a Master in the school yard and answer one by one. My position was therefore revealed in its somewhat invidious humility. It was the year 1887. Lord Randolph Churchill had only just resigned his position as Leader of the House of Commons and Chancellor of the Exchequer, and he still towered in the forefront of politics. In consequence large numbers of visitors of both sexes used to wait on the school steps, in order to see me march by; and I frequently heard the irreverent comment, "Why, he's last of all!"

I continued in this unpretentious situation for nearly a year. However, by being so long in the lowest form I gained an immense advantage over the cleverer boys. They all went on to learn Latin and Greek and splendid things like that. But I was taught English. We were considered such dunces that we could learn only English. Mr. Somervell—a most delightful man, to whom my debt is great—was charged with the duty of teaching the stupidest boys the most disregarded thing—namely, to write mere English. He knew how to do it. He taught it as no one else has ever taught it. Not only did we learn English parsing thoroughly, but we also practiced continually English analysis. Mr. Somervell had a system of his own. He took a fairly long sentence and broke it up into its components by means of black, red, blue and green inks. Subject, verb, object: Relative Clauses, Conditional Clauses, Conjunctive and Disjunctive Clauses! Each had its color and its bracket. It was a kind of drill. We did it almost daily. As I remained in the Third Fourth (β) three times as long as anyone else, I had three times as much of it. I learned it thoroughly. Thus I got into my bones the essential structure of the ordinary British sentence—which is a noble thing. And when in after years my schoolfellows who had won prizes and distinction for writing such beautiful Latin poetry and pithy Greek epigrams had to come down again to common English, to earn their living or make their way, I did not feel myself at any disadvantage. Naturally I am biassed in favor of boys learning English. I would make them all learn English: and then I would let the clever ones learn Latin as an honor, and Greek as a treat. But the only thing I would whip them for would be for not knowing English. I would whip them hard for that.

I first went to Harrow in the summer term. The school possessed the biggest swimming-bath I had ever seen. It was more like the bend of a river than a bath, and it had two bridges across it. Thither we used to repair for hours at a time and bask between our dips eating enormous buns on the hot asphalt margin. Naturally it was a good joke to come up behind some naked friend, or even enemy, and push him in. I made quite a habit of this with boys of my own size or less. One day when I had been no more than a month in the school, I saw a boy standing in a meditative posture wrapped in a towel on the very brink. He was no bigger than I was, so I thought him fair game. Coming stealthily behind I pushed him in, holding on to his towel out of humanity, so that it should not get wet. I was startled to see a furious face emerge from the foam, and a being evidently of enormous strength making its way by fierce strokes to the shore. I fled, but in vain. Swift as the wind my pursuer overtook me, seized me in a ferocious grip and hurled me into the deepest part of the pool. I soon scrambled out on the other side, and found myself surrounded by an agitated crowd of younger boys. "You're in for it," they said. "Do you know what you have done? It's Amery, he's in the Sixth Form. He is Head of his House; he is champion at Gym; he has got his football colors." They continued to recount his many titles to fame and reverence and to dilate upon the awful retribution that would fall upon me. I was convulsed not only with terror, but with the guilt of sacrilege. How could I tell his rank when he was in a bath-towel and so small? I determined to apologize immediately. I approached the potentate in lively trepidation. "I am very sorry," I said. "I mistook you for a Fourth Form boy. You are so small." He did not seem at all placated by this; so I added in a most brilliant recovery, "My father, who is a great man, is also small." At this he laughed, and after some general remarks about my "cheek" and how I had better be careful in the future, signified that the incident was closed.

I have been fortunate to see a good deal more of him, in times when three years' difference in age is not so important as it is at school. We were afterwards to be Cabinet colleagues for a good many years.

It was thought incongruous that while I apparently stagnated in the lowest form, I should gain a prize open to the whole school for reciting to the Headmaster twelve hundred lines of Macaulay's "Lays of Ancient Rome" without making a single mistake. I also succeeded in passing the preliminary examination for the Army while still almost at the bottom of the school. This examination seemed to have called forth a very special effort on my part, for many boys far above me in the school failed in it. I also had a piece of good luck. We knew that among other questions we should be asked to draw from memory a map of some country or other. The night before by way of final preparation I put the names of all the maps in the atlas into a hat and drew out New Zealand. I applied my good memory to the geography of that Dominion. Sure enough the first question in the paper was: "Draw a map of New Zealand." This was what is called at Monte Carlo an *en plein*, and I ought to have been paid thirty-five times my stake. However, I certainly got paid very high marks for my paper....

I spent nearly four and a half years at Harrow, of which three were in the Army class. To this I was admitted in consequence of having passed the preliminary examination. It consisted of boys of the middle and higher forms of the school and of very different ages, all of whom were being prepared either for the Sandhurst or the Woolwich examination. We were withdrawn from the ordinary movement of the school from form to form. In consequence I got no promotion or very little and remained quite low down upon the school list, though working alongside of boys nearly all in the Fifth Form. Officially I never got out of the Lower School, so I never had the privilege of having a fag of my own. When in the passage of time I became what was called "a three-yearer" I ceased to have to fag myself, and as I was older than other boys of my standing, I was appointed in my House to the position of Head of the Fags. This was my first responsible office, and the duties, which were honorary, consisted in keeping the roster of all the fags, making out the lists of their duties and dates and placing copies of these lists in the rooms of the monitors, football and cricket champions and other members of our aristocracy. I discharged these functions for upwards of a year, and on the whole I was resigned to my lot.

Meanwhile I found an admirable method of learning my Latin translations. I was always very slow at using a dictionary: it was just like using a telephone directory. It is easy to open it more or less at the right letter, but then you have to turn backwards and forwards and peer up and down the columns and very often find yourself three or four pages the wrong side of the word you want. In short I found it most laborious, while to other boys it seemed no trouble. But now I formed an alliance with a boy in the Sixth Form. He was very clever and could read Latin as easily as English. Caesar, Ovid, Virgil, Horace and even Martial's epigrams were all the same to him. My daily task was perhaps ten or fifteen lines. This would ordinarily have taken me an hour or an hour and a half to decipher, and then it would probably have been wrong. But my friend could in five minutes construe it for me word by word, and once I had seen it exposed, I remembered it firmly. My Sixth-Form friend for his part was almost as much troubled by the English essays he had to write for the Headmaster as I was by these Latin cross-word puzzles. We agreed together that he should tell me my Latin translations and that I should do his essays. The arrangement worked admirably. The Latin master seemed quite satisfied with my work, and I had more time to myself in the mornings. On the other hand once a week or so I had to compose the essays of my Sixth-Form friend. I used to walk up and down the room dictating—just as I do now—and he sat in the corner and wrote it down in long-hand. For several months no difficulty arose; but once we were nearly caught out. One of these essays was thought to have merit. It was "sent up" to the Headmaster who summoned my friend, commended him on his work and proceeded to discuss the topic with him in a lively spirit. "I was interested in this point you make here. You might I think have gone even further. Tell me exactly what you had in your mind." Dr. Welldon in spite of very chilling responses continued in this way for some time to the deep consternation of my confederate. However the Headmaster, not wishing to turn an occasion of praise into one of cavilling, finally let him go with the remark "You seem to be better at written than at oral work." He came back to me like a man who has had a very narrow squeak, and I was most careful ever afterwards to keep to the beaten track in essay-writing.

DISCUSSION AND WRITING

1. Define or explain: *cricket, declension, rigmarole, acrostic, rejoinder, solace, marshal* (vb.), *hale, precocious, preceptor, syntax, discernment, foolscap, invidious, irreverent, parsing, pithy, ferocious, potentate, incongruous, stagnate, fag, epigram, construe,*

consternation. What are the British "Public Schools"? Explain other references to British educational and political institutions.

2. Sir Winston mentions his training in English sentence structure. Examine and describe characteristic features of his own sentences. Pay attention to such matters of sentence style as length, variety, subordination, parallelism.

3. To what extent does the author let his present attitudes and judgments affect his account of childhood events? What is the tone of these childhood reminiscences? Is it self-conscious, nostalgic, resentful, amused? Give detailed examples.

4. Summarize the views about schools and teaching stated or implied in these pages. Present them in your own words, working them into a coherent picture.

5. How close to (or how remote from) American students today is the author's experience with uncongenial subject matter, authoritarian teachers, student potentates, examinations, successful or unsuccessful cheating? Compare and contrast relevant experiences of your own. Limit yourself to one major topic but develop it in detail.

6. How successful is Sir Winston's attempt to recover the perspective of childhood, to re-create authentically a child's perceptions, feelings, and attitudes? Compare and contrast this selection with Mrs. Hudson's "Children of the Harvest" in this respect. Or, compare and contrast the selections by Franklin and Churchill as revealing first-hand accounts of the private personalities of two great historical figures. What, if anything, do the two men have in common? How do they differ?

7. Discuss in detail one feature of your early schooling, school life, or school discipline of which you strongly approve or disapprove.

8. Attack or defend one of the following statements: a) For successful teaching, kindness is more important than discipline. b) Cheating by students is inevitable and should not be judged by ordinary moral standards. c) Students learn more about life in their dealings with their schoolmates than they do from their teachers.

9. How successful are American high schools in making history meaningful to their students? Cite detailed evidence from your own experience.

10. What do you consider the most essential qualification of a great man? Use detailed illustrations.

FURTHER READING

Among notable autobiographies are John Stuart Mill, *Autobiography* (1873); Henry Adams, *The Education of Henry Adams* (1907); Lincoln Steffens, *The Autobiography of Lincoln Steffens* (1931); and Alfred Kazin, *A Walker in the City* (1951).

3

Education in Utopia

If a nation expects to be ignorant and free, in a state of civilization, it expects what never was and never will be.
THOMAS JEFFERSON

The subject of education provides an ideal testing ground for our powers of generalization. When a discussion deals with teachers and schools, everyone has had some relevant experience (sometimes painful), and everyone has an opinion. The writers in this section all proceed beyond specific questions of content and method to underlying principles. Their concern is to sketch out the ideal to be approximated and the dangers to be avoided. They all adopt a long-range perspective, looking for answers that will survive this year's crash program and last year's startling technical innovations. The first selection goes to the heart of the matter: the power of education to mold a society in the image conceived by philosopher, church, or state. Plato, in a discussion famous for its bearing on censorship, develops for his ideal state an educational program single-minded in its pursuit of its moral aims. Rousseau, in a selection from a pioneer study of educational method, concentrates on the process of learning and the problem of motivation. Robert M. Hutchins, in "The University of Utopia," champions the cause of "liberal education" as against vocational training, vigorously promoting the "cultural" subjects as against the "practical." John Wain, in "The Dilemma of Youth," returns to the basic question raised by the selection from Plato's *Republic:* Should education promote a spirit of sceptical questioning, or should it promote loyalty to accepted ideals?

PLATO

Plato (428/7–348/7 B.C.) developed his philosophy in Athens, the most prominent of the ancient Greek city-states, in a period of factionalism, revolution, and war. In *The Republic,* he describes an ideal society, founded not in private ambition or brute force but in justice. In the following excerpt, Plato concerns himself with the early training of the "guardians," the military and political elite who will defend the state against external enemies and maintain internal order. After the completion of the training here described, a small number of the guardians are to be singled out for further training as "rulers." As in Plato's other writings, the discussion takes the form of a dialogue between Plato's teacher, Socrates, and some of the master's pupils—in this case, Plato's elder brothers, Glaucon and Adeimantus. The reader participates in an argument in progress, which forces him to reconsider, rethink, and recapitulate instead of allowing him to be a mere passive audience. The present translation, by F. M. Cornford, illustrates the work of contemporary scholars who are making important texts of classical antiquity available in vigorous and idiomatic modern English.

Educating the Guardians

Don't you think then, said I, that, for the purpose of keeping guard, a young man should have much the same temperament and qualities as a well-bred watch-dog? I mean, for instance, that both must have quick senses to detect an enemy, swiftness in pursuing him, and strength, if they have to fight when they have caught him.

Yes, they will need all those qualities.

And also courage, if they are to fight well.

Of course.

And courage, in dog or horse or any other creature, implies a spirited disposition. You must have noticed that a high spirit is unconquerable. Every soul possessed of it is fearless and indomitable in the face of any danger.

From *The Republic of Plato,* translated with introduction and notes by Francis Macdonald Cornford. Oxford University Press, 1941. Reprinted by permission.

Yes, I have noticed that.

So now we know what physical qualities our Guardian must have, and also that he must be of a spirited temper.

Yes.

Then, Glaucon, how are men of that natural disposition to be kept from behaving pugnaciously to one another and to the rest of their countrymen?

It is not at all easy to see.

And yet they must be gentle to their own people and dangerous only to enemies; otherwise they will destroy themselves without waiting till others destroy them.

True.

What are we to do, then? If gentleness and a high temper are contraries, where shall we find a character to combine them? Both are necessary to make a good Guardian, but it seems they are incompatible. So we shall never have a good Guardian.

It looks like it.

Here I was perplexed, but on thinking over what we had been saying, I remarked that we deserved to be puzzled, because we had not followed up the comparison we had just drawn.

What do you mean? he asked.

We never noticed that, after all, there are natures in which these contraries are combined. They are to be found in animals, and not least in the kind we compared to our Guardian. Well-bred dogs, as you know, are by instinct perfectly gentle to people whom they know and are accustomed to, and fierce to strangers. So the combination of qualities we require for our Guardian is, after all, possible and not against nature.

Evidently.

Do you further agree that, besides this spirited temper, he must have a philosophical element in his nature?

I don't see what you mean.

This is another trait you will see in the dog. It is really remarkable how the creature gets angry at the mere sight of a stranger and welcomes anyone he knows, though he may never have been treated unkindly by the one or kindly by the other. Did that never strike you as curious?

I had not thought of it before; but that certainly is how a dog behaves.

Well, but that shows a fine instinct, which is philosophic in the true sense.

How so?

Because the only mark by which he distinguishes a friendly and an unfriendly face is that he knows the one and does not know the other; and if a creature makes that the test of what it finds congenial or otherwise, how can you deny that it has a passion for knowledge and understanding?

Of course, I cannot.

And that passion is the same thing as philosophy—the love of wisdom.

Yes.

Shall we boldly say, then, that the same is true of human beings? If a man is to be gentle towards his own people whom he knows, he must have an instinctive love of wisdom and understanding.

Agreed.

So the nature required to make a really noble Guardian of our commonwealth will be swift and strong, spirited, and philosophic.

Quite so.

Given those natural qualities, then, how are these Guardians to be brought up and educated? First, will the answer to that question help the purpose of our whole inquiry, which is to make out how justice and injustice grow up in a state? We want to be thorough, but not to draw out this discussion to a needless length.

Glaucon's brother answered: I certainly think it will help.

If so, I said, we must not think of dropping it, though it may be rather a long business.

I agree.

Come on then. We will take our time and educate our imaginary citizens.

Yes, let us do so.

What is this education to be, then? Perhaps we shall hardly invent a system better than the one which long experience has worked out, with its two branches for the cultivation of the mind and of the body. And I suppose we shall begin with the mind, before we start physical training.

Naturally.

Under that head will come stories; and of these there are two kinds: some are true, others fictitious. Both must come in, but we shall begin our education with the fictitious kind.

I don't understand, he said.

Don't you understand, I replied, that we begin by telling children stories, which, taken as a whole, are fiction, though they contain some truth? Such story-telling begins at an earlier age than physical training; that is why I said we should start with the mind.

You are right.

And the beginning, as you know, is always the most important part, especially in dealing with anything young and tender. That is the time when the character is being molded and easily takes any impress one may wish to stamp on it.

Quite true.

Then shall we simply allow our children to listen to any stories that anyone happens to make up, and so receive into their minds ideas often the very opposite of those we shall think they ought to have when they are grown up?

No, certainly not.

It seems, then, our first business will be to supervise the making of fables and legends, rejecting all which are unsatisfactory; and we shall induce nurses and mothers to tell their children only those which we have approved, and to think more of molding their souls with these stories than they now do of rubbing their limbs to make them strong and shapely. Most of the stories now in use must be discarded.

What kind do you mean?

If we take the great ones, we shall see in them the pattern of all the rest, which are bound to be of the same stamp and to have the same effect.

No doubt; but which do you mean by the great ones?

The stories in Hesiod and Homer and the poets in general, who have at all times composed fictitious tales and told them to mankind.

Which kind are you thinking of, and what fault do you find in them?

The worst of all faults, especially if the story is ugly and immoral as well as false—misrepresenting the nature of gods and heroes, like an artist whose picture is utterly unlike the object he sets out to draw.

That is certainly a serious fault; but give me an example.

A signal instance of false invention about the highest matters is that foul story, which Hesiod repeats, of the deeds of Uranus and the vengeance of Cronos; and then there is the tale of Cronos's doings and of his son's treatment of him. Even if such tales were true, I should not have supposed they should be lightly told to thoughtless young people. If they cannot be altogether suppressed, they should only be revealed in a mystery, to which access should be as far as possible restricted by requiring the sacrifice, not of a pig, but of some victim such as very few could afford.

It is true: those stories are objectionable.

Yes, and not to be repeated in our commonwealth, Adeimantus. We shall not tell a child that, if he commits the foulest crimes or goes to any length in punishing his father's misdeeds, he will be doing nothing out of the way, but only what the first and greatest of the gods have done before him.

I agree; such stories are not fit to be repeated.

Nor yet any tales of warfare and intrigues and battles of gods against gods, which are equally untrue. If our future Guardians are to think it a disgrace to quarrel lightly with one another, we shall not let them embroider robes with the Battle of the Giants or tell them of all the other feuds of gods and heroes with their kith and kin. If by any means we can make them believe that no one has ever had a quarrel with a fellow citizen and it is a sin to have one, that is the sort of thing our old men and women should tell children from the first; and as they grow older, we must make the poets write for them in the same strain. Stories like those of Hera being bound by her son, or of Hephaestus flung from heaven by his father for taking his mother's part when she was beaten, and all those battles of the gods in Homer, must not be admitted into our state, whether they be allegorical or not. A child cannot distinguish the allegorical sense from the literal, and the ideas he takes in at that age are likely to become indelibly fixed; hence the great importance of seeing that the first stories he hears shall be designed to produce the best possible effect on his character.

Yes, that is reasonable. But if we were asked which of these stories in particular are of the right quality, what should we answer?

I replied: You and I, Adeimantus, are not, for the moment, poets, but founders of a commonwealth. As such, it is not our business to invent stories ourselves, but only to be clear as to the main outlines to be followed by the poets in making their stories and the limits beyond which they must not be allowed to go.

True; but what are these outlines for any account they may give of the gods?

Of this sort, said I. A poet, whether he is writing epic, lyric, or drama, surely ought always to represent the divine nature as it really is. And the truth is that that nature is good and must be described as such.

Unquestionably.

Well, nothing that is good can be harmful; and if it cannot do harm, it can do no evil; and so it cannot be responsible for any evil.

I agree.

Again, goodness is beneficent, and hence the cause of well-being.

Yes.

Goodness, then, is not responsible for everything, but only for what is as it should be. It is not responsible for evil.

Quite true.

It follows, then, that the divine, being good, is not, as most people say, responsible for everything that happens to mankind, but only for a small part; for the good things in human life are far fewer than the evil, and, whereas the good must be ascribed to heaven only, we must look elsewhere for the cause of evils.

I think that is perfectly true.

So we shall condemn as a foolish error Homer's description of Zeus as the "dispenser of both good and ill." We shall disapprove when Pandarus' violation of oaths and treaties is said to be the work of Zeus and Athena, or when Themis and Zeus are said to have caused strife among the gods. Nor must we allow our young people to be told by Aeschylus that "Heaven implants guilt in man, when his will is to destroy a house utterly." If a poet writes of the sorrows of Niobe or the calamities of the house of Pelops or of the Trojan war, either he must not speak of them as the work of a god, or, if he does so, he must devise some such explanation as we are now requiring: he must say that what the god did was just and good, and the sufferers were the better for being chastised. One who pays a just penalty must not be called miserable, and his misery then laid at heaven's door. The poet will only be allowed to say that the wicked were miserable because they needed chastisement, and the punishment of heaven did them good. If our commonwealth is to be well-ordered, we must fight to the last against any member of it being suffered to speak of the divine, which is good, being responsible for evil. Neither young nor old must listen to such tales, in prose or verse. Such doctrine would be impious, self-contradictory, and disastrous to our commonwealth.

I agree, he said, and I would vote for a law to that effect.

Well then, that shall be one of our laws about religion. The first principle to which all must conform in speech or writing is that heaven is not responsible for everything, but only for what is good.

I am quite satisfied.

Now what of this for a second principle? Do you think of a god as a sort of magician who might, for his own purposes, appear in various shapes, now actually passing into a number of different forms, now deluding us into believing he has done so; or is his nature simple and of all things the least likely to depart from its proper form?

I cannot say offhand.

Well, if a thing passes out of its proper form, must not the change come either from within or from some outside cause?

Yes.

Is it not true, then, that things in the most perfect condition are the least affected by changes from outside? Take the effect on the body of food and drink or of exertion, or the effect of sunshine and wind on a plant: the healthiest and strongest suffer the least change. Again, the bravest and wisest spirit is least disturbed by external influence. Even manufactured things— furniture, houses, clothes—suffer least from wear and tear when they are well made and in good condition. So this immunity to change from outside is characteristic of anything which, thanks to art or nature or both, is in a satisfactory state.

That seems true.

But surely the state of the divine nature must be perfect in every way, and would therefore be the last thing to suffer transformations from any outside cause.

Yes.

Well then, would a god change or alter himself?

If he changes at all, it can only be in that way.

Would it be a change for the better or for the worse?

It could only be for the worse; for we cannot admit any imperfection in divine goodness or beauty.

True; and that being so, do you think, Adeimantus, that anyone, god or man, would deliberately make himself worse in any respect?

That is impossible.

Then a god cannot desire to change himself. Being as perfect as he can be, every god, it seems, remains simply and forever in his own form.

That is the necessary conclusion.

If so, my friend, the poets must not tell us that "the gods go to and fro among the cities of men, disguised as strangers of all sorts from far countries"; nor must they tell any of those false tales of Proteus and Thetis transforming themselves, or bring Hera on the stage in the guise of a priestess collecting alms for "the life-giving children of Inachus, the river of Argos." Mothers, again, are not to follow these suggestions and scare young children with mischievous stories of spirits that go about by night in all sorts of outlandish shapes. They would only be blaspheming the gods and at the same time making cowards of their children.

No, that must not be allowed.

But are we to think that the gods, though they do not really change, trick us by some magic into believing that they appear in many different forms?

Perhaps.

What? said I; would a god tell a falsehood or act one by deluding us with an apparition?

I cannot say.

Do you not know that the true falsehood—if that is a possible expression—is a thing that all gods and men abominate?

What do you mean?

This, I replied: no one, if he could help it, would tolerate the presence of untruth in the most vital part of his nature concerning the most vital matters. There is nothing he would fear so much as to harbor falsehood in that quarter.

Still I do not understand.

Because you think I mean something out of the ordinary. All I mean is the presence of falsehood in the soul concerning reality. To be deceived about the truth of things and so to be in ignorance and error and to harbor untruth in the soul is a thing no one would consent to. Falsehood in that quarter is abhorred above everything.

It is indeed.

Well then, as I was saying, this ignorance in the soul which entertains untruth is what really deserves to be called the true falsehood; for the spoken falsehood is only the embodiment or image of a previous condition of the soul, not pure unadulterated falsity. Is it not so?

It is.

This real falsehood, then, is hateful to gods and men equally. But is the spoken falsehood always a hateful thing? Is it not sometimes helpful—in war, for instance, or as a sort of medicine to avert some fit of folly or madness that might make a friend attempt some mischief? And in those legends we were discussing just now, we can turn fiction to account; not knowing the facts about the distant past, we can make our fiction as good an embodiment of truth as possible.

Yes, that is so.

Well, in which of these ways would falsehood be useful to a god? We cannot think of him as embodying truth in fiction for lack of information about the past.

No, that would be absurd.

So there is no room in his case for poetical inventions. Would he need to tell untruths because he has enemies to fear?

Of course not.

Or friends who are mad or foolish?

No; a fool or a madman could hardly enjoy the friendship of the gods.

Gods, then, have no motive for lying. There can be no falsehood of any sort in the divine nature.

None.

We conclude, then, that a god is a being of entire simplicity and truthfulness in word and in deed. In himself he does not change, nor does he delude others, either in dreams or in waking moments, by apparitions or oracles or signs.

I agree, after all you have said.

You will assent, then, to this as a second principle to guide all that is to be said or written about the gods: that they do not transform themselves by any magic or mislead us by illusions or lies. For all our admiration of Homer, we shall not approve his story of the dream Zeus sent to Agamemnon; nor yet those lines of Aeschylus where Thetis tells how Apollo sang at her wedding:

> Boding good fortune for my child, long life
> From sickness free, in all things blest by heaven,
> His song, so crowned with triumph, cheered my heart.
> I thought those lips divine, with prophecy
> Instinct, could never lie. But he, this guest,
> Whose voice so rang with promise at the feast,
> Even he, has slain my son.

If a poet writes of the gods in this way, we shall be angry and refuse him the means to produce his play. Nor shall we allow such poetry to be used in educating the young, if we mean our Guardians to be godfearing and to reproduce the divine nature in themselves so far as man may.

I entirely agree with your principles, he said, and I would have them observed as laws.

So far, then, as religion is concerned, we have settled what sorts of stories about the gods may, or may not, be told to children who are to hold heaven and their parents in reverence and to value good relations with one another.

Yes, he said; and I believe we have settled right.

We also want them to be brave. So the stories they hear should be such as to make them unafraid of death. A man with that fear in his heart cannot be brave, can he?

Surely not.

And can a man be free from that fear and prefer death in battle to defeat and slavery, if he believes in a world below which is full of terrors?

No.

Here again, then, our supervision will be needed. The poets must be told to speak well of that other world. The gloomy descriptions they now give must be forbidden, not only as untrue, but as injurious to our future warriors. We shall strike out all lines like these:

> I would rather be on earth as the hired servant of another, in the house of a landless man with little to live on, than be king over all the dead;

or these:

> Alack, there is, then, even in the house of Death a spirit or a shade; but the wits dwell in it no more.

We shall ask Homer and the poets in general not to mind if we cross out all passages of this sort. If most people enjoy them as good poetry, that is all the more reason for keeping them from children or grown men who are to be free, fearing slavery more than death.

I entirely agree.

We must also get rid of all that terrifying language, the very sound of which is enough to make one shiver: "loathsome Styx," "the River of Wailing," "infernal spirits," "anatomies," and so on. For other purposes such language may be well enough; but we are afraid that fever consequent upon such shivering fits may melt down the fine-tempered spirit of our Guardians. So we will have none of it; and we shall encourage writing in the opposite strain.

Clearly.

Another thing we must banish is the wailing and lamentations of the famous heroes. For this reason: if two friends are both men of high character, neither of them will think that death has any terrors for his comrade; and so he will not mourn for his friend's sake, as if something terrible had befallen him.

No.

We also believe that such a man, above all, possesses within himself all that is necessary for a good life and is least dependent on others, so that he has less to fear from the loss of a son or brother or of his wealth or any other possession. When such misfortune comes, he will bear it patiently without lamenting.

True.

We shall do well, then, to strike out descriptions of the heroes bewailing the dead, and make over such lamentations to women (and not to women of good standing either) and to men of low character, so that the Guardians we are training for our country may disdain to imitate them.

Quite right.

Once more, then, we shall ask Homer and the other poets not to represent Achilles, the son of a goddess, as "tossing from side to side, now on his face, now on his back," and then as rising up and wandering distractedly on the seashore, or pouring ashes on his head with both hands, with all those tears and wailings the poet describes; nor to tell how Priam, who was near akin to the gods, "rolled in the dung as he made entreaty, calling on each man by name." Still more earnestly shall we ask them not to represent gods as lamenting, or at any rate not to dare to misrepresent the highest god by making him say: "Woe is me that Sarpedon, whom I love above all men, is fated to die at the hands of Patroclus." For if our young men take such unworthy descriptions seriously instead of laughing at them, they will hardly feel themselves, who are but men, above behaving in that way or repress any temptation to do so. They would not be ashamed of giving way with complaints and outcries on every trifling occasion; and that would be contrary to the principle we have deduced and shall adhere to, until someone can show us a better.

It would.

Again, our Guardians ought not to be overmuch given to laughter. Violent laughter tends to provoke an equally violent reaction. We must not allow poets to describe men of worth being overcome by it; still less should Homer speak of the gods giving way to "unquenchable laughter" at the sight of Hephaestus "bustling from room to room." That will be against your principles.

Yes, if you choose to call them mine.

Again, a high value must be set upon truthfulness. If we were right in saying that gods have no use for falsehood and it is useful to mankind only in the way of a medicine, obviously a medicine should be handled by no one but a physician.

Obviously.

If anyone, then, is to practice deception, either on the country's enemies or on its citizens, it must be the Rulers of the commonwealth, acting for its benefit; no one else may meddle with this privilege. For a private person to mislead such Rulers we shall declare to be a worse offense than for a patient to mislead his doctor or an athlete his trainer about his bodily condition, or for a seaman to misinform his captain about the state of the ship or of the crew. So, if anyone else in our commonwealth "of all that practice crafts, physician, seer, or carpenter," is caught not telling the truth, the Rulers will punish him for introducing a practice as fatal and subversive in a state as it would be in a ship.

It would certainly be as fatal, if action were suited to the word.

Next, our young men will need self-control; and for the mass of mankind that chiefly means obeying their governors, and themselves governing their appetite for the pleasures of eating and drinking and sex. Here again we shall disapprove of much that we find in Homer.

I agree.

Whereas we shall allow the poets to represent any examples of self-control and fortitude on the part of famous men, and admit such lines as these: "Odysseus smote his breast, chiding his heart: Endure, my heart; thou hast borne worse things than these."

Yes, certainly.

Nor again must these men of ours be lovers of money, or ready to take bribes. They must not hear that "gods and great princes may be won by gifts."

No, that sort of thing cannot be approved.

If it were not for my regard for Homer, I should not hesitate to call it downright impiety to make Achilles say to Apollo: "Thou hast wronged me, thou deadliest of gods; I would surely requite thee, if I had but the power." And all those stories of Achilles dragging Hector round the tomb of Patroclus and slaughtering captives on the funeral pyre we shall condemn as false, and not let our Guardians believe that Achilles, who was the son of a goddess and of the wise Peleus, third in descent from Zeus, and the pupil of the sage Chiron, was so disordered that his heart was a prey to two contrary maladies, mean covetousness and arrogant contempt of gods and men.

You are right.

We have now distinguished the kinds of stories that may and may not be told about gods and demigods, heroes, and the world below. There remains the literature concerned with human life.

Clearly.

We cannot lay down rules for that at our present stage.

Why not?

Because, I suspect, we shall find both poets and prose-writers guilty of the most serious misstatements about human life, making out that wrongdoers are often happy and just men miserable; that injustice pays, if not detected; and that my being just is to another man's advantage, but a loss to myself. We shall have to prohibit such poems and tales and tell them to compose others in the contrary sense. Don't you think so?

I am sure of it.

Well, as soon as you admit that I am right there, may I not claim that we shall have reached agreement on the subject of all this inquiry?

That is a fair assumption.

Then we must postpone any decision as to how the truth is to be told about human life, until we have discovered the real nature of justice and proved that it is intrinsically profitable to its possessor, no matter what reputation he may have in the eyes of the world.

That is certainly true....

One thing is easily settled, namely that grace and seemliness of form and movement go with good rhythm, ungracefulness and unseemliness with bad.

Naturally.

And again, good or bad rhythm and also tunefulness or discord in music go with the quality of the poetry; for they will be modelled after its form, if, as we have said, metre and music must be adapted to the sense of the words.

Well, they must be so adapted.

And the content of the poetry and the manner in which it is expressed depend, in their turn, on moral character.

Of course.

Thus, then, excellence of form and content in discourse and of musical expression and rhythm, and grace of form and movement, all depend on goodness of nature, by which I mean, not the foolish simplicity sometimes called by courtesy "good nature," but a nature in which goodness of character has been well and truly established.

Yes, certainly.

So, if our young men are to do their proper work in life, they must follow after these qualities wherever they may be found. And they are to be found in every sort of workmanship, such as painting, weaving, embroidery, architecture, the making of furniture; and also in the human frame and in all the works of nature: in all these grace and seemliness may be present or absent. And the absence of grace, rhythm, harmony is nearly allied to baseness of thought and expression and baseness of character; whereas their presence goes with that moral excellence and self-mastery of which they are the embodiment.

That is perfectly true.

Then we must not only compel our poets, on pain of expulsion, to make their poetry the express image of noble character; we must also supervise craftsmen of every kind and forbid them to leave the stamp of baseness, license, meanness, unseemliness, on painting and sculpture, or building, or any other work of their hands; and anyone who cannot obey shall not practice his art in our commonwealth. We would not have our Guardians grow up among representations of moral deformity, as in some foul pasture where, day after day, feeding on every poisonous weed they would, little by little, gather insensibly a mass of corruption in their very souls. Rather we must seek out those craftsmen whose instinct guides them to whatsoever is lovely and gracious; so that our young men, dwelling in a wholesome climate, may drink in good from every quarter, whence, like a breeze bearing health from happy regions, some influence from noble works constantly falls upon eye and ear from childhood upward, and imperceptibly draws them into sympathy and harmony with the beauty of reason, whose impress they take.

There could be no better upbringing than that.

Hence, Glaucon, I continued, the decisive importance of education in poetry and music: rhythm and harmony sink deep into the recesses of the soul and take the strongest hold there, bringing that grace of body and mind which is only to be found in one who is brought up in the right way. Moreover, a proper training in this kind makes a man quick to perceive any defect or ugliness in art or in nature. Such deformity will rightly disgust him. Approving all that is lovely, he will welcome it home with joy into his soul and, nourished thereby, grow into a man of a noble spirit. All that is ugly and disgraceful he will rightly condemn and abhor while he is still too young to understand the reason; and when reason comes, he will greet her as a friend with whom his education has made him long familiar.

I agree, he said; that is the purpose of education in literature and music....

Now, the ordinary athlete undergoes the rigors of training for the sake of muscular strength; but ours will do so rather with a view to stimulating the spirited element in their nature. So perhaps the purpose of the two established branches of education is not, as some suppose, the improvement of the soul in one case and of the body in the other. Both, it may be, aim chiefly at improving the soul.

How so?

Have you noticed how a life-long devotion to either branch, to the exclusion of the other, affects the mind, resulting in an uncivilized hardness in the one case, and an overcivilized softness in the other?

I have certainly noticed that unmitigated athletics produce a sort of ferocity, and a merely literary and musical education makes men softer than is good for them.

Surely that ferocity is the outcome of the spirited element in our nature. A proper training would produce courage; but if that element is overstrained, it naturally becomes hard and savage. Gentleness, on the other hand, is characteristic of the philosophic disposition. Here again, too much relaxation will result in oversoftness; the right training will produce a gentleness that is steady and disciplined. Now we agree that our Guardians must combine both these dispositions; and they will have to be harmonized so that courage and steadfastness may be united in a soul that would otherwise be either unmanly or boorish.

Certainly.

When a man surrenders himself to music, allowing his soul to be flooded through the channels of his ears with those sweet and soft and mournful airs we spoke of, and gives up all his time to the delights of song and melody, then at first he tempers the high-spirited part of his nature, like iron whose brittle hardness is softened to make it serviceable; but if he persists in subduing it to such incantation, he will end by melting it away altogether. He will have cut the sinews of his soul and made himself what Homer calls a faint-hearted warrior. Moreover, this result follows quickly in a temperament that is naturally spiritless; while a high-spirited one is rendered weak and unstable, readily flaring up and dying down again on slight provocation. Such men become rather irritable, bad-tempered, and peevish.

Quite so.

On the other hand, there are the consequences of hard bodily exercise and high living, with no attempt to cultivate the mind or use the intellect in study. At first, the sense of physical fitness fills a man with self-confidence and energy and makes him twice the man he was. But suppose he does nothing else and holds aloof from any sort of culture; then, even if there was something in him capable of desiring knowledge, it is starved of instruction and never encouraged to think for itself by taking part in rational discussion or intellectual pursuits of any kind; and so it grows feeble for lack of stimulus and nourishment, and deaf and blind because the darkness that clouds perception is never cleared away. Such a man ends by being wholly uncultivated and a hater of reason. Having no more use for reasonable persuasion, he gains all his ends by savage violence, like a brute beast, and he lives in a dull stupor of ignorance with no touch of inward harmony or grace.

That is exactly what happens.

There are, then, these two elements in the soul, the spirited and the philosophic; and it is for their sake, as I should say, and not (except incidentally) for the sake of soul and body, that heaven has given to mankind those two branches of education. The purpose is to bring the two elements into tune with one another by adjusting the tension of each to the right pitch. So one who can apply to the soul both kinds of education blended in perfect proportion will be master of a nobler sort of musical harmony than was ever made by tuning the strings of the lyre.

We may well say that, Socrates.

And our commonwealth will need the constant vigilance of such a master, to preserve its constitution.

Certainly, he will be indispensable.

So much, then, for the outlines of education and nurture. We need not go into all the details of their musical performances or of their hunting and athletic contests and races. Obviously these will follow from our principles and can easily be worked out.

Yes, easily.

DISCUSSION AND WRITING

1. For illustrations, Plato refers to Greek myth and legend as reflected in the cosmogony of Hesiod, the epics of Homer (*The Iliad* and *The Odyssey*), and a play by Aeschylus. In a dictionary of (or an introduction to) classical mythology and literature find a summary of some of the major themes alluded to: the revolt of Zeus against Cronos; Zeus's exploits as a lover; the role of Achilles and Hector in the Trojan War.

2. Socrates' argument relies heavily on analogy (for instance, the parallel between the state and a ship, or between the government and a physician). It further relies on detailed conclusions deduced from general principles (such as that of divine perfection). Discuss several examples of Socrates' use of logic and describe his method.

3. Summarize the steps in the argument, bringing out the major points or areas covered. State in your own words the view of education and of literature that underlies Plato's discussion.

4. What is the effect of Plato's use of the dialogue form? What can it do that ordinary exposition cannot do?

5. Discuss in detail some of the first books or stories that made a strong impression on your mind. Looking back, do you discover in them any moral or psychological implications? What kind of influence were they likely to exert on a child's attitudes?

6. Compare the practice of parents, teachers, and schools today with Plato's prescriptions concerning literature for young children. What is the tone and content of "approved" children's books? What kinds of reading are considered undesirable? Do you agree with the standards being applied?

7. To what extent does contemporary society approve of the government's privilege "to practice deception" for the benefit of the commonwealth? For instance, should the government withhold or "edit" news that affects national security?

8. Develop your answer to one of the following questions: To what extent should high-school teachers or librarians be influenced by Plato's principles in making literature available to adolescents? Discuss specific books that are sometimes withheld from young readers. Or, to what extent should American high schools follow Plato's principles in the teaching of American history? Show how his principles might apply to the treatment of specific historical events, figures, or issues.

9. Jonathan Swift, in the first book of *Gulliver's Travels,* describes the educational system of the Lilliputians. Along with their original laws and institutions, he exempts it from the censure he visits on many of their customs. Find the passage and compare and contrast the attitude toward education shown there with that of Plato.

10. When and how should education for the future leaders of society begin to differ from that of other students?

FURTHER READING

Since Plato's *Republic,* there have been many "Utopias," descriptions of imaginary ideal societies. Aldous Huxley's *Brave New World* (1932) was designed as a warning against the kind of thoroughly planned Utopian society that science was beginning to make possible. In *Brave New World Revisited* (1958), Huxley discussed current developments in the light of his earlier predictions.

JEAN-JACQUES ROUSSEAU

Jean-Jacques Rousseau (1712–1778), controversial and widely influential French writer, is best known for those of his books that promoted a spontaneous emotional response to nature and gave a strong impetus to the Romantic movement in literature. His name is associated with the eighteenth-century belief in the "perfectibility" of man, which played an important part in the French and American revolutions. Briefly, this belief implied that men are inherently good but that they are perverted and brutalized by unnatural customs and institutions. In histories of education, Rousseau appears with Pestalozzi and others as a forerunner of educational theories that found widespread acceptance in the twenties and thirties of this century and are often grouped together under the label of "progressive education." The following selection is from Rousseau's *Émile, or On Education* (1762), a complete account of the upbringing and schooling of an imaginary child. The brief excerpts here chosen deal with three major areas that continue to be frequent subjects of educational controversy. Rousseau discusses them with the missionary zeal and emphatic certitude of the true reformer.

On Education

Most actual and possible moral lessons for children can be reduced to this formula:

TEACHER: You must not do that.
CHILD: Why?
TEACHER: Because it is wrong.

CHILD: What is "wrong"?
TEACHER: Something you are told not to do.
CHILD: Why is it wrong to do things I am told not to do?
TEACHER: Because you will be punished.
CHILD: Then I'll do them without getting caught.
TEACHER: But I am going to watch you.
CHILD: Then I'll hide.
TEACHER: I am going to ask you what you were doing.
CHILD: Then I'll lie.
TEACHER: You must not lie.
CHILD: Why?
TEACHER: Because it is wrong, etc.

There you have the inevitable circle. Escape from it, and the child will no longer understand you. Does this sort of thing really do any good? I would like to know what could possibly be substituted for this dialogue. The great Locke himself would have exerted himself in vain. To know good and evil, to understand man's moral duties, is not for children.

Nature intends children to be children before they become adults. If we tamper with this sequence, our children will be precocious—premature fruit without flavor and easily spoiled. We shall have sage youths and childish old men. Childhood has its own ways of seeing, thinking, and feeling, and nothing is less sensible than to replace those ways with ours. I would as soon want a child to be five feet tall as expect him to be a reasoning being at ten years old. What good would reason be to him at that age? Reason is a restraint on our energies which the child does not yet need.

In trying to persuade your pupils that they owe you obedience, you add to this "persuasion" force and threats, or, worse, flattery and promises. Thus enticed or compelled, they pretend to be swayed by your arguments. They know very well that obedience is to their advantage and rebellion dangerous as soon as you become aware of it. But since everything you ask of them is unpleasant, and since it is always irksome to do someone else's bidding, they do as they please as soon as they are out of sight, at ease while they remain undetected but ready on being found out to confess to their crimes for fear of reprisal. Since the concept of moral duty is beyond their reach, no one can really make them grasp it; but fear of punishment, the hope of being forgiven, the insistence of the adults, and the difficulty of talking back to them force the children to say what they are expected to say. The adult thinks he has convinced them when he has only tormented and intimidated them.

What is the result of all this? First, in forcing on them duties that they do not understand, you prejudice them against your tyranny and turn their love away from you, while teaching them to dissemble, evade, and lie in order to be rewarded or escape punishment. In effect, in teaching them to disguise forever their real motives, you yourself supply them the means of perpetually deceiving you, of keeping you from knowing their true feelings, and of paying mere lip-service to your wishes and those of others. The laws, you will say, though morally binding, need the same sort of force to make them work with grown men. I agree. But then these grown men are merely children spoiled by education. That is exactly what needs to be changed. Use force on children and reasoning on adults; do things in their natural order—a wise man needs no laws.

Treat your pupil according to his age. From the beginning, put him in his proper place and keep him there so effectively that he no longer tries to depart from it. Then, before he knows what wisdom *is,* he will already observe its most important lesson. Never order him to do anything whatsoever. Never even let him imagine that you claim any authority over him. Merely let him realize that he is weak and you are strong, that because of your relative positions he is necessarily in your power—let him realize it, learn it, feel it; let him feel early on his stiff neck the heavy yoke that nature forces on man, the heavy yoke of necessity, to which every created being must submit. Let him ascribe that necessity to the way things are rather than to the whims of men; let the restraint that holds him back be that of force rather than of authority. Don't forbid things he should not do; simply stop him from doing them, without explanation or argument. What you allow him, allow when first asked, without pleading or whining and above all without conditions. Grant his requests with pleasure; refuse them reluctantly, but let your refusals be irrevocable. Let no insistence sway you; let your "No" be an iron wall, and the child will attack it with all his strength the first five or six times and then give up trying to budge it.

You will thus teach him to be patient, content, resigned, and calm even when he does not get his way; for it is human nature to submit patiently to physical necessity but not to human malice. The child never rebels against "There is none left"—unless he doubts it is true. . . . No one should teach children who cannot guide them solely by the laws of what is possible and what is not. Since the extent of either sphere is equally unknown to the child, the teacher can expand or narrow it at his will. He can restrain, urge on, or hold back his uncomplaining pupil by means of what has to be; he can make him flexible and cooperative merely by the power of circumstances with no occasion for the development of vicious traits, because passions do not arise as long as they are irrelevant.

Never rely on teaching that is merely verbal; the child has to learn from experience. Never punish him, because he does not know what it means to do wrong. Never make him ask to be forgiven, for he does not know how to offend. Since his actions have no moral significance, he can do nothing that is morally wrong, nothing that merits punishment or blame. . . .

In doing away with all the customary duties of children, I do away with the cause of their greatest misery: books. Reading is the curse of childhood, though almost the only occupation that adults can think of for children. At twelve years old, Émile will just barely know what a book is. But certainly, you will say, he must know how to read! I agree: He must know how to read when reading can be of use to him; until then it will only torment him.

If one must demand nothing of children on the grounds of obedience, it follows that they cannot learn anything unless they see immediate and present gain, whether pleasure or profit. What other motive could make them learn? The ability to speak to those absent and to hear them answer—to let them know without intermediary our feelings, wishes, and desires—is useful in a way a child can be made to see. What then has made this useful and pleasant art a torment for children? The practice of forcing it on them against their will and of putting it to uses they do not understand. A child is not eager to help perfect the instrument of his own torture; but make that instrument serve his pleasure and he will apply himself in spite of you.

There is a great to-do about finding the best methods for teaching reading; people invent alphabet games and cards and turn the nursery into a printing shop. Locke wants us to teach reading with alphabet dice. How is that for an ingenious invention? But alas! a much surer means, and the one always forgotten, is the desire to learn. Create this desire in the child, and put aside your games and dice—any method will serve.

Present interest—that is the key motive, the only one that works reliably and consistently. Now and then, Émile receives from his father, his mother, his relatives, or his friends, written invitations to a dinner, a walk, a trip by boat, a public celebration. These notes are short, clear, neat, and well written. He has to find someone to read them to him. The someone in question is not always at hand, or shows as little consideration as the child showed for him on some recent occasion. And thus the event, the precious moment passes. At last Émile hears the note read, but it is too late. Ah, if only he had known how to read himself! He receives other notes. They are so short—and so intriguing! He very much wants to decipher them. Sometimes he gets help, sometimes not. He tries hard and finally makes out part of a note: something about going somewhere tomorrow to eat something sweet—he cannot make out where or with whom. How hard he tries to read the rest! I don't think Émile will need any alphabet games. Should I go on to the teaching of writing? No, I am ashamed to play with these trifles in a treatise on education.

I merely add a few words that sum up an important principle: We usually obtain easily and quickly what we are in no great hurry to obtain. I am practically certain that Émile will read and write perfectly well before he is ten, precisely because it matters little to me whether he does before he is fifteen. But I would rather have him not read at all than have him learn this skill at the cost of everything that might make it useful. What good will reading do him if he has learned to hate it forever? "Above all we must see to it that he does not hate those studies which he is too young to love, and that their harshness, once perceived, does not keep him away from them beyond his unformed years...."

If you make your pupil observe the phenomena of nature, he will soon become curious; but in order to nourish that curiosity do not hurry to satisfy it. Put the problems within his reach and let him solve them. Let him believe something not because you said so but because he worked it out for himself. Instead of his "studying" science, let him discover it. If you ever allow him to substitute authority for independent thought, he will cease to think; he will be at the mercy of the beliefs of others.

You want to teach the child geography, and you get together globes, spheres, and maps: what apparatus! Why all these symbols? Why not start by showing him the thing itself, so that at least he will know what you are talking about!

One fine evening we go for a walk to a favorite spot, where the open horizon gives us a full view of the setting sun, and we observe objects that mark the point where it sets. The next morning, we return to the same spot before sunrise to enjoy the morning air. The sun announces its arrival from afar by fiery arrows it sends ahead. The arrows merge into a conflagration; the whole east seems on fire; its brilliance makes us expect the sun long before it shows itself. We constantly seem to see it appear; finally it is there. A glowing point appears like lightning and soon fills all space; the veil of darkness fades and disappears. Man recognizes his abode and finds it beautiful. The grass has gathered new strength during the night; in the light of dawn, the first rays that gild it show it to be covered by a glowing net of dew sparkling with light and color. Choirs of birds gather to hymn the father of life; not one of them is quiet at this hour. Their tweeting, still soft, is slower and sweeter than during the rest of the day; it reflects the languor of peaceful wakening. Together, these impressions create a feeling of freshness that seems to touch the very soul. Here is half an hour of enchantment that no one can resist; a spectacle of such grandeur, beauty, and delight cannot fail to move.

Full of his enthusiasm, the teacher wants to share it with the child; he thinks he can stir the child's emotions by pointing out the sensations that explain his own feelings. Pure nonsense! The beauty of nature lives in man's heart; to see it he must feel it. The child sees the same objects, but he cannot see how they are related, he cannot feel their sweet harmony. He has not had the experience, and he has not felt the emotions, that make possible the total impression to which all these sensations contribute. If he has not traversed endless arid plains, if the hot sand has not scorched his feet, if the stifling heat reflected by sun-drenched rocks has not oppressed him, how can he savor the fresh morning air? How can his senses revel in the fragrance of flowers, the charming green of the leaves, the moistness of the dew, the softness of the luxurious turf under his feet? How can the songbirds make him feel tender emotions if love and its pleasures are still far from his thoughts? Why should he derive joy from the sight of a beautiful morning if his imagination cannot yet paint the joys that can fill the day? Finally, how can the beauty of nature inspire him if he does not yet know whose hand has shaped it?

Do not subject the child to lectures that he cannot grasp. Do without descriptions, without eloquence, without figures of speech, without poetry. This is not the time for cultivating emotion or the sense of beauty. Continue to be clear, simple, and cold; the time for a different sort of language will come soon enough.

Brought up in keeping with our principles, accustomed to relying for help on himself and turning to others only after recognizing his own inadequacy, our pupil examines each new object in silence for a long time. He is thoughtful rather than inquisitive. Be content to bring things before him at their proper time; then, when his curiosity is sufficiently engaged, ask him some brief question that will put him on the way toward its solution.

On this occasion, after a good look at the rising sun, after pointing out to him the mountains and other sights, after letting him comment at his ease, be silent for a while like someone lost in thought, and then say: "It seems to me that last night the sun set over there, whereas this morning it rises over here. How can that be?" Add nothing else; if he asks questions, don't answer; change the subject. Leave him alone, and you may be sure that he will think about it.

If a child is to develop his powers of observation, and if he is to be strongly impressed with a tangible truth, he must undergo a few days of anxiety before he discovers it. If this particular truth is not obvious enough to him, you can make it more so by turning the question upside down. If he does not know how the sun travels from sunset to sunrise, he at least knows how it travels from sunrise to sunset; his eyes alone can tell him. Elucidate the first question by the second, and unless your pupil is plain stupid, the analogy will be too clear for him to miss. And that is his first lesson in astronomy. . . .

Different regions of the earth have different climates and different temperatures. As we approach the pole, variation in the seasons becomes more noticeable. All bodies contract when cooled and expand when heated; this effect is more obvious with liquids and even more so with spirits; hence the thermometer. Wind strikes our faces; air therefore is a body, a fluid; we feel it without being able to see it. Turn a glass upside down and immerse it in water, and the water will not fill it unless the air can in some way escape; air thus has the capacity of offering resistance. Immerse the glass more deeply, and the water will enter the space occupied by air without being able to fill it altogether; air therefore has the capacity of being compressed up to a certain point. A ball filled with compressed air bounces better than one filled with any other material; air is therefore elastic. Stretched out in your bath, lift your arms horizontally out of the water, and they will seem weighed down by a terrible load; therefore the air has weight. In establishing an equilibrium between air and other fluids, we can measure this weight; hence the barometer, the siphon, the air gun, and the air pump. All the laws of statics and hydrostatics can be deduced from such everyday observations. For none of this need we ever enter a laboratory; I dislike all that elaborate equipment. The scientific atmosphere kills true science. All these gadgets either frighten the child or by their external appearance divide and detract his attention from what they are supposed to demonstrate.

I want us to construct by ourselves whatever apparatus we need, and I don't want us to have the equipment first and the observation after. When we have more or less accidentally made the observation, we set about constructing equipment that will help us verify it. I would rather have instruments that are not perfect in every respect and have instead a clear idea of their purpose and the uses to which they will be put. For my first lesson in statics, instead of starting with a pair of scales, I balance a stick across the back of a chair. I measure the two parts of the stick, then at either end attach weights, sometimes equal sometimes unequal. Pushing the stick in either direction as necessary, I finally establish that equilibrium depends on the amount of weight being inversely proportional to the length of the lever. Already my little physicist knows how to adjust scales—without ever having seen any.

Undoubtedly we have a much clearer and more reliable knowledge of things that we thus learn on our own than of those we owe to someone else's teaching. Besides guarding our minds against the habit of servile submission to authority, we become more resourceful in discovering relations, establishing connections between ideas, and constructing equipment than when we accept everything that is handed to us and allow our mental powers to decay in indifferent ease, just as the limbs of someone who is always dressed and waited on by his servants and moved about by horses eventually lose their strength and flexibility. Boileau boasted that he taught Racine to write verse that demanded effort. With so many admirable methods for making the study of science easy, we greatly need someone who can provide a method of studying it with proper exertion.

The most obvious advantage of these slow and laborious researches is that they keep the child active and his limbs supple in the midst of intellectual pursuits and that they constantly train his hands for useful activity. An instrument designed to guide our observation and substitute for exact perception through our senses deprives them of their proper exercise.... The more ingenious our tools are, the clumsier our senses tend to become; after surrounding ourselves with external sources of assistance, we find fewer within ourselves.

However, when we employ in constructing our equipment the skill that served us in its stead and the intelligence that enabled us to do without it, we gain without corresponding loss; we make art supplement nature, becoming more resourceful without becoming less skilled. If instead of gluing a child to his books I keep him busy in a workshop, the work of his hands benefits his mind. He thinks he is a workman when in reality he is becoming a scholar.

DISCUSSION AND WRITING

1. Look up Locke, Boileau, and Racine and explain Rousseau's references to them.

2. Explain briefly the major principles of education stated or implied in these excerpts from Rousseau's book. Are they in any way connected?

3. The present translation attempts to reproduce the tone of the French original. How does Rousseau's tone and style affect the persuasiveness of his argument?

4. Like other innovators, Rousseau has been accused of pursuing paradoxes for their own sake. Define paradox and provide examples from Rousseau's discussion.

5. Compare and contrast Rousseau's program for his imaginary pupil with Churchill's account of his actual schooling.

6. Examine your own education in the light of the practices described in this selection. To what extent did your own teachers make use of Rousseau's principles? Limit your discussion to one major area or principle.

7. Discuss in detail possible objections to one major aspect of Rousseau's educational program. Take care not to oversimplify or distort his position.

8. Does modern American education teach students "to disguise forever their real motives"? To judge from your own experience and observation, how much candor is there typically between teacher and student in an American school?

9. After thinking about Plato's and Rousseau's comments on the moral teaching of children, what do you consider a feasible or responsible way of making moral values a part of education?

10. C. Wright Mills has described the difference between competition when there was room for many small independent businessmen and competition within the bureaucracy of a large business corporation: "Now the stress is on agility rather than ability, on 'getting along' in a context of associates, superiors, and rules, rather than 'getting ahead' across an open market." Of what kind is the competition among today's high school or college students? Is the stress on "getting along" or on "getting ahead"?

FURTHER READING

Among the best and most readable modern books on education are Jacques Barzun, *Teacher in America* (1945); John W. Gardner, *Excellence* (1961); Sidney Hook, *Education for Modern Man* (1963); and Bel Kaufman, *Up the Down Staircase* (1964). Study one of these to discover whether it has a major recurrent theme or central message.

ROBERT M. HUTCHINS

Among contemporary American educators, Robert M. Hutchins (born 1899) is one of the best known and the most influential. He was educated at Oberlin and Yale. As president and later chancellor of the University of Chicago, he instituted widely discussed experimental reforms in the curriculum. He became popularly known for his determination to substitute learning for football, with athletics devoted to stimulating "the urge to play for fun and health, instead of the urge to win at any cost." As director of the Ford Foundation's Fund for the Republic, Hutchins has continued to state his convictions on higher education in detail and with force. The following is the central portion of the chapter on "Philosophical Diversity" in his *The University of Utopia* (1953). Mr. Hutchins argues his case with the assurance of a writer used to controversy and not afraid to present new or unpopular views.

The University of Utopia

Education is the deliberate attempt to form men in terms of an ideal. It is the attempt of a society to produce the type of man that it wants. How does it determine the type of man it wants? If it does not know the type of man that it wants, how does it judge the educational efforts it makes? It may be said that the type of man a society wants is the product of many historical and psychological factors and that whatever philosophy enters into the formation of its vision of man is simply a rationalization of this largely unconscious product. But, even if this were so, we know that in every society there is some vision of man, his nature and his destiny, elaborated by philosophers living and dead, which interacts with the traditional view of the type of man desired and which amounts to a criticism of the tradition and the practices of the educational system. Education without a philosophy of education, that is, a coherent statement of the aims and possibilities of education, is impossible.

Of course a custodial system is possible without a philosophy of education or any other kind of philosophy. A custodial system may be regarded as the efflorescence of a society's despair that it can make no rational and coherent statement about the type of man that it wants to produce. It therefore decides to leave the matter to chance, providing harmless accommodation and occupation for the young until they reach maturity. This, I should be careful to point out, is an entirely different thing from saying that the kind of man we want is one who can think and act for himself and that therefore we are going to let him learn for himself while the educational system does little more for him than keep him out of harm's way.

Though I do not favor this philosophy of education, I admit that it is one. It is an adaptation of the laissez faire or free-enterprise system to education that approaches that popular at Harvard until the retirement of President Eliot. Vestiges of this philosophy still remain to plague the universities; and some versions of Progressive Education seem to be built on the same premises. The two most obvious disadvantages of it are, first, that it implies that teachers need not know, any more than their pupils, what an education is and, second, that it breaks up the community of learning that might exist among students and deprives them of the assistance of their fellow-students and of the ability to communicate with them during their schooling and with their fellow-men in later life.

A custodial system of that frank and open kind which American education seems bent on developing requires neither philosophy nor educational philosophy. The question is whether the philosophical diversity now rampant in the world leads inevitably to a custodial system. Must we say that because philosophers differ, and some even hold that there is no such thing as philosophy, we cannot have a philosophy of education, and hence not an educational system? I assume that we would like to have an educational system, rather than a custodial one, if we could.

If we are to have a philosophy of education, it has to rest on a rational conception of man and society. It also has to take into account the philosophical diversity characteristic of our time. It has to take account, moreover, of the fact that there is no authority that can decide among competing philosophies. The incredible number of school boards, legislatures, boards of regents, boards of trustees, together with principals, superintendents, presidents, chancellors, and faculties, are all more or less autonomous centers of educational decision. The business of raising ourselves by our own bootstraps into a new and rational world will not be easy.

Let us see what we can learn from Utopia. Utopia is singularly like the United States in that there is no central educational authority. Nevertheless, it has been able to develop a philosophy of education. It has been able to do this in spite of the fact that in Utopia, too, there is philosophical diversity. The Utopians even insist that philosophical diversity is a good thing. They say that it has always existed, even in those periods of history in which there has been a strong religious or political authority that nominally exercised control over the thoughts of men. The Utopians point out that such authorities have never succeeded in suppressing, and have usually not tried to suppress, philosophical diversity. The attempt to suppress such diversity has been a manifestation of modern progress and has appeared only with the totalitarian state.

Of course there are in Utopia no underspecialized institutions. The Utopians have never allowed themselves to be annoyed by such slogans as adjustment to the environment or meeting immediate needs, because they have sharply defined the purpose of their educational system. It is to promote the intellectual development of the people. The reason for the strength of the Utopian family and the Utopian church and the Utopian educational system is that each has its prescribed task. No Utopian, for example, would ever have been guilty of the proposition advanced to me the other day by an eminent bishop, who said that education should be limited to the elite and that the mass of the people should receive such culture as they need from the family and the church. The Utopians think that intellectual development is too important to be left to amateurs; and, since they are devoted to democracy, they do not see how they can maintain and improve their democracy unless every citizen has the chance to become as wise as he can.

The Utopians are sensible people. They have sense enough to know that children at the age of six cannot and should not do the kind of work in school that full-grown men should tackle. The Utopians know that physical and moral development are involved in intellectual development. Their educational system makes provision for the participation of educators in physical and moral development at the proper stages and in the proper ways, but never in such ways as to confuse anybody about who has the responsibility at every stage for intellectual development and who for moral and physical growth.

The Utopians believe that education is a conversation aimed at truth. Their object is to get everybody to take part in this conversation. They therefore start their children off by teaching them the techniques of communication. Those of you who have children may feel that this is a work of supererogation; but the Utopians think there is a great difference between chattering and conversing. The first ten years of the Utopian educational system is devoted primarily to reading, writing, and figuring. Because the Utopians are aware of the axiom that subjects that cannot be understood without experience should not be taught to those who are without experience, they do not bother inexperienced children with what are called the social studies. They want to fill their minds and touch their imaginations with the kind of knowledge suitable to their years. In the first ten years of his education, therefore, the young Utopian studies history, geography, and the greatest literature of the world. It is not supposed that he will understand all the implications of history and literature, but it is believed that he should be introduced to them in childhood and in such a way that he will want to continue to study them all his life. Since no one can understand his own language, or what a language is, by speaking or studying his own, every young Utopian masters a foreign language. And every young Utopian studies science; for this subject the Utopians regard as indispensable to understanding the modern world, and they believe that, as a subject that does not require experience, it is one that children can begin to study very early. In view of the celebrity that Utopians have achieved in the world of art and music, I need hardly add that all of them study these subjects.

By the age of sixteen the young Utopian has studied very few subjects; but he has studied all those appropriate to his time of life. The object has been to get him to go on studying them as long as he lives. The object has also been to fit him to understand any new idea or any new field that presents itself to him. And the great overruling object has been to prepare him to become a member of the republic of learning and of the political republic. Almost all the teaching in Utopia is conducted through discussion. The educational system is a paradigm of the conversation through which learning is advanced and through which a democracy works.

At the age of sixteen, or earlier if he is ready for it, the Utopian passes into the College. Here he continues to study history, geography, literature, science, music, and art, but the emphasis shifts from learning the techniques of communication to obtaining familiarity with the principal views of the world that men have developed and the leading ideas that have animated mankind. The curriculum from the beginning of the elementary school through the College is completely prescribed for all the students. The Utopians do not believe that any civilized man can omit any of the subjects that are included in the course of study. And they do not doubt that the educational profession is better qualified to say what children should study than the children themselves. The Utopians have heard of the American plan, by which a certain number of courses, whatever they are, finally add up to a degree, but the Utopians are, as I have said, a sensible people, and the credit system has never been introduced among them. This is one of the things that make the country Utopia.

Somewhere between the ages of eighteen and twenty, or whenever he is ready, the Utopian presents himself for examinations that cover the whole of his education up to that point. These examinations, which are constructed by an outside board, reflect what the educational profession of Utopia thinks of as a liberal education, the education appropriate to free men. If the student passes these examinations, he is awarded the degree of Bachelor of Arts. The Utopians have never been confused about the award of this degree at this stage, because the degree has never been debased into a certificate of time served, or credits accumulated, or a license to enter a graduate school, or a qualification for membership in the University Club. It has always stood for liberal education, and this is what the examinations at the end of the College of Utopia stand for too.

After leaving the College, the young Utopian has two courses open to him. He may enter upon the task of earning his living in the justly famous free-enterprise system of his country, or he may, if he is qualified, proceed to the University. But it never occurs to any Utopian that his education should stop when he leaves college. I have said that one of the premises upon which the educational program of Utopia is constructed is that subjects that cannot be understood without experience should not be taught to the inexperienced. History and literature are taught only by way of introduction in the schools and college of Utopia. The social sciences do not appear as such at all. Yet Utopians recognize that history, literature, and such knowledge as the social sciences have gained must be understood by civilized men. The Utopians also believe that a man must go on learning all his life, that he can do so if he is a man, and that, if he does not do so, he will cease to be one.

Therefore the whole country is dotted with centers of education for adults young and old, where the most important theoretical and practical questions are discussed. Some of these groups begin with the current issue of the *Utopian Times* and work backward to first principles. Some of them begin with Homer, who enjoys a considerable reputation in Utopia, and work forward to the pressing problems of the day. The object of these groups is not to confer social prestige or vocational advancement upon the members. It is to continue the intellectual development, the liberal education of the individual as a Utopian and a man.

The centers of adult education in Utopia are all residential. The Utopians have learned that the educational consequences of evening classes scattered over a period of weeks, though they are better than nothing at all, do not compare with those which can be achieved by having groups live together for a limited time and share in that continuous conversation about important subjects which to a Utopian is education. The industrial and agricultural life of the country revolves around the obligation that is felt by the whole community to spend some part of each year in organized study of this kind. No Utopian would think of taking a vacation in the American sense of the word, and the summer resorts, and even winter resorts, of that country are really centers of adult education.

The organization of the University of Utopia I have already roughly described. It is constituted of institutions of about twenty-five professors and two hundred and fifty students each. They are exclusively residential, for the same reason that the centers of adult education in Utopia are residential. Specialized study in Utopia begins only with the University. The University is built on the principle that men who must be intensively trained in the specialties must not lose their liberal education or their ability to communicate with other men or their interest in and capacity to understand ideas in any field of learning. All the major fields of learning are therefore represented in the faculties and among the students of the institutions of which the University of Utopia is composed. Because the Utopians recognize that the tendency of specialization is centrifugal and that every precaution must be taken against this tendency, they require the members of these institutions to live together.

The object of the University of Utopia is the clarification and reinterpretation of basic ideas. All ideas that can seriously pretend to be basic are discussed. The Utopians, because of the character of their liberal education, have little difficulty in assessing the pretensions of various ideas. Those ideas which underlie the learned professions are included. Those occupations which do not rest on any intellectual content or which have none in their own right are necessarily excluded; for how could those interested in them take part in the conversation? Persons who are interested only in the accumulation of data about some subject, even a subject of great importance, like the operations of government, or of the economic system, or of protons or proteins, are, unless they are able to think and communicate about the ideas involved in these phenomena, necessarily excluded, too.

The qualifications of the professors of the University of Utopia are strikingly different from those which prevail in the United States. With us the professor must only be eminent, or give promise of attaining eminence, in his field. In Utopia the professor must be eminent, or give promise of attaining eminence, in his field. This is taken as a matter of course. But unless in addition to meeting this requirement he is also willing and able to receive light from other fields and shed light from his own upon the basic problems that the University is discussing, he cannot be appointed. This conclusion follows remorselessly from the conception of a university that the Utopians entertain.

The students of the University of Utopia are not there because they do not want to go to work, or because they want to move a rung or two up the social ladder, or because they want to learn how to get ahead in some occupation, or because without the civilizing influence of the Dean of Men or the Dean of Women they might turn into juvenile delinquents. The students are there because they have intellectual interests and have shown in the program of liberal education they have passed through that they are capable of developing them. The University is not concerned with the question whether the studies of these students prepare them to carry on some specific activity in later life. Such a question would be incomprehensible to a Utopian. The Utopians have the conviction that intellectual activity and the discussion of the most important theoretical and practical problems is indispensable to a happy life and to the progress, and even the safety, of the state.

The University of Utopia was conceived and established as a center of independent thought. I have said enough to show in what sense it is a center: everybody can and will communicate with everybody else. I have perhaps said enough to suggest in what sense it deals with thought: anything that is not thought can have no place in it. By this I do not mean that the University is opposed to recreation or social life. The program of extra-curric-ulum activities is startling in its range and richness. All I mean is that the University has never confused these activities with the purpose of the institution. One reason for this is, perhaps, that intercollegiate football has never taken root—it has never even been thought of—in Utopia. As I have said, the Utopians are a sensible people.

Since they are sensible, they do not deny the value of the collection of information or data; nor do they deny the importance of technical training in many fields. And they would be the last to say that a society should not organize itself in some way to bring its knowledge and experience to bear on its urgent practical problems. All that the Utopians claim is that such activities, the collection of data, technical training, and the solution of immediate practical problems, cannot be conducted in a university without disrupting, or at least confusing, the institution. Since they regard the University as a highly specialized institution, they do not want it confused. They see confusion as the first step toward underspecialization and disinte-gration.

The Utopians understand, however, that men engaged in the collection of data, technical training at high levels, and the solution of urgent practical problems have much to gain from association with a center of independent thought. They also think that the University has much to gain from association with such men and with such undertakings. This is not because the professors are sensitive to the charge that they live in an ivory tower or have never met a payroll—such absurdities are never heard in Utopia—but because the Utopians recognize that anything worth thinking about has consequences in the practical order and that anything in the practical order may suggest something that is worth thinking about.

The Utopians have therefore surrounded the University with organiza-tions collecting data, giving technical training at high levels, and seeking the solution of urgent practical problems, and the interchange between these groups and the members of the University is very active. Neither side of the exchange is at all confused about what is the University and what is not. Neither side would wish to be the other. Each institution is specialized. These arrangements have worked remarkably well. I have heard that they were modeled after those between the Public Administration Clearing House and the University of Chicago.

I have now shown in what sense the University of Utopia is a center and in what sense it is dedicated to thought. In the next chapter I shall attempt to show in what sense it is independent and is therefore entitled to be called a center of independent thought. But I should say something now about the idea of independence as it affects the students of the University.

As you know, they enter the University between the ages of eighteen and twenty, having sought to obtain the beginnings of a liberal education in the

College. Their object in the University is to continue this education, to participate in the discussion that is the University, to understand the reasons for things, and to master the ideas in an important field of learning. The first difference that strikes us in looking at what they do and what the American student does lies in the negligible amount of formal instruction given to them. Twenty years ago, when I asked the chairman of the Economics Department at the University of Chicago why he had such large and frequent classes of graduate students, he replied, "Mr. Hutchins, my students cannot learn anything unless I am in the room." When I asked why he didn't get better students, he said, perhaps correctly, that there weren't any.

In Utopia this problem does not arise, because only those students who are qualified to do independent work and who are interested in doing it are admitted to the University. This is, in fact, one of the two great differences between the College and the University. The College does its work through formal instruction, and there is no specialization. In the University formal instruction is at a minimum, and one of the objects of the institution is to advance knowledge in special fields of learning. The College is in session for thirty-six weeks of the year; the University for only twenty-four. Since the Utopians pay no attention to time served as a criterion of intellectual progress, since, of course, there are no accrediting agencies in Utopia to tell the University that only time served can be such a criterion, and since the credit system has never been heard of, the Utopians have no difficulty in concluding that independent study and reflection should constitute the principal activity of the faculty and students of the University. In Utopia the student seldom attends formal class meetings more than four hours a week, and he is not required to attend those.

The method of instruction is chiefly discussion. The Professors in the University of Utopia never lecture, except about work that they have in progress. If that work has reached the stage at which it can be written down, it is written down, distributed among the students, and discussed. No Utopian professor would think of giving a course of lectures more than once. To do so would suggest that he had no work in progress or that he was not making any progress with it.

This brief survey of the organization and operation of the Utopian educational system enables us to see in what sense philosophical diversity is a hazard to education and in what sense it may be a positive advantage. Clearly if the educational system is thought of as a means by which society indoctrinates the young with a certain view of life and the world, then philosophical diversity is fatal and must be eliminated, if necessary by the most drastic methods. The drastic methods employed by Nazi Germany and those states which have officially embraced Marxism are known to all of us. If the University is thought of as performing, among other things, the task of training the so-called intelligentsia to preserve, interpret, and teach the official philosophy, then of course philosophical diversity cannot be tolerated. Educational systems and universities in countries that have militant official philosophies may be able to cope with industrialization and specialization by some of the methods practiced in Utopia. But they cannot cope with philosophical diversity. They cannot allow it. They have to take the view that the last word has been said, or at least the last important word, and that to permit the addition of another is to promote error and endanger the unity and safety of the state.

At first glance the problems raised by philosophical diversity in countries that are without an official philosophy seem insoluble. If there are many philosophies, how can we avoid having many educational philosophies? If there are many educational philosophies, how can we avoid having many educational systems, which is manifestly absurd? Yet the Utopian experience may suggest to us that it is possible to have one educational philosophy and many philosophies. The Utopian example may show that a country can have one educational system and one educational philosophy in the face of philosophical diversity.

The Utopians have accomplished this feat by making the consideration of philosophical diversity the primary concern of educational philosophy. A glance at the University of Utopia will show how this is done. The University is not a center of propaganda for an official doctrine. Still less is it an institution like many American universities that is not concerned with doctrine at all. It is concerned with all doctrines that can have any reasonable claim to be taken seriously. Its effort is to work toward a definition of the real points of agreement and disagreement among these doctrines, not in the hope of obtaining unanimity but in the hope of obtaining clarity. The object is not agreement but communication. The Utopians think it would be very boring to agree with one another. They think it helpful and interesting to understand one another. The University of Utopia, like the educational system as a whole, aims to bring together men of different attitudes, backgrounds, interests, temperaments, and philosophies for the purpose of promoting mutual comprehension. The University of Utopia is an understood diversity.

Thus the educational system of Utopia is a paradigm, or prototype, or model of the republic of learning and the world political republic for which the Utopians yearn. The civilization that the Utopians have established is one in which discussion takes the place of force, and consensus is the basis of action. In theoretical matters the Utopians believe that the continuous refinement of methods and ideas will lead to the development of new ideas and hence to the advancement of knowlededge. The Utopians are willing to examine the pretensions of any plan of action or of any theoretical proposition.

DISCUSSION AND WRITING

1. Define or explain: *efflorescence, laissez faire, vestige, rampant, autonomous, manifestation, elite, supererogation, axiom, paradigm, debase, centrifugal, pretension, eminent, remorseless, criterion, intelligentsia, militant, prototype, consensus.* Cite examples of simple, concrete, or popular phrases that keep Hutchins's style from becoming technical jargon.

2. Explain in your own words what Hutchins means by the "custodial system." In what sense is the University of Utopia "a highly specialized institution"? What is the meaning and what are the associations of the phrase "ivory tower"? What, in Hutchins's terms, does it mean to have "one educational philosophy and many philosophies"?

3. In one well-developed paragraph, sum up the author's definition of the nature and purposes of "liberal education."

4. Explain fully Hutchins's account of the relationship between education and democracy. Why is "liberal education" in his view incompatible with a totalitarian ideology?

5. Hutchins's style owes its force in part to his use of overstatement and sarcasm. Cite examples and discuss their effect.

6. Discuss specific points of agreement or disagreement between Hutchins's educational philosophy and the views of Plato and Rousseau reprinted in this section.

7. Weigh the arguments for or against one of the following statements: (a) Inexperienced children should not be bothered with social studies. (b) Every young American should master a foreign language. (c) The college curriculum should be completely prescribed. Use concrete illustrations and specific evidence.

8. To judge from your own experience, how well does the American high school prepare the future college student for "independent study and reflection"? Refer to specific subjects, assignments, teachers.

9. As far as you can tell, how successfully does your college bring together "men of different attitudes, backgrounds, interests, temperaments, and philosophies"? Compare and contrast from this point of view the members of the faculty that you have come to know.

10. Hutchins says that education is "the attempt of a society to produce the type of man that it wants." If you were defining the "type of man" that education today should produce, what would be his most essential characteristic? Use detailed illustrations.

FURTHER READING

Some articles by vigorous critics of American public education are Agnes E. Meyer, "Are Our Public Schools Doing Their Job?" *Atlantic,* February 1949; Arthur E. Bestor, Jr., "Aimlessness in Education," *Scientific Monthly,* August 1952; James B. Conant, "Education in the Western World," *Atlantic,* November 1957; Oscar Handlin, "Live Students and Dead Education," *Atlantic,* September 1961. Study these and one or two comparable more recent articles for recurrent complaints or characteristic trends.

JOHN WAIN

John Wain (born 1925) is a British novelist and poet who first became known as one of a group of writers called England's "Angry Young Men." His first novel, *Hurry on Down* (1953), has been called "a mordant commentary on the English academic world." A university lecturer in England for eight years, Mr. Wain resigned from teaching to devote full time to writing but has kept an "amateur's interest in education." The article here reprinted examines basic concepts of what education is; it has the vigorous style of a writer not afraid to generalize on the basis of his own experience and reading. Adopting a fresh and personal point of view, the author manages to give new life to two of the most frequently discussed subjects of our time: the values that guide or should guide our educational system, and the contrast between the Communist world and the West.

The Dilemma of Youth

In attitudes to education, as in most things, the world is divided. Many people in the West seem to believe that an educated person is somehow unworthy, little better than a traitor to the whole idea of education, unless he ranges himself pretty determinedly against the forces that propel his society along. This gives rise to the question, Can education legitimately aim at molding people into agreement with the basic assumptions of the society they live in, or is the only honourable role for the educated man that of rebel and disputant? Mr. David Riesman in a recent article has said roundly that "the relation of education to later life should be a dialectical and critical one." And speaking of the kind of student who makes the most favourable impression on faculty members, and finds himself recommended for fellowships, jobs, etc., he notes that the most favoured ones were "a bit rebellious, a bit off-beat . . . these were the students apt to appeal to a faculty member who had not entirely repressed a rebelliousness of his own that had led him to be a teacher in the first place."

The assumption here, that a main motive for devoting one's life to education is or can be "rebelliousness," is a widespread one in the West, though it must be virtually unknown in the Communist world, where the educational machine is seen as an assembly-line for producing good Communist citizens. But there are people in the West, also, who do not see education chiefly in terms of inciting people to challenge the society they live in, to overturn its assumptions, to rebel against its conventions. The word "convention" means "a coming together," and in every society there are important areas of thought and feeling on which men have come together. What is education primarily useful for? To strengthen this cohesion—to bind a society more closely together by presenting its basic assumptions in an acceptable form—or to weaken them by encouraging, in every sphere and over every issue, "rebellion"? Is the "rebel" thinking too much of himself and too little of others? Are there some things more important than the purity of one's spotless little intellectual integrity? We must be careful—the answer may be No.

Some societies, both today and in the past, have gone so far along the road towards an official, orthodox education that the very question we are discussing would seem to them meaningless. In the Middle Ages, European education was dominated by the Roman Catholic Church; theology was 'queen of the sciences' in every scheme of learning, and the question of an unorthodox (or anti-orthodox) teaching simply never arose.

As a matter of fact, the Middle Ages offer an interesting point of comparison with totalitarian modern societies. Their literary and scientific culture was based on the Greek and Latin past; when the highly trained, subtle, disputatious mediaeval scholar engaged in historical or literary teaching, he was working with material which dated from before the rise of his own society with its all-pervading Christian beliefs and assumptions. This set a problem which, during the mediaeval centuries, called forth some heroic solutions. A mediaeval scholar who loved, say Virgil—who responded to the majesty and beauty of Virgil's language and the nobility of his vision—was faced with the awkward fact that Virgil, having lived before Christ, was not a Christian writer, and therefore could not be used as an instrument of direct Christian teaching. If the mediaeval Christian scholars had been narrowly Philistine, they would have turned away from Virgil and concentrated entirely on their own Christian, neo-Latin culture. In fact, they did nothing of the kind; all the great Greek and Latin writers, in so far as the Middle Ages knew of their existence, were handed down with the utmost care, and every scrap of information about them was lovingly gathered.

To do this with the official backing of the Church was, of course, a matter of giving a Christian slant to the interpretation of the pagan classics, and this was accordingly done. Some of the interpretations we read about in a book like Comparetti's *Virgil in the Middle Ages* remind one of nothing so much as the efforts of presentday Soviet professors to "prove" that Shakespeare or

Goethe was "progressive," i.e. a Communist before his time. Their motive is a very strong one; being sensitive, intelligent readers, they want to go on being allowed to study these great poets and to spread a knowledge of them among their students; if this means dragging them across the ideological barrier, then drag they will. It is a mistake to mock at these men. If the Middle Ages had not performed the same service for Virgil and Ovid, not only would mediaeval culture have been much the poorer, but the works of these poets might have disappeared for ever.

The mediaeval church was no very hard task-master. In the absence of any strict standards of historical criticism, a scholar could get away with some very odd interpretations, if he had a strong enough motive to make him present his case vehemently. Thus, it was confidently asserted that the ancients were familiar with the Old Testament, so that they were already half-way to Christianity. Following on from this, the annotaters pounced on everything that would bear a Christian interpretation. Virgil's Fourth Eclogue, for instance, celebrates the prospective birth of a child to Pollio, a government official who was one of Virgil's early protectors. The poem pictures a new golden age of security and happiness which will date from this birth, and not unnaturally the early Christian commentators took this as a prophetic reference to the coming of the Messiah. It followed that Virgil must have been gifted with mystical powers of prophecy; and if he had them, might not others?

The important thing about the campaign is that it worked. Modern scholars are often puzzled to discern the exact degree of "sincerity" behind the mediaeval policy of reading all literary texts as if they were allegories, and making them yield the "right" meaning. Certainly they developed great skill at this kind of interpretation, and the exercise of that skill must have been a satisfaction in itself. But did the average mediaeval scholar, sitting down to expound a poem like the *Aeneid* or Ovid's *Metamorphoses* by splitting it up prismatically into a series of allegories, really believe that he was unwrapping a series of packages that had been deliberately tied by the author? Or did he not care about the author one way or another? Of course, the Middle Ages lacked the sense of history, as we now know it; they probably did not realise that an ancient Greek or Roman had an imagination attuned to a very different way of life from theirs, so different that the first step towards understanding his work would be to try to feel oneself back into his times. All they knew was that the ancients were "pagan," and must be made to yield a Christian message. Or was it "all they knew"? Did some of the more sensitive among them realise, as they compiled their vast commentaries in which every detail of the text had its allegorical "solution," like a puzzle, that their labours were essentially irrelevant, that they erected a superstructure of their own on the base provided by the author's words?

I fancy this thought must have strayed into their minds now and again, just as it must stray into the minds of Communist critics whose life-work is to provide every literary classic with a protective awning of "socialist realism." Sometimes very subtle and perceptive work can be produced even under these conditions; I have read Marxist analyses of Shakespeare plays which certainly provide interesting sidelights; the young English art critic Mr. John Berger is not so utterly insensitive to painting as you would think from reading his bald statement that "We can only make sense of art if we judge it by the criterion of whether or not it helps men to claim their social rights." This is exactly on a level with the mediaeval view that, since Christian truth is the only truth, any writing which cannot be made to yield a direct Christian message is simply falsehood. And yet mediaeval literary criticism is often profoundly interesting. (My own view, by the way, is the exact inversion of the mediaeval one; I think that if Christianity is true, then every good poem or novel is "Christian." And if Marxism, with its economic explanations and its relentless emphasis on the class struggle, really offered a satisfying explanation of human history, then all good writing would be Marxist writing; it would relate, in its own way, to the truth as Marx proclaimed it.)

Much has been written in the West about Soviet education, and violent arguments have sprung up between those who warn us that it is already ahead of our own, and those who, at the opposite extreme, maintain that the Soviet Union, not being interested in the cultivation of intellectual freedom and the spirit of enquiry, has no such thing as "education," in our Western sense, anywhere within its borders. The first group point to the colossal State expenditure on schools and colleges; the second to the heavily-slanted, doctrinaire nature of Soviet teaching.

Without wishing to open old wounds (for I have been involved in some of these arguments myself), I think it can be fairly said that Soviet education, admirably thorough as it is and enviably confident in the rightness of its own methods, is pre-eminently aimed at teaching its people to *know the answers*. All the answers: about medicine, about mathematics, about agriculture; about philosophy, about literature, about history and politics. The Soviet rulers do not encourage specialization, at any rate for undergraduates. They do not want historians or literary critics, they do not even want surgeons and engineers, who get on with the job according to their own lights, without much idea of the wider social implications of what they are doing. Their attitude is that all work is Communist work. A dam built by a Soviet engineer is not just a dam, it is a Communist dam. And so on down the line, until even the simplest tonsillectomy performed by a Soviet surgeon is a Communist tonsillectomy. Just as all literature, art and music produced by Soviet artists is required to be propaganda for the Soviet way of life, so all work is understood to be motivated first by a desire to serve that way of life and only secondly by love of the work itself.

This attitude, as everyone knows, is intensively fostered by Soviet teaching. The place occupied in eighteenth-century England by a simple assent to the Thirty-Nine Articles, which were drawn up by the English clergy in 1562 to unify Anglican worship, is occupied in the Soviet Union by a trio of formidable indoctrination courses, compulsory for all students, in whatever faculty, throughout the fifteen republics of the U.S.S.R. Thanks to the University of Michigan, we can now study the syllabus for these courses; in a thick pamphlet, *Administration of Teaching in Social Sciences in the U.S.S.R.*, they have published, in English translation, the requirements for three basic, compulsory courses: History of the Communist Party of the U.S.S.R., Political Economy, and Historical and Dialectical Materialism. The material is offered without comment, save for a short Introduction by Harlan H. Hatcher, setting out the circumstances—what the syllabi are, how they were obtained, and so forth. One sentence from this Introduction leaps into relief:

"Compulsory for all students, these courses constitute about eight to ten percent of the total instructional program of Soviet universities, technical schools, medical colleges and other institutions of higher education."

Obviously a system which compels every trained person, from a marine biologist to a lawyer, to spend one hour out of every ten during his or her college years in getting by heart the official doctrines of the State is determined on one thing at least: no one among the intelligentsia is going to be able to plead ignorance on any question of dogma. If anyone fails to live up to the full doctrinal requirements, the responsibility is entirely on his own shoulders, since his professional career was not at liberty to begin until he had shown himself word-perfect in the orthodoxy.

All this, in general terms, one knew already. From conversations with Soviet students and bureaucrats, I had come away with the impression of a flawlessly rehearsed catechism. What the Michigan pamphlet does is to reveal, step by step, how the indoctrination is done. Each subject is divided into "topics"; every topic has its official allotment of time, and its list of required reading. And the conclusions that must be reached are formulated in advance, there in the syllabus. Here, for example, is Topic 22 of the Political Economy course: "Completion of Territorial Division of World Among Great Powers and Struggle for its Redivision. Formation and Basic Features of Imperialism's Colonial System."

> 1. Imperialism as system of financial enslavement and colonial oppression. Completion of territorial division of world towards beginning of twentieth century. Struggle for redivision of divided world. Struggle of imperialists for world domination. Wars and militarization of national economy in capitalist countries.
>
> 2. Formation of imperialism's colonial system. Colonies and semi-colonies.
>
> Role of colonies in era of imperialism. Colonies as spheres for investing

capital. Colonies as markets for sales and as appendages supplying metropolitan countries with agricultural raw materials. One-sided character of development of national economy in colonial countries. Colonies as strategic military bases of imperialism.

And so on through two more articles.

That second section, when I read it, gave me a clue to the real nature of several conversations I had had in Moscow earlier in the year. Whenever "imperialism" was mentioned, the same arguments came out, no matter whom you were talking to. The basic position was, in each case, that there is only one kind of imperialism, i.e. planting your flag on the soil of another country and then proceeding to "exploit" that country. No distinction was admitted between old-style exploitation and modern mandate or protectorate systems; nor between countries which were being progressively educated towards self-government and those being held down by force. It was all "imperialism"—whereas the Soviet annexation of, say, Latvia was not imperialism because it didn't involve running up the Soviet flag. And having read Topic 22, I see it all. If one urged that the British action in Cyprus, say, was motivated not by a wish to "exploit" the Cypriots but by an obligation to NATO, that too had been forestalled, under the heading "Colonies as strategic military bases of imperialism."

I give this small and commonplace example to bring out the main point—that the Soviet educational system is succeeding in the basic task its rulers have imposed on it, which is to rehearse its entire bourgeoisie in an elaborate question-and-answer system of apologetics.

This is a form of "education for orthodoxy" which it is easy enough to reject as undesirable; one can't imagine any thoughtful person actually *wishing* to go in with such a system—though, no doubt, once enclosed in it most people would resign themselves and keep their mouths shut. When I propose for examination the question with which I started, about education for assent or dissent, I naturally had no intention of seriously recommending a giant processing-machine such as the Soviet Union has evolved. It isn't (in the West) necessary to muster all the arguments against such a system, but if I had to choose one argument that contains all the others I would merely point out that education is essentially a process of *launching*. An education, of whatever kind, has failed if it has not managed to stimulate in the student that kind of intellectual curiosity which will naturally lead him, year by year, to extend his knowledge. And also, it should go without saying, given him the necessary basic information to build on; not only factual information, but skills of a kind that do not show themselves in a parade of facts. How to find the knowledge he wants; how to marshal information; how to consider a subject dispassionately, brushing away the dust and cobwebs that will naturally form over any subject that has lain in one's mind for a few years, among the lumber of one's own prejudices and personal emphases. All this the student needs before he can begin. And he begins on the day he leaves college, just as the aviator begins on the day he first flies on his own.

By this test, the Soviet system of education fails. Its aim is not to launch people on a lifetime of original and developing thought, but to process them. By providing everyone with a shared background of information and argument, they may paper over the cracks in the Communist system, and in some cases actually cement them. But there is nothing here that can call itself education.

This kind of defect in the education of a totalitarian country is so glaringly obvious that one is sometimes driven close to the opposite extreme. It is tempting, after a look at the results of Communist orthodoxy in education, to throw the whole thing up and say that the sole duty of an educated person is to question, to probe, to protest, to rebel. Tempting, but in the end not satisfying.

All societies try to perpetuate themselves; we cannot deny them this right. Unless we take the extreme position represented by: "Communism is evil. Therefore anything that helps to strengthen a Communist society is evil. Therefore Communist education is evil," we can hardly quarrel with Russia or China for wanting to slant their educational systems towards orthodoxy. The West, naturally, does it too. In England, to take the example I know best, the State schools faithfully reflect the involvement of Church and Government which we symbolise by placing the Queen at the head of the Church of England. England is thus an 'officially' Christian country, in that the reigning monarch is identified with the Established Church. Proceeding downwards in a direct cause-and-effect chain, we get the compulsory religious teaching in schools. Every State-run school has to have religious instruction; it is the only compulsory subject, whereas there is no law which compels a school to teach, say arithmetic. And every such school must assemble once every day, teachers and pupils together, for religious worship. Both the instruction and the worship must be "undenominational"; there must be nothing to stir up the fierce warfare of the sects. But religion there must be. If a child's parents object—if they are Roman Catholics, or Orthodox Jews, or convinced atheists—the child is excused from these activities. But the school is not excused from the duty to provide them.

A Communist, then, could point out that we in England slant our education towards Christianity, which from his point of view is either a mere deception, aimed at keeping the poor in a proper state of resignation and holding back the wheels of change, or else a pitiable illusion. And however we chose to answer him, we could not deny that England has, in recent centuries, insisted on a definite show of orthodoxy from those entrusted with responsibility. The settlement of 1688, which came at the end of a long series of dangers and disasters provoked largely by Roman Catholic powers on the one hand, and the extreme revolutionary forms of Protestantism on the other, found a solution in the Thirty-Nine Articles. The Church of England, as a middle way, was deliberately used as a political instrument. From the 1680's until within living memory, it was impossible to hold a responsible position in England without assenting to the Thirty-Nine Articles—in other words, belonging to the Church of England. Without that assent, no one could hold Government office, be a Member of Parliament, study at Oxford or Cambridge or hold a commission in the army or navy.

What is more, this system remained firmly in place until the historical circumstances that produced it had finally withered away. It was never overthrown by determined opposition from below; it simply faded away of its own accord when it became out-of-date. (One of the last people to run up against it, incidentally, was H. G. Wells. As a boy, already sceptical in his views, he wanted to become a pupil-teacher in order to carry on with his education. The Thirty-Nine Articles were demanded; he writhed, raged, but gave in for the sake of going on increasing his knowledge. As a result, he hated religions, churches and priests till his dying hour.)

It is beyond my competence to settle, or even profitably discuss, the question, Was England right in taking this action, or wrong? I can see, of course, that the country entered a period of political stability in the 1680's such as the world has seldom seen, and continued in it until the twentieth century. And it seems reasonable to guess that the price that had to be paid for this stability was the Thirty-Nine Articles. But, as I say, the question lies outside my competence. The stability may have had other causes. What matters for our present purpose is that England, a country always known as a stronghold of political freedom, did find it necessary for over 150 years to impose on its citizens, or on such of them as sought to win authority and influence, a kind of Loyalty Oath.

This decision, however, did not bear very directly on English education. You had to be "Church of England" to get into Oxford or Cambridge, but once there you were not required to organize your studies along orthodox lines. (And if you were a Dissenter, there was, after the 1820's, the University of London offering first-class instruction—and there were always the Dissenting Academies, which play an honourable part in English educational history.) In other words, it was admitted that orthodoxy could not, in education, be forced on the student at every step. Compromise reigned; the comparison with modern Russia or China, or Nazi Germany, very soon breaks down. Shelley was sent down from Oxford for writing a pamphlet called "The Necessity of Atheism"; but if he had restrained his impatience for print, and merely *talked* about this necessity, he would have been left in peace.

The battle, in short, was never violently joined. Since the Church was at the heart of English institutional life, successive governments protected themselves by the simple bargain of requiring assent to the Thirty-Nine Articles from those who directed, or studied at, the country's chief centres of learning; but they did nothing to hinder the setting-up of rival centres, nor did they indulge in witch-hunting among the accepted. Both orthodox and unorthodox proceeded along the same traditional lines. They saw education as a matter of imparting a traditional body of wisdom. The three Classical languages, Latin, Greek and Hebrew, would enable a man to study, in the original, most of the texts on which the culture and ethics of Western society were based. Then there were the principal modern languages. Then there was history—mostly European history, since Europe was, effectively," the world" until the twentieth century, just as "philosophy" meant Western philosophy.

It was all rather like the process whereby old birds teach young birds to fly. The student was introduced to the texts in which the society's basic values were enshrined, and the implication was that if he made a mess of his life, or failed to be of use to the community, the responsibility would be his own.

Until the rise of mass communications, this system worked reasonably well. The target was a limited one; no attempt was made to educate an entire population, since it was assumed that decisions would be made by the educated class, and that values could be spread downwards, like butter soaking through a baked potato. Not until towards the end of the nineteenth century did successive shocks begin to weaken the traditional structure. First came industrialism with its demand for universal literacy. (No industrial society can be run by an illiterate working class. England, which became fully industrialized very early, was correspondingly early (1871) with compulsory free education, resulting in virtually 100% literacy. The ruling class of that time, like the Soviet ruling class of the present day, indulged in a good deal of boasting about its paternal generosity in teaching the people to read and write, but the more astute among them must have known that if they did not provide the funds for this instruction they would fall behind, in the race for trade, nations who *would* provide it.

From that hour, the older education was doomed. A literate people means a mass Press, challenging the values instilled by education with sensational and get-rich-quick values of its own. And within forty or fifty years, the Press was itself challenged by radio, cinema and, later, electronics. In every country where the entertainment and advertising industries are allowed a free hand, they spend money which makes the country's education budget look pitiable. They offer salaries to bright men which make the teacher's way of life, by comparison, reek of masochism. And they batter the minds of the people into insensibility before the vitalizing suggestions of literature, art or philosophy can begin to do their work.

It is at this point that we meet again, and in a sharper form, the initial question. Education for assent or dissent? For conformity or rebellion? In the East, there is no problem because both sides have been drawn into one central mass. The entertainment industry, the Press, the advertising copy-writers, have all been processed into the same solid block that contains the teacher and the writer. And Western visitors who feel disgust at the blatancy of their own ad-men and journalists often come back from Russia or China full of respect for the relative quietness and single-mindedness in the Communist atmosphere. Personally, I didn't. The bludgeoned conformity aroused my pity; the holier-than-thou attitude of official Communism, my impatience. This is not the way out. Better singing commercials than culture-squads raising hymns to Lenin by numbers.

And neither can that initial question admit of any simple answer. Should a society educate its members for assent?—Assent *to what?* The claim that a society can teach only "the values that it has" implies that those values are widely recognised and can be stated easily. In the Communist world, this is true, at least as far as the official values are concerned. But in a free society, values are continually forming, evolving, emerging into consciousness. If we say, for instance, that the twin sources of Western civilisation are still, in spite of all modern changes, Christianity and the classics, that does not close the discussion. It opens it. We see the Christian thread running through various attempts at social justice—Welfare States and the like. And we see the classical thread running through the efforts to preserve intellectual freedom (the gift of the Greek) and impartial, universally recognised laws (the gift of the Roman). But having noted these broad outlines, we are no nearer to answering the enormous number of questions thrust on us by day-to-day life, and which all resolve themselves into one basic question: Given that our values are these, how do we apply them in this situation?—and this?—and that which is coming towards us? For liberal democracy, unlike Communism, has no answer-book; we do not claim, as the Communists do, that the truth is immediately obvious. John Donne has told us in his Third Satire that

> On a huge hill,
> Cragged and steep, Truth stands, and he that will
> Reach her, about must, and about must go,

and we believe him, and are willing to go about and about, toiling up to where Truth stands.

And this, of course, puts a great strain on the teacher. In our kind of society, the teacher—any kind of teacher, from kindergarten to graduate school—is in an almost impossible position. In a society inclined to be sceptical about the practical use of education, except in so far as it channels the young into well-paid jobs, the teacher, who has no well-paid job, has to stand as a witness that education does confer riches and happiness. However modest he is, sooner or later he has to make the claim, "I have something to give your children. It will not bring them in big incomes and security; it will not solve their immediate personal problems. But I am offering it and I advise you to accept it on their behalf."And if society, still sceptical, with an eye on the teacher's low salary, few possessions, modest living-quarters, answers with the sneer,"You mean it will make them more like *you?*"then the teacher must find within himself, somewhere, the courage to say, "Yes." And let it go at that. Conscious as he is of his own inadequacies and limitations, of the many sacrifices he has accepted, of his own unsatisfied wants and irrational loves and hatreds, he must appear before the world as the representative of the free human mind. It is an almost impossible demand to make of anyone. And yet thousands accept it, and undertake the impossible, in every free country.

And having accepted it, they find themselves in the front line of attack. A society teaches "the values that it has," only by feeling its way concretely towards those values through the experience of living men and women. Both assent and dissent become merged in enquiry. For if we assent to the principle of intellectual freedom, we commit ourselves to fearless questioning. If we assent to the principle of the sacredness of the individual, we commit ourselves to the personal judgment. If we throw away the authority of the intellectual policeman on the corner, and substitute the right of appeal to the community of reasonable beings, we commit ourselves to respect for other people.

On either side of the fence, what we find is an education for assent. On the one side, assent to an authority which hands down values from above, and can alter them at will, and dictate exactly by what means they are to be put into practice. On the other, assent to a tradition of enquiry, of bringing even the least palatable truths into the open, and of making the practical application of those truths a matter for the individual conscience.

On the one side, assent to the tabulated and formally announced doctrines of a society. On the other, assent to the inner laws by whose authority the society came into being, and which, thwarted and fouled as they may be by individual acts of selfishness, still make themselves felt—as long as there is an education which frees the mind. To be free is, often, to be baffled by indecision; but a society whose education aims at banishing indecision will sooner or later find that truth, sanity and even loyalty have been banished as well.

DISCUSSION AND WRITING

1. Define or explain the following terms, paying attention to their history, associations, or typical uses. Are any of these terms used by the author in *untypical* ways? *Dialectical, convention, integrity, orthodox, totalitarian, disputatious, Philistine, ideological, allegory, expound, criterion, doctrinaire, propaganda, intelligentsia, dogma,*

bureaucrat, catechism, indoctrination, bourgeoisie, apologetics, dispassionate, astute, masochism, blatancy, palatable. Who were Virgil, Ovid, Goethe, H. G. Wells?

2. Find and explain half-a-dozen British terms or expressions used by the author—for instance, terms relating to British politics, British education, or British religious history. Are there any grammatical constructions or everyday expressions that strike you as British?

3. The author uses much vividly informal figurative language to render abstract concepts concrete and alive: "dragging them across the ideological barrier"; "a protective awning of 'socialist realism.'" Discuss these and four or five additional examples. What tends to be the general effect on the reader?

4. How much use does the author make of terse, striking statements, summing up in one short sentence a key concept? Note, for instance, "A dam built by a Soviet engineer is not just a dam, it is a Communist dam." Find additional examples and examine the way they are put together.

5. Examine the over-all structure and strategy of this essay. (Prepare a rough outline.) It is often said that a mature person avoids crude either-or, black-and-white choices. In talking about a subject like Communism, many writers fail to meet this criterion. How does Mr. Wain fare in this respect? How does his solution to this problem determine the structure of his argument as a whole?

6. In one solid paragraph, write a definition of education that might satisfy Mr. Wain. Try not to oversimplify the point of view that he represents.

7. What, in this essay, is the relationship between generalization and specifics? Does the author manage to bridge the gap between general statement and concrete example? What kinds of material does he draw on to help him substantiate his general conclusions?

8. Should American college education be "education for orthodoxy" or "education for dissent"? Anchor your discussion firmly to your own experience and reading.

9. Should teachers in American high schools be required to sign a loyalty oath? Examine in detail some of the possible justifications and objections. Refer to specific problems, concrete situations.

10. Would you call the United States an "officially" Christian country? If it isn't, should it be? Support your answer in detail.

FURTHER READING

Many modern British writers have made their reputations by satirizing aspects of English life that Americans often regard with nostalgia. Thus, Evelyn Waugh, writing in the thirties, produced an unforgettable portrait of latter-day aristocratic society in his novel *A Handful of Dust.* Kingsley Amis, writing in the fifties, provided in *Lucky Jim* a startling glimpse behind the ivied walls of an imaginary British university. In a similar vein, Angus Wilson satirized traditional scholarship in *Anglo-Saxon Attitudes* (1956).

4

The Writer's Tools

An education for freedom (and for the love and intelligence which are at once the conditions and the results of freedom) must be, among other things, an education in the proper uses of language. ALDOUS HUXLEY

A writer cannot be forever anxiously self-conscious about the means he uses to achieve his ends. Even when he fully exploits the resources of language, his use of them must seem spontaneous rather than calculating, inevitable rather than contrived. Sooner or later, nevertheless, every writer should take a careful look at the tools of his trade. More fully aware of the workings of language and of logic, he can learn to extend his control over both, to avoid the more obvious blind alleys, and to evaluate his work by realistic standards. The authors in this section discuss aspects of language and thought that have been the subject of extensive study and vigorous controversy. With a familiar lightness of touch, Stephen Leacock, in "Good and Bad Language," handles a basic feature of language: its richness and diversity, its refusal to stand still or to dwindle into something narrowly logical and one-dimensional. W. K. Wimsatt, Jr., in "When Is Variation 'Elegant'?", shows how a writer can be guided in his use of language, not by black-and-white rules, but by sensitivity to different stylistic effects. Monroe C. Beardsley, in an excerpt from a book that recognizes the close relationship between language and thought, studies the ways in which words acquire meaning and the kinds of meaning they acquire. Sir Francis Bacon, in his famous discussion of the "Idols of the Mind," examines perennial logical pitfalls and, by implication, some of the basic requirements of sound thinking.

STEPHEN LEACOCK

Stephen Leacock (1869–1944) was a Canadian economist and university teacher who had a knack for humorous writing with serious undertones. A native of England, he taught at McGill University and published a succession of volumes including *Literary Lapses* (1910), *Frenzied Fiction* (1917), and *Last Leaves* (1945). In the following chapter from a book giving advice to writers, Mr. Leacock takes the side of authorities who see in slang a symptom of the life and vigor of a growing and changing language. His essay shows an experienced writer's delight in the color and variety of language, in the richness of the writer's resources.

Good and Bad Language

Quite apart from the technical aspect of the art of narration, there is the broader general question of good and bad language, of where speech ends and slang begins. To what extent must the language of literature and cultivated discourse accept and assimilate the innovations, the irregularities and the corruptions that perpetually appear in all languages as spoken by the mass of the people? To what extent are we to think of our language as a moving current, never the same except in its identity, and to what extent should we wish to check the flow of the current, so that stiller waters may run deeper! Obviously there is a limit in each direction. A current totally arrested means stagnation. Waters that run too fast end in the sand. Somewhere there may be a happy mean between the two.

Now this question arises for all languages. But it has a very peculiar importance for the English language since here the current flows in two parts, the American and the British; and many people are inclined to think that one tends to run too fast and the other tends to slacken. In other words we have here the problem of the American language and American slang. Every now and then controversy breaks out in regard to British English and American English—or it used to before the war stilled all babble—and it sometimes had a rather nasty edge to it. It carried in it one of the last faint survivals of the Stamp Act and the Boston Tea Party. Great quarrels die

Reprinted by permission of Dodd, Mead & Company from *How to Write* by Stephen Leacock. Copyright 1943 by Dodd, Mead & Company, Inc.

away to leave only generous memories; little quarrels live on. Hence the question of "slang" as between England and America (England, not Scotland; the Scots are not worrying) keeps its edge; all the more so, in that a lot of Americans think in their hearts, that the reason why the English don't use much slang is that they can't make it up, and a lot of English people think that the Americans use slang because they weren't brought up properly—or, no, they don't think it, they know it. That's the provoking thing about the English (say the Americans); they don't think things, they know them. They did all their thinking years and years ago.

I can write on this controversy with the friendly neutrality of a Canadian. In Canada we have enough to do keeping up with two spoken languages without trying to invent slang, so we must go right ahead and use English for literature, Scotch for sermons and American for conversation.

Perhaps the highest point of controversy is reached in the discussion whether there is, whether there ought to be, whether it is a shame that there isn't, an "American" language. Some people feel very strongly on this point. They think that having your own language is a mark of independence like owning your own house, driving your own car and having your own shaving mug in the barber shop. Gangs of boys make themselves up a "language" and revel in its obscurity. The leading boys in this respect are the Irish, so anxious to have their own language that they are trying to learn Gaelic. If they are not careful, first thing they know they'll get to talk it and then they'll be sorry.

On the other hand, some people feel just the other way about it. A most interesting article appeared a little while ago in one of the leading British Quarterlies, written by an American, and deprecating all idea of the creation of an American language as dangerous to our mutual dependence and kinship.

My own feeling about this, if I may put it in slang, is "I should worry." Or, in other words, there is not the faintest chance of there ever being an American language as apart from English. The daily intercommunication of telegraph, telephone, literature and the press, fuses all forms of "English" toward one and the broadcast and the talking pictures even fuse the toned voice. In the world of today languages cannot separate. That process belonged to epochs of distance and silence unknown now. Even then it was long. It took Latin a thousand years to turn into French.

The situation in the world today is this: There is a language called "English." It is too bad, if you like, that one country should seem to have stolen or to monopolize the claim to the name. But if the English stole the name of a language, the "Americans" stole the whole of two continents. Humble people, like the Canadians, and the Eskimos, have to live in "America" and speak "English," without fretting about it.

English is spoken by the people in England; it also spoken by the Scots, by the unredeemed Irish, the Australians—a lot of other people than Americans. Who speaks it best, no one knows; it's a matter of taste. Personally I think I like best the speech of a cultivated Scot, and perhaps least a certain high-grade English which calls a railroad a "wailwoad." I myself talk Ontario English; I don't admire it, but it's all I can do; anything is better than affectation.

Now by slang is meant the unceasing introduction into language of new phrases, and especially new nouns as names for things. There is no doubt that this peculiar fermentation of language has reached in America higher proportions than ever known anywhere else. For example—and my authority here is Mr. Eric Partridge, who cannot be wrong—a test was taken not long ago in a Wisconsin high school to see how many different words the boys and girls employed to express a low opinion of a person. Their list reads, *mutt, bonehead, guy, carp, highbrow, tightwad, grafter, hayseed, hot-air artist, rube, tough-nut, chump* and *peanut.* Perhaps they thought of more after they got home; these no doubt were only some of the things they called their teachers.

Many people, without being students of language, have observed the extraordinary number of ways in which American slang can indicate that a man has had too much drink. The chief authority on the subject (I refer to American slang and don't want to be ambiguous), H. L. Mencken, gives a partial list, brought up to 1923, and including *piffled, fiddled, spiflicated, tanked, snooted, stewed, ossified, slopped, jiggered, edged, loaded, het up, frazzled, jugged, soused, cornered* and *jagged.*

Slang passes as it comes. It lives only when it deserves to live, when the word has something about it that does a real service. In the Wisconsin students' list above I can detect only two words that look permanent, *guy* and *highbrow. Guy* is a word with a history; it comes down to us from poor Guy Fawkes (Guido Faukes), tortured and executed for trying to blow up the English Parliament. His "Fifth of November" crime was kept alive in memory—still is—by toting around a tattered figure on a stick in a pro-cession with the cry, "Oh, please to remember the fifth of November, with gunpowder, treason and plot." So the word came to mean a tattered-looking person and then just a queer-looking person, like a professor. From that it began to mean just a person: *I was out with another guy last night.*

The fact is we are always hard up for neutral words to mean "just a person"; each new one gets spoiled and has to be replaced. Be careful how you call a woman a "woman," and a "lady" is apt to be worse; don't call a Frenchman an "individual," or an Englishman a "fellow." Hence the need for "guy," which will gradually rise from ridicule to respectability, as already indicated. At some future British coronation the Archbishop of Canterbury will say to the Queen, "Will you take this guy to be your husband?" And for all we know the queen will answer, "Sez-you."

The other word, *highbrow*, will live for another reason. We need it. It is a little different from *intellectual, learned, cultivated*. It started like most slang as a brilliant image, or metaphor, taken from the sweeping forehead, smooth as an egg, of a Shakespeare or a Hall Caine. But, with perhaps a change of spelling, the thought of *brow* will disappear and we shall use the term naturally and effectively—*a highbrow audience*, the *opinion of highbrows*, etc.

The making of slang is, as I say, a sort of living process of language like the scum on wine. Without it there is no wine, no life, no fermentation. Later on, the scum passes as dust and dregs and leaves behind the rich fluid of the wine. A language that has ceased to throw off slang has ceased to live. Thus came all our language. Every syllable of it since the dawn of speech has been rolled over and over in endless renewal. Our oldest words, our oldest names, were once bright with the colors of the morning, striking some new metaphor that brought into full relief the image of the thing seen. Centuries ago some Roman called his fellow-Roman's head a "pot" and put the word *testa* [tête] into the French language. His genius for seeing resemblances was no greater than that of his American successor who perceived that the human head was a *bean*.

Now, the process of creating slang is not confined to America. But I think the fermenting, slang-making process is livelier far in America than in England. This would seem to be the consequence of setting a language in a new country—with new lives, new scenes to turn it to, and with the débris of other languages jostling beside it. Under the wide canopy of heaven above the prairies a preacher became a *sky-pilot*. In England he remained, among other things, an *incumbent*, still sitting there. A newcomer in the West was a *tenderfoot* or a *greenhorn*, a locomotive an *iron horse*, and so on. Little snips of foreign idiom like the *something else again* of German, and *I should worry* of Yiddish, came snuggling into the language. *Yes, we have no bananas* carries with it the whole Mediterranean migration.

This process of change, like invention itself, became much more conscious in America than in England. What the English did for lazy convenience or by accident, the Americans did on purpose. Hence American slang contains a much greater percentage of cleverness than English. A lot of English slang words are just abbreviations. To call a professional at cricket a *pro*, or breakfast *brekker*, or political economy *pol. econ.*, saves time but that is all. To call a pair of trousers *bags* is a step up; there is a distinct intellectual glow of comparison. But it is only twilight as compared with such American effects as *lounge-lizard, rubber-neck, sugar-daddy, tangle-foot*, and *piece of calico*.

It is, moreover, a peculiar merit of American slang that a lot of it has the quality of vitality—vital force of renewed life. Take such words as a *hide-out* and *frame-up,* or a *tie-up* (on a railway). To make these involves the process of *starting over again,* forming language from the beginning. Compare *sob-stuff, fade-out, send-off, side-track,* and a host of others.

Everything, as the French say, has the defects of its merits. American slang forces the pace, and hence a lot of it *is* forced, pointless, of no literary or linguistic value. Especially tiresome is the supposed slang of the criminal class, as used in crime novels to heighten the reader's terror. Everyone recognizes such language, as *See here, pal, if the narks grab you for doing in that moll, the beak will send you up, see, and you'll burn.* I don't know whether any people really use this stuff. I hope not. If they must be criminals, they might at least talk like gentlemen. But in any case English crime stories often run to the same kind of stuff; indeed I am not sure just where the words above belong.

But no one need be afraid that slang will really hurt our language, here or in England. It cannot. There is no dictatorship behind it. Words and phrases live only on their worth; they survive only on their merits. Nor does slang tend to separate America and England. As a matter of fact, the rising generation in England reach out eagerly for American slang. If that means they're not rising but sinking, it's too bad. But anyway we'll sink together.

So much for the toleration of slang as bad language turning into good, or dying from its very badness. What are we to say of bad language in the other sense, the kind that really is bad? Are we to put it in or leave it out? When we write a story our characters, if they are what are called "red-blooded" men and women, are apt to get profane; and even if they are thin-blooded they are apt to get nasty, in fact the thinner the nastier. The problem which all writers of fiction have to try to solve, and none have solved, yet, is how to swear in print. Some writers of today think that they can solve the problem by ignoring it—just go ahead and swear. We open the pages of a typical novel and our eyes bounce off with a start at the expression . . . *You miserable bastard!* . . .

This is not said to the reader. It is what the hero says to, or rather *throws at* the villain, who has said something unbecoming in the presence of a girl, something that a girl ought not to hear. The hero is a splendid fellow. He has *guts.* The book says so. In fact that's why the girl likes him. It says, "She threw her arms about his neck and pressed her slim body close to him. 'You have guts,' she murmured." You see, she herself is so awfully slim that naturally—well, you get the idea. If not, you can read it all for yourself in any new book, under such a title as *Angel Whispers,* or *Undertones* or something like that, on the outside. On the inside it's full of *guts.* The new books are like that.

But we are not talking about any particular book but about the problem that is suggested—the question of how to deal with profanity in fiction—how can you swear in print?

We must, I fear, dismiss at once the old-fashioned Victorian expedient of telling the reader that one of the characters in the story said something "with a terrible oath." That won't do now-a-days. We want to hear it. What was it? This formula was the one used in the pirate stories written for boys and girls.

For example:

> "Har! har!" shouted the pirate with a foul oath. "They are in our power."
>
> "They certainly are," said the second pirate with an oath fouler than the first.
>
> "I'll say so," said the third pirate with an oath fouler still—a lot fouler.
>
> The fourth pirate remained silent. He couldn't make it.

Now that won't do. We'll judge for ourselves how foul the oath is. If you can't say it, just whisper it. It's got to be pretty foul to get past us.

And I need hardly say, that it won't do to fall back on that old-fashioned trick that is used in novels "laid" in the Middle Ages—I mean the trick of making up a lot of fanciful stuff and calling it swearing.

Here's how it runs:

> "Odd's piddlekins," cried Sir Gonderear, "by my halidome, thou art but a foul catiff. Let me not, or I'll have at you."
>
> "Nay, by the Belly of St. Mark," answered the Seneschal, "I fear thee not, false paynim . . . Have one on me!" (Or words to that effect.)

That was all right, as we shall see in the discussion of historical romances, from Sir Walter Scott. It won't do now. Such an epithet as *foul catiff* has been replaced by *you big stiff,* and a *paynim* is a *lobster.*

There used to be a special kind of swearing reserved by convention for the use of sailors in sea-stories. "Shiver my timbers!" cried the bosun, "you son of a swob! Lift a finger, you lobscouse, and I'll knock the dead lights out of you." After which he spat a quid—a *quid pro-quo*—into the lee scuppers.

Fenimore Cooper is a case in point. The public of his day was too strict in its ideas to allow a sailor even to shiver his timbers in print. A glance at any of Cooper's famous sea stories will reveal such terrible profanity as d——l, apparently hinting at *devil,* and d——e, which may be interpreted with a thrill as "damme." Oddly enough, in Cooper's day the word "bloody" had not yet taken on in America its later offensive connotation, so that Cooper was at liberty to write, "D——e," said the bosun, "what the d——l does the bloody fellow mean?" But we may leave that to Fenimore Cooper. At present you couldn't navigate even a car ferry with a truck on it on that language.

You see, it was much easier to get away with such things a hundred years ago, at the beginning of modern fiction, than it is now. Take the case of Charles Dickens. He couldn't, of course, put real swearing into his books, and anyway he wouldn't have wanted to. So he set up a sort of jargon that he took straight out of the blood and thunder of the cheap London theater of which, as an impecunious youth, he was inordinately fond.

An example is seen in the language used by Bill Sykes, the murderer, in *Oliver Twist*. There is a scene, in which he is just going to do the murder—no, has just done it and is trying to escape. A child has got in the way and Sykes says to his associates, "Open the door of some place where I can lock this screeching hell babe . . ." Why he didn't "bump the child off," I forget just now. The present point is the language he used. He would have had just as good a phrase for bumping it.

Compare the *hell's accursed,* and the *foul fiend,* and such mild phrases. With objurations of that sort you sometimes couldn't tell whether the characters were cursing or praying; in fact in origin the two are one.

That reminds me of the language I once heard used by a man showing a "picture panorama"—the kind of thing they used to have long ago before the real "pictures" replaced it. In these pictures, when the successive scenes were shown, there was a man who did the talking. "Here you see this," and "now you see that . . ." and so on, as the scene went by. The man I speak of was showing a scene representing a Swiss peasant, getting swallowed up in a morass, or nearly swallowed up, till an angel appeared to save him. I was quite unable, and I still am, to distinguish whether the Swiss peasant and the angel were praying or swearing. In fact I don't think the picture man had thought it out. He took a chance.

His talk ran:

> Here you see the Swiss Alps. In the foreground is one of those dangerous more-asses, where the treacherous surface, with all the aspect of firm ground, offers no real support. Here you see a Swiss peasant. Look! He is stepping out on the more-ass. The ground yields beneath his feet. He moves forward more rapidly to escape. He begins to sink. He tries in vain to withdraw his feet. He is slowly sinking to his doom. Look, he lifts his hands and cries aloud: "Oh, Heaven," he says, "get me out of this-more-ass. Oh, God, this is the damnedest more-ass. Christ! this is awful."
>
> His prayer is heard. An angel appears, bending out from the clouds, her hand outstretched. "You poor soul," she says in a voice vibrating with pity. "You poor nut, you poor bastard . . . give me your hand, and come up." She takes him to her bosom, and he is saved.

So he would be, of course.

But to turn back again to advice to writers. Don't think you can get away with swearing by putting something very close to it, something nearly as good and much cheaper, by a shift of a letter or two. Some writers try, for instance, to use "ruddy" to stand for "bloody." This is used especially in the mouths of English army sergeants and such. It is supposed to give a barrack-room touch. But it is really just a left-over piece of Victorian evasion. Rudyard Kipling used this trick, not so stale in his hey-day as it is now. One recalls his Soudanese negro Fuzzy-wuzzy, who was described as a "big, black, bounding beggar, who broke a British Square."

That's all right. Fuzzy-wuzzy was pretty close to that, but not just exactly that.

And here's another thing:

Don't try to get around the difficulty by turning the profanity into strokes (------), or making it into asterisks (***). That's just feeble.

Asterisks and dots and strokes are hopeless. You can't *swear* with those things. They won't read right . . . Read aloud, as they are, they would turn the pirate story into:

> "Three asterisks!" shouted the Pirate.
> "Four," shouted the next.
> "I'll make it six," yelled a third, adding a stroke and a colon.

A person still young and inexperienced might think—surely there is no problem here. The true method would be to write down the very words that an actual person would actually use, to put the swearing in the book exactly as people swear it. But that, of course, would never do. Leaving out all question of whether the law allows it, art forbids it. It wouldn't sound right. Try it. Put down a set of foul, profane, obscene words—not samples, but the whole set used in what is called a string of profanity. It would sound awful for one paragraph, flat and stale after two, and beyond that utterly nauseating—in fact just like swearing. And you know how that sounds.

The only advice that can be given to the writer is, don't go further than others do. In fact, keep just a little behind them. If they say "guts," you say "bowels of compassion."

DISCUSSION AND WRITING

1. Point out and discuss words and phrases that give Leacock's own language a colloquial tone. Discuss other features that contribute to the informality of his discussion.

2. Restate the author's definition of slang and sum up his attitude toward it.

3. Test Mr. Leacock's comments on the relative richness of American slang by collecting slang terms for one or more of the following: *money, policeman, girl, car, alcohol.* Point out other words for which slang furnishes a number of different terms.

4. Discuss recent slang expressions that illustrate the tendency of American slang toward striking metaphor, toward "a distinct intellectual glow of comparison."

5. Many children and adolescents delight in word play, word jokes, and made-up words. Examine examples from your own observation.

6. Can you provide examples of "affectation" in speech or in writing?

7. Parents sometimes vigorously object to the presence in high-school libraries of books making use of profane language. Do you consider such objections justified?

8. Investigate one of the following: trends in current high-school or college slang; use of slang and colloquial language in current advertising; use of language by your favorite disc jockey, comedian, or other radio or television performer. Give examples.

9. Investigate the treatment of the following words in half a dozen reference dictionaries, including *Webster's Third New International Dictionary* and dictionaries of usage: *ain't, can* and *may, enthuse, finalize, infer* and *imply, irregardless.* What conclusions can you draw about the way current dictionaries treat problems of "good and bad language"?

10. Are some kinds of speech or some varieties of usage a social or economic handicap? Limit your discussion to one area, such as college social life, business, or local politics.

FURTHER READING

The problem of "good and bad language" was widely debated in national magazines when the G. & C. Merriam Company published *Webster's Third New International Dictionary,* the third edition of the most authoritative American dictionary of the English language. Some notable contributions to this debate are Wilson Follett, "Sabotage in Springfield," *The Atlantic,* January 1962; Dwight Macdonald, "The String Untuned," *The New Yorker,* March 10, 1962; Bergen Evans, "But What's a Dictionary For?" *The Atlantic,* May 1962; Mario Pei, "The Dictionary as a Battlefront," *Saturday Review,* July 21, 1962; Jacques Barzun, "What Is a Dictionary?" *The American Scholar,* Spring 1963. What seem to be the two or three central issues that these articles tend to return to? Is there anything like an approximate consensus among the various writers? If so, how does it compare with the position taken by Leacock?

W. K. WIMSATT, JR.

W. K. Wimsatt, Jr. (born 1907), has been called one of the "toughest-minded" contemporary American critics of imaginative literature. His articles and books pay close attention to "what is there" on the printed page and at the same time to what gives a piece of writing its larger significance. In the following article, Mr. Wimsatt transfers this kind of attention from imaginative literature to expository prose. The result is the kind of thoughtful study of style that helps a writer go beyond simple black-and-white rules. Like H. W. Fowler (whom he quotes early in the article), Wimsatt here attempts not simply to "condemn" or "approve" but to "distinguish." Repetition, for instance, is in itself neither good nor bad—we may use it effectively for needed emphasis ("No! No! Not again!"), or we may repeat the same tired ideas yet once more because we have run out of things to say. Mr. Wimsatt's sensitivity to different stylistic effects can serve as a model to the writer who wants to make intelligent choices in his own use of language.

When Is Variation "Elegant"?

The term "elegant variation" is one which I believe we owe to *The King's English* of H. W. and F. G. Fowler. Their analytic wit and readiness with example seem to have brought recognition and a name to a rhetorical fault which formerly one shunned or cultivated only by intuition. Sir Arthur Quiller-Couch in his essay "On Jargon" has written humorously of the same fault. For some time now it has been a topic in textbooks for college English composition. H. W. Fowler's treatment in his *Modern English Usage* is perhaps the most concise and orderly. Here under the headings "Elegant Variation" and "Repetition of Words and Sounds" he illuminates complementary principles, which one may recall by considering only two of his examples.

> They dug their *own* clay, often in *front* of their *own front* doors.

> They spend a few weeks longer in their winter *home* than in their summer *habitat*.

"Diametrically opposed" faults, says Fowler, one of which consists in "carelessly repeating a word in a different application," the other in "carefully not repeating it in a similar application." Or, one might draw up two rules of thumb: When you mean different things, use different words. When you mean the same thing, use the same word.

To phrase the rules this way suggests at once a speculation which, I believe, can lead deep into the question of style and hence has a bearing on more central matters of rhetoric and poetry. "When do I mean different things?" "When do I mean the same thing?" In Fowler's words, when is the "application" different? When is it similar? Both these ways of phrasing harbor an ambiguity which must be resolved before the questions can be answered. A term means a thing, denotes it, refers to it. But also there is to

From *The Verbal Icon*. Copyright 1954 by the University of Kentucky Press. In the present version of this essay, part of the material in the author's original footnotes has been omitted.

be taken into consideration the class conception which usually accompanies the denoting, the aspect or quality under which the thing is denoted.

In examples of "elegant variation" one has always to consider not only the number of references or aspects but the number of things. There are examples of variation where several physically separable things (a southern part of the earth and a northern) are denoted under slightly different aspects (home and habitat), while the context indicates that the things are really thought of under one aspect (call it either home or habitat). But there are also examples where under different aspects only one thing is denoted. Fowler does not distinguish these two kinds, presenting examples of both but many more of the first kind, where two or more things are denoted. The second kind, however—the one-thing kind—is a better starting point for analysis. It is simpler and, as it appears to me, less frequently deserving of the derogatory name "elegant." One of Fowler's clearest examples of one-thing variation is this:

> Dr Tulloch was for a time *Dr Boyd's* assistant, & knew the *popular preacher* very intimately, & the picture he gives of the *genial essayist* is a very engaging one.

His name was Dr. Boyd; he was a popular preacher and a genial essayist, and he had certain relations with Dr. Tulloch. All this is predicated of a certain *him,* or, to cleanse our term as far as possible of residual predication, of a certain *it.* It is true that the predications are made in various ways; they are hung like Christmas-tree ornaments on various branches of a syntactic structure. But what then?

Predicates of propositions are not the only parts that have a predicative function. Almost all terms in a discourse manage to betray some predication, to assert something of something. "The barn is big. It is red." "Barn" predicates as much as and more than "big" and "red." Only the "it" is a pure subject, algebraically an $x,$ a pointer to the thing under discussion.

The usefulness of naming one thing under any number of aspects—asserting that it has these aspects—is, of course, not to be questioned. Such treatment of things is thinking; it is the basis of reflective and poetic discourse. Not to be questioned either is the logic and propriety of listing these aspects as a series, in formal parallel predicative positions. I find this noted in one textbook treatment of repetition. A "variation of emphatic repetition consists in repeating the idea but changing the words [rather in repeating the thing but slightly changing the idea]. 'The boys were tired— completely done up—dead on their feet.'" Furthermore, the subject of a proposition too may be a place for special deposits of predication—as in Homer or in our own *Time* magazine. "Much-enduring noble Odysseus heard him not." "Last week roly-poly (200 lb., 5 ft. 8 in.) Harry Gokey, 71, retired vaudeville trouper, made his bid for No. 1 U.S. professional Santa."

Sentences in *Time* tend to become a string of appositional predications with somewhere a finite verb which makes an assertion that does duty for the whole. What looks like a heavily weighted subject, all that comes before the assertion or copula, may turn out to be more of a predicate than what comes after. "A talented private secretary who, at 37, after her employer's wife died, finally married her 70-year-old boss not long before his death is the Dowager Marchioness of Reading."[1]

Neither of these uses, the multiple predicate and the epithetical cumulative subject, produces the effect of variation, for there is only one proposition, one copula or main finite verb. But the nearness of these to variation may be seen if one reflects how the various predications might be distributed through two or more propositions; that is, there might be two or more propositions where the subjects denoted the same thing, but either the subjects or predicates or both made different predications about this thing. Something like this, as a matter of fact, occurs in the Dr. Boyd example from Fowler. If we leave out of account parts of speech and varied syntax or think of them as reducible to the subject, copula, and predicate of propositions, we may find that something like variation occurs in many forms in many places. Poetry is a good place to look. And one of the best places that I have found is near the beginning of English poetry, in the Old English epic *Beowulf*.

> To *Hondscio* happened a hopeless contention,
> Death to the *doomed one,* dead he fell foremost,
> Girded *war-champion;* to him Grendel became then,
> To the *vassal-distinguished,* a tooth-weaponed murderer,
> The *well-beloved henchman's* body all swallowed.
>
>   The *sea-boat* resounded,
> The wind o'er the waters the *wave-floater* nowise
> Kept from its journey; the *sea-goer* traveled,
> The *foamy-necked vessel* floated forth o'er the currents,
> The *well-fashioned vessel* o'er the ways of the ocean.
> . . . .
>
>   The *wave-goer* hastened
> . . . .
>
> He bound to the bank then the *broad-bosomed vessel*
> Fast in its fetters, lest the force of the waters
> Should be able to injure the *ocean-wood winsome.*[2]

There are places in *Beowulf* where one might attribute a variation to metrical or alliterative necessity. But surely not here in these eight ways of

[1] *Time,* XXXVI (December 23, 1940), 56, 28.
[2] *Beowulf,* John Lesslie Hall, tr. (Boston, 1892), XXX, 43–47; XXVIII, 17–30.

naming the boat. Nor was the poet here merely afraid of a taboo, scrupulously observing a schoolboy's rule against using the same word in so many sentences or lines. Nor was he at Fowler's second stage, delighted with an ingenuity in kennings developed by observing the rule. He was delighted with the boat. He was eager to tell about it, as much about it as possible while telling what it did. Not only did it go, but it was a wave-floater and well fashioned and foamy necked. An opportunity for such interesting predications came each time the boat was denoted. So it was well to denote it many times, to repeat the fact that it went. (Better than piling all the predications in one proposition, because this other way the boat is kept moving.) Nay, the going itself has interesting aspects. The boat traveled, it floated, it hastened. Quite often, in fact, the poet of *Beowulf* has on his hands two or more variations at once. Not only the man but the sword he is wielding, or not only the swords but the monster they cleave. Not only the waves and the sea but the men and the boat.[3] And the effect of these multiple predications throughout this poem is much the same whether they appear in one proposition or in several. One of the most constant characters of the poem is the incrustation of ideas around single objects. An extreme example, in several propositions, like that of the boat, is felt as only a concentration of what occurs more casually on every page.

The contexts in which variation may function expressively are perhaps of as many kinds as one cares to discover or illustrate. Another example from *Beowulf* will suggest a widely familiar form.

> Lo! we blithely have brought thee, *bairn of Healfdene,*
> *Prince of the Scyldings,* these presents from ocean.

Here is multiple predication in the vocative—as in a litany. In a formal liturgical litany, like that of the Blessed Virgin in the Roman breviary, there may be more than forty predications, the same petition repeated after each. It would be impossible, of course, to think of this as elegant variation. In certain whimsical or emotional veins the essayist, showing his kinship with the poet, may offer us elaborate examples of variation. Lamb, for instance, begins "A Chapter on Ears" with ingenious playfulness:

> Nor imagine that I am by nature destitute of those exterior twin
> appendages, hanging ornaments, and (architecturally speaking) handsome
> volutes to the human capital.... I am, I think, rather delicately than
> copiously provided with those conduits; and I feel no disposition to envy
> the mule for his plenty, or the mole for her exactness, in those ingenious
> labyrinthine inlets—those indispensable side-intelligencers.

[3] J. R. R. Tolkien in his Prefatory Remarks to the 1940 edition of John R. Clark Hall's prose translation points out a passage of eighteen lines (210–28) in which there are six terms for boat, three for wave, five for men, and four for sea (pp. xxxvii–xl).

Or the novelist may employ variation to show the progress of a conception in the mind of a character.

> The distraught young man stood in the middle of the road and glared back at the town. He did not know the *reporter George Willard* and had no special feeling concerning *the tall boy who ran about town gathering the town news.* The *reporter* had merely come, by his presence in the office and in the printshop of the *Winesburg Eagle,* to stand for something in the young merchant's mind. He thought the *boy who passed and repassed Cowley and Son's Store and who stopped to talk to people in the street* must be thinking of him and perhaps laughing at him.[4]

One of the kinds of variation ridiculed by Sir Arthur Quiller-Couch is that employed by sports writers, and doubtless the ridicule is largely justified. An account of a football game is perhaps not often improved by the appearance of an "oval," a "pigskin," a "spheroid," a "big leather egg." But I believe that examples of condonable variation may easily be found. Let us consider an extreme and classical instance, the sports pages after the fight in June, 1935, between the Negro boxer Joe Louis and the giant Italian Primo Carnera. The writers had already exploited a great opportunity for antonomasia in each of these figures. Carnera was "ambling Alp," "Italian mastodon," "rudderless mammoth," "robot of the racketeers." Louis was "brown bomber," "dark destroyer," "black blizzard," "beige butcher," "sepia slugger," "dark dynamiter," "tan terror," "dusky Detroiter," "dark detonator," "killer from the cotton fields." And when these two met:

> The *frozen-faced, sloe-eyed Negro's* defeat of Carnera was enacted before 57,000 pairs of eyes red with blood lust. [Carnera] lacked only one thing—natural fighting ability, of which the *black Beowulf* had more than an abundance. The *imperturbable brown bear*... had whanged away under Carnera's guard... until the *jittery giant* had become very weary indeed.... The *sensational Senegambian* was pinned in a corner... the *lad with the petrified puss* was upon Carnera as he rose as wobbly as a punch-drunk fighter on stilts.... Crack, crack! went the right and left of this *calmly savage Ethiopian* to the head of the *battered derelict....* He reeled along the rig ropes, obviously begging that someone stop this *brown mechanism* that was so surely destroying him.... He feinted with his hands and the *vast Venetian* threw up his hands widely as his wits scattered.[5]

"Surfeit!" one cries (even though I have omitted a great deal), and one finds a certain crudity, an excess of horror and of alliteration. It is not always clear that expressiveness is put ahead of cleverness. Nevertheless, I submit

[4] Sherwood Anderson, *Winesburg, Ohio* (Modern Library ed.), 283.
[5] Washington *Post,* June 26, 1935.

that these bizarre variations do on the whole express something, that they are relevant to the violent conception, the picture of power and slaughter, which the writer certainly conveys. Without them the account would be much duller. These are his comments of admiration, of pity or contempt, as he tells the facts. These and similar devices (his variation is only part of a wild flair for metaphor) make him the bard, the popular narrator of heroic conflict. Another writer, on the same page, describing the same fight in a somewhat different style, exclaims: "Here was a two-fisted fighter, dealing out dynamite." Ðæt wæs gōd cyning! O Black Beowulf!

It would seem safe to say that variation is indigenous to and flourishes in writing that is dramatic and poetic. In poetry there is predication at every point. Every rift is to be packed with ore. The tone is that of trying to say as much as possible with every syllable. The more poetic a writing the more likely it is to employ variation of some sort. Even in more relaxed narrative prose, some more obvious form of variation is likely to crop out. One hardly objects to Meredith's occasional humor in calling one-legged Uncle Algernon "the dismembered Guardsman," or Tom Bakewell "Speed-the-Plough," or Richard Feverel "the hope of Raynham."

On the other hand, the less poetic a writing, the more logical and expository, the more likely an obvious or ingenious variation is to seem "elegant." Fowler's Dr. Boyd example was probably quite offensive in its context. In a purely scientific writing variation would be altogether out of place and incompatible with the purpose of the writing—which is to proceed from step to step with complete security as to what object or what aspect or abstraction is referred to. In a treatise on algebra, variation in verbal exposition would be as chaotic as the indication of a same quantity now by x and now by y. In philosophy the same would be true—or sometimes is. And a determination to avoid the fault makes some philosophers produce pages of a severely repetitious, mathematical character. Like algebraists or philophers—though with a difference too—the masters of the plain prose style have almost never resorted to poetic variation. Swift, for example, is scrupulous in this regard, especially in his satires, where the ironic effect depends on his sober, chill precision. So to a lesser degree are Dryden, Addison, and Steele. To study their prose is to see how variation may be avoided and how from this discipline a special prosaic beauty is achieved.

H. W. and F. G. Fowler have described a kind of variation which I believe may be legitimately distinguished from either the poetic or the elegant. This may be called "pronominal" variation, a usage by which the plain prose writer can sometimes solve the problem of how to secure reiterated reference without the reiterated emphasis commonly called "monotony" or "repetition." An object is named under a new aspect, but one more generic and hence less informative and less emphatic than that under which it has already been named. The "volume," the "story," the "author," the "hero," the "action," the "object," the "latter," the "former"—such generic levels regularly appear in unobtrusive instances of this arrangement. Yet the arrangement tends to make a kind of empty space in meaning and is perhaps not ideal. The secret of pure prose would seem to be a kind of economy, such a management of the parts of an argument that objects once named do not need to be named soon again—at least not explicitly and emphatically and as subjects of propositions. Loose thinking, fuzziness, and "elegant variation" go well together. There is a kind of unpretentious, unimaginative "elegant variation" which arises simply from one's not realizing the relations among objects discussed. The student of composition (if a pedagogic suggestion may be inserted here) might be persuaded to write a page on which the same things were rigorously denoted by the same words. Then might follow a surprising revelation of what the order of his thoughts ought to be—where pronouns could be used and where telescoping and ellipsis were called for.

II

But let us return to the other kind of variation described at the start of our discussion, that where two or more things are denoted. H. W. Fowler's examples would suggest that this is a more frequent and less obvious occurrence than one-thing variation. Two-thing variation, as Fowler's examples also show, readily invades all the parts of speech. Not nouns and adjectives only, which are easily seen as referring to the same or to different objects, but verbs (referring to objects as acting) or prepositions (referring to objects in their relations) or any parts of speech (referring to concrete or abstract objects in any of the possible ways) may readily be varied when two or more objects are present.

> France is now *going through* a similar experience *with regard to* Morocco to that which England had to *undergo with reference to* Egypt.

This is the kind of variation which finds its way into one's writing in countless complicated ways, sometimes in clearly isolable short phrases or words, sometimes in lack of parallel between phrases or clauses, sometimes in the whole structure of argument or order in which the ideas of a discourse are classified and presented. If one has in mind fifteen examples which show that romantic poets were interested in kinetic imagery, one does not state the case in an introductory paragraph and then list the examples; one achieves the appearance of complication by inventing fifteen ways to tie an example to the main theme. One writes fifteen introductory sentences, or fifteen paragraphs, which seem to say different things but, with relevance to the theme, say only one thing. Viewed this way, variation and its opposite are intrinsic to the very process of thinking. To avoid elegant variation is to achieve rightness, relevance, unity in the analysis and synthesis of our discourse.

When the difference between things and that between the aspects under which things are thought of are both great, there is not much difficulty in seeing that different words are wanted. That is the case when we mention almost any two things in nonparallel or oblique relation. The difficulty begins when we yoke things by parallel or contrast. Then widely different things may be referred to as alike. But it may also happen that different things are referred to as they are not alike, but almost alike; a more generic aspect in which they are alike is suggested by the naming of more specific aspects in which they are almost alike. Some such arrangement as this is common, particularly in narration and description, where different concepts are used in the mere naming of several objects and where the class concept of likeness is less often named by one general term than suggested by approximations, each approximation taking a variation from the thing to which it is attached. It does not matter to our argument what parts of speech are used to refer to likeness or to difference. In the following example from Conrad's *Heart of Darkness,* nouns refer to different objects under clearly different aspects, while adjectives refer to the same objects under aspects which approach one another and suggest a single generic aspect—for which perhaps there is no single word.

> A *small* flame would dart and vanish, a *little* white smoke would disappear, a *tiny* projectile would give a *feeble* screech.

Conrad describes a French man-of-war shelling the bush of the African coast. The action is futile—small and weak. He would make each part of the action contribute to the smallness and weakness in its own way. This is the method of concreteness, of narrative symbol as opposed to abstract science. This is basically the way in which the diverse concrete elements of any fiction gain relevance or unity.

Here is a kind of variation which is demanded by the context. If there is to be narrative, and not essay, the different things must be named and each must be small or weak in its own way, differently small or weak. The difference must be indicated verbally. Nevertheless—and this is a point which one may find it hard to grant—there need not be any clear or explicit propriety in the difference in words. It may be beyond the scope of the language to express such difference explicitly. In the home-habitat example the fault lay in implicit difference. In such an example as the above from Conrad the merit may be of the same sort. "Feeble" indicates exactly the way in which a "screech" is small, and "feeble" would not do so well for "projectile." But it might do for "flame." And "small" might do for "projectile," and "little" might do for "flame." But taken in a series, applied to these different objects, these different words for "small" do suggest accurate application and complete relevance. The reason is that flame, smoke, projectile, and screech really are small and weak in different ways, no matter whether there are words in our vocabulary to distinguish the ways accurately. A difference in the sound of words, a difference in their range of meaning, implicitly means the right difference. Let me lay myself open to a charge of insensitivity by citing a more famous instance:

> St. Agnes' Eve—Ah, bitter chill it was!
> The owl, for all his feathers, was a-cold.

"In the first Stanza," wrote Keats, "my copy reads . . . 'bitter *chill* it was' to avoid the echo cold in the second line." Certainly it is better to have the two words different. The air is cold or chill in one way; the owl in another. What seems more questionable is that the coldness of either could not (aside from the rhyme) be indicated equally well with either word. And somewhat the same can be said for the following line of *Paradise Lost:* "Horrid to think, how horrible to feel." There is a difference between "to think" and "to feel" which may be reflected or extended into the difference between "horrid" and "horrible," but (aside from meter and climax) it is difficult to see why the order of these adjectives might not be reversed.

A clearer propriety in difference of words may be discerned when objects are denoted under aspects that are parallel and nearly the same but nevertheless contrasted or antithetic. Wilde once read to Yeats from the proofs of *The Decay of Lying.*

> And when he came to the sentence: "Schopenhauer has analysed the pessimism that characterizes modern thought, but Hamlet invented it. The world has become sad because a puppet was once melancholy," I said, "Why do you change 'sad' to 'melancholy'?" He replied that he wanted a full sound at the close of his sentence.

But Wilde might have found a better reason. "World" and "puppet" refer to objects as they are different or contrasted; "sad" and "melancholy" refer to them as they are nearly the same. But there is a difference between "sad" and "melancholy," a modulation, which corresponds to the difference between "world" and "puppet." The world is sad, simply and actually sad. But the puppet, the player, is melancholy—sad in the Elizabethan, theatrical way, that of the whimsical, self-conscious malcontent. From the imitation has proceeded the reality. There is a parallel expressed in the nearness of the words "sad" and "melancholy" and at the same time a contrast and an oblique, causal relation expressed in their difference.

To close the cycle of our discussion, we need now only refer again to the clear difference between the aspects under which things are thought of when they are thought of in completely oblique or nonparallel relation to each other. Here belongs the example from Fowler quoted at the outset:

> They dug their *own* clay, often in *front* of their *own front* doors.

To use the same word in referring to nearly the same or parallel aspects of parallel things is to produce either emphasis or monotony—as Keats would have done if he had repeated "chill." But to use the same word in referring to objects in oblique relation is to produce a marked effect of impropriety, of wrong words. In such cases the need for different words, or for phrasal recasting, is urgent.

> Their clay they dug for themselves, often before their own front doors.

Here again, however, there is need less of exact propriety in difference than of difference implicitly expressed. This is particularly clear in the prepositional strings which Fowler quotes under "Repetition of Words and Sounds" and "Jingles."

> The observation *of* the facts *of* the geological succession *of* the forms *of* life.

The resources of the language are not adequate to express such a series of relationships with accurate explicit difference. One must resort either to complete recasting or to compression and *implicit* variation. It is less offensive to write:

> The observation of geological succession *in* the forms of life.

"In" may be less accurate than "of" at this juncture, but it serves to suggest the difference between the relationship to which it refers and the relationships referred to on either side of it. The same is true even of the syllabic jingles which Fowler quotes—*ly* adverbs or *ity* abstract nouns used in oblique or dependent relation.

> Their invalid*ity* was caused by a technical*ity*.
> It is probab*ly* general*ly* known.

Here some recasting is called for. Even down to these fractions of words the rule of thumb holds good: Use different words when you mean different things.

DISCUSSION AND WRITING

1. The author uses many terms that are of special interest to students of composition and literature. If you were to compile a brief glossary, how would you define or explain the following? *Concise, rhetoric, ambiguity, denote, context, derogatory, predication, syntactic, proposition, appositional, finite verb, copula, epithetical, cumulative, epic,*

alliterative, kenning, vocative, litany, breviary, antonomasia, metaphor, bard, reiterate, generic, ellipsis, kinetic, oblique, antithetic, modulation.

2. State as exactly as you can how Wimsatt modifies Fowler's treatment of "elegant" variation. How many kinds of variation does Wimsatt distinguish, and what are they?

3. The author compliments the Fowlers for "their analytic wit and readiness with example." Would his own style merit these same compliments? Are there other features of his style that you can point out and illustrate?

4. Like many modern specialists in the literary uses of language, the author discusses what may seem a minor technical matter but leads the reader to significant general observations about the workings of language. What are some of the things that this essay made you realize about the nature of language?

5. Discuss examples of humorous or whimsical variation that you have encountered in speech or writing.

6. Select a passage from a recent issue of *Time*. Write a detailed analysis of Timestyle. If you wish, develop your analysis by expanding or modifying Mr. Wimsatt's brief observations. Focus on major points; use detailed examples.

7. Find a passage of no more than 500 words in which a sportswriter employs variation and metaphor for genuine (though not necessarily sophisticated) dramatic effect. Discuss the writer's use of language in detail. (Your instructor may ask you to furnish a copy of the passage. Excerpt a longer passage if you wish.)

8. Write two versions of a passage (200–250 words) focused clearly on *one* object, person, or idea. In the first version, use "a plain prose style," with "the same things rigorously denoted by the same words." In the second version, use "poetic variation" for its expressiveness or dramatic effect. In each version, underline all words denoting the object, person, or idea that is the subject of the passage.

9. Write a brief guide to effective style for one of the following: a door-to-door or telephone salesman; a new neighborhood minister; a teacher of college freshmen. Give the kind of advice that would make the person's approach effective at least for a representative cross-section of his audience. Focus on a few major points directly involving the speaker's use of language. Use detailed illustrations.

10. In spite of their different subject matter, is there any basic similarity in the attitude toward language shown by Wimsatt and that shown by Leacock in "Good and Bad Language"? Compare and contrast the attitude toward language in the two essays.

FURTHER READING

H. L. Mencken once said that "with only one or two exceptions, all the books on prose style in English are by writers quite unable to write." Among some of the more obvious exceptions are H. W. Fowler, *A Dictionary of Modern English Usage* (1926; revised Second Edition, 1965); Bergen Evans and Cornelia Evans, *A Dictionary of Contemporary American Usage* (1957); and William Strunck, Jr., and E. B. White, *The Elements of Style* (1959). Find a problem of style treated in all three books; compare and contrast the treatment it receives at the hands of the different authors.

MONROE C. BEARDSLEY

Through the centuries, writers on language and logic have occasionally pointed out that the babble of conflicting voices heard in human societies derives in part from man's linguistic naïveté—his lack of awareness of the many subtle meanings and deceptive uses of words. In recent decades, students of "semantics" have devoted themselves with some success to the task of promoting greater awareness of the subtleties and pitfalls of language. Monroe C. Beardsley (born 1915) brings some of the findings of semantics to bear on the problem of teaching students to become more critical readers and more responsible writers. Professor of Philosophy at Swarthmore College, Mr. Beardsley is author or co-author of widely used college texts. The following selection is composed of excerpts from two key sections of his *Thinking Straight*. It shows a combination of systematic presentation with vivid illustration of key points which is the strength of many first-rate textbooks.

Meanings and Contexts

One of the fundamental facts about words is that the most useful ones in our language have many meanings. That is partly why they are so useful: they work overtime (but, as we shall see, not for nothing). Think of all the various things we mean by the word "foot" on different occasions: one of the lower extremities of the human body, a measure of verse, the ground about a tree, twelve inches, the floor in front of the stairs. The same is true of nearly every common noun or verb. The editors of *The American College Dictionary,* in their preliminary investigation of words most frequently used, found 55 distinct senses of the word "point" in 1,100 occurrences of the word, and they distinguished 109 different senses of the word "run."

Considering the number of ways of taking a particular word, the task of speaking clearly and being understood would seem pretty hopeless if it were not for another very important fact about language. Though a word may have many senses, these senses can be controlled, up to a point, by the *context* in which the word is used. When we find the word in a particular verbal setting—that is, take it with the words that come before and after it in

From Monroe C. Beardsley, *Thinking Straight: Principles of Reasoning for Readers and Writers,* 2nd ed. © 1956. Prentice-Hall, Inc., Englewood Cliffs, N.J. By permission.

a discourse—we can usually decide quite definitely which of the many senses of the word is relevant. If a poet says his verse has three feet, it doesn't occur to you that he could mean it's a yard long or is three-legged (unless perhaps you are a critic planning to puncture the poet with a pun about his "limping verse"). The context rules out these maverick senses quite decisively.

We might be puzzled if we read in a newspaper that "in the suicide's pocket the police found a large envelope full of bills." In this sentence, as it stands, the word "bills" can easily be taken in two very different senses. But if the context were expanded so as to read, "The police were surprised to find in the suicide's pocket a large envelope full of bills of various denominations," we should understand that "bills" meant *paper money,* and we might wonder whether it was indeed suicide or accident. Or if the context were expanded differently, so as to read, "The police were surprised to find in the suicide's pocket a large envelope full of unpaid bills," we should understand that "bills" meant *requests for payment of a debt,* and we might wonder whether that explains the suicide.

This is a rather simple illustration of the way in which the context of a word helps to pick out one of its senses and fix that sense. But of course "context" is used broadly here: it may be the rest of a sentence (the *immediate* context), a page, a whole book, or a newspaper file. A "shady street" is one thing; a "shady neighborhood" is something else. The word "strike" means one action on the front page of a paper and another action on the sports page; the words "liberal" and "patriotic" mean certain attitudes in *The New York Times* and mostly different ones in *The Chicago Tribune.* When some time ago a British physicist announced with pleasure that the hydrogen bomb is "safe," his statement caused gasps of surprise; in the technical talk of atomic scientists, "safe" apparently means that it couldn't set off a chain reaction that might destroy the earth itself. This is not the way the man in the street uses the word.

Many common words like "line," "pipe," "base," "stock," and "head," have acquired many serviceable meanings in different occupational contexts—say, in the shoptalk of plumbers, pitchers, or plastic engineers. Think of what the word "wing" means to a birdwatcher, an airman, a stagehand, a general, or an architect. But just because these meanings are so completely distinct—no one can confuse the wing of an airplane with the wing of a house—it is easy to control them by very light contextual pressure. A word or two makes it clear that it is the airman's wing rather than the architect's that is referred to. But when the differences between the senses of a word are slighter and subtler (they may be even more important, however), the most careful management of the context may be required to get and keep one sense in focus. The exact meaning of a word like "middle class" or "evolution" or "justice" may depend upon the whole book in which it appears.

That is why it is often easy to misrepresent what someone has said by quoting some of his remarks out of their context. The words may not, strictly speaking, be *mis*quoted, but their meaning has been changed. The political candidate's promise to obtain peace or balance the budget is echoed and attacked by his opponent—who is careful to leave out the conditions and qualifications that originally surrounded it. Even if a writer is scrupulous enough to put in dots to indicate that something has been left out, he may not be *quite* scrupulous enough to stick to the original meaning. You have seen advertisements of a new play, with a few words from a review. The phrase "...emotional subtlety...(Bridgeport *Post*)" may be from a sentence that goes: "It has all the emotional subtlety of a barroom brawl." The phrase "...great drama...(New Haven *Register*)" may be from a sentence that goes: "No doubt it was considered a great drama when it first appeared in 1927, but ..." And this is nothing to what a professional wiretapper can do if he records a telephone conversation and picks out words to rerecord on a new tape.

Representative Wayne L. Hays, a member of the Special House Committee set up by the 83rd Congress to investigate tax-exempt foundations, frequently argued during the committee's hearings that the "research directors" of the committee were willing to make judgments on passages torn out of contexts that might change their meanings considerably. He finally made a dramatic demonstration of this by producing three paragraphs which the associate research director testified were "closely comparable" with, and parallel to, Communist literature that he had read. They were excerpts from two papal encyclicals....

The importance of context in the interpretation of meaning varies from one discourse to another. In a technical article on mathematics or physics, most sentences can stand pretty much on their own feet and be well understood apart from their context. Scientific terms are designed to resist the influence of context so that they can pass from one context to another without changing their meaning. But sentences in ordinary discourse that contain pronouns often lean on other sentences that contain the antecedents of those pronouns. Moreover, some words in our language—and they are among the most useful, but the trickiest, ones—are so adaptable to their context, like chameleons, that they take most of their character from it, and when they are considered apart from any context, they have only the most indefinite meaning. Words like "efficient," "dangerous," "internal," "successful," "free," tell us very little unless we are told, for example, the *purpose* for which it is efficient, or the *standards* in terms of which the success is judged. Contexts like "free-handed," "free lunch," "free love," "free will," "freeborn," "free association," help to limit the word "free" to a somewhat more definite range of meaning, but even in such cases we often feel that we don't know exactly what the word "free" means unless the context provides answers to the questions: "Free *from* what?" "Free *for* what?" "Free *to do* what?"

Another thing that shows the importance of context is the fact that when people use the wrong word we sometimes know what word should have been used. When Mrs. Malaprop says, "I would by no means wish a daughter of mine to be a progeny of learning ... I would have her instructed in geometry, that she might know something of the contagious countries," we understand what she thought she was saying because the context so clearly tells us what words are called for if the sentences are to make sense. A malapropism is a word that is wrongly used in a sentence in place of another word that sounds somewhat like it. And if we couldn't tell from the context what the appropriate word would be, we could never recognize a malapropism....

The signification of a term in a particular context is the whole set of characteristics it refers to in that context. But some of these characteristics are more closely bound up with the word than others are; they become part of its signification in a variety of contexts, they get recorded in dictionaries, and speakers of English come to regard them as the central, or core, meaning of the word. And as this meaning is more widely established and stabilized, the other meanings become more variable, more responsive to the control of context, and more easy to overlook. The interplay between these two branches of the signification makes possible some of the most vital and useful, but also some of the most tricky and deceptive, ways of using language.

The distinction between these two levels of meaning, so to speak, needs to be well marked; its importance will become clear. We shall use the terms "designation" and "connotation" to make the distinction.

When we speak of the designation of a term, we shall mean a set of characteristics that has become a fairly standard or common signification of the term. If there are several standard senses, then the term has several designations. But lay that complication aside for the time being. When a term acquires a fairly fixed conventional meaning, it applies to a distinct set of things, and these things are its *comprehension*. They are grouped together in a class. But on what grounds? Well, ordinarily such a group is like a club or organization of some sort—there are rules of membership, or qualifications that each thing has to possess in order to be admitted. The class of *cots,* for example, includes all lightweight beds; in other words, to be included in this class, an object must be (1) a bed, or something you can sleep on, and (2) light in weight. This pair of characteristics marks off the class of cots from all other classes in the world, and we shall say that the term "cot" *designates* these two characteristics. The designation is *part* of its signification.

Of course, individual cots have a lot of other characteristics besides being light in weight and being a bed: some are wooden, some metal; some are stretched with canvas, some with wire mesh; some fold up, some don't; some are comfortable, some are not. But being light in weight and being a bed are the *indispensable* characteristics of cots, and only these two characteristics are involved in the standard, or customary, meaning of the term "cot." Even if it turned out that every cot that ever existed happened to be painted purple, we would probably not include this characteristic in the designation of "cot," for if someone decided to paint his cot yellow, we would still be willing to call it a "cot"; but if he boarded up the sides, filled it with dirt, and planted petunias, we would no doubt say that he had transformed it into something else.

It may at first give you a little trouble to find that in a number of books on English composition and rhetoric, the word "denotation" is used for what we have here called the "designation" of a term. This use of the word "denotation" is a shift from the sense universally assigned to it in logic books—just as the word "presently" in ordinary speech is gradually being shifted from its original meaning "shortly afterward" to "at present." Whenever you find the term "denotation" used in the sense of "dictionary meaning," you have only to subsitute the term "designation," to translate the terminology into the one used here.

But over and above the standard signification of a term (that is, its designation), there may be certain nuances of meaning that are more difficult to describe because they are less obtrusive or more dependent upon context than designation. Because cots are always, and by definition, light in weight, they are *generally,* though not always, readily portable; hence they tend to be moved about, and to be a relatively impermanent place to sleep. They are *likely* to be less expensive, less impressive, less handsome than fullfledged beds; a cot is therefore often thought of as the sort of bed slept in by a poor man, or a humble and unpretentious man, or a servant, or a man who does not expect to stay long. These characteristics are not part of the designation of the term, but some of them *are* part of its full signification in some contexts. We shall consider them, then, as part of the connotation of the term "cot," and we shall say that a term *connotes* those characteristics which, in one context or another, are part of its full signification but not part of its designation.

To make the notion of connotation as clear as possible, we have to draw two lines here, and neither of them can be very sharp.

Connotation, as just indicated, is bounded on one side by designation. It may be very difficult to tell on some occasions whether a characteristic belongs to the designation or the connotation of a word. But if the distinction can't be made with perfect precision, fortunately it does not need to be. What happens is that we find a pair of terms ("hurt" and "offended") or a whole set of them ("irritated," "annoyed," "cross," "mildly angry," "put out," "slightly burned up") whose significations overlap almost completely, but not quite. In some contexts you could substitute one for the other without doing any damage. But there are other contexts in which the difference, however subtle, might be tremendous. And this difference we are calling a difference in "connotation," to call attention to its importance.

Connotation is bounded on the other side by what we may call the *personal associations* that each one of us individually may come to attach to certain words. Some people are irrationally disturbed by snakes, or spiders, or cats; others are not. Individual childhood experiences or unconscious fears may give to certain words, because of the objects they refer to, certain special associations. But these are private associations; connotations are public in the sense that they can be recognized and understood by anyone who learns the language. Even if you were once chased by a cow, and the word "cow" is associated in your mind with danger and violence, you can perceive, at the same time, that in the common world of the English language "cow" connotes the opposite characteristics: friendliness, placidity, and gentleness. Of course, private associations may develop into public connotations in a neighborhood, region, or nation, and at any time there will be meanings, such as poets occasionally toy with, that are on the border. But the distinction is still useful, and, indeed, you can't do without it. For when you wish to communicate with others with the help of verbal connotations, you must know which of the meanings you *think* you are communicating are only in your own mind and which are understandable to your audience.

As some of the previous examples show, the connotation of a term is most clearly brought out by comparing it with a close synonym. The terms "brother" and "male sibling" are synonyms, for example, and in many books on psychology or child development you could use them interchangeably. But in "Am I my male sibling's keeper?" there is something missing. What is missing here is the connotation of "brother," which includes a number of characteristics that are not part of the dictionary meaning of "brother," but *are* part of its full meaning in the context of Genesis. This may seem like a farfetched example, but compare some of the famous phrases in the King James version of the Bible with the translations of them in the Revised Standard version that appeared a few years ago: "affliction" (Acts 7:34) has become "ill-treatment"; "whited sepulchres" (Matthew 23:27) has become "whitewashed tombs"; and in St. Paul's phrase (1 Corinthians 13), "sounding brass" has become "a noisy gong."

To work out the connotations of a term when it is important to do so, we have to consider four things on which they depend.

First, a term acquires some of its connotations from what is generally true, or from what is generally believed to be true, about the things it comprehends. Because most cots are rather temporary resting places, "cot" can connote impermanence, though it doesn't *designate* impermanence, since a cot doesn't *have* to be temporary by definition. Because most paper is white, "paper" can connote whiteness. Because most people *think* (however unjustly) that pigs are gross, lazy, greedy, dirty, and stupid, the word "pig" connotes grossness, laziness, greediness, dirtiness, and stupidity.

Thus we discover some of the connotations of a term (not that it can have all of them in a particular context) by finding out about the things it applies to, and also by finding out what people *believe* about those things. Of course these beliefs will vary from one sector of society to another in various ways: farmers will know more about pigs than city people, and they may have different beliefs about the weather from the meteorologist's. A term can take on special connotations if it is used by people of a certain social class, financial group, political persuasion, or occupation. Not all English words are specialized in that way: practically everyone, high or low, smart or dumb, drunk or sober, uses words like "house," "chair," and "pie." But it is usually a certain sort of person who calls magazines "books"; a housewife with certain attitudes who always refers to her house as her "home"; a man of a certain vocation (or avocation) who calls a rope a "line"; a person of rather definite opinions who always expresses his displeasure with a previous administration by the phrase "pinks and minks."

Second, then, a term acquires some of its connotations from its tendency (if any) to be used by people of a certain kind. So when we care to be really thorough in grasping the subtlest connotations of a term, we want to ask what sort of person would be likely to use this term in this context, and what sort of beliefs would such a person be likely to have about the situation or object to which the term is applied. Of course, for practical purposes, we seldom have to be this meticulous.

Third, a term acquires some of its connotations by implicit cross reference, so to speak, to other words with similar sounds. Even a combination of syllables that somebody has just made up (without yet assigning it any designation at all) can have connotations. Some of the sounds in our language that aren't words themselves turn up in several words with overlapping meanings. Take "sn" in

sneeze	snuff	snoot	sneer
snore	snoop	snooze	sniff
snort	snub	snicker	snivel

—they all have something to do with noses. (Or think of words beginning with "bl" that involve a sudden, or blurred, noise.) No wonder you can make up words beginning with "sn" that will connote some connection with noses, even if they have no designation. This is of course the secret of most of Lewis Carroll's Jabberwocky words, like "slithy" and "chortle." It also helps to explain the vague but undeniable connotations of words like "Pyrex" (something to do with fire and chemistry) and "Crisco" (crispness, cleanness, efficiency).

Fourth, a term acquires some of its connotations from the contexts in which it has been used in the past. "Sepulcher" and "tomb" must have nearly the same designations. But they have different histories as English words; they have appeared in different places in the Bible, in English poetry, in essays and sermons and novels; and now their connotations are different, too. The term "bread" has appeared in many memorable contexts:

> Give us this day our daily bread ...
> This is the bread of life ...
> Cast your bread upon the water ...
> Man cannot live by bread alone ...
> A jug of wine, a loaf of bread, and thou/ Beside me ...
> I *do* like a little bit of butter to my bread! ...

And "bread" has acquired an enormous range of potential connotation. They can't all be effective at the same time; in fact, some of the connotations of "bread" conflict. The *actual* characteristics connoted by the term in a particular context will be those that emerge from the whole context as the connotations of all the words clash, intersect, cancel out, or fuse together into a whole.

Thus each term has a range of possible connotations, but its actual connotations vary from context to context. And the range of possible connotations itself changes, of course, from time to time with the course of human history and of human knowledge. As people's beliefs about apples and ghosts change, as new stories are told, and poems are made, about them, the connotations of "apple" and "ghost" change too. You can see this clearly in the history of certain proper names. When the people who bear them have some prominent feature or some special behavior on which their fame rests, the names themselves acquire specific connotations. And if the names are often used in contexts that emphasize their connotations, the connotations become so familiar that the proper names lose their capitals and become general terms. So we get "pasteurize," "bowdlerize," "fletcherize," and "mesmerize," and "mae west" life belts. Some of these *eponyms* are given conventional definitions and hence standardized meanings, and come to *designate* fairly fixed characteristics: "boycott," "lynch," "quisling." Others seem to resist any such pinning-down, at least for a time: who can find a satisfactory conventional definition for "napoleonic" or "mccarthyism"?

Poetry is the best place to study word connotations. Indeed, what makes a poem a poem (not just verse) is in part the complexity and coherence of its connotations. But that, you might say, is an advanced course. For a general grasp of how they work, and how they can lead to confused thinking, we will do better to turn to the language of politics, and the language of advertising.

One of the important ideas in politics is that of *coming to terms with someone through willingness to modify one's original demands.* This way of putting it precisely makes it sound technical, but the basic situation it refers to can be illustrated in a thousand ways: for example, one child wants another to push him on a swing, and the other wants to be the one that gets pushed; they agree to take turns. Now, this very general idea is the common core of meaning in a whole series of familiar terms: "compromise," "mutual concessions," "mutual adjustment," "appeasement," "arbitration," "conciliation," "horse-trading," "give-and-take," "meeting each other half way." Not that all these terms have exactly the same designation, but their designations overlap, and in some cases coincide.

Now, the kernel of these terms is a process that nearly everyone can recognize to be a part of normal democratic human and social relations. But they have nice shades of difference in meaning as regards (1) the degree to which one party gives in to another, (2) the amount of advantage gained by giving in, (3) the extent to which threats of force are hinted at, (4) the amount of reasonable discussion and deliberate thought involved in the process. Now suppose the United States Government reaches an agreement with another government after negotiations in which each side has made some concessions to the other in order to achieve a working arrangement—on fishing rights, oil, armaments, air bases, or disputed boundaries. Several words might be used to describe this agreement, and they will all cover the essential facts. But each will also, unless the context guards against it, import a judgment about the case—that the United States gave in too far, or got too little in return, or was too spineless, or too hasty. These judgments, or some of them, may be true; the point to notice here, however, is that they are not stated explicitly so that they can be discussed on their merits; they are brought in slyly, via the connotations of the word selected, and they are easily overlooked by the unwary. Because the term "appeasement" is *roughly* apposite, its *extra* hints are accepted uncritically. Someone might call the agreement a "Munich," but that would be less subtle. Call it "appeasement" and people will half think of Munich without taking time to ask themselves exactly what are the respects in which it is, or is not, like Munich; call it "appeasement" and the damage may be done.

It is no wonder that sometimes, during a given election campaign or while a certain issue is before Congress, certain terms come to be repeated over and over by one side or another because their very useful connotations afford a chance to make all sorts of insinuations that would not survive careful scrutiny if they were baldly stated. After a time, of course, these words ("Isolationism," "New Dealism," "Fair Dealism") begin to wear thin; they are tossed about so carelessly that they no longer stand for anything very definite or identifiable. In the end they often wear out; but by that time a new set of terms has begun to take their place.

The same search for richly connotative words is carried on constantly by the advertising copywriters. Think of the names and descriptions of some of the most highly-touted products, and the key words of the most incessant commercials. What is meant by the injunction to be a "Dawn girl," to wear a "Dentosweet smile," to develop an "English complexion"? What is hinted at by saying that a cereal is "shot from guns," that a cigaret is "toasted," that a club soda has "pinpoint carbonation," or that a car has a "dynaflow" transmission or "floating power"? Without spelling things out, such words conjure up all sorts of desirable characteristics. Some words seem almost indispensable; whether you are selling pastes, lotions, oils, greases, or unguents, they must be called some kind of "cream": skin cream, hair cream, dental cream, or suntan cream.

For a more careful study of connotation, it is instructive to look among advertisements for groups of words that all have connotations of a similar sort. For example, there are the scientific-connotation terms: terms that carry with them the intimation that the product is the result of "laboratory research," is recommended or approved by doctors and druggists, is used by people "in the know," has been tested by the most delicate instruments and the tests coordinated by the most advanced statistical techniques, or contains some new, secret, complicated, marvellously effective ingredient. If you aren't a chemist, and if you haven't read impartial reports, say in *Consumer's Union*, you don't get much information (in terms of designation) when an advertisement tells you that something contains "Solium," "Solv-ex," "Dura-tex," "Aquasil," or *"Activated* Seismotite." Even if it gave the chemical formulas, that would mean nothing to most of us. Suppose a gasoline does contain platinum or "Petrox"; how do we know whether this is a good thing or a bad thing? Still, these terms have a strong flavor of the chemical laboratory and of industrial research, and they make a ready appeal to anyone who thinks that what is vaguely "scientific" must be good.

Now maybe that car, that hair lotion, or that whiskey actually does have not only the characteristics designated, but also the characteristics connoted, by the words used to describe it. But very often, of course, it does not. And if you were out to do a subtle and legally safe job of misrepresentation—if you wanted to promise more than you could deliver without making the promise open enough so that you could be held to it—you would pick your words largely for their connotations. It's no wonder that in some quarters the use of highly connotative words comes to be thought of as inevitably a form of lying, that people mistrust them and yearn for a plain unvarnished statement. But you don't have to be that cynical; you merely have to be a little wary. When you are asked to buy or do something on the ground that something is true, you always have a right to know what it is that is said to be true, and to know this clearly and fully you have to be aware of the connotations of the words in which it is stated.

DISCUSSION AND WRITING

1. Define or explain: *maverick, scrupulous, encyclical, rhetoric, nuance, meticulous, bowdlerize, apposite, insinuation, scrutiny, incessant, injunction, conjure, unguent, intimation.* In your own words, define and illustrate technical terms of interest to the student of language: *context, pun, shoptalk, malapropism, connotation, synonym, eponym.*

2. Without consulting your dictionary, list different meanings, in different contexts, of *point, run, hand, eye, green.*

3. Discuss in detail possible connotations of *bread, cottage, silk, snake, blonde, chapel, aristocratic, political boss, radical, artist.*

4. Collect as many synonyms (or near synonyms) as you can for the following terms: *courage, obedient, force, devout, strict.* Explore fully the differences in connotation within each group of synonyms.

5. Textbooks, like the one from which this selection was taken, are usually devoted to exceptionally systematic and foolproof exposition. Examine and discuss in detail the author's expository method—organization, development, selection and presentation of material. How successful is he in presenting fairly difficult material to his readers?

6. Present and explain to the layman as clearly and graphically as possible a number of key terms from the "shoptalk" of a special field, occupation, or hobby with which you are familiar.

7. In a passage here omitted, Professor Beardsley says that words like "freedom," "religion," and "democracy" have "many subtly different meanings." Choose one of the following terms and discuss the meanings of it that you have encountered: *democratic, conservative, liberal, modern, progressive, optimistic, pessimistic, intellectual.*

8. Compare and contrast a paragraph-length passage from the King James Version of the Bible with the same passage in one of several recently published modern versions. Discuss in detail differences in connotation.

9. Discuss in detail connotative terms used in the editorials of a newspaper (other than a college daily). Study recurrent terms in editorials published over a period of several weeks.

10. Collect and analyze several short passages (oral or written) in which what is stated is less important than what is implied.

FURTHER READING

Books that made semantics accessible to a large popular audience are S. I. Hayakawa, *Language in Action* (1941), revised as *Language in Thought and Action* (Second Edition, 1964); and Stuart Chase, *The Tyranny of Words* (1938), rewritten and brought up to date as *Power of Words* (1954).

FRANCIS BACON

Sir Francis Bacon (1561–1626) published a number of writings (in English and Latin) that make him a key figure in the history of philosophy and science. In working out a program for the extension of human knowledge, he stressed procedures that have since become commonplaces of scientific method: careful observation of natural phenomena and systematic collection of data; reliance on induction, that is, generalization from observed instances; verification, that is, testing of results, by experiment and practical application. Bacon's influence was widely felt and acknowledged by spokesmen of seventeenth- and eighteenth-century natural science, as well as of nineteenth-century industrial technology. Bacon has been highly praised for channeling philosophical inquiry into areas of immediate benefit to mankind. He has been criticized for neglecting the role of imagination in scientific discovery and for helping to create a climate of opinion in which views not based on rigorous scientific proof were likely to be brushed aside as mere superstition. The following selection is from Bacon's *Novum Organum,* or "new method," published in 1620. Its systematic organization and firm, businesslike tone are in harmony with Bacon's call for systematic and businesslike procedures for the extension of human knowledge.

Idols of the Mind

XXXVIII

The idols and false notions which are now in possession of the human understanding, and have taken deep root therein, not only so beset men's minds that truth can hardly find entrance, but even after entrance obtained, they will again in the very instauration of the sciences meet and trouble us, unless men being forewarned of the danger fortify themselves as far as may be against their assaults.

XXXIX

There are four classes of Idols which beset men's minds. To these for distinction's sake I have assigned names,—calling the first class *Idols of the Tribe;* the second, *Idols of the Cave;* the third, *Idols of the Market-place;* the fourth, *Idols of the Theatre.*

XL

The formation of ideas and axioms by true induction is no doubt the proper remedy to be applied for the keeping off and clearing away of idols. To point them out, however, is of great use; for the doctrine of Idols is to the Interpretation of Nature what the doctrine of the refutation of sophisms is to common Logic.

XLI

The Idols of the Tribe have their foundation in human nature itself, and in the tribe or race of men. For it is a false assertion that the sense of man is the measure of things. On the contrary, all perceptions, as well of the sense as of the mind, are according to the measure of the individual and not according to the measure of the universe. And the human understanding is like a false mirror, which, receiving rays irregularly, distorts and discolors the nature of things by mingling its own nature with it.

XLII

The Idols of the Cave are the idols of the individual man. For everyone (besides the errors common to human nature in general) has a cave or den of his own, which refracts and discolors the light of nature; owing either to his own proper and peculiar nature; or to his education and conversation with others; or to the reading of books, and the authority of those whom he esteems and admires; or to the differences of impressions, accordingly as they take place in a mind preoccupied and predisposed or in a mind indifferent and settled; or the like. So that the spirit of man (according as it is meted out to different individuals) is in fact a thing variable and full of perturbation, and governed as it were by chance. Whence it was well observed by Heraclitus that men look for sciences in their own lesser worlds, and not in the greater or common world.

XLIII

There are also Idols formed by the intercourse and association of men with each other, which I call Idols of the Market-place, on account of the commerce and consort of men there. For it is by discourse that men associate; and words are imposed according to the apprehension of the vulgar. And therefore the ill and unfit choice of words wonderfully obstructs the understanding. Nor do the definitions or explanations wherewith in some things learned men are wont to guard and defend themselves, by any means set the matter right. But words plainly force and overrule the understanding, and throw all into confusion, and lead men away into numberless empty controversies and idle fancies.

XLIV

Lastly, there are Idols which have immigrated into men's minds from the various dogmas of philosophies, and also from wrong laws of demonstration. These I call Idols of the Theatre; because in my judgment all the received systems are but so many stage-plays, representing worlds of their own creation after an unreal and scenic fashion. Nor is it only of the systems now in vogue, or only of the ancient sects and philosophies, that I speak; for many more plays of the same kind may yet be composed and in like artificial manner set forth; seeing that errors the most widely different have nevertheless causes for the most part alike. Neither again do I mean this only of entire systems, but also of many principles and axioms in science, which by tradition, credulity, and negligence have come to be received.

But of these several kinds of Idols I must speak more largely and exactly, that the understanding may be duly cautioned.

XLV

The human understanding is of its own nature prone to suppose the existence of more order and regularity in the world than it finds. And though there be many things in nature which are singular and unmatched, yet it devises for them parallels and conjugates and relatives which do not exist. Hence the fiction that all celestial bodies move in perfect circles; spirals and dragons being (except in name) utterly rejected. Hence too the element of Fire with its orb is brought in, to make up the square with the other three which the sense perceives. Hence also the ratio of density of the so-called elements is arbitrarily fixed at ten to one. And so on of other dreams. And these fancies affect not dogmas only, but simple notions also.

XLVI

The human understanding when it has once adopted an opinion (either as being the received opinion or as being agreeable to itself) draws all things else to support and agree with it. And though there be a greater number and weight of instances to be found on the other side, yet these it either neglects and despises, or else by some distinction sets aside and rejects; in order that by this great and pernicious predetermination the authority of its former conclusions may remain inviolate. And therefore it was a good answer that was made by one who when they showed him hanging in a temple a picture of those who had paid their vows as having escaped shipwreck, and would have him say whether he did not now acknowledge the power of the gods,—"Aye," asked he again, "but where are they painted that were drowned after their vows?" And such is the way of all superstition, whether in astrology, dreams, omens, divine judgments, or the like; wherein men, having a delight in such vanities, mark the events where they are fulfilled, but where they fail, though this happen much oftener, neglect and pass them by. But with far more subtlety does this mischief insinuate itself into philosophy and the sciences; in which the first conclusion colors and brings into conformity with itself all that come after, though far sounder and better. Besides, independently of that delight and vanity which I have described, it is the peculiar and perpetual error of the human intellect to be more moved and excited by affirmatives than by negatives; whereas it ought properly to hold itself indifferently disposed towards both alike. Indeed in the establishment of any true axiom, the negative instance is the more forcible of the two.

XLVII

The human understanding is moved by those things most which strike and enter the mind simultaneously and suddenly, and so fill the imagination; and then it feigns and supposes all other things to be somehow, though it cannot see how, similar to those few things by which it is surrounded. But for that going to and fro to remote and heterogeneous instances, by which axioms are tried as in the fire, the intellect is altogether slow and unfit, unless it be forced thereto by severe laws and overruling authority.

XLIX

The human understanding is no dry light, but receives an infusion from the will and affections; whence proceed sciences which may be called "sciences as one would." For what a man had rather were true he more readily believes. Therefore he rejects difficult things from impatience of research; sober things, because they narrow hope; the deeper things of nature, from superstition; the light of experience, from arrogance and pride, lest his mind should seem to be occupied with things mean and transitory; things not commonly believed, out of deference to the opinion of the vulgar. Numberless in short are the ways, and sometimes imperceptible, in which the affections color and infect the understanding.

LIII

The *Idols of the Cave* take their rise in the peculiar constitution, mental or bodily, of each individual; and also in education, habit, and accident. Of this kind there is a great number and variety; but I will instance those the pointing out of which contains the most important caution, and which have most effect in disturbing the clearness of the understanding.

LV

There is one principal and as it were radical distinction between different minds, in respect of philosophy and the sciences; which is this: that some minds are stronger and apter to mark the differences of things, others to mark their resemblances. The steady and acute mind can fix its contemplations and dwell and fasten on the subtlest distinctions; the lofty and discursive mind recognizes and puts together the finest and most general resemblances. Both kinds however easily err in excess, by catching the one at gradations the other at shadows.

LVI

There are found some minds given to an extreme admiration of antiquity, others to an extreme love and appetite for novelty; but few so duly tempered that they can hold the mean, neither carping at what has been well laid down by the ancients, nor despising what is well introduced by the moderns. This however turns to the great injury of the sciences and philosophy; since these affectations of antiquity and novelty are the humors of partisans rather than judgments; and truth is to be sought for not in the felicity of any age, which is an unstable thing, but in the light of nature and experience, which is eternal. These factions therefore must be abjured, and care must be taken that the intellect be not hurried by them into assent.

LVIII

Let such then be our provision and contemplative prudence for keeping off and dislodging the *Idols of the Cave,* which grow for the most part either out of the predominance of a favorite subject, or out of an excessive tendency to compare or to distinguish, or out of partiality for particular ages, or out of the largeness or minuteness of the objects contemplated. And generally let every student of nature take this as a rule,—that whatever his mind seizes and dwells upon with peculiar satisfaction is to be held in suspicion, and that so much the more care is to be taken in dealing with such questions to keep the understanding even and clear.

LIX

But the *Idols of the Market-place* are the most troublesome of all: idols which have crept into the understanding through the alliances of words and names. For men believe that their reason governs words; but it is also true that words react on the understanding; and this it is that has rendered philosophy and the sciences sophistical and inactive. Now words, being commonly framed and applied according to the capacity of the vulgar, follow those lines of division which are most obvious to the vulgar understanding. And whenever an understanding of greater acuteness or a more diligent observation would alter those lines to suit the true divisions of nature, words stand in the way and resist the change. Whence it comes to pass that the high and formal discussions of learned men end oftentimes in disputes about words and names; with which (according to the use and wisdom of the mathematicians) it would be more prudent to begin, and so by means of definitions reduce them to order. Yet even definitions cannot cure this evil in dealing with natural and material things; since the definitions themselves consist of words, and those words beget others: so that it is necessary to recur to individual instances, and those in due series and order; as I shall say presently when I come to the method and scheme for the formation of notions and axioms.

The idols imposed by words on the understanding are of two kinds. They are either names of things which do not exist (for as there are things left unnamed through lack of observation, so likewise are there names which result from fantastic suppositions and to which nothing in reality corresponds), or they are names of things which exist, but yet confused and ill-defined, and hastily and irregularly derived from realities. Of the former kinds are Fortune, the Prime Mover, Planetary Orbits, Element of Fire, and like fictions which owe their origin to false and idle theories. And this class of idols is more easily expelled, because to get rid of them it is only necessary that all theories should be steadily rejected and dismissed as obsolete.

But the other class, which springs out of a faulty and unskillful abstraction, is intricate and deeply rooted. Let us take for example such a word as *humid,* and see how far the several things which the word is used to signify agree with each other; and we shall find the word *humid* to be nothing else than a mark loosely and confusedly applied to denote a variety of actions which will not bear to be reduced to any constant meaning. For it both signifies that which easily spreads itself round any other body; and that which in itself is indeterminate and cannot solidize; and that which readily yields in every direction; and that which easily divides and scatters itself; and that which easily unites and collects itself; and that which readily flows and is put in motion; and that which readily clings to another body and wets it; and that which is easily reduced to a liquid, or being solid easily melts. Accordingly when you come to apply the word,—if you take it in one sense, flame is humid; if in another, air is not humid; if in another, fine dust is humid; if in another, glass is humid. So that it is easy to see that the notion is taken by abstraction only from water and common and ordinary liquids, without any due verification.

There are however in words certain degrees of distortion and error. One of the least faulty kinds is that of names of substances, especially of lowest species and well-deduced (for the notion of *chalk* and of *mud* is good, of *earth* bad); a more faulty kind is that of actions, as *to generate, to corrupt, to alter;* the most faulty is of qualities (except such as are the immediate objects of the sense) as *heavy, light, rare, dense,* and the like. Yet in all these cases some notions are of necessity a little better than others, in proportion to the greater variety of subjects that fall within the range of the human sense.

LXI

But the *Idols of the Theatre* are not innate, nor do they steal into the understanding secretly, but are plainly impressed and received into the mind from the play-books of philosophical systems and the perverted rules of demonstration. To attempt refutations in this case would be merely inconsistent with what I have already said: for since we agree neither upon principles nor upon demonstrations there is no place for argument. And this is so far well, inasmuch as it leaves the honor of the ancients untouched. For they are no wise disparaged—the question between them and me being only as to the way. For as the saying is, the lame man who keeps the right road outstrips the runner who takes a wrong one. Nay it is obvious that when a man runs the wrong way, the more active and swift he is the further he will go astray.

DISCUSSION AND WRITING

1. Define or explain: *axiom, induction, refutation, sophism, mete out, discourse, credulity, pernicious, inviolate, heterogeneous, felicity, faction, abjure, prime mover, disparage.* In context, what is the exact meaning of the italicized words: "education and *conversation* with others," "*commerce* and *consort* of men," "according to the *apprehension* of the *vulgar*," "after an unreal and *scenic* fashion," "in like *artificial* manner set forth," "parallels and *conjugates* and *relatives*," "*singular* and unmatched," "spirals and *dragons*," "infusion from the will and *affections*," "*humors* of *partisans*," "*sober* things, because they narrow hope," "rules of *demonstration*"?

2. What are the sources of error in the words *earth, heavy, rare, dense?*

3. Which of the following arguments can be identified and discussed with Bacon's help? Which of the logical fallacies illustrated here are familiar to you under modern names?

a. I know that many men reported missing by the Army don't return. But my son's case is different. My intuition as a mother tells me that he is still alive.

b. We are often told that the Nazis exterminated millions of Jews. But here is Professor X, who, though Jewish, was able to leave Germany in 1936 and is leading a happy and prosperous life!

c. Economists testifying before congressional committees invariably get bogged down in a mass of contradictory data and statistics. All they do is to obscure the simple workings of the economic system.

d. Any fool can see that the sun rises in the morning and sets in the evening. We don't need a lot of new-fangled theories about the alleged motion of the earth.

e. I have a strong conviction that our treasurer cannot be dishonest, and what I feel so strongly cannot be wrong.

f. The celestial bodies move in perfect circles because the circle is the most perfect geometrical figure, with the courses of the planets giving symbolic expression to divine perfection.

g. War must be understood in economic terms. Wars are started by have-not nations against those who have. It's as simple as that.

h. I have always claimed that most accidents are caused by woman drivers. Yesterday's fatal accident involving a woman driver only confirms my theory.

i. It would be rash to deny that dreams can predict the future. A woman I know dreamed that her father was going to die, and a week later he was killed in an accident.

j. Each civilization follows a predictable curve from youthful vigor through maturity to inevitable decay.

k. A person who calls himself a Christian communist is intellectually dishonest, for Christianity and communism are diametrically opposed philosophies and ways of life.

4. In an encyclopedia (or in an introduction to logic) look up the following common logical fallacies: *ad hominem, post hoc ergo propter hoc,* faulty or false analogy, false dilemma, hasty generalization. How, if at all, are these fallacies related to the "idols of the mind"?

5. Most of this selection consists of warnings against common tendencies toward error. In your own words, summarize the positive advice concerning sound thinking stated or implied by Bacon.

6. Does Bacon's *own* thinking follow any characteristic pattern? Use his account of other people's thought processes as a model for a study of his own.

7. Study current editorials in a local newspaper for evidence of logical problems or logical fallacies. Cite detailed evidence.

8. Bacon remarks that our view of the world is shaped in part by education and by the influence of others. Discuss a specific influence that helped determine your moral, political, or religious outlook.

9. What evidence have you encountered for the charge that "the human understanding is like a false mirror"?

10. Is it true that students consider "brains" a major handicap to popularity?

FURTHER READING

Among modern books on logical fallacies and popular prejudices are Bergen Evans, *The Natural History of Nonsense* (1946); Robert H. Thouless, *How to Think Straight* (1950); and Stuart Chase, *Guides to Straight Thinking* (1956). Report on the content, tone, and general approach of one of these books.

5

The Media and the Masses

The fact that your voice is amplified to the degree where it reaches from one end of the country to the other does not confer upon you greater wisdom or understanding than you possessed when your voice reached only from one end of the bar to the other. EDWARD R. MURROW

By studying the use of language in the mass media, we confront a basic problem encountered by everyone who has something to communicate. A writer sooner or later faces the problem of finding an audience and of establishing a degree of harmony between its tastes and capacities and his own. For people working in the mass media, the need to please the audience—and to adjust to its real or assumed level—is often an urgent requirement of economic survival. There is a constant temptation to avoid anything difficult, serious, demanding, unusual, disturbing, or controversial. The authors in this section take a look at some of the media. Joseph Addison, in an informal report on the infancy of modern advertising, reminds us first, however, of this primary source of revenue for all the major media of communication—newspapers, magazines, radio, television. Marya Mannes, in "The Conquest of Trigger Mortis," uses her satirical fable to raise some fundamental questions about the relationship between the make-believe world of television drama and the outlook and motives of its viewers. Otto Friedrich, in "How to Read a Tabloid," makes us re-examine our assumptions about what makes news news and "fit to print." Frederick Lewis Allen, in "The Ballyhoo Years," reviews trends in American newspapers during the twenties.

JOSEPH ADDISON

Early in the eighteenth century, Joseph Addison (1672–1719) and his collaborator, Richard Steele, developed the periodical essay as a vehicle for urbane comment on contemporary social mores. Their short, often humorous, articles in *The Tatler* and later in *The Spectator* treated subjects ranging from women's fashions to party politics and literary criticism. They developed a style designed to teach manners, to refine and edify a large public, not by vitriolic criticism but by constant good-humored nudging and civilized example. A modern variation of the type of informal essay they cultivated may still be found in such magazines as *Harper's, The Atlantic Monthly,* and *The New Yorker.* The following selection was first published in London in 1710. Spelling and capitalization have been modernized.

Advertisements

It is my custom in a dearth of news to entertain myself with those collections of advertisements that appear at the end of all our public prints. These I consider as accounts of news from the little world, in the same manner that the foregoing parts of the paper are from the great. If in one we hear that a sovereign prince is fled from his capital city, in the other we hear of a tradesman who has shut up his shop, and run away. If in one we find the victory of a general, in the other we see the desertion of a private soldier. I must confess, I have a certain weakness in my temper, that is often very much affected by these little domestic occurrences, and have frequently been caught with tears in my eyes over a melancholy advertisement.

But to consider this subject in its most ridiculous lights: advertisements are of great use to the vulgar: first of all, as they are instruments of ambition. A man that is by no means big enough for the Gazette may easily creep into the advertisements; by which means we often see an apothecary in the same paper of news with a plenipotentiary, or a running-footman with an ambassador. An advertisement from Piccadilly goes down to posterity with an article from Madrid; and John Bartlett of Goodman's Fields is celebrated in the same paper with the emperor of Germany. Thus the fable tells us that the wren mounted as high as the eagle, by getting upon his back.

A second use which this sort of writings have been turned to of late years has been the management of controversy, insomuch that above half the advertisements one meets with nowadays are purely polemical. The inventors of strops for razors have written against one another this way for several years, and that with great bitterness; as the whole argument pro and con in the case of the morning gowns is still carried on after the same manner. I need not mention the several proprietors of Dr. Anderson's Pills; nor take notice of the many satirical works of this nature so frequently published by Dr. Clark, who has had the confidence to advertise upon that learned knight, my very worthy friend, Sir William Read. But I shall not interpose in their quarrel; Sir William can give him his own in advertisements that, in the judgment of the impartial, are as well penned as the doctor's.

The third and last use of these writings is to inform the world where they may be furnished with almost everything that is necessary for life. If a man has pains in his head, colic in his bowels, or spots in his clothes, he may here meet with proper cures and remedies. If a man would recover a wife or a horse that is stolen or strayed; if he wants new sermons, electuaries, ass's milk, or anything else, either for his body or his mind, this is the place to look for them in.

The great art in writing advertisements is the finding out a proper method to catch the reader's eye; without which a good thing may pass over unobserved, or be lost among commissions of bankrupt. Asterisks and hands were formerly of great use for this purpose. Of late years, the *N.B.* has been much in fashion; as also little cuts and figures, the invention of which we must ascribe to the author of spring-trusses. I must not here omit the blind Italian character, which being scarce legible, always fixes and detains the eye, and gives the curious reader something like the satisfaction of prying into a secret.

But the great skill in an advertiser is chiefly seen in the style which he makes use of. He is to mention the universal esteem, or general reputation, of things that were never heard of. If he is a physician or astrologer, he must change his lodgings frequently, and (though he never saw anybody in them besides his own family) give public notice of it, "for the information of the nobility and gentry." Since I am thus usefully employed in writing criticisms on the works of these diminutive authors, I must not pass over in silence an advertisement which has lately made its appearance, and is written altogether in a Ciceronian manner. It was sent to me, with five shillings, to be inserted among my advertisements; but as it is a pattern of good writing in this way, I shall give it a place in the body of my paper.

> The highest compounded spirit of lavender, the most glorious (if the expression may be used) enlivening scent and flavor that can possibly be,

which so raptures the spirits, delights the gust, and gives such airs to the countenance, as are not to be imagined but by those that have tried it. The meanest sort of the thing is admired by most gentlemen and ladies; but this far more, as by far it exceeds it, to the gaining among all a more than common esteem. It is sold (in neat flint bottles fit for the pocket) only at the Golden-Key in Warton's-Court near Holborn-Bars, for 3 s. 6 d. with directions.

At the same time that I recommend the several flowers in which this spirit of lavender is wrapped up (if the expression may be used), I cannot excuse my fellow-laborers for admitting into their papers several uncleanly advertisements, not at all proper to appear in the works of polite writers. Among these I must reckon the Carminitive Wind-expelling Pills. If the doctor had called them only his Carminitive Pills, he had been as cleanly as one could have wished; but the second word entirely destroys the decency of the first. There are other absurdities of this nature so very gross that I dare not mention them; and shall therefore dismiss this subject, with a public admonition to Michael Parrot, that he not presume any more to mention a certain worm he knows of, which, by the way, has grown seven foot in my memory; for, if I am not much mistaken, it is the same that was but nine foot long about six months ago.

By the remarks I have here made, it plainly appears that a collection of advertisements is a kind of miscellany; the writers of which, contrary to all authors, except men of quality, give money to the booksellers who publish their copies. The genius of the bookseller is chiefly shown in his method of ranging and digesting these little tracts. The last paper I took up in my hands places them in the following order:

> The true Spanish blacking for shoes, etc.
>
> The beautifying cream for the face, etc.
>
> Pease and Plaisters, etc.
>
> Nectar and Ambrosia, etc.
>
> Four freehold tenements of 15 l. per annum, etc.
>
> ***The present state of England, etc.
>
> †††Annotations upon the Tatler, etc.
>
> A commission of bankrupt being awarded against B. L. Bookseller, etc.

DISCUSSION AND WRITING

1. Define or explain: *Gazette, plenipotentiary, running-footman, polemical, proprietor, interpose, gentry, diminutive, Ciceronian, countenance.* What, in the context of the essay, is the meaning of the italicized words: *"dearth* of news," "public *prints,"* "of great use to the *vulgar,"* "little *cuts* and figures," *"blind* Italian *character,"* *"polite* writers," "men of *quality,"* "the *genius* of the bookseller"?

2. Describe features of tone and style that give this essay an informal quality. Pay special attention to Addison's use of humor.

3. What advances has the art of advertising made since Addison's time? How does modern advertising compare in such matters as polemics against competitors; the use of attention-getting devices, superlatives, and flowery language; the observance of good taste? Use detailed illustrations.

4. Investigate and discuss the use of connotative language in current newspaper and magazine advertising.

5. From a national magazine, select a full-page advertisement that illustrates methods of persuasion characteristic of modern advertising. Examine and evaluate them in detail.

6. The success of advertising copy, more directly so than that of other kinds of writing, depends on the writer's accurate estimate of the intended audience. Study the advertising in a national magazine in order to arrive at a composite portrait of its readers as seen by its advertisers. What attitudes, interests, or ways of thinking do the advertisers count on in addressing their audience?

7. Examine several comparable short articles in the magazines mentioned in the headnote to this selection. To what extent do they preserve features of the informal essay as practiced by Addison?

8. While advertising can be shoddy or trite, it can also be imaginative. Discuss the use of design, color, humor, or similar features in current advertising of high quality.

9. Substantiate or refute *one* of the following charges: a) Current advertising does not help the customer interested in reliable factual information about a product; b) current advertising makes people pursue private luxuries while important public needs are neglected; c) current advertising deliberately exploits the customer's weaknesses.

10. J. B. Priestley once said, "One reason why even moderately intelligent people sink deeper and deeper into disillusion is that nothing now comes up to the advertisements." What illusions or what disillusion is current advertising responsible for?

FURTHER READING

Some critical studies of the modern advertiser's use of language are S. I. Hayakawa, "Poetry and Advertising," *Poetry: A Magazine of Verse*, January 1946; William H. Whyte, Jr., "The Language of Advertising," *Fortune*, September 1952; and Vance Packard, "The Growing Power of Admen," *Atlantic*, September 1957.

MARYA MANNES

The Reporter is a liberal magazine of opinion, founded as an "experiment in adult journalism" in 1949. Unlike the more familiar weekly newsmagazines, it passes by the varied spectacle of current news to explore underlying issues and long-range trends. Marya Mannes is *The Reporter's* television and drama critic. She has been playwright, feature editor for women's magazines, and radio scriptwriter. Known for her outspoken review articles and satirical verse, she is also the author of *The New York I Know* (1961), a "fierce, loving, and critical" portrait of her native New York City. The following article was first published in *The Reporter* in 1959. It illustrates a polemical journalistic style that can successfully stir up an apathetic public but that, overshooting the mark, may at the same time make fair discussion of the issues difficult.

The Conquest of Trigger Mortis

The ruling was passed in 1985, over the total opposition of the TV and radio networks and after years of controversy, six investigations, 483 juvenile murders, and the complete reorganization of the Federal Communications Commission. What finally pushed it through was the discovery of *trigger mortis* in a number of American children born in widely separated areas. In this malformation the index finger is permanently hooked, forcing partial contraction of the whole hand in the position required for grasping a revolver. "The gun," said a distinguished anthropologist, "has become an extension of the American arm."

This mutation had been suspected some time before by others, who had found it worthy of note that in 1959, for instance, American toy manufacturers had sold more than $60 million worth of guns and revolvers and that on any given day on television between one and ten o'clock there were more than fifteen programs devoted to violence, and that in each of these programs a gun was fired at least once and usually several times. The only difference between the programs was that in some the shooting was done out of doors and often from horses and that in others it was done in hotel rooms, bars, or apartments. The first category was called Western and was considered a wholesome fight between good men and bad men in healthy country; the second was called Crime and Detective and was considered salubrious in its repeated implication that "crime does not pay," although the women and the interiors shown were usually expensive and the criminal's life, though short, a rich one.

Although this wholesale preoccupation with killing by gun coincided for many years with the highest rate of juvenile crime ever known in this country, and with open access to firearms for all who desired them, television and radio violence was considered by most experts of minimal importance as a contributory cause of youthful killing. Psychiatrists, social workers, program directors, advertisers, and sponsors had a handy set of arguments to prove their point. These (with translation appended) were the most popular:

> Delinquency is a complex problem. No single factor is responsible. (Don't let's stick our necks out. Don't let's act. Don't let's lose money.)
>
> It's all a matter of the home. (Blame the parents. Blame the neighborhood. Blame poverty.)
>
> Crime and adventure programs are a necessary outlet for natural childhood aggressions. (Keep the little bastards quiet while Mummy fixes supper.)
>
> We don't really know what influences children. (Let's wait till they kill somebody.)
>
> Only disturbed or abnormal children are affected by what they see on programs. (And they are a minority. Let their psychiatrists worry about them.)

Everybody was very pleased with these conclusions, particularly the broadcasters, who could continue presenting thirty shootings a day secure in those sections of their old printed Code, which stated: ". . . such subjects as violence and sex shall be presented without undue emphasis and only as required by plot development or character delineation"; and "Television shall exercise care in . . . avoiding material which is excessively violent or would create morbid suspense, or other undesirable reactions in children. These same officials continued also to exercise care in not letting their own children look at the programs of violence which they broadcast.

So for years, and in spite of sporadic cries of alarm and protest from parents and a number of plain citizens, there were always enough experts to assure the public that crime and violence had nothing to do with crime and violence, and that gunplay was entertainment. Psychiatrists continued to say things like this about young killers: "The hostility, festering perhaps from the time he had been trained to the toilet, screamed for release," and educational groups came out periodically with reports on delinquency in which a suggested solution would be "to orient norm-violating individuals in the population towards a law-abiding lower-class way of life."

Dialogues like the following were frequent in Congressional investigations. This one occurred in a hearing of the Senate subcommittee on Juvenile Delinquency in 1954:

> SENATOR: "In your opinion, what is the effect of these Western movies on children?"
>
> EXPERT: "No one knows anything about it."
>
> SENATOR: "Well, of course, you know that little children 6, 7, 8 years old now have belts with guns. Do you think that is due to the fact that they are seeing these Western movies and seeing all this shooting?"
>
> EXPERT: "Oh, undoubtedly."

In the early 1950's, psychiatrist Fredric Wertham, from whose *The Circle of Guilt* the above was quoted, began a relentless campaign against what he called, in another book, *The Seduction of the Innocent*. Concentrating at first on horror and crime comics, the doctor moved inevitably into other fields of mass communication and provided impressive evidence along the way that although their gigantic dosage of violence could not be the sole factor in child criminality, it could certainly be considered a major one.

In attacking the slogan "It's all up to the home," he wrote: "Of course the home has a lot to do with it. But it is wrong to accuse the home as a cause in the usual abstract way, for the home is inseparable from other social circumstances to which it is itself vulnerable. . . . A hundred years ago the home could guard the children's safety; but with the new technological advances, the modern parent cannot possibly carry this responsibility. We need traffic regulations, school buses, school zones and police to protect children from irresponsible drivers. Who will guard the child today from irresponsible adults who sell him incentives, blueprints and weapons for delinquency?"

Wertham also countered the familiar claim that youthful violence was a result of wars by stating that it was not backed up by any scientific, concrete study and that neither the Second World War nor the Korean War explained the phenomenon: " . . . after the First World War the type of brutal violence currently committed on a large scale by the youngest children was almost unknown."

But Wertham was dismissed by many of his colleagues and much of the public as a man obsessed; too aggressively and intemperately committed to one cause—the rape of children's minds by mass communications—to be seriously considered. And the broadcasters and crime-comic publishers, first needled and exasperated by him, soon were able to view him with calm detachment as a crackpot. Thirty murders a day continued on the screen.

Then, early in 1959, the Nuffield Foundation in England put out a thick book called *Television and the Child,* by Hilde T. Himmelweit, A. N. Oppenheim, and Pamela Vince. For four years they examined thousands of children in five cities and of every class and background, and to this they joined a survey of American programming and viewing. They did not confine themselves to programming specifically for children, since it had long been obvious in England, as it was here, that children usually watched adult programs in preference. In more than four hundred pages of meticulous research, scientific detachment, and careful reasoning, they came to certain conclusions—the basis for a weight of further evidence that finally led to government intervention into broadcasting practices. Here are a few of their findings about the twenty per cent of programs seen by children in their peak viewing hours that are devoted to aggression and violence:

> At the center of preoccupation with violence is the gun. Everyone has a gun ready for immediate use—even the barbers and storekeepers, who are not cowboys. People in Westerns take guns for granted.... Finally, while guns are used mostly for killing, they are also let off for fun. Nevertheless, guns spell power, they make people listen, and force them to do what is wanted.
>
> It is said that these programmes have two main desirable effects; they teach the lesson that crime does not pay; and they provide a harmless outlet through fantasy for the child's hostile feelings. We shall take issue with both statements.... The lesson as taught in these programmes is entirely negative (it is best not to offend against the law).... To present such a one-sided view, repeated week after week, is contrary to the recognized educational principle that a moral lesson, to be effective, must teach what should be done as well as what should not be done.
>
> More serious is the fact that... the child may equally well learn other, less desirable lessons from these programmes; that to shoot, bully, and cheat is allowed, provided one is on the right side of the law; and that relationships among people are built not on loyalty and affection but on fear and domination....

As for being a "harmless outlet for aggressive feelings," the authors—quoting the testimony of Dr. Eleanor E. Maccoby of Harvard that this discharge in fantasy alters nothing in the child's real life and so has no lasting value—write that when aggressive feelings exist, "They are not as a rule discharged on viewing crime and violence." "We cite three sets of data . . . [which] show that aggressive feelings are just as likely to be aroused as to be lessened through viewing these programmes—indeed, this seems more often to be the case." And, quoting Dr. Maccoby again, "...the very children who are presumably using the movie as an outlet for their aggressive feelings are the ones who carry away the aggressive content in their memories, for how long we do not know."

Miss Himmelweit and her colleagues sum up as follows:

It is suggested that crime and violence programmes increase tension and anxiety, increase maladjustment and delinquent behaviour, teach children techniques of crime, blunt their sensitivity to suffering and, related to this, suggest to them that conflict is best solved by aggression.

Our findings and those of Maccoby suggest, then, that these programmes do not initiate aggressive, maladjusted, or delinquent behaviour, but may aid its expression. They may not affect a stable child, but they may evoke a response in the 5–10 per cent of all children who are disturbed or at least emotionally labile, 'a group to be reckoned with by all the responsible people in the field of mass communications.'

"We find...," says the Nuffield Report, closing this chapter, "evidence that [these programs] may retard children's awareness of the serious consequences of violence in real life and may teach a greater acceptance of aggression as the normal, manly solution of conflict. . . . Just as a nation improves public hygiene when the evidence *suggests, without necessarily proving it* [my italics], that harm may otherwise result, so, we think, there is need of remedial action here."

The Nuffield Report authors had obviously fallen into the error of blaming the industry instead of the child. For in most "acceptable" studies of television and its influence, wrote Wertham, "the assumption seems to be that when anything goes wrong the child must be morbid but the entertainment normal. Why not assume... that our children are normal, that they like adventure and imagination, that they can be stimulated to excitement, but that maybe something is wrong with what they are looking at? Why assume that they need death and destruction...?"

Voices, voices, voices. "Beefs," "squawks," the broadcasters called these surges of protest year after year. And they would point with pride to the one children's program out of ten that was educational, the one out of twenty that had no shooting.

But their biggest defense became, in the end, their undoing. They had assured themselves that by removing the physical effects of violence, the violence was stripped of its harm. They showed no blood, no close-ups of agony, no open wounds, no last convulsions of a riddled body. Men were shot, they clapped thier hands to their stomachs and either fell forwards or backwards as the camera panned away and returned to the gun. And while the broadcasters felt this a noble concession to the sensibilities of young viewers ("Brutality or physical agony," says the NBC Code, "is not presented in detail nor indicated by offensive sound or visual effects"), they were in actuality presenting, day after day, two great immoralities: that shooting is clean—and easy. To pull a trigger requires neither strength nor skill nor courage: it is the bullet that kills. And to kill with a gun is quick and painless. Hero or criminal, both were cowards who answered questions by pulling triggers. This was the daily lesson for sixty million children for twenty years.

Until, of course, the people finally rose. Some cool legal heads first managed to draft legislation banning the sale of pornographic and sensational printed material without in any way curbing individual liberty or preventing the sale of *Lady Chatterley's Lover* or Aristophanes. And then came the famous FCC ruling Bylaw A41-632. In effect, this gave the FCC, by then reorganized into a body of able and dedicated communications experts who functioned in areas of human values as well as in electronics, the power to revoke the license of any broadcaster showing fictionalized killing, whether by gun or knife or bludgeon, without also displaying the natural consequences to the person killed. The bill as originally drawn was a forthright ban on all fictionalized killing except by direct bodily means, without weapons: killing had to involve strength, skill, and direct physical involvement. But after long wrangling, the later version was adopted as being less tainted by censorship and more practicable. For if a program showing a killing had to show a head blown to bits at close range, or blood gushing from mouth and nose, or a jagged stomach wound—all natural results of shooting—the sponsor would not sell many goods. It was therefore far easier to cut out guns entirely.

Far easier, that is, for everyone but the writers. After the law was put into effect, there was mass unemployment among the television writers in Hollywood and New York. They had relied so long on their collaborator, the gun, that they were incapable of writing a plot without it. As Wertham quoted an experienced TV crime writer: "You have to work backwards. You're given a violent situation and you have to work within that framework." Start with the murder and then fit in the people. And suddenly the poor writers had to think up situations where people and ideas provided the excitement instead of a Colt .45. It was a period of anguish none of them will forget.

But for every ten writers who became alcoholics or joined insurance firms, one began to tap resources he had never used and to write well and truly for the first time. And after a hiatus of incredible sterility, when frantic producers threw in anything innocuous, however old and poor, to fill up the time formerly used by crime plays and Westerns, television slowly began to get better and better, more inventive both in the uses of realism and fantasy.

A new generation of American children grew up with no appetite for guns and no illusions about the fun of painless killing. Instead they learned judo or, through compulsory strenuous exercises then conducted daily by their schools, became a race of confident acrobats, able to show their prowess in feats of skill, daring, and endurance without knifing, stomping, or shooting anyone.

Disarmament—at least of the young—was finally a fact.

DISCUSSION AND WRITING

1. Define or explain: *malformation, mutation, salubrious, minimal, append, delineation, sporadic, intemperate, meticulous, labile, bludgeon, hiatus, innocuous.*

2. Examine the author's use of irony—point out statements that are clearly not meant to be taken literally or seriously. Marya Mannes has a gift for the striking, witty phrase. Cite examples. In what other ways does she use humor for purposes of persuasion?

3. Examine the author's use of emotive, connotative language. Cite examples of her describing familiar things so as to arouse emotion and imply condemnation or praise.

4. Examine the author's use of evidence. How effective is her use of quotations? The demands of persuasive writing often clash with those of dispassionate logic. What problems of logic, if any, arise in the course of this article?

5. In one well-developed paragraph, sum up the author's estimate of television programming. Be careful not to oversimplify or exaggerate her objections.

6. Examine some current television Westerns and crime shows in the light of the author's charges. Are they "immoral" in the sense in which she uses the word?

7. Discuss the quality of recent television programs devoted to one of the following: news background, history, the fine arts.

8. Science fiction programs enable writers and producers to adapt familiar expectations to radically new situations. Examine current programs of this kind for their moral and psychological implications, along the lines suggested by Miss Mannes' article.

9. Critics like Marya Mannes and John Crosby have vigorously condemned television's failure to live up to its cultural and educational potential. Follow the reviews of current television fare in a major newspaper or magazine and determine the critic's standards. Pay attention to his view both of the medium and of its audience.

10. From time to time proposals are made for financing television programs not through commercial advertising but through audience subscription. Instead of being forced to listen to commercials, people would pay for their entertainment, as they do when they go to see a movie. Would you favor such a plan?

FURTHER READING

Some articles evaluating the role of the mass media in American popular culture are Gilbert Seldes, "Radio, TV, and the Common Man," *Saturday Review,* August 1953; Walter Kerr, "What Good Is Television?" *Horizon,* March 1960; Martin Mayer, "How Good Is TV at Its Best?" *Harper's,* August–September 1960; Desmond Smith, "American Radio Today," *Harper's,* September 1964; Herbert Brucker, "Mass Man and Mass Media," *Saturday Review,* May 29, 1965. Examine several such articles for recurrent observations or common themes.

OTTO FRIEDRICH

The American Scholar is the quarterly published by Phi Beta Kappa. Otto Friedrich, who contributed the following article on some of the lesser-known aspects of news reporting, bases his observations on his experience as a staff member of a New York newspaper. The following article first appeared in *The American Scholar* in autumn 1959. It illustrates the strange mixture of horror and fascination with which the mass media are regarded by many of the people—writers, performers, technicians, critics—to whom they give employment.

A Vivacious Blonde Was Fatally Shot Today or *How to Read a Tabloid*

There is a joke among newspapermen that if a woman is pretty, she is called "beautiful"; if she is plain, she is called "attractive"; and if she is hideous, she is called "vivacious." Half the joke is the exaggeration; the other half is that this is no exaggeration at all. In describing a woman involved in a murder or a robbery or a divorce case, the same technique is generally applied to every aspect of her appearance. If she is tall, she is "statuesque." If she is short, the word is "petite." Thin women are "slender," while fat ones are "curvaceous." Physical appearance is not so important in a man, and the emphasis shifts to financial appearance. "Socially prominent" is a popular description of any man who is murdered by his wife. Bookies and gigolos may be identified as "sportsmen." And one connoisseur has defined "social-ite" as "a tabloid term meaning human being."

This form of wordmanship—the art of exaggerating without actually lying—is so common in tabloid newspapers that it may be termed tabloid prose, but it is by no means restricted to tabloids. Indeed, most newspapers and most wire services use it much of the time. Tabloid prose is not merely a corruption of the English language, however. Literary critics tell us that form cannot be disassociated from content, and since many writers of tabloid prose are intelligent and cultivated people, the reason for the use of a word such as "curvaceous" may be found in the mentality of the person for whom it is written. More accurately, the reason lies in the editor's concept of the mentality of the person who can be enticed by such words into surrendering his five or ten cents.

Despite all its pretenses of representing the public, the average newspaper is simply a business enterprise that sells news and uses that lure to sell advertising space. It is scarcely different from enterprises selling shoes or grass seed. Like any other business, a newspaper obeys the law of supply and demand, and most newspapers have discovered that a sex murder attracts more readers than does a French cabinet crisis. Murder, however, is a fairly commonplace event—one a day is the average in New York alone—and the tabloid editor therefore makes distinctions between what are known as "classy cases" and "cheap cases."

It is commonly believed that a reader's interest is attracted by a case with which he can identify himself—there but for the grace of God, et cetera. But if the average tabloid reader were murdered, his misfortune would not receive much coverage in the average tabloid. He would be a "cheap case." Essentially, a cheap case involves what tabloid editors consider to be cheap people. This includes all working-class people, such as factory hands, waitresses, and the unemployed. It also includes farmers, usually brushed aside as "hillbilly stuff." Alcoholics, whose antics are sometimes extremely entertaining, come under the same ban. So do Negroes, Mexicans, Puerto Ricans, and other "lesser breeds without the law." This causes some difficulties for the wire services since the current fashion is to delete any references to a criminal's race as "irrelevant." Thus an editor who might begin by showing great interest in a murder would cut the story down to a few paragraphs after learning that it involved a "Jig," but he would not publicly divulge the dread word that motivated his editing—and, of course, his editorial columns would continue to clamor for civil rights.

There is another subdivision of the cheap case that the editor generally describes as "too gruesome." Onto his spike go the stories, more common than the average reader realizes, of children being raped or chopped to pieces, stories of burglars torturing their victims to make them reveal their cache. Both cheap and gruesome, in the minds of most editors, is the subject of homosexuality. A traveling salesman strangled by a boy he brought up to his room at the Y.M.C.A. would never deserve one-tenth the tabloid attention that he would attain if his assassin had been a girl.

Sadism, sodomy, tortures, drunken stabbings, certain adulteries—these things happen every day, but in a kind of nether world that lies beneath what the tabloids like to consider their dignity. In contrast to all this, there is the "classy case." What gives a murder "class"? Rich men, beautiful women, yachts, racing stables—everything, in short, that forms part of the dreamworld of the gum-chewing tabloid reader. For the secret of the whole tabloid formula is that the "classy" murder case is not one with which the reader *can* identify himself but one with which he *would like* to identify himself. The New York *Times* and the *Herald Tribune* provide society pages for social climbers to read; the tabloids provide society columns for day-dreaming shopgirls. The concept of class, in other words, represents the Hollywood-fed, all-American fantasy, and yet the "news" about this dreamworld is always at least implicitly disastrous. The stockbroker is discovered in his "love nest"; the heiress is a "love slave"; the playboy is sued for "heart balm." Thus the lower orders, in buying the news about the upper ones, are given satisfying accounts of their objects of envy committing depravities and defalcations, of their imminent descent to the readers' own level. Although reader-criminal identification may seem farfetched here, one can assume that the tabloid reader would like to be in a position to *have* a "love nest," even if it meant eventually being "exposed."

Once in a decade there is a case like the shooting of Jim Fisk or the kidnapping of the Lindbergh baby, a case in which all the rules of the tabloid form fit into place and a famous story virtually writes itself. But the tabloids are printed every day, and every day the readers are hungry for a new taste of high-class sensations. That is why the homely waitress strangled on the beach becomes a "shapely blonde" (the favored term "blonde" can apply to almost any color of hair, although obviously unblonde women are often exoticized by terms such as "flame-haired" or "raven-tressed"). This is why the seedy sawbones who pinches his patients becomes a "distinguished physician" living in "a luxurious home in the fashionable suburb of Blank." Indeed, tabloid prose often reads like the same newspaper's real estate section for the simple reason that both the tabloid writer and the advertising writer are trying to make the shabby reality conform to the fantasy. Homes, in both cases, if not luxurious, are then spacious. Suburbs are always fashionable.

And houses are always "homes," for all the idealizing forces behind the tabloid writer require him to use the genteel euphemism in every case where the unidiomatic word will provide "class." Thus sons become heirs or scions. Doctors become physicians, carpenters become contracting executives, and even the lowest of the species may be "socially prominent."

The tabloid distortions represent so ubiquitous a fantasy that the tabloid writer occasionally discovers one of his subjects really acting out the transformation of human being into socialite. A few years ago, a New York millionaire was shot to death by his wife, and the tabloids set up a hue and cry for every detail of the story. One of the gaps was the background of the wife, who had been generally thought to be the orphaned daughter of a colonel. It took a tabloid reporter a considerable amount of time to determine that the colonel had never existed, and that the actual father was still very much alive as a streetcar motorman in Detroit. When the father was finally interviewed about his daughter's misfortunes, he expressed surprise that she had married a New York millionaire. He remembered that she had changed her name to become a model, but for many years he had been under the impression that his daughter was a well-known Hollywood actress with a similar *nom de guerre*. Here is a tabloid creation in the flesh.

Sex, as is well known, combines with crime to provide the tabloids with their huge circulations. But sex is as strangely distorted as crime, as strangely twisted to fit the American fantasies. The same bans apply—drunks, Negroes, workers, homosexuals, all these have no sex life of any news value. And yet the lowest "starlet" in Hollywood has her casual affairs broadcast to millions under such wonderful disguises as "friends wonder if so-and-so is secretly married to so-and-so." Disguise is the essence of sex chronicles, for although sex sells newspapers, even the most lurid tabloid schizophrenically considers itself a "family newspaper." Although it may seem strange to a casual reader, the tabloid editor's desire to stimulate sales is handcuffed by a criterion known as "good taste." This criterion is so mysterious, so much a matter of "feel," that it can best be illustrated by an example.

An enterprising young lady once tried to achieve fame by going to a Cannes film festival, accosting a popular actor, stripping off all her clothes above the waist, and embracing the rather embarrassed actor while photographers frantically took pictures that could never be printed. From reporters' accounts of the scene, the girl achieved a certain small notoriety, enough to get her to Hollywood, where her misfortunes were usually reported as an excuse to run pictures of her. One day, this aspiring actess—or could it have been some other specimen of the familiar type?—appeared in a two-column picture, wearing a tiny crucifix that dangled down into a resting place between her luxurious breasts. The editor, who had been out of the office when the picture was first printed, returned to his desk and cried out in horror. At considerable expense, the picture was treated with an airbrush, which sprayed flesh-colored paint over the crucifix, so that a new engraving of the voluptuous bosom could be portrayed in the next edition without violating "good taste."

Perhaps one more incident would illustrate this strange concept further. A few years ago, a teen-age youth in a suburb of Boston murdered a girl with whom he had just had sexual intercourse on the front seat of an automobile. When the youth confessed to the police, he proudly repeated over and over the details of how he had become a man in the parked car, and the words he used to express that experience were: "Then I scored and then I scored again, that's where I scored." The childish boast embarrassed the same editors who normally want to emphasize every implication of sex, and when the story was finally printed the youth was quoted as saying that "intimacies had occurred" in the spotted front seat of the car.

Intimacies. This is the tabloid word for sex. It turns up over and over again. If any ingenuous tabloid writer tries to use a word like "sex," on the theory that an accurate term is always in better taste than a euphemism, the more experienced copy desk will change it to "intimacies." The reason for this involves the same fantasies that dominate Hollywood: Miss Blank, who has had three husbands, is cast as an ingénue stranded overnight on a mountain top with Mr. Blank, who has had three wives. There is much giggling as they pitch their separate tents, but at the end they will get married. The movie will be advertised with twenty-foot-high posters of Miss Blank lying panting on the mountain top in her chemise while Mr. Blank crouches nearby in the attitude of a neurotic gorilla. The movie-goer knows that he will not be actually shown anything that could offend the local archbishop, but he will be allowed his snicker. The snicker, the leer, that nervous substitute for the thwarted need, is the American emotional response to the so-called "popular culture."

Although the tabloids and the movies provide much the same outlet for the need to snicker, the tabloids push the whole process one step further than is possible in the movies. With an almost baroque stylization, the tabloids would take Mr. Blank and Miss Blank to the mountain top, and then, instead of fading out like a discreet movie camera, they would quote Miss Blank as saying that "intimacies occurred." Nor is that the only dainty disguise. Mr. Blank may also be said to have been "dallying" with Miss Blank, or maybe he was "romancing" her. He is her "sweetheart." No, says she, they are "just good friends," and everybody gets a good healthy snicker out of it.

Curiously enough, the chief trouble for the tabloid writer occurs in supposed sex cases where no sex has been enjoyed, as far as can be determined. The problem arises, for instance, in the periodic story of the "nice" teen-age girl running off with a boy. The tabloid editors enjoy a vicarious thrill at the prospect of a young girl's availability, but the writer finds that everything he can say about the errant couple has already been tinged with the implications of past cases. Were they just "close friends"? Were they "intimate friends"? Had there been, all virginally, a "romance"? Every word revives echoes of the old euphemisms and the old snickers. Denials are accepted as lies. The English language has been wrung out.

Are the tabloids hopeless? Perhaps, but not on the grounds of sensationalism. Having already become rich, they hunger nowadays after finer things, such as respectability and political influence. In New York, where the *Times* fills its half-size brothers with awe, the tabloids feel compelled to tell their uninterested readers about such portentous events as a Senate debate on farm parity, largely because the *Times* has or inevitably will do so. It is almost with shock that today's tabloid writer, looking back through clippings on the Lindbergh case, finds Damon Runyon reporting the execution of Bruno Hauptmann in terms of near-hysteria: "The Wolf-man is dead." What amazement he feels, then, in looking at the old *Graphic's* faked pictures of

Peaches Browning in the bedroom with her aged husband, at the balloon that issues from Daddy's mouth and quotes him as quacking like a duck. To find such authentic trashiness now, one must leave America and take a look at the London *Mirror*, which is comparatively entertaining and consequently sells twice as many copies as its biggest New York counterpart. Although American tabloid circulations are in or near the millions, their sales are actually stagnant or declining, despite the increase in population. That is natural, however, when the popular touch has become the genteelism, when irreverence has given way to reverence, stuffiness, even pomposity.

One tabloid's saucy story about the preparations of a European princeling's long-anticipated marriage to a celebrated beauty was killed on the strength of a new managerial directive that the wedding had been handled too impertinently and was henceforth to be treated "with dignity." And so for one solid week, it printed fifteen "romantic" but "dignified" manuscript pages per day on one of the most laughable events of our time. The stories were laughable too, precisely because they accepted their subjects' social pretensions at face value. I wrote them myself.

DISCUSSION AND WRITING

1. Define or explain: *connoisseur, divulge, clamor, sadism, sodomy, defalcation, unidiomatic, ubiquitous, nom de guerre, lurid, schizophrenic, criterion, ingenuous, ingénue, baroque, stylization, vicarious, errant, portentous, genteelism.*

2. Study Friedrich's examples of euphemism and discuss its nature and typical uses. Collect and discuss further examples from newspapers and other sources.

3. Examine the organization of Friedrich's article, preparing a brief outline. Examine the effectiveness of introduction and conclusion, the adequacy of transitions.

4. In one well-developed paragraph, sum up the author's attitude toward the tabloids. Pay attention to his use of irony and connotative language, and to the development of the essay as a whole. Avoid oversimplification.

5. Study and evaluate one of the following features of a newspaper that you read regularly: society news, advice on personal or emotional problems, the "women's page," book reviews. Use detailed illustrations.

6. Study major illustrated feature articles in a family-type picture magazine of large circulation, such as *Life, Look,* or *The Saturday Evening Post.* Is there such a thing as a "typical" article? To what interests does it appeal? What attitudes or what outlook does it encourage?

7. To what extent have newsmagazines like *Time* or *Newsweek* adopted the tabloid formula described by Friedrich? For instance, is there any evidence of "the snicker, the leer, that nervous substitute for the thwarted need"? Or is there a predictable preoccupation with "European princelings" and other remnants of European aristocracy? Focus on *one major area* or point. Use detailed illustrations.

8. Do you agree that a newspaper is "simply a business enterprise"? Can or should it be? Why and how should it be different from other business enterprises? Argue your answer in detail.

9. Define and illustrate the standard of "good taste" that should be observed by one of the following: the editor of a high school or college newspaper; the editor of a college humor magazine; the director of a variety show produced by college students.

10. Have you ever adopted a style of expression or behavior that you personally considered "laughable," undesirable, or insincere? For instance, have you ever played a role as member or official of a group, or as a sales person, that did not really suit your true feelings or personality? What were the reasons, problems, results? What did you learn from the experience?

FURTHER READING

Among writers whose fiction in different ways preserves the popular touch of writing designed for newspapers and popular magazines are O. Henry, Ring Lardner, and Damon Runyon. Read several pieces by one of these. How close to, or how far removed from, current popular taste is his style?

FREDERICK LEWIS ALLEN

> Frederick Lewis Allen (1890–1954), magazine editor and social historian, wrote numerous articles and books on the American scene. In 1931, he published *Only Yesterday,* his account of the decade that had just come to an end—the period between the end of World War I and the beginning of the Great Depression. Allen based his book on a study of sources ranging from the work of outstanding sociologists and historians to newspaper articles and advertising. However, he combined his concern for authenticity with a journalist's verve, and his book restores color and life to a period known to younger readers only in fading popular stereotypes about the "roaring twenties." The following selection is an abridged version of the chapter in which Allen deals with the development of modern techniques in publicity.

The Ballyhoo Years

All nations, in all eras of history, are swept from time to time by waves of contagious excitement over fads or fashions or dramatic public issues. But the size and frequency of these waves are highly variable, as is the

nature of the events which set them in motion. One of the striking characteristics of the era of Coolidge Prosperity was the unparalleled rapidity and
unanimity with which millions of men and women turned their attention,
their talk and their emotional interest upon a series of tremendous trifles—a
heavyweight boxing-match, a murder trial, a new automobile model, a trans-
atlantic flight.

Most of the *causes célèbres* which thus stirred the country from end to end
were quite unimportant from the traditional point of view of the historian.
The future destinies of few people were affected in the slightest by the
testimony of the "pig woman" at the Hall-Mills trial or the attempt to rescue
Floyd Collins from his Kentucky cave. Yet the fact that such things could
engage the hopes and fears of unprecedented numbers of people was
anything but unimportant. No account of the Coolidge years would be
adequate which did not review that strange procession of events which a
nation tired of "important issues" swarmed to watch, or which did not take
account of that remarkable chain of circumstances which produced as the
hero of the age, not a great public servant, not a reformer, not a warrior, but
a stunt flyer who crossed the ocean to win a money prize.

By the time Calvin Coolidge reached the White House, the tension of the
earlier years of the Post-War Decade had been largely relaxed. Though
Woodrow Wilson still clung feebly to life in the sunny house in S Street, the
League issue was dead and only handfuls of irreconcilable idealists imagined
it to have a chance of resuscitation. The radicals were discouraged, the labor
movement had lost energy and prestige since the days of the Big Red Scare,
and under the beneficent influence of easy riches—or at least of easy Fords
and Chevrolets—individualistic capitalism had settled itself securely in the
saddle. The Ku Klux Klan numbered its millions, yet already it was beginning to lose that naïve ardor which had lighted its fires on a thousand
hilltops; it was becoming less of a crusade and more of a political racket.
Genuine public issues about which the masses of the population could be
induced to feel intensely, were few and far between. There was prohibition,
to be sure; anybody could get excited about prohibition; but because the
division of opinion on liquor cut across party lines, every national politician,
almost without exception, did his best to thrust this issue into the background. In the agricultural Northwest and Middle West there was a violent
outcry for farm relief but it could command only a scattered and halfhearted
interest throughout the rest of a nation which was becoming progressively
urbanized. Public spirit was at low ebb; over the World Court, the oil
scandals, the Nicaraguan situation, the American people as a whole refused
to bother themselves. They gave their energies to triumphant business, and
for the rest they were in holiday mood. "Happy," they might have said, "is
the nation which has no history—and a lot of good shows to watch." They
were ready for any good show that came along.

It was now possible in the United States for more people to enjoy the same good show at the same time than in any other land on earth or at any previous time in history. Mass production was not confined to automobiles; there was mass production in news and ideas as well. For the system of easy nation-wide communication which had long since made the literate and prosperous American people a nation of faddists was rapidly becoming more widely extended, more centralized, and more effective than ever before.

To begin with, there were fewer newspapers, with larger circulations, and they were standardized to an unprecedented degree by the increasing use of press-association material and syndicated features. Between 1914 and 1926, as Silas Bent has pointed out, the number of daily papers in the country dropped from 2,580 to 2,001, the number of Sunday papers dropped from 571 to 541, and the aggregate circulation per issue rose from somewhat over 28,000,000 to 36,000,000. The city of Cleveland, which a quarter of a century before had had three morning papers, now had but one; Detroit, Minneapolis, and St. Louis had lost all but one apiece; Chicago, during a period in which it had doubled in population, had seen the number of its morning dailies drop from seven to two. Newspapers all over the country were being gathered into chains under more or less centralized direction: by 1927 the success of the Hearst and Scripps-Howard systems and the hope of cutting down overhead costs had led to the formation of no less than 55 chains controlling 230 daily papers with a combined circulation of over 13,000,000.

No longer did the local editor rely as before upon local writers and cartoonists to fill out his pages and give them a local flavor; the central office of the chain, or newspaper syndicates in New York, could provide him with editorials, health talks, comic strips, sob-sister columns, household hints, sports gossip, and Sunday features prepared for a national audience and guaranteed to tickle the mass mind. Andy Gump and Dorothy Dix had their millions of admirers from Maine to Oregon, and the words hammered out by a reporter at Jack Dempsey's training-camp were devoured with one accord by real-estate men in Florida and riveters in Seattle.

Meanwhile, the number of national magazines with huge circulations had increased, the volume of national advertising had increased, a horde of publicity agents had learned the knack of associating their cause or product with whatever happened to be in the public mind at the moment, and finally there was the new and vastly important phenomenon of radio broadcasting, which on occasion could link together a multitude of firesides to hear the story of a World's Series game or a Lindbergh welcome. The national mind had become as never before an instrument upon which a few men could play. And these men were learning, as Mr. Bent has also shown, to play upon it in a new way—to concentrate upon *one tune at a time*.

Not that they put their heads together and deliberately decided to do this. Circumstances and self-interest made it the almost inevitable thing for them to do. They discovered—the successful tabloids were daily teaching them— that the public tended to become excited about one thing at a time. Newspaper owners and editors found that whenever a Dayton trial or a *Vestris* disaster took place, they sold more papers if they gave it all they had—their star reporters, their front-page display, and the bulk of their space. They took full advantage of this discovery: according to Mr. Bent's compila- tions, the insignificant Gray-Snyder murder trial got a bigger "play" in the press than the sinking of the *Titanic;* Lindbergh's flight, than the Armistice and the overthrow of the German Empire. Syndicate managers and writers, advertisers, press agents, radio broadcasters, all were aware that mention of the leading event of the day, whatever it might be, was the key to public interest. The result was that when something happened which promised to appeal to the popular mind, one had it hurled at one in huge headlines, waded through page after page of syndicated discussion of it, heard about it on the radio, was reminded of it again and again in the outpourings of publicity-seeking orators and preachers, saw pictures of it in the Sunday papers, and in the movies, and (unless one was a perverse individualist) enjoyed the sensation of vibrating to the same chord which thrilled a vast populace.

The country had bread, but it wanted circuses—and now it could go to them a hundred million strong. . . .

It was the tragedy of Floyd Collins, perhaps, which gave the clearest indication up to that time of the unanimity with which the American people could become excited over a quite unimportant event if only it were dramatic enough.

Floyd Collins was an obscure young Kentuckian who had been exploring an underground passage five miles from Mammoth Cave, with no more heroic purpose than that of finding something which might attract lucrative tourists. Some 125 feet from daylight he was caught by a cave-in which pinned his foot under a huge rock. So narrow and steep was the passage that those who tried to dig him out had to hitch along on their stomachs in cold slime and water and pass back from hand to hand the earth and rocks that they pried loose with hammers and blow-torches. Only a few people might have heard of Collins' predicament if W. B. Miller of the *Louisville Courier- Journal* had not been slight of stature, daring, and an able reporter. Miller wormed his way down the slippery, tortuous passageway to interview Collins, became engrossed in the efforts to rescue the man, described them in vivid dispatches—and to his amazement found that the entire country was turning to watch the struggle. Collins' plight contained those elements of dramatic suspense and individual conflict with fate which make a great news story, and every city editor, day after day, planted it on page one. When Miller arrived at Sand Cave he had found only three men at the entrance, warming themselves at a fire and wondering, without excitement, how soon their friend would extricate himself. A fortnight later there was a city of a hundred or more tents there and the milling crowds had to be restrained by barbed-wire barriers and State troops with drawn bayonets; and on February 17, 1925, even the *New York Times* gave a three-column page-one headline to the news of the dénouement:

FIND FLOYD COLLINS DEAD IN CAVE TRAP ON
18TH DAY; LIFELESS AT LEAST 24 HOURS; FOOT
MUST BE AMPUTATED TO GET BODY OUT

Within a month, as Charles Mertz later reminded the readers of the *New Republic,* there was a cave-in in a North Carolina mine in which 71 men were caught and 53 actually lost. It attracted no great notice. It was "just a mine disaster." Yet for more than two weeks the plight of a single commonplace prospector for tourists riveted the attention of the nation on Sand Cave, Kentucky. It was an exciting show to watch, and the dispensers of news were learning to turn their spotlights upon one show at a time.

Even the Collins thriller, however, was as nothing beside the spectacle which was offered a few months later when John Thomas Scopes was tried at Dayton, Tennessee, for teaching the doctrine of evolution in the Central High School.

The Scopes case had genuine significance. It dramatized one of the most momentous struggles of the age—the conflict between religion and science. Yet even this trial, so diligently and noisily was it ballyhooed, took on some of the aspects of a circus.

If religion lost ground during the Post-War Decade, the best available church statistics gave no sign of the fact. They showed, to be sure, a very slow growth in the number of churches in use; but this was explained partly by the tendency toward consolidation of existing churches and partly by the trend of population toward the cities—a trend which drew the church-going public into fewer churches with larger congregations. The number of church *members,* on the other hand, grew just about as fast as the population, and church wealth and expenditures grew more rapidly still. On actual attendance at services there were no reliable figures, although it was widely believed that an increasing proportion of the nominally faithful were finding other things to do on Sunday morning. Statistically, the churches apparently just about maintained their position in American life.

Yet it is difficult to escape the conclusion that they maintained it chiefly by the force of momentum—and to some extent, perhaps, by diligent attention to the things which are Caesar's: by adopting, here and there, the acceptable gospel according to Bruce Barton; by strenuous membership and money-raising campaigns (such as Bishop Manning's high-pressure drive in New York for a "house of prayer for all people," which proved to be a house of prayer under strictly Episcopal auspices); and by the somewhat secular lure of church theatricals, open forums, basketball and swimming pools, and muscular good fellowship for the young. Something spiritual had gone out of the churches—a sense of certainty that theirs was the way to salvation. Religion was furiously discussed; there had never been so many books on religious topics in circulation, and the leading divines wrote constantly for the popular magazines; yet all this discussion was itself a sign that for millions of people religion had become a debatable subject instead of being accepted without question among the traditions of the community.

If church attendance declined, it was perhaps because, as Walter Lippmann put it, people were not so certain that they were going to meet God when they went to church. If the minister's prestige declined, it was in many cases because he had lost his one-time conviction that he had a definite and authoritative mission. The Reverend Charles Stelzle, a shrewd observer of religious conditions, spoke bluntly in an article in the *World's Work*: the church, he said, was declining largely because "those who are identified with it do not actually believe in it." Mr. Stelzle told of asking groups of Protestant ministers what there was in their church programs which would prompt them, if they were outsiders, to say, "That is great; that is worth lining up for," and of receiving in no case an immediate answer which satisfied even the answerer himself. In the congregations, and especially among the younger men and women, there was an undeniable weakening of loyalty to the church and an undeniable vagueness as to what it had to offer them—witness, for example, the tone of the discussions which accompanied the abandonment of compulsory chapel in a number of colleges.

This loss of spiritual dynamic was variously ascribed to the general letdown in moral energy which followed the strain of the war; to prosperity, which encouraged the comfortable belief that it profited a man very considerably if he gained a Cadillac car and a laudatory article in the *American Magazine;* to the growing popularity of Sunday golf and automobiling; and to disapproval in some quarters of the political lobbying of church organizations, and disgust at the connivance of many ministers in the bigotry of the Klan. More important than any of these causes, however, was the effect upon the churches of scientific doctrines and scientific methods of thought.

The prestige of science was colossal. The man in the street and the woman in the kitchen, confronted on every hand with new machines and devices which they owed to the laboratory, were ready to believe that science could accomplish almost anything; and they were being deluged with scientific information and theory. The newspapers were given columns of space to inform (or misinform) them of the latest discoveries: a new dictum from Albert Einstein was now front-page stuff even though practically nobody could understand it. Outlines of knowledge poured from the presses to tell people about the planetesimal hypothesis and the constitution of the atom, to describe for them in unwarranted detail the daily life of the cave-man, and to acquaint them with electrons, endocrines, hormones, vitamins, reflexes, and psychoses. On the lower intellectual levels, millions of people were discovering for the first time that there was such a thing as the venerable theory of evolution. Those who had assimilated this doctrine without disaster at an early age were absorbing from Wells, Thomson, East, Wiggam, Dorsey, and innumerable other popularizers and interpreters of science a collection of ideas newer and more disquieting: that we are residents of an insignificant satellite of a very average star obscurely placed in one of who-knows-how-many galaxies scattered through space; that our behavior depends largely upon chromosomes and ductless glands; that the Hottentot obeys impulses similar to those which activate the pastor of the First Baptist Church, and is probably already better adapted to his Hottentot environment than he would be if he followed the Baptist code; that sex is the most important thing in life, that inhibitions are not to be tolerated, that sin is an out-of-date term, that most untoward behavior is the result of complexes acquired at an early age, and that men and women are mere bundles of behavior-patterns, anyhow. If some of the scientific and pseudo-scientific principles which lodged themselves in the popular mind contradicted one another, that did not seem to matter: the popular mind appeared equally ready to believe with East and Wiggam in the power of heredity and with Watson in the power of environment.

Of all the sciences it was the youngest and least scientific which most captivated the general public and had the most disintegrating effect upon religious faith. Psychology was king. Freud, Adler, Jung, and Watson had their tens of thousands of votaries; intelligence-testers invaded the schools in quest of I.Q.'s; psychiatrists were installed in business houses to hire and fire employees and determine advertising policies; and one had only to read the newspapers to be told with complete assurance that psychology held the key to the problems of waywardness, divorce, and crime.

The word science had become a shibboleth. To preface a statement with "Science teaches us" was enough to silence argument. If a sales manager wanted to put over a promotion scheme or a clergyman to recommend a charity, they both hastened to say that it was scientific.

The effect of the prestige of science upon churchmen was well summed up by Dr. Harry Emerson Fosdick at the end of the decade:

"The men of faith might claim for their positions ancient tradition, practical usefulness, and spiritual desirability, but one query could prick all such bubbles: Is it scientific? That question has searched religion for contraband goods, stripped it of old superstitions, forced it to change its categories of thought and methods of work, and in general has so cowed and scared religion that many modern-minded believers ... instinctively throw up their hands at the mere whisper of it. ... When a prominent scientist comes out strongly for religion, all the churches thank Heaven and take courage as though it were the highest possible compliment to God to have Eddington believe in Him. Science has become the arbiter of this generation's thought, until to call even a prophet and a seer scientific is to cap the climax of praise."

So powerful was the invasion of scientific ideas and of the scientific habit of reliance upon proved facts that the Protestant churches—which numbered in their membership five out of every eight adult church members in the United States—were broken into two warring camps. Those who believed in the letter of the Bible and refused to accept any teaching, even of science, which seemed to conflict with it, began in 1921 to call themselves Fundamentalists. The Modernists (or Liberals), on the other hand, tried to reconcile their beliefs with scientific thought; to throw overboard what was out of date, to retain what was essential and intellectually respectable, and generally to mediate between Christianity and the skeptical spirit of the age.

The position of the Fundamentalists seemed almost hopeless. The tide of all rational thought in a rational age seemed to be running against them. But they were numerous, and at least there was no doubt about where they stood. Particularly in the South they controlled the big Protestant denominations. And they fought strenuously. They forced the liberal Doctor Fosdick out of the pulpit of the Presbyterian church in which he had been preaching for years and back into his own Baptist fold (though there was no churchman in America more influential than he). They introduced into the legislatures of nearly half the states of the Union bills designed to forbid the teaching of the doctrine of evolution; in Texas, Louisiana, Arkansas, and South Carolina they pushed such bills through one house of the legislature only to fail in the other; and in Tennessee, Oklahoma, and Mississippi they actually succeeded in writing their anachronistic wishes into law.

The Modernists had the *Zeitgeist* on their side, but they were not united. Their interpretations of God—as the first cause, as absolute energy, as idealized reality, as a righteous will working in creation, as the ideal and goal toward which all that is highest and best is moving—were confusingly various and ambiguous. Some of these interpretations offered little to satisfy the worshipper: one New England clergyman said that when he thought of God he thought of "a sort of oblong blur." And the Modernists threw overboard so many doctrines in which the bulk of American Protestants had grown up believing (such as the Virgin birth, the resurrection of the body, and the Atonement) that they seemed to many to have no religious cargo left except a nebulous faith, a general benevolence, and a disposition to assure everyone that he was really just as religious as they. Gone for them, as Walter Lippmann said, was "that deep, compulsive, organic faith in an external fact which is the essence of religion for all but that very small minority who can live within themselves in mystical communion or by the power of their understanding." The Modernists, furthermore, had not only Fundamentalism to battle with, but another adversary, the skeptic nourished on outlines of science; and the sermons of more than one Modernist leader gave the impression that Modernism, trying to meet the skeptic's arguments without resorting to the argument from authority, was being forced against its will to whittle down its creed to almost nothing at all.

All through the decade the three-sided conflict reverberated. It reached its climax in the Scopes case in the summer of 1925.

The Tennessee legislature, dominated by Fundamentalists, passed a bill providing that "it shall be unlawful for any teacher in any of the universities, normals and all other public schools of the State, which are supported in whole or in part by the public school funds of the State, to teach any theory that denies the story of the Divine creation of man as taught in the Bible, and to teach instead that man has descended from a lower order of animals."

This law had no sooner been placed upon the books than a little group of men in the sleepy town of Dayton, Tennessee, decided to put it to the test. George Rappelyea, a mining engineer, was drinking lemon phosphates in Robinson's drug store with John Thomas Scopes, a likeable young man of twenty-four who taught biology at the Central High School, and two or three others. Rappelyea proposed that Scopes should allow himself to be caught red-handed in the act of teaching the theory of evolution to an innocent child, and Scopes—half serious, half in joke—agreed. Their motives were apparently mixed; it was characteristic of the times that (according to so friendly a narrator of the incident as Arthur Garfield Hays) Rappelyea declared that their action would put Dayton on the map. At all events, the illegal deed was shortly perpetrated and Scopes was arrested. William Jennings Bryan forthwith volunteered his services to the prosecution; Rappelyea wired the Civil Liberties Union in New York and secured for Scopes the legal assistance of Clarence Darrow, Dudley Field Malone, and Arthur Garfield Hays; the trial was set for July, 1925, and Dayton suddenly discovered that it was to be put on the map with a vengeance.

There was something to be said for the right of the people to decide what should be taught in their tax-supported schools, even if what they decided upon was ridiculous. But the issue of the Scopes case, as the great mass of newspaper readers saw it, was nothing so abstruse as the rights of taxpayers versus academic freedom. In the eyes of the public, the trial was a battle between Fundamentalism on the one hand and twentieth-century skepticism (assisted by Modernism) on the other. The champions of both causes were headliners. Bryan had been three times a candidate for the Presidency, had been Secretary of State, and was a famous orator; he was the perfect embodiment of old-fashioned American idealism—friendly, naïve, provincial. Darrow, a radical, a friend of the under-dog, an agnostic, had recently jumped into the limelight of publicity through his defense of Leopold and

Loeb. Even Tex Rickard could hardly have staged a more promising contest than a battle between these two men over such an emotional issue.

It was a strange trial. Into the quiet town of Dayton flocked gaunt Tennessee farmers and their families in mule-drawn wagons and ramshackle Fords; quiet, godly people in overalls and gingham and black, ready to defend their faith against the "foreigners," yet curious to know what this new-fangled evolutionary theory might be. Revivalists of every sort flocked there, too, held their meetings on the outskirts of the town under the light of flares, and tacked up signs on the trees about the courthouse—"Read Your Bible Daily for One Week," and "Be Sure Your Sins Will Find You Out."

Yet the atmosphere of Dayton was not simply that of rural piety. Hot-dog vendors and lemonade vendors set up their stalls along the streets as if it were circus day. Booksellers hawked volumes on biology. Over a hundred newspaper men poured into the town. The Western Union installed twenty-two telegraph operators in a room off a grocery store. In the courtroom itself, as the trial impended, reporters and camera men crowded alongside grim-faced Tennessee countrymen; there was a buzz of talk, a shuffle of feet, a ticking of telegraph instruments, an air of suspense like that of a first-night performance at the theater. Judge, defendant, and counsel were stripped to their shirt sleeves—Bryan in a pongee shirt turned in at the neck, Darrow with lavender suspenders, Judge Raulston with galluses of a more sober judicial hue—yet fashion was not wholly absent: the news was flashed over the wires to the whole country that the judge's daughters, as they entered the courtroom with him, wore rolled stockings like any metropolitan flapper's. Court was opened with a pious prayer—and motion-picture operators climbed upon tables and chairs to photograph the leading participants in the trial from every possible angle. The evidence ranged all the way from the admission of fourteen-year-old Howard Morgan that Scopes had told him about evolution and that it hadn't hurt him any, to the estimate of a zoölogist that life had begun something like six hundred million years ago (an assertion which caused gasps and titters of disbelief from the rustics in the audience). And meanwhile two million words were being telegraphed out of Dayton, the trial was being broadcast by the Chicago *Tribune's* station WGN, the Dreamland Circus at Coney Island offered "Zip" to the Scopes defense as a "missing link," cable companies were reporting enormous increases in trans-atlantic cable tolls, and news agencies in London were being besieged with requests for more copy from Switzerland, Italy, Germany, Russia, China, and Japan. Ballyhoo had come to Dayton.

It was a bitter trial. Attorney-General Stewart of Tennessee cried out against the insidious doctrine which was "undermining the faith of Tennessee's children and robbing them of their chance of eternal life." Bryan charged Darrow with having only one purpose, "to slur at the Bible." Darrow spoke of Bryan's "fool religion." Yet again and again the scene verged on farce. The climax—both of bitterness and of farce—came on the afternoon of July 20th, when on the spur of the moment Hays asked that the defense be permitted to put Bryan on the stand as an expert on the Bible, and Bryan consented.

So great was the crowd that afternoon that the judge had decided to move the court outdoors, to a platform built against the courthouse under the maple trees. Benches were set out before it. The reporters sat on the benches, on the ground, anywhere, and scribbled their stories. On the outskirts of the seated crowd a throng stood in the hot sunlight which streamed down through the trees. And on the platform sat the shirt-sleeved Clarence Darrow, a Bible on his knee, and put the Fundamentalist champion through one of the strangest examinations which ever took place in a court of law.

He asked Bryan about Jonah and the whale, Joshua and the sun, where Cain got his wife, the date of the Flood, the significance of the Tower of Babel. Bryan affirmed his belief that the world was created in 4004 B.C. and the Flood occurred in or about 2348 B.C.; that Eve was literally made out of Adam's rib; that the Tower of Babel was responsible for the diversity of languages in the world; and that a "big fish" had swallowed Jonah. When Darrow asked him if he had ever discovered where Cain got his wife, Bryan answered: "No, sir; I leave the agnostics to hunt for her." When Darrow inquired, "Do you say you do not believe that there were any civilizations on this earth that reach back beyond five thousand years?" Bryan stoutly replied, "I am not satisfied by any evidence I have seen." Tempers were getting frazzled by the strain and the heat; once Darrow declared that his purpose in examining Bryan was "to show up Fundamentalism . . . to prevent bigots and ignoramuses from controlling the educational system of the United States," and Bryan jumped up, his face purple, and shook his fist at Darrow, crying, "To protect the word of God against the greatest atheist and agnostic in the United States!"

It was a savage encounter, and a tragic one for the ex-Secretary of State. He was defending what he held most dear. He was making—though he did not know it—his last appearance before the great American public which had once done him honor (he died scarcely a week later). And he was being covered with humiliation. The sort of religious faith which he represented could not take the witness stand and face reason as a prosecutor.

On the morning of July 21st Judge Raulston mercifully refused to let the ordeal of Bryan continue and expunged the testimony of the previous afternoon. Scopes's lawyers had been unable to get any of their scientific evidence before the jury, and now they saw that their only chance of making the sort of defense they had planned for lay in giving up the case and bringing it before the Tennessee Supreme Court on appeal. Scopes was promptly found guilty and fined one hundred dollars. The State Supreme

Court later upheld the anti-evolution law but freed Scopes on a technicality, thus preventing further appeal.

Theoretically, Fundamentalism had won, for the law stood. Yet really Fundamentalism had lost. Legislators might go on passing anti-evolution laws, and in the hinterlands the pious might still keep their religion locked in a science-proof compartment of their minds; but civilized opinion everywhere had regarded the Dayton trial with amazement and amusement, and the slow drift away from Fundamentalism certainly continued.

The reporters, the movie men, the syndicate writers, the telegraph operators shook the dust of Dayton from their feet. This monkey trial had been a good show for the front pages, but maybe it was a little too highbrow in its implications. What next? ... How about a good clean fight without any biology in it?

The year 1925 drew slowly toward its close. The *Shenandoah*—a great navy dirigible—was wrecked, and for a few days the country supped on horror. The Florida real-estate boom reached its dizziest height. And then the football season revealed what the ballyhoo technic could do for a football star. Nobody needed a course in biology to appreciate Red Grange.

The Post-War Decade was a great sporting era. More men were playing golf than ever before—playing it in baggy plus-fours, with tassels at the knee and checked stockings. There were five thousand golf-courses in the United States, there were said to be two million players, and it was estimated that half a billion dollars was spent annually on the game. The ability to play it had become a part of the almost essential equipment of the aspiring business executive. The country club had become the focus of social life in hundreds of communities. But it was an even greater era for watching sports than for taking part in them. Promoters, chambers of commerce, newspaper-owners, sports writers, press agents, radio broadcasters, all found profit in exploiting the public's mania for sporting shows and its willingness to be persuaded that the great athletes of the day were supermen. Never before had such a blinding light of publicity been turned upon the gridiron, the diamond, and the prize ring.

Men who had never learned until the nineteen-twenties the difference between a brassie and niblick grabbed their five-star editions to read about Bobby Jones's exploits with his redoubtable putter, Calamity Jane. There was big money in being a successful golf professional: Walter Hagen's income for several years ranged between forty and eighty thousand dollars, and for a time he received thirty thousand a year and a house for lending the prestige of his presence and his name to a Florida real-estate development. World's Series baseball crowds broke all records. So intense was the excitement over football that stadia seating fifty and sixty thousand people were filled to the last seat when the big teams met, while scores of thousands more sat in warm living-rooms to hear the play-by-play story over the radio and to be told by Graham McNamee that it certainly was cold on the upper rim of the amphitheater. The Yale Athletic Association was said to have taken in over a million dollars in ticket money in a single season. Teams which represented supposed institutions of learning went barn-storming for weeks at a time, imbibing what academic instruction they might on the sleeping-car between the Yankee Stadium and Chicago or between Texas and the Tournament of Roses at Pasadena. More Americans could identify Knute Rockne as the Notre Dame coach than could tell who was the presiding officer of the United States Senate. The fame of star football players, to be sure, was ephemeral compared with that of Jones in golf, or of Ruth in baseball, or of Tilden in tennis. Aldrich, Owen, Bo McMillin, Ernie Nevers, Grange, the Four Horsemen, Benny Friedman, Caldwell, Cagle, and Albie Booth all reigned briefly. But the case of Red Grange may illustrate to what heights a hero of the stadium could rise in the consulship of Calvin Coolidge, when pockets were full and the art of ballyhoo was young and vigorous.

"Harold E. Grange—the middle name is Edward—was born in Forksville, Sullivan County, Pennsylvania, on June 13, 1903," announced a publicity item sent out to the press to put the University of Illinois on the map by glorifying its greatest product. "His father, Lyle N. Grange, in his youth had been the king of lumberjacks in the Pennsylvania mountains, being renowned for his strength, skill, and daring. His mother, a sweet and lovely girl, died when 'Red' was five years old, and it was this which determined his father to move from Pennsylvania to Wheaton, Illinois.... The father, who never married again, is deputy sheriff at Wheaton."

But the publicity item (which continues in this rhapsodic tone for many a paragraph) is perhaps too leisurely. Suffice it to say that Red Grange—the "Wheaton iceman," as they called him—played football exceedingly well for the University of Illinois, so well that at the end of the season of 1925 (his senior year) he decided not to bother any further with education at the moment, but to reap the harvest of his fame. Let a series of items summarizing the telegraphic press dispatches tell the story:

Nov. 2—Grange is carried two miles by students.

Nov. 3—His football jersey will be framed at Illinois.

Nov. 11—Admirers circulate petition nominating him for Congress despite his being under age. Is silent on $40,000 offer from New York Giants for three games.

Nov. 17—Is offered $120,000 a year by real-estate firm.

Nov. 21—Plays last game with Illinois, turns professional.

Nov. 22—Signs with Chicago Bears.

Nov. 26—Plays first professional game with Bears and collects $12,000.

Dec. 6—Collects $30,000 in first New York game.

Dec. 7—Signs movie contract with Arrow Picture Corporation; may earn $100,000 by June.

Dec. 8—Is presented to President Coolidge.

The public is fickle, however. Within a few months Gertrude Ederle and the first mother to swim the English Channel were being welcomed in New York with thunderous applause. Dempsey and Tunney were preparing for their Philadelphia fight, and the spotlight had left Red Grange. Five years later he was reported to be working in a night club in Hollywood, while that other hero of the backfield, Caldwell of Yale, was running a lunchroom in New Haven. *Sic transit....*

As 1925 gave way to 1926, the searchlight of public attention had shifted from Red Grange to the marriage of Irving Berlin and Ellin Mackay, showing that the curiosity of millions is no respecter of personal privacy; to the gallant rescue of the men of the steamship *Antinoë* in mid-ocean by Captain Fried of the *President Roosevelt;* to the exclusion from the United States of Vera, Countess Cathcart, on the uncomplimentary ground of moral turpitude; to Byrd's daring flight over the North Pole; and, as the summer of 1926 arrived, to the disappearance from a bathing beach of Aimee Semple McPherson, evangelist of a Four-Square Gospel made in California—a disappearance that was to prove the first of a series of opera-bouffe episodes which for years attracted wide-eyed tourists in droves to Mrs. McPherson's Angelus Temple.

The summer passed—the summer when the English Channel was full of swimmers, and the brown jacket of *The Private Life of Helen of Troy* ornamented thousands of cottage tables, girls in knee-length skirts and horizontally striped sweaters were learning to dance the Charleston, and the Philadelphia Sesquicentennial was sinking deeper and deeper into the red despite the aid of the Dempsey-Tunney fight. Toward the season's end there was a striking demonstration of what astute press-agentry could do to make a national sensation. A young man named Rudolph Alfonzo Raffaele Pierre Filibert Guglielmi di Valentina d'Antonguolla died in New York at the age of thirty-one. The love-making of Rudolph Valentino (as he had understandably preferred to call himself) had quickened the pulses of innumerable motion-picture addicts; with his sideburns and his passionate air, "the sheik" had set the standard for masculine sex appeal. But his lying in state in an undertaker's establishment on Broadway would hardly have attracted a crowd which stretched through eleven blocks if his manager had not arranged the scenes of grief with uncanny skill, and if Harry C. Klemfuss, the undertaker's press agent, had not provided the newspapers with everything they could desire—such as photographs, distributed in advance, of the chamber where the actor's body would lie, and posed photographs of the funeral cortège. (One of these latter pictures, according to Silas Bent, was on the streets in one newspaper before the funeral procession started.) With such practical assistance, the press gave itself to the affair so wholeheartedly that mobs rioted about the undertaker's and scores of people were injured. Sweet are the uses of publicity: Valentino had been heavily in debt when he died, but his posthumous films, according to his manager's subsequent testimony, turned the debt into a $600,000 balance to the credit of his estate.

Tunney beat Dempsey, a hurricane contributed the *coup-de-grâce* to the Florida boom. Queen Marie of Rumania sniffed the profits of ballyhoo from afar and made a royal visit to the United States; and then for months on end in the winter of 1926-27 the American people waded deep in scandal and crime.

It was four long years since the Reverend Edward W. Hall and Mrs. Eleanor R. Mills had been found murdered near the crab-apple tree by DeRussey's Lane outside New Brunswick, New Jersey. In 1922 the grand jury had found no indictment. But in 1926 a tabloid newspaper in search of more circulation dug up what purported to be important new evidence and got the case reopened. Mrs. Hall was arrested—at such an unholy hour of the night that the reporters and photographers of this tabloid got a scoop—and she and her two brothers, Henry and Willie Stevens, were brought to trial, thus providing thrills for the readers not only of the tabloid in question, but of every other newspaper in the United States.

The most sensational scene in this most sensational trial of the decade took place when Jane Gibson, the "pig woman," who was supposed to be dying, was brought from her hospital to the courtroom on a stretcher and placed on a bed facing the jury. Mrs. Gibson told a weird story. She had been pestered by corn-robbers, it seemed, and on the night of the murder, hearing the rattle of a wagon that she thought might contain the robbers, she saddled Jenny, her mule, and followed the wagon down DeRussey's Lane, "peeking and peeking and peeking." She saw a car in the Lane, with two people in it whom she identified as Mrs. Hall and Willie Stevens. She tethered Jenny to a cedar tree, heard the sound of a quarrel and a voice saying, "Explain these letters"; she saw Henry and Willie Stevens in the gleam of a flashlight, she heard shots, and then she fled in terror all the way home—only to find that she had left a moccasin behind. Despite her fear, she went all the way back to get that moccasin, and heard what she thought was the screeching of an owl, but found it was a woman crying—"a big white-haired woman doing something with her hand, crying something." She said this woman was Mrs. Hall. All this testimony the "pig woman" gave from her bed in a wailing voice, while trained nurses stood beside her and took her pulse; then, crying out to the defendants, "I have told the truth! So help me God! And you know I've told the truth!" she was borne from the room.

The testimony of the "pig woman" did not gain in force from what was brought out about her previous checkered career; it would have made even less impression upon the jury had they known that their "dying witness," whose appearance in the courtroom had been so ingeniously staged, was destined to live four years more. Mrs. Hall and her brothers came magnificently through their ordeal, slow-witted Willie Stevens in particular delighting millions of murder-trial fans by the way in which he stoutly resisted the efforts of Senator Simpson to bullyrag him into confusion. The new evidence dug up by the tabloid—consisting chiefly of a calling-card which was supposed to have Willie Stevens' fingerprints on it—did not impress the jury.

But though the prosecution's case thus collapsed, the reputation of the Stevens family had been butchered to make a Roman holiday of the first magnitude for newspaper readers. Five million words were written and sent from Somerville, New Jersey, during the first eleven days of the trial. Twice as many newspaper men were there as at Dayton. The reporters included Billy Sunday, the revivalist, and James Mills, the husband of the murdered choir-singer; and the man who had claimed the mantle of Bryan as the leader of Fundamentalism, the Reverend John Roach Straton, wrote a daily editorial moralizing about the case. Over wires jacked into the largest telegraph switchboard in the world traveled the tidings of lust and crime to every corner of the United States, and the public lapped them up and cried for more.

So insistently did they cry that when, a few short months later, an art editor named Albert Snyder was killed with a sash-weight by his wife and her lover, a corset salesman named Judd Gray, once more the forces of ballyhoo got into action. In this case there was no mystery, nor was the victim highly placed; the only excuses for putting the Snyder-Gray trial on the front page were that it involved a sex triangle and that the Snyders were ordinary people living in an ordinary New York suburb—the sort of people with whom the ordinary reader could easily identify himself. Yet so great was the demand for vicarious horrors that once more the great Western Union switchboard was brought into action, an even more imposing galaxy of special writers interpreted the sordid drama (including David Wark Griffith, Peggy Joyce, and Will Durant, as well as Billy Sunday and Doctor Straton), and once more the American people tasted blood.

In the interval between the Hall-Mills case and the Snyder-Gray case, they had had a chance to roll an even riper scandal on their tongues. Frances Heenan Browning, known to the multitude as "Peaches," brought suit for separation from Edward W. Browning, a New York real-estate man who had a penchant for giving to very young girls the delights of a Cinderella. Supposedly sober and reputable newspapers recited the unedifying details of "Daddy" Browning's adventures; and when the New York *Graphic,* a tabloid, printed a "composograph" of Browning in pajamas shouting "Woof! Woof! Don't be a goof!" to his half-clad wife because—according to the caption—she "refused to parade nude," even the *Daily News,* which in the past had shown no distaste for scandal, expressed its fear that if such things went on the public would be "drenched in obscenity."

A great many people felt as the *Daily News* did, and regarded with dismay the depths to which the public taste seemed to have fallen. Surely a change must come, they thought. This carnival of commercial degradation could not continue.

The change came—suddenly.

The owner of the Brevoort and Lafayette Hotels in New York, Raymond Orteig, had offered—way back in 1919—a prize of $25,000 for the first nonstop flight between New York and Paris. Only a few days after the conclusion of the Snyder-Gray trial, three planes were waiting for favorable weather conditions to hop off from Roosevelt Field, just outside New York, in quest of this prize: the *Columbia,* which was to be piloted by Clarence Chamberlin and Lloyd Bertaud; the *American,* with Lieutenant-Commander Byrd of North Pole fame in command; and the *Spirit of St. Louis,* which had abruptly arrived from the Pacific coast with a lone young man named Charles A. Lindbergh at the controls. There was no telling which of the three planes would get off first, but clearly the public favorite was the young man from the West. He was modest, he seemed to know his business, there was something particularly daring about his idea of making the perilous journey alone, and he was as attractive-looking a youngster as ever had faced a camera man. The reporters—to his annoyance—called him "Lucky Lindy" and the "Flying Fool." The spotlight of publicity was upon him. Not yet, however, was he a god.

On the evening of May 19, 1927, Lindbergh decided that although it was drizzling on Long Island, the weather reports gave a chance of fair skies for his trip and he had better get ready. He spent the small hours of the next morning in sleepless preparations, went to Curtiss Field, received further weather news, had his plane trundled to Roosevelt Field and fueled, and a little before eight o'clock—on the morning of May 20th—climbed in and took off for Paris.

Then something like a miracle took place.

No sooner had the word been flashed along the wires that Lindbergh had started than the whole population of the country became united in the exaltation of a common emotion. Young and old, rich and poor, farmer and stockbroker, Fundamentalist and skeptic, highbrow and lowbrow, all with one accord fastened their hopes upon the young man in the *Spirit of St. Louis.* To give a single instance of the intensity of their mood: at the Yankee Stadium in New York, where the Maloney-Sharkey fight was held on the evening of the 20th, forty thousand hard-boiled boxing fans rose as one man and stood with bared heads in impressive silence when the announcer asked them to pray for Lindbergh. The next day came the successive reports of

Lindbergh's success—he had reached the Irish coast, he was crossing over England, he was over the Channel, he had landed at Le Bourget to be enthusiastically mobbed by a vast crowd of Frenchmen—and the American people went almost mad with joy and relief. And when the reports of Lindbergh's first few days in Paris showed that he was behaving with charming modesty and courtesy, millions of his countrymen took him to their hearts as they had taken no other human being in living memory.

Every record for mass excitement and mass enthusiasm in the age of ballyhoo was smashed during the next few weeks. Nothing seemed to matter, either to the newspapers or to the people who read them, but Lindbergh and his story. On the day the flight was completed the Washington *Star* sold 16,000 extra copies, the St. Louis *Post-Dispatch* 40,000, the New York *Evening World* 114,000. The huge headlines which described Lindbergh's triumphal progress from day to day in newspapers from Maine to Oregon showed how thoroughly was public agreement with the somewhat extravagant dictum of the *Evening World* that Lindbergh had performed "the greatest feat of a solitary man in the records of the human race." Upon his return to the United States, a single Sunday issue of a single paper contained one hundred columns of text and pictures devoted to him. Nobody appeared to question the fitness of President Coolidge's action in sending a cruiser of the United States navy to bring this young private citizen and his plane back from France. He was greeted in Washington at a vast open-air gathering at which the President made—according to Charles Merz—"the longest and most impressive address since his annual message to Congress." The Western Union having provided form messages for telegrams of congratulations to Lindbergh on his arrival, 55,000 of them were sent to him—and were loaded on a truck and trundled after him in the parade through Washington. One telegram, from Minneapolis, was signed with 17,500 names and made up a scroll 520 feet long, under which ten messenger boys staggered. After the public welcome in New York, the Street Cleaning Department gathered up 1,800 tons of paper which had been torn up and thrown out of windows of office buildings to make a snowstorm of greeting—1,800 tons as against a mere 155 tons swept up after the premature Armistice celebration of November 7, 1918!

Lindbergh was commissioned Colonel, and received the Distinguished Flying Cross, the Congressional Medal of Honor, and so many foreign decorations and honorary memberships that to repeat the list would be a weary task. He was offered two and a half million dollars for a tour of the world by air, and $700,000 to appear in the films; his signature was sold for $1,600; a Texas town was named for him, a thirteen-hundred-foot Lindbergh tower was proposed for the city of Chicago, "the largest dinner ever tendered to an individual in modern history" was consumed in his honor, and a staggering number of streets, schools, restaurants, and corporations sought to share the glory of his name.

Nor was there any noticeable group of dissenters from all this hullabaloo. Whatever else people might disagree about, they joined in praise of him.

To appreciate how extraordinary was this universal outpouring of admiration and love—for the word love is hardly too strong—one must remind oneself of two or three facts.

Lindbergh's flight was not the first crossing of the Atlantic by air. Alcock and Brown had flown direct from Newfoundland to Ireland in 1919. That same year the N-C 4, with five men aboard, had crossed by way of the Azores, and the British dirigible R-34 had flown from Scotland to Long Island with 31 men aboard, and then had turned about and made a return flight to England. The German dirigible ZR-3 (later known as the *Los Angeles*) had flown from Friedrichshafen to Lakehurst, New Jersey, in 1924 with 32 people aboard. Two Round-the-World American army planes had crossed the North Atlantic by way of Iceland, Greenland, and Newfoundland in 1924. The novelty of Lindbergh's flight lay only in the fact that he went all the way from New York to Paris instead of jumping off from Newfoundland, that he reached his precise objective, and that he went alone.

Furthermore, there was little practical advantage in such an exploit. It brought about a boom in aviation, to be sure, but a not altogether healthy one, and it led many a flyer to hop off blindly for foreign shores in emulation of Lindbergh and be drowned. Looking back on the event after a lapse of years, and stripping it of its emotional connotations, one sees it simply as a daring stunt flight—the longest up to that time—by a man who did not claim to be anything but a stunt flyer. Why, then, this idolization of Lindbergh?

The explanation is simple. A disillusioned nation fed on cheap heroics and scandal and crime was revolting against the low estimate of human nature which it had allowed itself to entertain. For years the American people had been spiritually starved. They had seen their early ideals and illusions and hopes one by one worn away by the corrosive influence of events and ideas—by the disappointing aftermath of the war, by scientific doctrines and psychological theories which undermined their religion and ridiculed their sentimental notions, by the spectacle of graft in politics and crime on the city streets, and finally by their recent newspaper diet of smut and murder. Romance, chivalry, and self-dedication had been debunked; the heroes of history had been shown to have feet of clay, and the saints of history had been revealed as people with queer complexes. There was the god of business to worship—but a suspicion lingered that he was made of brass. Ballyhoo had given the public contemporary heroes to bow down before—but these contemporary heroes, with their fat profits from moving-picture contracts and ghost-written syndicated articles, were not wholly convincing. Something that people needed, if they were to live at peace with themselves and with the world, was missing from their lives. And all at once Lindbergh provided it. Romance, chivalry, self-dedication—here they were, embodied in a modern Galahad for a generation which had forsworn Galahads. Lindbergh did not accept the moving-picture offers that came his way, he did not sell testimonials, did not boast, did not get himself involved in scandal, conducted himself with unerring taste—and was handsome and brave withal. The machinery of ballyhoo was ready and waiting to lift him up where every eye could see him. Is it any wonder that the public's reception of him took on the aspects of a vast religious revival?

Lindbergh did not go back on his admirers. He undertook a series of exhibition flights and good-will flights—successfully and with quiet dignity. He married a daughter of the ambassador to Mexico, and in so doing delighted the country by turning the tables on ballyhoo itself—by slipping away with his bride on a motor-boat and remaining hidden for days despite the efforts of hundreds of newspaper men to spy upon his honeymoon. Wherever he went, crowds fought for a chance to be near him, medals were pinned upon him, tributes were showered upon him, his coming and going was news. He packed away a good-sized fortune earned chiefly as consultant for aviation companies, but few people grudged him that. Incredibly, he kept his head and his instinct for fine conduct.

And he remained a national idol.

Pretty good, one reflects, for a stunt flyer. But also, one must add, pretty good for the American people. They had shown that they had better taste in heroes than anyone would have dared to predict during the years which immediately preceded the 20th of May, 1927.

DISCUSSION AND WRITING

1. Define or explain: *cause célèbre, auspices, secular, laudatory, bigotry, dictum, votary, shibboleth, anachronistic, Zeitgeist, nebulous, provincial, insidious, expunge, hinterlands, rhapsodic, opera-bouffe, coup-de-grâce, carnival.* Examine these terms for connotations and ironic overtones.

2. Examine obviously connotative phrases such as "horde of publicity agents," "intelligence-testers invaded the schools," "public's mania for sporting shows." Find other examples: How do they affect the author's tone? How essential are they to revealing his attitude toward fundamentalism, toward athletic heroes?

3. Discuss Allen's use of metaphor ("The national mind had become as never before an instrument upon which a few men could play"). Discuss his use of literary and historical allusions, paying attention to their implications and appropriateness ("country had bread, but it wanted circuses"; "consulship of Calvin Coolidge").

4. Outline the way Allen has organized and presented his material, paying special attention to the selection and order of the major examples. Which of his sentences comes closest to summing up his central thesis?

5. In one well-developed paragraph, summarize the main features of "ballyhoo."

6. The twenties and thirties saw a great deal of "debunking," with writers delighting in the exposure of false heroes, hypocritical ideals, or popular illusions. Is Allen's general attitude too negative? Cite detailed evidence in support of your answer.

7. Examine the issues of a large newspaper over a period of time to see to what extent it practices the ballyhoo technique described by Allen. Limit your evidence to one major area, such as crime, sports, disaster, or show business.

8. Examine and discuss a recent case of "mass excitement" or "mass enthusiasm."

9. Critics sometimes charge that the typical newspaper reader can get sentimental over the plight of an individual but is usually indifferent to the sufferings or deprivations of large masses of men. Study recent issues of newspapers and popular magazines to determine whether they encourage or counteract this tendency.

10. Compare and evaluate the treatment of a grave political issue or recent crisis in several major newspapers. Do newspapers provide an adequate basis for responsible political judgments on the part of their readers?

FURTHER READING

Prominent among fictional treatments of the twenties and their aftermath are the writings of F. Scott Fitzgerald: his novel *The Great Gatsby* (1925), such short stories as "The Rich Boy" and "Babylon Revisited."

6

The American Experiment

*By the simple operation of constructing government on the
principles of society and the rights of man, every difficulty
retires, and all the parts are brought into cordial unison.*
THOMAS PAINE

With many topics, the writer has a genuine chance of observing
the familiar injunction to think for himself and to see with his
own eyes. With other topics, familiar assumptions—ideas we have
heard repeated hundreds of times—make any true firsthand
generalizing extremely difficult. When we write about the meaning of the American experiment, the purposes and distinctive
qualities of our country, it becomes almost impossible not to
follow the ruts left by the untold people who have traveled the
same route. The authors in this section are exceptionally well
equipped to break down the barriers erected by familiar phrases
and ideas repeated in countless schoolbooks and speeches. J. B.
Priestley, in "Midnight in the Desert," reports on life in the
American West with the quizzical eye of a foreign traveler who
represents neither the extreme of effusive friendship nor that of
stubborn prejudice. Jacques Barzun, in "Innocents at Home,"
defends his adopted country against familiar charges, drawing on
his knowledge of his native Europe for illuminating comparison
and contrast. John A. Kouwenhoven, in "What's American about
America?", ranges over a wide collection of data in his search for
a common denominator. Lewis Mumford, in "The Romanticism
of the Pioneer," examines the role of the pioneer, and the ideas
animating and surrounding him, in order to discover important
clues to this country's national identity.

J. B. PRIESTLEY

J. B. Priestley was born in Yorkshire in 1894 and served in the British Army for five years during World War I. He became one of the most productive and most widely known of British publicists and men of letters. He has had a varied and successful career as critic, essayist, novelist, playwright, producer, and lecturer. His novel *Angel Pavement* (1930) and his play *Dangerous Corner* (1932) are some of the more familiar titles from a long list. Characteristically, he has combined an interest in literature with an active concern for social and political questions. The present selection is a chapter from an autobiographical account of a winter spent in America in 1935–36. Mr. Priestley here takes a fresh and respectful look at the American cowboy, trusting his own observation rather than the picture of the American West created by Hollywood movies and popular novelists.

Midnight in the Desert

Arizona had been first recommended to us, as a place with a superb winter climate, by John Galsworthy, who used to come here, winter after winter. I think our chosen district, near Wickenburg, between Phoenix and Prescott, and about two thousand feet high, has the best winter climate in the state, which means that it has one of the best winter climates in the world, which is notoriously short of good winter climates. There are plenty of warm moist places—almost the whole range of the tropics—but not fairly warm dry ones. Here I prophesy that as transport becomes quicker, cheaper, easier, the Wickenburg district will become increasingly important, for a winter climate as good as this will prove a better gold-mine than the Old Vulture, which Henry Wickenburg discovered while chasing his burro, ever was. In short, there's gold in them thar hills, but the best of it is the January sunshine.

The air is enchanting, quite unlike any I have known before, being crystal clear and faintly but persistently aromatic. It is this air, strongly actinic, that gives the Arizona landscape its enduring charm. Seen close at hand, there is nothing very attractive about these hills, so prickly with cactus, or the savage rocky peaks behind them. There is no foreground prettiness here, as there is in California. The vast distances do the trick. This air seems to act like a powerful stereoscopic lens. Everything far away—and you can see scores of miles—is magically molded and colored. The mountains, solidly three-dimensional ranges and peaks, are an exquisite blue in the daytime, and then turn amethyst at sunset. Things near at hand are dusty green, grayish, brownish, rather drab, but everywhere towards the far horizon rise chunks of color, unbelievably sumptuous. And the nights are even more spacious than the days. No lid of darkness is clapped over you. The spaces are wider than ever, and are lit, night after night, with all the stars of the Northern Hemisphere, as precisely defined as the stars in a planetarium. To return to England is to feel like a man who is let down into a cellar after sunset. If Shakespeare had ever seen such nights of stars, he would have gone mad trying to improve upon his "Look, how the floor of heaven is thick inlaid with patines of bright gold!" But literature does not like too much encouragement, which is why some of the best lyrical poetry, ecstatic in its praise of nature, has been written by fellows shivering and fog-bound in dark attics. No real poetry has come out of Arizona yet, and not much painting. Nature is doing it all.

Now that the bad men have shut up their last saloon and we tourists are coming into Arizona, the copy-writers in the publicity departments of the railways and the local chambers of commerce are showering their adjectives on the place and gushing over it like new oil-wells. These professional enthusiasts are ruining travel for us. No reality can hope to compete with their purple eruptions. It is no use going to a nice little picturesque place if you have already had such rhapsodies about it pumped into you. What is this real world after those shiny folders, probably called *Wondrous Trails of Sheer Romance?* One reason why even moderately intelligent people sink deeper and deeper into disillusion is that nothing now comes up to the advertisements. We know there are no such razors, such soaps, such cigars, such shoes and ships and sealing-wax. Few things are advertised at greater expense and with more cunning than travel. Any tourists' agent will give you an armful of pictures of an ideal world. The light that never was on land or sea, the consecration and the poet's dream, shine from these booklets. You can make the round trip, in solid comfort and with the nicest people, to half a dozen Utopias. Now Arizona is having its share of this glittering and deceptive nonsense. One of the mildest descriptions of it is *This Wonderland of the Great Southwest.* This is enough to make any intelligent adult regard the place with the gravest suspicion. It must be a fraud on an impudently gigantic scale. And oddly enough, it isn't. For once these descriptions have an almost scientific precision. Nothing has been exaggerated. I am not a son of the state, have not ten cents invested in it, and am not being paid to boost it. Nevertheless, I declare that Arizona really is a wonderland. You ought to enter it by floating down a rabbit-hole.

It is filled with marvels. Wizardry has been at work here. In the north, where you are a mile and a half high, there is the Grand Canyon, which is enough in itself to clear a whole continent from the charge of being dull. But you also have the Painted Deserts and the Petrified Forests. The dinosaurs left their tracks in these parts. When the giant meteor decided to imbed itself in the earth, it chose Arizona, and you may see the crater it made, near Winslow. There are great tracts of virgin forest, as well as hundreds of miles of desert. There are mysterious Indian ruins all over the place. There are strange heights called the Superstition Mountains, where men have gone to look for lost gold-mines and have never returned. There is about the whole state a suggestion of the *Arabian Nights*. Its vegetation, with the immense pillars of Saguaro cactus dominating everything else, is fantastic. Its rocks hide treasures of gold, opals, and rubies, and are covered with ancient writing, perhaps Indian symbols for *Open Sesame*. Its moon, stars, and mountain peaks seem to be burnished by *genii*. Sinbad might have once passed this way, and there may come a morning when a riding-party will find a new valley and there disturb the Roc himself.

The old-timers here—the stringy old cowboys still rolling their cigarettes— the withered and dusty prospectors sitting by their piles of empty beancans— sound like the most stupendous liars, but you cannot be sure that they are not indulgently descending into the truth, for anything might have happened, and still might happen, in this vast empty state. Take the wrong turning here one morning, and you might never be heard of again. But what might happen to you, nobody knows. The clever fellows who sit in Chicago writing those *Wonderland of the Southwest* railway folders, thinking how cunningly they are taking us in again, do not know the half of it. One day they will come and lose themselves in Arizona, and be heard screaming among the hills for new and impossible adjectives. The Baghdad barber and all his six brothers will turn up here, sooner or later, and Scheherazade herself will be discovered in the beauty parlor of the Adams Hotel, Phoenix. It is not for nothing that the capital of the state is called Phoenix. And if this town does not match your mood, you can try Yuma and Buckeye, Ajo and Nogales and Tombstone. This was the last state to enter the Union, and if it is not the most fantastic of them all, I will eat my hat and it shall be a ten-gallon Stetson.

It was here in Arizona that I first met cowboys. Many of these cowboys now spend more time taking parties of ranch guests out for a morning ride than they do in rounding up cattle. Nevertheless, they are genuine cowboys.

As a rule they have known nothing but ranch life, and they have all the accomplishments of the legendary cowboy, except perhaps that famous marksmanship with a Colt. When not at work they practice for forthcoming rodeos or entertain themselves, and you, with that melancholy music, those long lugubrious strains, for which all men who lead an active open-air life seem to have a strange passion. Sedentary men may need gay cynical little tunes, but the cowboy, the sailor, the soldier, and their kind, ask for nothing better than a gloomy ballad of true love cut short by early death. The cowboy, who is a man of tradition, keeps the traditional tone in song, an odd and rather nasal little tone, which would drive any singing-master mad but somehow pleases the rest of us.

And like all healthy primitive males, the cowboy is a dressy fellow. Most of his pay still goes, as it always did, in tremendous hats and high-heeled boots, in belts and saddles and gaudy shirts. He is a peacock of a chap, unimpressed by any defeatist urban nonsense about quiet, respectable, drab clothes. The male in his natural state likes to show off, to blind the coy female, to stun her into admiration; and that is the cowboy.

He has the luck to live in a simple world. There are certain things he must be able to do well, or it is all up with him, and they cannot be faked, as politicians and professional men and directors of companies so often fake things. He cannot pretend to ride and rope, and get away with it. He has to be able to ride and rope really well, and to do a few other things, too; but once he has acquired the necessary skill, and the courage and endurance that match it, all is well with him. He lives a natural healthy life in a healthy uncomplicated world. He does not go to bed to worry himself sick about what the public, the debenture-holders, the board of directors, the departmental boss, will say. He does not feel like a piece of straw in a whirlpool. He does not grow fat and apoplectic, or thin and cancerous, at a desk, wondering what exactly it is that has wasted his manhood. He has not much money, but then neither has he many taxes, mortgages, insurance policies, and doctors' bills. If he has a wife, she does not regard him as a sagging, moody fraud of a fellow, whose mysterious and probably contemptible activities during the day have robbed him of all bright masculine virtue; but she knows exactly what he has to do, and respects him for the obvious skill and courage he brings to his tasks. If he has young children, he shines in their sight as a wise hero, and is therefore the perfect father. His life may be infinitely narrower than that of a saint or a philosopher, an artist or a scientist, but can it be said to be any narrower than the existences of all those pale-faced millions who go day after day to factories, warehouses, offices, and shops, the victims of all the cunningly deployed forces of publicity and salesmanship, of rubber-stamp opinions and artificially stimulated wants?

He is at peace with himself because his work allows free play to the strongest instincts of man. Unlike so many other men, he has not to pretend to be a short-sighted, deaf cripple all day to earn his living, and then to try and catch up with himself as a vital human being during the short hours of leisure allotted to him. His work is not without danger, and he is sustained by a sense of this, knowing that he has a certain fundamental dignity. This is true of other kinds of men, such as the miner and the sailor, men who are shabbily treated by the community they serve, but are often inwardly sustained by their sense of being engaged in an heroic calling. This is joined in the cowboy to an outward picturesqueness and a magnificent stage-setting.

There is still a good book to be written about the legend of the heroic West and the cowboy. The author would have to be a social philosopher as well as an historian. The legend has not been with us long. That West had a very short history. It did not begin until the 'sixties, and its Homeric age was over before the century ended. It was created by a passing set of economic circumstances, by cheap open grazing-land in the Southwest, and good prices on the hoof in Kansas City. It could not survive the invention of barbed wire. Yet what a legend it has created!

Cheap melodrama, whether in fiction, plays, or films, soon claimed that legend; yet there always remains a faint gleam of Homeric poetry, not in the monotonous and incredible fables of very good men and very bad men and doll-like heroines, but in the enduring image they give us of a man riding in the wilderness of desert and mountain, the solitary heroic figure. Here is one who seems to have escaped the economic slavery and universal degradation of our time; who does not compete except with charging animals and the hostile elements; who is seen as the strong free male, careless and smiling and bronzed, that essential male for whom all women have a tenderness. He is a man of our world who has contrived to live his life in an epic simplicity impossible to the rest of us, caught in a bewildering tangle of interests and loyalties.

All this is more than enough to explain the flood of popular stories, plays, and films about the cowboy. They are not so good as he was or still is. There has rarely been a genuine artistic impulse behind these things. The material has nearly always been better than the workmen. Indeed, many of the workmen have had no respect for the material, turning it into so much commercial hokum. Thus, the cowboy and his West, the whole sunlit legend, have been cynically distilled into what the more impatient and austere critics of our society call "dope." The heroic free man, they will tell us, has been used to stupefy the enslaved masses. This is true. But we must ask ourselves what disease it is that these masses are suffering from that demands this particular form of dope. Are they entranced by the cowboy simply because they do not own the means of production, because they belong to the exploited proletariat, because the profits of their factories are being handed over to capitalist shareholders? Change all this, and does this wistful admiration of the cowboy vanish at once? I doubt it.

The disease is not so easily diagnosed. It is less general and superficial, more personal to each man and woman, cutting deeper into the psychic; though I will readily admit that the make-up of our personalities owes more to economic and political conditions, capable of being completely changed in a few years, than most of us care to acknowledge. A free people, no longer feeling obscurely but deeply that their lives were undignified, unheroic, a waste of manhood, but conscious of the fact that every stone they lifted would be set in its place in the city wall, would smile with pleasure at the sight of the lean graceful cowboy, but would not hunger for every doped confection offered under his name. Yet I believe some wistfulness would remain; the men with the machines, in their air-conditioned factories, would be haunted by the vague image of the man with the horse and the camp fire.

From the first moment we met the cowboy and his folk we were impressed by their manners. While you are still a stranger, the cowboy observes with you an almost Spanish punctilio. His polite questions have an air of grave concern. He does not, in the actors' term, "throw away" his *Please* and *Thank you*. He listens carefully to what you have to say, and may be brief but is never offhand in his replies. His manners are very much like those of old-fashioned Americans in most parts of the country.

It is odd that American men are so frequently presented in European caricatures of the type, in fiction, plays, and films, as being extremely ill-mannered, loud, rough customers. Such Americans exist, of course, just as sneering Englishmen, bullying Teutons, insolent Latins, also exist. But it has always seemed to me that American manners in general tend to err on the side of formality and solemnity. They are rather like those of elderly English dons and clergymen. The ordinary English are much more casual. We do not take enough trouble, for example, with our introductions. Terrified of appearing pompous, we hastily mumble names, or hastily accept a mumble instead of names, so that our introductions do not serve their purpose, and often, not knowing to whom we are talking, we saunter into the most dreadful traps. The deliberate ceremony that most Americans make of introductions protects them from these dangers and errors.

I think the Far Western manner with strangers is like that which was common among all cultivated persons in the Eastern States a generation or two ago. But unless you deliberately make yourself unpleasant, you are not a stranger long in the West. The shell of grave formality is soon pierced, especially when the visitor is a man; and once you are through you find that the rancher and the cowboy are hearty and merry and easy in their manners. They live in a world of first names and nicknames: Jack and Smoky, Shorty and Hank. Where the older West still lingers, as it does around Wickenburg, where we have stayed, you have a pleasant glimpse of that classless society about which we hear so much now. The equality may be an illusion, but the manners do not hint at any suspicions of inferiority and superiority. To return to England, after a few months of this, is like dropping back into the feudal system.

Many Americans, usually people who have money and leisure, take to English country-house life as ducks to water, and tell us how enchanted they are by the good manners they find in this fading world of aristocratic land-owners and hat-touching tenants, and how delighted they are to have left behind their native democracy of bad manners. But if they had moved West—which would have been more sensible than coming to England to play charades all day—they might have discovered there a democracy of good manners. It is made up, as all such societies will have to be, of people who are reasonably sure of themselves, easy in their own minds, not galled by feelings of inferiority, and are ready to take others as they find them. And I prefer a classless society in which you are Smoky and he is Hank and I am Jack, to one in which we are all official comrades. I would rather be Mr. Priestley first, then Jack afterwards, than Comrade Priestley all the time. In fact, I don't want to be Comrade Priestley at all.

Thinking, then, of all those Arizona people around me, fast asleep while I smoked and ruminated in my hut, I considered—not too pompously, I hope—the little classless society they had temporarily evolved. How had they achieved this appearance of happy equality? There are not many of them, of course, and they all live very close to the desert and the mountains, and might still be called pioneers. There are no great inequalities of income or privilege. If most of these people sat down to the same dinner, some would not feel they were feasting while others felt they were fasting. There are few rags, fewer diamonds. The conventional Western clothes, adapted to the climate and to the conditions of work and play, are almost like a uniform, in spite of the cowboy's native dandyism; and this helps, too.

I sorted out these reasons not because I had any pretensions to be a social analyst of Western life, not because of any interest I had in that part of the world, but because the general problem seemed important. I had read and heard a good deal about it. We are always being offered systems of reform or revolution that will promptly remove all inequalities. The Communists talk to us about their classless society. We must remember, though, that they are thinking in terms of the Marxian dialectic and are referring to a world seen as a highly simplified economic structure. But obviously there can still be classes, and with them all the bitterness of inequality, even when the means of production have passed into the keeping of the state. In Russia, I gather, there is as yet no pretense of real equality. The old class distinctions have gone, but a new set, even more iron-bound, has taken their place. Because the Party official, occupying an important position, is not paid any more than most people, that does not prove he is no better off than they are; he may be given a number of pleasant things that would have to be bought and paid for in other countries. I have heard Bernard Shaw argue eloquently against the smallest inequalities in income, and demonstrate that anything short of a genuine equality of pay all around will keep us entangled in this sticky web of money, and poison all our relations with one another. But Shaw appears to believe in privilege. And this will not do. He has never lived in a society in which money did not mean much but privilege meant a great deal. And I have. I served over four and half years in the army, where money does not count for much and privilege, carefully adjusted according to rank and then very strongly enforced, counts for a lot. A wealthy private soldier is not allowed to be insolent to a poor officer. Money might bribe a little promotion, but that is all. Whereas there is a tremendous difference between what a private soldier is allowed to do and what a general is allowed to do. And to my mind this is far more galling than any difference of income, provided that that difference is above a certain level. Once the low level is raised, from starvation to decent comfort, the inequalities do not seem to me to matter very much. Henry Ford and the Duke of Westminster have more money that I can ever hope to have, but as I am not poor myself, have not to wonder where the next meal is coming from, I have never wasted a single second envying either of them.

This does not mean that I cannot see that an immensely rich man may have far more power than any private person in a so-called democracy has any right to possess, just as if he owned an army or navy of his own. But that is a different argument, belonging to politics and economics. What I maintain is that as soon as everybody has a little more than enough to live on decently, we should be better off with what inequalities of income there may be left than we should be with equal incomes under a system of state privilege, organized with military precision. Thus—to take a small example —most seats at the opera are expensive, and it may be said that as conditions are now in America or England, attendance at the opera is one of the privileges of the rich. Smith has a passion for opera and is not rich. What can he do? The answer is that it is hard luck, but that it might be worse, for at least he can save enough to buy an occasional seat. But under an equal-income-and-state-privilege system, though opera seats might cost nothing at all, they also might be strictly allotted as perquisites to members of one or two privileged classes, and if Smith—who may be always out of luck—did not happen to belong to those classes, he would never get near the opera. In England during the war, when Smith was a private soldier, he was never allowed, when in uniform, to enter the more comfortable rooms in many taverns. Now that he is out of uniform, he can at least decide for himself whether the extra comfort is worth the extra penny or so he will have to pay for his drink in the better room.

In short, equal income severely tempered by privilege would not enlarge, but further restrict, the liberty of the individual. What is needed is a juster distribution of wealth with as little privilege as possible. Owing to certain local and temporary conditions, a state like Arizona comes nearer to achieving this than the older communities do, with the result that it seems far nearer to our idea of a free and happy democracy.

DISCUSSION AND WRITING

1. Define or explain: *notorious, amethyst, sumptuous, ecstatic, eruption, rhapsody, consecration, opal, lugubrious, sedentary, defeatist, debenture, apoplectic, deploy, melodrama, stupefy, wistful, confection, punctilio, caricature, Teuton, don* (*n.*), *feudal.*

2. Examine the literary and mythological allusions. Explain "Homeric age," "Homeric poetry," and "epic simplicity" as applied to the American West and the cowboy's life. Explain the references to *Scheherazade, Open Sesame,* and *Phoenix.* How, in spite of a serious theme and the use of literary and sociological terminology, does the author maintain informality of tone?

3. Examine the initial paragraphs as examples of descriptive writing. Identify and illustrate features that make for graphic or effective description.

4. Throughout, the author makes use of comparison and contrast to clarify his points. Discuss characteristic examples.

5. What are the major qualities Mr. Priestley ascribes to the American cowboy? How valid or convincing is his account of them? Examine the order in which the cowboy's characteristics are introduced. What, if any, is the principle of organization or the strategy of presentation?

6. Does the author avoid the pitfalls often encountered in this kind of writing? Is he aware of the common temptations to hasty generalization, stereotyping, oversimplification? Examine the relationship between his general statements and specific example, between abstract idea and concrete personal experience.

7. Define or explain the term *Marxian dialectic.* What are the author's political preferences or sympathies, and how are they related to his topic? (Mr. Priestley's comments on social and political matters were first published in 1937. Do they seem dated?)

8. Compare and contrast the picture of the cowboy drawn by Priestley with that familiar to you from Western fiction, movies, or television dramas.

9. Have you ever observed or experienced a way of life that allows one "to live in a simple world" or that allows "free play to the strongest instincts of man"? Is such a way of life necessarily a thing of the past?

10. Write an essay on the characteristic manners of today's high-school or college student. Make use of detailed reference to actual people and incidents.

FURTHER READING

European travelers who have recorded their impressions of American life range from Charles Dickens to Simone de Beauvoir and Raymond Leopold Bruckberger. Report on a recent book in which a European writer or intellectual discusses his experiences in the United States. A convenient paperback collection of extracts from the reports of nineteenth-century European travelers is *America through Foreign Eyes: 1827–1842*, edited by Roland Bartel and Edwin R. Bingham (1956).

JACQUES BARZUN

Jacques Barzun, born in Paris in 1907, came to the United States at the age of twelve and has spent most of his adult life as student, teacher, and administrator at Columbia University. He has published several books on the intellectual and cultural backgrounds of modern society. Among his books on aspects of the current scene, *Teacher in America* (1945) and *The House of Intellect* (1960) have been widely read. "An American by law and by choice," he has described himself as a student of European history who since he came to these shores "has not ceased to observe with sympathy and wonder the civilization on both sides of the Atlantic." Mr. Barzun has been a vigorous defender of contemporary American civilization against charges ranging from "dollar imperialism" to "lack of culture." At the same time, he has shown himself seriously concerned with the price Americans pay for social equality and a high standard of living in increasing mechanization and standardization. The following are the opening pages of *God's Country and Mine*, first published in 1954.

Innocents at Home

The way to see America is from a lower birth about two in the morning. You've just left a station—it was the jerk of pulling out that woke you—and you raise the curtain a bit between thumb and forefinger to look out. You are in the middle of Kansas or Arizona, in the middle of the space where the freight cars spend the night and the men drink coffee out of cans. Then comes the signal tower, some bushes, a few shacks and—nothing. You see the last blue switch-light on the next track, and beyond is America—dark and grassy, or sandy, or rocky—and no one there. Nothing but the irrational universe with you in the center trying to reason it out. It's only ten, fifteen minutes since you've left a thriving town but life has already been swallowed up in that ocean of matter which is and will remain as wild as it was made.

Come daylight, the fear vanishes but not the awe or the secret pleasure. It is a perpetual refreshment to the soul to see that the country is so large, so indifferent to the uses we have put it to, so like a piece of the earth's crust and unlike any map. No names on it, no lines, no walls with guns through them. It is good that in this place at least there is more of just plain territory per square mile than anywhere else in the civilized world. Europe is lovely but it looks like a poodle cut—the trees are numbered, the flat parts divided like a checkerboard, the rivers as slim and well-behaved as the mercury in a thermometer. The towns, like dead men's bones on the line of a caravan, huddle white and dry, crowded behind defenses that have crumbled. And everywhere the steeples point to remind you that you must look upward if you want space and serenity.

Here space is ubiquitous, even on the Atlantic Coast, which by the country's own scale is shriveled and thick with human beings. But even here we have space enough to swallow up the worst signs of our busy nonchalance, the car dumps. And even here we refuse to follow the ways of the citified: suburban street signs leave you in the lurch, and houses forget or conceal their separate numbers. Nearby the wilderness exists and has been kept: the Adirondacks are a paradise of woods and waterfalls and luxuriant vegetation—and yet it's only a small state preserve for city campers playing Indians with canoes and grocery-store pemmican. The sand dunes of Cape Cod are as accessible and linked with city life as any suburb, yet they stretch most of the time as empty as the desert, and they are moved by giant storms that feel like the last shaping flick of the Creator's thumb.

Starting from the greatest city in the world, almost invisible on a fair-sized map of the continent, one must push the wheels for three quarters of a day before reaching the midland seas that are the country's crown. By that point, too, one has traveled but a short distance away (as soil and spirit mark it) from America's European shore. Clock time has moved one hour back to wait for the sun, and the world perspective has somewhat changed. The doings of other men on the rim of the vast saucer in whose hollow one stands do begin to seem remote. The space on all sides dwarfs the subdivisions that are so real to the many millions beyond the seas. From America's rich gestating center south of the Great Lakes, one seems merely to overhear the world while one broods on the permanent functions of the earth. And yet that center is not central. Like the human heart, the Middle West is to one side of the median line. To really find the west there is still the Mississippi to ford, the long plains to cross, the Rockies to climb and five, six other chains to pass over, with deserts between, before going down into the last valley and reaching the country's Asiatic shore. The clocks have turned back twice again for the slow sun, and the traveler who has been drinking space is reeling.

The memory cannot hold all he has seen, for there is no common measure between the human senses and the unfolded spectacle. Quick variety—yes, we have nets fine enough to catch and retain that. But variety on a cosmic scale is beyond us. We can name the valleys, mountains, and gorges but we hardly know them. Anywhere in the world we hold our breath at moments of beauty and unexpectedness. But we cannot hold our breath for the hundred miles of endlessly renewed beauty in the Feather River Canyon. We probably give up and call it dull, but we only are hiding the truth from ourselves. Any stretch before us makes us stare and hold our breath again. Even the wastes and crags, the wreckage of the furnace days in those gray workshops of nature where it seems as if the fairer regions had been forged, are transcendently beautiful. The eighteen thousand square miles of the Great Basin in Oregon show nothing but dun palisades sloping backwards into flats of broken rocks—once the scene of unimaginable upheavals, now dedicated to carrying into the abyss, by means of its underground rivers, the broken particles of the split atom.

Magnificent, but is it art? Certainly not. Art follows rules based on our tiny comprehension. Art has to be comfortable for family men and women's clubs. None of America was made to *please*. It was made perhaps to satisfy a Worker in the Sublime, who knew that by heaping up triumphs on a grand scale he would successfully escape detection. Every region, every state, has its mystery, its defiance of probability—the colors of the Southwest, the virtuosity of desert life, the immense salt sea, the giant redwoods, the lake that won't freeze (though miles up in a crater) and that stays fresh (though without visible outlet) ... When you think you've reached the end there is more—miles more—the source and the image of our abundance.

Only, in order to excuse so much exuberance of imagination, the Workman buried a treasure somewhere in the middle of his plot, and toward this he enticed men by decorating with small restful shapes and sights, in familiar greens and browns, the coast nearest the supply of active men.

At the same time, the artificer kept the weather congenial to his own robust frame and violent fancy. The solemn scientificos who call any spot in the United States part of the Temperate Zone are kidding. A change of thirty degrees between sunup and sundown, repeated without warning of season fifty times a year; highs of 90° to 120° in summer, with natural steam provided free; lows of zero and less in winter, with snowfalls and blizzards and ice-storms—none of these can be called temperate except in the sense of tempering. If they don't kill, they give a steel-like elasticity to the constitution.

But although the country is fertile, almost tropical in vegetation and rich in minerals, its food is bland. Everything that grows here is large but not luscious. The juices are not concentrated—as if to discourage self-indulgence through the belly. And just as there are but few delicate, man-size landscapes, so there is a lack of concentrated drama in the mountains. We have nothing like the Alps. Our bareness is diffuse, it is diluted—once again—in space. Our overwhelming masses of mountain timber are unbroken by any grassy islands that might give the scale through man's taking his cattle there. Our pure rock and eternal snows are remote, instead of rising from the midst of our daily life.

True, we can show stunning contrasts. The evergreen slopes around Lake Tahoe make a beautiful discord with the watery mass fringed by pale flowers. But the presence of man is not felt, even when you see him there relaxing from the toil of getting his Reno divorce nearby. The place keeps aloof, untouchable. The drama, so familiar elsewhere, of man master and victim of nature, is absent. Man here seems neither master nor victim but something which is at once more and less. He has not grown into and around the primal scene, but has either left it primitive or replaced it entirely by civilization. Maybe this is why he remains so innocent, his sense of struggle unembittered. The symbol of our relation to nature is the National Park, the State Reservation, where we go on purpose to see aboriginal America, and our amusement is to play at the hunting and fishing life with all the contraptions of technology at hand. Nature is not our context or background but solely our raw material and—for recreation—our plaything.

All this has a meaning that only those who live here can comprehend. Man on this continent does not "show" because he did not start primitive with it. He came prepared. And yet the task of establishing himself was so vast that the individual man who could typify the effort did not count. The saga had to be lived so many times that the single hero, the outstanding name, is lost in the mass. America was possessed and civilized by the mass; it was a community enterprise from the start, in which the leader leads and does not dominate. Even our discoverer bears a generic name: Cristobal Colón: The Colonizer. The feats of conquest and settlement were as memorable as any in history or legend, but being commanded wholesale by necessity they grew commonplace. Who remembers the amazing life of Dr. Marcus Whitman, except schoolboys in Walla Walla? What of David Thompson, John McLoughlin, Elijah White? John Jacob Astor lives in memory not by his strenuous deeds, but by his descendants' leisure. We all know Pike's Peak because of the jingle and the slogan, but who was Pike? One in a million can tell you that this youthful hero's first name was Zebulon, but whatever history says, tradition says no more.

True, it raises haunting visions to discover from a sign outside a gas station at Murphy, North Carolina, that here De Soto and his men encamped in 1540. One can imagine the swampy ground sloping toward the river—under the present concrete and asphalt that stretches to the bridge.

But for the ordinary traveler the reminiscence is barren. De Soto is a car and so is La Salle. They do not live in our imagination, for what they did many others did also, unknown soldiers of the conquest. There is no disloyalty in recognizing that by the very essence of America's greatness there can be no *national* American history as there is English or French history. What we have is state and county history rich, varied, and of the utmost liveliness and reality; complete with feuds, aristocrats, disasters, and leading roles. But on the greater scene the telling incidents and towering figures are simply not there. They may have existed but they have been dissolved away, not by time but by space and numbers.

You will say with some justice that I exaggerate. Yes, in early days, when America was still a colony of Europe, we can easily discern the great men, the chief founding fathers, but they live in us as myths and symbols rather than as flesh-and-blood people with distinct passions and errors, or cruel egos and dreadful deaths. Washington, Franklin, Hamilton, and Jefferson are wonderful legends—who will ever know or believe all that Jefferson did?— but match these names with Alexander Borgia, Henry VIII, Luther, or Napoleon, and our heroes pale into unreality. For one thing, they have no wickedness to speak of. All we can muster as villians are Benedict Arnold and Aaron Burr—a pitiful showing of borderline cases. Lincoln alone is vivid because in spite of his amazing saintliness he embodies the meaning of what happened here. He signifies not one great man, or even Man, but mankind—anonymous, humble and irresistible like the sweep of the Father of Waters.

What happened here on this enormous expanse of intact wildness is that mankind got out from under and spread out. From under what? From under the lid—everybody, from under all the lids—kings, churches, aristocracies, landlords, the military caste, the burgher class, the lawyers, the lesser nobility, the petty bourgeoisie—the piles of subclasses on top of subclasses that formed the structure of old Europe. They left an old world to stretch their limbs and spread out flat, with only the sky above them. Their goal was space. When the Eastern end thickened into layers for a new social pyramid, the underlayers slid out again to the West.

At first, a good many of the upper orders came over too, but they rarely kept their hold. The Revolution put an end to the English and Tory ruling class. If some of them salvaged their goods they remained as well-to-do citizens and that is all. Who can name offhand anybody descended from a colonial governor or bishop or major general? The connection, if known, would scarcely affect one's behavior toward him or his place in the community. It would be just a curious fact, possibly as funny as the "fact" that Theodore Roosevelt, according to the chart in his old house, was descended from Richard the Lion-Hearted. It is true that some of our leading citizens take genealogies very gravely. It's a thriving industry to dig them out of churchyards with the aid of a vaulting imagination. But pedigree has seldom helped any American to get elected mayor or to sell insurance; the Fuller Brush man does not introduce himself as a Son of the War of 1812—ask any ten people what the Order of Cincinnati is. Americans may love getting together in costumed brotherhoods, but these impress the membership much more than the nation.

The same is true of the social cliques that keep their barriers high. Movement in and out of these groups is constant, and their exclusivism is largely convivial—who goes to whose parties. It does not decide who runs corporations, schools, city government or anything else of importance. In fact, for all official and a good many unofficial posts, society manners and ways of speech are a handicap. Nor are the professions here encumbered by social pretensions as they still are abroad. Look at the names of our judges, doctors, scientists, men of letters, and university presidents. They do not have to be Cabot or Vanderhoof or Vere de Vere. They can be anything, pronounceable or not.

All of which says nothing against the proud inheritors of good old names. It only says something far more impressive for all the rest—which is that this country was peopled by underdogs, refugees, nobodies, and that it keeps on being run by them. The noble ancestors of the American people were, with negligible exceptions: starving peasants, poor mechanics, domestic servants, younger sons without prospects, unlucky youths who had to leave town in a hurry, adventurers and shady characters of all sorts—convicts too, for that matter—any kind of man or woman who for some reason found living in Europe intolerable. That also means, of course, men of faith and education who resented tyranny of one sort or another, like the original Puritans of 1620, the French Huguenots of 1685, the Liberal Germans of 1848 who wanted constitutional government, the Irish, driven by famine and hatred of England, and young nationals from all over who fled military service.

To say all this is nothing new. We know, the whole world knows, that the American people is in its origin a sampling of the peoples of Western Europe. America began by being the haven of the disinherited—the underside of Europe—and then two providential events took place. First, the Industrial Revolution broke out and destroyed the immemorial connection of wealth and power with land. Next, the search for new wealth from industry, mining, and railroads led the American capitalists of the nineteenth century to import labor from any and everywhere, of all colors and kinds, good or bad, literate or illiterate. In doing this they made the United States the testing ground of the possibility of mankind living together.

I harp on the idea of mankind because it is a sign of the future, not an exaggeration of the accomplished past. To begin with, we have here a complete Europe—Swedes cheek by jowl with Armenians, Hungarians with Poles, Germans with French, English with Italians, Jews with Christians,

Orthodox Greek with Baptists, and so on ad infinitum. No one can say that all is love and kisses in this grand mixture. In many a town there are two sides of the railroad track and on one side the poorer group, very likely ethnic in character, is discriminated against. But at what a rate these distinctions disappear! In Europe a thousand years of war, pogroms, and massacres settle nothing. Here two generations of common schooling, inter-marriage, ward politics, and labor unions create social peace.

Now turn from Europe to the world. The greed of the planters brought over the ancestors of our 15 million Negroes; that of the railroad builders brought the Chinese, by the tens of thousands, and the hundreds of thousands from Southern Europe, the Balkans, Greece, Asia Minor, and Russia. Not long after, at the end of our Spanish War, in came Puerto Ricans, Hawaiians, Filipinos, and Japanese. The Mexicans on our South-western border had long been drawn in for a similar exploitation. And the Indians we had always with us, from the days when we robbed them, killed them, and cheated them out of their ancestral lands.

That part by itself is not a pretty picture: we are only now and very slowly beginning to right a few of those wrongs. But the dark shadows are not all there is to see. We often overlook the real sweep of our democracy because we fail to add together what we know in fragments. We ignore the panorama and consider every item for our own ends or from our own tastes. We praise this and condemn that without noticing the connections and the meaning, and fail to see mankind all around us. We just read with curiosity the feature story that says Louisiana uses the Code Napoléon; that the Pennsylvania Dutch publish their own paper in their own inimitable English (this in a region they share with the descendants of their former persecutors); and that part of the ruling family of Tibet is now living in Baltimore. We never think that in loosing and mixing the masses we have all been civilized by the rubs and collisions—civilized not only from the top down, but from all parts interacting on one another, the humble teaching the proud in the literal way of the Gospels. It has proved a peculiar civilizing of the feelings for which there is as yet no name. But it is genuine and it is going on: the late war has for the hundredth time amplified our kaleido-scopic pattern of peoples, tongues, costumes, ideas, and religions.

All this has been, not automatic, but in the larger sense unplanned. How else could it have been, considering the steady dumping of the world's forgotten men—or surplus life—over here? The appearance of chaos is therefore true and important, though not in the way it is usually interpreted. We miss the central point if we think that great ideas like democracy become reality the way a blueprint becomes a car or a house, by an orderly arrangement of parts. Luck or Providence must intervene. And we must not expect the outcome to show perfect proportions frozen into place. History is movement, disarray as well as desirable direction. If the country had remained predominantly agricultural, the first comers would have taken all the land and kept down the rest of us as men had done elsewhere for seven thousand years. Once more a thin tough crust, with a deep-dish pie of human beings underneath. But every man's idea of escape to personal liberty, before or after he got here, combined with the needs of the industrial system to start an irresistible drive towards equalizing conditions. It is that drive, greater than any ideal of progress or party of resistance, that moves the world today, and we call it democracy.

This definition is no doubt incomplete. Every educated man who is a democrat at heart thinks first of the guarantees a true democracy gives to the individual—the vote, free speech, and free assembly. But most men outside the Western world are still largely indifferent to such rights. They want food, clothes, and shelter first and at all costs. Hence the dictatorships that trade on this desire by offering, say, a half-democracy, the democracy of rough equality. Here in America the thoughtful are properly concerned and most likely to dwell reproachfully on inequalities in wealth and opportunity, on injustices to unprotected persons and groups, on attempts to scoop up our individual rights and toss them to the winds of demagoguery. But while we resist being despoiled we must not lose faith in our combined industrial and emotional democracy. I call by that name our unpremeditated scheme which has an interest in pushing towards equality and fair treatment because that is the way we've learned to feel and because the scheme requires that we sell goods and keep our machinery going.

To those who decry this as "mere materialism" one need only ask when and where the world has seen a whole nation developing the habit, the tendency, of continually looking out for those who in one way or another are left out. We act abundantly on this strange motive, but let us be modest and call it but a tendency. If we had achieved the perfection of utopia and complete brotherhood, there would be nothing to talk about. Yet look at the subjects of unceasing agitation in our daily press: the rights of labor in bargaining, the fight for fair employment practices, for socialized medicine, against discrimination in Army and Navy, in colleges and hospitals, in restaurants, and places of public entertainment; in a word, the abolition of irrational privilege.

Millions, it is true, are against change. They condemn tryranny and act it out in their small, very small way. Inconsistency and resistance are to be expected. When one talks of mankind and its emergence on our soil, one must visualize men, not angels. But whatever the creature visualized one must not compare its behavior with an abstract ideal. One must compare it with the behavior of other men in the past. In the light of that contrast, it can be said that here in America, in spite of the vast problem of absorbing repeated injections of the world's peoples, the prevailing idea for a century has been, not the segregation or neutralization of these foreign bodies, but the abolition of differences, the equalizing of conditions. The reality in turn has taught the lesson that mankind is an inescapable fact. Instead of saying "Down with *them!* No, not *those!* Off with their heads!" we have not been afraid to take mankind out of hiding where we can look at it and deal with it as best we can, for the most part decently. There has been nothing like it since the wonderful hodgepodge of the late Roman Empire, and even there the common citizenship was theoretical and inoperative in far greater degree than it is with us.

One must immediately add that we have a thousand imperfections to blush for, heart-rending failures of justice manifested in lynchings, anti-Semitism, and racketeering; in cruelty to immigrants, to lunatics, to Indians, and to children. But before we rouse our energies to combat error we should from time to time restore our courage by taking in the whole scene, not in a detached but in a voluntarily calm spirit. The very things that upset us can be a source of strength, for aside from the effort to stem injustice and repress the oppressors, what is *the* most insistent theme of private mail and public press, of government posters and noncommercial ads, on radio and TV? Can it be denied that in a hundred different forms that theme is the fate of our fellow men? Floods break out along the Missouri or tornadoes in New England—the Red Cross is there and Federal and State aid pouring in. A polio epidemic—it's a rush of experts, nurses, and serum. The refugees, war brides, and homeless children from abroad, as well as our own minority groups, have not only spokesmen but disinterested outsiders who clamor ceaselessly into our ears that we help them bodily or fight for their rights: The native-born Japanese, cruelly displaced during the war, must be re-located. Farmers who have exhausted their soil must be allotted new lands and taught how to use them. We don't stop with the able-bodied. The blind, the paraplegics, the alcoholics, the insane, the sufferers from hookworm and deficiency diseases, those who lack dental care or eyeglasses, children without lunches—it's an endless round of reminders and requests. It's prenatal care for the unborn, vacations and play centers for the street boys, rehabilitation for victims of cerebral palsy or T.B., for the neurotic and sclerotic, cure for the venereal, employment for the ex-convicts, and occupational therapy for the jailed and the delinquent. You see business trucks carrying posters to say that the particular firm is ready to hire handicapped workers, and where these should apply for the names of other firms. Anyone who is hurt, anyone who feels or is inferior has a claim. One learns, for instance, by direct letter from a state senator, that there are half a million mentally retarded children in New York state alone. What is wanted is money for special schools, workships, clinics, and camps, so that this one three-hundredth of the national population will not turn into so many unhappy derelicts but men and women like the rest of us.

This is at last moral philosophy in action. We are no longer allowed to say

"Let the devil take the hindmost"; we say: "How can we bring these creatures into the fold?" No misfortune natural or acquired is any longer a bar to our sympathy or a sufficient cause for dismissal by the social conscience. We face all types of misery and misfitness and proclaim that they are equally entitled to our help, because mankind is what we aim to save. The first thing democracy has to be is inclusive. We worry about childhood, youth, the newly married, the middle-aged, the retired, the very old. We don't let God carry the burdens or the blame, *we* take them on. We don't let the kindly rich do a hand-to-mouth job of individual charity that perpetuates the evil, we try to organize the means to destroy it. No doubt the resources are inadequate and the services faulty, but the principle and the impulse are unheard-of in the only annals we have of the past, the annals of *in*humanity. There is an American Foundation for the Overseas Blind; we have yet to hear of a Foreign Foundation for the American Blind. But let us not grow self-righteous, let us rather acknowledge and thank God that there is in us a good honest selfish motive side by side with the kindly impulse, which otherwise would fester into pride of rectitude. The self-interest also shows that we have begun to estimate the waste, the loss in material output, the cost to us all, of prejudice and exclusion. That awareness is a lever to move the world.

DISCUSSION AND WRITING

1. What are the origin and history of the following words: *ubiquitous, nonchalance, pemmican, palisades, saga, slogan, legend, genealogy, pedigree, clique, kaleidoscopic, annals?* Explain the meaning and origin of historical terms like *caste, burgher, petty bourgeoisie, Tory, pogrom, utopia.* Explain historical references, such as the one to the late Roman Empire as a "wonderful hodgepodge." What use does the author make of words and phrases that are informal or popular rather than scholarly?

2. Examine figurative expressions for their implications and appropriateness. For instance, is the "ocean of matter" that swallows up the life of towns a good description of the American countryside? What attitude does Mr. Barzun convey by comparing the European countryside to a "poodle cut"?

3. Does the first sentence of this essay reveal anything about the author's skill as a writer? Examine the first sentence of each succeeding paragraph, commenting on its function and effectiveness. Comment on sentence length, parallel structure, variety, and other features that affect sentence style.

4. Why does it take the author so long to get to some of his major points? What is his general strategy in approaching his topic? Where and how does he begin; how and in what direction does he move the reader along?

5. At the end of the first half of this selection, Mr. Barzun says, "All this has a meaning that only those who live here can comprehend." In one well-developed paragraph, state that meaning as elaborated in the second half of the selection.

6. In your own words, restate the author's definition of democracy. How does it compare with more familiar definitions?

7. People who defend their country against criticism tend to overemphasize its virtues and gloss over its defects. Is this true of Mr. Barzun? Cite detailed evidence.

8. Compare Barzun's account of the role of human interest in the mass media with Friedrich's and Allen's. Which account seems closest to the truth?

9. What is the civilizing effect of the "mixing of the masses"? Have you had an opportunity to observe the assimilation (or lack of it) into American culture of people from different ethnic or cultural groups?

10. In your own experience, has equality of opportunity been a myth, a partially realized ideal, or an accomplished fact?

FURTHER READING

Among early books designed to explain the meaning of the American experiment to European readers are J. Hector St. John de Crèvecoeur, *Letters from an American Farmer* (1782), and Alexis de Tocqueville, *Democracy in America* (1835–1840). A magnificent reflection of the promise that America held out to Europe's oppressed minorities is Elia Kazan's film *America America* (1962), the turbulent story of a Greek boy's journey to the United States.

JOHN A. KOUWENHOVEN

Mere miscellaneous observation becomes tiresome and dull. We soon feel the need for something that brings the blurred sequence of details into focus. We look for something that imposes a pattern or a unifying mood, that reveals point or significance. John A. Kouwenhoven, in the article that follows, unifies a wide range of observations by systematic logical reasoning. His article demonstrates both the basic procedure and the inherent dangers of inductive thinking. Starting with specific facts and observations, induction discovers common features or prevailing patterns. It formulates the generalizations that the individual instances exemplify. In working out such generalizations, a writer is attracted by the satisfying unity of an overall pattern. He is held back by the stubborn resistance of facts that do not fit. The great temptation in inductive reasoning is to play down or ignore such facts and thus to oversimplify. Mr. Kouwenhoven (born 1909), college teacher and former magazine editor, has published numerous articles and books on American history and culture. He thus concerns himself with American civilization as an expert rather than as a casual observer.

What's American about America?

The discovery of America has never been a more popular pastime than it is today. Scarcely a week goes by without someone's publishing a new book of travels in the bright continent. The anthropologists, native and foreign, have discovered that the natives of Middletown and Plainville, U.S.A. are as amazing and as interesting as the natives of such better known communities as the Trobriand Islands and Samoa. Magazines here and abroad provide a steady flow of articles by journalists, historians, sociologists, and philosophers who want to explain America to itself, or to themselves, or to others.

The discoverers of America have, of course, been describing their experiences ever since Captain John Smith wrote his first book about America almost 350 years ago. But as Smith himself noted, not everyone "who hath bin at Virginia, understandeth or knowes what Virginia is." Indeed, just a couple of years ago the Carnegie Corporation, which supports a number of college programs in American Studies, entitled its Quarterly Report "Who Knows America?" and went on to imply that nobody does, not even "our lawmakers, journalists, civic leaders, diplomats, teachers, and others."

There is, of course, the possibility that some of the writers who have explored, vicariously or in person, this country's past and present may have come to understand or know what America really is. But how is the lay inquirer and the student to know which accounts to trust? Especially since most of the explorers seem to have found not one but two or more antipodal and irreconcilable Americas. The Americans, we are convincingly told, are the most materialistic of peoples, and, on the other hand, they are the most idealistic; the most revolutionary, and, conversely, the most conservative; the most rampantly individualistic, and, simultaneously, the most gregarious and herd-like; the most irreverent toward their elders, and, contrariwise, the most abject worshipers of "Mom." They have an unbridled admiration of everything big, from bulldozers to bosoms; and they are in love with everything diminutive, from the "small hotel" in the song to the little woman in the kitchen.

Maybe, as Henry James thought when he wrote *The American Scene,* it is simply that the country is "too large for any human convenience," too diverse in geography and in blood strains to make sense as any sort of unit. Whatever the reason, the conflicting evidence turns up wherever you look, and the observer has to content himself with some sort of pluralistic conception. The philosopher Santayana's way out was to say that the American mind was

From *Harper's Magazine,* July 1956. Reprinted by permission of the author.

split in half, one half symbolized by the skyscraper, the other by neat reproductions of Colonial mansions (with surreptitious modern conveniences).

"The American will," he concluded, "inhabits the skyscraper; the American intellect inherits the Colonial mansion." Mark Twain also defined the split in architectural terms, but more succinctly: American houses, he said, had Queen Anne fronts and Mary Anne behinds.

And yet, for all the contrarieties, there remains something which I think we all feel to be distinctively American, some quality or characteristic underlying the polarities which—as Henry James himself went on to say—makes the American way of doing things differ more from any other nation's way than the ways of any two other Western nations differ from each other.

I am aware of the risks of generalizing. And yet it would be silly, I am convinced, to assert that there are not certain things which are more American than others. Take the New York City skyline, for example—that ragged man-made Sierra at the eastern edge of the continent. Clearly, in the minds of immigrants and returning travelers, in the iconography of the ad-men who use it as a backdrop for the bourbon and airplane luggage they are selling, in the eyes of poets and of military strategists, it is one of the prime American symbols.

Let me start, then, with the Manhattan skyline and list a few things which occur to me as distinctively American. Then, when we have the list, let us see what, if anything, these things have in common. Here are a dozen items to consider:

1. The Manhattan skyline
2. The gridiron town plan
3. The skyscraper
4. The Model-T Ford
5. Jazz
6. The Constitution
7. Mark Twain's writing
8. Whitman's *Leaves of Grass*
9. Comic strips
10. Soap operas
11. Assembly-line production
12. Chewing gum

Here we have a round dozen artifacts which are, it seems to me, recognizably American, not likely to have been produced elsewhere. Granted that some of us take more pleasure in some of them than in others—that many people prefer soap opera to *Leaves of Grass* while others think Mark Twain's story-telling is less offensive than chewing gum—all twelve items are, I believe, widely held to be indigenous to our culture. The fact that many people in other lands like them too, and that some of them are nearly as acceptable overseas as they are here at home, does not in any way detract from their obviously American character. It merely serves to remind us that to be American does not mean to be inhuman—a fact which, in certain moods of self-criticism, we are inclined to forget.

What, then, is the "American" quality which these dozen items share? And what can that quality tell us about the character of our culture, about the nature of our civilization?

SKYLINES AND SKYSCRAPERS

Those engaged in discovering America often begin by discovering the Manhattan skyline, and here as well as elsewhere they discover apparently irreconcilable opposites. They notice at once that it doesn't make any sense, in human or aesthetic terms. It is the product of insane politics, greed, competitive ostentation, megalomania, the worship of false gods. Its products, in turn, are traffic jams, bad ventilation, noise, and all the other ills that metropolitan flesh is heir to. And the net result is, illogically enough, one of the most exaltedly beautiful things man has ever made.

Perhaps this paradoxical result will be less bewildering if we look for a moment at the formal and structural principles which are involved in the skyline. It may be helpful to consider the skyline as we might consider a lyric poem, or a novel, if we were trying to analyze its aesthetic quality.

Looked at in this way, it is clear that the total effect which we call "the Manhattan skyline" is made up of almost innumerable buildings, each in competition (for height, or glamor, or efficiency, or respectability) with all of the others. Each goes its own way, as it were, in a carnival of rugged architectural individualism. And yet—as witness the universal feeling of exaltation and aspiration which the skyline as a whole evokes—out of this irrational, unplanned, and often infuriating chaos, an unforeseen unity has evolved. No building ever built in New York was placed where it was, or shaped as it was, because it would contribute to the aesthetic effect of the skyline—lifting it here, giving it mass there, or lending a needed emphasis. Each was built, all those now under construction are being built, with no thought for their subordination to any over-all effect.

What, then, makes possible the fluid and everchanging unity which does, in fact, exist? Quite simply, there are two things, both simple in themselves, which do the job. If they were not simple, they would not work; but they are, and they do.

One is the gridiron pattern of the city's streets—the same basic pattern which accounts for Denver, Houston, Little Rock, Birmingham, and almost any American town you can name, and the same pattern which, in the form of square townships, sections, and quarter sections, was imposed by the Ordinance of 1785 on an almost continental scale. Whatever its shortcomings when compared with the "discontinuous street patterns" of modern planned communities, this artificial geometric grid—imposed upon the land without regard to contours or any preconceived pattern of social zoning—had at least the quality of rational simplicity. And it is this simple gridiron street pattern which, horizontally, controls the spacing and arrangement of the rectangular shafts which go to make up the skyline.

The other thing which holds the skyline's diversity together is the structural principle of the skyscraper. When we think of individual buildings, we tend to think of details of texture, color, and form, of surface ornamentation or the lack of it. But as elements in Manhattan's skyline, these things are of little consequence. What matters there is the vertical thrust, the motion upward; and that is the product of cage or skeleton, construction in steel—a system of construction which is, in effect, merely a three-dimensional variant of the gridiron street plan, extending vertically instead of horizontally.

The aesthetics of cage, or skeleton, construction have never been fully analyzed, nor am I equipped to analyze them. But as a lay observer, I am struck by fundamental differences between the effect created by height in the RCA building at Radio City, for example, and the effect created by height in Chartres cathedral or in Giotto's campanile. In both the latter (as in all the great architecture of the past) proportion and symmetry, the relation of height to width, are constituent to the effect. One can say of a Gothic cathedral, "This tower is too high"; of a Romanesque dome, "This is top-heavy." But there is nothing inherent in cage construction which would invite such judgments. A true skyscraper like the RCA building could be eighteen or twenty stories taller, or ten or a dozen stories shorter without changing its essential aesthetic effect. Once steel cage construction has passed a certain height, the effect of transactive upward motion has been established; from there on, the point at which you cut it off is arbitrary and makes no difference.

Those who are familiar with the history of the skyscraper will remember how slowly this fact was realized. Even Louis Sullivan—greatest of the early skyscraper architects—thought in terms of having to close off and climax the upward motion of the tall building with an "attic" or cornice. His lesser contemporaries worked for years on the blind assumption that the proportion and symmetry of masonry architecture must be preserved in the new technique. If with the steel cage one could go higher than with load-bearing masonry walls, the old aesthetic effects could be counterfeited by dressing the façade as if one or more buildings had been piled on top of another—each retaining the illusion of being complete in itself. You can still see such buildings in New York: the first five stories perhaps a Greco-Roman temple, the next ten a neuter warehouse, and the final five or six an Aztec pyramid. And that Aztec pyramid is simply a cheap and thoughtless equivalent of the more subtle Sullivan cornice. Both structures attempt to close and climax the upward thrust, to provide something similar to the *Katharsis* in Greek tragedy.

But the logic of cage construction requires no such climax. It has less to do with the inner logic of masonry forms than with that of the old Globe-Wernicke sectional bookcases, whose interchangeable units (with glass-flap fronts) anticipated by fifty years the modular unit systems of so-called modern furniture. Those bookcases were advertised in the 'nineties as "always complete but never finished"—a phrase which could with equal propriety have been applied to the Model-T Ford. Many of us remember with affection that admirably simple mechanism, forever susceptible to added gadgets or improved parts, each of which was interchangeable with what you already had.

Here, then, are the two things which serve to tie together the otherwise irrelevant components of the Manhattan skyline: the gridiron ground plan and the three-dimensional vertical grid of steel cage construction. And both of these are closely related to one another. Both are composed of simple and infinitely repeatable units.

THE STRUCTURE OF JAZZ

It was the French architect Le Corbusier who described New York's architecture as "hot jazz in stone and steel." At first glance this may sound as if it were merely a slick updating of Schelling's "Architecture ... is frozen music," but it is more than that if one thinks in terms of the structural principles we have been discussing and the structural principles of jazz.

Let me begin by making clear that I am using the term jazz in its broadest significant application. There are circumstances in which it is important to define the term with considerable precision, as when you are involved in discussion with a disciple of one of the many cults, orthodox or progressive, which devote themselves to some particular subspecies of jazz. But in our present context we need to focus upon what all the subspecies (Dixieland, Bebop, Swing, or Cool Jazz) have in common; in other words, we must neglect the by no means uninteresting qualities which differentiate one from another, since it is what they have in common which can tell us most about the civilization which produced them.

There is no definition of jazz, academic or otherwise, which does not acknowledge that its essential ingredient is a particular kind of rhythm. Improvisation is also frequently mentioned as an essential; but even if it were true that jazz always involves improvisation, that would not distinguish it from a good deal of Western European music of the past. It is the distinctive rhythm which differentiates all types of jazz from all other music and which gives to all of its types a basic family resemblance.

It is not easy to define that distinctive rhythm. Winthrop Sargeant has described it as the product of two superimposed devices: syncopation and polyrhythm, both of which have the effect of constantly upsetting rhythmical expectations. André Hodeir, in his recent analysis, *Jazz: Its Evolution and*

Essence, speaks of "an unending alternation" of syncopations and of notes played *on* the beat, which "gives rise to a kind of expectation that is one of jazz's subtlest effects."

As you can readily hear, if you listen to any jazz performance (whether of the Louis Armstrong, Benny Goodman, or Charlie Parker variety), the rhythmical effect depends upon there being a clearly defined basic rhythmic pattern which enforces the expectations which are to be upset. That basic pattern is the 4/4 or 2/4 beat which underlies all jazz. Hence the importance of the percussive instruments in jazz: the drums, the guitar or banjo, the bull fiddle, the piano. Hence too the insistent thump, thump, thump, thump which is so boring when you only half-hear jazz—either because you are too far away, across the lake or in the next room, or simply because you will not listen attentively. But hence also the delight, the subtle effects, which good jazz provides as the melodic phrases evade, anticipate, and return to, and then again evade the steady basic four-beat pulse which persists, implicitly or explicitly, throughout the performance.

In other words, the structure of a jazz performance is, like that of the New York skyline, a tension of cross-purposes. In jazz at its characteristic best, each player seems to be—and has the sense of being—on his own. Each goes his own way, inventing rhythmic and melodic patterns which, superficially, seem to have as little relevance to one another as the United Nations building does to the Empire State. And yet the outcome is a dazzlingly precise creative unity.

In jazz that unity of effect is, of course, the result of the very thing which each of the players is flouting: namely, the basic 4/4 beat—that simple rhythmic gridiron of identical and infinitely extendible units which holds the performance together. As Louis Armstrong once wrote, you would expect that if every man in a band "had his own way and could play as he wanted, all you would get would be a lot of jumbled up, crazy noise." But, as he goes on to say, that does not happen, because the players know "by ear and sheer musical instinct" just when to leave the underlying pattern and when to get back on it.

What it adds up to, as I have argued elsewhere, is that jazz that is the first art form to give full expression to Emerson's ideal of a union which is perfect only "when all the uniters are isolated." That Emerson's ideal is deeply rooted in our national experience need not be argued. Frederick Jackson Turner quotes a letter written by a frontier settler to friends back East, which in simple, unself-conscious words expresses the same reconciling of opposites. "It is a universal rule here," the frontiersman wrote, "to help one another, each one keeping an eye single to his own business."

One need only remember that the Constitution itself, by providing for a federation of separate units, became the infinitely extendible framework for the process of reconciling liberty and unity over vast areas and conflicting interests. Its seven brief articles, providing for checks and balances between interests, classes, and branches of the government, establish, in effect, the underlying beat which gives momentum and direction to a political process which Richard Hofstadter has called "a harmonious system of mutual frustration"—a description which fits a jazz performance as well as it fits our politics.

The aesthetic effects of jazz, as Winthrop Sargeant long ago suggested, have as little to do with symmetry and proportion as have those of a skyscraper. Like the skyscraper, a jazz performance does not build to an organically required climax; it can simply cease. The "piece" which the musicians are playing may, and often does, have a rudimentary Aristotelian pattern of beginning, middle, and end; but the jazz performance need not. In traditional Western European music, themes are developed. In jazz they are toyed with and dismantled. There is no inherent reason why the jazz performance should not continue for another 12 or 16 or 24 or 32 measures (for these are the rhythmic cages which in jazz correspond to the cages of a steel skeleton in architecture). As in the skyscraper, the aesthetic effect is one of motion, in this case horizontal rather than vertical.

Jazz rhythms create what can only be called momentum. When the rhythm of one voice (say the trumpet, off on a rhythmic and melodic excursion) lags behind the underlying beat, its four-beat measure carries over beyond the end of the underlying beat's measure into the succeeding one, which has already begun. Conversely, when the trumpet anticipates the beat, it starts a new measure before the steady underlying beat has ended one. And the result is an exhilarating forward motion which the jazz trumpeter Wingy Manone once described as "feeling an increase in tempo though you're still playing at the same tempo." Hence the importance in jazz of timing, and hence the delight and amusement of the so-called "break," in which the basic 4/4 beat ceases and a soloist goes off on a flight of rhythmic and melodic fancy which nevertheless comes back surprisingly and unerringly to encounter the beat precisely where it would have been if it had kept going.

Once the momentum is established, it can continue until—after an interval dictated by some such external factor as the conventional length of phonograph records or the endurance of dancers—it stops. And as if to guard against any Aristotelian misconceptions about an end, it is likely to stop on an unresolved chord, so that harmonically as well as rhythmically everything is left up in the air. Even the various coda-like devices employed by jazz performers at dances, such as the corny old "without a shirt" phrase of blessed memory, are harmonically unresolved. They are merely conventional ways of saying "we quit," not, like Beethoven's insistent codas, ways of saying, "There now; that ties off all the loose ends; I'm going to stop now; done; finished; concluded; signed, sealed, delivered."

TWAIN AND WHITMAN

Thus far, in our discussion of distinctively "American" things, we have focused chiefly upon twentieth-century items. But the references to the rectangular grid pattern of cities and townships and to the Constitution should remind us that the underlying structural principles with which we are concerned are deeply embedded in our civilization. To shift the emphasis, therefore, let us look at item number 7 on our list: Mark Twain's writing.

Mark's writing was, of course, very largely the product of oral influences. He was a born story-teller, and he always insisted that the oral form of the humorous story was high art. Its essential tool (or weapon), he said, is the pause—which is to say, timing. "If the pause is too long the impressive point is passed," he wrote, "and the audience have had time to divine that a surprise is intended—and then you can't surprise them, of course." In other words, he saw the pause as a device for upsetting expectations, like the jazz "break."

Mark, as you know, was by no means a formal perfectionist. In fact he took delight in being irreverent about literary form. Take, for example, his account of the way *Pudd'nhead Wilson* came into being. It started out to be a story called "Those Extraordinary Twins," about a youthful freak consisting, as he said, of "a combination of two heads and four arms joined to a single body and a single pair of legs—and I thought I would write an extravagantly fantastic little story with this freak of nature for hero—or heroes—a silly young miss [named Rowena] for heroine, and two old ladies and two boys for the minor parts."

But as he got to writing the tale, it kept spreading along and other people began intruding themselves—among them Pudd'nhead, and a woman named Roxana, and a young fellow named Tom Driscoll, who—before the book was half finished—had taken things almost entirely into their own hands and were "working the whole tale as a private venture of their own."

From this point, I want to quote Mark directly, because in the process of making fun of fiction's formal conventions he employs a technique which is the verbal equivalent of the jazz "break"—a technique of which he was a master.

> When the book was finished, and I came to look round to see what had become of the team I had originally started out with—Aunt Patsy Cooper, Aunt Betsy Hale, the two boys, and Rowena, the light-weight heroine—they were nowhere to be seen; they had disappeared from the story some time or other. I hunted about and found them—found them stranded, idle, forgotten, and permanently useless. It was very awkward. It was awkward all around; but more particularly in the case of Rowena, because there was a love match on, between her and one of the twins that constituted the freak, and I had worked it up to a blistering heat and thrown in a quite

dramatic love quarrel [now watch Mark take off like a jazz trumpeter flying off on his own in a fantastic break] wherein Rowena scathingly denounced her betrothed for getting drunk, and scoffed at his explanation of how it had happened, and wouldn't listen to it, and had driven him from her in the usual "forever" way; and now here she sat crying and broken-hearted; for she had found that he had spoken only the truth; that it was not he but the other half of the freak, that had drunk the liquor that made him drunk; that her half was a prohibitionist and had never drunk a drop in his life, and, although tight as a brick three days in the week, was wholly innocent of blame; and, indeed, when sober was constantly doing all he could to reform his brother, the other half, who never got any satisfaction out of drinking anyway, because liquor never affected him. [Now he's going to get back on the basic beat again.] Yes, here she was, stranded with that deep injustice of hers torturing her poor heart.

Now I shall have to summarize again. Mark didn't know what to do with her. He couldn't just leave her there, of course, after making such a to-do over her; he'd have to account to the reader for her somehow. So he finally decided that all he could do was "give her the grand bounce." It grieved him, because he'd come to like her after a fashion, "notwithstanding she was such an ass and said such stupid, irritating things and was so nauseatingly sentimental"; but it had to be done. So he started Chapter Seventeen with: "Rowena went out in the back yard after supper to see the fireworks and fell down the well and got drowned."

It seemed abrupt, [Mark went on] but I thought maybe the reader wouldn't notice it, because I changed the subject right away to something else. Anyway, it loosened up Rowena from where she was stuck and got her out of the way, and that was the main thing. It seemed a prompt good way of weeding out people that had got stalled, and a plenty good enough way for those others; so I hunted up the two boys and said they went out back one night to stone the cat and fell down the well and got drowned. Next I searched around and found Aunt Patsy Cooper and Aunt Betsy Hale where they were aground, and said they went out back one night to visit the sick and fell down the well and got drowned. I was going to drown some of the others, but I gave up the idea, partly because I believed that if I kept that up it would arouse attention,... and partly because it was not a large well and would not hold any more anyway.

That was a long excursion—but it makes the point: that Mark didn't have much reverence for conventional story structure. Even his greatest book, which is perhaps also the greatest book written on this continent—*Huckleberry Finn*—is troublesome. One can scarcely find a criticism of the book which does not object, for instance, to the final episodes, in which Tom rejoins Huck and they go through that burlesque business of "freeing" the old Negro Jim—who is, it turns out, already free. But, as T. S. Eliot was, I think, the first to observe, the real structure of *Huck Finn* has nothing to do with the traditional form of the novel—with exposition, climax, and resolution. Its structure is like that of the great river itself—without beginning and without an end. Its structural units, or "cages," are the episodes of which it is composed. Its momentum is that of the tension between the river's steady flow and the eccentric superimposed rhythms of Huck's flights from, and near recapture by, the restricting forces of routine and convention.

It is not a novel of escape; if it were, it would be Jim's novel, not Huck's. Huck is free at the start, and still free at the end. Looked at in this way, it is clear that *Huckleberry Finn* has as little need of a "conclusion" as has a skyscraper or a jazz performance. Questions of proportion and symmetry are as irrelevant to its structure as they are to the total effect of the New York skyline.

There is not room here for more than brief reference to the other "literary" items on our list: Whitman's *Leaves of Grass,* comic strips, and soap opera. Perhaps it is enough to remind you that *Leaves of Grass* has discomfited many a critic by its lack of symmetry and proportion, and that Whitman himself insisted: "I round and finish little, if anything; and could not, consistently with my scheme." As for the words of true poems, Whitman said in the "Song of the Answerer"—

> They bring none to his or her terminus or to be content and full,
> Whom they take they take into space to behold the birth of stars, to learn one of the meanings,
> To launch off with absolute faith, to sweep through the ceaseless rings and never be quiet again.

Although this is not the place for a detailed analysis of Whitman's verse techniques, it is worth noting in passing how the rhythm of these lines reinforces their logical meaning. The basic rhythmical unit, throughout, is a three-beat phrase of which there are two in the first line (accents falling on *none, his,* and *term . . . be, tent,* and *full*), three in the second and in the third. Superimposed upon the basic three-beat measure there is a flexible, nonmetrical rhythm of colloquial phrasing. That rhythm is controlled in part by the visual effect of the arrangement in long lines, to each of which the reader tends to give equal duration, and in part by the punctuation within the lines.

It is the tension between the flexible, superimposed rhythms of the rhetorical patterns and the basic three-beat measure of the underlying framework which unites with the imagery and the logical meaning of the words to give the passage its restless, sweeping movement. It is this tension and other analogous aspects of the structure of *Leaves of Grass* which give to the book that "vista" which Whitman himself claimed for it. If I may apply to it T. S. Eliot's idea about *Huckleberry Finn,* the structure of the *Leaves* is open at the end. Its key poem may well be, as D. H. Lawrence believed, the "Song of the Open Road."

As for the comics and soap opera, they too—on their own frequently humdrum level—have devised structures which provide for no ultimate climax, which come to no end demanded by symmetry or proportion. In them both there is a shift in interest away from the "How does it come out?" of traditional story-telling to "How are things going?" In a typical install-ment of Harold Gray's *Orphan Annie,* the final panel shows Annie walking purposefully down a path with her dog, Sandy, saying: "But if we're goin', why horse around? It's a fine night for walkin'...C'mon, Sandy...Let's go..." (It doesn't even end with a period, or full stop, but with the conventional three dots or suspension points, to indicate incompletion.) So too, in the soap operas, *Portia Faces Life,* in one form or another, day after day, over and over again. And the operative word is the verb *faces.* It is the process of facing that matters.

AMERICA IS PROCESS

Here, I think, we are approaching the central quality which all the diverse items on our list have in common. That quality I would define as a concern with process rather than with product—or, to re-use Mark Twain's words, a concern with the manner of handling experience or materials rather than with the experience or materials themselves. Emerson, a century ago, was fascinated by the way "becoming somewhat else is the perpetual game of nature." And this preoccupation with process is, of course, basic to modern science. "Matter" itself is no longer to be thought of as something fixed, but fluid and everchanging. Similarly, modern economic theory has abandoned the "static equilibrium" analysis of the neo-classic economists, and in philos-ophy John Dewey's instrumentalism abandoned the classic philosophical interest in final causes for a scientific interest in "the mechanism of occurrences"—that is, process.

It is obvious, I think, that the American system of industrial mass production reflects this same focus of interest in its concern with production rather than products. And it is the mass-production system, *not* machinery, which has been America's contribution to industry.

In that system there is an emphasis different from that which was characteristic of handicraft production or even of machine manufacture. In both of these there was an almost total disregard of the means of production. The aristocratic ideal inevitably relegated interest in the means exclusively to anonymous peasants and slaves; what mattered to those who controlled and administered production was, quite simply, the finished product. In a mass-production system, on the other hand, it is the process of production itself which becomes the center of interest, rather than the product.

If we are aware of this fact, we usually regard it as a misfortune. We hear a lot, for instance, of the notion that our system "dehumanizes" the worker, turning him into a machine and depriving him of the satisfactions of finishing anything, since he performs only some repetitive operation. It is true that the unit of work in mass production is not a product but an operation. But the development of the system, in contrast with Charlie Chaplin's wonderful but wild fantasy of the assembly line, has shown the intermediacy of the stage in which the worker is doomed to frustrating boredom. Merely repetitive work, in the logic of mass production, can and must be done by machine. It is unskilled work which is doomed by it, not the worker. More and more skilled workers are needed to design products, analyze jobs, cut patterns, attend complicated machines, and co-ordinate the processes which comprise the productive system.

The skills required for these jobs are different, of course, from those required to make handmade boots or to carve stone ornament, but they are not in themselves less interesting or less human. Operating a crane in a steel mill, or a turret lathe, is an infinitely more varied and stimulating job than shaping boots day after day by hand. A recent study of a group of workers on an automobile assembly line makes it clear that many of the men object, for a variety of reasons, to those monotonous, repetitive jobs which (as we have already noted) should be—but in many cases are not yet—done by machine; but those who *like* such jobs like them because they enjoy the process. As one of them said: "Repeating the same thing you can catch up and keep ahead of yourself ... you can get in the swing of it." The report of members of a team of British workers who visited twenty American steel foundries in 1949 includes this description of the technique of "snatching" a steel casting with a magnet, maneuvered by a gantry crane running on overhead rails:

> In its operation, the crane approaches a pile of castings at high speed with the magnet hanging fairly near floor level. The crane comes to a stop somewhere short of the castings, while the magnet swings forward over the pile, is dropped onto it, current switched on, and the hoist begun, at the same moment as the crane starts on its return journey. [And then, in words which might equally be applied to a jazz musician, the report adds:] The whole operation requires timing of a high order, and the impression gained is that the crane drivers derive a good deal of satisfaction from the swinging rhythm of the process.

This fascination with process has possessed Americans ever since Oliver Evans in 1785 created the first wholly automatic factory: a flour mill in

Delaware in which mechanical conveyors—belt conveyors, bucket conveyors, screw conveyors—are interlinked with machines in a continuous process of production. But even if there were no other visible sign of the national preoccupation with process, it would be enough to point out that it was an American who invented chewing gum (in 1869) and that it is the Americans who have spread it—in all senses of the verb—throughout the world. An absolutely nonconsumable confection, its sole appeal is the process of chewing it.

The apprehensions which many people feel about a civilization absorbed with process—about its mobility and wastefulness as well as about the "dehumanizing" effects of its jobs—derive, I suppose, from old habit and the persistence of values and tastes which were indigenous to a very different social and economic system. Whitman pointed out in *Democratic Vistas* more than eighty years ago that America was a stranger in her own house, that many of our social institutions, like our theories of literature and art, had been taken over almost without change from a culture which was not, like ours, the product of political democracy and the machine. Those institutions and theories, and the values implicit in them, are still around, though some (like collegiate gothic, of both the architectural and intellectual variety) are less widely admired than formerly.

Change, or the process of consecutive occurrences, is, we tend to feel, a bewildering and confusing and lonely thing. All of us, in some moods, feel the "preference for the stable over the precarious and uncompleted" which, as John Dewey recognized, tempts philosophers to posit their absolutes. We talk fondly of the need for roots—as if man were a vegetable, not an animal with legs whose distinction it is that he can move and "get on with it." We would do well to make ourselves more familiar with the idea that the process of development is universal, that it is "the form and order of nature." As Lancelot Law Whyte has said, in *The Next Development in Man*:

> Man shares the special form of the universal formative process which is common to all organisms, and herein lies the root of his unity with the rest of organic nature. While life is maintained, the component processes in man never attain the relative isolation and static perfection of inorganic processes ... The individual may seek, or believe that he seeks, independence, permanence, or perfection, but that is only through his failure to recognize and accept his actual situation.

As an "organic system" man cannot, of course, expect to achieve stability or permanent harmony, though he can create (and in the great arts of the past, has created) the illusion of them. What he can achieve is a continuing development in response to his environment. The factor which gives vitality to all the component processes in the individual and in society is "not permanence but development."

To say this is not to deny the past. It is simply to recognize that for a variety of reasons people living in America have, on the whole, been better able to relish process than those who have lived under the imposing shadow of the arts and institutions which Western man created in his tragic search for permanence and perfection—for a "closed system." They find it easy to understand what that very American philosopher William James meant when he told his sister that his house in Chocorua, New Hampshire, was "the most delightful house you ever saw; it has fourteen doors, all opening outwards." They are used to living in grid-patterned cities and towns whose streets, as Jean-Paul Sartre observed, are not, like those of European cities, "closed at both ends." As Sartre says in his essay on New York, the long straight streets and avenues of a gridiron city do not permit the buildings to "cluster like sheep" and protect one against the sense of space. "They are not sober little walks closed in between houses, but national highways. The moment you set foot on one of them, you understand that it has to go on to Boston or Chicago."

So, too, the past of those who live in the United States, like their future, is open-ended. It does not, like the past of most other people, extend downward into the soil out of which their immediate community or neighborhood has grown. It extends laterally backward across the plains, the mountains, or the sea to somewhere else, just as their future may at any moment lead them down the open road, the endless-vistaed street.

Our history is the process of motion into and out of cities; of westering and the counter-process of return; of motion up and down the social ladder—a long, complex, and sometimes terrifyingly rapid sequence of consecutive change. And it is this sequence, and the attitudes and habits and forms which it has bred, to which the term "America" really refers.

"America" is not a synonym for the United States. It is not an artifact. It is not a fixed and immutable ideal toward which citizens of this nation strive. It has not order or proportion, but neither is it chaos except as that is chaotic whose components no single mind can comprehend or control. America is process. And in so far as people have been "American"—as distinguished from being (as most of us, in at least some of our activities, have been) mere carriers of transplanted cultural traditions—the concern with process has been reflected in the work of their heads and hearts and hands.

DISCUSSION AND WRITING

1. Define or explain: *vicarious, antipodal, rampant, gregarious, abject, diminutive, pluralistic, surreptitious, succinct, polarities, iconography, artifact, indigenous, ostentation, megalomania, paradoxical, aesthetic, discontinuous, façade, orthodox, momentum, exhilarating, divine* (vb.), *burlesque* (adj.), *discomfit, colloquial, analogous, operative.*

2. In developing and illustrating his points, the author uses a wide range of literary, cultural, or historical allusions: "Middletown," "Gothic cathedral," "Romanesque dome," *"Katharsis* in Greek *tragedy,"* "syncopation and polyrhythm," *"Beethoven's* insistent codas," "John Dewey's instrumentalism," "collegiate gothic." Investigate one of these and explain its full implications. Summarize briefly how the range of reference and allusion helps determine the level of difficulty and the tone of the article. To what extent does the author leaven his more scholarly references with the familiar, the colloquial, the humorous?

3. What evidence is there in the essay of freshness of observation? What use does the author make of expressive, graphic, concrete words? What is the role of figurative language, of imaginative parallels?

4. Typically, induction derives general conclusions from at first apparently disconnected observations. In outlining the essay, show in detail how the inductive method determines its structure.

5. Select any one page of this essay and trace in detail its pattern of argument: generalization, qualification, contrast, objection and refutation. Pay special attention to the use of transitional devices.

6. Develop in your own words the contrast between the "traditional" structural principles of proportion and symmetry and those that the author suggests are typical of many facets of American culture.

7. In what way do Barzun and Kouwenhoven agree, or how do they differ, in their account of the American scene? Work out a detailed comparison and contrast, concentrating on one significant area of agreement and disagreement.

8. Describe as graphically as you can common features of (a) modern subdivisions, (b) current big-city architecture, (c) deteriorating sections of major cities, (d) Victorian houses in an older section of a town.

9. Assume that you are to address a group of foreign students on "Things I Consider Distinctively American." What would you nominate to head the list? Choose a feature of American life that a foreign visitor could observe or verify; discuss it in detail. Or, select several distinctive features of the American scene and show what they have in common.

10. Select one of the author's generalizations or analogies that you feel qualified to support, challenge, or modify. Or discuss fully one prominent aspect of the current American scene that does not fit into the author's general pattern. Use detailed evidence from your own observation or reading.

FURTHER READING

Mr. Kouwenhoven comments on the "steady flow" of magazine articles designed to "explain America." Find a number of recent articles dealing with the contemporary American scene and examine them for current trends or recurrent themes. Possible examples are Mary McCarthy, "America the Beautiful," *New Directions 10* (1948); Oscar Mandel, "Nobility and the United States," *The American Scholar,* Spring 1958; Leslie Fiedler, "The Un-Angry Young Men: America's Post-War Generation," *Encounter,* January 1958.

LEWIS MUMFORD

At a time when the specialist enjoys increasing influence and prestige, Lewis Mumford (born 1895) is a "generalist," who considers culture as more than the sum of special skills and disciplines and is concerned "to produce a unified image out of a vast welter of details." He is best known for his books on architecture and city planning, ranging from *Sticks and Stones* (1924) to *The City in History* (1961). Mr. Mumford's studies of American cultural history go beyond the mere record of political and historical fact, drawing for instance on imaginative literature as an expression or reflection of national experience. The present selection, which deals with a crucial factor in that experience, is part of a chapter from *The Golden Day,* first published in 1926. The American philosopher George Santayana called this book "the best book about America, if not the best American book that I have read." Like other influential studies published during the twenties and thirties, *The Golden Day* substituted a searching look at the American past for patriotic platitudes.

The Romanticism of the Pioneer

I

The pioneer has usually been looked upon as a typical product of the American environment; but the truth is that he existed in the European mind before he made his appearance here. Pioneering may in part be described as the Romantic movement in action. If one wishes to fathom the pioneer's peculiar behavior, one must not merely study his relations with the Indians, with the trading companies, and with the government's land policies: one must also understand the main currents of European thought in the Eighteenth Century. In the episode of pioneering, a new system of ideas wedded itself to a new set of experiences: the experiences were American, but the ideas themselves had been nurtured in Savoy, in the English lake country, and on the Scots moors. Passing into action, these ideas became queerly transmogrified, so that it now takes more than a little digging to see the relation between Chateaubriand and Mark Twain, or Rousseau and

William James. The pioneer arose out of an external opportunity, an unopened continent, and out of an inward necessity. It is the inward necessity that most of our commentators upon him have neglected.

In the Eighteenth Century, Europe became at last conscious of the fact that the living sources of its older culture had dried up; and it made its first attempt to find a basis for a new culture. Many of its old institutions were already hollow and rotten. The guilds had become nests of obsolete privileges, which stood doggedly in the way of any technical improvement. The church, in England and in France, had become an institution for providing support to the higher ranks of the clergy, who believed only in the mundane qualities of bread and wine. In fact, all the remains of medieval Europe were in a state of pitiable decay; they were like venerable apple trees, burgeoned with suckers and incapable of bearing fruit. A mere wind would have been enough to send the old structure toppling; instead of it, a veritable tempest arose, and by the time Voltaire had finished with the Church, Montesquieu and Rousseau with the State, Turgot and Adam Smith with the old corporations, there was scarcely anything left that an intelligent man of the Eighteenth Century would have cared to carry away. Once the old shelters and landmarks were gone, where could people turn? The classic past had already been tried, and had been found—dull. Medievalism was not yet quite dead enough to be revived; *chinoiseries* were merely amusing. There remained one great and permanent source of culture, and with a hundred different gestures the Eighteenth Century acclaimed it—Nature.

The return to Nature occurred at the very climax of an arranged and artificial existence: trees had been clipped, hedges had been deformed, architecture had become as cold and finicking as a pastrycook's icing, the very hair of the human head had been exchanged for the white wig of senility. Precisely at this moment, when a purely urbane convention seemed established forever, a grand retreat began. In the Middle Ages such a retreat would have led to the monastery: it now pushed back to the country, by valiant mountain paths, like Rousseau's, or by mincing little country lanes, like that which led Marie Antoinette to build an English village in Versailles, and play at being a milkmaid. Nature was the fashion: "every one did it." If one had resources, one laid out a landscape park, wild like the fells of Yorkshire, picturesque like the hills of Cumberland, the whole atmosphere heightened by an artificial ruin, to show dramatically the dominance of Nature over man's puny handiwork. If one were middle class, one built a villa, called Idle Hour, or The Hermitage; at the very least, one took country walks, or dreamed of a superb adventurous manhood in America.

In the mind of the great leader of this movement, Jean-Jacques Rousseau, Nature was not a fresh element in the tissue of European culture: it was a complete substitute for the existing institutions, conventions, habits, and histories. Rousseau began his career with an essay on the question whether the restoration of the arts and sciences had the effect of purifying or corrupting public morals: he won the prize offered by the academy at Dijon by affirming their tendency to corrupt; and from that time onward (1750) he continued to write, with better sense but with hardly any decrease in his turbulent conviction, upon the worthlessness of contemporary civilization in Europe. His prescription was simple: return to Nature: shun society; enjoy solitude. Rousseau's Nature was not Newton's Nature—a system of matter and motion, ordered by Providence, and established in the human mind by nice mathematical calculations. By Nature Rousseau meant the mountains, like those which shoulder across the background of his birthplace; he meant the mantle of vegetation, where one might botanize, and see "eternity in a grain of sand, and heaven in a wild flower"; he meant the fields, like those of Savoy, where a simple peasantry practiced the elementary routine of living.

The return to Nature, in Rousseau's sense, was not a new injunction; nor was it an unsound one. As an aid to recovery in physical illness and neurosis, its value was recognized at least as early as Hippocrates, and as a general social formula it has played a part in the life and literature of every finished civilization. The Georgics, the Bucolics, and the idylls of classic culture belong to its sophisticated moments: after the formalities of the Confucian period Lao-tse's philosophy developed a similar creed and persuaded its individualistic adherents to renounce the sterile practices of the court and the bureaucracy and bury themselves in the Bamboo Grove. Nature almost inevitably becomes dominant in the mind when the powers of man himself to mold his fortunes and make over his institutions seem feeble—when, in order to exist at all, it is necessary to accept the wilderness of Nature and human passion as "given," without trying to subdue its disorder.

What made the authority of Rousseau's doctrine so immense, what made it play such a presiding part in European life, echoing through the minds of Goethe, Herder, Kant, Wordsworth, and even, quite innocently, Blake, was the fact that there awaited the European in America a Nature that was primitive and undefiled. In the purely mythical continent that uprose in the European mind, the landscape was untainted by human blood and tears, and the Red Indian, like Atala, led a life of physical dignity and spiritual austerity: the great Sachem was an aborigine with the stoic virtues of a Marcus Aurelius. Rousseau's glorification of peasant life was after all subject to scrutiny, and by the time the French Revolution came, the peasant had a word or two to say about it himself; but the true child of Nature in the New World, uncorrupted by the superstitions of the Church, could be idealized to the heart's content: his customs could be attributed to the unhindered spontaneity of human nature, his painfully acquired and transmitted knowledge might be laid to instinctive processes; in short, he became a pure ideal. Even William Blake could dream of liberty on the banks of the Ohio, if not on the banks of the Thames.

In America, if society was futile, one had only to walk half a day to escape it; in Europe, if one walked half a day one would be in the midst of another society. In Europe one had to *plan* a retreat: in America one simply encountered it. If Nature was, as Wordsworth said, a world of ready wealth, blessing our minds and hearts with wisdom and health and cheerfulness, what place could be richer than America? Once Romanticism turned its eyes across the ocean, it became a movement indeed. It abandoned culture to return to Nature; it left a skeleton of the past for an embryo of the future; it renounced its hoarded capital and began to live on its current income; it forfeited the old and the tried for the new and the experimental. This transformation was, as Nietzsche said, an immense physiological process, and its result was "the slow emergence of an essentially super-national and nomadic species of man, who possesses, physiologically speaking, a maximum of the art and power of adaptation as his typical distinction."

The Romantic Movement was thus the great formative influence which produced not merely the myth of pioneering, but the pioneer. But it was not the sole influence upon the scene. Human society was divided. in the Eighteenth Century between those who thought it perfectible, and those who thought that the existing institutions were all essentially rotten: the Benthams and the Turgots were on one side, the Rousseaus and Blakes on the other, and the great mass of people mixed these two incompatible doctrines in varying proportions. The perfectionists believed in progress, science, laws, education, and comfort; progress was the mode and comfort the end of every civil arrangement. The followers of Rousseau believed in none of these things. Instead of sense, they wanted sensibility; instead of education, spontaneity; instead of smokeless chimneys and glass windows and power-looms, a clear sky and an open field.

If the pioneer was the lawfully begotten child of the Romantic Movement, he belonged to the other school by adoption. He wanted Nature; and he wanted comfort no less. He sought to escape the conventions of society; yet his notion of a free government was one that devoted itself to a perpetual process of legislation, and he made no bones about appealing to the Central Government when he wanted inland waterways and roads and help in exterminating the Indian. Society was effete: its machinery could be perfected—the pioneer accepted both these notions. He believed with Rousseau that "man is good naturally, and that by institutions only is he made bad." And if the Yankees who first settled in Illinois were looked upon as full of "notions" because they were wont to take thought for the morrow and to multiply mechanical devices, these habits, too, were quickly absorbed. As Nature grew empty, progress took its place in the mind of the pioneer. Each of these ideas turned him from the past, and enabled him to speculate, in both the commercial and philosophic senses of the word, on the future.

II

In America the return to nature set in before there was any physical necessity for filling up the raw lands of the West. The movement across the Alleghenies began long before the East was fully occupied: it surged up in the third quarter of the Eighteenth Century, after the preliminary scouting and road-building by the Ohio Company, and by the time the Nineteenth Century was under way, the conquest of the Continent had become the obsession of every progressive American community.

This westward expansion of the pioneer was, without doubt, furthered by immediate causes, such as the migration of disbanded soldiers after the Revolution, endowed with land-warrants; but from the beginning, the movement was compulsive and almost neurotic; and as early as 1837 Peck's *New Guide to the West* recorded that "migration has become almost a habit." External matters of fact would perhaps account for the New England migration to Ohio: they cease to be relevant, however, when they are called upon to explain the succession of jumps which caused so many settlers to pull up stakes and move into Illinois—and then into Missouri—and so beyond, until finally the Pacific Coast brought the movement temporarily to an end. This restless search was something more than a prospecting of resources; it was an experimental investigation of Nature, Solitude, The Primitive Life; and at no stage of the journey, however much the story may be obscured by land-booms and Indian massacres and gold rushes, did these things drop out of the pioneer's mind. Charles Fenno Hoffmann, in *A Winter in the West* (1835), was only echoing the unconscious justification of the pioneer when he exclaimed: "What is the echo of roofs that a few centuries since rung with barbaric revels, or of aisles that pealed the anthems of painted pomp, to the silence which has reigned in these dim groves since the first fiat of Creation was spoken?"

Mark the difference between this movement and that which first planted the colonists of Massachusetts or Pennsylvania in the New World. In the first period of the seaboard settlement, America was a place where the European could remain more nearly his proper self, and keep up the religious practices which were threatened by economic innovations and political infringements in Europe. The Puritans, the Moravians, the Dunkers, the Quakers, the Catholics, sought America as a refuge in which they could preserve in greater security what they dearly valued in Europe. But with the drift to the West, America became, on the contrary, a place where the European could be swiftly transformed into something different: where the civil man could become a hardy savage, where the social man could become an "individual," where the settled man could become a nomad, and the family man could forget his old connections. With pioneering, America ceased to be an outpost of Europe. The Western communities relapsed into an earlier and more primitive type of occupation; they reverted to the crude practices of the hunter, the woodman, and the miner. Given the occasion and the environment, these were necessary occupations; the point to be noted, however, is that, uninfluenced by peasant habits or the ideas of an old culture, the work of the miner, woodman, and hunter led to unmitigated destruction and pillage. What happened was just the reverse of the old barbarian invasions, which turned the Goths and the Vandals into Romans. The movement into backwoods America turned the European into a barbarian.

The grisly process of this settlement was described by Crèvecœur and Cooper long before Professor Turner summed them up in his classic treatise on the passing of the frontier. "In all societies," says Crèvecœur, "there are off-casts; this impure part serves as our precursors or pioneers.... By living in or near the woods, their actions are regulated by the neighborhood. The deer often come to eat their grain, the wolves to destroy their sheep, the bears to kill their hogs, the foxes to catch their poultry. The surrounding hostility immediately puts the gun into their hands; they watch these animals; they kill some; and thus, by defending their property, they soon become professed hunters; this is the progress; once hunters, farewell to the plow. The chase renders them ferocious, gloomy, unsociable; a hunter wants no neighbors, he rather hates them because he dreads competition."

Equipped with his ax and his rifle, the two principal weapons of the pioneer, he carried on his warfare against Nature, cutting down the forest and slaughtering its living creatures. Instead of seeking Nature in a wise passiveness, as Wordsworth urged, he raped his new mistress in a blind fury of obstreperous passion. No one who has read *The Pioneers* can forget Cooper's account of the sickening massacre of wild pigeons, carried on long after the need for food had been satisfied. In these practices, the ordinary farmer and tradesman of the old country went back to a phase of European experience which had lingered on chiefly in the archaic hunts of a predatory aristocracy; and in the absence of any restraints or diversions, these primitive practices sank more deeply into the grain.

The apology for this behavior was based upon the noblest grounds; one can scarcely pick up a contemporary description of the pioneering period without finding a flowery account of the new life, put in contrast to wretched, despotic, foolishly beautiful Europe; and this animus was echoed even in the comments that Hawthorne and Emerson, to say nothing of such a real pioneer as Mark Twain, made upon the institutions of the Old World. Let me put the contemporary apology and criticism side by side. The first is from a pamphlet by George Lunt called *Three Eras of New England* (1857):

> Whenever this is the state of man the impertinent fictions and sophisms of life die out. The borrowings and lendings of the human creature fall

away from him under the rigid discipline of primeval necessities, as the encrusting dirt, which bedimmed the diamond, is removed by the hard process which reveals and confirms its inestimable price. The voice of the mountain winds would mock at the most indispensable and best recognized trappings of polished society as they rent them away and fastened them fluttering in the crevices of a cliff, or bore them onwards to the unknown wilderness, and would hail its very discomforts with the shout and laughter of derision. . . . So far, therefore, as our familiar and inherent characteristics, which form the foundation of our nature, and make us good and make us great, are liable to become diluted or perverted by the sophistications of social being, they may require an actual refreshment and renewal, under the severe and inevitable trials of colonial existence. . . . This, then, is the absolute law of all legitimate migration, that it leaves behind it the weaknesses, the concretions and superfluities of artificial life, and founds its new existence upon an appeal to the primordial elements of natural society.

Against this apology for the deprivations of the pioneer life, let me set the comment of a young English settler named Fordham, who had come face to face with the untrammeled Children of Nature; this passage occurs on the page after that in which he records the amiable slaughter of six Indians, men and women, on English Prairie, in the spring of 1817:

Instead of being more virtuous, as he is less refined, I am inclined to think that man's virtues are like the fruits of the earth, only excellent when subjected to culture. The force of the simile you will never feel, until you ride in these woods over wild strawberries, which dye your horses' fetlocks like blood, yet are insipid in flavor; till you have seen wagon-loads of grapes, choked by the brambles and the poisonous vine; till you find peaches, tasteless as a turnip, and roses throwing their leaves of every shade upon the wind, with scarcely a scent upon them. 'Tis the hand of man that makes the wilderness shine.

The hand of man was of course busy, and here and there, particularly in Ohio, Kentucky and Tennessee, villages and cities grew up which carried on, for a generation or so in the Nineteenth Century, the tradition that the seaboard knew in an earlier day; but like a river that, rushing onwards, deposits its heaviest burdens first, the best people and the soundest traditions tended to be deposited in the tracts that adjoined the original colonies, and as the stream moved further west, the traditions of a civil life disappeared, and the proportion of scalawags, cut-throats, bruisers, bullies, and gamblers tended to increase, and the wilderness got the upper hand. There are plenty of exceptions to this generalization, it goes without saying; but Texas and Nevada were the poles towards which pioneer effort tended to run. The original process has been obscured in many places by a second and third wave of agriculturists: but it is not hard to get below the surface and see what the original reality was.

III

The shock of the pioneer's experience left its mark in one or two gestures of anticipation, and in an aftermath of regretful reminiscence. The post-Civil War writers who deal with *Roughing It, A Son of the Middle Border,* or *A Hoosier Schoolmaster,* to mention only a few examples, had already abandoned the scene of the pioneer's efforts and had returned to the East: they made copy of their early life, but, though they might be inclined to sigh after it, because it was associated with their youth, they had only a sentimental notion of continuing it. For them, the pioneering experience could be recapitulated in a night around a camp-fire or a visit to the Wild West Show, which the astute Barnum had introduced to the denizens of New York in a day when the West was still in fact wild. A genuine culture and a relevant way of life do not lose their significance so easily; and the thin-skinnedness of the pioneer in the face of criticism, and the eagerness of the post-pioneer generation to identify themselves with the culture of the past, shows, I think, that at bottom the pioneer realized that his efforts had gone awry.

One is faced by the paradox that the formative elements in the pioneer's career expressed themselves in literature almost at the very outset of the movement, in the works of men who were in fact almost as aloof from the realities of the western exodus as Chateaubriand himself; and although the pioneer types and the pioneer adventures have been repeated in literature of the rubber-stamp pattern from Gustave Aimard to Zane Grey, what was valid and what was peculiar in the pioneer regime was embodied, once for all, by James Fenimore Cooper. These new contacts, these new scenes, these adventures, served to create just three genuine folk-heroes. In these heroes, the habits of the pioneer were raised to the plane of a pattern.

Cooper's Leatherstocking was the new *Natur-Mensch*,[1] established on a platform of simple human dignity. He was versed in the art of the woods, with the training of the aborigine himself; he shared the reticence and shyness that the Amerind perhaps showed in the company of strangers; and above the tender heart he exhibited mutely in *The Deerslayer,* he disclosed a leathery imperturbability. His eye was unerring; and it was only in instinct that Chingachgook, the Indian, sometimes surpassed this great hunter and warrior. Leatherstocking's bullet, which drives the bullet that has already hit the bull's eye still deeper into the target, is of course no ordinary bullet: it shared the inevitable enlargement of the hero's powers. Not every pioneer, needless to say, was a Natty Bumppo; but the shy, reserved, taciturn, dryly

---

[1] [Natural man.]

humorous hunter was the sort of being the pioneer tended, under the first stress of his new association, to become. Cooper himself painted other pioneer types, the sullen squatter, Ishmael, the fur trader, the frontier soldier, the woodman, the bee-hunter; but the fact that he had already outlined the character of Leatherstocking in the equally shrewd and reserved Spy of the Neutral Ground, Harvey Birch, showed, I believe, that this figure had become a property of his unconscious.

First a hunter, then a scout, then a trapper, Leatherstocking encompassed the chief pioneering experiences; it required a generation or two before the trader became the boomtown manufacturer, and the manufacturer the realtor and financier, dealing only with the tokens of industry. Like the first pioneers, Leatherstocking fled before the smoke of the settler's domestic fire, as before the prairie fire itself. With all the shoddiness of Cooper's imaginative constructions, he was plainly seized by a great character: his novels live solely through their central conception of Leatherstocking. The hard man, a Sir Giles Overreach, or the cunning man, Ulysses, had been portrayed before in literature; but the hardness and craft of Leatherstocking brought forth a new quality, which came directly from the woods and the prairies. When the pioneer called his first political hero Old Hickory he poetically expressed this new truth of character: barbarians or outlaws they might be, these pioneers, but their heroes grew straight. This straightness is the great quality one feels in Lincoln. It was as if, after centuries of clipping and pruning, we had at last allowed a tree to grow to its full height, shaped only by snow, rain, sun, wind, frost. A too timid and complacent culture may sacrifice the inner strength to an agreeable conformity to a common mold, a little undersized. These Old Hickories, on the other hand, grew a little scraggly and awkward; but in their reach, one would catch, occasionally, a hint of the innate possibilities of the species.

In the course of the Nineteenth Century, Leatherstocking was joined by an even more authentic folk-hero, Paul Bunyan, whose gigantic shape, partly perhaps derived from Gargantua through his French-Canadian forebears, took form over the fire in the logger's shack. Paul Bunyan, properly enough, was an axman; and, as if to complete the symbolism and identify himself more completely with the prime activities of the new American type, he was also a great inventor. He figures on a continental scale. All his prowess and strength is based upon the notion that a thing becomes a hundred times as important if it is a hundred times as big. The habit of counting and "calculating" and "figuring" and "reckoning" and "guessing"—the habit, that is, of exchanging quality for number—is expressed in nearly all of Bunyan's exploits. In a day when no one dared point to the string of shacks that formed the frontier town as a proof of the qualitative beauties and delights of a pioneer community, the popular imagination took refuge in a statistical criterion of value: they counted heads: they counted money: they counted miles: they counted anything that lent itself to large figures.

This habit grew to such an extent that people began to appreciate its comic quality; in the Bunyan tales it is a device of humor as well as of heroic exaggeration. For many years, as the legend was quietly growing and expanding, Paul Bunyan lurked under the surface of our life: we lived by his light, even if we were ignorant of his legend. He, too, like Leatherstocking, was aloof from women; and this fact is not without significance; for with the woman the rough bachelor life must come to an end, and though the pioneer might carry his family with him, bedstead, baby, and all, they were sooner or later bound to domesticate him, and make him settle down. Woman was the chief enemy of the pioneer: she courageously rose to the burdens of the new life, and demanded her place side by side in the legislature: but in the end she had her revenge, in temperance clubs, in anti-vice societies, or in the general tarnation tidiness of Tom Sawyer's aunt. When Whitman sang of the Perfect Comrade, he did not at first think of woman: so far from indicating a special sexual anomaly in Whitman, it is rather a tribute to his imaginative identification with the collective experience of his generation.

At the same time, another folk-hero arose in literature, at first sight an incomprehensible one. He was neither heroic, nor, on the surface, a pioneer; and the story that brought him forth was a rather commonplace fantasy of an earlier day. Yet the history of Rip Van Winkle shows that he has had a deep hold on the American mind: Irving's tale itself remains a popular legend, and the play that was written about him as early as the eighteen-thirties was remodeled by succeeding generations of American actors. How did this happen? The reason, I think, was that Rip's adventures and disappointments stood for that of the typical American of the pioneer period. Inept at consecutive work, harried by his wife, and disgusted with human society, he retires to the hills with his dog and his gun. He drinks heavily, falls asleep, and becomes enchanted. At the end of twenty years he awakes to find himself in a different society. The old landmarks have gone; the old faces have disappeared; all the outward aspects of life have changed. At the bottom, however, Rip himself has not changed; for he has been drunk and lost in a dream, and for all that the calendar and the clock records, he remains, mentally, a boy.

There was the fate of a whole generation: indeed, is it not still the fate of perhaps the great majority of Americans, lost in their dreams of a great fortune in real estate, rubber, or oil? In our heroic moments, we may think of ourselves as Leatherstockings, or two-fisted fellows like Paul Bunyan; but in the bottom of our hearts, we are disconsolate Rips. In this process of uneasy transition, in the endless experimentalism and externality of the American scheme, the American came to feel that something was wrong. He saw no way of rectifying the fact itself; the necessity to be "up and moving" seemed written in the skies. In his disappointment and frustration, he became maudlin. It is no accident that our most sentimental popular songs all date back to the earlier half of the Nineteenth Century. At the moment when the eagle screamed loudest, when the words Manifest Destiny were put into circulation, when Colonel Diver, the fire-eater, Jefferson Brick, the editor of the Rowdy Journal, and Scadder, the real-estate gambler, were joining voices in a Hallelujah of triumph,—it was then that the tear of regret and the melancholy clutch of the Adam's apple made their way into the ballad.

The great song of the mid-century was "Don't you remember Sweet Alice, Ben Bolt?" but the truth is that Alice was merely a name to start the tears rolling. It was not over the fate of Alice that the manly heart grieved: what hurt was the fact that in the short space of twenty years, the mill-wheel had fallen to pieces, the rafters had tumbled in, the cabin had gone to ruin, the tree had been felled, and "where once the lord of the forest waved" were grass and golden grain. In short, ruin and change lay in the wake of the pioneer, as he went westering. "There is change in the things I loved, Ben Bolt, they have changed from the old to the new," and somehow this progressive generation had an uneasy suspicion that they were not changing altogether for the better. What a conflict was in the pioneer's bosom! He pulls up stakes, to the tune of Home Sweet Home. He sells his parcel of real estate to the next gambler who will hold it, still sighing "there is no place like home." He guts out the forest: "Woodman, spare that tree, touch not a single bough, in youth it sheltered me, and I'll protect it now." And in the struggle of scalping one of the Red Varmints he is driving to the Land of the Sunset the Song of Hiawatha slips from his hip-pocket.

Does this seem to exaggerate the conflict? Be assured that it was there. The Mark Twains, Bret Hartes, and Artemus Wards would not have found the old solidities of Europe so ingratiating, taught as they were to despise Europe's cities and institutions as the relics of a miserable and feudal past, if the life they had known had not too often starved their essential humanity.

DISCUSSION AND WRITING

1. Define or explain: *transmogrify, guild, mundane, veritable, medievalism, chinoiseries, urbane, puny, injunction, idyll, sachem, perfectible, sensibility, effete, fiat, infringement, nomad, obstreperous, predatory, animus, sophism, primeval, inestimable, derision, concretion, primordial, scalawag, denizen, exodus, taciturn, prowess, disconsolate, rectify, maudlin, ingratiate.* Explain literary and historical references: *Marie Antoinette, Georgics, Bucolics, Moravians, Dunkers, Gargantua, Manifest Destiny.*

2. Among writers and philosophers mentioned briefly by Mumford are François-René de Chateaubriand, William James, Voltaire, Adam Smith, Lao-tse, Johann Wolfgang

von Goethe, Immanuel Kant, William Wordsworth, William Blake, Marcus Aurelius, Jeremy Bentham, J. Hector St. John de Crèvecœur, Zane Grey, Bret Harte, Artemus Ward. Trace three of these and spell out in some detail what ideas, tendencies, or conventions their names stand for *in this essay.*

3. Explain in your own words the contribution made to Mumford's concept of the role and significance of the pioneer by Jean-Jacques Rousseau, James Fenimore Cooper, the folk tale of Paul Bunyan, and Washington Irving.

4. Write a paragraph outline of the argument in Section I of the essay, summing up in one sentence the major point of each paragraph.

5. In a key sentence early in the essay, Mumford says that "in the episode of pioneering, a new system of ideas wedded itself to a new set of experiences." In your own words, identify the "ideas" and the "experiences" involved.

6. What is the major contrast between Mumford's account of the pioneer and previous impressions you derived from history courses, books, and other sources? Limit yourself to one major point or one essential difference.

7. Compare and contrast Mumford and Barzun on their interpretation of or reaction to one important aspect of the American experiment. Or, compare and contrast the attitude of Mumford and Kouwenhoven toward what is "distinctively American."

8. Discuss a fictional or legendary figure who seems to you symbolic of some essential element in the American national character.

9. To judge from your own experience and reading, which view seems closer to the truth: Rousseau's view that "man is good naturally" and that "by institutions only is he made bad" or the opposing view that "man's virtues are like the fruits of the earth, only excellent when subjected to culture"?

10. Unlike the pioneer, the modern American is often described as gregarious, unable to preserve privacy or enjoy solitude. How much truth is there in this description?

FURTHER READING

An outstanding historical account of the pioneering movement by a contemporary is Francis Parkman, *The California and Oregon Trail* (1849). The significance of the frontier experience and its effect on Old World ideas and traditions are treated in Frederick Jackson Turner's famous essay "The Significance of the Frontier in American History" (1893) and in Walter Prescott Webb's *The Great Frontier* (1952). Compare and contrast the picture of the pioneer as it emerges from one of these or a similar historical study with the picture drawn by Mumford.

7

The Definition of Culture

Perfection—as culture from a thorough disinterested study of human nature and human experience learns to conceive it—is a harmonious expansion of all the powers which make the beauty and worth of human nature. MATTHEW ARNOLD

Culture is the kind of large abstraction that is more often used as a term of vague praise than as a term whose substance is clearly defined. Like other large abstractions, it has various rather distinct areas of application and is used by different people for different, and sometimes incompatible ends. The essays in the following group indicate some of the areas and some of the issues that a comprehensive definition of culture would have to take into account. Russell Lynes deals with what comes first to mind when we speak of the "cultural program" of a city or when we call a city "an island of culture." He talks about the artist who creates or performs, and about his problems in finding an audience in contemporary society. Santha Rama Rau shifts our attention to what is involved when we speak about people from "different cultures." In talking about her native India, she tries to get at the essence of a way of life, with its traditional ways of thinking and of doing things, with its familiar patterns of work and leisure that may yet seem strange to the outsider. Ralph Waldo Emerson turns to what often threatens to make culture something thin or artificial—the separation of art and beauty from the everyday "practical" world. Matthew Arnold, in discussing major currents in the history of Western civilization, shares Emerson's concern with culture as something that embraces the whole of life.

RUSSELL LYNES

Russell Lynes (born 1910) has for a long time been known to readers of *Harper's* as managing editor of and regular contributor to the magazine. He has taken a special interest in the role of the performing arts in contemporary American society. In addition to his numerous articles, he has published several books, including *A Surfeit of Honey, The Taste-makers,* and *The Domesticated Americans. Harper's Magazine,* founded in 1850, is one of several magazines addressing themselves to an educated audience and paying serious attention to political and cultural issues. At the same time, its success in the world of American journalism depends at least in part on its ability to meet familiar journalistic criteria: to entertain as well as to instruct the reader; to be up to date, giving especially full coverage to current interests and current fashions; above all, to provide a new batch of reading matter, some outstanding and some mere routine, in time for each new inescapable deadline. The following article by Mr. Lynes was first published in *Harper's* in November 1963. In an amusing and instructive way, it presents the impressions and opinions of a knowledge-able observer on matters of current significance.

Is Kindness Killing the Arts?

Something is obviously wrong with the audience for the arts in America, but the trouble is not, as a great many people devoted to the arts think, that it is not serious enough. Never have so many people been so solemn about the serious arts or so serious about the frivolous arts. A joke about the arts today is in almost as bad taste as a joke about a minority group, and there is no surer way to lose cultural caste (which is very much the same thing today as social caste) than to utter a frivolous word at Art's expense.

This new solemnity which has affected so many Americans is the reflec-tion of a carefully nurtured bad conscience about culture. The shepherds of the public taste have gone to great pains to impress on everyone his duty toward the arts, with the result that even those who are not interested bear a weight of aesthetic guilt. The disinterested are quick to admit that they ought to care, and a great many hardened Philistines try to buy aesthetic salvation by contributing to artistic institutions that mean nothing to them. Our cultural bishops are in the business of selling aesthetic indulgences. And yet, paradoxically, while the audience for the arts grows in size and solemnity, the artists today are in full flight from those who profess to revere them most.

By no means the entire audience for the arts is solemn about them, and solemnity is not the only thing that keeps the artist and the audience at loggerheads. The audience is sharply divided into nearly exclusive segments, each with its own kind of proprietary attitude toward the arts or, in the case of those who are neither involved nor guilty, its own way of shrugging its shoulders at them.

There are four principal segments in what can loosely be called "the audience," each of which brings pressure to bear on the arts of our time, each in a distinct manner. For the sake of convenience (rather than accuracy— individuals are not generalities, after all) I shall give each of the segments a name: the Hard Core audience, the Genteel audience, the "Who, me?" audience, and the Tastemakers, or Missionary, audience.

Let me explain in more detail who they are, how they think, and what effect they have on the artist.

The Hard Core audience is a relatively small group to whom the arts are meat and drink and who give their whole hearts to them—a handful of scholars and critics, a coterie of hard-working dilettantes (I use the word in its real, not in its pejorative, sense), the professional artists themselves, and the aspiring young. To them the arts are a way of life. They eat them, drink them, quarrel about them, accuse each other of compromises with integrity, and talk of little else. There is often a worshipful quality in the young among them, but it changes from solemnity to productive seriousness if they remain part of this group of professionals and do not slip off into the larger congregation on the fringe of the arts.

A few of the regular members of this part of the audience maintain some sort of missionary zeal, especially those who reside in what they consider the wastelands of academe, and spread their gospel among the undergraduate heathen. Most of them, however, are concerned with the practical problems of being able to perform, to talk the language of the arts with their peers, to create or interpret, to refine their skills, and to concentrate their vision. But the fact that they perform on their individual stages does not mean that they are not also part of the audience for the arts. They are, indeed, the most critical, often dogmatic, and intensely concerned audience for which the arts perform. They are the first to perceive the slightest shifts in the winds of style, and the first to lambaste what they disapprove of or suspect of being incompatible with their hard-bought ideals. But, if they are likely to be the most critical audience, they are often the most avid one, not only for the arts they primarily practice or preach but for other arts as well. Their respect for artists working in other media from their own is based not on any distant vision of the artist and his problems and aspirations but on the itch in their own fingers. The painter who is struggling to evolve new forms on canvas may not understand the twelve-tone scale, but he understands the composer's need to wrestle with it and to turn it to his own ends. If on the other hand he is a traditionalist, intent on preserving accepted values as he understands them, he does not consider the artist who has thrown over those values as a fool or a sport, but as a knave and a betrayer. He cannot stand aside, for his most passionate beliefs are involved.

This segment of the audience for the arts has expanded considerably in the last decade, and it will grow still more. Part of this growth is the result of disenchantment with the values of materialism, though I do not think it is a very significant part. Far more important is the amount of money that has been flowing into the arts—more scholarships and fellowships are available to young artists; colleges and universities have been busy establishing elaborate theatres. (The directors of college drama departments at the University of Kansas, at Harvard, and at Williams, for example, work with equipment that makes the lot of the professional theatre people seem sorry indeed.) Many communities have recently built art centers, organized concert series, turned over galleries and stages to give local talent the chance to be seen and heard. The Hard Core of the audience, in other words, has been receiving, if not every encouragement, at least kinds of encouragement which twenty-five years ago were almost unheard of. The result is, not surprisingly, that the thirst of the artist has been whetted, and not slaked. As opportunities are spread before him, his appetites grow and his demands become more insistent. As his status rises, so does his ambition for more status and more opportunities, a situation equally true of steam fitters, physicians, and marine biologists.

The Genteel audience approaches the arts in a very different frame of mind from the doers and interpreters, of course; there is a chasm of mystery that separates the arts from the Genteel audience and keeps it at arm's length. The most solemn part of the Genteel audience attaches itself loosely to the Hard Core and the institutions that display the arts, and they often become part of the volunteer machinery of art and music and theatre. They are the joiners of the art world, and they are engaged in a flirtation with the arts without ever quite daring to come to grips with them. They keep the arts without demanding much of anything in return except the privilege of being in their company. They are respectful, indulgent, patient, and often puzzled. They are generous, forbearing, and eager to learn. They go through the rituals; they learn their catechisms; they wrestle with the dogma, and they do their utmost to keep up. More of them are women than men, and I like to think of these women as the Culturettes, who, like the farmerettes of the first world war, tilled the soil so that the seed might grow. They sell books as volunteers in museum bookstores on their Thursday mornings; they organize parties for young people to "get them interested" in the civic theatre; they sit on boards or they run errands for those who do; they sell tickets and they take tickets; they meet visiting lecturers at airports, and they paste labels on the backs of paintings at "promote your local artists" exhibitions. They serve tea.

They are repaid for their servitude by dining with visiting celebrities, by being on a first-name basis with orchestra conductors and museum directors, and by being identified with "culture" in a way that makes it "work." Because of their intimate association with the arts they often wear jewelry (copies of ancient pieces) sold at the museum reception desk and they sit on the floor and drink wine with the cast of the local theatre group after opening nights. Sometimes one wonders why they give so much of their time to the arts, but there is no one intimately connected with any local cultural activity who isn't delighted that they do. They are handmaidens keeping the house of art wholesome in the eyes of those members of the community who think there is something a little disreputable about the arts, a little immoral, a little suspect.

These handmaidens (and their male counterparts, the hand-misters)—a modest and for the most part unassuming group—constitute only a small portion of the Genteel audience in our expanding and expansive society. The largest part of the Genteel audience is an aesthetically floating population. Their heads are not in the clouds and their feet are not firmly planted on the path to the promised land where their lives will be enriched by an appreciation of what an earlier, and presumably less sophisticated, generation used to call "the finer things." They are the conscientious parents who traipse their footsore children through museums on Sunday afternoons, and who deposit them with a get-culture-or-else attitude at children's concerts on Saturday mornings, in much the same spirit and for the same reasons that they deposit them at dancing school. An acquaintance with Art—all the arts—is a part of social accomplishment, though it is not necessary to know them well. The process of being exposed to them, however, is important.

It is widely believed today that it is a solemn part of one's duty as a responsible member of a democratic society to evince some concern for those things which used to be more or less the province of the aristocracy. But for the most part it is sufficient to be able to drop a few names less well-known than Rembrandt or van Gogh, possibly to be on an opus-number basis with a few composers, and to know how to avoid the most obvious artistic gaffes. There are those, of course, who go a good deal further than this, who travel abroad in order to be able to capture cathedrals and temples with their

Leicas, who visit the homes of long-dead poets in order to send postcards to their friends but who, of course, haven't necessarily read the work of the poet whose house, among other things, they have gone three thousand miles to look at. But these people make the turnstiles in museums spin, the statistics of culture become heady, and the flirtation seem like a genuine affair of the heart. They seem to make the efforts of the trustees, treasurers, and public-relations people of our cultural institutions worth the trouble.

It is in this segment of the Genteel audience that one finds the group whom artists, Culturettes, and the Missionaries consider the "enemies of art," the true-blue Philistines. They do not, of course, think of themselves as enemies, but as the defenders of "traditional values." They have poked around just enough in museums and art books and have seen enough repro-ductions in *Life* and *Horizon* and listened to just enough concerts to know that Raphael and Brahms were right and that "these modern fellows" are "trying to pull the public's leg." (There is the other side of this coin—those whose near-sightedness takes the form of contending that there was no art or music before Picasso and Stravinsky.) They hold their opinions strongly out of a conviction that a democratic society requires of everyone that he have an opinion on cultural matters. In this sense Philistinism is the creation of those who demand that every aesthetic soul be saved. The Philistines have listened to these demands (or at least are conscious of them); and, to the dismay of those who try to purvey the arts, some of their breed not infrequently turn up on the governing boards of cultural institutions. They are zealous in their conviction that our cultural heritage should be preserved, and believe that the way to preserve it is to protect it from live artists.

By all odds the largest audience for the arts (and it is actual rather than potential) is the "Who, me?" audience. It does not think of itself as con-cerned with the arts at all; it can take them or leave them strictly alone, not on the basis of whether they are art but on the basis of whether it finds them interesting. To those who believe in an elite culture, they are the culturally unwashed and unwashable and might just as well be left in their state of indifference. But to those who look upon mass culture as the hope of a new kind of leisure-blessed civilization they are at one and the same time the promised land and the desert desperately in need of irrigation. It is this audience whose intelligence many believe is vastly underestimated by those who control mass communication. Pablum and treacle, mayhem and maso-chism are their daily fare, and they deserve better, it is said. But in any event, no one says that this vast audience is engaged in a flirtation with culture, much less an affair with it.

For this very reason it commands a respect from the artist that the self-seeking and flirtatious do not command. It is not seduced by aesthetic blandishments; it is not interested in artistic snobberies; it cannot be con-sidered Philistine because it is not in the least interested in attacking the arts or in talking back to its intellectual betters, and it makes no pretense at being interested in what it is not interested in. It is a frightful problem for the conscientious Missionaries, especially in our time, because it can well afford better taste than all the evidence seems to indicate that it has. It is easily seduced by the garish and the gaudy, by shiny surfaces that conceal shoddy workmanship, and is subject to whims and fads. But then, let it be said, so are all but a very few of those who feel it incumbent upon them to tell the biggest of audiences what it should like. The most dangerous kind of shoddiness is often the most sophisticated and the most "artistic."

In some respects the fourth segment of the audience, the Tastemakers, is its most self-indulgent and influential part, more influential than the Hard Core, more self-indulgent than the Genteel. The numbers of people directly influenced by the opinions of the Hard Core would be negligible were it not for the missionaries and merchants who spread the word. They are beholden to the artists for their function, and their affair with the arts is often a genuine and dedicated one. They draw their nourishment and their solace (and frequently their livelihood) from daily involvement in the arts, and they feel impelled to share their private satisfactions and pleasures with others and to encourage others to enter into their bower and breathe the same sweet and tangy air. But they also know that the way of the arts is not without its thorny paths and its oubliettes, that the arts are tough, often uncompromising, and usually demanding. It is easy for the historian of taste to laugh at their mistakes and misjudgments, at the false trails that they have followed with such vigor and conviction, at the traps they have laid for the unwary and then fallen into themselves. Today's hindsight is likely to be extremely condescending to yesterday's foresight, but instead of making today's Tastemakers modest it is likely to do just the opposite; it makes them arrogant. But then every generation of Tastemakers must have the egocentricity of its convictions or taste would stand still, and so, perhaps, would the arts.

The Tastemakers think of themselves not as part of the audience for the arts but as watchdogs and entrepreneurs, as the public conscience and the purveyors of the word. They are the product of industrial democracy, a relatively new breed, a new kind of participating audience that appeared along with the revolutionary idea of universal literacy as an essential prerequisite for an informed electorate. The idea that it should be anyone's problem to worry about everybody's taste was certainly no concern of the Middle Ages or of the Renaissance or of the age of the Baroque or the Rococo. Worry about everyone's soul, however humble, was indeed a concern, but it was not until the nineteenth century that anyone began to fret about the notion that it was necessary to save Everyman from the sin of bad taste, set his feet upon the paths of good taste, and thus rescue him—and the society of which he was a part—from eternal aesthetic damnation. This religion of taste, this conviction that in our kind of society everyone should be raised from indifference to appreciation has spread like wildfire until it has become one of the major industries of democratic societies. Taste is very big business indeed, and I would like to suggest that it is the Tastemakers who have caused the segmentation of the audience that I have described, who have split it into handmaidens and hand-misters, into a Hard Core of artists at loggerheads with those whose pursuit of the arts is the pursuit of social acceptability. They have done this by making art mysterious, by making it chic, and by making it class-conscious.

How did this come to pass?

The consumption of art in America has long been associated with the genteel tradition, which is a by-product of democracy and the antithesis of aristocratic tradition. Gentility does not know what it will think next and never holds strong opinions about anything except what it considers "vulgar." The cult of gentility in America began as a reaction against the so-called First Age of the Common Man in the 1830s when Andrew Jackson brought "the ruffians" into the White House. Ideas of egalitarianism (then called the republican spirit) ran strong and, as so often happens, those who could afford to put on airs and graces did so in order to make themselves as unequal as possible in a society that paid more than just lip service to equality. Part of the pose of gentility was a nodding acquaintance with the arts, and taste became a facet of gentility and a badge of class.

If the tame arts were socially acceptable, artists were not, though some of them became so as the century moved on and it became evident that an artist, like a businessman or a lawyer, could command high prices for his talents. But the artist was not in the least happy about the way in which society treated the arts, and if he was unacceptable to society, society was equally unacceptable to him. He deplored the way that Everyman considered himself a connoisseur whether he knew anything or not, and he scorned what was considered to be genteel taste. The split between the artist and the world that prided itself on its gentility was a chasm that there seemed to be no way to bridge, though the Missionaries have been trying ever since. They sought to build a span between the artist and the consumer, and they did it by appealing to the moneyed classes to recognize their responsibility for promoting culture on this new continent. They had an idea that if the leisure classes could be made to have taste, it would filter down to the poorer and busier classes. The rich, it turned out, had no better taste than the poor, but they did have the money to enable them to take the advice of the missionaries of taste: they filled their houses, copied from European palaces, with bonded European masterpieces. Genteel taste became a taste for the works of long-dead artists.

There were obviously many forces besides the efforts of the art missionaries that segmented the audience for the arts in the last century, and keep
them segmented today. Thomas Cole was right when he said in the 1830s
that the "tide of utility sets against the fine arts." He might also have said that
the tide of priggishness set against them, as did the excitements of opening a
new continent, of evolving new ways to distribute the riches of the soil, of
creating literate rather than illiterate masses. Utility was not the only, or even
the first, enemy of the arts; other intellectual preoccupations, equally valid,
were also their enemies, as they are their enemies today.

There is, however, one vast change in the audience for the arts which has
thrown the whole structure of the arts in our society into a new perspective
and which has started spirited, indeed sometimes bloodletting, arguments
among those who are most involved in the arts. It is simply that there is no
leisure class anymore, or, to put it another way, nearly everybody belongs to
the leisure class. Now that the work week has dropped from sixty hours to
forty and for most white-collar workers to thirty-five and promises in another decade to be twenty hours for almost everyone not in the professions,
the jobholder works scarcely any longer today than it used to take the
mistress of a household to order her meals, plan the work of her servants,
and drop cards on her friends. Suddenly (for it seems to be suddenly) that
portion of the populace who used to work long hours and who, we believed,
had earned an afternoon at the ball park or the racetrack becomes a problem
not only in ethics but in aesthetics. Suddenly many conscientious Americans
are worried about the citizen's sensibilities instead of his body; worried about
all that time he has on his hands (more worried than he is), about how he
should improve each shining hour of his time off, or if not each hour at least
some hours which have come to be called, in the vernacular of television,
"prime time."

The argument which this benighted creature of automation and reform
has set off is the argument of class culture versus mass culture. I do not mean
to precipitate myself into the vortex of this argument here; to do so is a little
like jumping into a cultural automatic clothes washer in which the froth
very quickly obscures the dirty linen at hand. Briefly stated, the class-culture
partisans view with alarm the nature of the material with which the mass
media provide the mass audience, as well as the attempts to provide what
they believe to be a watered-down version of culture. They believe that
culture should be preserved from such contamination. They deplore the
corruption of "standards." Those who see in mass culture the hope of the
future are inclined to believe that there is splendid evidence (most of it
statistical) that the masses are taking culture to heart, or at least that all this
flirtation may someday come to grips with reality and breed something other

than a monster. Both groups believe that the root of our cultural problem is in the audience, and that the solution will be found in how it can be wooed or guided, bullied or cajoled, made to toe the mark or pursue the cultural carrot.

I wonder. I wonder if we are not too worried about the audience and about leading it by the hand or dragging it by the heels to culture. It has been amply demonstrated that our society can create audiences for the arts by public relations, by display techniques, by snobbery, by civic and even national pride. We have learned hundreds of tricks for making art fashionable; we know all the wiles of beguilement and seduction, and having used them so successfully, we want to entice everybody into the boudoir of art. We talk about making the arts "meaningful" (whatever that means) to everybody, not just as an ornament of leisure but as a force of life. In a prosperous society everyone has time for culture of some sort; everyone should have a chance to have his sights raised, his sensibilities sharpened, and his mind stretched. It would be anti-democratic to quarrel with that. It is a Utopian idea, but then most good ideas usually are, or were in their origins.

But there is a catch in it, and the catch is the artist.

It is a paradox of our society that artists are deeply suspicious of the very methods by which they are exposed to the public. I do not know a painter or a writer or a composer (I exempt actors and other interpreting artists from this) who is not cynical about the ballyhoo and the publicity that butters his bread, though he enjoys his butter as much as anybody and exploits the opportunities that are offered him to get it. He is suspicious of the popularity he enjoys; he mistrusts the public that pays him extravagant lip service. It is characteristic of our time that no matter how hard he tries to escape from his audience into a world of his own and his peers (whose opinion really matters to him), no matter how abstruse or abstract he becomes, the culturettes and the hand-misters and the Tastemakers come panting after him in a perpetual game of hide and seek. One cannot help wondering if the artist of our time is not being understood to death—overinterpreted, overcriticized, overexploited, and overwhelmed with self-consciousness. He is a man in perpetual flight from a society that insists on discovering corners of his soul that he has not yet discovered for himself.

We seem to be bent on the creation of the audience for the arts at the expense of the arts and the artist. In our determination to nurture the audience we create an enthusiasm less for the arts than for being part of the right audience, and we endow those who qualify with social diplomas that guarantee their rights and privileges to stand up and be counted among the cultured. We are creating our own, twentieth-century forms of genteel appreciation, and by doing so we are keeping the artist at loggerheads with the public. We insist that art is "nice" when art is not nice at all. It is tough;

it is explosive; it is often upsetting; and only when it is not art is it dreary. It tries to be honest, and honesty in our public-relations-ridden society is, as everyone knows, the worst policy. We try halfheartedly—by insisting on proper labeling—to overcome the blandishments of those manufacturers who would deceive us with their products. We hope to get the same protection in art by labeling our artists.

It seems to me possible, just barely possible, that if we were to desist from making everybody think that he ought to like art and that art is good for him, the serious artist might have more respect for his audience. He might even think that the audience was a respectable thing to pursue if he were not pursued by an audience he does not and cannot respect. We should, perhaps, call a moratorium on taste entirely and reconsider the concept of pleasure— the pleasure of surprise, the pleasure of understanding, of discovery, of shared experience, of stretching the imagination.

DISCUSSION AND WRITING

1. Define or explain, paying attention to the associations of a word as well as its dictionary meaning: *frivolous, caste, aesthetic, revere, proprietary, coterie, academe, dogmatic, avid, chasm, evince, purvey, mayhem, blandishment, incumbent* (adj.), *beholden, solace, bower, egocentricity, antithesis, egalitarianism, vernacular, vortex, abstruse, moratorium*. What is the origin and meaning of *gaffe, oubliette, entrepreneur, connoisseur, boudoir*? What does *dilettante* mean when used "in its real, not in its pejorative" sense?

2. Explain the allusions in "the *shepherds* of the public taste" and "our cultural bishops are in the business of selling *aesthetic indulgences*." Can you show other instances in the text where the same basic analogy is used? What is the effect for the tone of the essay as a whole? Are there any other recurrent analogies underlying the author's use of figurative language in this essay?

3. Many educated readers turn for information and entertainment to a kind of journalism marked by a combination of familiar features: an introduction, or "lead," that will arrest the reader's attention; vivid figurative language; striking and if possible paradoxical formulas; a frequently facetious tone resulting from an informal and occasionally disrespectful treatment of subjects often treated more seriously; colloquialisms used for their humorous effect and technical or foreign terms used as evidence of sophistication. Show by detailed examples to what extent the article lives up to this formula.

4. Examine the scheme of classification that provides the basic structure of the essay. Describe in your own words the four major groups and any sub-groups. How appropriate or convincing are they?

5. How does the division into four groups serve the author's overall argument? What logical progression or argumentative drive is there in the essay as a whole? What is the author's thesis?

6. Examine the author's use of the following terms: *materialism, genteel, elite, mass culture, snobbery*. Choose one of these and prepare an extended definition in which you examine its history, meanings, associations, and typical uses (or abuses).

7. Using this essay as a model, write a paper in which you establish three or four major categories for people associated with an occupation, organization, institution, or area of public life. Make use of vivid detail to help make your distinctions clear and convincing.

8. Which of the author's four categories do *you* belong to? Is the author's description of the group fair, instructive, helpful?

9. Would you call your own home community a cultural wasteland or a cultural oasis? Use detailed evidence in support of your answer. Make sure the evidence is clearly relevant to your own implied or stated definition of culture.

10. Is it really true that the American mass audience "is easily seduced by the garish and the gaudy, by shiny surfaces that conceal shoddy workmanship, and is subject to whims and fads"? Limit your discussion to one major area, or to one major part of this question, and support your answer with detailed use of examples.

FURTHER READING

Mr. Lynes's magazine articles range from shorter casual pieces like "Is There a Gentleman in the House?" (*Look*, June 9, 1959) to more serious topical articles like "Who Wants Art?" (*Harper's*, July 1965). Study these and several other comparable articles by Mr. Lynes. Do they share basic common features? What advice would you give to someone who wants to emulate Mr. Lynes's success as a writer of magazine prose?

SANTHA RAMA RAU

Travel is said to be educational, and indeed occasionally is so. The traveler in search of education is fortunate when he finds as sensitive a guide as Santha Rama Rau, who in talking about cultural traditions of her native India helps us escape from that amused condescension that isolates us from the different and the new. Daughter of an Indian diplomat, Miss Rau was educated in England and the United States and has traveled widely in other countries. She has published numerous articles and books, among them her autobiographical *Gifts of Passage* (1961). The following article first appeared in *The Reporter* in June 1960. It illustrates the author's gift for taking the reader beyond the first surface impression to closer understanding.

Return to India

During the three months that my husband and I and our small son were in the Soviet Union, we lost count of the number of times Russians asked us, "Don't you think our life here is very good?"

"Yes, very good," we always replied, politely refraining from adding "for the Russians."

Inevitably the point would be pressed a little further. Life in the Soviet Union was not only good, we would be assured, but was getting better every day. Certainly on the evidence of the past few years, this was no more than the truth. Usually after this kind of opening exchange, the Russians we met proved to be intensely inquisitive about life in America, my husband's country, and the questions ranged from the price of nylons to American intentions for nuclear war. Sometimes they even showed a faintly patronizing interest in my country, India.

On one such occasion I had a brief and uninspired conversation with a chance Russian acquaintance that I was to remember much later with quite a different feeling. A young man, noticing across a restaurant dining room that I wore a sari, came over to the table where my husband and I were sitting. *"Hindi-Russki bhai-bhai!"* he announced proudly—a phrase Russians learned when Prime Minister Nehru visited their country, a phrase they love to use, which means in Hindi, "Indians and Russians are brothers."

"Hindi-Russki bhai-bhai," I replied dutifully, and then, after the usual opening formalities, the young man started to ask me—or rather, to tell me—about life in India.

With my husband interpreting for us, he remarked, "The Indian people are very poor."

"Yes, they are."

"I have seen photographs. They have few clothes and many have no shoes."

"That's true."

"Most of them are uneducated."

"Yes."

"Many beggars on the streets."

"Yes."

"It must be very distressing to live in such a country."

"No—" I began, suddenly feeling homesick.

From *The Reporter*, June 9, 1960. Copyright © 1960 by Santha Rama Rau. Reprinted by permission of *The Reporter* and the author.

But the young man was finished with the subject of India. "In Russia we have a very good life . . ."

After our stay in Russia, I returned with my son to visit my family in India. We flew from Uzbekistan in the far south of Russia, over the magnificent expanse of the Himalayas to New Delhi. The plane arrived after dark and by the time we reached my uncle's house it was quite late at night and we were too tired to do much talking or to pay much attention to our surroundings.

The next morning, with my first glimpse of the newspapers, I was sharply aware not so much that I was in India as that I was out of Russia. One paragraph was enough to convince me. It ran, as I remember, something like this: "Yesterday the Prime Minister opened the debate in parliament on the Second Five-Year Plan with a two-hour speech in his usual diffuse style." I read, and reread, and *reread* the words "his usual diffuse style," remembering the monotonously reverential tone of all Russian newspapers toward all Russian leaders—the ones in favor, that is.

This was trivial enough as an incident, but in the course of that first day a number of other moments—equally minor, equally transient—began to acquire a collective force. I had offered to help with the household shopping, partly because I always enjoy bazaars and partly because I wanted to show my son a little of the city. We started in the fruit market, which I'm afraid my Russian friends would have found hopelessly disorganized. No orderly queues, no rationing, no fixed prices, no stern-faced women with string shopping bags waiting in line, dutifully reading signs saying, "Drink fruit juices. They are good for you."

To me an Indian bazaar is a source of endless delight and excitement. It is usually a series of plain wooden stalls on which are piled, with unconscious artistry, brightly colored fruits, vegetables, spices, gleaming silver jewelry, brilliant silks and cottons, or charming, grotesque painted wooden toys. The vendors who can't afford a stall sit on the sidewalk outside the market, their baskets stacked behind them, their wives in vivid cotton saris crouching in the shade, and in front of them are spread carpets of scarlet chillies drying in the sun, small hills of saffron, turmeric, coriander, ginger, cinnamon—all the magical names from the old days of the spice trade with the Indies. With a worn stone mortar and pestle the vendor or his wife will grind your spices for you, blending them according to your particular taste, and weigh them in tiny brass scales strung on twine and balanced delicately in one hand. In all transactions you receive a pleasantly individual attention—nothing is standardized.

The vegetable and fruit and flower merchants are surrounded by baskets of purple eggplant, green peppers, strings of tiny silvery onions, heads of bitter Indian spinach, and a dozen Indian vegetables for which I don't even know the English names. I had forgotten about the profusion of fruit in

India—it is only during the brief, intense summer that you see much variety of fruit in Moscow. In Russia as winter approaches, all vegetables except for potatoes and the pervasive cabbage in soup seem to disappear from the menus.

My son was enjoying himself, pouncing on the stacks of bananas—unobtainable in Russia—regarding with some suspicion the papayas and *chikus* which he had not remembered from his last stay in India. He prodded a pile of the tiny, sharp Indian limes to see if they would collapse, an action for which he would have been severely reprimanded in Russia. I was reminded of the evening when we had run into an official of the Ministry of Culture in the lobby of the Metropole, our hotel in Moscow. He had come to the hotel to buy a lemon. It seemed like an extraordinary place to come for such an item, but he explained that there were too few lemons in the winter, so that they were saved for the tourists and the foreigners and could only be obtained, if you were lucky, at an Intourist hotel.

Flowers. This was something I missed very much in Russia, where flowers are a real luxury. I can remember standing at a street corner in Russia, astonished by the sight of a flowerwoman sitting in the middle of a splash of color in those gray streets. The Russians stopped to look too. Not many of them bought the flowers—too costly—but a surprising number paused in the rush to get home from offices, factories, and shops in the shadowy autumn twilight just to feast for a moment on the rare color of a few stiff bunches of chrysanthemums on a street corner.

All around us, in Delhi, there were flowers. Yes, it is a tropical country, and yes, the climate makes this possible—but there was a personal pride and feminine joy in the countrywomen who tucked a marigold casually into their hair, who wove roses into small hoops to wear more formally around the knot of hair on the back of the head. I realized then that I had missed all this in Russia; the pleasure of women in being women, a sense of decoration, an unquestioned right of anyone to the small, cheap luxuries and gaieties.

But most impressive—to me anyway—are the people in an Indian bazaar. First of all there is the inquisitiveness that often embarrasses foreigners. When you are engaged on an errand as prosaic as buying potatoes, in the course of the transaction your vendor may well ask you any variety of what my American friends would call personal questions. How old are you? How many children do you have? Only one? (A commiserating shake of the head.) Better hurry and have another before you are too old. Where do you live? Is your mother-in-law alive? Inevitably I made the comparison with Russia, where this kind of passing, interested exchange (between Russians) is so suspect. The right to express ordinary human curiosity about a fellow countryman came to seem like an unusual privilege.

Meanwhile, the brisk, canny routine of bargaining would be going on, and the whole performance would be interspersed with jokes and cracks and comments. Next to me a man, bargaining for a basket of tangerines, remarked to the old woman standing behind the stall, "Clearly you believe in the soak-the-rich program." This was the popular description of India's new taxation policy. The woman looked amused and replied drily, "Give me your income and I will gladly pay your taxes." And the bargaining went on without rancor—it was all very Indian, or rather, un-Russian.

We finished our shopping and summoned a boy to carry our purchases out of the bazaar—another small, cheap luxury.

On our way out of the market, we had to pass the familiar barrage of beggars on the sidewalk and, as usual, gave them the small change left over from shopping. Even my son was struck with the contrast to Moscow. "Why are they asking for money, Mummy?"

"Because they are poor, darling."

"Why are they poor, Mummy?"

"India is a poor country, darling. Too many people and not enough food."

"We could give them some of our fruit."

"Well, that's what we've done in another way. We've given them some money to buy whatever they choose."

Then I was left wondering, as so often in the past, about the ethics of begging and giving. It is easy to win approval from foreigners by deploring two elements of Indian life—the caste structure and begging for a livelihood. The best that can be said about either of them is that it is gradually disappearing. However, it would be less than honest to pretend that social malaise is all that is involved in either system. The goals in the Hindu view of life are not the same as those of Russia or the western world. Indeed, India's highest caste, the Brahmans, are traditionally sworn to poverty. Ambition, getting ahead, comfort, success are obstacles, not aims, in the Hindu concept of a good life. Enlightenment is reached, if it is reached, when you have detached yourself from worldly considerations and emotional drives of any sort, so it is not surprising that many of India's most respected "holy men" are, in fact, beggars, or perhaps live on unsolicited contributions from strangers, disciples, casual visitors.

What in the West is almost always a degrading occupation can, in India, be a high achievement. Not, of course, that all beggars are religious mendicants. Many are simply poor, or sick, or unemployed, or seeking a little extra income. If, to a westerner, they are an embarrassment or raise guilts about his own privileged life, to an Asian they are more likely to engender a down-to-earth recognition of conditions as they are and an urge to contribute in a small way to a social responsibility. This is combined with the knowledge that there is no society, including the Russian, in which privilege is unknown. Money, birth, education, accomplishment, something makes a class (or caste) structure. The Hindu view is not to rise to a higher level of privilege but to rise beyond the concern with privilege and levels altogether.

It is hard enough to explain this attitude to a sympathetic, philosophic westerner; it is impossible to describe to the average Russian, to whom spiritual values seem to be mysterious, unacceptable, or discredited.

Could the Indian government, like the Russian or the Chinese, abolish beggars with a sweeping compulsory measure? I suppose it could. Would the cost in undemocratic forcefulness be too high? I think it might. We are committed to raising the standard of living in India, but by different methods, at a different pace—a pace designed to preserve other important aspects of our life. Although a number of these thoughts occurred to me that day at the bazaar, luckily I hadn't the time to try and explain many of them to my son because he was thirsty and was more concerned with demanding a *limonad* of the sort he had liked in Russia. We stopped at a nearby coffee shop.

An Indian coffeehouse, like an Indian bazaar, has its own peculiar atmosphere. It is a cheerful, unpretentious place in which to dawdle, encounter friends, talk, discuss, gossip. Students make fiery speeches to each other; women meet for a break in a morning's shopping; idlers stop by for a rest, to watch the world go by, to pick up a chance colleague. The actual drinking of coffee is the least important part of the whole affair. Looking around at the animated groups of uninhibited talkers at the tables, I couldn't help thinking that this particular sort of place doesn't exist in Moscow. There, one can find restaurants (mostly rather expensive by any standard), or "Parks of Culture and Rest," or hotel dining rooms, and several varieties of bar ranging from the *pivnaya,* where as a rule you can't even sit down, where women are seldom seen, and where the customers walk to the bar, order a drink, down it and leave, all within the space of five minutes, to the *stolovoye,* which is considered more refined, more suitable for women, and where ordinary vodka is not served, though wines and brandy are brought to your table. But India is not a drinking country—even in the states where there is no prohibition. The sight of drunks being thrown out of restaurants with the offhand ruthlessness that the Russians employ for such occasions is extremely rare in India.

Indians meet in public places for sociability, and though poor housing contributes, as it does in Russia, to the life of cafés and restaurants and street corners, still Indians do not meet for the dedicated purpose of getting drunk. They are incurable talkers. At the coffeehouse I found myself once again cozy and amused in the endless stream of comment, criticism, scandal, anecdote, and analysis that accompanies one's days in any Indian society. I like the idea that one can be interested, amused, or disapproving of the activities or remarks of one's neighbors, friends, and acquaintances, or of political figures, college professors, taxi drivers, and artists. I like the idea that one's concern, malicious or pleasant, in one's fellow countrymen cannot lead to their political harassment.

Listening that morning in the coffeehouse to the flurry of debate that rose from the students' tables about the latest political controversy, interspersed with the social chit-chat of the ladies or the shop talk of secretaries, office workers, and clerks, I thought of the sad, sly exchanges we had shared with our Russian acquaintances. I remembered the way conversation with a Russian in a restaurant would stop cold whenever a waiter came to the table or strangers walked by. At first I was astonished to find that Russians are much more willing to talk than I had expected, that people will come up to you in parks, restaurants, on the street, drawn by curiosity to a foreigner, eager to ask and answer questions. But we soon learned, after hearing some deeply intimate confidences from Russians we scarcely knew, that our relations with them were very much in the nature of a shipboard romance. It can be intimate because it is so brief. "I can talk to you frankly," one of our friends said, not wistfully, merely as a statement of fact, "because you are in Moscow only a short time. Soon you will go and we will never meet again."

I remembered a waiter at the Metropole Hotel who had seen us so often in the dining room that one day he drifted unobtrusively over to our table to ask us in muttered conversation and scribbled notes about foreign writers. In return for whatever fragments of information we could give him, he told us about his favorite poet, Valery Bryusov. We had never heard of him, and then learned that he was banned in the Soviet Union. "You see," the waiter whispered, "he is a symbolist." In the rowdy air of the coffeehouse, it seemed incredible that there were places where poetry, even symbolist poetry, was considered too dangerous for the fragile human intellect.

After those early days in India, both the novelty of being home and the continual contrasts with Russia began to wear thin. Soon I slipped back in the slow pace and familiar daily life of India. My son no longer noticed beggars. I no longer thought of a trip to the bazaar or the coffeehouse as an occasion. I even remembered the cold blue evenings of Moscow with some nostalgia as the Indian climate warmed up to its early spring. But once during that time I had reason to think of my trip to Moscow and of India as a nation with a shock of rediscovery. It was during the Independence Day parade that takes place in New Delhi every January 26.

It is an immense celebration and villagers from all the surrounding areas of the city had been walking into town or arriving in their bullock carts for days before. As the day grew closer all the open spaces of New Delhi were gradually filled with impromptu camps. Carts were unhitched, oxen grazed in the parks, the evening air was filled with the haze of open-air cooking fires for the scanty dinners of the travelers. On the streets you saw everywhere the brilliantly colored full anklelength skirts and tight bodices of the village women. Each footstep (yes, barefoot, I would have had to admit to my Russian acquaintance) was emphasized by the metallic clink of silver anklets or toe rings. Every time a small child was hitched into a more comfortable position on his mother's hip, the sound of silver bracelets would accompany the movement. The fathers, proudly carrying sons on a tour of the city's sights or carefully washing their oxen at a public fountain, were less decorative but good-humored and ready for a festival. The streets were full of color and excitement and nobody checked the wanderings of the villagers as they looked around their capital.

In Russia you need a permit to travel even within the country, an identity card and an official permit before you may stay at a hotel. For most non-Muscovites, the only way to get to Moscow is to come, as a reward for outstanding service, on a brief "workers' tour" or as a member of some delegation. Chekhov's yearning phrase "To Moscow, to Moscow..." has just as intense a meaning now.

The day of the parade brought thousands of villagers and citizens of Delhi to the parade route, lining the roads in a dense, active crowd of mothers, fathers, children, babies, donkeys, oxen. Many families had their lunches tied up in pieces of cloth. Children clutched balloons or candy sticks. Little stalls selling nuts, tea, sweets, and fruit sprang up everywhere. I was lucky enough to have a seat on one of the bleachers outside the president's house where the procession started, and next to me was an old man in a worn khaki sweater and army trousers. A faded patch on his arm said "Engineers." He was obviously a veteran, obviously now retired, and obviously he had never been higher in rank than the equivalent of a sergeant.

When the procession began with the arrival of the Indian president, the old man stood up to get a better view. All the pomp and ceremony of viceregal days surrounded the appearance of the president—the outriders, the cavalry escort, the great coach drawn by matched horses, guarded by lancers. Out of the coach stepped a small thin man in a brown *achkan* (the Indian jacket), narrow trousers wrinkled at the ankles, a Gandhi cap on his head. He looked embarrassed by the flashy display that surrounded him. Smiling shyly, he brought his hands together in a *namaskar,* the Indian greeting, and hurried to his place on the reviewing platform. This in no way discouraged the old man next to me. He raised his hands in a *namaskar* above the heads of the people around him. With tears streaming down his face, he yelled (apparently convinced that the president could hear him), *"Namaste ji! Jai Hind!"* and continued with such fervor that the rest of us near him suddenly found ourselves joining in a tribute from an Indian who had spent all his life in the British Army to an Indian who represented, at last, the fact that all this and India itself belonged to all of us.

The parade was splendid as such things go—a vast cavalcade of camels, elephants, ski troops, horsemen, the tough Gurkhas, the bearded colorful Sikhs—all the diversity and pageantry of India. But I am not really very keen on parades. They worry and depress me, and while this fantastic procession was going on, in my mind I had slipped back to the day of the fortieth anniversary of the Russian Revolution in Moscow. Another parade. Of a very different sort. There were no crowds lining the sidewalks—the streets had been cleared for security reasons. There was none of the good-humored pushing and shoving and wriggling of small children to get to the front where they could see best. Color? Pageantry? No, a few people in the factory workers' groups in the procession carried paper flowers, and one realized in a moment how seldom one saw color on the streets in Moscow, how rarely the drab grays and browns of the city were ever lightened by even so much as a pretty shop window. Mostly the Russian parade was grimly military, tanks and guns and huge rockets, and ranks and ranks of marching soldiers.

At the end of our parade the tribesmen from the Naga hills came by to do a dance in the street in front of the president. Predictably (it couldn't happen in Russia), they were late in getting started. Consequently they clashed with the flypast of the new Indian jets. Watching the two performances simultaneously, I could only think I would never have been able to explain to that anonymous Russian acquaintance of mine the appeal of Indian casualness, of the need for color, ease, humor—the joy of an Indian festival.

Poor and undernourished and undereducated, yes. But in India, people turn out every election day in a larger percentage than anywhere else in the world to *choose* a government. They make a real holiday of it, decorating their oxcarts and dressing in their best clothes to go to the polls. Certainly one cannot pretend that there is nothing in India that needs to be changed, but somewhere in all this is a confidence and pleasure in being Indian, and in the country's ways. And, yes, those ways are very different from Russian ways.

Well, it never fails: one always sounds sentimental in trying to say things like this. Perhaps it is just as well that I never got a chance to explain to that remote young man in Moscow how I feel about India.

DISCUSSION AND WRITING

1. Define or explain: *inquisitive, patronize, sari, expanse, diffuse, transient* (adj.), *grotesque, profusion, pervasive, prosaic, commiserate, canny, interspersed, rancor, ethics, malaise, disciple, mendicant, engender, anecdote, viceregal, fervor, cavalcade, diversity.*

2. The author emphasizes the distinctive nature of the ways and attitudes of her native India. Describe these ways and attitudes in your own words.

3. Sum up the author's impressions of Russia and her attitude toward Russian ways of thinking and the Russian way of life.

4. A writer can hardly be expected to discuss a subject as close to him as the ways and traditions of his native country with complete objectivity. To what extent is Miss Rau's article colored by nostalgia, loyalty, or bias?

5. Discuss the author's use of comparison and contrast in presenting and organizing her material. Are her comparisons effective, revealing, arbitrary, artificial, one-sided?

6. Visitors from India sometimes claim that Russian and American civilization have more in common than Americans realize. What truth is there in this claim? To what extent, and in what form, would a person like Miss Rau find in the United States the things she missed in Russia? Limit yourself to one major question, such as the role of color and diversity in American life.

7. Write a paper conveying the pervading spirit or dominant impression of an unusual place—an open-air market, an auctioneer's hall, a revivalist's tent. Use vivid authentic detail.

8. Develop the contrast between two different environments or ways of life: high school as against college, city as against countryside, one part of the country as against another, life abroad as against life at home.

9. What is the role in American life of symbols, of "pomp and ceremony," that express national unity and national pride? Are they worthy or adequate? Are they deficient or neglected? Are such symbols obsolete in a modern society?

10. Is it true that "ambition, getting ahead, comfort, success" are the goals of the American way of life?

FURTHER READING

E. M. Forster's novel *A Passage to India* (1924) is a famous treatment of the theme of misunderstanding between East and West—between the educated, Westernized native and the representatives of colonial English rule. To many Americans, the spirit of India was summed up in the figure of Mahatma Gandhi. Critical evaluations of his role and influence are George Orwell's essay "Reflections on Gandhi" (in *A Collection of Essays*, 1954) and Bertrand Russell's "Mahatma Gandhi," *Atlantic*, December 1952. These and other studies of Gandhi published in the West after his death in 1948 show the contrasting reactions of writers of different convictions to Gandhi as a "modern saint."

RALPH WALDO EMERSON

Ralph Waldo Emerson (1803–1882) is the foremost of American writers in the nineteenth century who helped "domesticate" the rich cultural traditions of Western Europe in their new setting while at the same time serving as spokesmen of a self-reliant native American culture. Coming from a family of New England clergymen, Emerson was trained at Harvard Divinity School and became a Unitarian minister. Like other prominent writers of the nineteenth century looking for new religious forms, Emerson soon broke with the church, resigning his ministry in order to find the living spirit of religion outside established institutions. In several volumes of essays, often based on his successful public lectures, Emerson became the leading spokesman of American transcendentalism, a philosophy indebted to German philosophers like Kant and English writers like Wordsworth and Carlyle. The aim of the transcendentalist was to find, and to cherish and develop, the hints of an underlying spiritual reality present everywhere in nature and the life of man. To the transcendentalist, material reality was not mechanical and dead but imbued with profound spiritual significance. The task of the writer, the artist, or the philosopher was to "transcend" material reality, to go beyond its surface to find its true meaning. Emerson influenced and befriended a number of important American writers, the most prominent being Henry David Thoreau and Walt Whitman. The following essay is characteristic of Emerson's work in its tendency to discuss all reality in terms of the ideal to which it aspires, the moral and philosophical meaning it implies. The essay was first published in 1841, appearing in the same volume with Emerson's well-known essays on "The Over-Soul" and "Self-Reliance."

Art

Give to barrows, trays and pans
Grace and glimmer of romance,
Bring the moonlight into noon
Hid in gleaming piles of stone;
On the city's pavéd street
Plant gardens lined with lilac sweet,
Let spouting fountains cool the air,
Singing in the sun-baked square.
Let statue, picture, park and hall,
Ballad, flag and festival,
The past restore, the day adorn
And make each morrow a new morn.
So shall the drudge in dusty frock
Spy behind the city clock

Retinues of airy kings,
Skirts of angels, starry wings,
His fathers shining in bright fables
His children fed at heavenly tables
'T is the privilege of Art
Thus to play its cheerful part.
Man in Earth to acclimate
And bend the exile to his fate,
And, moulded of one element
With the days and firmament,
Teach him on these as stairs to climb
And live on even terms with Time;
Whilst upper life the slender rill
Of human sense doth overfill.

Because the soul is progressive, it never quite repeats itself, but in every act attempts the production of a new and fairer whole. This appears in works both of the useful and fine arts, if we employ the popular distinction of works according to their aim either at use or beauty. Thus in our fine arts, not imitation but creation is the aim. In landscapes the painter should give the suggestion of a fairer creation than we know. The details, the prose of nature he should omit and give us only the spirit and splendor. He should know that the landscape has beauty for his eye because it expresses a thought which is to him good; and this because the same power which sees through his eyes is seen in that spectacle; and he will come to value the expression of nature and not nature itself, and so exalt in his copy the features that please him. He will give the gloom of gloom and the sunshine of sunshine. In a portrait he must inscribe the character and not the features, and must esteem the man who sits to him as himself only an imperfect picture or likeness of the aspiring original within.

What is that abridgment and selection we observe in all spiritual activity, but itself the creative impulse? for it is the inlet of that higher illumination which teaches to convey a larger sense by simpler symbols. What is a man but nature's finer success in self-explication? What is a man but a finer and compacter landscape than the horizon figures—nature's eclecticism? and what is his speech, his love of painting, love of nature, but a still finer success—all the weary miles and tons of space and bulk left out, and the spirit or moral of it contracted into a musical word, or the most cunning stroke of the pencil?

But the artist must employ the symbols in use in his day and nation to convey his enlarged sense to his fellow-men. Thus the new in art is always formed out of the old. The Genius of the Hour sets his ineffaceable seal on the work and gives it an inexpressible charm for the imagination. As far as the spiritual character of the period overpowers the artist and finds expression in his work, so far it will retain a certain grandeur, and will represent to future beholders the Unknown, the Inevitable, the Divine. No man can quite exclude this element of Necessity from his labor. No man can quite emancipate himself from his age and country, or produce a model in which the education, the religion, the politics, usages and arts of his times shall have no share. Though he were never so original, never so wilful and fantastic, he cannot wipe out of his work every trace of the thoughts amidst which it grew. The very avoidance betrays the usage he avoids. Above his will and out of his sight he is necessitated by the air he breathes and the idea on which he and his contemporaries live and toil, to share the manner of his times, without knowing what that manner is. Now that which is inevitable in the work has a higher charm than individual talent can ever give, inasmuch as the artist's pen or chisel seems to have been held and guided by a gigantic hand to inscribe a line in the history of the human race. This circumstance gives a value to the Egyptian hieroglyphics, to the Indian, Chinese and Mexican idols, however gross and shapeless. They denote the height of the human soul in that hour, and were not fantastic, but sprung from a necessity as deep as the world. Shall I now add that the whole extant product of the plastic arts has herein its highest value, as *history;* as a stroke drawn in the portrait of that fate, perfect and beautiful, according to whose ordinations all beings advance to their beatitude?

Thus, historically viewed, it has been the office of art to educate the perception of beauty. We are immersed in beauty, but our eyes have no clear vision. It needs, by the exhibition of single traits, to assist and lead the dormant taste. We carve and paint, or we behold what is carved and painted, as students of the mystery of Form. The virtue of art lies in detachment, in sequestering one object from the embarrassing variety. Until one thing comes out from the connection of things, there can be enjoyment, contemplation, but no thought. Our happiness and unhappiness are unproductive. The infant lies in a pleasing trance, but his individual character and his practical power depend on his daily progress in the separation of things, and dealing with one at a time. Love and all the passions concentrate all existence around a single form. It is the habit of certain minds to give an all-excluding fulness to the object, the thought, the word they alight upon, and to make that for the time the deputy of the world. These are the artists, the orators, the leaders of society. The power to detach and to magnify by detaching is the essence of rhetoric in the hands of the orator and the poet. This rhetoric, or power to fix the momentary eminency of an object—so remarkable in Burke, in Byron, in Carlyle—the painter and sculptor exhibit in color and in stone. The power depends on the depth of the artist's insight of that object he contemplates. For every object has its roots in central nature, and may of course be so exhibited to us as to represent the world. Therefore each work of genius is the tyrant of the hour and concentrates attention on itself. For the time, it is the only thing worth naming to do that—be it a sonnet, an opera, a landscape, a statue, an oration, the plan of a temple, of a campaign, or of a voyage of discovery. Presently we pass to some other object, which rounds itself into a whole as did the first; for example a well-laid garden; and nothing seems worth doing but the laying out of gardens. I should think fire the best thing in the world, if I were not acquainted with air, and water, and earth. For it is the right and property of all natural objects, of all genuine talents, of all native properties whatsoever, to be for their moment the top of the world. A squirrel leaping from bough to bough and making the wood but one wide tree for his pleasure, fills the eye not less than a lion—is beautiful, self-sufficing, and stands then and there for nature. A good ballad draws my ear and heart whilst I listen, as much as an epic has done before. A dog, drawn by a master, or a litter of pigs, satisfies and is a reality not less than the frescoes of Angelo. From this succession of excellent objects we learn at last the immensity of the world, the opulence of human nature, which can run out to infinitude in any direction. But I also learn that what astonished and fascinated me in the first work, astonished me in the second work also; that excellence of all things is one.

The office of painting and sculpture seems to be merely initial. The best pictures can easily tell us their last secret. The best pictures are rude draughts of a few of the miraculous dots and lines and dyes which make up the ever-changing "landscape with figures" amidst which we dwell. Painting seems to be to the eye what dancing is to the limbs. When that has educated the frame to self-possession, to nimbleness, to grace, the steps of the dancing-master are better forgotten; so painting teaches me the splendor of color and the expression of form, and as I see many pictures and higher genius in the art, I see the boundless opulence of the pencil, the indifferency in which the artist stands free to choose out of the possible forms. If he can draw every thing, why draw any thing? and then is my eye opened to the eternal picture which nature paints in the street, with moving men and children, beggars and fine ladies, draped in red and green and blue and gray; long-haired, grizzled, white-faced, black-faced, wrinkled, giant, dwarf, expanded, elfish—capped and based by heaven, earth and sea.

A gallery of sculpture teaches more austerely the same lesson. As picture teaches the coloring, so sculpture the anatomy of form. When I have seen fine statues and afterwards enter a public assembly, I understand well what he meant who said, "When I have been reading Homer, all men look like giants." I too see that painting and sculpture are gymnastics of the eye, its training to the niceties and curiosities of its function. There is no statue like this living man, with his infinite advantage over all ideal sculpture, of perpetual variety. What a gallery of art have I here! No mannerist made these varied groups and diverse original single figures. Here is the artist himself improvising, grim and glad, at his block. Now one thought strikes him, now another, and with each moment he alters the whole air, attitude and expression of his clay. Away with your nonsense of oil and easels, of marble and chisels; except to open your eyes to the masteries of eternal art, they are hypocritical rubbish.

The reference of all production at last to an aboriginal Power explains the traits common to all works of the highest art—that they are universally intelligible; that they restore to us the simplest states of mind, and are religious. Since what skill is therein shown is the reappearance of the original soul, a jet of pure light, it should produce a similar impression to that made by natural objects. In happy hours, nature appears to us one with art; art perfected—the work of genius. And the individual in whom simple tastes and susceptibility to all the great human influences overpower the accidents of a local and special culture, is the best critic of art. Though we travel the world over to find the beautiful, we must carry it with us, or we find it not. The best of beauty is a finer charm than skill in surfaces, in outlines, or rules of art can ever teach, namely a radiation from the work of art, of human character—a wonderful expression through stone, or canvas, or musical sound, of the deepest and simplest attributes of our nature, and therefore most intelligible at last to those souls which have these attributes. In the sculptures of the Greeks, in the masonry of the Romans, and in the pictures of the Tuscan and Venetian masters, the highest charm is the universal language they speak. A confession of moral nature, of purity, love, and hope, breathes from them all. That which we carry to them, the same we bring back more fairly illustrated in the memory. The traveller who visits the Vatican and passes from chamber to chamber through galleries of statues, vases, sarcophagi and candelabra, through all forms of beauty cut in the richest materials, is in danger of forgetting the simplicity of the principles out of which they all sprung, and that they had their origin from thoughts and laws in his own breast. He studies the technical rules on these wonderful remains, but forgets that these works were not always thus constellated; that they are the contributions of many ages and many countries; that each came out of the solitary workshop of one artist, who toiled perhaps in ignorance of the existence of other sculpture, created his work without other model save life, household life, and the sweet and smart of personal relations, of beating hearts, and meeting eyes; of poverty and necessity and hope and fear. These were his inspirations, and these are the effects he carries home to your heart and mind. In proportion to his force, the artist will find in his work an outlet for his proper character. He must not be in any manner pinched or hindered by his material, but through his necessity of imparting himself the adamant will be wax in his hands, and will allow an adequate communication of himself, in his full stature and proportion. He need not cumber himself with a conventional nature and culture, nor ask what is the mode in Rome or in Paris, but that house and weather and manner of living which poverty and the fate of birth have made at once so odious and so dear, in the gray unpainted wood cabin, on the corner of a New Hampshire farm, or in the log-hut of the backwoods, or in the narrow lodging where he has endured the constraints and seeming of a city poverty, will serve as well as any other condition as the symbol of a thought which pours itself indifferently through all.

I remember when in my younger days I had heard of the wonders of Italian painting, I fancied the great pictures would be great strangers; some surprising combination of color and form; a foreign wonder, barbaric pearl and gold, like the spontoons and standards of the militia, which play such pranks in the eyes and imaginations of school-boys. I was to see and acquire I knew not what. When I came at last to Rome and saw with eyes the pictures, I found that genius left to novices the gay and fantastic and ostentatious, and itself pierced directly to the simple and true; that it was familiar and sincere; that it was the old, eternal fact I had met already in so many forms—unto which I lived; that it was the plain *you and me* I knew so well—had left at home in so many conversations. I had had the same experience already in a church at Naples. There I saw that nothing was changed with me but the place, and said to myself—"Thou foolish child, hast thou come out hither, over four thousand miles of salt water, to find that which was perfect to thee there at home?" That fact I saw again in the Academmia at Naples, in the chambers of sculpture, and yet again when I came to Rome and to the paintings of Raphael, Angelo, Sacchi, Titian, and Leonardo da Vinci. "What, old mole! workest thou in the earth so fast?" It had travelled by my side; that which I fancied I had left in Boston was here in the Vatican, and again at Milan and at Paris, and made all travelling ridiculous as a treadmill. I now require this of all pictures, that they domesticate me, not that they dazzle me. Pictures must not be too picturesque. Nothing astonishes men so much as common-sense and plain dealing. All great actions have been simple, and all great pictures are.

The Transfiguration, by Raphael, is an eminent example of this peculiar merit. A calm benignant beauty shines over all this picture, and goes directly to the heart. It seems almost to call you by name. The sweet and sublime face of Jesus is beyond praise, yet how it disappoints all florid expectations! This familiar, simple, home-speaking countenance is as if one should meet a friend. The knowledge of picture dealers has its value, but listen not to their criticism when your heart is touched by genius. It was not painted for them, it was painted for you; for such as had eyes capable of being touched by simplicity and lofty emotions.

Yet when we have said all our fine things about the arts, we must end with a frank confession that the arts, as we know them, are but initial. Our best praise is given to what they aimed and promised, not to the actual result. He has conceived meanly of the resources of man, who believes that the best age of production is past. The real value of the Iliad or the Transfiguration is as signs of power; billows or ripples they are of the stream of tendency; tokens of the everlasting effort to produce, which even in its worst estate the soul betrays. Art has not yet come to its maturity if it do not put itself abreast with the most potent influences of the world, if it is not practical and moral, if it do not stand in connection with the conscience, if it do not make the poor and uncultivated feel that it addresses them with a voice of lofty cheer. There is higher work for Art than the arts. They are abortive births of an imperfect or vitiated instinct. Art is the need to create; but in its essence, immense and universal, it is impatient of working with lame or tied hands, and of making cripples and monsters, such as all pictures and statues are. Nothing less than the creation of man and nature is its end. A man should find in it an outlet for his whole energy. He may paint and carve only as long as he can do that. Art should exhilarate, and throw down the walls of circumstance on every side, awakening in the beholder the same sense of universal relation and power which the work evinced in the artist, and its highest effect is to make new artists.

Already History is old enough to witness the old age and disappearance of particular arts. The art of sculpture is long ago perished to any real effect. It was originally a useful art, a mode of writing, a savage's record of gratitude or devotion, and among a people possessed of a wonderful perception of form this childish carving was refined to the utmost splendor of effect. But it is the game of a rude and youthful people, and not the manly labor of a wise and spiritual nation. Under an oak-tree loaded with leaves and nuts, under a sky full of eternal eyes, I stand in a thoroughfare; but in the works of our plastic arts and especially of sculpture, creation is driven into a corner. I cannot hide from myself that there is a certain appearance of paltriness, as of toys and the trumpery of a theatre, in sculpture. Nature transcends all our moods of thought, and its secret we do not yet find. But the gallery stands at the mercy of our moods, and there is a moment when it becomes frivolous. I do not wonder that Newton, with an attention habitually engaged on the paths of planets and suns, should have wondered what the Earl of Pembroke found to admire in "stone dolls." Sculpture may serve to teach the pupil how deep is the secret of form, how purely the spirit can translate its meanings into that eloquent dialect. But the statue will look cold and false before that new activity which needs to roll through all things, and is impatient of counterfeits and things not alive. Picture and sculpture are the celebrations and festivities of form. But true art is never fixed, but always flowing. The sweetest music is not in the oratorio, but in the human voice when it speaks from its instant life tones of tenderness, truth, or courage. The oratorio has already lost its relation to the morning, to the sun, and the earth, but that persuading voice is in tune with these. All works of art should not be detached, but extempore performances. A great man is a new statue in every attitude and action. A beautiful woman is a picture which drives all beholders nobly mad. Life may be lyric or epic, as well as a poem or a romance.

A true announcement of the law of creation, if a man were found worthy to declare it, would carry art up into the kingdom of nature, and destroy its separate and contrasted existence. The fountains of invention and beauty in modern society are all but dried up. A popular novel, a theatre, or a ballroom makes us feel that we are all paupers in the almshouse of this world, without dignity, without skill or industry. Art is as poor and low. The old tragic Necessity, which lowers on the brows even of the Venuses and the Cupids of the antique, and furnishes the sole apology for the intrusion of such anomalous figures into nature—namely that they were inevitable; that the artist was drunk with a passion for form which he could not resist, and which vented itself in these fine extravagances—no longer dignifies the chisel or the pencil. But the artist and the connoisseur now seek in art the exhibition of their talent, or an asylum from the evils of life. Men are not well pleased with the figure they make in their own imaginations, and they flee to art, and convey their better sense in an oratorio, a statue, or a picture. Art makes the same effort which a sensual prosperity makes; namely to detach the beautiful from the useful, to do up the work as unavoidable, and, hating it, pass on to enjoyment. These solaces and compensations, this division of beauty from use, the laws of nature do not permit. As soon as beauty is sought, not from religion and love but for pleasure, it degrades the seeker. High beauty is no longer attainable by him in canvas or in stone, in sound, or in lyrical construction; an effeminate, prudent, sickly beauty, which is not beauty, is all that can be formed; for the hand can never execute any thing higher than the character can inspire.

The art that thus separates is itself first separated. Art must not be a superficial talent, but must begin farther back in man. Now men do not see nature to be beautiful, and they go to make a statue which shall be. They abhor men as tasteless, dull, and inconvertible, and console themselves with color-bags and blocks of marble. They reject life as prosaic, and create a death which they call poetic. They despatch the day's weary chores, and fly to voluptuous reveries. They eat and drink, that they may afterwards execute the ideal. Thus is art vilified; the name conveys to the mind its secondary and bad senses; it stands in the imagination as somewhat contrary to nature, and struck with death from the first. Would it not be better to begin higher up—to serve the ideal before they eat and drink; to serve the ideal in eating and drinking, in drawing the breath, and in the functions of life? Beauty must come back to the useful arts, and the distinction between the fine and the useful arts be forgotten. If history were truly told, if life were nobly spent, it would be no longer easy or possible to distinguish the one from the other. In nature, all is useful, all is beautiful. It is therefore beautiful because it is alive, moving, reproductive; it is therefore useful because it is symmetrical and fair. Beauty will not come at the call of a legislature, nor will it repeat in England or America its history in Greece. It will come, as always, un-announced, and spring up between the feet of brave and earnest men. It is in vain that we look for genius to reiterate its miracles in the old arts; it is its instinct to find beauty and holiness in new and necessary facts, in the field and road-side, in the shop and mill. Proceeding from a religious heart it will raise to a divine use the railroad, the insurance office, the joint-stock com-pany; our law, our primary assemblies, our commerce, the galvanic battery, the electric jar, the prism, and the chemist's retort; in which we seek now only an economical use. Is not the selfish and even cruel aspect which belongs to our great mechanical works, to mills, railways, and machinery, the effect of the mercenary impulses which these works obey? When its errands are noble and adequate, a steamboat bridging the Atlantic between Old and New England and arriving at its ports with the punctuality of a planet, is a step of man into harmony with nature. The boat at St. Petersburg, which plies along the Lena by magnetism, needs little to make it sublime. When science is learned in love, and its powers are wielded by love, they will appear the supplements and continuations of the material creation.

DISCUSSION AND WRITING

1. Define or explain: *eclecticism, hieroglyphics, beatitude, sequester, opulence, austere, novice, transfiguration, benignant, florid, countenance* (n.), *vitiate, paltriness, trumpery, lower* (vb.), *anomalous, prosaic, voluptuous, reiterate, mercenary.* In context, what is the meaning of "the *genius* of the hour," "the *accidents* of a local and special culture," the *"standards* of the militia"? Can you find half a dozen words and grammatical constructions that sound like nineteenth-century rather than twentieth-century English?

2. To what extent are you familiar with the terminology of art and art history employed by the author? Compile a glossary of a dozen technical terms—terms for types of works, features of form, details of artistic production and the like. Select those that you think the general reader is least likely to know. Explain each term briefly to the layman.

3. Like other nineteenth-century writers, Emerson had a preference for the kind of memorable sentence that sums up an important idea in a striking form. Study the following examples and find similar ones on your own. Do they have anything in common—word choice, grammatical construction, sentence style, tone? What features do these sentences have that make Emerson one of the "sentence-makers" of nineteenth-century American prose?

 a. Painting seems to be to the eye what dancing is to the limbs.

 b. Pictures must not be too picturesque.

 c. Nothing astonishes men so much as common sense and plain dealing.

 d. There is higher work for Art than the arts.

 e. A beautiful woman is a picture which drives all beholders nobly mad.

 f. In nature all is useful, all is beautiful.

4. Emerson shares with other successful lecturers of his time the tendency to build an essay around a few key ideas restated in many different variations and applications. What are the key ideas in this essay, and where are they most clearly stated?

5. In spite of the intentional repetition of key ideas, is there any logical progression from paragraph to paragraph? Prepare a paragraph outline, indicating roughly the contribution of each paragraph to the essay as a whole. Does the essay have a definite design, a deliberate strategy, an overall argument?

6. What does Emerson mean when he says that "all works of the highest art" are "religious"?

7. Modern disciples of Emerson often claim that culture is not what we see in museums—"not what is displayed behind drawn curtains in dark rooms but what is displayed for all to see": street signs, street lamps, newsstands, shop windows—the everyday scene through which people move. Examine, from this point of view, the cultural quality of a city you know well.

8. Would Emerson approve of modern art, or rather of some particular *kind* of modern art that you know from first-hand observation? Discuss some specific works in the light of Emerson's criteria and preferences.

9. Some people feel, with Emerson, that the great and beautiful in art makes us see and appreciate the great and beautiful in life. ("When I have been reading Homer, all men look like giants.") Others feel that the great and beautiful in art makes everyday

life seem petty and ugly by contrast. ("When I have been reading Homer, ordinary men look like dwarfs.") Does your own experience with art tend to have an inspiring or a disillusioning effect?

10. Is it true of contemporary American culture as you know it that we tend "to detach the beautiful from the useful, to do up the work as unavoidable, and, hating it, pass on to enjoyment"?

FURTHER READING

In a collection of Emerson's writing, find his address on "The American Scholar." Write an essay in which you discuss the ideal of American culture envisioned by Emerson in this famous lecture.

MATTHEW ARNOLD

Matthew Arnold (1822–1888) was an English spokesman of the humanities whose influence is still strong in our time. Like his contemporaries Thomas Carlyle and John Ruskin, Arnold reached a large audience through magazine essays and public lectures. In addition to his work as poet, critic, and lecturer, he was a government inspector of schools and for ten years taught at the University of Oxford. Trained as a classical scholar, Arnold read widely in English and continental European literature. His concern with literature and culture thus went beyond narrow national boundaries. He effectively championed the concerns of culture against overemphasis on the practical on the one hand and narrow specialization in the sciences on the other. "Sweetness and Light" was first published in 1867. In the section omitted from this version of the essay, Arnold evaluates contemporary religious and political trends in the light of his standards. Like his American contemporary Emerson, Arnold depends on deliberate repetition and variation to reinforce key terms and key ideas.

Sweetness and Light

The disparagers of culture make its motive curiosity; sometimes, indeed, they make its motive mere exclusiveness and vanity. The culture which is supposed to plume itself on a smattering of Greek and Latin is a culture which is begotten by nothing so intellectual as curiosity; it is valued either out of sheer vanity and ignorance or else as an engine of social and class distinction, separating its holder, like a badge or title, from other people who have not got it. No serious man would call this *culture*, or attach any value to it, as culture, at all. To find the real ground for the very different estimate which serious people will set upon culture, we must find some motive for culture in the terms of which may lie a real ambiguity; and such a motive the word *curiosity* gives us.

I have before now pointed out that we English do not, like the foreigners, use this word in a good sense as well as in a bad sense. With us the word is always used in a somewhat disapproving sense. A liberal and intelligent eagerness about the things of the mind may be meant by a foreigner when he speaks of curiosity, but with us the word always conveys a certain notion of frivolous and unedifying activity. In the *Quarterly Review,* some little time ago, was an estimate of the celebrated French critic M. Sainte-Beuve, and a very inadequate estimate it in my judgment was. And its inadequacy consisted chiefly in this: that in our English way it left out of sight the double sense really involved in the word *curiosity,* thinking enough was said to stamp M. Sainte-Beuve with blame if it was said that he was impelled in his operations as a critic by curiosity, and omitting either to perceive that M. Sainte-Beuve himself, and many other people with him, would consider that this was praiseworthy and not blameworthy, or to point out why it ought really to be accounted worthy of blame and not of praise. For as there is a curiosity about intellectual matters which is futile, and merely a disease, so there is certainly a curiosity,—a desire after the things of the mind simply for their own sakes and for the pleasures of seeing them as they are,—which is, in an intelligent being, natural and laudable. Nay, and the very desire to see things as they are implies a balance and regulation of mind which is not often attained without fruitful effort, and which is the very opposite of the blind and diseased impulse of mind which is what we mean to blame when we blame curiosity. Montesquieu says: "The first motive which ought to impel us to study is the desire to augment the excellence of our nature, and to render an intelligent being yet more intelligent." This is the true ground to assign for the genuine scientific passion, however manifested, and for culture, viewed simply as a fruit of this passion; and it is a worthy ground, even though we let the term *curiosity* stand to describe it.

But there is of culture another view, in which not solely the scientific passion, the sheer desire to see things as they are, natural and proper in an intelligent being, appears as the ground of it. There is a view in which all the love of our neighbor, the impulses towards action, help, and beneficence, the desire for removing human error, clearing human confusion, and diminishing human misery, the noble aspiration to leave the world better and happier than we found it,—motives eminently such as are called social,—come in as part of the grounds of culture, and the main and preeminent part. Culture is then properly described not as having its origin in curiosity, but as having its origin in the love of perfection; it is *a study of perfection*. It moves by the force, not merely or primarily of the scientific passion for pure knowledge, but also of the moral and social passion for doing good. As, in the first view of it, we took for its worthy motto Montesquieu's words: "To render an intelligent being yet more intelligent!" so, in the second view of it, there is no better motto which it can have than these words of Bishop Wilson: "To make reason and the will of God prevail!"

Only, whereas the passion for doing good is apt to be over-hasty in determining what reason and the will of God say, because its turn is for acting rather than thinking and it wants to be beginning to act; and whereas it is apt to take its own conceptions, which proceed from its own state of development and share in all the imperfections and immaturities of this, for a basis of action; what distinguishes culture is that it is possessed by the scientific passion as well as by the passion of doing good; that it demands worthy notions of reason and the will of God, and does not readily suffer its own crude conceptions to substitute themselves for them. And knowing that no action or institution can be salutary and stable which is not based on reason and the will of God, it is not so bent on acting and instituting, even with the great aim of diminishing human error and misery ever before its thoughts, but that it can remember that acting and instituting are of little use, unless we know how and what we ought to act and to institute....

And religion, the greatest and most important of the efforts by which the human race has manifested its impulse to perfect itself,—religion, that voice of the deepest human experience,—does not only enjoin and sanction the aim which is the great aim of culture, the aim of setting ourselves to ascertain what perfection is and to make it prevail; but also, in determining generally in what human perfection consists, religion comes to a conclusion identical with that which culture,—culture seeking the determination of this question through *all* the voices of human experience which have been heard upon it, of art, science, poetry, philosophy, history, as well as of religion, in order to give a greater fullness and certainty to its solution,—likewise reaches. Religion says: *The kingdom of God is within you;* and culture, in like manner, places human perfection in an *internal* condition, in the growth and predominance of our humanity proper, as distinguished from our animality. It places it in the ever-increasing efficacy and in the general harmonious expansion of those gifts of thought and feeling, which make the peculiar dignity, wealth, and happiness of human nature. As I have said on a former occasion: "It is in making endless additions to itself, in the endless expansion of its powers, in endless growth in wisdom and beauty, that the spirit of the human race finds its ideal. To reach this ideal, culture is an indispensable aid, and that is the true value of culture." Not a having and a resting, but a growing and a becoming, is the character of perfection as culture conceives it; and here, too, it coincides with religion.

And because men are all members of one great whole, and the sympathy which is in human nature will not allow one member to be indifferent to the rest or to have a perfect welfare independent of the rest, the expansion of our humanity, to suit the idea of perfection which culture forms, must be a *general* expansion. Perfection, as culture conceives it, is not possible while the individual remains isolated. The individual is required, under pain of being stunted and enfeebled in his own development if he disobeys, to carry others along with him in his march towards perfection, to be continually doing all he can to enlarge and increase the volume of the human stream sweeping thitherward. And here, once more, culture lays on us the same obligation as religion, which says, as Bishop Wilson has admirably put it, that "to promote the kingdom of God is to increase and hasten one's own happiness."

But, finally, perfection,—as culture from a thorough disinterested study of human nature and human experience learns to conceive it,—is a harmonious expansion of *all* the powers which make the beauty and worth of human nature, and is not consistent with the over-development of any one power at the expense of the rest. Here culture goes beyond religion, as religion is generally conceived by us.

If culture, then, is a study of perfection, and of harmonious perfection, general perfection, and perfection which consists in becoming something rather than in having something, in an inward condition of the mind and spirit, not in an outward set of circumstances,—it is clear that culture, instead of being a frivolous and useless thing, has a very important function to fulfill for mankind. And this function is particularly important in our modern world, of which the whole civilization is, to a much greater degree than the civilization of Greece and Rome, mechanical and external, and tends constantly to become more so. But above all in our own country has culture a weighty part to perform, because here that mechanical character, which civilization tends to take everywhere, is shown in the most eminent degree. Indeed nearly all the characters of perfection, as culture teaches us to fix them, meet in this country with some powerful tendency which thwarts them and sets them at defiance. The idea of perfection as an *inward* condition of the mind and spirit is at variance with the mechanical and material civilization in esteem with us, and nowhere, as I have said, so much in esteem as with us. The idea of perfection as a *general* expansion of the human family is at variance with our strong individualism, our hatred of all limits to the unrestrained swing of the individual's personality, our maxim of "every man for himself." Above all, the idea of perfection as a *harmonious* expansion of human nature is at variance with our want of flexibility, with our inaptitude for seeing more than one side of a thing, with our intense energetic absorption in the particular pursuit we happen to be following. So culture has a rough task to achieve in this country. Its preachers have, and are likely long to have, a hard time of it, and they will much oftener be regarded, for a great while to come, as elegant or spurious Jeremiahs than as friends and benefactors. That, however, will not prevent their doing in the end good service if they persevere. And, meanwhile, the mode of action they have to pursue, and the sort of habits they must fight against, ought to be made quite clear for everyone to see, who may be willing to look at the matter attentively and dispassionately.

Faith in machinery is, I said, our besetting danger; often in machinery most absurdly disproportioned to the end which this machinery, if it is to do any good at all, is to serve; but always in machinery, as if it had a value in and for itself. What is freedom but machinery? what is population but machinery? what is coal but machinery? what are railroads but machinery? what is wealth but machinery? what are, even, religious organizations but machinery? Now almost every voice in England is accustomed to speak of these things as if they were precious ends in themselves, and therefore had some of the characters of perfection indisputably joined to them. I have before now noticed Mr. Roebuck's stock argument for proving the greatness and happiness of England as she is, and for quite stopping the mouths of all gainsayers. Mr. Roebuck is never weary of reiterating this argument of his, so I do not know why I should be weary of noticing it. "May not every man in England say what he likes?"—Mr. Roebuck perpetually asks; and that, he thinks, is quite sufficient, and when every man may say what he likes, our aspirations ought to be satisfied. But the aspirations of culture, which is the study of perfection, are not satisfied, unless what men say, when they may say what they like, is worth saying,—has good in it, and more good than bad. In the same way the *Times,* replying to some foreign strictures on the dress, looks, and behavior of the English abroad, urges that the English ideal is that everyone should be free to do and to look just as he likes. But culture indefatigably tries, not to make what each raw person may like the rule by which he fashions himself; but to draw ever nearer to a sense of what is indeed beautiful, graceful, and becoming, and to get the raw person to like that.

And in the same way with respect to railroads and coal. Everyone must have observed the strange language current during the late discussions as to the possible failure of our supplies of coal. Our coal, thousands of people were saying, is the real basis of our national greatness; if our coal runs short, there is an end of the greatness of England. But what *is* greatness?—culture makes us ask. Greatness is a spiritual condition worthy to excite love, interest, and admiration; and the outward proof of possessing greatness is that we excite love, interest, and admiration. If England were swallowed up by the sea tomorrow, which of the two, a hundred years hence, would most excite the love, interest, and admiration of mankind,—would most, therefore, show the evidences of having possessed greatness,—the England of the last twenty years, or the England of Elizabeth, of a time of splendid spiritual effort, but when our coal, and our industrial operations depending on coal, were very little developed? Well, then, what an unsound habit of mind it must be which makes us talk of things like coal or iron as constituting the greatness of England, and how salutary a friend is culture, bent on seeing things as they are, and thus dissipating delusions of this kind and fixing standards of perfection that are real!

Wealth, again, that end to which our prodigious works for material advantage are directed,—the commonest of commonplaces tells us how men are always apt to regard wealth as a precious end in itself; and certainly they have never been so apt thus to regard it as they are in England at the present time. Never did people believe anything more firmly than nine Englishmen out of ten at the present day believe that our greatness and welfare are proved by our being so very rich. Now, the use of culture is that it helps us, by means of its spiritual standard of perfection, to regard wealth as but machinery, and not only to say as a matter of words that we regard wealth as but machinery, but really to perceive and feel that it is so. If it were not for this purging effect wrought upon our minds by culture, the whole world, the future as well as the present, would inevitably belong to the Philistines. The people who believe most that our greatness and welfare are proved by our being very rich, and who most give their lives and thoughts to becoming rich, are just the very people whom we call Philistines. Culture says: "Consider these people, then, their way of life, their habits, their manners, the very tones of their voice; look at them attentively; observe the literature they read, the things which give them pleasure, the words which come forth out of their mouths, the thoughts which make the furniture of their minds: would any amount of wealth be worth having with the condition that one was to become just like these people by having it?" And thus culture begets a dissatisfaction which is of the highest possible value in stemming the common tide of men's thoughts in a wealthy and industrial community, and which saves the future, as one may hope, from being vulgarized, even if it cannot save the present....

But bodily health and vigor, it may be said, are not to be classed with wealth and population as mere machinery; they have a more real and essential value. True; but only as they are more intimately connected with a perfect spiritual condition than wealth or population are. The moment we disjoin them from the idea of a perfect spiritual condition, and pursue them, as we do pursue them, for their own sake and as ends in themselves, our worship of them becomes as mere worship of machinery, as our worship of wealth or population, and as unintelligent and vulgarizing a worship as that is. Everyone with anything like an adequate idea of human perfection has distinctly marked this subordination to higher and spiritual ends of the cultivation of bodily vigor and activity. "Bodily exercise profiteth little; but godliness is profitable unto all things," says the author of the Epistle to Timothy. And the utilitarian Franklin says just as explicitly:—"Eat and drink such an exact quantity as suits the constitution of thy body, *in reference to the services of the mind*." But the point of view of culture, keeping the mark of human perfection simply and broadly in view, and not assigning to this perfection, as religion or utilitarianism assigns to it, a special and limited character, this point of view, I say, of culture is best given by these words of Epictetus: "It is a sign of ἀφυΐα," says he,—that is, of a nature not finely tempered,—"to give yourselves up to things which relate to the body; to make, for instance, a great fuss about exercise, a great fuss about eating, a great fuss about drinking, a great fuss about walking, a great fuss about riding. All these things ought to be done merely by the way: the formation of the spirit and character must be our real concern." This is admirable; and, indeed, the Greek word εὐφυΐα, a finely tempered nature, gives exactly the notion of perfection as culture brings us to conceive it: a harmonious perfection, a perfection in which the characters of beauty and intelligence are both present, which unites "the two noblest of things,"—as Swift, who of one of the two, at any rate, had himself all too little, most happily calls them in his *Battle of the Books*,—"the two noblest of things, *sweetness and light*." The εὐφυής is the man who tends toward sweetness and light; the ἀφυής, on the other hand, is our Philistine. The immense spiritual significance of the Greeks is due to their having been inspired with this central and happy idea of the essential character of human perfection; and the misconception of culture, as a smattering of Greek and Latin, comes itself, after all, from this wonderful significance of the Greeks having affected the very machinery of our education, and is in itself a kind of homage to it.

In thus making sweetness and light to be characters of perfection, culture is of like spirit with poetry, follows one law with poetry. Far more than on our freedom, our population, and our industrialism, many amongst us rely upon our religious organizations to save us. I have called religion a yet more important manifestation of human nature than poetry, because it has worked on a broader scale for perfection, and with greater masses of men. But the idea of beauty and of a human nature perfect on all its sides, which is the dominant idea of poetry, is a true and invaluable idea, though it has not yet had the success that the idea of conquering the obvious faults of our animality, and of a human nature perfect on the moral side,—which is the dominant idea of religion,—has been enabled to have; and it is destined, adding to itself the religious idea of a devout energy, to transform and govern the other.

The best art and poetry of the Greeks, in which religion and poetry are one, in which the idea of beauty and of a human nature perfect on all sides adds to itself a religious and devout energy, and works in the strength of that, is on this account of such surpassing interest and instructiveness for us, though it was,—as, having regard to the human race in general, and, indeed, having regard to the Greeks themselves, we must own,—a premature attempt, an attempt which for success needed the moral and religious fiber in humanity to be more braced and developed than it had yet been. But Greece did not err in having the idea of beauty, harmony, and complete human perfection, so present and paramount. It is impossible to have this idea too present and paramount; only, the moral fiber must be braced too. And we, because we have braced the moral fiber, are not on that account in the right way, if at the same time the idea of beauty, harmony, and complete human perfection, is wanting or misapprehended amongst us; and evidently it *is* wanting or misapprehended at present. . . .

The pursuit of perfection, then, is the pursuit of sweetness and light. He who works for sweetness and light, works to make reason and the will of God prevail. He who works for machinery, he who works for hatred, works only for confusion. Culture looks beyond machinery, culture hates hatred; culture has one great passion, the passion for sweetness and light. It has one even yet greater!—the passion for making them *prevail*. It is not satisfied till we *all* come to a perfect man; it knows that the sweetness and light of the few must be imperfect until the raw and unkindled masses of humanity are touched with sweetness and light. If I have not shrunk from saying that we must work for sweetness and light, so neither have I shrunk from saying that we must have a broad basis, must have sweetness and light for as many as possible. Again and again I have insisted how those are the happy moments of humanity, how those are the marking epochs of a people's life, how those are the flowering times for literature and art and all the creative power of genius, when there is a *national* glow of life and thought, when the whole of society is in the fullest measure permeated by thought, sensible to beauty, intelligent and alive. Only it must be *real* thought and *real* beauty; *real* sweetness and *real* light. Plenty of people will try to give the masses, as they call them, an intellectual food prepared and adapted in the way they think proper for the actual condition of the masses. The ordinary popular literature is an example of this way of working on the masses. Plenty of people will try to indoctrinate the masses with the set of ideas and judgments constituting the creed of their own profession or party. Our religious and political organizations give an example of this way of working on the masses. I condemn neither way; but culture works differently. It does not try to teach down to the level of inferior classes; it does not try to win them for this or that sect of it own, with ready-made judgments and watchwords. It seeks to do away with classes; to make the best that has been thought and known in the world current everywhere; to make all men live in an atmosphere of sweetness and light, where they may use ideas, as it uses them itself, freely,—nourished, and not bound by them.

This is the *social idea;* and the men of culture are the true apostles of equality. The great men of culture are those who have had a passion for diffusing, for making prevail, for carrying from one end of society to the other, the best knowledge, the best ideas of their time; who have labored to divest knowledge of all that was harsh, uncouth, difficult, abstract, professional, exclusive; to humanize it, to make it efficient outside the clique of the cultivated and learned, yet still remaining the *best* knowledge and thought of the time, and a true source, therefore, of sweetness and light. Such a man was Abelard in the Middle Ages, in spite of all his imperfections; and thence the boundless emotion and enthusiasm which Abelard excited. Such were Lessing and Herder in Germany, at the end of the last century; and their services to Germany were in this way inestimably precious. Generations will pass, and literary monuments will accumulate, and works far more perfect than the works of Lessing and Herder will be produced in Germany; and yet the names of these two men will fill a German with a reverence and enthusiasm such as the names of the most gifted masters will hardly awaken. And why? Because they *humanized* knowledge; because they broadened the basis of life and intelligence; because they worked powerfully to diffuse sweetness and light, to make reason and the will of God prevail. With Saint Augustine they said: "Let us not leave thee alone to make in the secret of thy knowledge, as thou didst before the creation of the firmament, the division of light from darkness; let the children of thy spirit, placed in their firmament, make their light shine upon the earth, mark the division of night and day, and announce the revolution of the times; for the old order is passed, and the new arises; the night is spent, the day is come forth; and thou shalt crown the year with thy blessing, when thou shalt send forth laborers into thy harvest sown by other hands than theirs; when thou shalt send forth new laborers to new seed-times, whereof the harvest shall be not yet."

DISCUSSION AND WRITING

1. Define or explain: *disparage, frivolous, edify, laudable, augment, predominance, spurious, gainsayer, reiterate, stricture, indefatigable, salutary, prodigious, Philistine, disjoin, utilitarian, homage, paramount, permeate, diffuse* (vb.), *uncouth.* Explain the meaning of the italicized terms in context: "*plume* itself on a *smattering* of Greek and Latin"; "*engine* of social and class distinction"; "*at variance* with the mechanical and material civilization"; "regarded as elegant, or spurious *Jeremiahs*"; "bent on *dissipating* delusions."

2. In what sense is freedom "but machinery"? What view of freedom of speech and conduct is implied in Arnold's discussion? In what sense is wealth "but machinery"?

3. In a well-developed paragraph, summarize Arnold's definition of culture. What, in Arnold's view, is the relation of culture to science and religion?

4. Outline the development of Arnold's argument, locating the key idea (or ideas) of each paragraph. Describe and illustrate Arnold's characteristic style or method as a lecturer.

5. How strong is the impulse toward "perfection" in contemporary American society? To what extent is it thwarted by obstacles similar to those Arnold describes?

6. How does Arnold's view of the "scientific passion" compare with the account given of science by T. H. Huxley? Or, compare and contrast Arnold's definition of religion with William James's.

7. Is there a common basis for Emerson's definition of "Art" and Arnold's definition of "culture"? Trace in detail any essential parallels and significant differences.

8. Argue one of the following theses: American education does (does not) develop disinterested curiosity. American education does (does not) recognize an ideal of perfection.

9. Write an essay attacking or defending the Philistine. Use concrete illustrations.

10. Define national greatness and show whether or how your definition applies to the United States.

FURTHER READING

For fuller development of Arnold's view of the relationship between science and culture, compare his essay on "Literature and Science" (1885).

8

The Twinkle in the Eye

Life everywhere furnishes an accurate observer with the ridiculous. HENRY FIELDING

The most obvious function of humor is to help us escape from the deadly seriousness that at times befalls the best of us. Humor provides the kind of detachment that makes grim literal fact bearable. It reminds us that man is not altogether the slave of circumstance, that he has spiritual resources that can give him a measure of independence from raw reality. At the same time, this detachment may enable him to see things in their more general perspective, to attain a view perhaps truer and more revealing than that of the mere humorless, literal-minded, "realistic" observer. The authors in this section are all humorists who know how to entertain their audiences while letting show through, more or less clearly, their serious intentions. Samuel Clemens (Mark Twain), the most widely known and translated of American authors, combines the American humorist's traditional preference for broad exaggeration, for outrageous overstatement, with the deadly accuracy of aim of the born satirist. Ben Hecht combines a boisterous kind of humor, a thorn in the side of gentility, with a capacity for intense conviction and stubborn loyalty. James Thurber, the best known of a number of outstanding contemporary American humorists associated with *The New Yorker,* shows that humor need not become any less barbed for changing into a lower key. Leszek Kolakowski, schooled in ideological combat, illustrates the irreverence of a brilliant intellectual kind of wit and the destructive potential of ridicule.

SAMUEL CLEMENS

Samuel Langhorne Clemens (1835–1910), whose pen name was Mark Twain, grew up in Hannibal, Missouri, on the banks of the Mississippi. The river, then a main artery of trade and of national expansion, was well known to him as a boy and later as an apprentice pilot. It plays a dominant role in several of his books, including *Life on the Mississippi* (1883). Mark Twain became famous as a writer of humorous sketches for newspapers and of humorous travel books like *The Innocents Abroad* (1869), in which he drew upon a brand of American folk humor using broad exaggeration. In spite of its exuberance, Mark Twain's humor often had overtones of personal bitterness. Among his later stories, *The Man That Corrupted Hadleyburg* (1900) and *The Mysterious Stranger* (1916) are sardonic commentaries on human pretensions and illusions. The "Pudd'nhead Wilson Maxims" are here collected from *Pudd'nhead Wilson* and *Following the Equator*.

The Pudd'nhead Wilson Maxims

There is no character, howsoever good and fine, but it can be destroyed by ridicule, howsoever poor and witless. Observe the ass, for instance: his character is about perfect, he is the choicest spirit among all the humbler animals, yet see what ridicule has brought him to. Instead of feeling complimented when we are called an ass, we are left in doubt.

Adam was but human—this explains it all. He did not want the apple for the apple's sake, he wanted it only because it was forbidden. The mistake was in not forbidding the serpent; then he would have eaten the serpent.

Training is everything. The peach was once a bitter almond; cauliflower is nothing but cabbage with a college education.

Let us endeavor so to live that when we come to die even the undertaker will be sorry.

Habit is habit and not to be flung out of the window by any man but coaxed down-stairs a step at a time.

The holy passion of Friendship is of so sweet and steady and loyal and enduring a nature that it will last through a whole lifetime, if not asked to lend money.

If you pick up a starving dog and make him prosperous, he will not bite you. This is the principal difference between a dog and a man.

Few things are harder to put up with than the annoyance of a good example.

Noise proves nothing. Often a hen who has merely laid an egg cackles as if she had laid an asteroid.

We should be careful to get out of an experience only the wisdom that is in it—and stop there; lest we be like the cat that sits down on a hot stove-lid. She will never sit down on a hot stove-lid again, and that is well; but also she will never sit down on a cold one any more.

There are those who scoff at the school-boy, calling him frivolous and shallow. Yet it was the school-boy who said, "Faith is believing what you know ain't so."

Truth is stranger than Fiction, but it is because Fiction is obliged to stick to possibilities; Truth isn't.

It is by the goodness of God that in our country we have those three unspeakably precious things: freedom of speech, freedom of conscience, and the prudence never to practice either of them.

Man is the only animal that blushes. Or needs to.

When people do not respect us we are sharply offended; yet deep down in his private heart no man much respects himself.

The man with a new idea is a Crank until the new idea succeeds.

There are several good protections against temptations but the surest is cowardice.

Prosperity is the best protector of principle.

The old saw says, "Let a sleeping dog lie." Right. Still, when there is much at stake it is better to get a newspaper to do it.

Simple rules for saving money: To save half, when you are fired by an eager impulse to contribute to charity, wait and count forty. To save three-quarters, count sixty. To save it all, count sixty-five.

There are two times in a man's life when he should not speculate: when he can't afford it and when he can.

Often, the surest way to convey misinformation is to tell the strict truth.

In the first place God made idiots. This was for practice. Then He made School Boards.

Everyone is a moon and has a dark side which he never shows to anybody.

The very ink with which all history is written is merely fluid prejudice.

There isn't a Parallel of Latitude but thinks it would have been the Equator if it had had its rights.

DISCUSSION AND WRITING

1. Identify or explain some of the techniques or types of humor that Twain employs in this selection. How effective are they? Do any of them seem out of fashion, ineffectual, or objectionable?

2. Samuel Clemens is one of the most quotable of American writers. Among these maxims, select those that you consider the most memorable or quotable. Describe and illustrate the features of diction and of sentence style that help make them so.

3. State in one well-developed paragraph the attitude toward life or toward people that predominates in these maxims. Do you find it congenial, defensible, appealing?

4. Select one of the maxims with which you agree or disagree. Develop its implications and support or attack the point of view it represents.

5. Using these maxims as a model, compose half a dozen maxims derived from your own experience and observation. Make use of humor, irony, and satire.

6. Examine and discuss the nature and use of satire in the comic strips of Al Capp, Walt Kelly, or some other contemporary cartoonist known for his use of social or political satire.

7. Discuss the characteristic brand of humor of one of several contemporary American comedians known for their satirical treatment of political, social, or racial questions.

8. Where do you draw the line between things that can be legitimately treated in a humorous manner and those that should not be made the subject of humor, satire, or ridicule? Use detailed examples.

9. How much a part of everyday American life is humor? Use detailed illustrations.

10. Samuel Clemens is a master of the aphorism, the short memorable statement of a striking truth. Compare his use of this form with its use by one of the following: Blaise Pascal, in *Pensées;* Benjamin Franklin, in *Poor Richard's Almanac;* Ambrose Bierce, in *The Devil's Dictionary.*

FURTHER READING

Of Mark Twain's books, *Tom Sawyer* (1876) and *Huckleberry Finn* (1885) became classics of worldwide fame, effectively contradicting his own definition of a "classic" as "a book which people praise and don't read."

BEN HECHT

In the world of journalism and popular entertainment, Ben Hecht (1893–1964) represented an almost extinct breed, marked by boisterous noncomformity and articulate intelligence. Born in New York as the son of immigrants from southern Russia, he had a varied and successful career as journalist, editor, columnist, novelist, playwright, and producer. In his autobiography, *A Child of the Century* (1954), he describes his years as a newspaperman and foreign correspondent, his success as a scriptwriter in Hollywood, and his contribution to the efforts of the Jewish underground in Palestine. The following brief selection illustrates Hecht's gusto as a narrator and his gift for broad humor.

At Home on Misty Mountain

Each time we went to Hollywood we took with us most of our Nyack ménage. Lester Bartow, our driver, rode them across country in the car. Lester became our driver in his teens. Being the only member of our household who could drive a car, repair electric lights, remember appointments, understand plumbing and mail letters, he posed during these years as an admirable Crichton and fancied himself the keystone of my existence—which, possibly, in sundry ways he was.

With Lester on the coast-to-coast treks went my strongman trainer, Elmore Cole, under whose eye for twenty years every morning at eight I punched the bag, did mat work and grunted lifting weights; our French poodle, Googie, named after the fine Russian writer Nikolai Gogol; and our three old ladies, Gertie, Jo and Hilja. Twenty suitcases, six trunks, oil paintings, our radios and phonograph records, and favorite window drapes went each time by freight. Rose and I took the train.

Lying in a drawing room for three days reading mystery books, having neither to bathe, shave nor dress, and without the Homeric Elmore and his punching bag to torment me, without telephones, pencils or problems, was always a time of fetal bliss. Nevertheless, I often flew to Hollywood—a mode of travel that has never failed to terrify me.

Roaring through the sky in the always precarious plane, I would wonder what perversity or weakness it was that made me risk my life and sweat nervously through a dozen hours in the air instead of riding peacefully and lethargically in the drawing room of my dreams. Once, waiting for my plane to take off in Buenos Aires and fly over the Andes to Santiago, I was given insight into what sent me off on trips through the sky.

I had thought before that it was the cowardice of conformity. Most of the people I knew flew to and from Hollywood. Obviously, I did not want to stand out as someone fearful of flying. Rather than have people think that of me, I submitted myself to the bumps and palpitations of aerial transport.

I became aware in Buenos Aires that I had explained myself incorrectly. Sitting in the plane that was going to hop over the Andes—in that year still an enterprising thing to do—the word "jeopardy" came to me. I was not in the plane because of social fears. I was in it because of the lure of jeopardy, the same jeopardy that makes men risk their well-being on the roll of dice or fall of cards.

The small boy, ancestor of such jeopardy hunters, likes to see how close to the railroad track he can stand without being run over by the train. The engine roaring past him, spraying his face with cinders but leaving him still in one piece, fills the small boy with a sense of victory. He has tested his courage and won. He has also done something else. With his feat of daring and danger, he has atoned for certain boyish sins. By offering himself as a possible sacrifice to the thundering locomotive, he feels himself punished for those sins, and thus cleansed of them.

I am willing to believe that to rid myself of the guilt of going to Hollywood I punished myself by flying there.

I return to Lester and his non-perilous cavalcade. The ménage he transported made movieland more palatable to me. Magically, my home and its many familiar faces appeared there.

Gertie was the oldest lady of our ménage. She was in her seventies and was one of our cooks and cleaners. She was five feet tall, deaf, red-cheeked, weather-beaten and radiant-eyed. She teetered and clomped through the day like a redskin on the warpath. Dust was the enemy.

Gertie had been a scrub lady and washerwoman since her childhood. At eight she had begun to clean floors in Germany. Come to Brooklyn, she had been early widowed and left with five small sons. Of her husband she said, "Ooh! He wash no goot! All the time drink. Und he was hit me, too. He died in Bellfew Hoshpital. No goot, dat feller."

Left alone, she had toiled eighteen hours a day bringing up her five sons to become policemen. They ate well in their boyhood. She had never made complaint and had worshiped God amid her scrub pails and washtubs.

She was in her fifties when we found her "schroobing" in a Henry Street house where we had gone to live among the noises, smells and hazards of the slums. I had induced Rose to move to Henry Street after a year in New York. I thought it would be good to taste the city's squalor.

Gertie, discovered in this squalor, was to remain with us until she died in her eighties, never to stop teetering and clomping, whooping and schroobing till she was ridden off to the hospital to die. "Gott ish goot zu me," she announced proudly when in a reminiscent mood. "He always gived me woik to do."

She went to church once a year on Christmas Eve and contributed ten cents toward the maintenance of the Catholic faith, which she revered. "Ish enough fer dem. Dem priests got lotsh money. Oho!"

Rose sat beside Gertie in the hospital when she was dying and told her she would ask the priest in St. Patrick's Cathedral to say a mass to take away the pain. Gertie was dying of cancer. "A high mass," said Rose, weeping. "No Mish Heck," Gertie gasped, "high mass cosht ten dollar. Too much. Better make low mass. Cosht one dollar." She held up a gnarled finger. "Must nit t'rown money away."

"No, Gertie," said Rose. "It will be a high mass, for ten dollars."

In St. Patrick's Cathedral the priest refused the money, after hearing the story of Gertie. He said a high mass for nothing. A stranger was found to light the candles in front of St. Anne, Gertie's favorite intercessor. The stranger in the big cathedral whispered, "Tell her I will know her when we meet in Heaven."

Gertie's stinginess was deep and touching, to friends as well as to priest and stranger. It was like a battle trauma. It told of the days of eighteen-hour toil, of penny by penny earned over her scrub pails to feed her sons. In Nyack her hand would reach into the bathroom and switch off the light while I was shaving.

On her first trip across the country with Lester she demanded each night before retiring that he fetch her a pail of water, soap and brush. She scrubbed the floors of each of the motels in which she slept. During the day she whooped with anguish at the prices charged by restaurants. Lolling in the back seat of the Cadillac she would look for poor people all along the way to California. A dusty figure in the road would set her to clucking, "Poor people. All alone und so hungry."

Rose gave her fancy hats and silk dresses and sent her off with Lester to the theater. She returned always with a drunken air and whooping that she had seen, "Lots fine t'ings. Lobely goils! All neked! Whee! Real lobely! But nit so goot like the Mish Heck! No, neber! The Mish Heck ish the best von all of them!" And she would push her head against Rose's head and laugh boisterously. A portrait of Gertie painted by Billy Brice hangs in our entrance hall in Nyack. Gertie looks moodier on canvas than she did in life, but her small deep eyes still twinkle on our home.

Our second oldest lady, Jo, was Gertie's relative. Their children had married each other. Jo was also cook and cleaner. She had come out of the same Henry Street basement that had given us Gertie. When we had lived in Henry Street, Gertie and Jo used to wait for us on the curb to come home in a taxi. They would stand surrounded by howling kids and neighborhood toughs, their arms loaded with apples and flowers.

Jo's voice was hoarse and to be heard frequently in moans of despair or foghorn sighs of such sadness as to tear the heart. She mourned some mysterious past. Yet Jo loved lively doings. When guests were laughing and music played in our house, she would seize her friend Gertie and waltz with her in the kitchen. In her seventies Jo was not quite as powerful as Gertie, due to a trouble with her hip. Her toil was less demoniac. But when she was unable to walk up the stairs she continued to polish the woodwork as high as she could reach on tiptoe. Gertie and Jo loved each other with sneers and grimaces, and they loved the home in which they worked as if it were a roost in Eden.

Hilja, our third old lady, was from Finland. She was a gentle and mystic figure with a canary-bird tweet for a voice. Her face was white and childlike. She would stand for an hour in front of the sink, motionless and smiling into space, and attentive only to the dream in her head. The dream was divided between Jesus and the snails, bugs and birds in the garden. She spoke to Jesus in silence, but addressed the little garden life openly, kneeling before snails and beetles and speaking sweetly to them in Finnish. Hilja had been a hotel chambermaid before joining our home, where she was to live till she died many years later. In her girlhood in Finland she had written poetry, dreamed of becoming an actress, and come upon a great grief. The grief, never known to us, had left her gentle and abstracted all the rest of her life.

Lester and his troop arrived at the newly rented Beverly Hills palazzo on the day Rose and I got there in May, 1939. So did a van full of suitcases, trunks, paintings and other impedimenta. Credit for this fine timing was shared between Rose and Lester. We all started poking into new rooms and uncovering fresh wonders, for we had come this time on an actual castle. It had been built by Fred Niblo, one of the early geniuses of the town. Old palace rooms had been brought from Italy and reassembled inside it. There were carved beams and carved and painted high ceilings, ancient panelings, antique stairways and stained-glass windows. A large Roman pool with arbors at each end lay beyond the house. Sweeping lawns and curling driveways were in front of it. But most exciting about our new abode was that it was built on top of the highest hill in Hollywood. The hill was called Misty Mountain. A perilous and winding road called Angelo Drive, after climbing Misty Mountain, ended in our wide driveway, lit by old Italian lanterns. Toward evening a mist sometimes covered the hillsides ending a few yards below our buttressed stone house. On such evenings we seemed to

perch over a vanished world. Inside the house we felt ourselves drifting away
in an extravagant balloon.

Glass walls enclosed half the dining room. From our table we saw far
below the lighted city of Hollywood that looked no larger than a blazing
chandelier.

As we were sitting down to our first meal, our Western retainers began to
appear, having read of our arrival in some movie column. There was no
question of whether or not they were to work in our new home. They had
bolted whatever jobs they had, appearing with bulging suitcases like relatives
moving in.

The most constant of our Western retainers was Lucy, who was tall and in
her seventies. She was as proud as a top sergeant, bold-eyed and noisy with
dreams of love. She was a Croatian and spoke an English too incredible for
recording. Her happily squealing voice filled the kitchen like a calliope. She
stood over the stove and sink swooning with anecdotes of life undaunted, of
lovers entwined in each other's arms leaping to their deaths, or murders and
suicides rising out of thwarted passions. Her tales of Croatian, Bulgarian and
Egyptian romances held Jo spellbound. Jo would stand motionless with a
broom in her hand for an hour listening agape and crying out hoarsely at
intervals, "Balogny!" Hilja, who heard nothing but the sounds of Heaven
and the converse of snails and beetles, was unable to make head or tail out of
Lucy's high whistle of talk. But Gertie, who could hear nothing lower than a
yell, nevertheless got the sense of it. She would swing a wash rag at Lucy
and scold, "Dosh aber terrible! An olt lady mit a big nose talkin' doity talk!
My Gotness!" Lucy would answer in her lusty squeal, "Oh mine soul! Mine
body ees olt—but mine heart ees yoong!"

Lucy brought her tales into the dining room. She would stand near the
table while we ate, her ancient face aglow, and tell us of men and women she
had seen die of love. "Love ees only t'eeng in woild, Mahdam. Ees wonful!
Oh, oh, mine Heaven, when I was yoong—when I was yoong!" One day she
asked in a solemn voice, "Mahdam, weech way ees dot Alatzka? You know,
Alatzka, weet bears, the white ones?"

We pointed to the north, Lucy darted to a window, crying out, "Mahdam,
mine man ees gone Alatzka! I meet him by park. He has beautiful eyes! I
love heem! But he go Alatzka. I waiting now. Ooh, mine God in Heaven,
how I love heem!"

We asked his name.

"What I want name for?" Lucy cried. "He is Irishman. Ees enough for
me!" Her seventy-five-year-old face flushed with romance and she blew a kiss
to the north.

When alone with her Mahdam, Lucy would offer to make her love spells.
She had two spells she eagerly recommended. One was done with the aid of
a piece of knotted string. It guaranteed my impotence while away from

home. The other spell would make every man who looked at Mahdam quake with sexual desire and sink to the floor to kiss her feet. This one was made with herbs. Rose scorned both spells, and Lucy, hugging her, cried out, "Mahdam, you yoong! Beaudeeful! You no need spell. I make spell for the Esther. He need." Esther was Lester, whose name, along with a thousand other names, she always mispronounced.

Screams from Lucy's room roused the house often in the middle of the night. No one ever moved to investigate; for we all knew it was Lucy wrestling with the Devil again. In the morning she would say, "He come to me last night thot Deevil! I fight weet heem for whole hour. Today I go in church, make novena."

I sat one evening in the kitchen of our *palazzo* on the Misty Mountain and watched our three cooks and their helper Hilja prepare a dinner party for twenty. Gertie was cooking her favorite veal stew, a dish she always brought to the table regardless of what had been requested. She was also preparing her favorite salad ("cosht notting"), which I never tasted for twenty years. Jo was tending ducks in the oven. Soup was steaming on the stove, a soup that took almost forever to cook but when eaten was guaranteed to double male virility, according to Lucy. The smells of seven different desserts baked by Lucy—cakes, tortes, strudels and *dampfnudels*—filled the mountain air. Lucy was making chicken sausages for appetizers. She had ground up the meat of five chickens into a paste and was stuffing them into skins of dough.

"I cooka for Kaizer tees sausagen in Port Said," Lucy cried out.

"Go wan!" Jo pushed her. "You never seen no Kaiser, Balogny!"

"What you talk! You crazy!" Lucy squealed rapturously. "Before Heaven, I seen heem! He says to me, 'Lucia, you best cook in whole Europa. You come home by me.' I tell him, 'You fine man. Fine eyes. I like your eyes. But I no like work for Germans.' Ho, ho, thot Kaizer! He squeazie mine hand."

Gertie heard nothing. Her eyes glared again at the shelves piled with cakes and strudels. She shuddered and cried out, "You aber crazy! Truly Gott, you verrickt! All dot stuff! The Mish Heck gonna holler, you t'rowen away the money!"

"On me, holler! Who? Never! I love mine Mahdam. I love her with mine soul!" Lucy yelled in rebuttal.

"Mish Heck ish best woman in the woild," Gertie retorted. "She nit shmoked und she nit goed out mid oder man. I cut mine head off on dat!"

Lucy was reminded of a story. She had worked once for a Croatian general. One night the general had come home unexpectedly and discovered his young bride being kissed by a colonel of hussars. The general had drawn his sword and run the colonel through. Then with one swoop of that weapon he had cut off his wife's beautiful head. A moment later the general, still madly in love with his bride, had picked her head up off the floor and sat weeping and kissing it. The colonel had revived for a moment, screamed with jealousy at this sight, and shot the general dead. Then he had uttered a last cry of love and fallen dead himself.

Jo listened with her mouth open in wonder, crying out hoarsely now and then, "Balogny!" Gertie had dropped to her knees unexpectedly and was giving the floor a schroobing. Hilja sliced vegetables and smiled dreamily into the sink. I left to get dressed for dinner.

We had no butler, Rose having decided it would be an affront to her retainers to introduce one into the house, let alone the impossibility of finding a butler who would tolerate our kitchen circus. As a result, despite our numerous staff, there was never anyone to answer the doorbell or the telephone. None of our ladies could speak over the instrument. They usually unhooked it slyly and let the receiver lie untouched till it had stopped rumbling.

This night, as on other nights, our guests let each other in and ultimately came to the dining table. One of the guests was Charles Chaplin, at the time under a cloud of unfavorable publicity.

I had always considered Chaplin the best actor, the best scenario writer and one of the best directors in the movies. The fact that he had never received or even been mentioned for any sort of an Academy Oscar was a measure of the sad cowardice of the movie people. They were afraid to honor the great artist among them because the press called him wicked or traitorous. I have never known a less wicked man than Chaplin (in Hollywood at least) or one who contributed more riches to the country in which he lived.

Socially Chaplin lived in Hollywood like a hermit. He was seldom to be seen at any of its cafés or parties. I was pleased to have this moody man at our table. The dinner started. We never had bells on our table to summon servants. Rose preferred to bring them on with a friendly cry that reached the kitchen. Such a cry sounded, the pantry door opened and Gertie and Jo entered. Rose had bought them black taffeta dresses and small white aprons for the occasion. Our two old ladies sidled in like a pair of musical-comedy characters. They carried platters of Lucy's chicken sausages. Beholding the dressed-up guests, Gertie paused to titter and pay homage with a drawn out "ooh." Jo advised her hoarsely to behave herself and they both started around the table with the appetizers.

Gertie suddenly stopped. Her small eyes were peering excitedly at one of the guests.

"Ya, it's der Sharlie!" she cried out, pointing and going into a half-crouch. "Oh mine gotness! Der Sharlie Shaplin!"

Jo, forgetting her social schooling, came running for a look. Her face lit up as brightly as Gertie's and her voice foghorned, "God. It's him! Charlie Chaplin. What d'ya know!"

Both old ladies stood beaming and speechless. Lucy, peering in to see how her sausages were going, spied Chaplin and came squealing into the room.

"Ooh, mine Charlie!" she cried. "Oh, how I lovin' thot man! Meester Charlie, you mine sweetheart! I lovin' you!"

Gertie smiled shyly as Chaplin stood up, his hand held out to her.

"Ya," she whispered, "I seen him lotsh times in der nickel shows. Ya, lotsh times. Wonerful! Truly Gott!"

Jo croaked, "How do you do, Mr. Chaplin. We are proud to have you eat from us. Thanks."

She curtsied to him, as before a king.

After Chaplin had shaken their hands, Gertie and Jo returned flushed and giggling to the kitchen. Lucy remained in the pantry doorway wringing her hands and uttering cries of love.

Since that evening I have never worried over the fact that the movies have failed ever to honor their greatest artist, Charlie Chaplin.

DISCUSSION AND WRITING

1. Examine the effects of Hecht's use of broken English. Why are foreign accents and imperfect English funny? What kind of humor do they illustrate?

2. Discuss in detail features other than language that give Hecht's account a broad comic touch. What do they reveal concerning the nature of humor?

3. Humor can range from biting ridicule to expansive joviality. What is Hecht's attitude toward the people he describes?

4. Tastes in humor change. Describe and illustrate the type of humor popular with your own high-school or college generation.

5. How much of a handicap in contemporary American society is a foreign accent or a foreign appearance? Or, what attitude do Americans have toward "old country" customs and mannerisms?

6. Describe the kind of humor employed in one of the comedy classics of the silent screen—for instance, a movie with Charles Chaplin, Buster Keaton, or Harold Lloyd. Use detailed illustrations.

7. Choose one of the most popular television comedians of the last ten or twenty years. What seems to be the secret of his popularity? Discuss his appeal as concretely as you can.

8. What contemporary movie actor or actress comes close to meriting a description as the movies' "greatest artist" and as having "contributed more riches to the country in which he lived" than anyone you know?

9. Discuss in detail a recent motion picture that struck you as a serious treatment of a meaningful theme. Avoid the appearance of a mere plot summary.

10. Hollywood is sometimes accused of giving moviegoers in foreign countries a distorted view of American life. To judge from recent American films, how much justice is there in this charge?

FURTHER READING

For more on Chaplin, see Al Capp, creator of *L'il Abner,* on "The Comedy of Charlie Chaplin," *Atlantic,* February 1950. An evocation of the Hollywood setting much less nostalgic than Hecht's, and a drastic rewriting of the Hollywood dream, is Nathanael West's novel *The Day of the Locust* (1939).

JAMES THURBER

For many years, James Thurber (1894–1961), writer and cartoonist, observed and patiently chronicled modern man's struggle to maintain some minimal dignity in the face of nuclear explosions, cold-war alarums, and domineering wives. Like other outstanding American humorists, he was for many years a contributor to *The New Yorker* magazine. Some of his best work has been collected in volumes like *My Life and Hard Times* (1933) and *The Thurber Carnival* (1945). In the following selection, he uses the ancient device of the beast fable, where, as in Aesop's time, the sly fox, the rapacious tiger, the timid hare, and other animals act out the drama of human motives, schemes, and illusions.

Fables for Our Time

THE FAIRLY INTELLIGENT FLY

A large spider in an old house built a beautiful web in which to catch flies. Every time a fly landed on the web and was entangled in it the spider devoured him, so that when another fly came along he would think the web was a safe and quiet place in which to rest. One day a fairly intelligent fly buzzed around above the web so long without lighting that the spider appeared and said, "Come on down." But the fly was too clever for him and said, "I never light where I don't see other flies and I don't see any other flies in your house." So he flew away until he came to a place where there were a great many other flies. He was about to settle down among them when a bee buzzed up and said, "Hold it, stupid, that's flypaper. All those flies are trapped." "Don't be silly," said the fly, "they're dancing." So he settled down and became stuck to the flypaper with all the other flies.

Moral: There is no safety in numbers, or in anything else.

THE BAT WHO GOT THE HELL OUT

A colony of bats living in a great American cave had got along fine for a thousand generations, flying, hanging head down, eating insects, and raising young, and then one year a male named Flitter, who had fluttered secretly out of his room at night and flown among the haunts of men, told his father that he had decided to get the hell out. The shocked father sent Flitter to Fleder, the great-great-grandfather of all the bats in the cave.

"You should be proud of being a bat among bats," said old Fleder, "for we are one of the oldest species on the planet, much older than Man, and the only mammal capable of true flight."

The discontented young bat was not impressed. "I want to live like a man among men," he said. "Men have the best food, and the most fun, and the cutest females."

At this, old Fleder stormed about the cave, squeaking unintelligibly. Then he recovered his calm and continued his talk. "A man got into my room one night," he said, "and managed somehow to tangle me in his hair. It was a shattering experience, from which I shall never completely recover."

"When men die they go to Heaven, but when bats are dead they are dead," said Flitter. "I want to go to Heaven when I die."

This amused old Fleder in a gaunt and gloomy sort of way, and he chittered, quickered, and zickered for some moments before he could say, "You have no more soul than a moose, or a mouse, or a mole. You should be glad that you will never become an angel, for angels do not have true flight. One wants to *sleep* through eternity, not bumble and flap about forever like a bee or a butterfly."

But Flitter had made up his mind, and the old bat's words of wisdom were in vain. That night, the discontented young bat quit the bat colony, and flickered out of the cave, in the confident hope of giving up his membership in the Chiroptera and joining the happy breed of men. Unfortunately for his dream, he spent his first night hanging head down from the rafters of an auditorium in which a best-selling Inspirationalist was dragging God down to the people's level. Ushers moved silently among the rapt listeners, selling copies of the speaker's books: *Shake Hands with the Almighty, You Can Be Jehovah's Pal* and *Have You Taken Out Eternity Insurance?* The speaker was saying, "Have a little talk with the Lord while you're waiting for a bus, or riding to work, or sitting in the dentist's chair. Have comfy chats with the Lord in the little cozy corners of spare time."

Flitter decided that there was something the matter with the acoustics, or with his tragus, caused by hanging head down in the presence of the Eternal Species, but when he began flying about the auditorium, there was no change in the nature of the English sentences. "Tell the Lord to put it there," the inspired man went on. "Give him your duke." The speaker waved clasped hands above his head and gazed up at the ceiling. "Keep pitching, God," he said. "You've got two strikes on Satan."

Flitter, who had never felt sick before in his life, felt sick, and decided to get the air. After he had got the air, he realized that he did not want to become a member of the species *Homo sapiens,* because of the danger of bumbling or flapping into the Inspirationalist after they had both become angels. And so Flitter returned to the cave, and everybody was astonished to see him, and nobody said anything, and for a time there was a great silence.

"I've come the hell back," said Flitter, meekly. And he resumed, without discontent, the immemorial life of the Chiroptera, flying, hanging head down, eating insects, and raising young.

Moral: By decent minds is he abhorred who'd make a Babbitt of the Lord.

THE BRAGDOWDY AND THE BUSYBODY

A female hare, who had been born with a foot in everybody's affairs, became known in her community as "that big Belgian busybody." She was always listening to the thumpings of her neighbors. "You're all ears," her mate snarled one day. "For God's sake, get some *laissez faire.*" There was no answer, for she had hopped next door to exhort, reproach, and upbraid a female guinea pig who had borne one hundred and seventy-three young and then let herself go. She had become a bragdowdy, and spent her time weeping over *True Pigtales.*

"Where is your civic spirit?" demanded Mrs. Hare. "And your country, state, federal, and global spirit? Look at me. I am president, or chairwoman, of practically everything, and founder of the Listening Post, an organization of eight hundred females with their ears to the ground."

The male guinea pig, who had been lying on a lettuce leaf, taking it easy, tried to hide from his nosy neighbor, but she came into the room, buttocky buttocky, before he could get out of bed.

"A big strapping male like you," she scoffed, "lying around the house when you ought to be at the laboratory, having injections to see whether some new serum is deadly or not." The male guinea pig's teeth began to chatter, and when a male guinea pig's teeth chatter it doesn't mean he's afraid, it means he's mad. But the Belgian busybody didn't care how anybody felt except herself. "You and your mate should join things and do things!" she exclaimed. "Shoulder to the wheel, nose to the grindstone, best foot forward, finger in the pie, knee on the chest!"

Before many weeks had passed, Mrs. Pig developed a guilt complex that manifested itself in an activity compulsion. She gave up reading *True Pigtales,* took her mate's edible bed away from him, straightened up the house, and joined twenty-four up-and-coming organizations. She became famous for keeping everybody on his toes, whether that's where he wanted to be or not. She was made chairman of the Bear a Basket of Babies Committee, secretary of the Get Behind Your Mate and Push Movement, treasurer of the Don't Let Dad Dawdle League, inventor of its slogan, "He can do twice as much in half the time if he puts your mind to it," and, in the end, national president of the Daughters of Ambitious Rodents.

The now celebrated Mrs. Pig also found time to bear thirty-seven more offspring, which was thirty-seven more than her mate had wanted. They drove him to Distraction, where he found the male Belgian hare, who had been driven there by his own mate's private and public projects, pryings, proddings, and pushings. The two males had such a quiet and peaceful time together without their mates that they decided to keep it that way. Representatives of ninety-six different organizations—the seventy-two Mrs. Hare belonged to and Mrs. Pig's twenty-four—argued with them in vain. They ran away one night while their mates were addressing the He Could If He Wanted To, He's Just Not Trying Club, without so much as a fare-thee-well or a note on a pillow, and leaving no forwarding address. They decided to go to Tahiti to forget, but long before they reached Tahiti they had forgot.

Moral: Thou shalt not convert thy neighbor's wife, nor yet louse up thy neighbor's life.

THE TURTLE WHO CONQUERED TIME

A turtle appeared in a meadow one summer's day and attracted the attention of all the creatures in the grass and in the trees, because the date 44 B.C. was carved on his shell. "Our meadow is honored indeed," exclaimed a grasshopper, "for our visitor is the oldest of all living creatures."

"We must build a pavilion in his honor," said a frog, and the catbirds and the swallows and the other birds built a stately pleasure dome out of twigs and leaves and blossoms for the very important turtle. An orchestra of crickets played music in his honor, and a wood thrush sang. The sounds of jubilee were heard in nearby fields and woods, and as more and more creatures turned up from farther and farther away to have a look at the ancient turtle, the grasshopper decided to charge admission to the pavilion.

"I will be the barker," said the frog, and, with the help of the grasshopper, he composed an impressive spiel. "Yesterday and yesterday and yesterday," it began, "creeps in this carapace from day to day to the first syllable of recorded time. This great turtle was born two thousand years ago, the year the mighty Julius Caesar died. Horace was twenty-one in 44 B.C., and Cicero had but a single year to live." The bystanders did not seem very much interested in the turtle's ancient contemporaries, but they gladly paid to go in and have a look at his ancient body.

Inside the pavilion, the grasshopper continued the lecture. "This remarkable turtle is a direct descendant of one of the first families of Ooze," he chanted. "His great-grandfather may have been the first thing that moved in the moist and muddy margins of this cooling planet. Except for our friend's ancestors, there was nothing but coal and blobs of glob."

One day a red squirrel who lived in a neighboring wood dropped in to look at the turtle and to listen to the ballyhoo. "Forty-four B.C., my foot!" scoffed the squirrel, as he glared at the grasshopper. "You are full of tobacco juice, and your friend the frog is full of lightning bugs. The carving of an ancient date on the carapace of a turtle is a common childish prank. This creep was probably born no earlier than 1902."

As the red squirrel ranted on, the spectators who had paid to get into the pavilion began departing quietly, and there was no longer a crowd listening to the frog out front. The crickets put away their instruments and disappeared as silently as the Arabs, and the wood thrush gathered up his sheet music and flew off and did not return. The sounds of jubilee were no longer heard in the once merry meadow, and the summer seemed to languish like a dying swan.

"I knew all the time he wasn't two thousand years old," admitted the grasshopper, "but the legend pleased the people, young and old, and many smiled who had not smiled for years."

"And many laughed who had not laughed for years," said the frog, "and many eyes sparkled and many hearts were gay." The turtle shed a turtle tear at this and crawled away.

"The truth is not merry and bright," said the red squirrel. "The truth is cold and dark. Let's face it." And, looking smug and superior, the iconoclast scampered impudently back to his tree in the wood. From the grass of the meadow voices once carefree and gay joined in a rueful and lonely chorus, as if someone great and wonderful had died and was being buried.

Moral: Oh, why should the shattermyth have to be a crumplehope and a dampenglee?

DISCUSSION AND WRITING

1. Compare "The Fairly Intelligent Fly" with such familiar Aesopian fables as that of the ant and the grasshopper. How are they similar; how are they different?

2. Examine Thurber's use of verbal humor—his puns, made-up words, twisted clichés, parodies of familiar expressions and arguments.

3. Describe your own experience with the kind of popular religion encountered by "The Bat Who Got the Hell Out." Is Thurber's treatment of it justified? Is there something to be said *in defense* of bringing God "to the people's level"?

4. What is Thurber's satirical technique in "The Bragdowdy and the Busybody"? What are the targets of his satire?

5. What is the point of "The Turtle Who Conquered Time"? Can you think of any specific cases to which it would apply?

6. Compare and contrast Thurber's satirical technique with that of Mark Twain in "The Pudd'nhead Wilson Maxims."

7. Though both are extremely successful as humorous writers, James Thurber and Ben Hecht appeal to different audiences. Discuss as concretely as you can the differences in taste that would set the two audiences apart.

8. Discuss—support, attack, modify—the moral of one of Thurber's fables.

9. Write a "fable for our time" on some contemporary phenomenon that you feel invites satirical treatment.

10. In giving us the bat's-eye view of the Inspirationalist, Thurber uses the old technique of making the reader look at familiar things from a completely new perspective. Write an account of something familiar in which you employ a similar extreme change in point of view.

FURTHER READING

Several other outstanding American humorists became famous through their association with *The New Yorker*: E. B. White contributed regularly to its "Talk of the Town"; his best pieces are available in *One Man's Meat* (1942) and *The Second Tree from the Corner* (1948). S. J. Perelman, who reports of himself that "under a forehead roughly comparable to that of the Javanese or the Piltdown Man are visible a pair of tiny pig eyes, lit up alternately by greed and concupiscence," has made available such memorable instances of Perelmania as "Second-Class Matter" and "Beat Me, Post-Impressionist Daddy" in *The Best of S. J. Perelman* (1947). Examine humorous pieces by Thurber, White, and Perelman to determine whether there is such a thing as a *New Yorker* brand of humor.

LESZEK KOLAKOWSKI

Leszek Kolakowski (born 1927), Polish philosopher and satirist, was educated in a Catholic school and has published major historical studies in the philosophy of religion. During the German occupation of Poland, his father became a victim of the Gestapo. After the death of Stalin, Kolakowski emerged as an effective critic of the rigid official ideology. He became the hero and spokesman of other post-Stalinist Communist intellectuals who, no longer content to parrot whatever current wisdom the authorities had decreed, insisted on the freedom to read, to argue, and to doubt. The following fables were first written in 1957 but not printed in Poland until 1964. In these fables, Kolakowski plays the role of the bitter fool, who uses the license traditionally granted to someone in his motley garb to say things that would be dangerous to say soberly and outright. As one of his readers has pointed out, Kolakowski is the kind of satirist who is "more concerned to preserve humane values than the fences built for the protection of institutions." The views he expresses or implies are his own, and any similarity with those held by the Polish government, the Catholic Church, or the editor of the present volume is entirely coincidental.

The Key to Heaven

GOD, OR THE RELATIVITY OF MERCY

This fable is very short and simple; it offers only a point of departure, a question, and a moral.

Point of departure: The psalmist says of the Lord (Psalm 136, 10 and 15) that he smote Egypt in their firstborn—for his mercy endureth forever; that he overthrew Pharaoh and his host in the Red Sea—for his mercy endureth forever.

Question: What opinion do Egypt and Pharaoh hold concerning the mercy of the Lord?

Moral: Mercy and benevolence cannot exist for everyone simultaneously. When we use these words, we should always specify for *whom*. And when we do act benevolently toward nations, let us also inquire into *their* opinion. Remember Egypt.

RAHAB, OR SOLITUDE REAL AND IMAGINED

The book of Joshua recounts the familiar story of espionage (also involving public morals, the history of music, and the annals of murder) that took place in the city of Jericho. It seems that Joshua had divine assurance that he would conquer the city of Jericho as well as further territory. For reasons unknown however Joshua did not rest content with this promise—though he could certainly have slept soundly in the firm expectation of victory—but instead, to be quite safe, before the beginning of the siege sent two intelligence agents into the city, who as is customary in such cases carried ample provision of the local currency. These were two quite capable but somewhat unreliable young fellows. They had hardly entered the city when they decided not to miss the various joys of civilization that in the military service they had to do without. Since they had considerable cash in their pockets, they spent the evening roaming the streets in search of the red light district. There were several relevant institutions, the city being one of remarkable cultural attainments. Soon the boys found their desired goal and, guided by supernatural intuition, fell in with a lady by the name of Rahab. This was a person of ill repute, for she earned her living through the sale of her physical charms. Unfortunately these charms were rapidly wilting, so that the fat and somewhat antiquated Rahab had to work for lower prices and with the poorer type of client, earning each time progressively less. After the rough life of the barracks, however, the two boys were not choosy and took a liking to the wilting haetera. Having had a few drinks, they started to brag and talked about their espionage mission. Too late they realized what they had done. They were at Rahab's mercy. They implored her to take pity on them, but someone of Rahab's profession experiences too little pity herself to be able to share it with others. Rahab thought quickly:

"It is nearly certain that the enemy will occupy the city, for I know that he is allied with God. This must serve as the premise. And now for the alternatives: Either I hand the spies over to the police, gaining the favor of the prince and showing my loyalty to the city, but then am destroyed upon the triumph of the enemy. Or I hide the two and later ask for the protection of the occupying forces, but risk my life until they arrive. It is true that in hiding two of our enemies I may seem disloyal to the city and to the prince, but perhaps these scruples are superfluous. Do I really owe loyalty to this my home town, where people have always spit in my face and would, should they survive, let me starve to death a few years hence? As it is, I am living here quite alone, as if in a deserted city. The qualms of conscience felt by moralists are none of my concern. It follows that my choice is between possible death during the next few weeks and certain death after the city has been taken. This is not an easy decision, since certain death is mitigated by its somewhat distant date, whereas I am incurring the risk of possible death at this very minute. It is impossible to choose rationally between the possibility of evil now and the certainty of evil later. I shall therefore choose blindly: I shall save the spies. A few weeks of fear—and then, what a life! Fur coats, jewels, Halvah every day, visits to the opera—perhaps one of their generals will marry me. For those barbarians I am still good enough."

Having thus thought the matter through, Rahab concluded the following agreement with her scouts: She was ready to hide the two and help them escape, provided they would in turn save her upon the conquest of the city by Joshua. They arranged for a token that would help the conquerors recognize her house. Here ends the part of the story concerning espionage and public morals.

Now for the part relevant to the history of music. God had planned the siege of the city in every detail, and Joshua conscientiously followed his instructions. Where common sense would have advised surrounding the city with engines of war and cannon, Joshua assembled a brass band of clergymen and made it march around the city walls, playing martial music. Behind them was carried the ark of the covenant; in front of them marched a military contingent. The priests blew their trumpets for seven days until they were totally exhausted, suffering from sore throats and distended lungs, priests too being after all human. The soldiers were grumbling and discontented, believing that it was their commander's purpose to make them seem ridiculous. The people of Jericho on the walls laughed heartily at their enemies and swore they were mad, one and all. On the seventh day, the band blew so powerfully that the priests' eyes started from their sockets. Simultaneously the army, following orders, set up such a tremendous shout that the city walls miraculously fell down and scattered as if made of dust.

Now for the murderous part of the story: Upon God's orders the warriors each penetrated straight into the city and there murdered, as the book says, "both man and woman, young and old, and ox, and sheep, and ass, with the edge of the sword." The treasures of the city were taken over by the priests, and the city itself, with the exception of one single house, was burned to the ground. This was the house of Rahab. The army kept its promise, sparing the harlot's quarters, furniture, and family. It is true some of the officers had designs upon her virtue, but Rahab complained to the high command and was duly indemnified. Then the troops left, and Rahab threw herself on the ground in tears. She was left behind in the deserted city, in the only house still standing among the ruins. She was alone with the corpses, with the rubble and smell of burning, without friends, solicitude, or customers. No one gave her any fur coats, or jewels, or Halvah; no one asked her to visit the opera; no general wanted to marry her. There was nothing but a lonely, empty life among ruins. This was the end.

One thing is especially remarkable about this story: It is physically impossible to make the walls of a city fall down by warlike shouts and the sound of seven trumpets—therefore we are dealing with a miracle. If however it was God's purpose to produce a miracle anyway, why did he let the army wear itself out for a whole week and incur everyone's ridicule? Why did he let the priests ruin their health and risk their authority with the people? For who will respect priests who play in a military band? Why, I ask, and discovered two possible answers:

Either he was so fond of the music of military bands that he had a sudden desire to hear as much of it as he could, or the whole matter was an *acte gratuit,* a surrealistic joke he indulged in with his creatures. Assuming the second possibility, he would have shown a lively sense of humor, but from what I infer concerning his temperament I incline toward the first possibility. A pity—such taste, with such a potential!

Indeed—in later times also he has frequently gone out of his way in order to hear as much military music as possible. His preference for it continues to this day.

Now for some of the moral implications of this story:

First Moral: The situation of Rahab.

In order to save one's skin during a great upheaval, physical prostitution is not enough.

Second Moral: The situation of the spies.

Providence leads men to the weirdest places, but there is always a hidden reason, significant for the welfare of humanity.

Third Moral: The situation of Rahab.

Let us not rashly assert that we are "lonely in a crowd." When we are really lonely, we will notice the difference.

Fourth Moral: The general situation.

Let us blow as hard as we can—perhaps there will be a miracle.

NOAH, OR THE TEMPTATIONS OF SOLIDARITY

When God—too late!—came to regret having created man and decided, appalled by the results of his rashness, to drown those made unsuccessfully in his image, he considered Noah as we know the one specimen worthy of being saved. In acting on this decision, however, he may be accused of both a lack of foresight and an injustice.

Lack of foresight—he should have known man well enough to foresee that everything would start all over again if even a single human couple survived on this earth, and that all the old worries would return in a few years.

Injustice—since only the crimes of man had annoyed him, why use this opportunity to destroy the innocent animals? But let us leave these speculations. Our real interest is elsewhere—in Noah.

Noah knew how to fawn on authority. If a teacher known to be violent, envious, irascible and vindictive scolds all his students except one that he heaps praises on, it is easy to guess at the subservience of this model pupil.

But Noah did have a rudimentary sense of honor. As long as the Lord's measures were limited to scoldings and threats, Noah gained his confidence by flattery and obsequiousness. But finally Noah realized that matters were coming to a head: The survival of humanity was at stake.

Noah studied his situation carefully. On the one hand, his natural sense of human solidarity did not permit him to turn his back on his brothers and sisters about to be destroyed, and to take advantage of the good will of a dictator about to wipe out all his relatives and friends. A decent individual, so he told himself, must in such a situation cast in his lot with the doomed and share their suffering instead of entering into the service of their persecutor. Even if they were guilty, there would be something indecent about deserting them in their misfortune in order to save one's own skin. Ultimately, so he thought, I am after all more human than divine and must thus recognize the bonds of human solidarity.

On the other hand, so Noah continued, the only chance for the survival of humanity is now in my hands. (God had made it quite clear that he had no intention of exempting anyone from the pogrom except Noah and his immediate family, his brothers and sisters not included.) If therefore I should decide on suicide in the name of brotherhood, so Noah argued, I thus destroy the sole possibility for a survival of mankind. Even if this is not the best of all possible worlds, it nevertheless deserves to continue in existence.

Noah's dilemma was having to decide what was better: to betray his friends, or to be responsible for the utter destruction of mankind.

No one had ever faced such a cruel decision, a situation in which the future of humanity lay literally in his hands, while at the same time its salvation could be bought only at the price of his personal ignominy.

It is true, so Noah thought, that I would hurt no one if I should decide to die and thus ethically save face. For it would not be logical to assert that I would hurt my nonexisting descendants by preventing their existence. It would be naive to assume that I was acting wrong in the year 1749 after the creation of the world (this being the exact date of the deluge) or in the year 2011 B.C. because in the year 1957 A.D., or 3706 years later, there will be no one to chronicle my heroism. Therefore it would probably be best to do the decent thing and at the same time put an end to this botched affair once and for all.

At the same time, however, I cannot help thinking that the survival of humanity is a worthy goal in itself. It is true I cannot logically prove this, and I cannot offhand think of good reasons why it should be true, but I carry this conviction with me deep down inside and cannot get rid of it.

After much hesitation Noah decided to take upon himself the terrible dishonor of betraying his fellow men if indeed this was the only way to save humanity. From this moment on he was a different person. He was ashamed of his earlier obsequiousness and realized the wrongness and folly of his past behavior. He honestly believed that he would have carried the burden of his ignominy much more gladly if it had not been he who was destined to save the world and if he had not stood to gain personal advantage by his deed. Would people believe that his actions were *not* motivated by the desire to save himself? The reputation he had gained willy-nilly made this impossible.

Noah's posture was a truly heroic one—he was ready to carry his own dishonor deliberately even further. When he told his brothers and acquaintances of his decision, they merely turned away from him in disgust, thinking that Noah had simply remained what he had always been, an incorrigible lickspittle. No one realized how dramatic his decision had been. Noah suffered in silence. He merely determined that he would avenge himself upon the tyrant: He would educate his children in such a fashion that all the rebellions and lawlessness of times past would seem pale when compared with the doings of the new generations. His descendants would be a race of incorrigible rebels, of notorious scoffers, whose existence would be an everlasting thorn to the Almighty.

This is exactly what happened—though Noah did not live to see it come about.

He now boarded the ark, betrayed his friends, his country, and his brothers. . . .

Moral: Let us remember that at times we may have to submit obsequiously to the mighty and betray our comrades—but only if we are absolutely sure that this course is the only way of saving all humanity. So far Noah has been the only one to face such a dilemma.

DISCUSSION AND WRITING

1. Compare these three stories with their Biblical version. What if anything does the author preserve of the original? What kind of twist does he give the original material? Is it the same or similar in all three stories?

2. Satire is typically indirect. What are the targets of Kolakowski's satire? Study the stories for possible clues. For instance, what is the meaning and history of the term *pogrom?* What other terms and expressions seem revealing?

3. What evidence of your own can you supply that in using the words *mercy* and *benevolence* "we should always specify for *whom*"? In your own experience, what other abstraction or abstractions seem most urgently in need of similar treatment?

4. Examine the arguments in the stories about Rahab and Noah. How good is the logic in these arguments? What function do they serve in the stories?

5. (a) Describe the humor in these stories, using detailed examples. What is your reaction to it? Is there any room for humor in relation to religious subjects at all, in your opinion? If so, what would be the proper relationship between humor and religion? (b) Compare and contrast Kolakowski's kind of humor with that of James Thurber in "Fables for Our Time."

6. It is often said that fables derive much of their charm and impact from their drastically simplified situations and the simplified motives of the major characters. To what extent do these fables seem simplified? What are some of the things that make them complicated?

7. Like other postwar European writers, Kolakowski has had censorship problems on both sides of the Iron Curtain. In West Germany, for instance, a planned broadcast of one of his texts was canceled when Catholic groups objected to it as blasphemous. What is the definition of blasphemy? How is it different from mere irreverence? Write a paper in which you justify or attack a hypothetical banning of the above fables because of their possible blasphemous character.

8. Kolakowski once said that the only important fruits of philosophical thinking are "kindness without sentimentality, courage without fanaticism, hope without illusion." Do the fables help to produce any of these effects?

9. Kolakowski was accused by the Polish Communist party of "ideological confusion." To judge from what you know about Communist ideology, which attitudes expressed or hinted at in these stories might be compatible with it? Which might seem alien to or incompatible with it?

10. In a famous series of essays, Kolakowski called the typical Communist of the Stalin era "the man without alternative"—the person who on every political, moral, and ideological question believed what he had been told; whose key virtue was conformity to prevailing attitudes; who saw the world in terms of good (his side) and evil (any opposing side); who had no real conception of the possibility that an opposing view might be right; who had lost the capacity for independent judgment. To what extent is the typical American student of your own generation a person "without alternative"?

FURTHER READING

Humor varies from culture to culture, from period to period, from group to group. Study a characteristic brand of humor as exhibited in one of the following: (1) several issues of *Punch,* the British humor magazine (which has been called "as British as vegetable marrow"); (2) a humorous treatment of university life, such as Kingsley Amis's *Lucky Jim* or Vladimir Nabokov's *Pnin;* (3) several issues of a current college humor magazine.

9

The Voice of Protest

*Here I stand—I cannot act otherwise. May God help me.
Amen.* MARTIN LUTHER

Protest is often a lonely and dangerous undertaking. Rewards and recognition often go to the writer who confirms expectations, who endorses established values, who puts the practices of the community in the best possible light. The writer raising the voice of protest may find that society is impatient even with polite criticism, and sometimes strikes back viciously at the spokesman of open discontent. The essays in this section show that there is ultimately for the serious writer a higher goal than satisfying his audience: the goal of satisfying his own conscience and of speaking his mind. Each of the four writers in this section grapples in his own way with the problem of how to address people who are in no mood to listen. Thomas Mann's "Letter to the Dean" reflects the deliberateness of a man who after long grim silence finally speaks out against intolerable evil. André Gide, in "Return from the Soviet Union," speaks with the eloquence of a man passionately involved in a cause betrayed, profoundly loyal to the victims of injustice. Henry David Thoreau, in his famous essay "On the Duty of Civil Disobedience," speaks with the stubborn insistence of the nineteenth-century American individualist asserting his own sense of what is right against the pressures to do what is practical, popular, respectable, and patriotic. H. L. Mencken, finally, attacks the recalcitrant reader with the weapons of the satirist: outrageous overstatement, cutting irony, well-aimed abuse.

THOMAS MANN

When Hitler and his party set out to discredit and suppress all German literature that they considered un-German or subversive, Thomas Mann (1875–1955) was among their principal targets. Mann's novel *Budden-brooks* had received the Nobel prize for literature in 1929. *The Magic Mountain,* first published in 1924, remains one of the milestones of modern literature. Mann's cosmopolitanism required a loyalty to ideals transcending narrow national boundaries. It thus was in direct conflict with the kind of patriotism that insists on a fanatical belief in the God-given superiority and unique mission of one's own country. Furthermore, Mann's irony required the kind of detachment that goes counter to the unquestioning conformity demanded by a totalitarian regime. After the Nazis came to power, Thomas Mann had emigrated, first to Switzerland and then to the United States. The Nazi government stripped him of his German citizenship, and in 1936 the University of Bonn sent him a letter announcing its withdrawal of the honorary doctorate it had earlier granted him. The following letter is Mann's reply to this announcement. The documentary value of this letter lies in Mann's attempt to define the nature of the political catastrophe that had overtaken his country and to define the responsibility of the writer in such a situation. The literary and human value of the letter lies in its attempt to do the almost impossible: to exercise rational restraint in addressing an audience deaf to the voice of reason.

Letter to the Dean

To the Dean of the Philosophical Faculty
of the University of Bonn:

I have received the melancholy communication which you addressed to me on the nineteenth of December. Permit me to reply to it as follows:

The German universities share a heavy responsibility for all the present distresses which they called down upon their heads when they tragically misunderstood their historic hour and allowed their soil to nourish the

From *The Thomas Mann Reader,* edited by Joseph Warner Angell, translated by H. T. Lowe-Porter. Copyright 1937 by Alfred A. Knopf, Inc. Reprinted by permission.

ruthless forces which have devastated Germany morally, politically, and economically. This responsibility of theirs long ago destroyed my pleasure in my academic honour and prevented me from making any use of it whatever. Moreover, I hold today an honorary degree of Doctor of Letters conferred upon me more recently by Harvard University. I cannot refrain from explaining to you the grounds upon which it was conferred. My diploma contains a sentence which, translated from the Latin, runs as follows: "... we the President and Fellows with the approval of the honorable Board of Overseers of the University in solemn session have designated and appointed as honorary Doctor of Letters Thomas Mann, famous author, who has interpreted life to many of our fellow-citizens and together with a very few contemporaries sustains the high dignity of German culture; and we have granted to him all the rights and privileges appertaining to this degree."

In such terms, so curiously contradictory to the current German view, do free and enlightened men across the ocean think of me—and, I may add, not only there. It would never have occurred to me to boast of the words I have quoted; but here and today I may, nay, I must repeat them. If you, Herr Dean (I am ignorant of the procedure involved), have posted a copy of your communication to me on the bulletin board of your university, it would gratify me to have this reply of mine receive the same honour. Perhaps some member of the university, some student or professor, may be visited by a sudden fear, a dismaying and swiftly suppressed presentiment, on reading a document which gives him in his disgracefully enforced isolation and ignorance a brief revealing glimpse of the free world of the intellect that still exists outside.

Here I might close. And yet at this moment certain further explanations seem to me desirable or at least permissible. I made no statement when my loss of civil rights was announced, though I was more than once asked to do so. But I regard the academic divestment as a suitable occasion for a brief personal declaration. I would beg you, Herr Dean (I have not even the honour of knowing your name), to regard yourself as merely the chance recipient of a communication not designed for you in a personal sense.

I have spent four years in an exile which it would be euphemistic to call voluntary since if I had remained in Germany or gone back there I should probably not be alive today. In these four years the odd blunder committed by fortune when she put me in this situation has never once ceased to trouble me. I could never have dreamed, it could never have been prophesied of me at my cradle, that I should spend my later years as an émigré, expropriated, outlawed, and committed to inevitable political protest. From the beginning of my intellectual life I had felt myself in happiest accord with the temper of my nation and at home in its intellectual traditions. I am better suited to represent those traditions than to become a martyr for them; far more fitted to add a little to the gaiety of the world than to foster conflict and hatred in it. Something very wrong must have happened to make my life take so false and unnatural a turn. I tried to check it, this very wrong thing, so far as my weak powers were able—and in so doing I called down on myself the fate which I must now learn to reconcile with a nature essentially foreign to it.

Certainly I challenged the wrath of these despots by remaining away and giving evidence of my irrepressible disgust. But it is not merely in the last four years that I have done so. I felt thus long before and was driven to it because I saw—earlier than my now desperate countrymen—who and what would emerge from all this. But when Germany had actually fallen into those hands I thought to keep silent. I believed that by the sacrifice I had made I had earned the right to silence; that it would enable me to preserve something dear to my heart, the contact with my public within Germany. My books, I said to myself, are written for Germans, for them above all; the outside world and its sympathy have always been for me only a happy accident. They are, these books of mine, the product of a mutually nourishing bond between nation and author and depend on conditions which I myself have helped to create in Germany. Such bonds as these are delicate and of high importance; they ought not to be rudely sundered by politics. Though there might be impatient ones at home who, muzzled themselves, would take ill the silence of a free man, I was still able to hope that a great majority of Germans would understand my reserve, perhaps even thank me for it.

These were my assumptions. They were not justified. I could not have lived or worked, I should have suffocated, had I not been able now and again to cleanse my heart, so to speak, to give from time to time free vent to my abysmal disgust at what was happening at home—the contemptible words and still more contemptible deeds. Justly or not, my name had once and for all been connected for the world with the conception of a Germany which it loved and honoured. The disquieting challenge rang in my ears: that I and no other must in clear terms contradict the ugly falsification which this conception of Germany was now suffering. That challenge disturbed all the free-flowing creative fancies to which I would so gladly have yielded. It was a challenge hard to resist for one to whom it had always been given to express himself, to release himself through language, to whom experience had always been one with the purifying and preserving Word.

The mystery of the Word is great; the responsibility for it and its purity is of a symbolic and spiritual kind; it has not only an artistic but also a general ethical significance; it is responsibility itself, human responsibility quite simply, also the responsibility for one's own people, the duty of keeping pure its image in the sight of humanity. In the Word is involved the unity of humanity, the wholeness of the human problem, which permits nobody, and today less than ever, to separate the intellectual and artistic from the political and social and to isolate himself within the ivory tower of the "cultural" alone. This true totality is equated with humanity itself, and anyone—whoever he be—is making a criminal attack upon humanity when he undertakes to "totalize" a segment of human life: I mean politics, I mean the State.

A German author accustomed to this responsibility of the Word, a German whose patriotism, perhaps naïvely, expresses itself in a belief in the infinite moral significance of whatever happens in Germany—should he be silent, wholly silent, in the face of the inexpiable evil that is done daily in my country to bodies, souls, and minds, to right and truth, to men and mankind? And should he be silent in the face of the frightful danger to the whole continent presented by this soul-destroying régime, which exists in abysmal ignorance of the hour that has struck today in the world? It was not possible for me to be silent. And so, contrary to my intention, came the utterances, the unavoidably compromising gestures which have now resulted in the absurd and deplorable business of my national excommunication. The mere knowledge of who these men are who happen to possess the pitiful outward power to deprive me of my German birthright is enough to make the act appear in all its absurdity. I, forsooth, am supposed to have dishonoured the Reich, Germany, in acknowledging that I am against *them!* They have the incredible effrontery to confuse themselves with Germany! When, after all, perhaps the moment is not far off when it will be of supreme importance to the German people not to be confused with them.

To what a pass, in less than four years, have they brought Germany! Ruined, sucked dry body and soul by armaments with which they threaten the whole world, holding up the whole world and hindering it in its real task of peace, loved by nobody, regarded with fear and cold aversion by all, it stands on the brink of economic disaster, while its "enemies" stretch out their hands to snatch back from the abyss so important a member of the future family of nations, to help it, if only it will come to its senses and try to understand the real needs of the world at this hour, instead of dreaming dreams about mythical "sacred necessities." Yes, after all, it must be helped by those whom it hinders and menaces, in order that it may not drag down the rest of the continent with it and unleash the war upon which as the *ultima ratio* it keeps its eyes ever fixed. The mature and cultural states—by which I mean those which understand the fundamental fact that war is no longer permissible—treat this endangered and endangering country, or rather the impossible leaders into whose hands it has fallen, as doctors treat a sick man: with the utmost tact and caution, with inexhaustible if not very flattering patience. But it thinks it must play politics—the politics of power and hegemony—with the doctors. That is an unequal game. If one side plays politics when the other no longer thinks of politics but of peace, then for a time the first side reaps certain advantages. Anachronistic ignorance of the fact that war is no longer permissible results for a while of course in "successes" against those who are aware of the truth. But woe to the people which, not knowing what way to turn, at last actually seeks its way out through the abomination of war, hated of God and man! Such a people will be lost. It will be so vanquished that it can never rise again.

The meaning and purpose of the National-Socialist State is this alone and can be only this: to put the German people in readiness for the "coming war" by ruthless repression, elimination, extirpation of every stirring of opposition; to make of them an instrument of war, infinitely compliant, without a single critical thought, driven by a blind and fanatical ignorance. Any other meaning and purpose, any other excuse this system cannot have; all the sacrifices of freedom, justice, human happiness, including the secret and open crimes for which it has blithely been responsible, can be justified only by the end—absolute fitness for war. If the idea of war as an aim in itself disappeared, the system would mean nothing but the exploitation of the people; it would be utterly senseless and superfluous.

Truth to tell, it *is* both of these, senseless and superfluous, not only because war will not be permitted it, but also because its leading idea, the absolute readiness for war, will result in precisely the opposite of what it is striving for. No other people on earth is today so utterly incapable of war, so little in condition to endure one. That Germany would have no allies, not a single one in the world, is the first consideration but the smallest. Germany would be forsaken—terrible of course even in her isolation—but the really frightful thing would be the fact that she had forsaken herself. Intellectually reduced and humbled, morally gutted, inwardly torn apart by her deep mistrust of her leaders and the mischief they have done her in these years, profoundly uneasy herself, ignorant of the future, of course, but full of forebodings of evil, she would go into war not in the condition of 1914 but, even physically, of 1917 or 1918. The ten per cent of direct beneficiaries of the system—half even of them fallen away—would not be enough to win a war in which the majority of the rest would only see the opportunity of shaking off the shameful oppression that has weighed upon them so long—a war, that is, which after the first inevitable defeat would turn into a civil war.

No, this war is impossible; Germany cannot wage it; and if its dictators are in their senses, then their assurances of readiness for peace are not tactical lies repeated with a wink at their partisans; they spring from a faint-hearted perception of just this impossibility. But if war cannot and shall not be—then why these robbers and murderers? Why isolation, world hostility, lawlessness, intellectual interdict, cultural darkness, and every other evil? Why not rather Germany's voluntary return to the European system, her reconciliation with Europe, with all the inward accompaniments of freedom, justice, well-being, and human decency and a jubilant welcome from the rest of the world? Why not? Only because a régime which in word and deed denies the rights of man, which wants above all else to remain in power, would stultify itself and be abolished, if, since it cannot make war, it actually made peace!

I had forgotten, Herr Dean, that I was actually addressing you. Certainly I may console myself with the reflection that you long since ceased to read this letter, aghast at language which in Germany has long been unspoken, terrified because somebody dares use the German tongue with the ancient freedom. I have not spoken out of arrogant presumption, but out of a concern and a distress from which your usurpers did not release me when they decreed that I was no longer a German—a mental and spiritual distress from which for four years not an hour of my life has been free, and struggling with which I have had to accomplish my creative work day by day. The pressure was great. And as a man who out of diffidence in religious matters will seldom or never either by tongue or pen let the name of the Deity escape him, yet in moments of deep emotion cannot refrain, let me—since after all one cannot say everything—close this letter with a brief and fervent prayer: *God help our darkened and desecrated country and teach it to make its peace with the world and with itself!*

DISCUSSION AND WRITING

1. Define or explain: *presentiment, divestment, émigré, expropriate, despot, inexpiable, excommunication, effrontery,* ultima ratio, *hegemony, anachronistic, abomination, extirpation, compliant, interdict, jubilant, stultify, usurper, diffidence, desecrate.*

2. Mann's prose is read by many for the rich texture of his style—his exploitation of nuances in word choice, his elaborately constructed sentences. Are any of these features reflected in this translation? Discuss several detailed examples. (If your instructor desires, select a paragraph from a translation of one of Mann's short stories or novels and compare its style with that of the present selection.)

3. What is Mann's tone? What stance does he adopt toward his audience? Is the prevailing note one of passionate indictment, biting scorn, helpless rage, grim determination, indiscriminate abuse? What effect does Mann's chosen tone have on the reader? Discuss several examples in detail.

4. Restate in your own words Mann's account of his motives and responsibilities as a writer. Why was it impossible for him to insulate himself in the sphere of culture or to accept a totalitarian philosophy?

5. The following are routine examples of Nazi propaganda, of the type that were found daily in newspapers, textbooks, and the like. (The first two are excerpts from Hitler's speeches.) Describe some of the characteristic features of these selections. To judge from these samples, what would make it difficult to *counteract* this type of propaganda effectively?

a. Germany wants peace. We assure the world that Germany's whole desire is to live in peace and friendship with all nations. The peace treaty (of 1919) is based on the allegation that Germany caused the war. A weak generation signed this document, afraid of renewed blackmail and oppression. Today we know that it would have been a blessing for the whole German people if it had been represented by men with the courage to stand before the world and declare: We are ready to accept any kind of peace, but we shall never, against our own better knowledge, use our signature to perpetuate a lie and to surrender our national honor.

b. As you are assembled here, my young comrades, our whole nation must be assembled in spirit and feel that we belong together. Unfortunately it was not always thus. We must cherish this insight: We must be animated by one single will, we must form one single unity, we must be inspired by one single spirit of obedience and subordination. When this insight is transformed into a sacred obligation, then the spirit animating us here today will spread and weld together our whole people into one single being of unified will and tremendous power. You are the Germany of the future; you are our hope.

c. The decisive element in true leadership is personal responsibility, that is, authority in dealing with those below and responsibility toward those above. Responsibility requires more than doing one's duty, it requires complete dedication to the work at hand and the decisions it requires. What is expected of each of us is a personal commitment to the rebuilding of our society and to its leader, a determination to serve our people and our country beyond the call of duty, with inner joy and from deep conviction.

d. The law ordering the role of labor in our nation is based on the leadership principle as applied to economic life. It abolishes the conflicts that pit one social class against the other and emphasizes the principle of honor in economic management. Management represents leadership; the staff and the workers are the followers. All work together to accomplish the purposes of the organization and to benefit the nation and the country. The relationship of the worker to management involves loyalty. There is no longer any such thing as an "employee."

e. In placing people in newly developed communities, we must determine whether the requirements of racial hygiene have been met—whether the families have a record of good heredity and numerous children. The absence of mental illness and hereditary defects is a necessary requirement in addition to the obvious personal criteria, such as proven effectiveness in one's chosen occupation and a decent and healthy life.

6. Young people in postwar Germany often carried their disillusionment with Nazi ideals to the point of refusing to accept *any* large idealistic abstractions. To what extent is Mann's language "idealistic"? What values does he appeal to? Are they familiar? Are they handled in predictable ways? How effective is Mann as a spokesman for these values?

7. Is today's typical college student temperamentally inclined to be a spokesman rather than a martyr?

8. Is it possible or desirable today to separate the intellectual and artistic from the political and social? Is today's artist or writer still torn between a yearning for serenely independent art and the duty of "inevitable political protest"?

9. Thomas Mann once said, "In Germany, those critical of the German character have always been the most truly German." Could this statement be adapted to describe what it means to be "truly American"? Attack, defend, or discuss the proposition that "True Americanism requires the ability to be critical of one's own country."

10. Write "A Letter to . . ." on a subject that for you has serious moral implications. State your position in such a way that it will prove intelligible, and perhaps persuasive, to someone who may strongly disagree with your views.

FURTHER READING

Recent German literature reflects the attempt of many younger writers to come to terms with the Nazi past and to find honest answers to its problems of guilt and responsibility. The works of these writers are increasingly being translated into English. Check the card catalogue of your college library for translations of works by Günter Grass, Heinrich Böll, Max Frisch, Uwe Johnson, Siegfried Lenz. Check the last five years or so of the *Book Review Digest* for discussions of some of their books.

ANDRÉ GIDE

André Gide (1869–1951) is one of the most widely known and influential of modern French authors. Born into a wealthy family and financially independent, he early devoted himself to writing. In books like *The Immoralist* (1902) and *Les Faux Monnayeurs* (1925), he explored new areas of thought, emotion, and form. His *Journals,* completed during the last years of his life, found a wide audience. In the early thirties, Gide, like other artists and intellectuals, was strongly attracted to communism. He proclaimed his sympathy for the communist ideal, influenced less by the economic or historical doctrines of Marx than by the hope for an end to social injustice and abuses. He visited Russia in 1936 and registered his disillusionment in two books, from which the following account has been adapted. The publication of his *Return from the Soviet Union* was a milestone in a general movement of disaffection, which over the years cost the Soviet state most of the sympathy it had originally enjoyed among the intellectual and cultural elite of western Europe. The present selection is an outstanding example of an argument developed, not from prejudice, but *against* the author's own original inclination.

Return from the Soviet Union

Homer relates how the great goddess Demeter, in her wanderings in search of her daughter, came to the court of Celeus. No one recognized her in the disguise of a nurse, and a newborn child—the boy

Demophoön—was entrusted to her care. At night, with the doors closed and while the household slept, Demeter used to lift Demophoön from his warm soft cradle and, with seeming cruelty—though in reality inspired by great love and the desire to transform the child into a god—she would lay him naked on a bed of glowing coals, and bend lovingly over her bonny nursling, as if over the incarnation of future mankind. He endured the heat of the embers and this ordeal by fire made him strong and glorious beyond all dreams and hopes. Demeter, however, was not permitted to complete her daring endeavor. Metaneira, the mother—so the legend relates—anxious for the safety of her child, burst one night into the room, and, thrusting aside the goddess, scattered the embers with all the superhuman virtues which were being wrought and, in order to save the child, sacrificed the god.

Some years ago I wrote of my love and admiration for the Soviet Union, where an unprecedented experiment was being attempted, the thought of which inflamed my heart with expectation and from which I hoped a tremendous advance, an impulse capable of sweeping along the whole of humanity. It was certainly worth-while to be alive at such a moment to be able to witness this rebirth and to give one's whole life to further it. In my heart I bound myself resolutely, in the name of future culture, to the fortunes of the Soviet Union.

Four days after my arrival in Russia I declared, at the funeral of Gorky, in the Red Square at Moscow, that the fate of culture was linked, in my mind, with the future of the Soviet Union. "Culture," I said, "had long remained the prerogative of a privileged class, and leisure was necessary for its development. One whole section of society had toiled in order to allow a small number of people to enjoy life, while the garden of culture, literature and art had long remained a private enclosed property to which only the most intelligent could ever hope to have access—those who from childhood had been sheltered from need. It is of course true that ability does not necessarily accompany wealth and in French literature Molière, Diderot and Rousseau had risen from the people, but their readers had been men of leisure. When the October Revolution stirred up the deep masses of the Russian people, it was said in the West, oft repeated and universally believed, that this tidal wave would swamp all art. As soon as literature ceased being the privilege of one class would it not—it was asked—then constitute a danger? It was to answer that accusation that writers from all countries grouped themselves together with the firm conviction of accomplishing an urgent duty. It is true that culture was menaced—but the peril did not come from the revolutionary and liberating forces; it came, on the contrary, from the parties which were trying to subjugate these forces and to break them. It is war which most threatens culture, war toward which national forces inspired by hate and envy drive us. It is the great international and revolutionary forces on which the duty is laid to protect culture and to make it illustrious. Its fate is bound up, in my mind, with the fate of the Soviet Union and it shall be defended."

This speech belonged to the early part of my visit, to the time when I still believed—still had the naïveté to believe—that one could seriously discuss questions of culture with the Russians. I wish that I could still believe it. If I was mistaken at first, it is only right that I should recognize my error as soon as possible, because I am responsible for those at home whom my opinions might lead astray. No personal pride must hinder me—I have little in any case—there are matters far more important than myself and my personal pride, more important than the Soviet Union. The future of humanity and the fate of its culture are at stake.

As long as my tour in Russia was conducted everything seemed to me wonderful. In direct contact with the working people, in their workshops, in their factories, in their recreation centers, I was able to enjoy moments of deep joy. Nowhere are human relationships as easily formed as in the Soviet Union, nor as warm or deep. Friendships are quickly made—often a mere glance suffices—and strong bonds of sympathy are instantly forged. I verily believe that nowhere as much as in the Soviet Union does one enjoy so deep a feeling of humanity, an immediate up-surge of brotherly love. My heart swelled and tears came into my eyes through excess of joy—tears of love and affection. The children whom I saw in the camps were well-fed, well-cared-for, cherished and happy. Their eyes were clear and full of confidence and hope. This expression of illumined happiness I saw also on the faces of workers in the recreation centers, where they assembled, in the evening, when their work was done. Each town in the Soviet Union has now its recreation center and its kindergarten. Like many other visitors, I saw model factories, clubs, pleasure grounds, at which I marveled. I asked for nothing better than to be carried away with admiration and to convert others as well. And so, as it is very pleasant to be enraptured and to persuade others, if I protest against all this enchantment, I must have serious grounds for doing so. I only began to see clearly when, abandoning the government transport, I traveled alone through the country in order to be able to get into direct contact with the people. I had read too much Marxist literature to feel a fish out of water in Russia, but I had also read too many accounts of idyllic trips and too many enthusiastic apologies. My mistake, at first, was to believe all the praise that I heard, and everything which might have enlightened me was always said in a spiteful tone of voice. It happens too often that the friends of the Soviet Union refuse to see anything bad there—or at least to recognize it—so it happens that truth is spoken with hatred and falsehood with love. My mind is constituted in such a way that my greatest severity is directed especially toward those of whom I would like always to approve, and I do not think that it is the best way to express one's love to be content with praise alone. I think that I do more service to the cause which the

Soviet Union represents by speaking without pretense and without too much circumspection and consideration. I certainly had personally nothing to complain of in the course of my trip, in spite of all the spiteful explanations which were invented subsequently to invalidate my criticism, which was too often interpreted as the result and expression of personal pique and disappointment—this is most absurd of all. For never have I traveled in greater or more luxurious ease—I had the most comfortable cars everywhere, a private coach on the train, the best rooms and meals in all the hotels—always the best was offered me and what a reception I received everywhere! I was acclaimed and fêted. Nothing was considered too good for me. I could not fail to carry away with me a most wonderful memory of the welcome I had received, but nevertheless all these favors reminded me constantly of the privileges and differences where I had hoped to find equality. When I escaped from officials and went amongst the workers, I discovered that most of them lived in the direst poverty, while I was offered a ceremonial banquet every evening, at which the variety, richness and quantity of the hors d'oeuvres alone were sufficient to sate the appetite before the main part of the meal had even begun—a dinner of six courses which lasted four hours. Never having had to settle a bill while I was in Russia, I cannot form an estimate of the cost of such a feast, but one of my friends who knows the range of prices in the Soviet Union, told me that it would cost two or three hundred roubles a head, and the workers whom I had seen earned only five roubles a day and had to be content with black bread and dried fish. During our stay in Russia we were not exactly the guests of the government, but of the wealthy Society of Soviet Authors. When I think of all they spent on us—and there were six of us, with our guides, and often as many hosts as guests! Of course they had counted on a different return for their money, and I think that part of the resentment of *Pravda* came from the fact that I was so poor an investment. Certainly it seemed to me quite natural that they should want to receive a guest as well as possible and to show him the best of everything, but nevertheless it surprised me to find so great a difference between the best and the common lot, such excessive privileges beside such depths of poverty. It is on account of my admiration for the Soviet Union and the marvels she has already accomplished by herself, that my criticism is going to be severe: because of what we expect from her and what she gave us reason to hope from her. I trusted her and so, in Russia, what distressed me most was not what was not yet perfect, but rather to find there everything from which I had always fled at home—the privileges which I had hoped abolished forever.

Who can ever say what the Soviet Union had been for me? Far more than the country of my choice, an example and an inspiration, it represented what I had always dreamed of but no longer dared hope—it was something toward which all my longing was directed—it was a land where I imagined

Utopia was in process of becoming reality. The Soviet Union is, however, at an early stage of construction—that needs to be remembered constantly—and we are present at the parturition of the future. There are both good and bad points—I should say both the best and the worst; one moves from the brightest to the darkest with alarming and disconcerting suddenness. Much has already been accomplished which has filled our hearts with joy and this, doubtless, made me exacting. It seemed at first to me as if the most difficult had already been achieved, and I was ready to throw myself with all my heart into the contract, as it were, into which I had entered with the Soviet Union in the name of all suffering mankind. I felt myself so much committed that failure was not to be contemplated.

I admired particularly in Russia the extraordinary impulse toward education and culture. But the sad thing is that the education the people receive only informs them on what leads them to flatter themselves on the present state of affairs and to believe in the Soviet Union *Ave Spes Unica*.[1] Culture is directed toward one aim only, the glorification of the Soviet Union; it is not disinterested, and critical discrimination is entirely lacking. I know well that they make a parade of self-criticism and, at first, I believed and hoped in that, thinking that it might lead to great results if it was applied with integrity; but I soon discovered that criticism consists solely in inquiring whether such or such a work is in agreement with the Party line. It is not the Party line which is discussed or criticized, but only the question whether a certain theory tallies or not with this sacred line. No state of mind is more dangerous than this, nor more likely to imperil real culture. Soviet citizens remain in the most complete ignorance of everything outside their own country and—what is worse—have been persuaded that everything abroad is vastly inferior to everything at home. On the other hand, although they are not interested in what prevails outside their country, they are very much interested in what foreigners think of them. What they are very anxious to know is whether they are sufficiently admired abroad; what they fear above all else is that foreigners may not be sufficiently well-informed concerning their merits; what they want from them is praise and not information.

I happened to visit a model collective—it is one of the finest and most prosperous in the Soviet Union—and I went into several of the houses. I wish that I could give some conception of the uniformly depressing impression which is communicated by each of the dwellings, that of a total absence of individuality. In each there are the same ugly pieces of furniture, the same picture of Stalin and absolutely nothing else—not the smallest vestige of ornament or personal belonging. Any house could be exchanged for any other without the tenant being aware of the alteration. Of course the members of a collective take all their pleasures in common, and their homes

[1] [Hail Our Only Hope.]

are only, as it were, lairs to sleep in; the whole interest of their lives is centered in the club. Doubtless the happiness of all can most easily be achieved by the sacrifice of the individuality of each, through conformity. But can it be called progress, this loss of individuality, this uniformity, toward which everything in Russia is now tending? I cannot believe that it is. In the Soviet Union it is accepted once and for all that on every subject —whatever may be the issue—there can only be one opinion, the right one. And each morning *Pravda* tells the people what they need to know, and must believe and think. When I was in the Soviet Union, I was astonished to see no mention in the papers of the Civil War in Spain which, at the time, was causing much troubled anxiety in democratic circles. I expressed my pained surprise to my interpreter and noticed some embarrassment on his part, but he thanked me for my observations and said that he would transmit them to the correct quarter. That evening, at the usual ceremonial dinner, there were many speeches and toasts according to the usual custom. When the health of all the guests and hosts had been drunk, one of my party, Jef Last, rose to his feet and, in Russian, proposed a toast to the triumph of the Red cause on the Spanish Front. The company applauded with some embarrassment and lack of cordiality, I thought, and replied immediately with a toast to Stalin. When my turn came, I lifted my glass to the political prisoners in Germany. This time the toast was vociferously applauded and with no halfhearted enthusiasm—answered again by another toast to Stalin. All present knew what to think about the victims of Fascism in Germany and what attitude to adopt. But on the Spanish question *Pravda* had not yet made any official pronouncement and they did not dare risk approval without getting a lead and knowing what they were expected to think. It was only a few days later, when we had arrived at Sebastopol, that an immense wave of sympathy unfurled from the Red Square in Moscow and, through *Pravda,* swept across the whole country. By now the minds of the people are so well-trained in conformity that compliance has become natural and easy for them—I do not believe that it is hypocrisy—so that each time you speak with one Russian it is as if you had spoken with all.

The disappearance of capitalism has not brought freedom to the Soviet workers—it is essential that the proletariat abroad should realize this fully. It is of course true that they are no longer exploited by shareholding capitalists, but nevertheless they are exploited, and in so devious, subtle and twisted a manner that they do not know any more whom to blame. The largest number of them live below the poverty line, and it is their starvation wages which permit the swollen pay-packets of the privileged workers—the pliant yes-men. One cannot fail to be shocked by the indifference shown by those in power toward their inferiors, and the servility and obsequiousness on the part of the latter—I almost said the poor. Granted that there are no longer any classes nor class distinctions in the Soviet Union; but the poor are still with them—and there are far too many of them. I had hoped to find none—or more exactly, it was precisely in order to find none that I went to the Soviet Union. But poverty there is frowned upon—one might imagine that it was indelicate and criminal—it does not arouse pity or charity, only contempt. Those who parade themselves so proudly are those whose prosperity has been bought at the price of this infinite poverty. It is not that I object to inequality of wages—I agree that it is a necessary and inevitable measure—but there ought to be some way of relieving the most grievous disparities. I am afraid that all this means a return to a form of working-class bourgeoisie, gratified and hence conservative—too like the petty bourgeoisie at home for my taste. I see the symptoms already. There is no doubt that all the bourgeois vices and failings still lie dormant, in spite of the Revolution in many. Man cannot be reformed from the outside—a change of heart is necessary—and I feel anxious when I observe all the bourgeois instincts flattered and encouraged in the Soviet Union, and all the old layers of society forming again—if not precisely social classes, at least a new kind of aristocracy, and not an aristocracy of intellect or ability, but an aristocracy of right-thinkers and conformists. In the next generation it may well be an aristocracy of money. Are my fears exaggerated? I sincerely hope so.

When I visited Sotchi I marveled at the number of sanatoria and rest-houses that are being erected for the workers. These hostels are most pleasant, with beautiful gardens and private bathing beaches. It is praise-worthy that all this semi-luxury should be provided for the use of the workers; nevertheless those who enjoy this comfort are all too often the new privileged class. It is true that those in need of rest or treatment are given priority—but always provided that they agree with the Party line. And it is lamentable to see nearby the men employed in building these very rest-houses so badly paid and parked in such sordid encampments.

If I am full of admiration for the rest-houses at Sotchi, what can I say about the hotel at Sinop, near Soukhoum, where I stayed, so vastly superior to anything else that it can be compared only to the most comfortable and luxurious hotels abroad. Each room has its own bathroom, its private balcony, the furnishings are of the finest and the cooking equal to first class anywhere. Near the hotel is a model farm to supply it with produce, comprising model stables, cowsheds, pigsties and an enormous hencote provided with the latest contrivances. But, if you cross the stream which marks the boundary of the farm, you come across a row of mean hovels in which each small room of six square feet houses four people at a rent of two roubles a month per person.

Although the long-heralded Dictatorship of the Proletariat has not materialized, there is nevertheless dictatorship of one kind—dictatorship of the Soviet bureaucracy. It is essential to recognize this and not to allow oneself to be bamboozled. This is not what was hoped for—one might almost say that it is precisely the last thing in the world that was hoped. The workers have no longer even the liberty of electing their own representatives to defend their threatened interests. Free ballot—open or secret—is a derision and a sham; the voters have merely the right of electing those who have been chosen for them beforehand. The workers are cheated, muzzled and bound hand and foot, so that resistance has become wellnigh impossible. The game has been well played by Stalin, and Communists the whole world over applaud him, believing that in the Soviet Union at least they have gained a glorious victory, and they call all those who do not agree with them public enemies and traitors. But in Russia this has led to treachery of a new sort. An excellent way of earning promotion is to become an informer; that puts you on good terms with the dangerous police which protect you while using you. Once you have started on that easy, slippery slope, no question of friendship or loyalty can intervene to hold you back; on every occasion you are forced to advance, sliding further into the abyss of shame. The result is that everyone is suspicious of everyone else and the most innocent remarks—even of children—can bring destruction, so that everyone is on his guard and no one lets himself go.

During my tour I was taken to see the model town of Bolchevo, which is unique of its kind since all its inhabitants are convicts—housebreakers, pickpockets and murderers. It started as a small penal settlement founded in the belief that criminals are only invalids or neurotic misfits whom proper treatment, sympathetic kindness and a normal life would cure and turn into valuable, contented citizens, but it has grown into a large and flourishing town in which not only factories are found, but also libraries, rest-centers and clubs. When I visited it, it seemed to me one of the noblest and most successful experiments in the Soviet Union and a great achievement. It was only later that I discovered, what I did not know at first, that only informers—those who had betrayed their fellow-convicts to the authorities—were granted the privilege of living in this model settlement. Could moral cynicism sink lower than this?

The unfortunate Soviet worker is tied to his factory—just as the agricultural worker is tied to his collective—like Ixion to his wheel. If the worker for some personal reason—either because he imagines, or hopes, that he will elsewhere be better off, or less badly off, or merely because he would welcome a change—thinks of leaving his job, then, classified and regimented as he is, he runs the risk of obtaining no employment anywhere. And even if, whilst remaining in the same town, he leaves his factory, he is deprived of the living quarters, to which his work gave him the right—hard to find elsewhere—and for which moreover he had been paying rent. He also discovers that he forfeits, on leaving, a considerable part of his wages and loses the whole of the accumulated profits from his collective work. On the other hand, if his transfer is considered necessary by the authorities, he cannot refuse to leave. He is free neither to go when he wishes nor to stay where his affections and personal interests are centered. Then, if he does not belong to the Party, those who do outstrip him in promotion. Yet all who desire cannot become Party members, and moreover everyone does not possess the requisite qualities of flattery, obsequiousness and submission. If, on the other hand, he is lucky enough to be a Party member, he cannot resign without losing all the advantages his employment gave him, and he is also liable to suspicion and reprisals. Why, it is asked, should anyone want to leave a Party which grants such substantial rewards in return for mere acquiescence and obedience? Why, besides, should anyone want to think for himself since it is universally agreed that everything is for the best in the best of all possible worlds? To think for oneself is to run the risk of being accused of being counter-revolutionary, and then—if one is a Party member—one is expelled and there follows the probability of Siberia. This impoverishment of the human stock is all the more tragic since it passes unobserved and those who disappear—or are made to disappear—are amongst the bravest and most independent of those who distinguish themselves from the masses and hinder uniformity and mediocrity. These deportees—thousands of them— who have been unable to be humble or to bend the knee—it seems to me that I hear them in the darkness around me: it is the cries of these countless victims which rouse me in the long watches of the night; it is their unwilling silence which urges me to speech today; it is thinking of these martyrs that I now pen these lines; and recognition from them—if my words could ever reach them—would be more sweet and precious to me than all the incense from *Pravda*. No one intervenes on their behalf, and those who are responsible for justice and liberty are silent, while the masses of the people are blinded. When I raise my voice in their favor I am told—again in the name of Marx—that these deportations, the poverty of the workers and the abolition of suffrage, all these are only provisional measures and are the necessary price to pay for the gains of 1917. It is, however, terrifying to see abandoned, one after the other, all the benefits gained at the price of so much suffering. It is time that eyes should be opened to this tragic failure in which all our hopes have foundered. One might perhaps have accepted the absence of personal and intellectual freedom in Russia today, if at least there had been evidence that the material progress of the masses was being gradually, if slowly, achieved, but this if far from being the case and, on the contrary, it is evident that all the worst and most reprehensible features of capitalist society are being re-established. That petty-bourgeois mentality, to which I have previously referred, which I greatly fear is on the increase, is, in my opinion, profoundly and fundamentally counter-revolutionary. Yet what they call counter-revolutionary is precisely that revolutionary spirit, that surging torrent, which, at first, tore through the rotting and crumbling dikes of the

Czarist world. One would like to be able to believe that love still filled their hearts to overflowing—or at least a passionate need for justice—but once the Revolution was accomplished, it all vanished and the generous ardor which had inspired the first revolutionaries became, as it were, the rusting debris of tools whose utility is done. Now that the Revolution has become established, it parleys with iniquity; and those in whom the rebel spirit still burns, those for whom all these successive concessions are compromises, these are disregarded or liquidated. Would it not then be better to cease quibbling and to recognize that the inspiration of the Revolution no longer prevails, since what is expected is submission and conformity? What is demanded is approbation of everything done by the government. The slightest opposition and the merest criticism exposes its agent to the severest penalties and is, moreover, instantly suppressed. From top to bottom of the reformed social ladder, those with the best references are the most servile, and those who stand out independently are mown down or deported. Soon, in that heroic race which has deserved so well of our love and admiration, there will be left only the profiteers, the executioners and the victims. The small, independent worker has become a hunted animal, starved, broken and finally eliminated. I doubt whether in any country in the world—not even in Hitler's Germany —have the mind and spirit ever been less free, more bent, more terrorized over and indeed vassalized—than in the Soviet Union. Yet the suppression of the opposition in a country—or even the curtailing of its expression—is a very dangerous thing, an invitation to terrorism. If all the citizens in a state thought alike, it would no doubt spare the government much trouble, but, faced with such a prospect, can one then talk of culture? Real wisdom consists in listening to opposition views—in fostering them even whilst preventing them from harming the common weal.

Humanity is complex and not all of a piece—that must be accepted—and every attempt at simplification and regimentation, every effort from the outside to reduce everything and everyone to the same common denominator, will always be reprehensible, pernicious and dangerous.

With artists it is still more sinister than with the ordinary citizen. I believe that the real value of an author consists in his revolutionary force, or more exactly—for I am not foolish enough to credit the Left alone with intellectual and artistic powers—in his quality of opposition. A great artist is of necessity a "nonconformist" and he must swim against the current of his day. But what will eventually happen in the Soviet Union when the transformed state has removed from the artist all need for opposition? What will happen to the artist when there will be no longer any possibility even of opposition? Will the only course left to him then be to drift with the current? Doubtless, as long as the struggle persists and victory has not been wholly achieved, he will be able to lead the revolution and, by fighting himself, assure its victory. But what is to happen then? It is precisely this which makes me look with so much anxiety toward the Soviet Union; that was the vital question which I had been asking myself before I went to Russia and to which I found no satisfactory answer. Furthermore, what is to happen to the subtle and truly original artist? One painter whom I met in Russia told me that subtlety and originality were no longer what the country wanted, not what was now needed. He said that an opera was no use to the workers if, on leaving the theater, there were no tunes that they could whistle. What was now needed, he insisted, were works which could be immediately apprehended and understood. I protested that the greatest works—and even those which later became popular—were never appreciated when they were first heard—or were only appreciated by a small and select public. He admitted that even Beethoven would have found it impossible, in the Soviet Union, to make a come-back after an initial failure. "You see," he said, "an artist here must first and foremost be in the Party line—otherwise even the highest works will be considered examples of mere 'formalism.'" That is the expression now used in Russia to designate everything which they do not care to see or hear. "We intend," he went on, "to create a new art worthy of the great people that we have now become." I answered that this would oblige all the artists to be "conformists" and that the best and most original would never consent to debase their art and to bow to such a *diktat;* they would therefore be reduced to silence. Then the very culture which the leaders were anxious to further, illustrate and glorify would spurn them and despise them. He said that I was only talking as a bourgeois and that he, for his part, was convinced that Marxism, which in so many other fields had achieved great things, would also produce great works of art. He claimed that the only thing which prevented their emergence was the excessive importance still attributed by artists to outworn forms of art. He was speaking in an ever rising voice and seemed to be delivering a lecture or else to be reciting a lesson by rote. I could not listen any longer in patience and left him without answering. Some time later, however, he came to my room and admitted that, at heart, he agreed with me but that, in the lounge downstairs, he was being overheard, that he was opening a one-man show in the near future and needed official support and approval.

When I arrived in the Soviet Union, the general public had not yet resolved the thorny controversy about "formalism." I tried to understand what was meant by the expression and discovered that the works which were accused of "formalism" were those by artists who had laid more emphasis on form than on content. I might, however, add that only one content was considered worthy of consideration—or indeed tolerated—the right one, and every work was held to be "formalist" which did not point in that one direction. It is enough to make one weep to realize that this is the spirit which inspires all criticism in the Soviet Union. Such sectarianism may once have been politically useful, but one certainly cannot describe it as culture. Culture will always be in peril where criticism cannot be freely practiced. In Russia a work which is not in the Party line is condemned, and beauty is considered a bourgeois aberration. However great may be the talent of an artist, if he does not follow the Party line he labors unknown and unrecognized—if he is allowed to labor at all—but if he conforms, he receives recompense and praise. It is easy to see what advantage can accrue to a government from singling out for reward an artist who can sing the praises of the regime. Conversely, it is easy to see the advantages which accrue to the artist himself if he is prepared to sing the praises of the government which gives him so goodly a heritage.

Amongst all workers and artisans in the Soviet Union it is the writer who is most favored and indulged. The immense privileges that I was offered amazed and terrified me and I was afraid of being seduced and corrupted. I did not go to the Soviet Union for the sake of benefits, and those that I saw were glaring; but that did not prevent my criticism, since the most favored position enjoyed by writers in Russia—better than in any other country in the world—was granted only to the right-thinking. That was a danger signal to me and I was immediately on my guard. The price exacted is the total surrender of all opposition, and opposition in the Soviet Union is merely the exercise of free criticism. I discovered that a certain distinguished member of the Academy of Sciences had just been released from prison, whose sole crime had been independence of judgment, and when foreign scientists tried to get in touch with him, they were always told that he was indisposed. Another was dismissed from his professorship and denied laboratory facilities for having expressed scientific opinions which did not tally with current Soviet doctrine, and he was obliged to write a public letter of recantation to avoid deportation. It is a characteristic trait of despotism to be unable to suffer independence and to tolerate only servility. However just his brief, woe betide the Soviet lawyer who rises to defend an accused whom the authorities wish to see convicted. Stalin allows only praise and approbation, and soon he will be surrounded only by those who cannot put him in the wrong since they have no opinions whatsoever. His portrait is seen everywhere, his name is on everyone's lips and praise of him occurs in every public speech. Is all this the result of worship, love or fear? Who can say? I remember, on the way to Tiflis, as we went through Gori, the little village where he was born, I thought it would be a kind and courteous attention to send him a personal message as an expression of gratitude for the warm welcome we had received in the Soviet Union, where we had been treated everywhere with lavish hospitality. I thought that no better opportunity would occur again, so I had the car stopped at the post office and I handed in a telegram which began: "Passing through Gori on our wonderful trip I feel the impulse to send you—" But here the translator paused and said that he could not transmit such a message, that "you," when addressed to Stalin, was not sufficient. It was not decent, he declared, and something must be added. He suggested "You leader of the workers" or else "You Lord of the people." It seemed to me absurd and I said that Stalin must surely be above such flattery, but all in vain. Nothing would budge him, and he would not transmit the telegram unless I agreed to the emendation. I reflected sadly that such formalities contribute to erect an insuperable barrier between Stalin and his subjects. I was also frequently obliged to make additions or alterations in the speeches I delivered in the course of my visit. They explained to me that a word like "destiny" must always be preceded by the epithet "glorious" when it referred to the destiny of the Soviet Union; on the other hand they requested me to delete the adjective "great" when it qualified a king, since a monarch can never be "great"! At Leningrad I was invited to address a society of students and writers and I submitted my script beforehand to the committee, but I was informed that what I had intended to say would be considered unseemly since it was not in the Party line. The ensuing difficulties were so many and so tortuous, that I eventually abandoned the project of the address, which ran as follows:

> I have often been invited to give my views on Contemporary Soviet Literature, and I would like to explain why I have hitherto refused to express an opinion. This will permit me to clarify and amplify certain statements which I made in the Red Square in Moscow on the occasion of Gorky's funeral. I spoke then of the new problems which the very success of the Revolution had provoked, and I said it would be to the eternal credit of the Soviet Union to have resuscitated them for our consideration. As the future of civilization is closely linked with whatever solution is found for them in Russia, it seems to me profitable to raise them again here. The majority, even when it comprises the best elements, never appreciates what is new or difficult in a work of art, but only what can readily be recognized—that is to say, what is most commonplace. It must be remembered that there are revolutionary as well as bourgeois commonplaces and clichés. It is also essential to realize that what gives quality to a work of art and brings it immortality, is never what comes from the revolution nor what reflects its doctrine, however noble it may be. A work of art will survive only by what is truly original in it, by the new questions it asks or anticipates, and by the answers that it gives to questions which have not yet been formulated. I greatly fear that many of the works of art impregnated with the purest Marxist doctrine—to which indeed they owe their contemporary success—will, for posterity, smack only of the laboratory. The only works of art which will survive oblivion are those which

have risen superior to contemporary preoccupations. Now that the Revolution is triumphant, art runs a grave risk—as grave as any under the most calamitous oppressions—the danger of becoming an orthodoxy. What triumphant revolution needs to grant, above all else, to the artist, is freedom. Without complete freedom, art loses all its significance and worth. And, since the applause of the majority means success, reward and fame will go to those works which the public can grasp and understand at the first attempt. I often ask myself anxiously whether a Keats, a Baudelaire or a Rimbaud[2] may not languish unknown today in the Soviet Union who, by reason of their originality and power, have not yet been heard. It is they who interest me most, those who, at first, were despised and neglected—the Baudelaires, the Rimbauds and the Keatses—those whom posterity will single out for immortality. You may argue perhaps that we do not need nowadays a Keats, a Baudelaire or a Rimbaud, that they are significant only insofar as they reflect the decadent and dying society of which they were the sorry products; you may say that if they cannot prevail, so much the worse for them and so much the better for us, since we have nothing further to learn from their like, and the writers who can teach us something today are those who, in the new society, feel perfectly at home—in other words, those who approve and flatter the regime. But I personally believe that it is precisely the works which flatter and approve which are of poor educational worth, and that a culture, if it is to progress, must ignore them. As for the literature which confines itself to reflecting society, I have already said what I think of it. To remain in constant self-contemplation and self-admiration may be one stage in the development of a young society, but it would indeed be regrettable and tragic if this first stage were to remain the final and only one.

As long as man is oppressed and downtrodden, as long as the compulsion of social injustice keeps him in subjection, we are at liberty to hope much from what has not yet had opportunity to burgeon, from all the latent fertility in the fallow classes. Just as we hope much from children who may eventually grow up into quite commonplace people, in the same way we often have the illusion that the masses are composed of men of a finer clay than the rest of disappointing humanity. I think that they are merely less corrupt and less decadent than the others, that is all. I see already a new bourgeoisie developing in the Soviet Union from these untried masses, with exactly the same faults and vices as ours. No sooner have they risen above the poverty line, than they despise the poor and become jealous and possessive of the belongings of which they were so long deprived; they know how to acquire them now and how to keep them. Are these really the people who

[2] [Baudelaire, author of *Flowers of Evil*, and Rimbaud were outstanding and controversial French poets of the nineteenth century.]

made the Revolution? No! They are merely those who have turned it to their own selfish advantage. They may well still be members of the Communist Party, but they are no longer Communist at heart. I blame the Soviet Union not for having failed to achieve more—I see now that nothing better could have been accomplished in that time, the country had started from too low—what I complain of is the extent of their bluff, that they boasted that the situation in the Soviet Union was desirable and enviable—this from the country of my hopes and trust was painful to me.

I blame the Communists in France—and elsewhere too—and I do not mean those who were duped in all good faith, but those who knew—or ought to have known—better, and yet lied to the workers abroad while all the time seeking political aims. It is time that the workers outside the Soviet Union should realize that they have been bamboozled and led astray by the Communist Party, just as the Russian workers were duped before them.

Deplorable and unsatisfactory as the state of affairs in the Soviet Union is, I would have remained silent if I could have been assured of any faint progress toward something better. It is because I have reached the firm conviction that the Soviet Union is sliding down the slope that I had hoped to see it ascend, and because it has abandoned, one after another—and always for the most specious reasons—the liberties gained by the great Revolution after so much hardship and bloodshed. It is because I see it dragging in its wake to irreparable chaos the Communist Parties of other countries, that I consider it my duty to speak openly.

No question of Party loyalty can restrain me from speaking frankly for I place truth above the Party. I know well that in Marxist doctrine there is no such thing as truth—at least not in any absolute sense—there is only relative truth. I believe, however, that in so serious a matter it is criminal to lead others astray, and urgent to see matters as they are, not as we would wish them to be or had hoped that they might be. The Soviet Union has deceived our fondest hopes and shown us tragically in what treacherous quicksand an honest revolution can founder. The same old capitalist society has been re-established, a new and terrible despotism crushing and exploiting man, with all the abject and servile mentality of serfdom. Russia, like Demophoön, has failed to become a god and she will never now arise from the fires of the Soviet ordeal.

DISCUSSION AND WRITING

1. Define or explain: *prerogative, illustrious, naïveté, invalidate, pique, fêted, parturition, disinterested, discrimination, devious, pliant, servility, obsequiousness, acquiescence, reprehensible, iniquity, approbation, pernicious, sinister, diktat, aberration, recantation, emendation, insuperable, epithet, tortuous, calamitous, decadent, specious, serfdom.* Identify the writers and historical events Gide mentions.

2. Examine Gide's use or application of key terms like "culture," "petty-bourgeois mentality," "bourgeoisie," "conformity," "orthodoxy," "sectarianism," "Marxist doctrine," "capitalism."

3. André Gide's account is the sort of writing that is seriously misleading when read incompletely or quoted out of context. Why doesn't he get straight to the point? How effective or persuasive is his approach? Whom is he trying to persuade?

4. Where does Gide first reveal his over-all attitude? What sentence or passage comes closest to summing up his theme? What are some of the basic assumptions that underlie his discussion? Describe his own political outlook as implied in this account.

5. Select a passage that you consider exceptionally telling, eloquent, or persuasive. Explain in detail what makes it so.

6. Compare and contrast Gide's reaction to Soviet society of the thirties with Miss Rau's reaction to that of the fifties. Or, compare and contrast Gide's view of the relationship between the writer and society with that of Mann.

7. How great is the difference in contemporary American society between "the best and the common lot"? Are there "excessive privileges" beside "depths of poverty"?

8. Discuss American politics as reflected in editorials, political speeches, and similar sources to answer one of the following: How much is there in American politics of that "real wisdom" that "consists in listening to opposition views"? Or, how much of a tendency is there in American life to grant freedom of expression only to the "right-thinking"? Refer to concrete instances.

9. What evidence have you encountered for the view that "humanity is complex and not all of a piece" and that every attempt at simplification and regimentation "will always be reprehensible, pernicious and dangerous"?

10. What ideas, influences, or experiences have shaped your own political views? Limit yourself to one major point or to one important area.

FURTHER READING

Of the many books registering the disillusionment of idealistic foreign observers with the promise of the Soviet utopia, two of the most sobering and most telling are Arthur Koestler's *Darkness at Noon* (1941), a novel based on the author's close personal involvement, and *Animal Farm* (1946), George Orwell's biting satirical fable. How much basic agreement is there in the two authors' indictment of Stalinist Russia?

HENRY DAVID THOREAU

Henry David Thoreau (1817–1862), one of the great masters of American prose, is best known for his *Walden* (1854), the record of his attempt to "live deliberately, to front only the essential facts of life"; to rediscover

truly worthy human aims obscured by an external and superficial civilization. He first published "On the Duty of Civil Disobedience" in 1849, at a
time when allegiance to established political institutions was tested by
slavery and the Mexican War. Many Northerners disapproved of slavery in
the South but in effect helped it survive through commercial and political
collaboration with the Southern states. The Fugitive Slave Law, for
example, made it a crime for a New Englander like Thoreau to aid
Negroes who had escaped from their Southern owners. The war against
Mexico had followed the annexation of Texas and eventually brought
California and large areas of the Southwest into the Union. Many
Americans considered this territorial expansion an inevitable stage in the
country's "Manifest Destiny." Others, including Thoreau, considered the
conflict an aggressive and imperialistic war on the discredited European
pattern, as well as a means of strengthening the slave-holding South.
Thoreau expressed his convictions as a speaker at abolitionist rallies,
through active aid to fugitive slaves, and through refusal to pay taxes
toward the upkeep of a government condoning injustice. Thoreau's views
have influenced modern advocates of peaceful resistance to unjust governments, notably India's Mahatma Gandhi. The section omitted in the
following version of Thoreau's essay contains his account of a night spent
in Concord jail upon his refusal to pay the poll tax.

On the Duty of Civil Disobedience

I heartily accept the motto,—"That government is best which
governs least"; and I should like to see it acted up to more rapidly and
systematically. Carried out, it finally amounts to this, which also I believe,—
"That government is best whch governs not at all"; and when men are
prepared for it, that will be the kind of government which they will have.
Government is at best but an expedient; but most governments are usually,
and all governments are sometimes, inexpedient. The objections which have
been brought against a standing army, and they are many and weighty, and
deserve to prevail, may also at last be brought against a standing government.
The standing army is only an arm of the standing government. The government itself, which is only the mode which the people have chosen to execute
their will, is equally liable to be abused and perverted before the people can
act through it. Witness the present Mexican war, the work of comparatively
a few individuals using the standing government as their tool; for, in the
outset, the people would not have consented to this measure.

This American government,—what is it but a tradition, though a recent
one, endeavoring to transmit itself unimpaired to posterity, but each instant
losing some of its integrity? It has not the vitality and force of a single living

man; for a single man can bend it to his will. It is a sort of wooden gun to the people themselves. But it is not the less necessary for this; for the people must have some complicated machinery or other, and hear its din, to satisfy that idea of government which they have. Governments show thus how successfully men can be imposed on, even impose on themselves, for their own advantage. It is excellent, we must all allow. Yet this government never of itself furthered any enterprise, but by the alacrity with which it got out of its way. *It* does not keep the country free. *It* does not settle the West. *It* does not educate. The character inherent in the American people has done all that has been accomplished; and it would have done somewhat more, if the government had not sometimes got in its way. For government is an expedient by which men would fain succeed in letting one another alone; and, as has been said, when it is most expedient, the governed are most let alone by it. Trade and commerce, if they were not made of India-rubber, would never manage to bounce over the obstacles which legislators are continually putting in their way; and, if one were to judge these men wholly by the effects of their actions and not partly by their intentions, they would deserve to be classed and punished with those mischievous persons who put obstructions on the railroads.

But, to speak practically and as a citizen, unlike those who call themselves no-government men, I ask for, not at once no government, but *at once* a better government. Let every man make known what kind of government would command his respect, and that will be one step toward obtaining it.

After all, the practical reason why, when the power is once in the hands of the people, a majority are permitted, and for a long period continue, to rule is not because they are most likely to be in the right, nor because this seems fairest to the minority, but because they are physically the strongest. But a government in which the majority rule in all cases cannot be based on justice, even as far as men understand it. Can there not be a government in which majorities do not virtually decide right and wrong, but conscience?— in which majorities decide only those questions to which the rule of expediency is applicable? Must the citizen ever for a moment, or in the least degree, resign his conscience to the legislator? Why has every man a conscience, then? I think that we should be men first, and subjects afterward. It is not desirable to cultivate a respect for the law, so much as for the right. The only obligation which I have a right to assume is to do at any time what I think right. It is truly enough said, that a corporation has no conscience; but a corporation of conscientious men is a corporation *with* a conscience. Law never made men a whit more just; and, by means of their respect for it, even the well-disposed are daily made the agents of injustice. A common and natural result of an undue respect for law is, that you may see a file of soldiers, colonel, captain, corporal, privates, powder-monkeys, and all, marching in admirable order over hill and dale to the wars, against their wills, ay, against their common sense and consciences, which makes it very steep marching indeed, and produces a palpitation of the heart. They have no doubt that it is a damnable business in which they are concerned; they are all peaceably inclined. Now, what are they? Men at all? or small movable forts and magazines, at the service of some unscrupulous man in power? Visit the Navy Yard, and behold a marine, such a man as an American government can make, or such as it can make a man with its black arts,—a mere shadow and reminiscence of humanity, a man laid out alive and stand-ing, and already, as one may say, buried under arms with funeral accom-paniments, though it may be,—

> "Not a drum was heard, not a funeral note,
>   As his corse to the rampart we hurried;
> Not a soldier discharged his farewell shot
>   O'er the grave where our hero we buried."

The mass of men serve the state thus, not as men mainly, but as machines, with their bodies. They are the standing army, and the militia, jailers, con-stables, *posse comitatus,* etc. In most cases there is no free exercise whatever of the judgment or of the moral sense; but they put themselves on a level with wood and earth and stones; and wooden men can perhaps be manu-factured that will serve the purpose as well. Such command no more respect than men of straw or a lump of dirt. They have the same sort of worth only as horses and dogs. Yet such as these even are commonly esteemed good citizens. Others—as most legislators, politicians, lawyers, ministers, and office-holders—serve the state chiefly with their heads; and, as they rarely make any moral distinctions, they are as likely to serve the devil, without *intending* it, as God. A very few, as heroes, patriots, martyrs, reformers in the great sense, and *men,* serve the state with their consciences also, and so necessarily resist it for the most part; and they are commonly treated as enemies by it. A wise man will only be useful as a man, and will not submit to be "clay," and "stop a hole to keep the wind away," but leave that office to his dust at least:—

> "I am too high-born to be propertied,
>   To be a secondary at control,
>   Or useful serving-man and instrument
> To any sovereign state throughout the world."

He who gives himself entirely to his fellow-men appears to them useless and selfish; but he who gives himself partially to them is pronounced a benefactor and philanthropist.

How does it become a man to behave toward this American government today? I answer, that he cannot without disgrace be associated with it. I cannot for an instant recognize that political organization as *my* government which is the *slave's* government also.

All men recognize the right of revolution; that is, the right to refuse allegiance to, and to resist, the government, when its tyranny or its inefficiency are great and unendurable. But almost all say that such is not the case now. But such was the case, they think, in the Revolution of '75. If one were to tell me that this was a bad government because it taxed certain foreign commodities brought to its ports, it is most probable that I should not make an ado about it, for I can do without them. All machines have their friction; and possibly this does enough good to counterbalance the evil. At any rate, it is a great evil to make a stir about it. But when the friction comes to have its machine, and oppression and robbery are organized, I say, let us not have such a machine any longer. In other words, when a sixth of the population of a nation which has undertaken to be the refuge of liberty are slaves, and a whole country is unjustly overrun and conquered by a foreign army, and subjected to military law, I think that it is not too soon for honest men to rebel and revolutionize. What makes this duty the more urgent is the fact that the country so overrun is not our own, but ours is the invading army....

Practically speaking, the opponents to a reform in Massachusetts are not a hundred thousand politicians at the South, but a hundred thousand merchants and farmers here, who are more interested in commerce and agriculture than they are in humanity, and are not prepared to do justice to the slave and to Mexico, *cost what it may*. I quarrel not with far-off foes, but with those who, near at home, cooperate with, and do the bidding of, those far away, and without whom the latter would be harmless. We are accustomed to say, that the mass of men are unprepared; but improvement is slow, because the few are not materially wiser or better than the many. It is not so important that many should be as good as you, as that there be some absolute goodness somewhere; for that will leaven the whole lump. There are thousands who are *in opinion* opposed to slavery and to the war, who yet in effect do nothing to put an end to them; who, esteeming themselves children of Washington and Franklin, sit down with their hands in their pockets, and say that they know not what to do, and do nothing; who even postpone the question of freedom to the question of free-trade, and quietly read the prices-current along with the latest advices from Mexico, after dinner, and, it may be, fall asleep over them both. What is the price-current of an honest man and patriot today? They hesitate, and they regret, and sometimes they petition; but they do nothing in earnest and with effect. They will wait, well disposed, for others to remedy the evil, that they may no longer have it to regret. At most, they give only a cheap vote, and a feeble countenance and God-speed, to the right, as it goes by them. There are nine hundred and ninety-nine patrons of virtue to one virtuous man. But it is easier to deal with the real possessor of a thing than with the temporary guardian of it.

All voting is a sort of gaming, like checkers or backgammon, with a slight moral tinge to it, a playing with right and wrong, with moral questions; and betting naturally accompanies it. The character of the voters is not staked. I cast my vote, perchance, as I think right; but I am not vitally concerned that that right should prevail. I am willing to leave it to the majority. Its obligation, therefore, never exceeds that of expediency. Even voting *for the right* is *doing* nothing for it. It is only expressing to men feebly your desire that it should prevail. A wise man will not leave the right to the mercy of chance, nor wish it to prevail through the power of the majority. There is but little virtue in the action of masses of men. When the majority shall at length vote for the abolition of slavery, it will be because they are indifferent to slavery, or because there is but little slavery left to be abolished by their vote. *They* will then be the only slaves. Only *his* vote can hasten the abolition of slavery who asserts his own freedom by his vote.

I hear of a convention to be held at Baltimore, or elsewhere, for the selection of a candidate for the Presidency, made up chiefly of editors, and men who are politicians by profession; but I think, what is it to any independent, intelligent, and respectable man what decision they may come to? Shall we not have the advantage of his wisdom and honesty, nevertheless? Can we not count upon some independent votes? Are there not many individuals in the country who do not attend conventions? But no: I find that the respectable man, so called, has immediately drifted from his position, and despairs of his country, when his country has more reason to despair of him. He forthwith adopts one of the candidates thus selected as the only *available* one, thus proving that he is himself *available* for any purposes of the demagogue. His vote is of no more worth than that of any unprincipled foreigner or hireling native, who may have been bought. O for a man who is a *man,* and, as my neighbor says, has a bone in his back which you cannot pass your hand through! Our statistics are at fault: the population has been returned too large. How many *men* are there to a square thousand miles in this country? Hardly one. Does not America offer any inducement for men to settle here? The American has dwindled into an Odd Fellow,—one who may be known by the development of his organ of gregariousness, and a manifest lack of intellect and cheerful self-reliance; whose first and chief concern, on coming into the world, is to see that the almshouses are in good repair; and, before yet he has lawfully donned the virile garb, to collect a fund for the support of the widows and orphans that may be; who, in short, ventures to live only by the aid of the Mutual Insurance company, which has promised to bury him decently.

It is not a man's duty, as a matter of course, to devote himself to the eradication of any, even the most enormous wrong; he may still properly have other concerns to engage him; but it is his duty, at least, to wash his hands of it, and, if he gives it no thought longer, not to give it practically his support. If I devote myself to other pursuits and contemplations, I must first see, at least, that I do not pursue them sitting upon another man's shoulders. I must get him off first, that he may pursue his contemplations too. See what gross inconsistency is tolerated. I have heard some of my townsmen say, "I should like to have them order me out to help put down an insurrection of the slaves, or to march to Mexico;—see if I would go"; and yet these very men have each, directly by their allegiance, and so indirectly, at least, by their money, furnished a substitute. The soldier is applauded who refuses to serve in an unjust war by those who do not refuse to sustain the unjust government which makes the war; is applauded by those whose own act and authority he disregards and sets at naught; as if the state were penitent to that degree that it hired one to scourge it while it sinned, but not to that degree that it left off sinning for a moment. Thus, under the name of Order and Civil Government, we are all made at last to pay homage to and support our own meanness. After the first blush of sin, comes its indifference; and from immoral it becomes, as it were, *un*moral, and not quite unnecessary to that life which we have made.

The broadest and most prevalent error requires the most disinterested virtue to sustain it. The slight reproach to which the virtue of patriotism is commonly liable, the noble are most likely to incur. Those who, while they disapprove of the character and measures of a government, yield to it their allegiance and support, are undoubtedly its most conscientious supporters, and so frequently the most serious obstacles to reform. Some are petitioning the state to dissolve the Union, to disregard the requisitions of the President. Why do they not dissolve it themselves,—the union between themselves and the state,—and refuse to pay their quota into its treasury? Do not they stand in the same relation to the state that the state does to the Union? And have not the same reasons prevented the state from resisting the Union which have prevented them from resisting the state?

How can a man be satisfied to entertain an opinion merely, and enjoy *it*? Is there any enjoyment in it, if his opinion is that he is aggrieved? If you are cheated out of a single dollar by your neighbor, you do not rest satisfied with knowing that you are cheated, or with saying that you are cheated, or even with petitioning him to pay you your due; but you take effectual steps at once to obtain the full amount, and see that you are never cheated again. Action from principle, the perception and the performance of right, changes things and relations; it is essentially revolutionary, and does not consist wholly with anything which was. It not only divides states and churches, it divides families; ay, it divides the *individual,* separating the diabolical in him from the divine.

Unjust laws exist: shall we be content to obey them, or shall we endeavor to amend them, and obey them until we have succeeded, or shall we transgress them at once? Men generally, under such a government as this, think that they ought to wait until they have persuaded the majority to alter them. They think that, if they should resist, the remedy would be worse than the evil. But it is the fault of the government itself that the remedy *is* worse than the evil. *It* makes it worse. Why is it not more apt to anticipate and provide for reform? Why does it not cherish its wise minority? Why does it cry and resist before it is hurt? Why does it not encourage its citizens to be on the alert to point out its faults, and *do* better than it would have them? Why does it always crucify Christ, and excommunicate Copernicus and Luther, and pronounce Washington and Franklin rebels?

One would think, that a deliberate and practical denial of its authority was the only offense never contemplated by government; else, why has it not assigned its definite, its suitable and proportionate penalty? If a man who has no property refuses but once to earn nine shillings for the state, he is put in prison for a period unlimited by any law that I know, and determined only by the discretion of those who placed him there; but if he should steal ninety times nine shillings from the state, he is soon permitted to go at large again.

If the injustice is part of the necessary friction of the machine of government, let it go, let it go; perchance it will wear smooth,—certainly the machine will wear out. If the injustice has a spring, or a pulley, or a rope, or a crank, exclusively for itself, then perhaps you may consider whether the remedy will not be worse than the evil; but if it is of such a nature that it requires you to be the agent of injustice to another, then, I say, break the law. Let your life be a counter friction to stop the machine. What I have to do is to see, at any rate, that I do not lend myself to the wrong which I condemn.

As for adopting the ways which the state has provided for remedying the evil, I know not of such ways. They take too much time, and a man's life will be gone. I have other affairs to attend to. I came into this world, not chiefly to make this a good place to live in, but to live in it, be it good or bad. A man has not everything to do, but something; and because he cannot do *everything,* it is not necessary that he should do *something* wrong. It is not my business to be petitioning the Governor or the Legislature any more than it is theirs to petition me; and if they should not hear my petition, what should I do then? But in this case the state has provided no way: its very Constitution is the evil. This may seem to be harsh and stubborn and unconciliatory; but it is to treat with the utmost kindness and consideration the only spirit that can appreciate or deserves it. So is all change for the better, like birth and death, which convulse the body.

I do not hesitate to say, that those who call themselves Abolitionists should at once effectually withdraw their support, both in person and property, from the government of Massachusetts and not wait till they constitute a majority of one, before they suffer the right to prevail through them. I think that it is enough if they have God on their side, without waiting for that other one. Moreover, any man more right than his neighbors constitutes a majority of one already.

I meet this American government, or its representative, the state government, directly, and face to face, once a year—no more—in the person of its tax-gatherer; this is the only mode in which a man situated as I am necessarily meets it; and it then says distinctly, Recognize me; and the simplest, the most effectual, and, in the present posture of affairs, the indispensablest mode of treating with it on this head, of expressing your little satisfaction with and love for it, is to deny it then. My civil neighbor, the tax-gatherer, is the very man I have to deal with,—for it is, after all, with men and not with parchment that I quarrel,—and he has voluntarily chosen to be an agent of the government. How shall he ever know well what he is and does as an officer of the government, or as a man, until he is obliged to consider whether he shall treat me, his neighbor, for whom he has respect, as a neighbor and well-disposed man, or as a maniac and disturber of the peace, and see if he can get over this obstruction to his neighborliness without a ruder and more impetuous thought or speech corresponding with his action. I know this well, that if one thousand, if one hundred, if ten men whom I could name,—if ten *honest* men only,—ay, if *one* HONEST man, in this State of Massachusetts, *ceasing to hold slaves,* were actually to withdraw from this copartnership, and be locked up in the county jail therefor, it would be the abolition of slavery in America. For it matters not how small the beginning may seem to be: what is once well done is done forever. But we love better to talk about it: that we say is our mission. Reform keeps many scores of newspapers in its service, but not one man. . . .

I have never declined paying the highway tax, because I am as desirous of being a good neighbor as I am of being a bad subject; and, as for supporting schools, I am doing my part to educate my fellow-countrymen now. It is for no particular item in the tax-bill that I refuse to pay it. I simply wish to refuse allegiance to the state, to withdraw and stand aloof from it effectually. I do not care to trace the course of my dollar, if I could, till it buys a man or a musket to shoot one with,—the dollar is innocent,—but I am concerned to trace the effects of my allegiance. In fact, I quietly declare war with the state, after my fashion, though I will still make what use and get what advantage of her I can, as is usual in such cases.

If others pay the tax which is demanded of me, from a sympathy with the state, they do but what they have already done in their own case, or rather they abet injustice to a greater extent than the state requires. If they pay the tax from a mistaken interest in the individual taxed, to save his property, or prevent his going to jail, it is because they have not considered wisely how far they let their private feelings interfere with the public good.

This, then, is my position at present. But one cannot be too much on his guard in such a case, lest his action be biased by obstinacy, or an undue regard for the opinions of men. Let him see that he does only what belongs to himself and to the hour.

I think sometimes, Why, this people mean well, they are only ignorant; they would do better if they knew how: why give your neighbors this pain to treat you as they are not inclined to? But I think again, This is no reason why I should do as they do, or permit others to suffer much greater pain of a different kind. Again, I sometimes say to myself, When many millions of men, without heat, without ill will, without personal feeling of any kind, demand of you a few shillings only, without the possibility, such is their constitution, of retracting or altering their present demand, and without the possibility, on your side, of appeal to any other millions, why expose yourself to this overwhelming brute force? You do not resist cold and hunger, the winds and the waves, thus obstinately; you quietly submit to a thousand similar necessities. You do not put your head into the fire. But just in proportion as I regard this as not wholly a brute force, but partly a human force, and consider that I have relations to those millions as to so many millions of men, and not of mere brute or inanimate things, I see that appeal is possible, first and instantaneously, from them to the Maker of them, and, secondly, from them to themselves. But, if I put my head deliberately into the fire, there is no appeal to fire or to the Maker of fire, and I have only myself to blame. If I could convince myself that I have any right to be satisfied with men as they are, and to treat them accordingly, and not according, in some respects, to my requisitions and expectations of what they and I ought to be, then, like a good Mussulman and fatalist, I should endeavor to be satisfied with things as they are, and say it is the will of God. And, above all, there is this difference between resisting this and a purely brute or natural force, that I can resist this with some effect; but I cannot expect, like Orpheus, to change the nature of the rocks and trees and beasts.

I do not wish to quarrel with any man or nation. I do not wish to split hairs, to make fine distinctions, or set myself up as better than my neighbors. I seek rather, I may say, even an excuse for conforming to the laws of the land. I am but too ready to conform to them. Indeed I have reason to suspect myself on this head; and each year, as the tax-gatherer comes round, I find myself disposed to review the acts and position of the general and state governments, and the spirit of the people, to discover a pretext for conformity.

I believe that the state will soon be able to take all my work of this sort out of my hands, and then I shall be no better a patriot than my fellow-countrymen. Seen from a lower point of view, the Constitution, with all its faults, is very good; the law and the courts are very respectable; even this state and this American government are, in many respects, very admirable, and rare things, to be thankful for, such as a great many have described them; but seen from a point of view a little higher, they are what I have described them; seen from a higher still, and the highest, who shall say what they are, or that they are worth looking at or thinking of at all?

However, the government does not concern me much, and I shall bestow the fewest possible thoughts on it. It is not many moments that I live under a government, even in this world. If a man is thought-free, fancy-free, imagination-free, that which *is not* never for a long time appearing *to be* to him, unwise rulers or reformers cannot fatally interrupt him.

I know that most men think differently from myself; but those whose lives are by profession devoted to the study of these or kindred subjects content me as little as any. Statesmen and legislators, standing so completely within the institution, never distinctly and nakedly behold it. They speak of moving society, but have no resting-place without it. They may be men of a certain experience and discrimination, and have no doubt invented ingenious and even useful systems, for which we sincerely thank them; but all their wit and usefulness lie within certain not very wide limits. They are wont to forget that the world is not governed by policy and expediency. Webster never goes behind government, and so cannot speak with authority about it. His words are wisdom to those legislators who contemplate no essential reform in the existing government; but for thinkers, and those who legislate for all time, he never once glances at the subject. I know of those whose serene and wise speculations on this theme would soon reveal the limits of his mind's range and hospitality. Yet, compared with the cheap professions of most reformers, and the still cheaper wisdom and eloquence of politicians in general, his are almost the only sensible and valuable words, and we thank Heaven for him. Comparatively, he is always strong, original, and, above all, practical. Still, his quality is not wisdom, but prudence. The lawyer's truth is not Truth, but consistency or a consistent expediency. Truth is always in harmony with herself, and it is not concerned chiefly to reveal the justice that may consist with wrong-doing. He well deserves to be called, as he has been called, the Defender of the Constitution. There are really no blows to be given by him but defensive ones. He is not a leader, but a follower. His leaders are the men of '87. "I have never made an effort," he says, "and never propose to make an effort; I have never countenanced an effort, and never mean to countenance an effort, to disturb the arrangement as originally made, by which the various states came into the Union." Still thinking of the sanction which the Constitution gives to slavery, he says, "Because it was a part of the original compact,—let it stand." Notwithstanding his special acuteness and ability, he is unable to take a fact out of its merely political relations, and behold it as it lies absolutely to be disposed of by the intellect,—what, for instance, it behooves a man to do here in America today with regard to slavery,—but ventures, or is driven, to make some such desperate answer as the following, while professing to speak absolutely, and as a private man,—from which what new and singular code of social duties might be inferred? —"The manner," says he, "in which the governments of those states where slavery exists are to regulate it, is for their own consideration, under their responsibility to their constituents, to the general laws of propriety, humanity, and justice, and to God. Associations formed elsewhere, springing from a feeling of humanity, or any other cause, have nothing whatever to do with it. They have never received any encouragement from me, and they never will."

They who know of no purer sources of truth, who have traced up its stream no higher, stand, and wisely stand, by the Bible and the Constitution, and drink at it there with reverence and humility; but they who behold where it comes trickling into this lake or that pool, gird up their loins once more, and continue their pilgrimage toward its fountain-head.

No man with a genius for legislation has appeared in America. They are rare in the history of the world. There are orators, politicians, and eloquent men, by the thousand; but the speaker has not yet opened his mouth to speak who is capable of settling the much-vexed questions of the day. We love eloquence for its own sake, and not for any truth which it may utter, or any heroism it may inspire. Our legislators have not yet learned the comparative value of free-trade and of freedom, of union, and of rectitude, to a nation. They have no genius or talent for comparatively humble questions of taxation and finance, commerce and manufactures and agriculture. If we were left solely to the wordy wit of legislators in Congress for our guidance, uncorrected by the seasonable experience and the effectual complaints of the people, America would not long retain her rank among the nations. For eighteen hundred years, though perchance I have no right to say it, the New Testament has been written; yet where is the legislator who has wisdom and practical talent enough to avail himself of the light which it sheds on the science of legislation?

The authority of government, even such as I am willing to submit to,—for I will cheerfully obey those who know and can do better than I, and in many things even those who neither know nor can do so well,—is still an impure one: to be strictly just, it must have the sanction and consent of the governed. It can have no pure right over my person and property but what I concede to it. The progress from an absolute to a limited monarchy, from a limited monarchy to a democracy, is a progress toward a true respect for the individual. Even the Chinese philosopher was wise enough to regard the individual as the basis of the empire. Is a democracy, such as we know it, the last improvement possible in government? Is it not possible to take a step further towards recognizing and organizing the rights of man? There will never be a really free and enlightened state until the state comes to recognize the individual as a higher and independent power, from which all its own power and authority are derived, and treats him accordingly. I please myself with imagining a state at last which can afford to be just to all men, and to treat the individual with respect as a neighbor; which even would not think it inconsistent with its own repose if a few were to live aloof from it, not meddling with it, nor embraced by it, who fulfilled all the duties of neighbors and fellow-men. A state which bore this kind of fruit, and suffered it to drop off as fast as it ripened, would prepare the way for a still more perfect and glorious state, which also I have imagined, but not yet anywhere seen.

DISCUSSION AND WRITING

1. Report on the origin, history, and meaning of the following words: *motto, expedient, impair, posterity, alacrity, fain, palpitation, posse comitatus, martyr, demagogue, gregarious, virile, homage, prevalent, excommunicate, abet, lest, inanimate, fatalist, behoove*. What, in context, is the meaning of the following: *"standing* army," "give a feeble *countenance* to the right," "my *civil* neighbor," "governed by *policy*," "part of the original *compact"?*

2. Thoreau has a reputation as one of the great "sentence-makers" of American prose. Select a paragraph that shows exceptionally well Thoreau's mastery of the written word. Discuss his use of stylistic resources, paying special attention to matters that affect sentence style.

3. In your own words, develop fully Thoreau's definition of "freedom" and "justice." Explain and illustrate his distinction between "justice" and "expediency" or between "wisdom" and "prudence" as governing principles of political action.

4. Thoreau says, "All men recognize the right of revolution." On what premises or arguments is this right founded? How is it related to Thoreau's view of the nature of social organization and the individual's allegiance to society?

5. Some readers consider Thoreau a representative of true American individualism; others consider his ideas dangerous or subversive. To what extent do Thoreau's ideas agree with political principles that are familiar or widely accepted? How or why does he depart from them?

6. Examine the tone of Thoreau's essay. Consider, for instance, his statement that he is only "too ready to conform" to the laws of the land and indeed suspects himself on this head. Examine the tone of his references to his fellow citizens, to political leaders, to the Constitution. How does his tone affect the persuasiveness of his argument?

7. Discuss an example (or several related ones) of conflict between majority opinion and individual conviction, or between government authority and individual conscience. For instance, what course should one follow if he disapproves of majority sentiment about integrated schools or housing, state laws helping to perpetuate segregation, discriminatory clauses in the constitutions of clubs and fraternal organizations?

8. Jacques Barzun once said that true self-government "does not mean the government of everyone by himself, but the government of each by all." In the light of Thoreau's arguments, which of these alternatives seems to you more nearly right?

9. Emerson, Thoreau's older contemporary and close associate, said, "Whoso would be a man, must be a nonconformist." How valid or appropriate is this statement in contemporary American society?

10. At what point, if at all, does civil disobedience become justified? Make use of concrete illustration.

FURTHER READING

Among other famous statements of the American creed of individualism and non-conformity is Ralph Waldo Emerson's "Self-Reliance" (1841). The classic statement on the limits of political authority is *On Liberty* (1859) by the British philosopher John Stuart Mill.

H. L. MENCKEN

H. L. Mencken (1880–1956), representing the sturdy independence of the American journalist of past decades, developed brilliant invective into a fine art and a way of life. He started his career as a journalist in 1899, and for many years was active as a reporter, columnist, editor, and critic. To many of his readers in the twenties and in the thirties, he personified the colorful local journalism that was becoming obsolete through the spread of large newspaper chains and the adoption of tried-and-true journalistic formulas. Mencken achieved national fame by his boisterous, irreverent attacks on what he considered the failings of middle-class Americans: their timid respectability, their ostentatious prosperity, their complacent patriotism, their general lack of backbone and common sense. As a scholar and critic, Mencken championed a vigorous American language and literature, independent of European traditions. The following selection was first published in a Baltimore newspaper in 1923.

The Anglo-Saxon

When I speak of Anglo-Saxons, of course, I speak inexactly and in the common phrase. Even within the bounds of that phrase the American of the dominant stock is Anglo-Saxon only partially, for there is probably just as much Celtic blood in his veins as Germanic, and his norm is to' be found, not south of the Tyne and west of the Severn, but on the two sides of the northern border. Among the first English colonists there were many men of almost pure Teutonic stock from the east and south of England, and their influence is yet visible in many characteristic American folkways, in certain traditional American ideas—some of them now surviving only in national hypocrisies—and, above all, in the fundamental peculiarities of the American dialect of English. But their Teutonic blood was early diluted by Celtic strains from Scotland, from the north of Ireland, from Wales, and from the west of England, and today those Americans who are regarded as being most thoroughly Anglo-Saxons—for example, the mountaineers of the Appalachian slopes from Pennsylvania to Georgia—are obviously far more Celtic than Teutonic, not only physically but also mentally. They are leaner and taller than the true English, and far more given to moral obsessions and religious fanaticism. A Methodist revival is not an English phenomenon; it is Welsh. So is the American tendency, marked by every foreign student of our history, to turn all political combats into moral crusades. The English themselves, of course, have been greatly polluted by Scotch, Irish and Welsh blood during the past three centuries, and for years past their government has been largely in the hands of Celts, but though this fact, by making them more like Americans, has tended to conceal the difference that I am discussing, it has certainly not sufficed to obliterate it altogether. The English notion of humor remains different from the American notion, and so does the English view of personal liberty, and on the same level of primary ideas there are many other obvious differences.

But though I am thus convinced that the American Anglo-Saxon wears a false label, and grossly libels both of the great races from which he claims descent, I can imagine no good in trying to change it. Let him call himself whatever he pleases. Whatever he calls himself, it must be plain that the term he uses designates a genuinely distinct and differentiated race—that he is separated definitely, in character and habits of thought, from the men of all other recognizable strains—that he represents, among the peoples of the earth, almost a special species, and that he runs true to type. The traits that he developed when the first mixture of races took place in colonial days are the traits that he still shows; despite the vast changes in his material environment, he is almost precisely the same, in the way he thinks and acts, as his forefathers were. Some of the other great races of men, during the past two centuries, have changed very noticeably, but the American Anglo-Saxon has stuck to his hereditary guns. Moreover, he tends to show much less variation than other races between man and man. No other race, save it be the Chinese, is so thoroughly regimented.

The good qualities of this so-called Anglo-Saxon are many, and I am certainly not disposed to question them, but I here pass them over without apology, for he devotes practically the whole of his literature and fully a half of his oral discourse to celebrating them himself, and so there is no danger that they will ever be disregarded. No other known man, indeed, is so violently the blowhard, save it be his English kinsman. In this fact lies the first cause of the ridiculous figure he commonly cuts in the eyes of other people: he brags and blusters so incessantly that, if he actually had the combined virtues of Socrates, the Cid and the Twelve Apostles, he would still go beyond the facts, and so appear a mere Bombastes Furioso. This habit, I believe, is fundamentally English, but it has been exaggerated in the Americano by his larger admixture of Celtic blood. In late years in America it has taken on an almost pathological character, and is to be explained, perhaps, only in terms of the Freudian necromancy. Braggadocio, in the 100% American—"we won the war," "it is our duty to lead the world," and so on—is probably no more than a protective mechanism erected to conceal an inescapable sense of inferiority.

That this inferiority is real must be obvious to any impartial observer. Whenever the Anglo-Saxon, whether of the English or of the American variety, comes into sharp conflict with men of other stocks, he tends to be worsted, or, at best, to be forced back upon extraneous and irrelevant aids to assist him in the struggle. Here in the United States his defeat is so palpable that it has filled him with vast alarms, and reduced him to seeking succor in grotesque and extravagant devices. In the fine arts, in the sciences and even in the more complex sorts of business the children of the later immigrants are running away from the descendants of the early settlers. To call the roll of Americans eminent in almost any field of human endeavor above the most elemental is to call a list of strange and often outlandish names; even the panel of Congress presents a startling example. Of the Americans who have come into notice during the past fifty years as poets, as novelists, as critics, as painters, as sculptors and in the minor arts, less than half bear Anglo-Saxon names, and in this minority there are few of pure Anglo-Saxon blood. So in the sciences. So in the higher reaches of engineering and technology. So in philosophy and its branches. So even in industry and agriculture. In those areas where the competition between the new and the old bloodstreams is most sharp and clearcut, say in New York, in seaboard New England and in the farming states of the upper Middle West, the defeat of the so-called Anglo-Saxon is overwhelming and unmistakable. Once his predominance everywhere was actual and undisputed; today, even where he remains superior numerically, it is largely sentimental and illusory.

The descendants of the later immigrants tend generally to move upward; the descendants of the first settlers, I believe, tend plainly to move downward, mentally, spiritually and even physically. Civilization is at its lowest mark in the United States precisely in those areas where the Anglo-Saxon still presumes to rule. He runs the whole South—and in the whole South there are not as many first-rate men as in many a single city of the mongrel North. Wherever he is still firmly in the saddle, there we look for such pathological phenomena as Fundamentalism, Prohibition and Ku Kluxery, and there they flourish. It is not in the northern cities, with their mixed population, that the death-rate is highest, and politics most corrupt, and religion nearest to voodooism, and every decent human aspiration suspect; it is in the areas that the recent immigrations have not penetrated, where "the purest Anglo-Saxon blood in the world" still flows. I could pile up evidences, but they are not necessary. The fact is too plain to be challenged. One testimony will be sufficient: it comes from two inquirers who made an exhaustive survey of a region in southeastern Ohio, where "the people are more purely Americans than in the rest of the State":

> Here gross superstition exercises strong control over the thought and action of a large proportion of the people. Syphilitic and other venereal diseases are common and increasing over whole counties, while in some communities nearly every family is afflicted with inherited or infectious disease. Many cases of incest are known; inbreeding is rife. Imbeciles, feeble-minded, and delinquents are numerous, politics is corrupt, and selling of votes is common, petty crimes abound, the schools have been badly managed and poorly attended. Cases of rape, assault, and robbery are of almost weekly occurrence within five minutes' walk of the corporation limits of one of the county seats, while in another county political control is held by a self-confessed criminal. Alcoholic intemperance is excessive. Gross immorality and its evil results are by no means confined to the hill districts, but are extreme also in the towns.[1]

As I say, the American of the old stock is not unaware of this steady, and, of late, somewhat rapid deterioration—this gradual loss of his old mastery in the land his ancestors helped to wring from the Indian and the wildcat. He senses it, indeed, very painfully, and, as if in despair of arresting it in fact, makes desperate efforts to dispose of it by denial and concealment. These efforts often take grotesque and extravagant forms. Laws are passed to hobble and cage the citizen of newer stocks in a hundred fantastic ways. It is made difficult and socially dangerous for him to teach his children the speech of his fathers, or to maintain the cultural attitudes that he has inherited from them. Every divergence from the norm of the low-cast Anglo-Saxon is treated as an *attentat* against the commonwealth, and punished with eager ferocity.

It so happens that I am myself an Anglo-Saxon—one of far purer blood, indeed, than most of the half-bleached Celts who pass under the name in the United States and England. I am in part Angle and in part Saxon, and what else I am is safely white, Nordic, Protestant and blond. Thus I feel free, without risk of venturing into bad taste, to regard frankly the *soi-disant*

---

[1] Since the above was written there has been unqualified confirmation of it by a distinguished English authority, to wit, Arnold J. Toynbee. See his *Study of History*, Vol. I, pp. 466–67, and Vol. II, pp. 311–12.

Anglo-Saxon of this incomparable Republic and his rather less dubious cousin of the Motherland. How do the two appear to me, after years spent largely in accumulating their disfavor? What are the characters that I discern most clearly in the so-called Anglo-Saxon type of man? I may answer at once that two stick out above all others. One is his curious and apparently incurable incompetence—his congenital inability to do any difficult thing easily and well, whether it be isolating a bacillus or writing a sonata. The other is his astounding susceptibility to fears and alarms—in short, his hereditary cowardice.

To accuse so enterprising and successful a race of cowardice, of course, is to risk immediate derision; nevertheless, I believe that a fair-minded examination of its history will bear me out. Nine-tenths of the great feats of derring-do that its sucklings are taught to venerate in school—that is, its feats as a race, not the isolated exploits of its extraordinary individuals, most of them at least partly of other stocks—have been wholly lacking in even the most elementary gallantry. Consider, for example, the events attending the extension of the two great empires, English and American. Did either movement evoke any genuine courage and resolution? The answer is plainly no. Both empires were built up primarily by swindling and butchering unarmed savages, and after that by robbing weak and friendless nations. Neither produced a hero above the average run of those in the movies; neither exposed the folks at home to any serious danger of reprisal. Almost always, indeed, mercenaries have done the Anglo-Saxon's fighting for him— a high testimony to his common sense, but scarcely flattering, I fear, to the truculence he boasts of. The British empire was won mainly by Irishmen, Scotchmen and native allies, and the American empire, at least in large part, by Frenchmen and Spaniards. Moreover, neither great enterprise cost any appreciable amount of blood; neither presented grave and dreadful risks; neither exposed the conqueror to the slightest danger of being made the conquered. The British won most of their vast dominions without having to stand up in a single battle against a civilized and formidable foe, and the Americanos won their continent at the expense of a few dozen puerile skirmishes with savages. The total cost of conquering the whole area from Plymouth Rock to the Golden Gate and from Lake George to the Everglades, including even the cost of driving out the French, Dutch, English and Spaniards, was less than the cost of defending Verdun.

So far as I can make out there is no record in history of any Anglo-Saxon nation entering upon any great war without allies. The French have done it, the Dutch have done it, the Germans have done it, the Japs have done it, and even such inferior nations as the Danes, the Spaniards, the Boers and the Greeks have done it, but never the English or Americans. Can you imagine the United States resolutely facing a war in which the odds against it were as huge as they were against Spain in 1898? The facts of history are wholly against any such fancy. The Anglo-Saxon always tries to take a gang with him when he goes into battle, and even when he has it behind him he is very uneasy, and prone to fall into panic at the first threat of genuine danger. Here I put an unimpeachably Anglo-Saxon witness on the stand, to wit, the late Charles W. Eliot. I find him saying, in an article quoted with approbation by the *Congressional Record,* that during the Revolutionary War the colonists now hymned so eloquently in the school-books "fell into a condition of despondency from which nothing but the steadfastness of Washington and the Continental army *and the aid from France* saved them," and that "when the War of 1812 brought grave losses a considerable portion of the population experienced a moral collapse, from which they were rescued only by the exertions of a few thoroughly patriotic statesmen and the exploits of three or four American frigates on the seas"—to say nothing of an enterprising Corsican gentleman, Bonaparte by name.

In both these wars the Americans had enormous and obvious advantages, in terrain, in allies and in men; nevertheless, they fought, in the main, very badly, and from the first shot to the last a majority of them stood in favor of making peace on almost any terms. The Mexican and Spanish Wars I pass over as perhaps too obscenely ungallant to be discussed at all; of the former, U. S. Grant, who fought in it, said that it was "the most unjust war ever waged by a stronger against a weaker nation." Who remembers that, during the Spanish War, the whole Atlantic Coast trembled in fear of the Spaniards' feeble fleet—that all New England had hysterics every time a strange coal-barge was sighted on the sky-line, that the safe-deposit boxes of Boston were emptied and their contents transferred to Worcester, and that the Navy had to organize a patrol to save the coast towns from depopulation? Perhaps those Reds, atheists and pro-Germans remember it who also remember that during World War I the entire country went wild with fear of an enemy who, without the aid of divine intervention, obviously could not strike it a blow at all—and that the great moral victory was gained at last with the assistance of twenty-one allies and at odds of eight to one.[2]

But the American Civil War remains? Does it, indeed? The almost unanimous opinion of the North, in 1861, was that it would be over after a few small battles; the first soldiers were actually enlisted for but three months. When, later on, it turned unexpectedly into a severe struggle, recruits had to be driven to the front by force, and the only Northerners remaining in favor of going on were Abraham Lincoln, a few ambitious generals and the profiteers. I turn to Dr. Eliot again. "In the closing year of the war," he says, "large portions of the Democratic party in the North *and*

[2] The case of World War II was even more striking. The two enemies that the United States tackled had been softened by years of a hard struggle with desperate foes, and those foes continued to fight on. Neither enemy could muster even a tenth of the materials that the American forces had the use of. And at the end both were outnumbered in men by odds truly enormous.

of the Republican party, advocated surrender to the Confederacy, *so down-hearted were they."* Downhearted at odds of three to one! The South was plainly more gallant, but even the gallantry of the South was largely illusory. The Confederate leaders, when the war began, adopted at once the traditional Anglo-Saxon device of seeking allies. They tried and expected to get the aid of England, and they actually came very near succeeding. When hopes in that direction began to fade (i.e., when England concluded that tackling the North would be dangerous), the common people of the Confederacy threw up the sponge, and so the catastrophe, when it came at last, was mainly internal. The South failed to bring the quaking North to a standstill because, to borrow a phrase that Dr. Eliot uses in another connection, it "experienced a moral collapse of unprecedented depth and duration." The folks at home failed to support the troops in the field, and the troops in the field began to desert. Even so early as Shiloh, indeed, many Confederate regiments were already refusing to fight.

This reluctance for desperate chances and hard odds, so obvious in the military record of the English-speaking nations, is also conspicuous in times of peace. What a man of another and superior stock almost always notices, living among so-called Anglo-Saxons, is (a) their incapacity for prevailing in fair rivalry, either in trade, in the fine arts or in what is called learning—in brief, their general incompetence, and (b) their invariable effort to make up for this incapacity by putting some inequitable burden upon their rivals, usually by force. The Frenchman, I believe, is the worst of chauvinists, but once he admits a foreigner to his country he at least treats that foreigner fairly, and does not try to penalize him absurdly for his mere foreignness. The Anglo-Saxon American is always trying to do it; his history is a history of recurrent outbreaks of blind rage against peoples who have begun to worst him. Such movements would be inconceivable in an efficient and genuinely self-confident people, wholly assured of their superiority, and they would be equally inconceivable in a truly gallant and courageous people, disdaining unfair advantages and overwhelming odds. Theoretically launched against some imaginary inferiority in the non-Anglo-Saxon man, either as patriot, as democrat or as Christian, they are actually launched at his general superiority, his greater fitness to survive in the national environment. The effort is always to penalize him for winning in fair fights, to handicap him in such a manner that he will sink to the general level of the Anglo-Saxon population, and, if possible, even below it. Such devices, of course, never have the countenance of the Anglo-Saxon minority that is authentically superior, and hence self-confident and tolerant. But that minority is pathetically small, and it tends steadily to grow smaller and feebler. The communal laws and the communal *mores* are made by the folk, and they offer all the proof that is necessary, not only of its general inferiority, but also of its alarmed awareness of that inferiority. The normal American of the "pure-blooded" majority goes to rest every night with an uneasy feeling that there is a burglar under the bed, and he gets up every morning with a sickening fear that his underwear has been stolen.

This Anglo-Saxon of the great herd is, in many important respects, the least civilized of white men and the least capable of true civilization. His political ideas are crude and shallow. He is almost wholly devoid of esthetic feeling. The most elementary facts about the visible universe alarm him, and incite him to put them down. Educate him, make a professor of him, teach him how to express his soul, and he still remains palpably third-rate. He fears ideals almost more cravenly than he fears men. His blood, I believe, is running thin; perhaps it was not much to boast of at the start; in order that he may exercise any functions above those of a trader, a pedagogue or a mob orator, it needs the stimulus of other and less exhausted strains. The fact that they increase is the best hope of civilization in America. They shake the old race out of its spiritual lethargy, and introduce it to disquiet and experiment. They make for a free play of ideas. In opposing the process, whether in politics, in letters or in the ages-long struggle toward the truth, the prophets of Anglo-Saxon purity and tradition only make themselves ridiculous.

DISCUSSION AND WRITING

1. Define or explain: *Celtic, Teutonic, obliterate, regimented, braggadocio, necromancy, palpable, succor, illusory, pathological, Fundamentalism, voodooism, attentat, soidisant, congenital, susceptibility, derision, gallantry, truculence, puerile, unimpeachable, approbation, despondency, frigate, inequitable, chauvinist, devoid, esthetic, craven, pedagogue.* Generally, is Mencken's tone slangy, colloquial, formal? What are the sources and characteristic effects of his diction?

2. Mencken was a master (and, in turn, a frequent target) of abusive language. Cite examples of abusive or insulting phrases, assertions, implications; examine their direction and effect.

3. Among the weapons in the arsenal of the satirist are irony, paradox (statements apparently absurd or contradictory but found to be meaningful on reflection), parody (reducing a literary style or line of argument to absurdity by exaggerating its ridiculous traits), understatement, overstatement. Which of these does Mencken use, and how? With what effects?

4. What, if any, is Mencken's major target? To what extent is his treatment of it justified? Examine the validity of some of his charges.

5. Mencken is the kind of writer who can be vitriolic in his criticism of society while at the same time enjoying himself immensely. What seems to be his major purpose in this selection—to criticize and reform; to ridicule and denounce; to provide boisterous entertainment for readers who share his views?

6. Mencken was the kind of man who has loyal admirers and unforgiving enemies. Read some of the obituaries and critical reviews that appeared in newspapers and

magazines after his death in 1956. What do they reveal about the reactions of different readers to Mencken as a satirist?

7. Is it true that Americans have a tendency toward self-praise, toward self-congratulation, both in speech and writing? Examine evidence from such sources as newspaper editorials, advertising, or political speeches.

8. Have you had close contact with people from a particular ethnic group, such as Americans of Italian, Polish, or Irish descent? Can you identify some common trait or characteristic of this group? Use detailed examples—beware of stereotypes.

9. When confronted with some outstanding example of pompousness or gullibility, many an observer has muttered to himself, "Mencken, thou shouldst be living at this hour." Write a denunciation, in the Mencken style, of some current piece of foolishness.

10. Compare and contrast Mencken's brand of humor with that of one of the writers in the section "The Twinkle in the Eye."

FURTHER READING

Some of Mencken's best pieces have been reprinted in such collections as *The Vintage Mencken* (1955). Other famous satirical attacks on middle-class smugness and small-town boosterism are the novels of Sinclair Lewis, the most widely read and influential being *Main Street* (1920) and *Babbitt* (1922).

10

The Art of Persuasion

I am no orator, as Brutus is;
But, as you know me all, a plain, blunt man.

SHAKESPEARE, *Julius Caesar*

When persuasion becomes the central goal of a writer, he needs to shift a major part of his attention from the substance of what he has to say to its probable effect on the reader. The requirements of persuasive writing confront the writer with difficult problems: whether to tell the reader what he should hear or what he would like to hear; whether to appeal primarily to logic or to emotion; where to draw the line in exploiting the resources of language for making the worse appear the better reason. The essays in this section each solve these problems in a somewhat different way. The first two selections in this group at a critical time helped to crystallize sentiment and determine the course of political action. Thomas Paine, in "The American Crisis," exhorts the American colonists of the War of Independence with the passionate zeal of a man for whom war does not admit of qualified objectives and mixed feelings. Edmund Burke, in his "Reflections" on the French Revolution, mobilizes the attachment of men to cherished traditions and conventions. William James's "The Will to Believe," famous for its closely argued analysis of the problem of faith and reason, aims at the reader who is willing to think a problem through to its conclusion and who will settle for nothing less than the truth. Walter Lippmann, in "The Renewal of the Public Philosophy," shows his familiar ability to make the reader face up to the implications of his own premises and seriously consider some of the more unpalatable answers to old vexing questions.

THOMAS PAINE

Thomas Paine (1737–1809), an Englishman who had come to America in 1774, became the most effective and widely known spokesman for the cause of American independence. The conflict between the American colonists and the mother country had originally centered on objections to taxes not approved by the colonial assemblies. As the conflict developed into the War of Independence, American opinion was divided between the Revolutionists or "Whigs," and the loyalists or "Tories," who favored compromise and continued association with Britain. General Howe commanded one major contingent of the British forces, consisting in large part of "Hessians," German mercenaries who, unlike the American citizen army, fought neither for country nor for revolutionary ideals. The following selection is the first of a series of pamphlets published between 1776 and 1783; it appeared at a time of reversal for Washington's forces and is credited with restoring their morale. After the end of the war, Paine continued to champion his revolutionary political convictions. Indicted in England as a traitor, imprisoned by the French revolutionaries as an advocate of moderate policies, reviled in America for his alleged atheism, he died in obscurity. Paine's writing illustrates the kind of passionate appeal that in times of crisis can sway masses of men. He was a master of the kind of inflammatory rhetoric that can incite those already half convinced but that at the same time is likely to earn the writer the unforgiving hatred of those he attacks.

The American Crisis

NUMBER I

These are the times that try men's souls. The summer soldier and the sunshine patriot will, in this crisis, shrink from the service of his country; but he that stands it NOW, deserves the love and thanks of man and woman. Tyranny, like hell, is not easily conquered; yet we have this consolation with us, that the harder the conflict, the more glorious the triumph. What we obtain too cheap, we esteem too lightly: 'tis dearness only that gives everything its value. Heaven knows how to put a proper price upon its good; and it would be strange indeed, if so celestial an article as FREEDOM should not be highly rated. Britain, with an army to enforce her tyranny, has declared that she has a right (*not only to* TAX) but "to BIND *us in* ALL CASES WHATSOEVER," and if being *bound in that manner* is not slavery, then is there not such a thing as slavery upon earth. Even the expression is impious, for so unlimited a power can belong only to God.

Whether the independence of the continent was declared too soon, or delayed too long, I will not now enter into as an arguemnt; my own simple opinion is, that had it been eight months earlier, it would have been much better. We did not make a proper use of last winter, neither could we, while we were in a dependent state. However, the fault, if it were one, was all our own; we have none to blame but ourselves. But no great deal is lost yet; all that Howe has been doing for this month past is rather a ravage than a conquest, which the spirit of the Jerseys a year ago would have quickly repulsed, and which time and a little resolution will soon recover.

I have as little superstition in me as any man living, but my secret opinion has ever been, and still is, that God Almighty will not give up a people to military destruction, or leave them unsupportedly to perish, who have so earnestly and so repeatedly sought to avoid the calamities of war, by every decent method which wisdom could invent. Neither have I so much of the infidel in me as to suppose that He has relinquished the government of the world, and given us up to the care of devils; and as I do not, I cannot see on what grounds the king of Britain can look up to Heaven for help against us: a common murderer, a highwayman, or a house-breaker has as good a pretense as he.

'Tis surprising to see how rapidly a panic will sometimes run through a country. All nations and ages have been subject to them: Britain has trembled like an ague at the report of a French fleet of flat bottomed boats; and in the fourteenth century the whole English army, after ravaging the kingdom of France, was driven back like men petrified with fear; and this brave exploit was performed by a few broken forces collected and headed by a woman, Joan of Arc. Would that heaven might inspire some Jersey maid to spirit up her countrymen, and save her fair fellow sufferers from ravage and ravishment! Yet panics, in some cases, have their uses; they produce as much good as hurt. Their duration is always short; the mind soon grows through them, and acquires a firmer habit than before. But their peculiar advantage is that they are the touchstones of sincerity and hypocrisy, and bring things and men to light which might otherwise have lain forever undiscovered. In fact, they have the same effect on secret traitors which an imaginary apparition would have upon a private murderer. They sift out the hidden thoughts of man, and hold them up in public to the world. Many a disguised Tory has lately shown his head, that shall penitentially solemnize with curses the day on which Howe arrived upon the Delaware.

As I was with the troops at Fort Lee, and marched with them to the edge of Pennsylvania, I am well acquainted with many circumstances which those who live at a distance know but little or nothing of. Our situation there was exceedingly cramped, the place being a narrow neck of land between the North River and the Hackensack. Our force was inconsiderable, being not one-fourth so great as Howe could bring against us. We had no army at hand to have relieved the garrison, had we shut ourselves up and stood on the defense. Our ammunition, light artillery, and the best part of our stores had been removed, on the apprehension that Howe would endeavor to penetrate the Jerseys, in which case Fort Lee could be of no use to us: for it must occur to every thinking man, whether in the army or not, that these kind of field forts are only for temporary purposes, and last in use no longer than the enemy directs his force against the particular object which such forts are raised to defend. Such was our situation and condition at Fort Lee on the morning of the 20th of November, when an officer arrived with information that the enemy with two hundred boats had landed about seven or eight miles above: Major General Green, who commanded the garrison, immediately ordered them under arms, and sent express to his excellency, General Washington, at the town of Hackensack, distant by the way of the ferry, six miles. Our first object was to secure the bridge over the Hackensack, which laid up the river between the enemy and us, about six miles from us, and three miles from them. General Washington arrived in about three-quarters of an hour, and marched at the head of the troops towards the bridge, which place I expected we should have a brush for; however, they did not choose to dispute it with us, and the greatest part of our troops went over the bridge, the rest over the ferry, except some which passed at a mill on a small creek, between the bridge and the ferry, and made their way through some marshy grounds up to the town of Hackensack, and there passed the river. We brought off as much baggage as the wagons could contain, the rest was lost. The simple object was to bring off the garrison, and to march them on till they could be strengthened by the Jersey or Pennsylvania militia, so as to be enabled to make a stand. We stayed four days at Newark, collected in our out-posts with some Jersey militia, and marched out twice to meet the enemy, on being informed that they were advancing, though our numbers were greatly inferior to theirs. Howe, in my little opinion, committed a great error in generalship in not throwing a body of forces off from Staten Island through Amboy, by which means he might have seized all our stores at Brunswick and intercepted our march into Pennsylvania: but if we believe the power of hell to be limited, we must likewise believe that their agents are under some providential control.

I shall not now attempt to give all the particulars of our retreat to the Delaware; suffice it for the present to say, that both officers and men, though greatly harassed and fatigued, frequently without rest, covering, or provision, the inevitable consequences of a long retreat, bore it with a manly and martial spirit. All their wishes centered in one, which was, that the country would turn out and help them to drive the enemy back. Voltaire has remarked that King William never appeared to full advantage but in difficulties and in action; the same remark may be made on General Washington, for the character fits him. There is a natural firmness in some minds which cannot be unlocked by trifles, but which, when unlocked, discovers a cabinet of fortitude; and I reckon it among those kind of public blessings, which we do not immediately see, that God hath blest him with uninterrupted health and given him a mind that can even flourish upon care.

I shall conclude this paper with some miscellaneous remarks on the state of our affairs; and shall begin with asking the following question: Why is it that the enemy have left the New England provinces, and made these middle ones the seat of war? The answer is easy: New England is not infested with Tories, and we are. I have been tender in raising the cry against these men, and used numberless arguments to show them their danger, but it will not do to sacrifice a world to either their folly or their baseness. The period is now arrived in which either they or we must change our sentiments, or one or both must fall. And what is a Tory? Good God! what is he? I should not be afraid to go with a hundred Whigs against a thousand Tories, were they to attempt to get into arms. Every Tory is a coward; for servile, slavish, self-interested fear is the foundation of Toryism; and a man under such influence, though he may be cruel, never can be brave.

But, before the line of irrecoverable separation be drawn between us, let us reason the matter together: your conduct is an invitation to the enemy, yet not one in a thousand of you has heart enough to join him. Howe is as much deceived by you as the American cause is injured by you. He expects you will all take up arms, and flock to his standard, with muskets on your shoulders. Your opinions are of no use to him, unless you support him personally, for 'tis soldiers, and not Tories, that he wants.

I once felt all that kind of anger which a man ought to feel against the mean principles that are held by the Tories: a noted one, who kept a tavern at Amboy, was standing at his door, with as pretty a child in his hand, about eight or nine years old, as I ever saw, and, after speaking his mind as freely as he thought was prudent, finished with this unfatherly expression, *"Well! give me peace in my day."* Not a man lives on the continent but fully believes that a separation must sometime or other finally take place, and a generous parent should have said, *"If there must be trouble, let it be in my day, that my child may have peace";* and this single reflection, well applied, is sufficient to awaken every man to duty. Not a place upon earth might be so happy as America. Her situation is remote from all the wrangling world, and she has nothing to do but to trade with them. A man can easily distinguish in himself between temper and principle, and I am as confident, as I am that God governs the world, that America will never be happy till she gets clear of foreign dominion. Wars, without ceasing, will break out till that period arrives, and the continent must in the end be conqueror; for though the flame of liberty may sometimes cease to shine, the coal can never expire.

America did not, nor does not want force; but she wanted a proper application of that force. Wisdom is not the purchase of a day, and it is no wonder that we should err at the first setting off. From an excess of tenderness, we were unwilling to raise an army, and trusted our cause to the temporary defense of a well-meaning militia. A summer's experience has now taught us better; yet with those troops, while they were collected, we were able to set bounds to the progress of the enemy, and, thank God! they are again assembling. I always considered militia as the best troops in the world for a sudden exertion, but they will not do for a long campaign. Howe, it is probable, will make an attempt on this city; should he fall on this side the Delaware, he is ruined: if he succeeds, our cause is not ruined. He stakes all on his side against a part on ours; admitting he succeeds, the consequence will be, that armies from both ends of the continent will march to assist their suffering friends in the middle states; for he cannot go everywhere; it is impossible. I consider Howe as the greatest enemy the Tories have; he is bringing a war into their country, which, had it not been for him and partly for themselves, they had been clear of. Should he now be expelled, I wish with all the devotion of a Christian that the names of Whig and Tory may never more be mentioned; but should the Tories give him encouragement to come, or assistance if he come, I as sincerely wish that our next year's arms may expel them from the continent, and the congress appropriate their possessions to the relief of those who have suffered in well-doing. A single successful battle next year, will settle the whole. America could carry on a two years' war by the confiscation of the property of disaffected persons, and be made happy by their expulsion. Say not that this is revenge, call it rather the soft resentment of a suffering people, who, having no object in view but the *good* of *all*, have staked their *own all* upon a seemingly doubtful event. Yet is is folly to argue against determined hardness; eloquence may strike the air, and the language of sorrow draw forth the tear of compassion, but nothing can reach the heart that is steeled with prejudice.

Quitting this class of men, I turn with the warm ardor of a friend to those who have nobly stood, and are yet determined to stand the matter out: I call not upon a few, but upon all: not on *this* state or *that* state, but on *every* state; up and help us; lay your shoulders to the wheel; better have too much force than too little, when so great an object is at stake. Let it be told to the future world, that in the depth of winter, when nothing but hope and virtue could survive, that the city and the country, alarmed at one common danger, came forth to meet and to repulse it. Say not that thousands are gone, turn out your tens of thousands; throw not the burden of the day upon Providence, but *"show your faith by your works,"* that God may bless you. It matters not where you live, or what rank of life you hold, the evil or the blessing will reach you all. The far and the near, the home counties and the back, the rich and the poor, will suffer or rejoice alike. The hart that feels not now, is dead: the blood of his children will curse his cowardice, who shrinks back at a time when a little might have saved the whole, and made *them* happy. I love the man that can smile in trouble, that can gather strength from distress, and grow brave by reflection. 'Tis the business of little minds to shrink; but he whose heart is firm, and whose conscience approves his conduct, will pursue his principles unto death. My own line of reasoning is to myself as straight and clear as a ray of light. Not all the treasures of the world, so far as I believe, could have induced me to support an offensive war, for I think it murder; but if a thief breaks into my house, burns and destroys my property, and kills or threatens to kill me, or those that are in it, and to *"bind me in all cases whatsoever"* to his absolute will, am I to suffer it? What signifies it to me whether he who does it is a king or a common man; my countryman or not my countryman: whether it be done by an individual villain, or an army of them? If we reason to the root of things we shall find no difference; neither can any just cause be assigned why we should punish in the one case and pardon in the other. Let them call me rebel, and welcome, I feel no concern from it; but I should suffer the misery of devils were I to make a whore of my soul by swearing allegiance to one whose character is that of a sottish, stupid, stubborn, worthless, brutish man. I conceive likewise a horrid idea in receiving mercy from a being who at the last day shall be shrieking to the rocks and mountains to cover him, and fleeing with terror from the orphan, the widow, and the slain of America.

There are cases which cannot be overdone by language, and this is one. There are persons too who see not the full extent of the evil which threatens them; they solace themselves with hopes that the enemy, if they succeed, will be merciful. It is the madness of folly to expect mercy from those who have refused to do justice; and even mercy, where conquest is the object, is only a trick of war; the cunning of the fox is as murderous as the violence of the wolf; and we ought to guard equally against both. Howe's first object is, partly by threats and partly by promises, to terrify or seduce the people to deliver up their arms and receive mercy. The ministry recommended the same plan to Gage, and this is what the Tories call making their peace, *"a peace which passeth all understanding"* indeed! A peace which would be the immediate forerunner of a worse ruin than any we have yet thought of. Ye men of Pennsylvania, do reason upon these things! Were the back counties to give up their arms, they would fall an easy prey to the Indians, who are all armed: this perhaps is what some Tories would not be sorry for. Were the home counties to deliver up their arms, they would be exposed to the resentment of the back counties, who would then have it in their power to chastise their defection at pleasure. And were any one state to give up its arms, *that* state must be garrisoned by all Howe's army of Britons and Hessians to preserve it from the anger of the rest. Mutual fear is the principal link in the chain of mutual love, and woe be to that state that breaks the compact. Howe is mercifully inviting you to barbarous destruction, and men must be either rogues or fools that will not see it.

I dwell not upon the powers of imagination; I bring reason to your ears: and in language as plain as A,B,C hold up truth to your eyes.

I thank God that I fear not. I see no real cause for fear. I know our situation well, and can see the way out of it. While our army was collected, Howe dared not risk a battle, and it is no credit to him that he decamped from the White Plains, and waited a mean opportunity to ravage the defenseless Jerseys; but it is great credit to us that, with a handful of men, we sustained an orderly retreat for near a hundred miles, brought off our ammunition, all our field pieces, the greatest part of our stores, and had four rivers to pass. None can say that our retreat was precipitate, for we were near three weeks in performing it, that the country might have time to come in. Twice we marched back to meet the enemy, and remained out till dark. The sign of fear was not seen in our camp, and had not some of the cowardly and disaffected inhabitants spread false alarms through the country, the Jerseys had never been ravaged. Once more we are again collected and collecting, our new army at both ends of the continent is recruiting fast, and we shall be able to open the next campaign with sixty thousand men, well armed and clothed. This is our situation, and who will may know it. By perseverance and fortitude we have the prospect of a glorious issue; by cowardice and submission, the sad choice of a variety of evils—a ravaged country, a depopulated city, habitations without safety, and slavery without hope, our homes turned into barracks and bawdy-houses for Hessians, and a future race to provide for, whose fathers we shall doubt of. Look on this picture and weep over it! and if there yet remains one thoughtless wretch who believes it not, let him suffer it unlamented.

DISCUSSION AND WRITING

1. Define or explain: *impious, ravage, celestial, infidel, relinquish, ague, petrify, solemnize, harass, servile, irrecoverable, dominion, disaffected, repulse, sottish, precipitate* (adj.).

2. How does Paine's language differ from that of the historian interested primarily in objective fact? For instance, what is the effect of phrases like "summer soldier" and

"sunshine patriot"? Examine the history and exact denotation of terms like *tyranny* and *slavery*. How appropriate or justified is Paine's use of them?

3. Examine the features of Paine's pamphlet that contribute most to its persuasive effect. Which of his arguments illustrate generally applicable methods of persuasion or familiar appeals? Cite detailed passages from the essay.

4. What is Paine's strategy in developing his pamphlet? Does he lead up to a climax? Is there any change in tone or in the direction of the argument as he proceeds?

5. At one time, Paine makes his appeal to the "heart," at another time to "reason." Which of these predominates in the essay?

6. Compare the spirit of Paine's essay with the revolutionary spirit shown by English poets like Robert Burns in "Scots, Wha Hae wi' Wallace Bled" and "A Man's a Man for A' That" or Percy Bysshe Shelley in "Song to the Men of England" and "England in 1819." Or, compare Paine's technique with that of Mark Antony's funeral speech in Shakespeare's *Julius Caesar*.

7. From a current newspaper or magazine, select an editorial that relies heavily on emotional appeals. Analyze it, distinguishing between its factual and logical substance and the emotional appeals employed.

8. What principles should guide the work of people assigned to help build or maintain morale in a modern American army? Are soldiers entitled to the unvarnished factual truth? What efforts should be made to inspire patriotism or courage?

9. Examine in detail features that make for eloquence and persuasiveness in a speech (or a group of short speeches) of major historical significance: Abraham Lincoln's inaugural addresses and the Gettysburg Address (1861–1865); Woodrow Wilson's Pueblo speech on the League of Nations (1919); Franklin Roosevelt's first inaugural address (1933) or the "Four Freedoms" speech (1941); Winston Churchill's "Dunkirk" speech (1940).

10. Where do you draw the line between legitimate political persuasion and misleading propaganda? Make detailed use of recent examples.

FURTHER READING

Compare and contrast the account of the causes of the American War of Independence given by an American historian like Henry Steele Commager and by a British historian like G. M. Trevelyan. Is there any evidence of a one-sided perspective or national basis?

EDMUND BURKE

Edmund Burke (1729–1797) was a long-time member of the British parliament who continues to exercise an influence on contemporary political thought. He championed such causes as the abolition of the slave trade and the protection of the natives of India against exploitation by British administrators. Before and during the American War of Independence, Burke defended the rights of the colonists and criticized Britain's colonial policies. His *Reflections on the Revolution in France* (1790) was addressed to a Frenchman who had asked for Burke's opinion on recent developments in that country. Early in 1789, the French States-General—an assembly representing the three "estates": the clergy, the nobles, and the common people—had met in an attempt to limit the absolute power of the French king and to institute constitutional government. Later the same year, a popular uprising had overthrown the French monarchy, liberating political prisoners held in the Bastille and destroying the power and wealth of the privileged aristocratic families. The ideology of the French Revolution was derived from such French writers as Rousseau and Voltaire; its program of "Liberty, Equality, Fraternity" had earlier influenced events in America through the writings of men like Thomas Jefferson and Thomas Paine. In contrast with his sympathy with the American revolution, Burke was one of the first prominent Englishmen to condemn both the principles and the actions of the French revolutionaries. The following are brief excerpts from a long and carefully prepared indictment that turned out to be prophetic of later developments in France. The strength of Burke's political writing is his recognition of loyalties that are hard to put into words, and that may run counter to abstract principles, but that powerfully influence the political behavior of men.

Reflections on the Revolution in France

You will observe that from Magna Carta to the Declaration of Right it has been the uniform policy of our constitution to claim and assert our liberties as an *entailed inheritance* derived to us from our forefathers, and to be transmitted to our posterity—as an estate specially belonging to the people of this kingdom, without any reference whatever to any other more general or prior right. By this means our constitution preserves a unity in so great a diversity of its parts. We have an inheritable crown, an inheritable peerage, and a House of Commons and a people inheriting privileges, franchises, and liberties from a long line of ancestors.

This policy appears to me to be the result of profound reflection, or rather the happy effect of following nature, which is wisdom without reflection, and above it. A spirit of innovation is generally the result of a selfish temper and confined views. People will not look forward to posterity, who never look backward to their ancestors. Besides, the people of England well know that the idea of inheritance furnishes a sure principle of conservation and a sure principle of transmission, without at all excluding a principle of improvement. It leaves acquisition free, but it secures what it acquires, whatever advantages are obtained by a state proceeding on these maxims are locked fast as in a sort of family settlement, grasped as in a kind of mortmain forever. By a constitutional policy, working after the pattern of nature, we receive, we hold, we transmit our government and our privileges in the same manner in which we enjoy and transmit our property and our lives. The institutions of policy, the goods of fortune, the gifts of providence are handed down to us, and from us, in the same course and order. Our political system is placed in a just correspondence and symmetry with the order of the world and with the mode of existence decreed to a permanent body composed of transitory parts, wherein, by the disposition of a stupendous wisdom, molding together the great mysterious incorporation of the human race, the whole, at one time, is never old or middle-aged or young, but, in a condition of unchangeable constancy, moves on through the varied tenor of perpetual decay, fall, renovation, and progression. Thus, by preserving the method of nature in the conduct of the state, in what we improve we are never wholly new; in what we retain we are never wholly obsolete. By adhering in this manner and on those principles to our forefathers, we are guided not by the superstition of antiquarians, but by the spirit of philosophic analogy. In this choice of inheritance we have given to our frame of polity the image of a relation in blood, binding up the constitution of our country with our dearest domestic ties, adopting our fundamental laws into the bosom of our family affections, keeping inseparable and cherishing with the warmth of all their combined and mutually reflected charities our state, our hearths, our sepulchres, and our altars.

Through the same plan of a conformity to nature in our artificial institutions, and by calling in the aid of her unerring and powerful instincts to fortify the fallible and feeble contrivances of our reason, we have derived several other, and those no small, benefits from considering our liberties in the light of an inheritance. Always acting as if in the presence of canonized forefathers, the spirit of freedom, leading in itself to misrule and excess, is tempered with an awful gravity. This idea of a liberal descent inspires us with a sense of habitual native dignity which prevents that upstart insolence almost inevitably adhering to and disgracing those who are the first acquirers of any distinction. By this means our liberty becomes a noble freedom. It carries an imposing and majestic aspect. It has a pedigree and illustrating ancestors. It has its bearings and its ensigns armorial. It has its gallery of portraits, its monumental inscriptions, its records, evidences, and titles. We procure reverence to our civil institutions on the principle upon which nature teaches us to revere individual men: on account of their age and on account of those from whom they are descended. All your sophisters cannot produce anything better adapted to preserve a rational and manly freedom than the course that we have pursued, who have chosen our nature rather than our speculations, our breasts rather than our inventions, for the great conservatories and magazines of our rights and privileges. . . .

[The] opposed and conflicting interests which you considered as so great a blemish in your old and in our present constitution interpose a salutary check to all precipitate resolutions. They render deliberation a matter, not of choice, but of necessity; they make all change a subject of *compromise,* which naturally begets moderation; they produce *temperaments* preventing the sore evil of harsh, crude, unqualified reformations and rendering all the headlong exertions of arbitrary power, in the few or in the many, forever impracticable. Through that diversity of members and interests, general liberty had as many securities as there were separate views in the several orders, whilst, by pressing down the whole by the weight of a real monarchy, the separate parts would have been prevented from warping, and starting from their allotted places.

You had all these advantages in your ancient states, but you chose to act as if you had never been molded into civil society and had everything to begin anew. You began ill, because you began by despising everything that belonged to you. You set up your trade without a capital. If the last generations of your country appeared without much luster in your eyes, you might have passed them by and derived your claims from a more early race of ancestors. Under a pious predilection for those ancestors, your imaginations would have realized in them a standard of virtue and wisdom beyond the vulgar practice of the hour; and you would have risen with the example to whose imitation you aspired. Respecting your forefathers, you would have been taught to respect yourselves. You would not have chosen to consider the French as a people of yesterday, as a nation of low-born servile wretches until the emancipating year of 1789. In order to furnish, at the expense of your honor, an excuse to your apologists here for several enormities of yours, you would not have been content to be represented as a gang of Maroon slaves suddenly broke loose from the house of bondage, and therefore to be pardoned for your abuse of the liberty to which you were not accustomed and ill fitted. Would it not, my worthy friend, have been wiser to have you thought, what I, for one, always thought you, a generous and gallant nation, long misled to your disadvantage by your high and romantic sentiments of fidelity, honor, and loyalty; that events had been unfavorable to you, but that you were not enslaved through any illiberal or servile disposition; that in your most devoted submission you were actuated by a principle of public spirit, and that it was your country you worshiped in the person of your king? Had you made it to be understood that in the delusion of this amiable error you had gone further than your wise ancestors, that you were resolved to resume your ancient privileges, whilst you preserved the spirit of your ancient and your recent loyalty and honor; or if, diffident of yourselves and not clearly discerning the almost obliterated constitution of your ancestors, you had looked to your neighbors in this land who had kept alive the ancient principles and models of the old common law of Europe meliorated and adapted to its present state—by following wise examples you would have given new examples of wisdom to the world. You would have rendered the cause of liberty venerable in the eyes of every worthy mind in every nation. You would have shamed despotism from the earth by showing that freedom was not only reconcilable, but, as when well disciplined it is, auxiliary to law. You would have had an unoppressive but a productive revenue. You would have had a flourishing commerce to feed it. You would have had a free constitution, a potent monarchy, a disciplined army, a reformed and vener-ated clergy, a mitigated but spirited nobility to lead your virtue, not to overlay it; you would have had a liberal order of commons to emulate and to recruit that nobility; you would have had a protected, satisfied, laborious, and obedient people, taught to seek and to recognize the happiness that is to be found by virtue in all conditions; in which consists the true moral equality of mankind, and not in that monstrous fiction which, by inspiring false ideas and vain expectations into men destined to travel in the obscure walk of laborious life, serves only to aggravate and embitter that real inequality which it never can remove, and which the order of civil life establishes as much for the benefit of those whom it must leave in a humble state as those whom it is able to exalt to a condition more splendid, but not more happy. You had a smooth and easy career of felicity and glory laid open to you, beyond anything recorded in the history of the world, but you have shown that difficulty is good for man.

Compute your gains: see what is got by those extravagant and presump-tuous speculations which have taught your leaders to despise all their predecessors, and all their contemporaries, and even to despise themselves until the moment in which they become truly despicable. By following those false lights, France has bought undisguised calamities at a higher price than any nation has purchased the most unequivocal blessings! France has bought poverty by crime! France has not sacrificed her virtue to her interest, but she has abandoned her interest, that she might prostitute her virtue. All other nations have begun the fabric of a new government, or the reformation of an old, by establishing originally or by enforcing with greater exactness some rites or other of religion. All other people have laid the foundations of civil freedom in severer manners and a system of a more austere and masculine morality. France, when she let loose the reins of regal authority, doubled the license of a ferocious dissoluteness in manners and of an insolent irreligion in opinions and practice, and has extended through all ranks of life, as if she were communicating some privilege or laying open some secluded benefit, all the unhappy corruptions that usually were the disease of wealth and power. This is one of the new principles of equality in France. . . .

Far am I from denying in theory, full as far is my heart from withholding in practice (if I were of power to give or to withhold) the *real* rights of men. In denying their false claims of right, I do not mean to injure those which are real, and are such as their pretended rights would totally destroy. If civil society be made for the advantage of man, all the advantages for which it is made become his right. It is an institution of beneficence; and law itself is only beneficence acting by a rule. Men have a right to live by that rule; they have a right to do justice, as between their fellows, whether their fellows are in public function or in ordinary occupation. They have a right to the fruits of their industry and to the means of making their industry fruitful. They have a right to the acquisitions of their parents, to the nourishment and improvement of their offspring, to instruction in life, and to consolation in death. Whatever each man can separately do, without trespassing upon others, he has a right to do for himself; and he has a right to a fair portion of all which society, with all its combinations of skill and force, can do in his favor. In this partnership all men have equal rights, but not to equal things. He that has but five shillings in the partnership has as good a right to it as he that has five hundred pounds has to his larger proportion. But he has not a right to an equal dividend in the product of the joint stock; and as to the share of power, authority, and direction which each individual ought to have in the management of the state, that I must deny to be amongst the direct original rights of man in civil society, for I have in my contemplation the civil social man, and no other. It is a thing to be settled by convention.

If civil society be the offspring of convention, that convention must be its law. That convention must limit and modify all the descriptions of constitution which are formed under it. Every sort of legislative, judicial, or executory power are its creatures. They can have no being in any other state of things; and how can any man claim under the conventions of civil society rights which do not so much as suppose its existence—rights which are absolutely repugnant to it? One of the first motives to civil society, and which becomes one of its fundamental rules, is *that no man should be judge in his own cause.* By this each person has at once divested himself of the first fundamental right of uncovenanted man, that is, to judge for himself and to assert his own cause. He abdicates all right to be his own governor. He inclusively, in a great measure, abandons the right of self-defense, the first law of nature. Men cannot enjoy the rights of an uncivil and of a civil state together. That he may obtain justice, he gives up his right of determining what it is in points the most essential to him. That he may secure some liberty, he makes a surrender in trust of the whole of it.

Government is not made in virtue of natural rights, which may and do exist in total independence of it, and exist in much greater clearness and in a much greater degree of abstract perfection; but their abstract perfection is their practical defect. By having a right to everything they want everything. Government is a contrivance of human wisdom to provide for human *wants.* Men have a right that these wants should be provided for by this wisdom. Among these wants is to be reckoned the want, out of civil society, of a sufficient restraint upon their passions. Society requires not only that the passions of individuals should be subjected, but that even in the mass and body, as well as in the individuals, the inclinations of men should frequently be thwarted, their will controlled, and their passions brought into subjection. This can only be done *by a power out of themselves,* and not, in the exercise of its function, subject to that will and to those passions which it is its office to bridle and subdue. In this sense the restraints on men, as well as their liberties, are to be reckoned among their rights. But as the liberties and the restrictions vary with times and circumstances and admit to infinite modifi- cations, they cannot be settled upon any abstract rule; and nothing is so foolish as to discuss them upon that principle.

The moment you abate anything from the full rights of men, each to govern himself, and suffer any artificial, positive limitation upon those rights, from that moment the whole organization of government becomes a con- sideration of convenience. This it is which makes the constitution of a state and the due distribution of its powers a matter of the most delicate and complicated skill. It requires a deep knowledge of human nature and human necessities, and of the things which facilitate or obstruct the various ends which are to be pursued by the mechanism of civil institutions. The state is to have recruits to its strength, and remedies to its distempers. What is the use of discussing a man's abstract right to food or medicine? The question is upon the method of procuring and administering them. In that deliberation I shall always advise to call in the aid of the farmer and the physician rather than the professor of metaphysics.

The science of constructing a commonwealth, or renovating it, or reform- ing it, is, like every other experimental science, not to be taught *a priori.* Nor is it a short experience that can instruct us in that practical science, because the real effects of moral causes are not always immediate; but that which in the first instance is prejudicial may be excellent in its remoter operation, and its excellence may arise even from the ill effects it produces in the beginning. The reverse also happens: and very plausible schemes, with very pleasing commencements, have often shameful and lamentable conclusions. In states there are often some obscure and almost latent causes, things which appear at first view of little moment, on which a very great part of its prosperity or adversity may most essentially depend. The science of government being therefore so practical in itself and intended for such practical purposes—a matter which requires experience, and even more experience than any person can gain in his whole life, however sagacious and observing he may be—it is with infinite caution that any man ought to venture upon pulling down an edifice which has answered in any tolerable degree for ages the common purposes of society, or on building it up again without having models and patterns of approved utility before his eyes....

History will record that on the morning of the 6th of October, 1789, the king and queen of France, after a day of confusion, alarm, dismay, and slaughter, lay down, under the pledged security of public faith, to indulge nature in a few hours of respite and troubled, melancholy repose. From this sleep the queen was first startled by the sentinel at her door, who cried out to her to save herself by flight—that this was the last proof of fidelity he could give—that they were upon him, and he was dead. Instantly he was cut down. A band of cruel ruffians and assassins, reeking with his blood, rushed into the chamber of the queen and pierced with a hundred strokes of bayonets and poniards the bed, from whence this persecuted woman had but just time to fly almost naked, and, through ways unknown to the murderers, had escaped to seek refuge at the feet of a king and husband not secure of his own life for a moment.

This king, to say no more of him, and this queen, and their infant children (who once would have been the pride and hope of a great and generous people) were then forced to abandon the sanctuary of the most splendid palace in the world, which they left swimming in blood, polluted by massacre and strewed with scattered limbs and mutilated carcasses. Thence they were conducted into the capital of their kingdom.

Two had been selected from the unprovoked, unresisted, promiscuous slaughter, which was made of the gentlemen of birth and family who composed the king's body guard. These two gentlemen, with all the parade of an execution of justice, were cruelly and publicly dragged to the block and beheaded in the great court of the palace. Their heads were stuck upon spears and led the procession, whilst the royal captives who followed in the train were slowly moved along, amidst the horrid yells, and shrilling screams, and frantic dances, and infamous contumelies, and all the unutterable abominations of the furies of hell in the abused shape of the vilest of women.

After they had been made to taste, drop by drop, more than the bitterness of death in the slow torture of a journey of twelve miles, protracted to six hours, they were, under a guard composed of those very soldiers who had thus conducted them through this famous triumph, lodged in one of the old palaces of Paris now converted into a bastille for kings. . . .

It is now sixteen or seventeen years since I saw the queen of France, then the dauphiness, at Versailles, and surely never lighted on this orb, which she hardly seemed to touch, a more delightful vision. I saw her just above the horizon, decorating and cheering the elevated sphere she just began to move in—glittering like the morning star, full of life and splendor and joy. Oh! what a revolution! and what a heart must I have to contemplate without emotion that elevation and that fall! Little did I dream when she added titles of veneration to those of enthusiastic, distant, respectful love, that she should ever be obliged to carry the sharp antidote against disgrace concealed in that bosom, little did I dream that I should have lived to see such disasters fallen upon her in a nation of gallant men, in a nation of men of honor and of cavaliers. I thought ten thousand swords must have leaped from their scabbards to avenge even a look that threatened her with insult. But the age of chivalry is gone. That of sophisters, economists, and calculators has succeeded, and the glory of Europe is extinguished forever. Never, never more shall we behold that generous loyalty to rank and sex, that proud submission, that dignified obedience, that subordination of the heart which kept alive, even in servitude itself, the spirit of an exalted freedom. The unbought grace of life, the cheap defense of nations, the nurse of manly sentiment and heroic enterprise, is gone! It is gone—that sensibility of principle, that charity of honor which felt a stain like a wound, which inspired courage whilst it mitigated ferocity, which ennobled whatever it touched, and under which vice itself lost half its evil by losing all its grossness.

This mixed system of opinion and sentiment had its origin in the ancient chivalry; and the principle, though varied in its appearance by the varying state of human affairs, subsisted and influenced through a long succession of generations even to the time we live in. If it should ever be totally extinguished, the loss I fear will be great. It is this which has given its character to modern Europe. It is this which has distinguished it under all its forms of government, and distinguished it to its advantage, from the states of Asia and possibly from those states which flourished in the most brilliant periods of the antique world. It was this which, without confounding ranks, had produced a noble equality and handed it down through all the gradations of social life. It was this opinion which mitigated kings into companions and raised private men to be fellows with kings. Without force or opposition, it subdued the fierceness of pride and power, it obliged sovereigns to submit to the soft collar of social esteem, compelled stern authority to submit to elegance, and gave a dominating vanquisher of laws to be subdued by manners.

But now all is to be changed. All the pleasing illusions which made power gentle and obedience liberal, which harmonized the different shades of life, and which, by a bland assimilation, incorporated into politics the sentiments which beautify and soften private society, are to be dissolved by this new conquering empire of light and reason. All the decent drapery of life is to be rudely torn off. All the superadded ideas, furnished from the wardrobe of a moral imagination, which the heart owns and the understanding ratifies as necessary to cover the defects of our naked, shivering nature, and to raise it to dignity in our own estimation, are to be exploded as a ridiculous, absurd, and antiquated fashion.

On this scheme of things, a king is but a man, a queen is but a woman; a woman is but an animal, and an animal not of the highest order. All homage paid to the sex in general as such, and without distinct views, is to be regarded as romance and folly. Regicide, and parricide, and sacrilege are but fictions of superstition, corrupting jurisprudence by destroying its simplicity. The murder of a king, or a queen, or a bishop, or a father are only common homicide; and if the people are by any chance or in any way gainers by it, a sort of homicide much the most pardonable, and into which we ought not to make too severe a scrutiny.

On the scheme of this barbarous philosophy, which is the offspring of cold hearts and muddy understandings, and which is as void of solid wisdom as it is destitute of all taste and elegance, laws are to be supported only by their own terrors and by the concern which each individual may find in them from his own private speculations or can spare to them from his own private interests. In the groves of *their* academy, at the end of every vista, you see nothing but the gallows. Nothing is left which engages the affections on the part of the commonwealth. On the principles of this mechanic philosophy, our institutions can never be embodied, if I may use the expression, in persons so as to create in us love, veneration, admiration, or attachment. But that sort of reason which banishes the affections is incapable of filling their place. These public affections, combined with manners, are required sometimes as supplements, sometimes as correctives, always as aids to law. The precept given by a wise man, as well as a great critic, for the construction of poems is equally true as to states:—*Non satis est pulchra esse poemata, dulcia sunto.*[1] There ought to be a system of manners in every nation which a well-informed mind would be disposed to relish. To make us love our country, our country ought to be lovely.

But power, of some kind or other, will survive the shock in which manners and opinions perish; and it will find other and worse means for its support. The usurpation which, in order to subvert ancient institutions, has destroyed ancient principles will hold power by arts similar to those by which it has acquired it. When the old feudal and chivalrous spirit of *fealty,*

---

[1] [It isn't enough that poems should be beautiful; they ought to be sweet.]

which, by freeing kings from fear, freed both kings and subjects from the precautions of tyranny, shall be extinct in the minds of men, plots and assassinations will be anticipated by preventive murder and preventive confiscation, and that long roll of grim and bloody maxims which form the political code of all power not standing on its own honor and the honor of those who are to obey it. Kings will be tyrants from policy when subjects are rebels from principle.

When ancient opinions and rules of life are taken away, the loss cannot possibly be estimated. From that moment we have no compass to govern us; nor can we know distinctly to what port we steer. Europe, undoubtedly, taken in a mass, was in a flourishing condition the day on which your revolution was completed. How much of that prosperous state was owing to the spirit of our old manners and opinions is not easy to say; but as such causes cannot be indifferent in their operation, we must presume that on the whole their operation was beneficial.

DISCUSSION AND WRITING

1. Define or explain: *entail, maxim, polity, sepulchre, canonize, interpose, salutary, predilection, illiberal, obliterate, meliorate, emulate, felicity, beneficence, abate, a priori, sagacious, respite, contumely, cavalier, mitigate, regicide, parricide, fealty.* In context, what is the meaning of "varied *tenor* of perpetual decay, fall, renovation . . ."; "*ensigns* armorial"; "generous and *gallant* nation"; "fruits of their *industry*"; "*uncovenanted* man"? Explain *Magna Carta, Declaration of Right, peerage, House of Commons,* and other references to British history or politics.

2. Discuss in detail the principles, attitudes, and emotions to which Burke appeals. Which of them are familiar? How, if at all, are they related?

3. Edmund Burke was a member of the Whig, or liberal, party; yet he is admired and respected by modern conservatives. On the evidence of these excerpts, in what sense and to what extent is Burke a political conservative?

4. Examine Burke's use of extended analogies and parallels. What is their persuasive effect or logical force?

5. Analyses of persuasive writing often distinguish between discussion of issues as against attack on personalities, appeal to logic as against emotion, the use of objective as against emotive language. Examine Burke's *Reflections* in the light of these criteria. How relevant or valid do these criteria seem when applied to Burke's writing?

6. In *The Rights of Man,* Thomas Paine said that Burke "pities the plumage, but forgets the dying bird" and believes that governments must depend on "show and parade to fascinate the vulgar." How much justice is there in Paine's charge?

7. What room is there in contemporary political life for the sentiments, emotions, or "pleasing illusions" that Burke considers necessary "to cover the defects of our naked, shivering nature"? For instance, does the American political system succeed in

producing leaders that "create in us love, veneration, admiration, or attachment"? Limit yourself to one major point.

8. Compare and contrast Thomas Paine and Edmund Burke as masters of political rhetoric.

9. Drawing on your own experience or observation, discuss a case (or several related ones) of conflict between "tradition" and "innovation."

10. Define a current trend in political thought. For instance, what is a "new conservative," a "pragmatic liberal," or a "modern Republican"? Give a coherent, well-illustrated account of his principles or convictions.

FURTHER READING

One of the best-known fictional accounts of the revolutionary terror in France is Dickens's *A Tale of Two Cities* (1859). For short excerpts, see Orwell's essay on "Charles Dickens" in this volume.

WILLIAM JAMES

William James's "The Will to Believe" illustrates the kind of argument that has a powerful persuasive effect on readers who expect rational discussion rather than emotional appeals. A writer addressing himself to such readers advances his thesis as a tentative assertion to be fully examined later. He carefully defines his terms, considers precedents, weighs alternatives, examines objections. He follows a systematic analysis through to its logical conclusion. William James (1842–1910) ranks with John Dewey as the most prominent of American philosophers. Trained as a physician at Harvard Medical School, he combined scientific training with a strong interest in religion. He became a pioneer in the new science of psychology, publishing his *Principles of Psychology* in 1890. As a philosopher, he was an early advocate of pragmatism, often called the most characteristic American contribution to philosophy. The pragmatist judges ideas by their results; as James says, "belief is measured by action." Thus, the pragmatist reinforces the traditional American faith in the practical and in effective effort. Like his English contemporary T. H. Huxley, William James had a gift for making difficult technical matters understandable to the educated layman. He first delivered "The Will to Believe" as a lecture and later included it in a collection of "essays in popular philosophy" published in 1897. In the present version of the essay, a portion reviewing different definitions of truth and evidence has been omitted.

The Will to Believe

In the recently published Life by Leslie Stephen of his brother, Fitz-James, there is an account of a school to which the latter went when he was a boy. The teacher, a certain Mr. Guest, used to converse with his pupils in this wise: "Gurney, what is the difference between justification and sanctification?—Stephen, prove the omnipotence of God!" etc. In the midst of our Harvard freethinking and indifference we are prone to imagine that here at your good old orthodox College conversation continues to be somewhat upon this order; and to show you that we at Harvard have not lost all interest in these vital subjects, I have brought with me tonight something like a sermon on justification by faith to read to you—I mean an essay in justification *of* faith, a defense of our right to adopt a believing attitude in religious matters, in spite of the fact that our merely logical intellect may not have been coerced. "The Will to Believe," accordingly, is the title of my paper.

I have long defended to my own students the lawfulness of voluntarily adopted faith; but as soon as they have got well imbued with the logical spirit, they have as a rule refused to admit my contention to be lawful philosophically, even though in point of fact they were personally all the time chock-full of some faith or other themselves. I am all the while, however, so profoundly convinced that my own position is correct, that your invitation has seemed to me a good occasion to make my statements more clear. Perhaps your minds will be more open than those with which I have hitherto had to deal. I will be as little technical as I can, though I must begin by setting up some technical distinctions that will help us in the end.

I

Let us give the name of *hypothesis* to anything that may be proposed to our belief; and just as the electricians speak of live and dead wires, let us speak of any hypothesis as either *live* or *dead*. A live hypothesis is one which appeals as a real possibility to him to whom it is proposed. If I ask you to believe in the Mahdi, the notion makes no electric connection with your nature—it refuses to scintillate with any credibility at all. As an hypothesis it is completely dead. To an Arab, however (even if he be not one of the Mahdi's followers), the hypothesis is among the mind's possibilities: it is alive. This shows that deadness and liveness in an hypothesis are not intrinsic properties, but relations to the individual thinker. They are measured by his willingness to act. The maximum of liveness in an hypothesis means willingness to act irrevocably. Practically, that means belief; but there is some believing tendency wherever there is willingness to act at all.

Next, let us call the decision between two hypotheses an *option*. Options may be of several kinds. They may be—1, *living* or *dead;* 2, *forced* or *avoidable;* 3, *momentous* or *trivial;* and for our purposes we may call an option a *genuine* option when it is of the forced, living, and momentous kind.

1. A living option is one in which both hypotheses are live ones. If I say to you: "Be a theosophist or be a Mohammedan," it is probably a dead option, because for you neither hypothesis is likely to be alive. But if I say: "Be an agnostic or be a Christian," it is otherwise: trained as you are, each hypothesis makes some appeal, however small, to your belief.

2. Next, if I say to you: "Choose between going out with your umbrella or without it," I do not offer you a genuine option, for it is not forced. You can easily avoid it by not going out at all. Similarly, if I say, "Either love me or hate me," "Either call my theory true or call it false," your option is avoidable. You may remain indifferent to me, neither loving nor hating, and you may decline to offer any judgment as to my theory. But if I say, "Either accept this truth or go without it," I put on you a forced option, for there is no standing place outside of the alternative. Every dilemma based on a complete logical disjunction, with no possibility of not choosing, is an option of this forced kind.

3. Finally, if I were Dr. Nansen and proposed to you to join my North Pole expedition, your option would be momentous; for this would probably be your only similar opportunity, and your choice now would either exclude you from the North Pole sort of immortality altogether or put at least the chance of it into your hands. He who refuses to embrace a unique opportunity loses the prize as surely as if he tried and failed. *Per contra,*[1] the option is trivial when the opportunity is not unique, when the stake is insignificant, or when the decision is reversible if it later prove unwise. Such trivial options abound in the scientific life. A chemist finds an hypothesis live enough to spend a year in its verification; he believes in it to that extent. But if his experiments prove inconclusive either way, he is quit for his loss of time, no vital harm being done.

It will facilitate our discussion if we keep all these distinctions well in mind.

II

The next matter to consider is the actual psychology of human opinion. When we look at certain facts, it seems as if our passional and volitional nature lay at the root of all our convictions. When we look at

---

[1] [By contrast.]

others, it seems as if they could do nothing when the intellect had once said its say. Let us take the latter facts up first.

Does it not seem preposterous on the very face of it to talk of our opinions being modifiable at will? Can our will either help or hinder our intellect in its perceptions of truth? Can we, by just willing it, believe that Abraham Lincoln's existence is a myth, and that the portraits of him in *McClure's Magazine* are all of someone else? Can we, by any effort of our will, or by any strength of wish that it were true, believe ourselves well and about when we are roaring with rheumatism in bed, or feel certain that the sum of the two one-dollar bills in our pocket must be a hundred dollars? We can *say* any of these things, but we are absolutely impotent to believe them; and of just such things is the whole fabric of the truths that we do believe in made up—matters of fact, immediate or remote, as Hume said, and relations between ideas, which are either there or not there for us if we see them so, and which if not there cannot be put there by any action of our own.

In Pascal's *Thoughts* there is a celebrated passage known in literature as Pascal's wager. In it he tries to force us into Christianity by reasoning as if our concern with truth resembled our concern with the stakes in a game of chance. Translated freely his words are these: You must either believe or not believe that God is—which will you do? Your human reason cannot say. A game is going on between you and the nature of things which at the day of judgment will bring out either heads or tails. Weigh what your gains and your losses would be if you should stake all you have on heads, or God's existence: if you win in such case, you gain eternal beatitude; if you lose, you lose nothing at all. If there were an infinity of chances, and only one for God in this wager, still you ought to stake your all on God; for though you surely risk a finite loss by this procedure, any finite loss is reasonable, even a certain one is reasonable, if there is but the possibility of infinite gain. Go, then, and take holy water, and have masses said; belief will come and stupefy your scruples—*Cela vous fera croire et vous abêtira.*[2] Why should you not? At bottom, what have you to lose?

You probably feel that when religious faith expresses itself thus, in the language of the gaming-table, it is put to its last trumps. Surely Pascal's own personal belief in masses and holy water had far other springs; and this celebrated page of his is but an argument for others, a last desperate snatch at a weapon against the hardness of the unbelieving heart. We feel that a faith in masses and holy water adopted wilfully after such a mechanical calculation would lack the inner soul of faith's reality; and if we were ourselves in the place of the Deity, we should probably take particular pleasure in cutting off believers of this pattern from their infinite reward. It is evident that unless there be some pre-existing tendency to believe in masses and holy

[2] [That will make you believe and stultify you.]

water, the option offered to the will by Pascal is not a living option. Certainly no Turk ever took to masses and holy water on its account; and even to us Protestants these means of salvation seem such foregone impossibilities that Pascal's logic, invoked for them specifically, leaves us unmoved. As well might the Mahdi write to us, saying, "I am the Expected One whom God has created in his effulgence. You shall be infinitely happy if you confess me; otherwise you shall be cut off from the light of the sun. Weigh, then, your infinite gain if I am genuine against your finite sacrifice if I am not!" His logic would be that of Pascal; but he would vainly use it on us, for the hypothesis he offers us is dead. No tendency to act on it exists in us to any degree.

The talk of believing by our volition seems, then, from one point of view, simply silly. From another point of view it is worse than silly, it is vile. When one turns to the magnificent edifice of the physical sciences, and sees how it was reared; what thousands of disinterested moral lives of men lie buried in its mere foundations; what patience and postponement, what choking down of preference, what submission to the icy laws of outer fact are wrought into its very stones and mortar; how absolutely impersonal it stands in its vast augustness—then how besotted and contemptible seems every little sentimentalist who comes blowing his voluntary smoke-wreaths, and pretending to decide things from out of his private dream! Can we wonder if those bred in the rugged and manly school of science should feel like spewing such subjectivism out of their mouths? The whole system of loyalties which grow up in the schools of science go dead against its toleration; so that it is only natural that those who have caught the scientific fever should pass over to the opposite extreme, and write sometimes as if the incorruptibly truthful intellect ought positively to prefer bitterness and unacceptableness to the heart in its cup.

> It fortifies my soul to know
> That though I perish, Truth is so—

sings Clough, while Huxley exclaims: "My only consolation lies in the reflection that, however bad our posterity may become, so far as they hold by the plain rule of not pretending to believe what they have no reason to believe, because it may be to their advantage so to pretend [the word 'pretend' is surely here redundant], they will not have reached the lowest depth of immorality." And that delicious *enfant terrible* Clifford writes: "Belief is desecrated when given to unproved and unquestioned statements for the solace and private pleasure of the believer.... Whoso would deserve well of his fellows in this matter will guard the purity of his belief with a very fanaticism of jealous care, lest at any time it should rest on an unworthy object, and catch a stain which can never be wiped away.... If [a] belief has been accepted on insufficient evidence [even though the belief be true, as Clifford on the same page explains] the pleasure is a stolen one.... It is sinful because it is stolen in defiance of our duty to mankind. That duty is to guard ourselves from such beliefs as from a pestilence which may shortly master our own body and then spread to the rest of the town.... It is wrong always, everywhere, and for everyone, to believe anything upon insufficient evidence."

III

All this strikes one as healthy, even when expressed, as by Clifford, with somewhat too much of robustious pathos in the voice. Free will and simple wishing do seem, in the matter of our credences, to be only fifth wheels to the coach. Yet if anyone should thereupon assume that intellectual insight is what remains after wish and will and sentimental preference have taken wing, or that pure reason is what then settles our opinions, he would fly quite as directly in the teeth of the facts.

It is only our already dead hypotheses that our willing nature is unable to bring to life again. But what has made them dead for us is for the most part a previous action of our willing nature of an antagonistic kind. When I say "willing nature," I do not mean only such deliberate volitions as may have set up habits of belief that we cannot now escape from—I mean all such factors of belief as fear and hope, prejudice and passion, imitation and partisanship, the circumpressure of our caste and set. As a matter of fact we find ourselves believing, we hardly know how or why. Mr. Balfour gives the name of "authority" to all those influences, born of the intellectual climate, that make hypotheses possible or impossible for us, alive or dead. Here in this room, we all of us believe in molecules and the conservation of energy, in democracy and necessary progress, in Protestant Christianity and the duty of fighting for "the doctrine of the immortal Monroe," all for no reasons worthy of the name. We see into these matters with no more inner clearness, and probably with much less, than any disbeliever in them might possess. His unconventionality would probably have some grounds to show for its conclusions; but for us, not insight, but the *prestige* of the opinions, is what makes the spark shoot from them and light up our sleeping magazines of faith. Our reason is quite satisfied, in nine hundred and ninety-nine cases out of every thousand of us, if it can find a few arguments that will do to recite in case our credulity is criticized by someone else. Our faith is faith in someone else's faith, and in the greatest matters this is most the case. Our belief in truth itself, for instance, that there is a truth, and that our minds and it are made for each other—what is it but a passionate affirmation of desire, in which our social system backs us up? We want to have a truth; we want to believe that our experiments and studies and discussions must put us in a continually better and better position towards it; and on this line we agree to fight out our thinking lives. But if a Pyrrhonistic sceptic asks us *how we know* all this, can our logic find a reply? No! certainly it cannot. It is just one volition against another—we willing to go in for life upon a trust or assumption which he, for his part, does not care to make.

As a rule we disbelieve all facts and theories for which we have no use. Clifford's cosmic emotions find no use for Christian feelings. Huxley belabors the bishops because there is no use for sacerdotalism in his scheme of life. Newman, on the contrary, goes over to Romanism, and finds all sorts of reasons good for staying there, because a priestly system is for him an organic need and delight. Why do so few "scientists" even look at the evidence for telepathy, so called? Because they think, as a leading biologist, now dead, once said to me, that even if such a thing were true, scientists ought to band together to keep it suppressed and concealed. It would undo the uniformity of Nature and all sorts of other things without which scientists cannot carry on their pursuits. But if this very man had been shown something which as a scientist he might *do* with telepathy, he might not only have examined the evidence, but even have found it good enough. This very law which the logicians would impose upon us—if I may give the name of logicians to those who would rule out our willing nature here—is based on nothing but their own natural wish to exclude all elements for which they, in their professional quality of logicians, can find no use.

Evidently, then, our non-intellectual nature does influence our convictions. There are passional tendencies and volitions which run before and others which come after belief, and it is only the latter that are too late for the fair; and they are not too late when the previous passional work has been already in their own direction. Pascal's argument, instead of being powerless, then seems a regular clincher, and is the last stroke needed to make our faith in masses and holy water complete. The state of things is evidently far from simple; and pure insight and logic, whatever they might do ideally, are not the only things that really do produce our creeds.

IV

Our next duty, having recognized this mixed-up state of affairs, is to ask whether it be simply reprehensible and pathological, or whether, on the contrary, we must treat it as a normal element in making up our minds. The thesis I defend is, briefly stated, this: *Our passional nature not only lawfully may, but must, decide an option between propositions, whenever it is a genuine option that cannot by its nature be decided on intellectual grounds; for to say, under such circumstances, "Do not decide, but leave the question open," is itself a passional decision—just like deciding yes or no—and is attended with the same risk of losing the truth....*

VIII

...I fear here that some of you my hearers will begin to scent danger, and lend an inhospitable ear. Two first steps of passion you have indeed had to admit as necessary—we must think so as to avoid dupery, and we must think so as to gain truth; but the surest path to those ideal consummations, you will probably consider, is from now onwards to take no further passional step.

Well, of course, I agree as far as the facts will allow. Wherever the option between losing truth and gaining it is not momentous, we can throw the chance of *gaining truth* away, and at any rate save ourselves from any chance of *believing falsehood,* by not making up our minds at all till objective evidence has come. In scientific questions, this is almost always the case; and even in human affairs in general, the need of acting is seldom so urgent that a false belief to act on is better than no belief at all. Law courts, indeed, have to decide on the best evidence attainable for the moment, because a judge's duty is to make law as well as to ascertain it, and (as a learned judge once said to me) few cases are worth spending much time over: the great thing is to have them decided on *any* acceptable principle, and got out of the way. But in our dealings with objective nature we obviously are recorders, not makers, of the truth; and decisions for the mere sake of deciding promptly and getting on to the next business would be wholly out of place. Throughout the breadth of physical nature facts are what they are quite independently of us, and seldom is there any such hurry about them that the risks of being duped by believing a premature theory need be faced. The questions here are always trivial options, the hypotheses are hardly living (at any rate not living for us spectators), the choice between believing truth or falsehood is seldom forced. The attitude of sceptical balance is therefore the absolutely wise one if we would escape mistakes. What difference, indeed, does it make to most of us whether we have or have not a theory of the Röntgen rays, whether we believe or not in mind-stuff, or have a conviction about the causality of conscious states? It makes no difference. Such options are not forced on us. On every account it is better not to make them, but still keep weighing reasons *pro et contra* with an indifferent hand.

I speak, of course, here of the purely judging mind. For purposes of discovery such indifference is to be less highly recommended, and science would be far less advanced than she is if the passionate desires of individuals to get their own faiths confirmed had been kept out of the game. On the other hand, if you want an absolute duffer in an investigation, you must, after all, take the man who has no interest whatever in its results: he is the warranted incapable, the positive fool. The most useful investigator, because the most sensitive observer, is always he whose eager interest in one side of the question is balanced by an equally keen nervousness lest he become deceived. Science has organized this nervousness into a regular *technique,* her so-called method of verification; and she has fallen so deeply in love with the method that one may even say she has ceased to care for truth by itself at all. It is only truth as technically verified that interests her. The truth of truths might come in merely affirmative form, and she would decline to touch it. Such truth as that, she might repeat with Clifford, would be stolen in defiance of her duty to mankind. Human passions, however, are stronger than technical rules. *"Le cœur a ses raisons,"* as Pascal says, *"que la raison ne connaît pas,"*[3] and however indifferent to all but the bare rules of the game the umpire, the abstract intellect, may be, the concrete players who furnish him the materials to judge are usually, each one of them, in love with some pet "live hypothesis" of his own. Let us agree, however, that wherever there is no forced option, the dispassionately judicial intellect with no pet hypothesis, saving us, as it does, from dupery at any rate, ought to be our ideal.

The question next arises: Are there not somewhere forced options in our speculative questions, and can we (as men who may be interested at least as much in positively gaining truth as in merely escaping dupery) always wait with impunity till the coercive evidence shall have arrived? It seems *a priori* improbable that the truth should be so nicely adjusted to our needs and powers as that. In the great boarding-house of nature, the cakes and the butter and the syrup seldom come out so even and leave the plates so clean. Indeed, we should view them with scientific suspicion if they did.

IX

Moral questions immediately present themselves as questions whose solution cannot wait for sensible proof. A moral question is a question not of what sensibly exists, but of what is good, or would be good if it did exist. Science can tell us what exists; but to compare the *worths,* both of what exists and of what does not exist, we must consult not science, but what Pascal calls our heart. Science herself consults her heart when she lays it down that the infinite ascertainment of fact and correction of false belief are the supreme goods for man. Challenge the statement, and science can only repeat it oracularly, or else prove it by showing that such ascertainment and correction bring man all sorts of other goods which man's heart in turn declares. The question of having moral beliefs at all or not having them is decided by our will. Are our moral preferences true or false, or are they only odd biological phenomena, making things good or bad for *us,* but in themselves indifferent? How can your pure intellect decide? If your heart does not *want* a world of moral reality, your head will assuredly never make you believe in one. Mephistophelian scepticism, indeed, will satisfy the head's play-instincts much better than any rigorous idealism can. Some men (even at the student age) are so naturally cool-hearted that the moralistic hypoth-

---

[3] [The heart has reasons which reason knows nothing of.]

esis never has for them any pungent life, and in their supercilious presence the hot young moralist always feels strangely ill at ease. The appearance of knowingness is on their side, of *naïveté* and gullibility on his. Yet, in the inarticulate heart of him, he clings to it that he is not a dupe, and that there is a realm in which (as Emerson says) all their wit and intellectual superiority is no better than the cunning of a fox. Moral scepticism can no more be refuted or proved by logic than intellectual scepticism can. When we stick to it that there *is* truth (be it of either kind), we do so with our whole nature, and resolve to stand or fall by the results. The sceptic with his whole nature adopts the doubting attitude; but which of us is the wiser, Omniscience only knows.

Turn now from these wide questions of good to a certain class of questions of fact, questions concerning personal relations, states of mind between one man and another. *Do you like me or not?*—for example. Whether you do or not depends, in countless instances, on whether I meet you halfway, am willing to assume that you must like me, and show you trust and expectation. The previous faith on my part in your liking's existence is in such cases what makes your liking come. But if I stand aloof, and refuse to budge an inch until I have objective evidence, until you shall have done something apt, as the absolutists say, *ad extorquendum assensum meum,*[4] ten to one your liking never comes. How many women's hearts are vanquished by the mere sanguine insistence of some man that they *must* love him! he will not consent to the hypothesis that they cannot. The desire for a certain kind of truth here brings about that special truth's existence; and so it is in innumerable cases of other sorts. Who gains promotions, boons, appointments, but the man in whose life they are seen to play the part of live hypotheses, who discounts them, sacrifices other things for their sake before they have come, and takes risks for them in advance? His faith acts on the powers above him as a claim, and creates its own verification.

A social organism of any sort whatever, large or small, is what it is because each member proceeds to his own duty with a trust that the other members will simultaneously do theirs. Wherever a desired result is achieved by the cooperation of many independent persons, its existence as a fact is a pure consequence of the precursive faith in one another of those immediately concerned. A government, an army, a commercial system, a ship, a college, an athletic team, all exist on this condition, without which not only is nothing achieved, but nothing is even attempted. A whole train of passengers (individually brave enough) will be looted by a few highwaymen, simply because the latter can count on one another, while each passenger fears that if he makes a movement of resistance, he will be shot before anyone else backs him up. If we believed that the whole car-full would rise at once with

4 [To force me to assent.]

us, we should each severally rise, and train-robbing would never even be attempted. There are, then, cases where a fact cannot come at all unless a preliminary faith exists in its coming. *And where faith in a fact can help create the fact,* that would be an insane logic which should say that faith running ahead of scientific evidence is the "lowest kind of immorality" into which a thinking being can fall. Yet such is the logic by which our scientific absolutists pretend to regulate our lives!

X

In truths dependent on our personal action, then, faith based on desire is certainly a lawful and possibly an indispensable thing.

But now, it will be said, these are all childish human cases, and have nothing to do with great cosmical matters, like the question of religious faith. Let us then pass on to that. Religions differ so much in their accidents that in discussing the religious question we must make it very generic and broad. What then do we now mean by the religious hypothesis? Science says things are; morality says some things are better than other things; and religion says essentially two things.

First, she says that the best things are the more eternal things, the over-lapping things, the things in the universe that throw the last stone, so to speak, and say the final word. "Perfection is eternal"—this phrase of Charles Secrétan seems a good way of putting this first affirmation of religion, an affirmation which obviously cannot yet be verified scientifically at all.

The second affirmation of religion is that we are better off even now if we believe her first affirmation to be true.

Now, let us consider what the logical elements of this situation are *in case the religious hypothesis in both its branches be really true.* (Of course, we must admit that possibility at the outset. If we are to discuss the question at all, it must involve a living option. If for any of you religion be a hypothesis that cannot, by any living possibility, be true, then you need go no farther. I speak to the "saving remnant" alone.) So proceeding, we see, first, that religion offers itself as a *momentous* option. We are supposed to gain, even now, by our belief, and to lose by our non-belief, a certain vital good. Secondly, religion is a *forced* option, so far as that good goes. We cannot escape the issue by remaining sceptical and waiting for more light, because, although we do avoid error in that way *if religion be untrue,* we lose the good, *if it be true,* just as certainly as if we positively chose to disbelieve. It is as if a man should hesitate indefinitely to ask a certain woman to marry him because he was not perfectly sure that she would prove an angel after he brought her home. Would he not cut himself off from that particular angel-possibility as decisively as if he went and married someone else? Scepticism, then, is not avoidance of option; it is option of a certain particular kind of risk. *Better risk loss of truth than chance of error*—that is your faith-vetoer's exact

position. He is actively playing his stake as much as the believer is; he is
backing the field against the religious hypothesis, just as the believer is
backing the religious hypothesis against the field. To preach scepticism to us
as a duty until "sufficient evidence" for religion be found, is tantamount
therefore to telling us, when in presence of religious hypothesis, that to yield
to our fear of its being error is wiser and better than to yield to our hope that
it may be true. It is not intellect against all passions, then; it is only intellect
with one passion laying down its law. And by what, forsooth, is the supreme
wisdom of this passion warranted? Dupery for dupery, what proof is there
that dupery through hope is so much worse than dupery through fear? I, for
one, can see no proof; and I simply refuse obedience to the scientist's
command to imitate his kind of option, in a case where my own stake is
important enough to give me the right to choose my own form of risk. If
religion be true and the evidence for it be still insufficient, I do not wish, by
putting your extinguisher upon my nature (which feels to me as if it had
after all some business in this matter), to forfeit my sole chance in life of
getting upon the winning side—that chance depending, of course, on my
willingness to run the risk of acting as if my passional need of taking the
world religiously might be prophetic and right.

All this is on the supposition that it really may be prophetic and right, and
that, even to us who are discussing the matter, religion is a live hypothesis
which may be true. Now, to most of us religion comes in a still further way
that makes a veto on our active faith even more illogical. The more perfect
and more eternal aspect of the universe is represented in our religions as
having personal form. The universe is no longer a mere *It* to us, but a *Thou,*
if we are religious; and any relation that may be possible from person to
person might be possible here. For instance, although in one sense we are
passive portions of the universe, in another we show a curious autonomy, as
if we were small active centres on our own account. We feel, too, as if the
appeal of religion to us were made to our own active good-will, as if evidence
might be forever withheld from us unless we met the hypothesis half-way.
To take a trivial illustration: just as a man who in a company of gentlemen
made no advances, asked a warrant for every concession, and believed no
one's word without proof, would cut himself off by such churlishness from
all the social rewards that a more trusting spirit would earn—so here, one
who should shut himself up in snarling logicality and try to make the gods
extort his recognition willy-nilly, or not get it at all, might cut himself off
forever from his only opportunity of making the gods' acquaintance. This
feeling, forced on us we know not whence, that by obstinately believing that
there are gods (although not to do so would be so easy both for our logic
and our life) we are doing the universe the deepest service we can, seems
part of the living essence of the religious hypothesis. If the hypothesis *were*
true in all its parts, including this one, then pure intellectualism, with its veto

on our making willing advances, would be an absurdity; and some participation of our sympathetic nature would be logically required. I, therefore, for one, cannot see my way to accepting the agnostic rules for truth-seeking, or wilfully agree to keep my willing nature out of the game. I cannot do so for this plain reason, that *a rule of thinking which would absolutely prevent me from acknowledging certain kinds of truth if those kinds of truth were really there, would be an irrational rule.* That for me is the long and short of the formal logic of the situation, no matter what the kinds of truth might materially be.

I confess I do not see how this logic can be escaped. But sad experience makes me fear that some of you may still shrink from radically saying with me, *in abstracto,*[5] that we have the right to believe at our own risk any hypothesis that is live enough to tempt our will. I suspect, however, that if this is so, it is because you have got away from the abstract logical point of view altogether, and are thinking (perhaps without realizing it) of some particular religious hypothesis which for you is dead. The freedom to "believe what we will" you apply to the case of some patent superstition; and the faith you think of is the faith defined by the schoolboy when he said, "Faith is when you believe something that you know ain't true." I can only repeat that this is misapprehension. *In concreto,*[6] the freedom to believe can only cover living options which the intellect of the individual cannot by itself resolve; and living options never seem absurdities to him who has them to consider. When I look at the religious question as it really puts itself to concrete men, and when I think of all the possibilities which both practically and theoretically it involves, then this command that we shall put a stopper on our heart, instincts, and courage, and *wait*—acting of course meanwhile more or less as if religion were *not* true[7]—till doomsday, or till such time as our intellect and senses working together may have raked in evidence enough—this command, I say, seems to me the queerest idol ever manufactured in the philosophic cave. Were we scholastic absolutists, there might be more excuse. If we had an infallible intellect with its objective certitudes, we might feel ourselves disloyal to such a perfect organ of knowledge in not trusting to it exclusively, in not waiting for its releasing word. But if we are empiricists, if we believe that no bell in us tolls to let us know for certain

[5] [In abstract terms.]

[6] [In concrete terms.]

[7] Since belief is measured by action, he who forbids us to believe religion to be true, necessarily also forbids us to act as we should if we did believe it to be true. The whole defense of religious faith hinges upon action. If the action required or inspired by the religious hypothesis is in no way different from that dictated by the naturalistic hypothesis, then religious faith is a pure superfluity, better pruned away, and controversy about its legitimacy is a piece of idle trifling, unworthy of serious minds. I myself believe, of course, that the religious hypothesis gives to the world an expression which specifically determines our reactions, and makes them in a large part unlike what they might be on a purely naturalistic scheme of belief.

when truth is in our grasp, then it seems a piece of idle fantasticality to preach so solemnly our duty of waiting for the bell. Indeed we *may* wait if we will—I hope you do not think that I am denying that—but if we do so, we do so at our peril as much as if we believed. In either case we *act,* taking our life in our hands. No one of us ought to issue vetoes to the other, nor should we bandy words of abuse. We ought, on the contrary, delicately and profoundly to respect one another's mental freedom: then only shall we bring about the intellectual republic; then only shall we have that spirit of inner tolerance without which all our outer tolerance is soulless, and which is empiricism's glory; then only shall we live and let live, in speculative as well as in practical things.

I began by a reference to Fitz-James Stephen; let me end by a quotation from him. "What do you think of yourself? What do you think of the world? ... These are are questions with which all must deal as it seems good to them. They are riddles of the Sphinx, and in some way or other we must deal with them.... In all important transactions of life we have to take a leap in the dark.... If we decide to leave the riddles unanswered, that is a choice; if we waver in our answer, that, too, is a choice: but whatever choice we make, we make it at our peril. If a man chooses to turn his back altogether on God and the future, no one can prevent him; no one can show beyond reasonable doubt that he is mistaken. If a man thinks otherwise and acts as he thinks, I do not see that anyone can prove that *he* is mistaken. Each must act as he thinks best; and if he is wrong, so much the worse for him. We stand on a mountain pass in the midst of whirling snow and blinding mist, through which we get glimpses now and then of paths which may be deceptive. If we stand still we shall be frozen to death. If we take the wrong road we shall be dashed to pieces. We do not certainly know whether there is any right one. What must we do? 'Be strong and of a good courage.' Act for the best, hope for the best, and take what comes.... If death ends all, we cannot meet death better."

DISCUSSION AND WRITING

1. Define or explain: *coerce, imbue, Mahdi, scintillate, intrinsic, irrevocable, momentous, theosophist, agnostic, logical disjunction, reversible, verification, passional, volitional, beatitude, effulgence, august, besotted, redundant, desecrate, credence, credulity, Pyrrhonistic, sacerdotalism, Romanism, reprehensible, duffer, impunity, a priori, oracular, Mephistophelian, pungent, supercilious, sanguine, generic, tantamount, autonomy, scholastic, empiricism, Sphinx.* In context, what is the meaning of "admit my *contention*," "light up our sleeping *magazines* of faith," "some *patent* superstition," "*naturalistic* hypothesis"?

2. Identify the writers quoted by James. (The Huxley referred to is T. H. Huxley; Balfour is the English statesman, also noted as an essayist. William Clifford was an English, Charles Secrétan a French nineteenth-century philosopher.)

3. Examine James's use of concrete examples and analogies. How do they contribute to the effectiveness of the essay?

4. In a well-developed paragraph, sum up James's definition of science and religion.

5. Outline the major steps in James's argument. Describe generally the logical pattern or the method of argument that James employs.

6. One editor has called this essay a "magnificently reasoned and convincing analysis." Does it convince *you?* Why or why not? Identify features that contribute to or interfere with the persuasive effect of the essay.

7. What kind of faith is a "live option" for today's college student?

8. James claims that we all hold basic moral and political beliefs "for no reasons worthy of the name." Select one of your basic convictions and defend it against James's charge. Rely on detailed logical argument rather than on emotional assertion.

9. How much room is there for logical argument and the weighing of probabilities in true faith? Do you believe in "our right to adopt a believing attitude in religious matters, in spite of the fact that our merely logical intellect may not have been coerced"?

10. Can you think of any information or theory that would make you say that "even if such a thing were true" it should be kept "suppressed or concealed"?

FURTHER READING

William James developed his "justification of faith" more fully in *The Varieties of Religious Experience* (1902). Other books aiming at a reconciliation of science and faith are Henri Bergson, *Creative Evolution* (1907), and Lecomte Du Noüy, *Human Destiny* (1947).

WALTER LIPPMANN

Although the word "principle" frequently occurs in political debate, thorough re-examination of political principles, divorced from short-range objectives, is rare. Walter Lippmann (born 1889) is one close observer of current politics who has also found time to think through some of the problems inherent in the structure of contemporary democratic societies. A graduate of Harvard, Mr. Lippmann worked as writer and editor for *The New Republic,* the *New York World,* and the *New York Herald Tribune.* He is the author of *A Preface to Politics* (1913), *A Preface to Morals* (1929), and *The Good Society* (1937). Widely known for his literate and informed comments on public affairs, he has through the decades seen his newspaper column grow into a national institution and minor oracle. The following excerpt is taken from *The Public Philosophy* (1955). It forces the reader to think through basic political issues often obscured by a fog of vague self-congratulatory phrases.

The Renewal of the Public Philosophy

1. THE CAPACITY TO BELIEVE

The freedom which modern men are turned away from, not seldom with relief and often with enthusiasm, is the hollow shell of freedom. The current theory of freedom holds that what men believe may be important to them but that it has almost no public significance. The outer defenses of the free way of life stand upon the legal guarantees against the coercion of belief. But the citadel is vacant because the public philosophy is gone, and all that the defenders of freedom have to defend in common is a public neutrality and a public agnosticism.

Yet when we have demonstrated the need for the public philosophy, how do we prove that the need can be satisfied? Not, we may be sure, by exhortation, however eloquent, to rise to the enormity of the present danger, still less by lamentations about the glory and the grandeur that are past. Modern men, to whom the argument is addressed, have a low capacity to believe in the invisible, the intangible, and the imponderable.

Exhortation can capture the will to believe. But of the will to believe there is no lack. The modern trouble is in a low capacity to believe in precepts which restrict and restrain private interests and desire. Conviction of the need of these restraints is difficult to restore once it has been radically impaired. Public principles can, of course, be imposed by a despotic government. But the public philosophy of a free society cannot be restored by fiat and by force. To come to grips with the unbelief which underlies the condition of anomy, we must find a way to re-establish confidence in the validity of public standards. We must renew the convictions from which our political morality springs.

In the prevailing popular culture all philosophies are the instruments of some man's purpose, all truths are self-centered and self-regarding, and all principles are the rationalizations of some special interest. There is no public criterion of the true and the false, of the right and the wrong, beyond that which the preponderant mass of voters, consumers, readers, and listeners happen at the moment to be supposed to want.

There is no reason to think that this condition of mind can be changed until it can be proved to the modern skeptic that there are certain principles which, when they have been demonstrated, only the willfully irrational can deny, that there are certain obligations binding on all men who are committed to a free society, and that only the willfully subversive can reject them. . . .

3. FOR EXAMPLE: FREEDOM OF SPEECH

Only within a community which adheres to the public philosophy is there sure and sufficient ground for the freedom to think and to ask questions, to speak and to publish. Nobody can justify in principle, much less in practice, a claim that there exists an unrestricted right of anyone to utter anything he likes at any time he chooses. There can, for example, be no right, as Mr. Justice Holmes said, to cry "Fire" in a crowded theater. Nor is there a right to tell a customer that the glass beads are diamonds, or a voter that the opposition candidate for President is a Soviet agent.

Freedom of speech has become a central concern of the Western society because of the discovery among the Greeks that dialectic, as demonstrated in the Socratic dialogues, is a principal method of attaining truth, and particularly a method of attaining moral and political truth. "The ability to raise searching difficulties on both sides of a subject will," said Aristotle, "make us detect more easily the truth and error about the several points that arise."[1] The right to speak freely is one of the necessary means to the attainment of the truth. That, and not the subjective pleasure of utterance, is why freedom is a necessity in the good society.

This was the ground on which Milton in the *Areopagitica* opposed the order of Parliament (1643) that no book should be printed or put on sale unless it had first been licensed by the authorities:

> As therefore the state of man now is; what wisdom can there be to choose, what continence to forbear without the knowledge of evil? Since therefore the knowledge and survey of vice is in this world necessary to the constituting of human virtue, and the scanning of evil, to the confirmation of truth, how can we more safely, and with less danger, scout into the regions of sin and falsity than by reading all manner of tractates and hearing all manner of reason?[2]

The method of dialectic is to confront ideas with opposing ideas in order that the pro and the con of the dispute will lead to true ideas. But the dispute must not be treated as a trial of strength. It must be a means of elucidation.

---

[1] *Topics,* Bk. I, Ch. 1, 101a35.
[2] Milton's *Areopagitica* (Oxford University Press, 1949), pp. 18–19.

In a Socratic dialogue the disputants are arguing co-operatively in order to acquire more wisdom than either of them had when he began. In a sophistical argument the sophist is out to win a case, using rhetoric and not dialectic. "Both alike," says Aristotle, "are concerned with such things as come, more or less, within the general ken of all men and belong to no definite science."[3] But while "dialectic is a process of criticism wherein lies the path to the principle of all inquiries,"[4] "rhetoric is concerned with the modes of persuasion."[5]

Divorced from its original purpose and justification, as a process of criticism, freedom to think and speak are not self-evident necessities. It is only from the hope and the intention of discovering truth that freedom acquires such high public significance. The right of self-expression is, as such, a private amenity rather than a public necessity. The right to utter words, whether or not they have meaning, and regardless of their truth, could not be a vital interest of a great state but for the presumption that they are the chaff which goes with the utterance of true and significant words.

But when the chaff of silliness, baseness, and deception is so voluminous that it submerges the kernels of truth, freedom of speech may produce such frivolity, or such mischief, that it cannot be preserved against the demand for a restoration of order or of decency. If there is a dividing line between liberty and license, it is where freedom of speech is no longer respected as a procedure of the truth and becomes the unrestricted right to exploit the ignorance, and to incite the passions, of the people. Then freedom is such a hullabaloo of sophistry, propaganda, special pleading, lobbying, and salesmanship that it is difficult to remember why freedom of speech is worth the pain and trouble of defending it.

What has been lost in the tumult is the meaning of the obligation which is involved in the right to speak freely. It is the obligation to subject the utterance to criticism and debate. Because the dialectical debate is a procedure for attaining moral and political truth, the right to speak is protected by a willingness to debate.

In the public philosophy, freedom of speech is conceived as the means to a confrontation of opinion—as in a Socratic dialogue, in a schoolmen's disputation, in the critiques of scientists and savants, in a court of law, in a representative assembly, in an open forum.

> Even at the canonization of a saint, [says John Stuart Mill] the church admits and listens patiently to a "devil's advocate." The holiest of men, it appears, cannot be admitted to posthumous honors, until all that the devil could say against him is known and weighed. If even the Newtonian

[3] *Rhetoric*, Bk. I, Ch. 1, 1354a1–3.
[4] *Topics*, Bk. I, Ch. 2, 101b3–4.
[5] *Rhetoric*, Bk. I, Ch. 1, 1355a4.

philosophy were not permitted to be questioned, mankind could not feel as complete assurance of its truth as they now [1859] do. The beliefs which we have most warrant for, have no safeguard to rest on, but a standing invitation to the whole world to prove them unfounded. If the challenge is not accepted, or is accepted and the attempt fails, we are far enough from certainty still; but we have done the best that the existing state of human reason admits of; we have neglected nothing that could give the truth the chance of reaching us: if the lists are kept open, we may hope that if there be a better truth, it will be found when the human mind is capable of receiving it; and in the meantime we may rely on having attained such approach to truth, as is possible in our day. This is the amount of certainty attainable by a fallible being, and this is the sole way of attaining it.[6]

And because the purpose of the confrontation is to discern truth, there are rules of evidence and of parliamentary procedure, there are codes of fair dealing and fair comment, by which a loyal man will consider himself bound when he exercises the right to publish opinions. For the right to freedom of speech is no license to deceive, and willful misrepresentation is a violation of its principles. It is sophistry to pretend that in a free country a man has some sort of inalienable or constitutional right to deceive his fellow men. There is no more right to deceive than there is a right to swindle, to cheat, or to pick pockets. It may be inexpedient to arraign every public liar, as we try to arraign other swindlers. It may be a poor policy to have too many laws which encourage litigation about matters of opinion. But, in principle, there can be no immunity for lying in any of its protean forms.

In our time the application of these fundamental principles poses many unsolved practical problems. For the modern media of mass communication do not lend themselves easily to a confrontation of opinions. The dialectical process for finding truth works best when the same audience hears all the sides of the disputation. This is manifestly impossible in the moving pictures: if a film advocates a thesis, the same audience cannot be shown another film designed to answer it. Radio and television broadcasts do permit some debate. But despite the effort of the companies to let opposing views be heard equally, and to organize programs on which there are opposing speakers, the technical conditions of broadcasting do not favor genuine and productive debate. For the audience, tuning on and tuning off here and there, cannot be counted upon to hear, even in summary form, the essential evidence and the main arguments on all the significant sides of a question. Rarely, and on very few public issues, does the mass audience have the benefit of the process by which truth is sifted from error—the dialectic of debate in which there is immediate challenge, reply, cross-examination, and

[6] J. S. Mill, *On Liberty*. In *On Liberty, Representative Government, The Subjection of Women* (London, Oxford University Press, 1946), Ch. II, pp. 28–29.

rebuttal. The men who regularly broadcast the news and comment upon the news cannot—like a speaker in the Senate or in the House of Commons—be challenged by one of their listeners and compelled then and there to verify their statements of fact and to re-argue their inferences from the facts.

Yet when genuine debate is lacking, freedom of speech does not work as it is meant to work. It has lost the principle which regulates it and justifies it—that is to say, dialectic conducted according to logic and the rules of evidence. If there is no effective debate, the unrestricted right to speak will unloose so many propagandists, procurers, and panderers upon the public that sooner or later in self-defense the people will turn to the censors to protect them. An unrestricted and unregulated right to speak cannot be maintained. It will be curtailed for all manner of reasons and pretexts, and to serve all kinds of good, foolish, or sinister ends.

For in the absence of debate unrestricted utterance leads to the degradation of opinion. By a kind of Gresham's law the more rational is overcome by the less rational, and the opinions that will prevail will be those which are held most ardently by those with the most passionate will. For that reason the freedom to speak can never be maintained merely by objecting to interference with the liberty of the press, of printing, of broadcasting, of the screen. It can be maintained only by promoting debate.

In the end what men will most ardently desire is to suppress those who disagree with them and, therefore, stand in the way of the realization of their desires. Thus, once confrontation in debate is no longer necessary, the toleration of all opinions leads to intolerance. Freedom of speech, separated from its essential principle, leads through a short transitional chaos to the destruction of freedom of speech.

It follows, I believe, that in the practice of freedom of speech, the degree of toleration that will be maintained is directly related to the effectiveness of the confrontation in debate which prevails or can be organized. In the Senate of the United States, for example, a Senator can promptly be challenged by another Senator and brought to an accounting. Here among the Senators themselves the conditions are most nearly ideal for the toleration of all opinions.[7] At the other extreme there is the secret circulation of anonymous allegations. Here there is no means of challenging the author, and without any violation of the principles of freedom, he may properly be dealt with by detectives, by policemen, and the criminal courts. Between such extremes there are many problems of toleration which depend essentially upon how effective is the confrontation in debate. Where it is inefficient, as in the standard newspaper press taken as a whole, freedom is largely unrestricted by law. Where confrontation is difficult, as in broadcasting, there is also an acceptance of the principle that some legal regulation is necessary—for example, in order to insure fair play for political parties. When confrontation

---

[7] For non-Senators attacked by Senators the case is different.

is impossible, as in the moving picture, or in the so-called comic books, there will be censorship.

4. THE LIMITS OF DISSENT

The counterrevolutionary movements have subjected the liberal democracies to severe stresses and strains: how to insure their security and survival without abandoning their liberties. They are faced with popular movements, aided and abetted by unfriendly foreign powers, and employing the machinery of democratic governments to capture it and in order to abolish it. When they are working to attain power and before they do attain it, the fascist and communist parties invoke all the guarantees of the bill of rights, all the prerogatives of popular parties, of elections, of representation of the assemblies, of tenure in the civil service. But when they attain power, they destroy the liberal democratic institutions on which, as on a broad staircase, they climbed to power.

This exploitation of free institutions is, it seems to me, compelling proof that these institutions are inseparable from the public philosophy. If the connection is forgotten, as is so generally the case in the contemporary democracies, free institutions are poorly defended by the liberal democracies. They are the easy prey of their enemies. Either the fascists seize power in order to forestall the communists, or the communists seize power to forestall the fascists.

There is no equivocation in the public philosophy about the principle of the defense of free institutions. The rule is that the right to enjoy them and the duty to maintain them are inseparable. The right to these institutions is, that is to say, for those who adhere to them.

The criterion of loyalty is an indubitable commitment to defend and preserve the order of political and civil rights. The question of whether the liberal democratic states should outlaw, or in other ways contain, counter-revolutionary movements is not one of principle but of expediency and practical prudence. There is no doubt about the principle: that the counter-revolutionary movements are enemies of the state, and must be defeated.

In applying the principle the specific question of whether this party or that individual is or is not loyal is a matter to be determined by due process. For while there can be no right to destroy the liberal democratic state, there is an inalienable right to have the question adjudicated justly in all particular cases as to whether this person or that is an enemy of the state. This right cannot be denied to those who have not been proved guilty without denying it to all who would be proved not guilty.

The limits of dissent are not too difficult to fix when we are dealing with avowedly revolutionary parties like the communists and the fascists. The borderline between sedition and radical reform is between the denial and the acceptance of the sovereign principle of the public philosophy: that we live in a rational order in which by sincere inquiry and rational debate we can distinguish the true and the false, the right and wrong. The counterrevolutionists, who suppress freedom in order to propagate the official doctrine, reject the procedure by which in the free society official policy is determined. Rational procedure is the ark of the covenant of the public philosophy. There is no set of election laws or constitutional guarantees which are unchangeable. What is unchangeable is the commitment to rational determination, the commitment to act in public life on the assumption which C. S. Peirce stated as follows:

> Human opinion universally tends in the long run to a definite form, which is the truth. Let any human being have enough information and exert enough thought upon any question, and the result will be that he will arrive at a certain definite conclusion, which is the same that any other mind will reach under sufficiently favorable circumstances. . . . There is, then, to every question a true answer, a final conclusion, to which the opinion of every man is constantly gravitating. He may for a time recede from it, but give him more experience and time for consideration, and he will finally approach it. The individual may not live to reach the truth; there is a residuum of error in every individual's opinions. No matter; it remains that there is a definite opinion to which the mind of man is, on the whole and in the long run, tending. On many questions the final agreement is already reached, on all it will be reached if time enough is given. The arbitrary will or other individual peculiarities of a sufficiently large number of minds may postpone the general agreement in that opinion indefinitely; but it cannot affect what the character of that opinion shall be when it is reached. This final opinion then is independent, not indeed of thought in general, but of all that is arbitrary and individual in thought; is quite independent of how you, or I, or any number of men, think.[8]

It is not possible to reject this faith in the efficacy of reason and at the same time to believe that communities of men enjoying freedom could govern themselves successfully.

5. THE MIRROR OF HISTORY

We find, then, that the principle of freedom of speech, like that of private property, falls within the bounds of the public philosophy. It can be justified, applied, regulated in a plural society only by adhering to the postulate that there is a rational order of things in which it is possible, by sincere inquiry and rational debate, to distinguish the true and the false, the

---

[8] Cited in Herbert W. Schneider, *A History of American Philosophy* (1946), p. 517. From a review of Fraser's *Works of George Berkeley* in *North American Review*, Vol. CXIII (1871), pp. 455–456.

right and the wrong, the good which leads to the realization of human ends and the evil which leads to destruction and to the death of civility.

The free political institutions of the Western world were conceived and established by men who believed that honest reflection on the common experience of mankind would always cause men to come to the same ultimate conclusions. Within the Golden Rule of the same philosophy for elucidating their ultimate ends, they could engage with confident hope in the progressive discovery of truth. All issues could be settled by scientific investigation and by free debate if—but only if—all the investigators and the debaters adhered to the public philosophy; if, that is to say, they used the same criteria and rules of reason for arriving at the truth and for distinguishing good and evil.

Quite evidently, there is no clear sharp line which can be drawn in any community or among communities between those who adhere and those who do not adhere to the public philosophy. But while there are many shades and degrees in the spectrum, the two ends are well-defined. When the adherence of the whole body of people to the public philosophy is firm, a true community exists; where there is division and dissent over the main principles the result is a condition of latent war.

In the maintenance and formation of a true community the articulate philosophy is, one might say, like the thread which holds the pieces of the fabric together. Not everyone can have mastered the philosophy; most people, presumably, may have heard almost nothing about it. But if among the people of light and leading the public philosophy has, as the Chinese say, the Mandate of Heaven, the beliefs and the habits which cause men to collaborate will remain whole. But if the public philosophy is discarded among them, being treated as reactionary or as nonsensical, then the stitches will have been pulled out and the fabric will come apart.

The fabrics in the metaphor are the traditions of how the good life is lived and the good society is governed. When they come apart, as they have in the Western democracies, the result is tantamount to a kind of collective amnesia. The liberal democracies have been making mistakes in peace and in war which they would never have made were they not suffering from what is a failure of memory. They have forgotten too much of what their predecessors had learned before them. The newly enfranchised democracies are like men who have kept their appetites but have forgotten how to grow food. They have the perennial human needs for law and order, for freedom and justice, for what only good government can give them. But the art of governing well has to be learned. If it is to be learned, it has to be transmitted from the old to the young, and the habits and the ideas must be maintained as a seamless web of memory among the bearers of the tradition, generation after generation.

When the continuity of the traditions of civility is ruptured, the community is threatened: unless the rupture is repaired, the community will break down into factional, class, racial and regional wars. For when the continuity is interrupted, the cultural heritage is not being transmitted. The new generation is faced with the task of rediscovering and re-inventing and relearning, by trial and error, most of what the guardians of a society need to know.

No one generation can do this. For no one generation of men are capable of creating for themselves the arts and sciences of a high civilization. Men can know more than their ancestors did if they start with a knowledge of what their ancestors had already learned. They can do advanced experiments if they do not have to learn all over again how to do the elementary ones. That is why a society can be progressive only if it conserves its traditions. The generations are, as Bernard of Chartres said, "like dwarfs seated on the shoulders of giants," enabled, therefore, to "see more things than the Ancients and things more distant."[9]

But traditions are more than the culture of the arts and sciences. They are the public world to which our private worlds are joined. This continuum of public and private memories transcends all persons in their immediate and natural lives and it ties them all together. In it there is performed the mystery by which individuals are adopted and initiated into membership in the community.

The body which carries this mystery is the history of the community, and its central theme is the great deeds and the high purposes of the great predecessors. From them the new men descend and prove themselves by becoming participants in the unfinished story.

"Where I belong," says Jaspers, "and what I am living for, I first learned in the mirror of history."[10] When the individual becomes civilized he acquires a second nature. This second nature is made in the image of what he is and is living for and should become. He has seen the image in the mirror of history. This second nature, which rules over the natural man, is at home in the good society. This second nature is no proletarian but feels itself to be a rightful proprietor and ruler of the community. Full allegiance to the community can be given only by a man's second nature, ruling over his first and primitive nature, and treating it as not finally himself. Then the disciplines and the necessities and the constraints of a civilized life have ceased to be alien to him, and imposed from without. They have become his own inner imperatives.

DISCUSSION AND WRITING

1. Define or explain: *citadel, agnosticism, imponderable, exhortation, anomy, rationalization, preponderant, elucidation, amenity, critique, posthumous, arraign, litigation,*

[9] Cited in Étienne Gilson, *The Spirit of Medieval Philosophy* (1940), p. 426.
[10] Karl Jaspers, *Origin and Goal of History* (1953), p. 271.

protean, equivocation, indubitable, adjudicate, sedition, residuum, postulate, latent, tantamount, continuum, transcend, imperative. Explain "Gresham's law," "ark of the covenant."

2. What sentence in the introductory paragraphs provides the clue to the author's later treatment of freedom of speech? Defend your choice.

3. In your own words, restate Lippmann's definition of "freedom of speech"—his account of its nature, purpose, and limitations. Explain his distinction between "rhetoric" and "dialectic" and between "liberty" and "license." What other, more specific terms are important to the reader's understanding of these distinctions?

4. Explain the nature and implications of Lippmann's "faith in the efficacy of reason." Show how this faith is related to his definition of "loyalty," his account of civilized man's allegiance to society.

5. Describe the characteristic style and manner of Lippmann's argument. What is there about the way he writes that would help explain the influence and respect he enjoys?

6. What evidence have you encountered that the "current theory of freedom holds that what men believe may be important to them but that it has almost no public significance"?

7. Discuss obstacles to or abuses of freedom of speech that you have encountered in your own experience or reading. What is your own definition of "free speech"?

8. Compare Lippmann's view of the relationship between "dialectic" and democracy with that expressed by Robert M. Hutchins in "The University of Utopia." Or, compare and contrast Lippmann's position on freedom of speech and censorship with that of other authors in this volume: Plato, Marya Mannes, André Gide.

9. College students are sometimes accused of opposition merely for the sake of opposition; of opposition that is merely wrongheaded, negative, or destructive. To judge from such evidence as current campus controversies, student government, or campus journalism, are these charges justified?

10. Formulate the "public philosophy" that seems to underlie the current treatment of political issues in a magazine devoted to a considerable extent to political comment or opinion: *Time, The New Republic, The American Mercury, The Reporter, The Nation, Commonweal, Commentary.* Study editorials and articles in a number of recent issues.

FURTHER READING

For an appraisal of Lippmann's role in American journalism—and for a critical analysis of *The Public Philosophy*—see Marquis Childs and James Reston (eds.), *Walter Lippmann and His Times* (1959). To study other political commentators influential in recent decades, consult your library catalogue, periodical indexes, or newspaper files for material by or about Norman Cousins, Elmer Davis, David Lawrence, Kingsley Martin, or James Reston.

11

The Mirror of Man

What a piece of work is man! How noble in reason! How infinite in faculty! In form and moving how express and admirable! In action how like an angel! In apprehension how like a god! The beauty of the world! The paragon of animals! And yet, to me, what is this quintessence of dust?

SHAKESPEARE, *Hamlet*

At one extreme, expository prose is factual and technical, bristling with data. At the other extreme, it is abstract and philosophical, addressing itself to basic questions about man's nature and the meaning of life. The same basic resources of language that serve the technical writer in a factual, impersonal, businesslike report serve the writer who eloquently states the assumptions that give life purpose or direction. The writers in this group explore, from widely different perspectives, the question of man's view of himself. Jeremy Taylor, the seventeenth-century churchman, preaches the vanity and insecurity of human life, thus encouraging man to look to the salvation of his soul. Thomas Hobbes, though a contemporary of Taylor, anticipates the modern tendency to trace man's values and institutions to roots in his biological condition. T. H. Huxley, in his often reprinted essay "On the Advisableness of Improving Natural Knowledge," documents the revolutionary impact of nineteenth-century science on traditional beliefs and illustrates the confidence of its followers in its power to serve not only technological but also moral and spiritual needs. Robert Louis Stevenson, in "An Apology for Idlers," makes us re-examine our definition of success by stressing the intangibles that make for vitality, zest, contentment.

JEREMY TAYLOR

The literature of the seventeenth century is rich in sermons, devotional tracts, works of theology, and pamphlets devoted to religious controversy. One of the most eloquent of religious writers was Jeremy Taylor (1613–1667), an Anglican priest who for a time was chaplain to King Charles I. He wrote some of his best-known works after losing his position and suffering imprisonment during the temporary Puritan victory over the monarchy and the established Church. The following is the opening section of his *The Rule and Exercises of Holy Dying* (1651). It shows the otherworldliness of the orthodox churchman, exhorting men to recognize the vanity of human wishes in view of certain death. At the same time, this selection illustrates a "baroque" style: a love for rich ornament and elaborate pattern.

On the Vanity and Shortness of Man's Life

A man is a bubble, said the Greek proverb; which Lucian represents with advantages and its proper circumstances to this purpose, saying that all the world is a storm, etc., and men rise up in their several generations, like bubbles descending *a Jove pluvio*,[1] from God and the dew of heaven, from a tear and drop of man, from nature and providence; and some of these instantly sink into the deluge of their first parent, and are hidden in a sheet of water, having had no other business in the world but to be born that they might be able to die; others float up and down two or three turns, and suddenly disappear and give their place to others; and they that live longest upon the face of the waters are in perpetual motion, restless and uneasy, and, being crushed with the great drop of a cloud, sink into flatness and a froth; the change not being great, it being hardly possible it should be more a nothing than it was before.

So is every man: he is born in vanity and sin; he comes into the world like morning mushrooms, soon thrusting up their heads into the air, and conversing with their kindred of the same production, and as soon they turn into dust and forgetfulness; some of them without any other interest in the affairs of the world but that they made their parents a little glad and very sorrow-

---

[1] [From rain-giving Jupiter.]

ful; others ride longer in the storm, it may be until seven years of vanity be expired, and then peradventure the sun shines hot upon their heads and they fall into the shades below, into the cover of death and darkness of the grave to hide them. But if the bubble stands the shock of a bigger drop, and outlives the chances of a child, of a careless nurse, of drowning in a pail of water, of being overlaid by a sleepy servant, or such little accidents, then the young man dances like a bubble, empty and gay, and shines like a dove's neck or the image of a rainbow, which hath no substance and whose very imagery and colors are fantastical; and so he dances out the gaiety of his youth, and is all the while in a storm, and endures only because he is not knocked on the head by a drop of bigger rain, or crushed by the pressure of a load of indigested meat, or quenched by the disorder of an ill-placed humor. And to preserve a man alive in the midst of so many chances and hostilities is as great a miracle as to create him; to preserve him from rushing into nothing, and at first to draw him up from nothing, were equally the issues of an almighty power. And therefore the wise men of the world have contended who shall best fit man's condition with words signifying his vanity and short abode. Homer calls a man "a leaf," the smallest, the weakest piece of a short-lived, unsteady plant. Pindar calls him "the dream of a shadow"; another, "the dream of the shadow of smoke." But St. James spake by a more excellent spirit, saying, "Our life is but a vapor," *viz.,* drawn from the earth by a celestial influence; made of smoke, or the lighter parts of water, tossed with every wind, moved by the motion of a superior body, without virtue in itself, lifted up on high or left below, according as it pleases the sun, its foster-father. But it is lighter yet; it is but "appearing"; a fantastic vapor, an apparition, nothing real: it is not so much as a mist, not the matter of a shower, nor substantial enough to make a cloud; but it is like Cassiopeia's chair, or Pelops' shoulder, or the circles of heaven, φαινόμενα,[2] than which you cannot have a word that can signify a verier nothing. And yet the expression is one degree more made diminutive: a "vapor," and "fantastical," or a "mere appearance," and this but for a little while neither; the very dream, the phantasm disappears in a small time, "like the shadow that departeth"; or "like a tale that is told"; or "as a dream when one awaketh." A man is so vain, so unfixed, so perishing a creature, that he cannot long last in the scene of fancy: a man goes off, and is forgotten, like the dream of a distracted person. The sum of all is this: that thou art a man, than whom there is not in the world any greater instance of heights and declensions, of lights and shadows, of misery and folly, of laughter and tears, of groans and death.

And because this consideration is of great usefulness and great necessity to many purposes of wisdom and the spirit, all the succession of time, all the

---

[2] [Phenomena, appearances.]

changes in nature, all the varieties of light and darkness, the thousand thousands of accidents in the world, and every contingency to every man, and to
every creature doth preach our funeral sermon, and calls us to look and see
how the sexton Time throws up the earth and digs a grave where we must
lay our sins or our sorrows, and sow our bodies, till they rise again in a fair,
or in an intolerable, eternity. Every revolution which the sun makes about
the world divides between life and death; and death possesses both those
portions by the next morrow; and we are dead to all those months which we
have already lived, and we shall never live them over again.

And still God makes little periods of our age. First we change our world,
when we come from the womb to feel the warmth of the sun. Then we sleep
and enter into the image of death, in which state we are unconcerned in all
the changes of the world; and if our mothers or our nurses die, or a wild
boar destroy our vineyards, or our king be sick, we regard it not, but during
that state are as disinterested as if our eyes were closed with the clay that
weeps in the bowels of the earth. At the end of seven years our teeth fall and
die before us, representing a formal prologue to the tragedy; and still every
seven years it is odds but we shall finish the last scene. And when nature, or
chance, or vice takes our body in pieces, weakening some parts and loosing
others, we taste the grave and the solemnities of our own funerals, first in
those parts that ministered to vice, and next in them that served for ornament; and in a short time even they that served for necessity become useless
and entangled like the wheels of a broken clock. Baldness is but a dressing to
our funerals, the proper ornament of mourning, and of a person entered very
far into the regions and possession of death; and we have many more of the
same signification: gray hairs, rotten teeth, dim eyes, trembling joints, short
breath, stiff limbs, wrinkled skin, short memory, decayed appetite. Every
day's necessity calls for a reparation of that portion which death fed on all
night, when we lay in his lap and slept in his outer chambers. The very
spirits of a man prey upon the daily portion of bread and flesh, and every
meal is a rescue from one death and lays up for another; and while we think
a thought, we die; and the clock strikes and reckons on our portion of
eternity; we form our words with the breath of our nostrils, we have the less
to live upon for every word we speak.

Thus nature calls us to meditate of death by those things which are the
instruments of acting it, and God by all the variety of His providence makes
us see death everywhere, in all variety of circumstances, and dressed up for
all the fancies and the expectation of every single person. Nature hath given
us one harvest every year, but death hath two; and the spring and the
autumn send throngs of men and women to charnel-houses; and all the
summer long men are recovering from their evils of the spring, till the dog-
days come, and the Srian star makes the summer deadly; and the fruits of

autumn are laid up for all the year's provision, and the man that gathers them eats and surfeits, and dies and needs them not, and himself is laid up for eternity; and he that escapes till winter only stays for another opportunity, which the distempers of that quarter minister to him with great variety. Thus death reigns in all the portions of our time; the autumn with its fruits provides disorders for us, and the winter's cold turns them into sharp diseases, and the spring brings flowers to strew our hearse, and the summer gives green turf and brambles to bind upon our graves. Calentures and surfeit, cold and agues, are the four quarters of the year, and all minister to death; and you can go no whither but you tread upon a dead man's bones.

The wild fellow in Petronius that escaped upon a broken table from the furies of a shipwreck, as he was sunning himself upon the rocky shore espied a man rolled upon his floating bed of waves, ballasted with sand in the folds of his garment, and carried by his civil enemy, the sea, towards the shore to find a grave; and it cast him into some sad thoughts: that peradventure this man's wife in some part of the continent, safe and warm, looks next month for the good man's return; or, it may be, his son knows nothing of the tempest; or his father thinks of that affectionate kiss which still is warm upon the good old man's cheek ever since he took a kind farewell; and he weeps with joy to think how blessed he shall be when his beloved boy returns into the circle of his father's arms. These are the thoughts of mortals, this is the end and sum of all their designs: a dark night and an ill guide, a boisterous sea and a broken cable, a hard rock and a rough wind dashed in pieces the fortune of a whole family, and they that shall weep loudest for the accident are not yet entered into the storm and yet have suffered shipwreck. Then, looking upon the carcass, he knew it, and found it to be the master of the ship, who the day before cast up the accounts of his patrimony and his trade, and named the day when he thought to be at home. See how the man swims who was so angry two days since; his passions are becalmed with the storm, his accounts cast up, his cares at an end, his voyage done, and his gains are the strange events of death, which, whether they be good or evil, the men that are alive seldom trouble themselves concerning the interest of the dead.

But seas alone do not break our vessel in pieces: everywhere we may be shipwrecked. A valiant general, when he is to reap the harvest of his crowns and triumphs, fights unprosperously, or falls into a fever with joy and wine, and changes his laurel into cypress, his triumphal chariot to a hearse, dying the night before he was appointed to perish in the drunkenness of his festival joys. It was a sad arrest of the loosenesses and wilder feasts of the French court, when their King Henry the Second was killed really by the sportive image of a fight. And many brides have died under the hands of paranymphs and maidens, dressing them for uneasy joy, the new and undiscerned chains of marriage; according to the saying of Bensirah, the wise Jew, "the bride went into her chamber, and knew not what should befall her there." Some have been paying their vows, and giving thanks for a prosperous return to their own house, and the roof hath descended upon their heads, and turned their loud religion into the deeper silence of a grave. And how many teeming mothers have rejoiced over their swelling wombs, and pleased themselves in becoming the channels of blessing to a family, and the midwife hath quickly bound their heads and feet, and carried them forth to burial? Or else the birthday of an heir hath seen the coffin of the father brought into the house, and the divided mother hath been forced to travail twice, with a painful birth, and a sadder death.

There is no state, no accident, no circumstance of our life but it hath been soured by some sad instance of a dying friend; a friendly meeting often ends in some sad mischance and makes an eternal parting; and when the poet Aeschylus was sitting under the walls of his house, an eagle hovering over his bald head mistook it for a stone, and let fall his oyster, hoping there to break the shell, but pierced the poor man's skull.

Death meets us everywhere, and is procured by every instrument and in all chances, and enters in at many doors: by violence and secret influence; by the aspect of a star and the stink of a mist; by the emissions of a cloud and the meeting of a vapor; by the fall of a chariot and the stumbling at a stone; by a full meal or an empty stomach; by watching at the wine or by watching at prayers; by the sun or the moon; by a heat or a cold; by sleepless nights or sleeping days; by water frozen into the hardness and sharpness of a dagger, or water thawed into the floods of a river; by a hair or a raisin; by violent motion or sitting still; by severity or dissolution; by God's mercy or God's anger; by everything in providence and everything in manners; by everything in nature and everything in chance. *Eripitur persona, manet res;*[3] we take pains to heap up things useful to our life and get our death in the purchase; and the person is snatched away, and the goods remain. And all this is the law and constitution of nature; it is a punishment to our sins, the unalterable event of providence and the decree of heaven. The chains that confine us to this condition are strong as destiny and immutable as the eternal laws of God.

I have conversed with some men who rejoiced in the death or calamity of others, and accounted it as a judgment upon them for being on the other side and against them in the contention; but within the revolution of a few months the same man met with a more uneasy and unhandsome death; which when I saw, I wept and was afraid; for I knew that it must be so with all men, for we also shall die and end our quarrels and contentions by passing to a final sentence.

---

[3] [The person is snatched away; the thing remains.]

DISCUSSION AND WRITING

1. Define or explain: *deluge, abode, celestial, diminutive, phantasm, contingency, sexton, prologue, charnel house, surfeit, distemper, calenture, ague, peradventure, patrimony, paranymph, mischance, emission, immutable, contention.* What, in context, is the meaning of the italicized words: "born in *vanity* and sin," "signify a *verier* nothing," "heights and *declensions*," "the *sportive* image of a fight," "forced to *travail* twice," "by the *aspect* of a star," "within the *revolution* of a few months"?

2. Like other seventeenth-century divines, Taylor makes constant use of figurative language. Explain passages like "representing a formal prologue to the tragedy," "changes his laurel into cypress." Discuss typical examples of metaphor and simile, of imaginative parallels and analogies.

3. Pindar and Petronius are poets of classical antiquity. What other sources does Taylor rely on for illustrations, parallels, examples?

4. Sum up the essential points in Taylor's view of man.

5. Taylor relies on insistent repetition and variation of a central idea. Describe in detail the way the central idea is developed in this selection.

6. Illustrate and discuss Taylor's use of repetition and parallelism in sentence structure. Analyze a number of typical examples.

7. Is Taylor's rich, elaborate style out of keeping with his somber message? How, if at all, are form and content related in this selection? Argue your answer in detail.

8. How strong is the emphasis on the vanity and shortness of life in contemporary religion, or in your own church?

9. Study the style of a well-known contemporary preacher or evangelist. What is his characteristic method of presenting his message? How effective or persuasive is it?

10. Magazine articles critical of the present state of religion in America range from such general criticisms as Harry C. Meserve, "The New Piety" (*Atlantic,* June 1955) or Curtis Cate, "God and Success" (*Atlantic,* April 1957) to more specific articles like Edward Wakin and Fr. Joseph F. Scheuer, "The American Nun" (*Harper's,* August 1965). Review one of these or a similar article, giving an account of its purpose, a summary and interpretation of its findings, and an estimate of its validity.

FURTHER READING

Famous examples of the devotional literature of the seventeenth century are John Donne's *Devotions upon Emergent Occasions* (1623–1624). A famous example of a baroque prose style is Chapter V of Sir Thomas Browne's *Hydriotaphia, or Urn-Burial* (1658).

THOMAS HOBBES

More than one reader of the British philosophers has found that "besides being philosophers they were uncommonly good writers." One vigorous (if not the most polished) writer among the British philosophers is Thomas Hobbes, whose *Leviathan,* published in 1651, is famous for developing a system of ethics and politics based on enlightened self-interest. Hobbes (1588–1679) was concerned to find a secure foundation for political institutions at a time of civil war and religious controversy. In England, political and religious disunity had led to the temporary overthrow of the monarchy and the establishment of Puritan rule. Influenced in part by scientific and philosophical trends represented earlier by Sir Francis Bacon, Hobbes turned away from traditional views and attempted a radical reconstruction of basic principles. Hobbes has been widely criticized for his unflattering view of human nature. He has been admired for the independence and rigorous internal logic of his thought; for "the gruff, downright John Bullishness of his personality." The following selection is a key chapter in the first part of *Leviathan, or the Matter, Form, and Power of a Commonwealth Ecclesiastical and Civil.*

On the Natural Condition of Mankind

Nature has made men so equal in the faculties of the body and mind as that, though there be found one man sometimes manifestly stronger in body or of quicker mind than another, yet, when all is reckoned together, the difference between man and man is not so considerable as that one man can thereupon claim to himself any benefit to which another may not pretend as well as he. For as to the strength of body, the weakest has strength enough to kill the strongest, either by secret machination or by confederacy with others that are in the same danger with himself.

And as to the faculties of the mind, setting aside the arts grounded upon words, and especially that skill of preceding upon general and infallible rules called science—which very few have and but in few things, as being not a native faculty born with us, nor attained, as prudence, while we look after somewhat else—I find yet a greater equality among men than that of strength. For prudence is but experience, which equal time equally bestows on all men in those things they equally apply themselves unto. That which may perhaps make such equality incredible is but a vain conceit of one's own wisdom, which almost all men think they have in a greater degree than the vulgar—that is, than all men but themselves and a few others whom, by fame or for concurring with themselves, they approve. For such is the nature of men that howsoever they may acknowledge many others to be more witty or more eloquent or more learned, yet they will hardly believe there be many so wise as themselves; for they see their own wit at hand and other men's at a distance. But this proves rather that men are in that point equal than unequal. For there is not ordinarily a greater sign of the equal distribution of anything than that every man is contented with his share.

From this equality of ability arises equality of hope in the attaining of our ends. And therefore if any two men desire the same thing, which nevertheless they cannot both enjoy, they become enemies; and in the way to their end, which is principally their own conservation, and sometimes their delectation only, endeavor to destroy or subdue one another. And from hence it comes to pass that where an invader has no more to fear than another man's single power, if one plant, sow, build, or possess a convenient seat, others may probably be expected to come prepared with forces united to dispossess and deprive him, not only of the fruit of his labor, but also of his life or liberty. And the invader again is in the like danger of another.

And from this diffidence of one another there is no way for any man to secure himself so reasonable as anticipation—that is, by force or wiles to master the persons of all men he can, so long till he see no other power great enough to endanger him; and this is no more than his own conservation requires, and is generally allowed. Also, because there be some that take pleasure in contemplating their own power in the acts of conquest, which they pursue farther than their security requires, if others that otherwise would be glad to be at ease within modest bounds should not by invasion increase their power, they would not be able, long time, by standing only on their defense, to subsist. And by consequence, such augmentation of dominion over men being necessary to a man's conservation, it ought to be allowed him.

Again, men have no pleasure, but on the contrary a great deal of grief, in keeping company where there is no power able to overawe them all. For every man looks that his companion should value him at the same rate he sets upon himself; and upon all signs of contempt or undervaluing naturally endeavors, as far as he dares (which among them that have no common power to keep them in quiet is far enough to make them destroy each other), to extort a greater value from his contemners by damage and from others by the example.

So that in the nature of man we find three principal causes of quarrel: first, competition; secondly, diffidence; thirdly, glory.

The first makes men invade for gain, the second for safety, and the third for reputation. The first use violence to make themselves masters of other men's persons, wives, children, and cattle; the second, to defend them; the third, for trifles, as a word, a smile, a different opinion, and any other sign of undervalue, either direct in their persons or by reflection in their kindred, their friends, their nation, their profession, or their name.

Hereby it is manifest that, during the time men live without a common power to keep them all in awe, they are in that condition which is called war, and such a war as is of every man against every man. For war consists not in battle only, or the act of fighting, but in a tract of time wherein the will to contend by battle is sufficiently known; and therefore the notion of *time* is to be considered in the nature of war as it is in the nature of weather. For as the nature of foul weather lies not in a shower or two of rain but in an inclination thereto of many days together, so the nature of war consists not in actual fighting but in the known disposition thereto during all the time there is no assurance to the contrary. All other time is peace.

Whatsoever, therefore, is consequent to a time of war where every man is enemy to every man, the same is consequent to the time wherein men live without other security than what their own strength and their own invention shall furnish them withal. In such condition there is no place for industry, because the fruit thereof is uncertain: and consequently no culture of the earth; no navigation nor use of the commodities that may be imported by sea; no commodious building; no instruments of moving and removing such things as require much force; no knowledge of the face of the earth; no account of time; no arts; no letters; no society; and, which is worst of all, continual fear and danger of violent death; and the life of man solitary, poor, nasty, brutish, and short.

It may seem strange to some man that has not well weighed these things that nature should thus dissociate and render men apt to invade and destroy one another; and he may therefore, not trusting to this inference made from the passions, desire perhaps to have the same confirmed by experience. Let him therefore consider with himself—when taking a journey he arms himself and seeks to go well accompanied, when going to sleep he locks his doors, when even in his house he locks his chests, and this when he knows there be laws and public officers, armed, to revenge all injuries shall be done him—what opinion he has of his fellow subjects when he rides armed, of his fellow citizens when he locks his doors, and of his children and servants when he locks his chests. Does he not there as much accuse mankind by his actions as I do by my words? But neither of us accuse man's nature in it. The desires and other passions of man are in themselves no sin. No more are the actions that proceed from those passions till they know a law that forbids them, which, till laws be made, they cannot know, nor can any law be made till they have agreed upon the person that shall make it.

It may peradventure be thought there was never such a time nor condition of war as this, and I believe it was never generally so over all the world; but there are many places where they live so now. For the savage people in many places of America, except the government of small families, the concord whereof depends on natural lust, have no government at all and live at this day in that brutish manner as I said before. Howsoever, it may be perceived what manner of life there would be where there were no common power to fear by the manner of life which men that have formerly lived under a peaceful government use to degenerate into in a civil war.

But though there had never been any time wherein particular men were in a condition of war one against another, yet in all times kings and persons of sovereign authority, because of their independency, are in continual jealousies and in the state and posture of gladiators, having their weapons pointing and their eyes fixed on one another—that is, their forts, garrisons, and guns upon the frontiers of their kingdoms, and continual spies upon their neighbors—which is a posture of war. But because they uphold thereby the industry of their subjects, there does not follow from it that misery which accompanies the liberty of particular men.

To this war of every man against every man, this also is consequent: that nothing can be unjust. The notions of right and wrong, justice and injustice, have there no place. Where there is no common power, there is no law; where no law, no injustice. Force and fraud are in war the two cardinal virtues. Justice and injustice are none of the faculties neither of the body nor mind. If they were, they might be in a man that were alone in the world, as well as his senses and passions. They are qualities that relate to men in society, not in solitude. It is consequent also to the same condition that there be no propriety, no dominion, no *mine* and *thine* distinct; but only that to be every man's that he can get, and for so long as he can keep it. And thus much for the ill condition which man by mere nature is actually placed in, though with a possibility to come out of it consisting partly in the passions, partly in his reason.

The passions that incline men to peace are fear of death, desire of such things as are necessary to commodious living, and a hope by their industry to obtain them. And reason suggests convenient articles of peace, upon which men may be drawn to agreement. These articles are they which otherwise are called the Laws of Nature.

DISCUSSION AND WRITING

1. Define or explain: *machination, confederacy, infallible, delectation, augmentation, contend, consequent, commodious, peradventure, concord, posture, gladiator, cardinal* (adj.), *propriety, dominion.* Hobbes sometimes uses a familiar word in an unfamiliar or unusual sense. For the following, find the meaning that best fits the context: *conceit,*

vulgar, wit, conservation, seat, tract, cattle, industry, culture, articles. List features of Hobbes's diction and grammatical usage that are archaic or old-fashioned.

2. Hobbes has a reputation for rigorously systematic exposition. Outline his argument, paying special attention to logical continuity and transition.

3. Examine Hobbes's use and definition of such familiar abstractions as "equality," "peace," "sin," and "justice." Compare his definitions with those you consider widely accepted or with your own.

4. In one paragraph, sum up Hobbes's view of man and society.

5. Summarize Hobbes's account of war and martial glory. To what extent does his description apply to international relations in modern times? Are there, or should there be, codes of warfare different from those described by Hobbes?

6. Should Hobbes's view of human nature be called "realistic" or "cynical"?

7. Compare and contrast Hobbes's view of man with that implied in Lippmann's "The Renewal of the Public Philosophy" or in Thoreau's "On the Duty of Civil Disobedience."

8. What would a modern society, or a modern system of laws, be like if it took full account of Hobbes's view of "the natural condition of mankind"? Refer to specific passages from the essay for support.

9. Of the three natural causes for quarrel cited by Hobbes, how important as a motive in American life is the desire for glory or reputation?

10. Is there such a thing as a prevailing popular view of man's nature in contemporary American society? How does it compare with that developed by Hobbes?

FURTHER READING

For two contrasting nineteenth-century views of the "natural condition of mankind" see John Stuart Mill's essay on "Nature" (in *Three Essays on Religion*) and Robert Louis Stevenson's "Pulvis et Umbra" (in *Memories and Portraits*). A modern fable taking a grim view of man in a state of nature is William Golding's novel *Lord of the Flies* (1955).

THOMAS HENRY HUXLEY

Thomas Henry Huxley (1825–1895) was the kind of popularizer who is the "liaison officer between the world's thinkers and mankind at large." Trained as a physician, he established a firm reputation through his field work in zoology as an assistant ship's surgeon and through his studies in comparative anatomy as a teacher and lecturer in later years. Huxley became an effective spokesman for the natural sciences at a time when they were under attack as a threat to established religion and to the cultural values of traditional liberal education. More than any one man, he was successful in making popular opinion regard Darwin's theory of evolution no longer as a slur on man's dignity but as a fruitful hypothesis. Apart from his participation in specific controversies, however, Huxley offers an important alternative to the picture of the man of science as a narrow-minded specialist. He represents the scientist of impressive intellectual integrity and humane temperament, whom the humanities banish from their ranks at their peril. "On the Advisableness of Improving Natural Knowledge" was first delivered as a lecture in 1866. It has the careful organization, deliberate pace, and straightforward tone of the nineteenth-century lecture at its best.

On the Advisableness of Improving Natural Knowledge

This time two hundred years ago—in the beginning of January, 1666—those of our forefathers who inhabited this great and ancient city, took breath between the shocks of two fearful calamities: one not quite past, although its fury had abated; the other to come.

Within a few yards of the very spot on which we are assembled, so the tradition runs, that painful and deadly malady, the plague, appeared in the latter months of 1664; and, though no new visitor, smote the people of England, and especially of her capital, with a violence unknown before, in the course of the following year. The hand of a master has pictured what happened in those dismal months; and in that truest of fictions, "The History of the Plague Year," Defoe shows death, with every accompaniment of pain and terror, stalking through the narrow streets of old London, and changing their busy hum into a silence broken only by the wailing of the mourners of fifty thousand dead; by the woeful denunciations and mad prayers of fanatics; and by the madder yells of despairing profligates.

But, about this time in 1666, the death-rate had sunk to nearly its ordinary amount; a case of plague occurred only here and there, and the richer citizens who had flown from the pest had returned to their dwellings. The remnant of the people began to toil at the accustomed round of duty, or of pleasure; and the stream of city life bid fair to flow back along its old bed, with renewed and uninterrupted vigor.

The newly kindled hope was deceitful. The great plague, indeed, returned no more; but what it had done for the Londoners, the great fire, which broke out in the autumn of 1666, did for London; and, in September of that year, a heap of ashes and the indestructible energy of the people were all that remained of the glory of five-sixths of the city within the walls.

Our forefathers had their own ways of accounting for each of these calamities. They submitted to the plague in humility and in penitence, for they believed it to be the judgment of God. But, towards the fire they were furiously indignant, interpreting it as the effect of the malice of man,—as the work of the Republicans, or of the Papists,[1] according as their prepossessions ran in favor of loyalty or of Puritanism.

It would, I fancy, have fared but ill with one who, standing where I now stand, in what was then a thickly-peopled and fashionable part of London, should have broached to our ancestors the doctrine which I now propound to you—that all their hypotheses were alike wrong; that the plague was no more, in their sense, Divine judgment, than the fire was the work of any political, or of any religious, sect; but that they were themselves the authors of both plague and fire, and that they must look to themselves to prevent the recurrence of calamities, to all appearance so peculiarly beyond the reach of human control—so evidently the result of the wrath of God, or of the craft and subtlety of an enemy.

And one may picture to one's self how harmoniously the holy cursing of the Puritan of that day would have chimed in with the unholy cursing and the crackling wit of the Rochesters and Sedleys,[2] and with the revilings of the political fanatics, if my imaginary plain dealer had gone on to say that, if the return of such misfortunes were ever rendered impossible, it would not be in virtue of the victory of the faith of Laud,[3] or that of Milton; and, as little, by the triumph of republicanism, as by that of monarchy. But that the one thing needful for compassing this end was that the people of England should second the efforts of an insignificant corporation, the establishment of which a few years before the epoch of the great plague and the great fire, had been as little noticed, as they were conspicuous.

Some twenty years before the outbreak of the plague a few calm and thoughtful students banded themselves together for the purpose, as they phrased it, of "improving natural knowledge." The ends they proposed to attain cannot be stated more clearly than in the words of one of the founders of the organization:—

> Our business was (precluding matters of theology and state affairs) to discourse and consider of philosophical enquiries, and such as related thereunto:—as Physick, Anatomy, Geometry, Astronomy, Navigation, Staticks, Magneticks, Chymicks, Mechanicks, and Natural Experiments;

[1] [The anti-monarchical Puritans or the Roman Catholics, both assumed to be conspiring against the existing order in church and state.]

[2] [Courtiers and poets famous for cynicism and loose living.]

[3] [Anglican archbishop, foe of the Puritans.]

with the state of these studies and their cultivation at home and abroad. We then discoursed of the circulation of the blood, the valves in the veins, the venæ lacteæ,[4] the lymphatic vessels, the Copernican hypothesis, the nature of comets and new stars, the satellites of Jupiter, the oval shape (as it then appeared) of Saturn, the Spots on the sun and its turning on its own axis, the inequalities and selenography of the moon, the several phases of Venus and Mercury, the improvement of telescopes and grinding of glasses for that purpose, the weight of air, the possibility or impossibility of vacuities and nature's abhorrence thereof, the Torricellian[5] experiment in quicksilver, the descent of heavy bodies and the degree of acceleration therein, with divers other things of like nature, some of which were then but new discoveries, and others not so generally known and embraced as now they are; with other things appertaining to what hath been called the New Philosophy, which, from the times of Galileo at Florence, and Sir Francis Bacon (Lord Verulam) in England, hath been much cultivated in Italy, France, Germany, and other parts abroad, as well as with us in England.

The learned Dr. Wallis, writing in 1696, narrates, in these words, what happened half a century before, or about 1645. The associates met at Oxford, in the rooms of Dr. Wilkins, who was destined to become a bishop; and subsequently coming together in London, they attracted the notice of the king. And it is a strange evidence of the taste for knowledge which the most obviously worthless of the Stuarts shared with his father and grandfather, that Charles the Second was not content with saying witty things about his philosophers, but did wise things with regard to them. For he not only bestowed upon them such attention as he could spare from his poodles and his mistresses, but, being in his usual state of impecuniosity, begged for them of the Duke of Ormond; and, that step being without effect, gave them Chelsea College, a charter, and a mace: crowning his favors in the best way they could be crowned, by burdening them no further with royal patronage or state interference.

Thus it was that the half-dozen young men, studious of the "New Philosophy," who met in one another's lodgings in Oxford or in London, in the middle of the seventeenth century, grew in numerical and in real strength, until, in its latter part, the "Royal Society for the Improvement of Natural Knowledge" had already become famous, and had acquired a claim upon the veneration of Englishmen, which it has ever since retained, as the principal focus of scientific activity in our islands, and the chief champion of the cause it was formed to support.

It was by the aid of the Royal Society that Newton published his "Prin-

4 [Lacteal veins.]
5 [Torricelli was an Italian physicist.]

cipia." If all the books in the world, except the "Philosophical Transactions," were destroyed, it is safe to say that the foundations of physical science would remain unshaken, and that the vast intellectual progress of the last two centuries would be largely, though incompletely, recorded. Nor have any signs of halting or of decrepitude manifested themselves in our own times. As in Dr. Wallis's days, so in these, "our business is, precluding theology and state affairs, to discourse and consider of philosophical enquiries." But our "Mathematick" is one which Newton would have to go to school to learn; our "Staticks, Mechanicks, Magneticks, Chymicks, and Natural Experiments" constitute a mass of physical and chemical knowledge, a glimpse at which would compensate Galileo for the doings of a score of inquisitorial cardinals; our "Physick" and "Anatomy" have embraced such infinite varieties of being, have laid open such new worlds in time and space, have grappled, not unsuccessfully, with such complex problems, that the eyes of Vesalius[6] and of Harvey might be dazzled by the sight of the tree that has grown out of their grain of mustard seed.

The fact is perhaps rather too much, than too little, forced upon one's notice, nowadays, that all this marvelous intellectual growth has a no less wonderful expression in practical life; and that, in this respect, if in no other, the movement symbolized by the progress of the Royal Society stands without a parallel in the history of mankind.

A series of volumes as bulky as the "Transactions of the Royal Society" might possibly be filled with the subtle speculations of the Schoolmen; not improbably, the obtaining a mastery over the products of medieval thought might necessitate an even greater expenditure of time and of energy than the acquirement of the "New Philosophy"; but though such work engrossed the best intellects of Europe for a longer time than has elapsed since the great fire, its effects were "writ in water," so far as our social state is concerned.

On the other hand, if the noble first President of the Royal Society could revisit the upper air and once more gladden his eyes with a sight of the familiar mace, he would find himself in the midst of a material civilization more different from that of his day, than that of the seventeenth was from that of the first century. And if Lord Brouncker's native sagacity had not deserted his ghost, he would need no long reflection to discover that all these great ships, these railways, these telegraphs, these factories, these printing-presses, without which the whole fabric of modern English society would collapse into a mass of stagnant and starving pauperism,—that all these pillars of our State are but the ripples and the bubbles upon the surface of that great spiritual stream, the springs of which only, he and his fellows were privileged to see; and seeing, to recognize as that which it behooved them above all things to keep pure and undefiled.

6 [Belgian anatomist.]

It may not be too great a flight of imagination to conceive our noble *revenant* not forgetful of the great troubles of his own day, and anxious to know how often London had been burned down since his time, and how often the plague had carried off its thousands. He would have to learn that, although London contains tenfold the inflammable matter that it did in 1666; though, not content with filling our rooms with woodwork and light draperies, we must needs lead inflammable and explosive gases into every corner of our streets and houses, we never allow even a street to burn down. And if he asked how this had come about, we should have to explain that the improvement of natural knowledge has furnished us with dozens of machines for throwing water upon fires, any one of which would have furnished the ingenious Mr. Hooke, the first "curator and experimenter" of the Royal Society, with ample materials for discourse before half a dozen meetings of that body; and that, to say truth, except for the progress of natural knowledge, we should not have been able to make even the tools by which these machines are constructed. And, further, it would be necessary to add, that although severe fires sometimes occur and inflict great damage, the loss is very generally compensated by societies, the operations of which have been rendered possible only by the progress of natural knowledge in the direction of mathematics, and the accumulation of wealth in virtue of other natural knowledge.

But the plague? My Lord Brouncker's observation would not, I fear, lead him to think that Englishmen of the nineteenth century are purer in life, or more fervent in religious faith, than the generation which could produce a Boyle, an Evelyn,[7] and a Milton. He might find the mud of society at the bottom, instead of at the top, but I fear that the sum total would be as deserving of swift judgment as at the time of the Restoration. And it would be our duty to explain once more, and this time not without shame, that we have no reason to believe that it is the improvement of our faith, nor that of our morals, which keeps the plague from our city; but, again, that it is the improvement of our natural knowledge.

We have learned that pestilences will only take up their abode among those who have prepared unswept and ungarnished residences for them. Their cities must have narrow, unwatered streets, foul with accumulated garbage. Their houses must be ill-drained, ill-lighted, ill-ventilated. Their subjects must be ill-washed, ill-fed, ill-clothed. The London of 1665 was such a city. The cities of the East, where plague has an enduring dwelling, are such cities. We, in later times, have learned somewhat of Nature, and partly obey her. Because of this partial improvement of our natural knowledge and of that fractional obedience, we have no plague; because that knowledge is still very imperfect and that obedience yet incomplete, typhoid is our com-

[7] [John Evelyn, diarist noted for his piety.]

panion and cholera our visitor. But it is not presumptuous to express the belief that, when our knowledge is more complete and our obedience the expression of our knowledge, London will count her centuries of freedom from typhoid and cholera, as she now gratefully reckons her two hundred years of ignorance of that plague which swooped upon her thrice in the first half of the seventeenth century.

Surely, there is nothing in these explanations which is not fully borne out by the facts? Surely, the principles involved in them are now admitted among the fixed beliefs of all thinking men? Surely, it is true that our countrymen are less subject to fire, famine, pestilence, and all the evils which result from a want of command over and due anticipation of the course of Nature, than were the countrymen of Milton; and health, wealth, and well-being are more abundant with us than with them? But no less certainly is the difference due to the improvement of our knowledge of Nature, and the extent to which that improved knowledge has been incorporated with the household words of men, and has supplied the springs of their daily actions.

Granting for a moment, then, the truth of that which the depreciators of natural knowledge are so fond of urging, that its improvement can only add to the resources of our material civilization; admitting it to be possible that the founders of the Royal Society themselves looked for no other reward than this, I cannot confess that I was guilty of exaggeration when I hinted, that to him who had the gift of distinguishing between prominent events and important events, the origin of a combined effort on the part of mankind to improve natural knowledge might have loomed larger than the Plague and have outshone the glare of the Fire; as a something fraught with a wealth of beneficence to mankind, in comparison with which the damage done by those ghastly evils would shrink into insignificance.

It is very certain that for every victim slain by the plague, hundreds of mankind exist and find a fair share of happiness in the world, by the aid of the spinning jenny. And the great fire, at its worst, could not have burned the supply of coal, the daily working of which, in the bowels of the earth, made possible by the steam pump, gives rise to an amount of wealth to which the millions lost in old London are but as an old song.

But spinning jenny and steam pump are, after all, but toys, possessing an accidental value; and natural knowledge creates multitudes of more subtle contrivances, the praises of which do not happen to be sung because they are not directly convertible into instruments for creating wealth. When I contemplate natural knowledge squandering such gifts among men, the only appropriate comparison I can find for her is to liken her to such a peasant woman as one sees in the Alps, striding ever upward, heavily burdened, and with mind bent only on her home; but yet, without effort and without thought, knitting for her children. Now stockings are good and comfortable things, and the children will undoubtedly be much the better for them; but surely it would be short-sighted, to say the least of it, to depreciate this toiling mother as a mere stocking-machine—a mere provider of physical comforts.

However, there are blind leaders of the blind, and not a few of them, who take this view of natural knowledge, and can see nothing in the bountiful mother of humanity but a sort of comfort-grinding machine. According to them, the improvement of natural knowledge always has been, and always must be, synonymous with no more than the improvement of the material resources and the increase of the gratifications of men.

Natural knowledge is, in their eyes, no real mother of mankind, bringing them up with kindness, and, if need be, with sternness, in the way they should go, and instructing them in all things needful for their welfare; but a sort of fairy godmother, ready to furnish her pets with shoes of swiftness, swords of sharpness, and omnipotent Aladdin's lamps, so that they may have telegraphs to Saturn, and see the other side of the moon, and thank God they are better than their benighted ancestors.

If this talk were true, I, for one, should not greatly care to toil in the service of natural knowledge. I think I would just as soon be quietly chipping my own flint ax after the manner of my forefathers a few thousand years back, as be troubled with the endless malady of thought which now infests us all, for such reward. But I venture to say that such views are contrary alike to reason and to fact. Those who discourse in such fashion seem to me to be so intent upon trying to see what is above Nature, or what is behind her, that they are blind to what stares them in the face in her.

I should not venture to speak thus strongly if my justification were not to be found in the simplest and most obvious facts,—if it needed more than an appeal to the most notorious truths to justify my assertion that the improvement of natural knowledge, whatever direction it has taken and however low the aims of those who may have commenced it, has not only conferred practical benefits on men but, in so doing, has effected a revolution in their conceptions of the universe and of themselves, and has profoundly altered their modes of thinking and their views of right and wrong. I say that natural knowledge, seeking to satisfy natural wants, has found the ideas which can alone still spiritual cravings. I say that natural knowledge, in desiring to ascertain the laws of comfort, has been driven to discover those of conduct, and to lay the foundations of a new morality.

Let us take these points separately; and first, what great ideas has natural knowledge introduced into men's minds?

I cannot but think that the foundations of all natural knowledge were laid when the reason of man first came face to face with the facts of Nature; when the savage first learned that the fingers of one hand are fewer than those of both; that it is shorter to cross a stream than to head it; that a stone stops where it is unless it be moved, and that it drops from the hand which lets it go; that light and heat come and go with the sun; that sticks burn away in a fire; that plants and animals grow and die; that if he struck his fellow savage a blow he would make him angry, and perhaps get a blow in return, while if he offered him a fruit he would please him, and perhaps receive a fish in exchange. When men had acquired this much knowledge, the outlines, rude though they were, of mathematics, of physics, of chemistry of biology, of moral, economical, and political science, were sketched. Nor did the germ of religion fail when science began to bud. Listen to words which, though new, are yet three thousand years old:—

> ". . . When in heaven the stars about the moon
> Look beautiful, when all the winds are laid,
> And every height comes out, and jutting peak
> And valley, and the immeasurable heavens
> Break open to their highest, and all the stars
> Shine, and the shepherd gladdens in his heart."

If the half savage Greek could share our feelings thus far, it is irrational to doubt that he went further, to find as we do, that upon that brief gladness there follows a certain sorrow,—the little light of awakened human intelligence shines so mere a spark amidst the abyss of the unknown and unknowable; seems so insufficient to do more than illuminate the imperfections that cannot be remedied, the aspirations that cannot be realized, of man's own nature. But in this sadness, this consciousness of the limitation of man, this sense of an open secret which he cannot penetrate, lies the essence of all religion; and the attempt to embody it in the forms furnished by the intellect is the origin of the higher theologies.

Thus it seems impossible to imagine but that the foundations of all knowledge—secular or sacred—were laid when intelligence dawned, though the superstructure remained for long ages so slight and feeble as to be compatible with the existence of almost any general view respecting the mode of governance of the universe. No doubt, from the first, there were certain phenomena which, to the rudest mind, presented a constancy of occurrence, and suggested that a fixed order ruled, at any rate, among them. I doubt if the grossest of Fetish worshipers ever imagined that a stone must have a god within it to make it fall, or that a fruit had a god within it to make it taste sweet. With regard to such matters as these, it is hardly questionable that mankind from the first took strictly positive and scientific views.

But, with respect to all the less familiar occurrences which present themselves, uncultured man, no doubt, has always taken himself as the standard of comparison, as the center and measure of the world; nor could he well avoid doing so. And finding that his apparently uncaused will has a powerful effect in giving rise to many occurrences, he naturally enough ascribed other and greater events to other and greater volitions, and came to look upon the world and all that therein is, as the product of the volitions of persons like himself, but stronger, and capable of being appeased or angered, as he himself might be soothed or irritated. Through such conceptions of the plan and working of the universe all mankind have passed, or are passing. And we may now consider what has been the effect of the improvement of natural knowledge on the views of men who have reached this stage, and who have begun to cultivate natural knowledge with no desire but that of "increasing God's honor and bettering man's estate."

For example, what could seem wiser, from a mere material point of view, more innocent, from a theological one, to an ancient people, than that they should learn the exact succession of the seasons, as warnings for their husbandmen; or the position of the stars, as guides to their rude navigators? But what has grown out of this search for natural knowledge of so merely useful a character? You all know the reply. Astronomy,—which of all sciences has filled men's minds with general ideas of a character most foreign to their daily experience, and has, more than any other, rendered it impossible for them to accept the beliefs of their fathers. Astronomy,—which tells them that this so vast and seemingly solid earth is but an atom among atoms, whirling, no man knows whither, through illimitable space; which demonstrates that what we call the peaceful heaven above us, is but that space, filled by an infinitely subtle matter whose particles are seething and surging, like the waves of an angry sea; which opens up to us infinite regions where nothing is known, or ever seems to have been known, but matter and force, operating according to rigid rules; which leads us to contemplate phenomena the very nature of which demonstrates that they must have had a beginning, and that they must have an end, but the very nature of which also proves that the beginning was, to our conceptions of time, infinitely remote, and that the end is as immeasurably distant.

But it is not alone those who pursue astronomy who ask for bread and receive ideas. What more harmless than the attempt to lift and distribute water by pumping it; what more absolutely and grossly utilitarian? Yet out of pumps grew the discussions about Nature's abhorrence of a vacuum; and then it was discovered that Nature does not abhor a vacuum, but that air has weight; and that notion paved the way for the doctrine that all matter has weight, and that the force which produces weight is co-extensive with the universe,—in short, to the theory of universal gravitation and endless force. While learning how to handle gases led to the discovery of oxygen, and to modern chemistry, and to the notion of the indestructibility of matter.

Again, what simpler, or more absolutely practical, than the attempt to keep the axle of a wheel from heating when the wheel turns round very fast?

How useful for carters and gig drivers to know something about this; and how good were it, if any ingenious person would find out the cause of such phenomena, and thence educe a general remedy for them. Such an ingenious person was Count Rumford; and he and his successors have landed us in the theory of the persistence, or indestructibility, of force. And in the infinitely minute, as in the infinitely great, the seekers after natural knowledge of the kinds called physical and chemical, have everywhere found a definite order and succession of events which seem never to be infringed.

And how has it fared with "Physick" and Anatomy? Have the anatomist, the physiologist, or the physician, whose business it has been to devote themselves assiduously to that eminently practical and direct end, the alleviation of the sufferings of mankind,—have they been able to confine their vision more absolutely to the strictly useful? I fear they are the worst offenders of all. For if the astronomer has set before us the infinite magnitude of space, and the practical eternity of the duration of the universe; if the physical and chemical philosophers have demonstrated the infinite minuteness of its constituent parts, and the practical eternity of matter and of force; and if both have alike proclaimed the universality of a definite and predictable order and succession of events, the workers in biology have not only accepted all these, but have added more startling theses of their own. For, as the astronomers discover in the earth no center of the universe, but an eccentric speck, so the naturalists find man to be no center of the living world, but one amidst endless modifications of life; and as the astronomer observes the mark of practically endless time set upon the arrangements of the solar system so the student of life finds the records of ancient forms of existence peopling the world for ages, which, in relation to human experience, are infinite.

Furthermore, the physiologist finds life to be as dependent for its manifestation on particular molecular arrangements as any physical or chemical phenomenon; and wherever he extends his researches, fixed order and unchanging causation reveal themselves, as plainly as in the rest of Nature.

Nor can I find that any other fate has awaited the germ of Religion. Arising, like all other kinds of knowledge, out of action and interaction of man's mind with that which is not man's mind, it has taken the intellectual coverings of Fetishism or Polytheism; of Theism or Atheism; of Superstition or Rationalism. With these, and their relative merits and demerits, I have nothing to do; but this it is needful for my purpose to say, that if the religion of the present differs from that of the past, it is because the theology of the present has become more scientific than that of the past; because it has not only renounced idols of wood and idols of stone, but begins to see the necessity of breaking in pieces the idols built up of books and traditions and fine-spun ecclesiastical cobwebs: and of cherishing the noblest and most human of man's emotions, by worship "for the most part of the silent sort" at the altar of the Unknown.

Such are a few of the new conceptions implanted in our minds by the improvement of natural knowledge. Men have acquired the ideas of the practically infinite extent of the universe and of its practical eternity; they are familiar with the conception that our earth is but an infinitesimal fragment of that part of the universe which can be seen; and that, nevertheless, its duration is, as compared with our standards of time, infinite. They have further acquired the idea that man is but one of innumerable forms of life now existing in the globe, and that the present existences are but the last of an immeasurable series of predecessors. Moreover, every step they have made in natural knowledge has tended to extend and rivet in their minds the conception of a definite order of the universe—which is embodied in what are called, by an unhappy metaphor, the laws of Nature—and to narrow the range and loosen the force of men's belief in spontaneity, or in changes other than such as arise out of that definite order itself.

Whether these ideas are well or ill founded is not the question. No one can deny that they exist, and have been the inevitable outgrowth of the improvement of natural knowledge. And if so, it cannot be doubted that they are changing the form of men's most cherished and most important convictions.

And as regards the second point—the extent to which the improvement of natural knowledge has remodeled and altered what may be termed the intellectual ethics of men,—what are among the moral convictions most fondly held by barbarous and semi-barbarous people?

They are the convictions that authority is the soundest basis of belief; that merit attaches to a readiness to believe; that the doubting disposition is a bad one, and scepticism a sin; that when good authority has pronounced what is to be believed, and faith has accepted it, reason has no further duty. There are many excellent persons who yet hold by these principles, and it is not my present business, or intention, to discuss their views. All I wish to bring clearly before your minds is the unquestionable fact, that the improvement of natural knowledge is effected by methods which directly give the lie to all these convictions, and assume the exact reverse of each to be true.

The improver of natural knowledge absolutely refuses to acknowledge authority, as such. For him, scepticism is the highest of duties; blind faith the one unpardonable sin. And it cannot be otherwise, for every great advance in natural knowledge has involved the absolute rejection of authority, the cherishing of the keenest scepticism, the annihilation of the spirit of blind faith; and the most ardent votary of science holds his firmest convictions, not because the men he most venerates hold them; not because their verity is testified by portents and wonders; but because his experience teaches him that whenever he chooses to bring these convictions into contact with their primary source, Nature—whenever he thinks fit to test them by appealing to experiment and to observation—Nature will comfirm them. The man of science has learned to believe in justification, not by faith, but by verification.

Thus, without for a moment pretending to despise the practical results of the improvement of natural knowledge, and its beneficial influence on material civilization, it must, I think, be admitted that the great ideas, some of which I have indicated, and the ethical spirit which I have endeavored to sketch, in the few moments which remained at my disposal, constitute the real and permanent significance of natural knowledge.

If these ideas be destined, as I believe they are, to be more and more firmly established as the world grows older; if that spirit be fated, as I believe it is, to extend itself into all departments of human thought, and to become coextensive with the range of knowledge; if, as our race approaches its maturity, it discovers, as I believe it will, that there is but one kind of knowledge and but one method of acquiring it; then we, who are still children, may justly feel it is our highest duty to recognize the advisableness of improving natural knowledge, and so to aid ourselves and our successors in our course towards the noble goal which lies before mankind.

DISCUSSION AND WRITING

1. Define or explain: *profligate, penitence, prepossession, broach, propound, revile, selenography, impecunious, mace, veneration, decrepitude, inquisitorial, engross, sagacity, behoove, revenant, depreciator, fraught, gratification, superstructure, fetish, volition, utilitarian, educe, polytheism, theism, rationalism, infinitesimal, votary, verity.* Explain the meaning in context of "for *compassing* this end," "speculations of the *Schoolmen*," "*fractional* obedience," "the most *notorious* truths," "strictly *positive*."

2. Explain historical references. Among the patron saints of modern science mentioned in the essay are Copernicus, Galileo, Sir Francis Bacon, Sir Isaac Newton, and William Harvey. Look them up and describe briefly their significance and contribution.

3. Summarize Huxley's view of the essential features of science as a method of controlling external nature. Then restate in your own words his account of the moral and philosophical dimensions of science, its influence on modern man's view of himself and the universe. What over-all definition of science or the "scientific spirit" emerges from the essay?

4. What are Huxley's views on the essence, origin, and historical role of religion? Would you call him "irreligious" or "hostile to religion"? Cite detailed evidence.

5. What does this essay show about Huxley's skill and effectiveness as a speaker and writer? Examine the organization of the essay, the choice and presentation of material, the use of forceful language. What is Huxley's strategy as a persuasive writer?

6. Compare and contrast Huxley's view of science and religion with that of William James in "The Will to Believe."

7. How prevalent in contemporary American society is the view of science as "a sort of fairy godmother"? Or, to what extent does American education recognize Huxley's principle that "scepticism is the highest of duties"?

8. W. T. Stace said, "It matters little what the doctors of science or the doctors of philosophy think, believe, or say among themselves in their cloisters. What humanity thinks and believes—that is what matters." To what extent have the ideas developed in Huxley's essay become part of the thought and belief of the average newspaper reader or voter?

9. In 1928, J. B. S. Haldane claimed that the results of scientific research "have always taken the public and the politicians completely by surprise. The present disturbed condition of humanity is largely the result of this unpreparedness." Have events since tended to support or to invalidate Haldane's charge? In what ways?

10. If a student wants to understand some basic principles of modern science and its role in the modern world, which natural science should he study? Why?

FURTHER READING

Among authors who have written on science and its role in the modern world are James B. Conant, *On Understanding Science* (1947), and C. P. Snow, *The Two Cultures and the Scientific Revolution* (1959). Some discussions of the relationship between science and faith are Bertrand Russell, "A Free Man's Worship," in *Mysticism and Logic* (1929); Albert Einstein, "Science and Religion," in *Science, Philosophy, and Religion: A Symposium* (1941); W. T. Stace, "Man against Darkness," *Atlantic,* September 1948; and Arthur H. Compton, "Science and Man's Freedom," *Atlantic,* October 1957.

ROBERT LOUIS STEVENSON

Robert Louis Stevenson (1850–1894) is best known as the author of *Treasure Island* (1883) and *The Strange Case of Dr. Jekyll and Mr. Hyde* (1886). In addition to being a famous story-teller, Stevenson was a master of the informal essay, a literary form traditionally devoted to personal reflection in a style colored by humor or whimsy though not ruling out an underlying serious purpose. In spite of continuous bad health (he died of tuberculosis), Stevenson became known as a representative of a positive, zestful attitude toward life that has little in common with the more superficial modern varieties of "positive thinking." Stevenson's style, which may strike the modern reader as quaint at first glance, in its gusto and richness of color reflects the personality the author assumes in his essays.

An Apology for Idlers

BOSWELL: We grow weary when idle.

JOHNSON: That is, sir, because others being busy, we want company; but if we were all idle, there would be no growing weary; we should all entertain one another.

Just now, when everyone is bound, under pain of a decree in absence convicting them of *lèse*-respectability, to enter on some lucrative profession, and labor therein with something not far short of enthusiasm, a cry from the opposite party, who are content when they have enough, and like to look on and enjoy in the meanwhile, savors a little of bravado and gasconade. And yet this should not be. Idleness so called, which does not consist in doing nothing, but in doing a great deal not recognized in the dogmatic formularies of the ruling class, has as good a right to state its position as industry itself. It is admitted that the presence of people who refuse to enter in the great handicap race for sixpenny pieces, is at once an insult and a disenchantment for those who do. A fine fellow (as we see so many) takes his determination, votes for sixpences, and in the emphatic Americanism 'goes for' them. And while such a one is ploughing distressfully up the road, it is not hard to understand his resentment, when he perceives cool persons in the meadows by the wayside, lying with a handkerchief over their ears and a glass at their elbow. Alexander is touched in a very delicate place by the disregard of Diogenes. Where was the glory of having taken Rome for those tumultuous barbarians, who poured into the Senate-house, and found the Fathers sitting silent and unmoved by their success? It is a sore thing to have labored along and scaled the arduous hilltops, and when all is done find humanity indifferent to your achievement. Hence physicists condemn the unphysical; financiers have only a superficial toleration for those who know little of stocks; literary persons despise the unlettered; and people of all pursuits combine to disparage those who have none.

But though this is one difficulty of the subject, it is not the greatest. You could not be put in prison for speaking against industry, but you can be sent to Coventry for speaking like a fool. The greatest difficulty with most subjects is to do them well; therefore, please to remember this is an apology. It is certain that much may be judiciously argued in favor of diligence; only there is something to be said against it, and that is what, on the present occasion, I have to say. To state one argument is not necessarily to be deaf to all others, and that a man has written a book of travels in Montenegro, is no reason why he should never have been to Richmond.

It is surely beyond a doubt that people should be a good deal idle in youth. For though here and there a Lord Macaulay may escape from school honors with all his wits about him, most boys pay so dear for their medals that they never afterwards have a shot in their locker, and begin the world bankrupt. And the same holds true during all the time a lad is educating himself, or suffering others to educate him. It must have been a very foolish old gentleman who addressed Johnson at Oxford in these words: 'Young man, ply your book diligently now, and acquire a stock of knowledge; for when years come upon you, you will find that poring upon books will be but an irksome task.' The old gentleman seems to have been unaware that many other things besides reading grow irksome, and not a few become impossible, by the time a man has to use spectacles and cannot walk without a stick. Books are good enough in their own way, but they are a mighty bloodless substitute for life. It seems a pity to sit like the Lady of Shalott, peering into a mirror with your back turned on all the bustle and glamor of reality. And if a man reads very hard, as the old anecdote reminds us, he will have little time for thought.

If you look back on your own education, I am sure it will not be the full, vivid, instructive hours of truantry that you regret; you would rather cancel some lack-luster periods between sleep and waking in the class. For my own part, I have attended a good many lectures in my time. I still remember that the spinning of a top is a case of Kinetic Stability. I still remember that Emphyteusis is not a disease, nor Stillicide a crime. But though I would not willingly part with such scraps of science, I do not set the same store by them as by certain other odds and ends that I came by in the open street while I was playing truant. This is not the moment to dilate on that mighty place of education, which was the favorite school of Dickens and of Balzac, and turns out yearly many inglorious masters in the Science of the Aspects of life. Suffice it to say this: if a lad does not learn in the streets, it is because he has no faculty of learning. Nor is the truant always in the streets, for if he prefers, he may go out by the gardened suburbs into the country. He may pitch on some tuft of lilacs over a burn, and smoke innumerable pipes to the tune of the water on the stones. A bird will sing in the thicket. And there he may fall into a vein of kindly thought, and see things in a new perspective. Why, if this be not education, what is? We may conceive Mr. Worldly Wiseman accosting such a one, and the conversation that should thereupon ensue:

'How now, young fellow, what dost thou here?'

'Truly, sir, I take mine ease.'

'Is not this the hour of the class? and should'st thou not be plying thy Book with diligence, to the end thou mayest obtain knowledge?'

'Nay, but thus also I follow after Learning, by your leave.'

'Learning, quotha! After what fashion, I pray thee? Is it mathematics?'

'No, to be sure.'

'Is it metaphysics?'

'Nor that.'

'Is it some language?'

'Nay, it is no language.'

'Is it a trade?'

'Nor a trade neither.'

'Why, then, what is't?'

'Indeed, sir, as time may soon come for me to go upon Pilgrimage, I am desirous to note what is commonly done by persons in my case, and where are the ugliest Sloughs and Thickets on the Road; as also, what manner of staff is of the best service. Moreover, I lie here, by this water, to learn by root-of-heart a lesson which my master teaches me to call Peace, or Contentment.'

Hereupon Mr. Worldly Wiseman was much commoved with passion, and shaking his cane with a very threatful countenance, broke forth upon this wise: 'Learning, quotha!' said he: 'I would have all such rogues scourged by the Hangman!'

And so he would go his way, ruffling out his cravat with a crackle of starch, like a turkey when it spreads its feathers.

Now this, of Mr. Wiseman's, is the common opinion. A fact is not called a fact, but a piece of gossip, if it does not fall into one of your scholastic categories. An inquiry must be in some acknowledged direction, with a name to go by; or else you are not inquiring at all, only lounging; and the workhouse is too good for you. It is supposed that all knowledge is at the bottom of a well, or the far end of a telescope. Sainte-Beuve, as he grew older, came to regard all experience as a single great book, in which to study for a few years ere we go hence; and it seemed all one to him whether you should read in chapter xx, which is the differential calculus, or in chapter xxxix, which is hearing the band play in the gardens. As a matter of fact, an intelligent person, looking out of his eyes and hearkening in his ears, with a smile on his face all the time, will get more true education than many another in a life of heroic vigils. There is certainly some chill and arid knowledge to be found upon the summits of formal and laborious science; but it is all round about you, and for the trouble of looking, that you will acquire the warm and palpitating facts of life. While others are filling their memory with a lumber of words, one-half of which they will forget before the week be out, your truant may learn some really useful art: to play the fiddle, to know a good cigar, or to speak with ease and opportunity to all varieties of men. Many who have 'plied their book diligently,' and know all about some one branch or another of accepted lore, come out of the study with an ancient and owl-like demeanor, and prove dry, stockish, and dyspeptic in all the better and brighter parts of life. Many make a large fortune, who remain underbred and pathetically stupid to the last. And meanwhile there goes the idler, who began life along with them—by your leave, a different picture. He has had time to take care of his health and his spirits; he has been a great deal in the open air, which is the most salutary of all things for both body and mind; and if he has never read the great Book in very recondite places, he has dipped into it and skimmed it over to excellent purpose. Might not the student afford some Hebrew roots, and the business man some of his half-crowns, for a share of the idler's knowledge of life at large, and Art of Living? Nay, and the idler has another and more important quality than these. I mean his wisdom. He who has much looked on at the childish satisfaction of other people in their hobbies will regard his own with only a very ironical indulgence. He will not be heard among the dogmatists. He will have a great and cool allowance for all sorts of people and opinions. If he finds no out-of-the-way truths, he will identify himself with no very burning falsehood. His way takes him along a by-road, not much frequented, but very even and pleasant, which is called Common-place Lane and leads to the Belvedere of Common-sense. Thence he shall command an agreeable, if not very noble prospect; and while others behold the East and West, the Devil and the Sunrise, he will be contentedly aware of a sort of morning hour upon all sublunary things, with an army of shadows running speedily and in many different directions into the great daylight of Eternity. The shadows and the generations, the shrill doctors and the plangent wars, go by into ultimate silence and emptiness; but underneath all this, a man may see, out of the Belvedere windows, much green and peaceful landscape; many firelit parlors; good people laughing, drinking, and making love as they did before the Flood or the French Revolution; and the old shepherd telling his tale under the hawthorn.

Extreme *busyness,* whether at school or college, kirk or market, is a symptom of deficient vitality; and a faculty for idleness implies a catholic appetite and a strong sense of personal identity. There is a sort of dead-alive, hackneyed people about, who are scarcely conscious of living except in the exercise of some conventional occupation. Bring these fellows into the country or set them aboard ship, and you will see how they pine for their desk or their study. They have no curiosity; they cannot give themselves over to random provocations; they do not take pleasure in the exercise of their faculties for its own sake; and unless Necessity lays about them with a stick, they will even stand still. It is no good speaking to such folk: they *cannot* be idle, their nature is not generous enough: and they pass those hours in a sort of coma, which are not dedicated to furious moiling in the gold-mill. When they do not require to go to office, when they are not hungry and have no mind to drink, the whole breathing world is a blank to them. If they have to wait an hour or so for a train, they fall into a stupid trance with their eyes open. To see them, you would suppose there was nothing to look at and no one to speak with; you would imagine they were paralyzed or alienated: and yet very possibly they are hard workers in their own way, and have good eyesight for a flaw in a deed or a turn of the market. They have been to school and college, but all the time they had their eye on the medal; they have gone about in the world and mixed with clever people, but all the time they were thinking of their own affairs. As if a man's soul were not too small to begin with, they have dwarfed and narrowed theirs by a life of all work and no play; until here they are at forty, with a listless attention, a mind vacant of all material of amusement, and not one thought to rub against another, while they wait for the train. Before he was breeched, he might have clambered on the boxes; when he was twenty, he would have stared at the girls; but now the pipe is smoked out, the snuff-box empty, and my gentleman sits bolt upright upon a bench, with lamentable eyes. This does not appeal to me as being Success in Life.

But it is not only the person himself who suffers from his busy habits, but his wife and children, his friends and relations, and down to the very people he sits with in a railway-carriage or an omnibus. Perpetual devotion to what a man calls his business is only to be sustained by perpetual neglect of many other things. And it is not by any means certain that a man's business is the most important thing he has to do. To an impartial estimate it will seem clear that many of the wisest, most virtuous, and most beneficent parts that are to be played upon the Theatre of Life are filled by gratuitous performers, and pass, among the world at large, as phases of idleness. For in that Theatre, not only the walking gentlemen, singing chambermaids, and diligent fiddlers in the orchestra, but those who look on and clap their hands from the benches do really play a part and fulfil important offices towards the general result.

You are no doubt very dependent on the care of your lawyer and stockbroker, of the guards and signalmen who convey you rapidly from place to place, and the policemen who walk the streets for your protection; but is there not a thought of gratitude in your heart for certain other benefactors who set you smiling when they fall in your way, or season your dinner with good company? ... Though Falstaff was neither sober nor very honest, I think I could name one or two long-faced Barabbases whom the world could better have done without. Hazlitt mentions that he was more sensible of obligation to Northcote, who had never done him anything he could call a service, than to his whole circle of ostentatious friends; for he thought a good companion emphatically the greatest benefactor. I know there are people in the world who cannot feel grateful unless the favor has been done them at the cost of pain and difficulty. But this is a churlish disposition. A man may send you six sheets of letter-paper covered with the most entertaining gossip, or you may pass half an hour pleasantly, perhaps profitably, over an article of his; do you think the service would be greater if he had made the manuscript in his heart's blood, like a compact with the devil? Do you really fancy you should be more beholden to your correspondent if he had been damning you all the while for your importunity? Pleasures are more beneficial than duties because, like the quality of mercy, they are not strained, and they are twice blest. There must always be two to a kiss, and there may be a score in a jest; but wherever there is an element of sacrifice, the favor is conferred with pain, and, among generous people, received with confusion.

There is no duty we so much underrate as the duty of being happy. By being happy we sow anonymous benefits upon the world, which remain unknown even to ourselves, or, when they are disclosed, surprise nobody so much as the benefactor. The other day, a ragged, barefoot boy ran down the street after a marble, with so jolly an air that he set everyone he passed into a good humor; one of these persons, who had been delivered from more than usually black thoughts, stopped the little fellow and gave him some money with this remark: 'You see what sometimes comes of looking pleased.' If he had looked pleased before, he had now to look both pleased and mystified. For my part, I justify this encouragement of smiling rather than tearful children; I do not wish to pay for tears anywhere but upon the stage; but I am prepared to deal largely in the opposite commodity. A happy man or woman is a better thing to find than a five-pound note. He or she is a radiating focus of good will; and their entrance into a room is as though another candle had been lighted. We need not care whether they could prove the forty-seventh proposition; they do a better thing than that, they practically demonstrate the great Theorem of the Liveableness of Life. Consequently, if a person cannot be happy without remaining idle, idle he should remain. It is a revolutionary precept; but, thanks to hunger and the workhouse, one not easily to be abused; and within practical limits, it is one of the most incontestable truths in the whole Body of Morality. Look at one of your industrious fellows for a moment, I beseech you. He sows hurry and reaps indigestion; he puts a vast deal of activity out to interest, and receives a large measure of nervous derangement in return. Either he absents himself entirely from all fellowship, and lives a recluse in a garret, with carpet slippers and a leaden inkpot; or he comes among people swiftly and bitterly, in a contraction of his whole nervous system, to discharge some temper before he returns to work. I do not care how much or how well he works, this fellow is an evil feature in other people's lives. They would be happier if he were dead. They could easier do without his services in the Circumlocution Office than they can tolerate his fractious spirits. He poisons life at the well-head. It is better to be beggared out of hand by a scapegrace nephew, than daily hag-ridden by a peevish uncle.

And what, in God's name, is all this pother about? For what cause do they embitter their own and other people's lives? That a man should publish three or thirty articles a year, that he should finish or not finish his great allegorical picture, are questions of little interest to the world. The ranks of life are full; and although a thousand fall, there are always some to go into the breach. When they told Joan of Arc she should be at home minding women's work, she answered there were plenty to spin and wash. And so, even with your own rare gifts! When nature is 'so careless of the single life,' why should we coddle ourselves into the fancy that our own is of exceptional importance? Suppose Shakespeare had been knocked on the head some dark night in Sir Thomas Lucy's preserves, the world would have wagged on better or worse, the pitcher gone to the well, the scythe to the corn, and the student to his book; and no one been any the wiser of the loss. There are not many works extant, if you look the alternative all over, which are worth the price of a pound of tobacco to a man of limited means. This is a sobering reflexion for the proudest of our earthly vanities. Even a tobacconist may, upon consideration, find no great cause for personal vainglory in the phrase; for although tobacco is an admirable sedative, the qualities necessary for retailing it are neither rare nor precious in themselves. Alas and alas! you may take it how you will, but the services of no single individual are indispensable. Atlas was just a gentleman with a protracted nightmare! And yet you see merchants who go and labor themselves into a great fortune, and thence into the bankruptcy court; scribblers who keep scribbling at little articles until their temper is a cross to all who come about them, as though Pharaoh should set the Israelites to make a pin instead of a pyramid; and fine young men who work themselves into a decline, and are driven off in a hearse with white plumes upon it. Would you not suppose these persons had been whispered, by the Master of the Ceremonies, the promise of some momentous destiny? and that this lukewarm bullet on which they play their farces was the bull's-eye and centerpoint of all the universe? And yet it is not so. The ends for which they gave away their priceless youth, for all they know, may be chimerical or hurtful; the glory and riches they expect may never come, or may find them indifferent; and they and the world they inhabit are so inconsiderable that the mind freezes at the thought.

DISCUSSION AND WRITING

1. Define or explain: *formulary, unlettered, cravat, hearken, vigil, salutary, recondite, dogmatist, plangent, moil, listless, gratuitous, ostentatious, beholden, importunity, recluse, fractious, pother, allegorical, momentous.* In context, what is the meaning of "have a *shot* in their locker," "lilacs over a *burn*," "a *catholic* appetite," "paralyzed or *alienated*," "a *compact* with the devil"? Study the history of the following words to explain their origin, meaning, and associations: *lucrative, bravado, gasconade, belvedere, sublunary, kirk, churlish, chimerical.* Explain a coinage like *lèse-respectability,* an idiom

like "sent to Coventry." Generally, what are characteristic features of Stevenson's diction?

2. Like other nineteenth-century essayists, Stevenson makes free use of literary, historical, and mythological allusions. Explain or trace as many of these as you can.

3. Stevenson makes constant use of figurative language and of concrete and colorful illustrations. Discuss some typical examples and show how they affect the style of the essay as a whole.

4. In much nineteenth-century writing, paragraphs tend to be long if not, by modern standards, interminable. Examine the structure of some of Stevenson's longer paragraphs. Prepare a rough paragraph outline showing the contribution of each major paragraph to the essay as a whole. How systematic is the over-all development of the essay, how logical its over-all progression?

5. Is Stevenson merely paraphrasing familiar ideas about the limitations of "book-learning," about "all work and no play," about "successful" but unhappy businessmen? What does he contribute that would go beyond such stereotypes?

6. In your own words, summarize how Stevenson modifies conventional definitions of the "really useful," of "success," and of "duty." How serious is he? Is his main purpose to entertain or to convince?

7. Compare and contrast Stevenson's attitude toward education with that of Hutchins in "The University of Utopia." Which writer seems to you closer to the truth? How much is there to be said for the other side?

8. Select one of Stevenson's statements with which you strongly sympathize or disagree. Defend or attack, bringing in supporting detail from your own observation or experience.

9. Using Stevenson's essay as a model, write "An Apology for . . ." or "A Defense of . . ." some conventionally frowned upon character trait, form of behavior, or kind of life.

10. Does American life as you know it encourage people to follow Stevenson's precepts? Focus your discussion on one major area or point. For instance, is there in American life too much of that extreme "busyness" that kills vitality, curiosity, zest? Or, is it true that our Puritan heritage makes it hard for us to find happiness and contentment in well-spent leisure? Or, is there in Stevenson's positive attitude toward life something that actually has close parallels in prevailing American attitudes?

FURTHER READING

Other well-known late-nineteenth-century essays are Robert Louis Stevenson's "Aes Triplex" (1878), Thomas Henry Huxley's "Science and Culture" (1880), and Matthew Arnold's "Literature and Science" (1882). These essays and such examples of the modern magazine essay as the articles by Krutch, Jacobson, and Mrs. Hudson reprinted in this volume provide material for a comparison of nineteenth- and twentieth-century prose styles.

12

The Function of Literature

A good book is the precious lifeblood of a master spirit, embalmed and treasured up on purpose to a life beyond life. JOHN MILTON

Critical discussions of literature impose upon the critic a discipline salutary for any writer. Even more than other writers, the critic must resist the tendency toward premature generalization, toward a mere restatement of long-standing prejudices. He must learn to stay close to the text of the literary work he is discussing. He must become involved in its purposes and strategy; he must respond to nuances of tone and details of form. He must be competent in dealing with technical points and yet capture something of the spirit of the whole. The writers in this section are well equipped to make the general reader more sensitive to both the substance and the spirit of literature. Aldous Huxley, in trying to set tragedy apart from other kinds of literature, reopens the ancient controversy about the relationship between the truth of life and the truth of fiction. George Orwell examines Charles Dickens, one of the most widely read of all authors, from the point of view of a critic stressing the writer's social conscience and moral responsibilities. Arthur Miller, in "The American Theater," explores the fascination that the stage has for playwright and actor. John Ciardi, in "The Act of Language," explores the ways in which the meaning of poetry differs from more familiar kinds of meaning.

ALDOUS HUXLEY

Aldous Huxley (1894–1963) had to an outstanding degree the qualities of the true intellectual: an incisive mind, breadth of knowledge, and a mature concern for human problems and dilemmas. He published many successful books, and his influence as novelist, essayist, and lecturer has been widely felt. His novel *Point Counter Point* (1928) dramatized the clash of conflicting ideologies and was for a long time required reading for the campus sophisticate. His best-known novel, *Brave New World* (1932), remains a frighteningly up-to-date preview of a future society shaped by dehumanized science. In the following essay, Mr. Huxley discusses the relationship between life and literature, truth and art. A critic writing for the common reader, he uses only the most necessary technical terms and makes use of detailed reference to actual literary works.

Tragedy and the Whole Truth

There were six of them, the best and bravest of the hero's companions. Turning back from his post in the bows, Odysseus was in time to see them lifted, struggling, into the air, to hear their screams, the desperate repetition of his own name. The survivors could only look on, helplessly, while Scylla "at the mouth of her cave devoured them, still screaming, still stretching out their hands to me in the frightful struggle." And Odysseus adds that it was the most dreadful and lamentable sight he ever saw in all his "explorings of the passes of the sea." We can believe it; Homer's brief description (the too poetical simile is a later interpolation) convinces us.

Later, the danger passed, Odysseus and his men went ashore for the night, and, on the Sicilian beach, prepared their supper—prepared it, says Homer, "expertly." The Twelfth Book of the Odyssey concludes with these words: "When they had satisfied their thirst and hunger, they thought of their dear companions and wept, and in the midst of their tears sleep came gently upon them."

The truth, the whole truth and nothing but the truth—how rarely the older literatures ever told it! Bits of the truth, yes; every good book gives us bits of the truth, would not be a good book if it did not. But the whole truth, no. Of the great writers of the past incredibly few have given us that. Homer—the Homer of the *Odyssey*—is one of those few.

"Truth?" you question. "For example, $2 + 2 = 4$? Or Queen Victoria came to the throne in 1837? Or light travels at the rate of 187,000 miles a second?" No, obviously, you won't find much of that sort of thing in literature. The "truth" of which I was speaking just now is in fact no more than an acceptable verisimilitude. When the experiences recorded in a piece of literature correspond fairly closely with our own actual experiences, or with what I may call our potential experiences—experiences, that is to say, which we feel (as the result of a more or less explicit process of inference from known facts) that we might have had—we say, inaccurately, no doubt: "This piece of writing is true." But this, of course, is not the whole story. The record of a case in a textbook of psychology is scientifically true, in so far as it is an accurate account of particular events. But it might also strike the reader as being 'true' with regard to himself—that is to say, acceptable, probable, having a correspondence with his own actual or potential experiences. But a textbook of psychology is not a work of art—or only secondarily and incidentally a work of art. Mere verisimilitude, mere correspondence of experience recorded by the writer with experience remembered or imaginable by the reader, is not enough to make a work of art seem 'true.' Good art possesses a kind of super-truth—is more probable, more acceptable, more convincing than truth itself. Naturally; for the artist is endowed with a sensibility and a power of communication, a capacity to "put things across," which events and the majority of people to whom events happen, do not possess. Experience teaches only the teachable, who are by no means as numerous as Mrs. Micawber's papa's favorite proverb would lead us to suppose. Artists are eminently teachable and also eminently teachers. They receive from events much more than most men receive, and they can transmit what they have received with a peculiar penetrative force, which drives their communication deep into the reader's mind. One of our most ordinary reactions to a good piece of literary art is expressed in the formula: "This is what I have always felt and thought, but have never been able to put clearly into words, even for myself."

We are now in a position to explain what we mean when we say that Homer is a writer who tells the Whole Truth. We mean that the experiences he records correspond fairly closely with our own actual or potential experiences—and correspond with our experiences not on a single limited sector, but all along the line of our physical and spiritual being. And we also mean that Homer records these experiences with a penetrative artistic force that makes them seem peculiarly acceptable and convincing.

So much, then, for truth in literature. Homer's, I repeat, is the Whole Truth. Consider how almost any other of the great poets would have concluded the story of Scylla's attack on the passing ship. Six men, remember, have been taken and devoured before the eyes of their friends. In any other poem but the *Odyssey,* what would the survivors have done? They would, of course, have wept, even as Homer made them weep. But would they previously have cooked their supper, and cooked it, what's more, in a masterly fashion? Would they previously have drunk and eaten to satiety? And after weeping, or actually while weeping, would they have dropped quietly off to sleep? No, they most certainly would not have done any of these things. They would simply have wept, lamenting their own misfortune and the horrible fate of their companions, and the canto would have ended tragically on their tears.

Homer, however, preferred to tell the Whole Truth. He knew that even the most cruelly bereaved must eat; that hunger is stronger than sorrow and that its satisfaction takes precedence even of tears. He knew that experts continue to act expertly and to find satisfaction in their accomplishment, even when friends have just been eaten, even when the accomplishment is only cooking the supper. He knew that, when the belly is full (and only when the belly is full) men can afford to grieve, and that sorrow after supper is almost a luxury. And finally he knew that, even as hunger takes precedence of grief, so fatigue, supervening, cuts short its career and drowns it in a sleep all the sweeter for bringing forgetfulness of bereavement. In a word, Homer refused to treat the theme tragically. He preferred to tell the Whole Truth.

Another author who preferred to tell the Whole Truth was Fielding. *Tom Jones* is one of the very few Odyssean books written in Europe between the time of Aeschylus and the present age; Odyssean, because never tragical; never—even when painful and disastrous, even when pathetic and beautiful things are happening. For they do happen; Fielding, like Homer, admits all the facts, shirks nothing. Indeed, it is precisely because these authors shirk nothing that their books are not tragical. For among the things they don't shirk are the irrelevancies which, in actual life, always temper the situations and characters that writers of tragedy insist on keeping chemically pure. Consider, for example, the case of Sophy Western, that most charming, most nearly perfect of young women. Fielding, it is obvious, adored her (she is said to have been created in the image of his first, much-loved wife). But in spite of his adoration, he refused to turn her into one of those chemically pure and, as it were, focused beings who do and suffer in the world of tragedy. That innkeeper who lifted the weary Sophia from her horse—what need had he to fall? In no tragedy would he (nay, could he) have collapsed beneath her weight. For, to begin with, in the tragical context weight is an irrelevance; heroines should be above the law of gravitation. But that is not all; let the reader now remember what were the results of his fall. Tumbling flat on his back, he pulled Sophia down on top of him—his belly was a cushion, so that happily she came to no bodily harm—pulled her down head first. But head first is necessarily legs last; there was a momentary display of the most ravishing charms; the bumpkins at the inn door grinned or guffawed; poor Sophia, when they picked her up, was blushing in an agony of embarrassment and wounded modesty. There is nothing intrinsically improbable about this incident, which is stamped, indeed, with all the marks of literary truth. But however true, it is an incident which could never, never have happened to a heroine of tragedy. It would never have been allowed to happen. But Fielding refused to impose the tragedian's veto; he shirked nothing—neither the intrusion of irrelevant absurdities into the midst of romance or disaster, nor any of life's no less irrelevantly painful interruptions of the course of happiness. He did not want to be a tragedian. And, sure enough, that brief and pearly gleam of Sophia's charming posterior was sufficient to scare the Muse of Tragedy out of *Tom Jones* just as, more than five and twenty centuries before, the sight of stricken men first eating, then remembering to weep, then forgetting their tears in slumber had scared her out of the *Odyssey*.

In his *Principles of Literary Criticism* Mr. I. A. Richards affirms that good tragedy is proof against irony and irrelevance—that it can absorb anything into itself and still remain tragedy. Indeed, he seems to make of this capacity to absorb the untragical and the anti-tragical a touchstone of tragic merit. Thus tried, practically all Greek, all French and most Elizabethan tragedies are found wanting. Only the best of Shakespeare can stand the test. So, at least, says Mr. Richards. Is he right? I have often had my doubts. The tragedies of Shakespeare are veined, it is true, with irony and an often terrifying cynicism; but the cynicism is always heroic idealism turned neatly inside out, the irony is a kind of photographic negative of heroic romance. Turn Troilus's white into black and all his blacks into white and you have Thersites. Reversed, Othello and Desdemona became Iago. White Ophelia's negative is the irony of Hamlet, is the ingenuous bawdry of her own mad songs; just as the cynicism of mad King Lear is the black shadow-replica of Cordelia. Now, the shadow, the photographic negative of a thing, is in no sense irrelevant to it. Shakespeare's ironies and cynicism serve to deepen his tragic world, but not to widen it. If they had widened it, as the Homeric irrelevancies widened out the universe of the *Odyssey*—why, then, the world of Shakespearean tragedy would automatically have ceased to exist. For example, a scene showing the bereaved Macduff eating his supper, growing melancholy over the whisky, with thoughts of his murdered wife and children, and then, with lashes still wet, dropping off to sleep, would be true enough to life; but it would not be true to tragic art. The introduction of such a scene would change the whole quality of the play; treated in this Odyssean style, *Macbeth* would cease to be a tragedy. Or take the case of Desdemona. Iago's bestially cynical remarks about her character are in no sense, as we have seen, irrelevant to the tragedy. They present us with negative images of her real nature and of the feelings she has for Othello. These negative images are always *hers,* are always recognizably the property of the heroine-victim of a tragedy. Whereas, if, springing ashore at Cyprus, she had tumbled, as the no less exquisite Sophia was to tumble, and revealed the inadequacies of sixteenth-century underclothing, the play would no longer be the *Othello* we know. Iago might breed a family of little cynics and the existing dose of bitterness and savage negation be doubled and trebled; *Othello* would still remain fundamentally *Othello.* But a few Field-ingesque irrelevancies would destroy it—destroy it, that is to say, as a tragedy; for there would be nothing to prevent it from becoming a magnificent drama of some other kind. For the fact is that tragedy and what I have called the Whole Truth are not compatible; where one is, the other is not. There are certain things which even the best, even Shakespearean tragedy, cannot absorb into itself.

To make a tragedy the artist must isolate a single element out of the totality of human experience and use that exclusively as his material. Tragedy is something that is separated out from the Whole Truth, distilled from it, so to speak, as an essence is distilled from the living flower. Tragedy is chemically pure. Hence its power to act quickly and intensely on our feelings. All chemically pure art has this power to act upon us quickly and intensely. Thus, chemically pure pornography (on the rare occasions when it happens to be written convincingly, by someone who has the gift of "putting things across") is a quick-acting emotional drug of incomparably greater power than the Whole Truth about sensuality, or even (for many people) than the tangible and carnal reality itself. It is because of its chemical purity that tragedy so effectively performs its functions of catharsis. It refines and corrects and gives a style to our emotional life, and does so swiftly, with power. Brought into contact with tragedy, the elements of our being fall, for the moment at any rate, into an ordered and beautiful pattern, as the iron filings arrange themselves under the influence of the magnet. Through all its individual variations, this pattern is always fundamentally of the same kind. From the reading or the hearing of a tragedy we rise with the feeling that

> *Our friends are exultations, agonies,*
> *And love, and man's unconquerable mind;*

with the heroic conviction that we too would be unconquerable if subjected to the agonies, that in the midst of the agonies we too should continue to love, might even learn to exult. It is because it does these things to us that tragedy is felt to be so valuable. What are the values of Wholly-Truthful art? What does it do to us that seems worth doing? Let us try to discover.

Wholly-Truthful art overflows the limits of tragedy and shows us, if only by hints and implications, what happened before the tragic story began, what will happen after it is over, what is happening simultaneously elsewhere (and "elsewhere" includes all those parts of the minds and bodies of the protagonists not immediately engaged in the tragic struggle). Tragedy is an arbitrarily isolated eddy on the surface of a vast river that flows on majestically, irresistibly, around, beneath, and to either side of it. Wholly-Truthful art contrives to imply the existence of the entire river as well as of the eddy. It is quite different from tragedy, even though it may contain, among other constituents, all the elements from which tragedy is made. (The "same thing" placed in different contexts loses its identity and becomes, for the perceiving mind, a succession of different things.) In Wholly-Truthful art the agonies may be just as real, love and the unconquerable mind just as admirable, just as important, as in tragedy. Thus, Scylla's victims suffer as painfully as the monster-devoured Hippolytus in *Phèdre;* the mental anguish of Tom Jones when he thinks he has lost his Sophia, and lost her by his own fault, is hardly less than that of Othello after Desdemona's murder. (The fact that Fielding's power of "putting things across" is by no means equal to Shakespeare's is, of course, merely an accident.) But the agonies and indomitabilities are placed by the Wholly-Truthful writer in another, wider context, with the result that they cease to be the same as the intrinsically identical agonies and indomitabilities of tragedy. Consequently, Wholly-Truthful art produces in us an effect quite different from that produced by tragedy. Our mood when we have read a Wholly-Truthful book is never one of heroic exultation; it is one of resignation, of acceptance. (Acceptance can also be heroic.) Being chemically impure, Wholly-Truthful literature cannot move us as quickly and intensely as tragedy or any other kind of chemically pure art. But I believe that its effects are more lasting. The exultations that follow the reading or hearing of a tragedy are in the nature of temporary inebriations. One being cannot long hold the pattern imposed by tragedy. Remove the magnet and the filings tend to fall back into confusion. But the pattern of acceptance and resignation imposed upon us by Wholly-Truthful literature, though perhaps less unexpectedly beautiful in design, is (for that very reason perhaps) more stable. The catharsis of tragedy is violent and apocalyptic; but the milder catharsis of Wholly-Truthful literature is lasting.

In recent times literature has become more and more acutely conscious of the Whole Truth—of the great oceans of irrelevant things, events and thoughts stretching endlessly away in every direction from whatever island point (a character, a story) the author may choose to contemplate. To impose the kind of arbitrary limitations, which must be imposed by anyone who wants to write a tragedy, has become more and more difficult—is now indeed, for those who are at all sensitive to contemporaneity, almost impossible. This does not mean, of course, that the modern writer must confine himself to a merely naturalist manner. One can imply the existence of the

Whole Truth without laboriously cataloguing every object within sight. A book can be written in terms of pure phantasy and yet, by implication, tell the Whole Truth. Of all the important works of contemporary literature not one is a pure tragedy. There is no contemporary writer of significance who does not prefer to state or imply the Whole Truth. However different one from another in style, in ethical, philosophical and artistic intention, in the scales of values accepted, contemporary writers have this in common, that they are interested in the Whole Truth. Proust, D. H. Lawrence, André Gide, Kafka, Hemingway—here are five obviously significant and important contemporary writers. Five authors as remarkably unlike one another as they could well be. They are at one only in this: that none of them has written a pure tragedy, that all are concerned with the Whole Truth.

I have sometimes wondered whether tragedy, as a form of art, may not be doomed. But the fact that we are still profoundly moved by the tragic masterpieces of the past—that we can be moved, against our better judgment, even by the bad tragedies of the contemporary stage and film—makes me think that the day of chemically pure art is not over. Tragedy happens to be passing through a period of eclipse, because all the significant writers of our age are too busy exploring the newly discovered, or re-discovered, world of the Whole Truth to be able to pay any attention to it. But there is no good reason to believe that this state of things will last forever. Tragedy is too valuable to be allowed to die. There is no reason, after all, why the two kinds of literature—the Chemically Impure and the Chemically Pure, the literature of the Whole Truth and the literature of Partial Truth—should not exist simultaneously, each in its separate sphere. The human spirit has need of both.

DISCUSSION AND WRITING

1. Define or explain, paying special attention to the exact technical (as against the loose popular) meanings of literary terms: *interpolation, verisimilitude, inference, satiety, canto, supervene, pathetic, intrusion, Muse, ingenuous, carnal, catharsis, indomitable, intrinsic, exultation, inebriation, apocalyptic, contemporaneity, naturalistic.*

2. Of Huxley's literary allusions, select one that is familiar to you. Explain fully the use he makes of it and examine the validity of his interpretation.

3. In your own words, explain and illustrate Huxley's view of the difference between "tragic" and "wholly truthful" literature. Show why "irony" would play a different role in the two kinds of literature.

4. Select a novel or a play that you know well and discuss it in the light of Huxley's distinction between "tragedy" and "the whole truth."

5. Can Huxley's criteria be applied to arts other than literature? Give examples.

6. In an anthology of modern poetry (or in a collection of Mr. Auden's poems), find W. H. Auden's poem "Musée des Beaux Arts." Examine the parallels and differences between the theme of Huxley's essay and that of Auden's poem.

7. Have you ever felt in reading a book or seeing a play, "This is what I have always felt and thought"? Discuss in detail a book or play that lived up, or came close, to this standard.

8. How much truth, and what kind, do we require in books we read mainly for entertainment: historical novels, detective novels, science fiction? Limit yourself to one of these areas.

9. A master of the expository essay, Huxley demonstrates the effectiveness of generalizations backed up by detailed illustrations, by carefully defined key terms, by illuminating comparison and contrast. Prepare a detailed analysis of this essay, describing as fully as you can its organization, strategy, and style.

10. Is the modern reader (or spectator) prepared to have the tragic mingle with the comic without having the one destroy the other?

FURTHER READING

Read Homer's *Odyssey,* or parts thereof suggested by your instructor. How well does your reading bear out Huxley's contention that Homer tells the "whole truth"?

GEORGE ORWELL

George Orwell (1903–1950), whose original name was Eric Blair, was a British socialist who combined a rare capacity for compassion and moral indignation with a clear analytical mind. At a time when "propaganda" had become synonymous with the tawdry and the corrupt, his writings demonstrated the persuasive force of a message strongly felt and stated with integrity and force. His early political education took place when service with the Imperial Police in British Burma brought him face to face with inequality and exploitation. He fought in the Spanish Civil War on the Loyalist side; his *Homage to Catalonia* (1938) documents the betrayal of the Spanish working-class movement by the Western democracies and Stalinist Russia. His *Animal Farm* (1946) is a devastating satire of Russian communism under Stalin. His best-known book is *1984,* a novel describing a totalitarian society of the future and deriving its horror not so much from the external trappings of totalitarianism as from Orwell's understanding of the psychological mechanisms that make it a nightmarish menace. In his literary essays, Orwell examined the moral and political implications of literature, without ever becoming a mere partisan measuring the politics of a writer by his conformity to simple-minded formulas. The following is the first part of a long essay on Dickens that Orwell wrote in 1939. Its style is that of a lifelong champion and practitioner of clear, vigorous prose.

Charles Dickens

Dickens is one of those writers who are well worth stealing. Even the burial of his body in Westminster Abbey was a species of theft, if you come to think of it.

When Chesterton wrote his introduction to the Everyman Edition of Dickens's works, it seemed quite natural to him to credit Dickens with his own highly individual brand of medievalism, and more recently a Marxist writer, Mr. T. A. Jackson, has made spirited efforts to turn Dickens into a bloodthirsty revolutionary. The Marxist claims him as "almost" a Marxist, the Catholic claims him as "almost" a Catholic, and both claim him as a champion of the proletariat (or "the poor," as Chesterton would have put it). On the other hand, Nadezhda Krupskaya, in her little book on Lenin, relates that towards the end of his life Lenin went to see a dramatized version of *The Cricket on the Hearth,* and found Dickens's "middle-class sentimentality" so intolerable that he walked out in the middle of a scene.

Taking "middle class" to mean what Krupskaya might be expected to mean by it, this was probably a truer judgment than those of Chesterton and Jackson. But it is worth noticing that the dislike of Dickens implied in this remark is something unusual. Plenty of people have found him unreadable, but very few seem to have felt any hostility towards the general spirit of his work. Some years ago Mr. Bechhofer Roberts published a full-length attack on Dickens in the form of a novel (*This Side Idolatry*), but it was a merely personal attack, concerned for the most part with Dickens's treatment of his wife. It dealt with incidents which not one in a thousand of Dickens's readers would ever hear about, and which no more invalidate his work than the second-best bed invalidates *Hamlet.* All that the book really demonstrated was that a writer's literary personality has little or nothing to do with his private character. It is quite possible that in private life Dickens was just the kind of insensitive egoist that Mr. Bechhofer Roberts makes him appear. But in his published work there is implied a personality quite different from this, a personality which has won him far more friends than enemies. It might well have been otherwise, for even if Dickens was a bourgeois, he was certainly a subversive writer, a radical, one might truthfully say a rebel.

Everyone who has read widely in his work has felt this. Gissing, for instance, the best of the writers on Dickens, was anything but a radical himself, and he disapproved of this strain in Dickens and wished it were not there, but it never occurred to him to deny it. In *Oliver Twist, Hard Times, Bleak House, Little Dorrit,* Dickens attacked English institutions with a ferocity that has never since been approached. Yet he managed to do it without making himself hated, and, more than this, the very people he attacked have swallowed him so completely that he has become a national institution himself. In its attitude towards Dickens the English public has always been a little like the elephant which feels a blow with a walking-stick as a delightful tickling. Before I was ten years old I was having Dickens ladled down my throat by schoolmasters in whom even at that age I could see a strong resemblance to Mr. Creakle, and one knows without needing to be told that lawyers delight in Serjeant Buzfuz and that *Little Dorrit* is a favorite in the Home Office. Dickens seems to have succeeded in attacking everybody and antagonizing nobody. Naturally this makes one wonder whether after all there was something unreal in his attack upon society. Where exactly does he stand, socially, morally and politically? As usual, one can define his position more easily if one starts by deciding what he was *not*.

In the first place he was *not,* as Messrs. Chesterton and Jackson seem to imply, a "proletarian" writer. To begin with, he does not write about the proletariat, in which he merely resembles the overwhelming majority of novelists, past and present. If you look for the working classes in fiction, and especially English fiction, all you find is a hole. This statement needs qualifying, perhaps. For reasons that are easy enough to see, the agricultural laborer (in England a proletarian) gets a fairly good showing in fiction, and a great deal has been written about criminals, derelicts and, more recently, the working-class intelligentsia. But the ordinary town proletariat, the people who make the wheels go round, have always been ignored by novelists. When they do find their way between the covers of a book, it is nearly always as objects of pity or as comic relief. The central action of Dickens's stories almost invariably takes place in middle-class surroundings. If one examines his novels in detail one finds that his real subject-matter is the London commercial bourgeoisie and their hangers-on—lawyers, clerks, tradesmen, inn-keepers, small craftsmen and servants. He has no portrait of an agricultural worker, and only one (Stephen Blackpool in *Hard Times*) of an industrial worker. The Plornishes in *Little Dorrit* are probably his best picture of a working-class family—the Peggottys, for instance, hardly belong to the working class—but on the whole he is not successful with this type of character. If you ask any ordinary reader which of Dickens's proletarian characters he can remember, the three he is almost certain to mention are Bill Sykes, Sam Weller and Mrs. Gamp. A burglar, a valet and a drunken midwife—not exactly a representative cross-section of the English working class.

Secondly, in the ordinary accepted sense of the word, Dickens is not a "revolutionary" writer. But his position here needs some defining.

Whatever else Dickens may have been, he was not a hole-and-corner soul-saver, the kind of well-meaning idiot who thinks that the world will be perfect if you amend a few by-laws and abolish a few anomalies. It is worth comparing him with Charles Reade, for instance. Reade was a much better-informed man than Dickens, and in some ways more public-spirited. He really hated the abuses he could understand, he showed them up in a series of novels which for all their absurdity are extremely readable, and he probably helped to alter public opinion on a few minor but important points. But it was quite beyond him to grasp that, given the existing form of society, certain evils *cannot* be remedied. Fasten upon this or that minor abuse, expose it, drag it into the open, bring it before a British jury, and all will be well—that is how he sees it. Dickens at any rate never imagined that you can cure pimples by cutting them off. In every page of his work one can see a consciousness that society is wrong somewhere at the root. It is when one asks "Which root?" that one begins to grasp his position.

The truth is that Dickens's criticism of society is almost exclusively moral. Hence the utter lack of any constructive suggestion anywhere in his work. He attacks the law, parliamentary government, the educational system and so forth, without ever clearly suggesting what he would put in their places. Of course it is not necessarily the business of a novelist, or a satirist, to make constructive suggestions, but the point is that Dickens's attitude is at bottom not even *de*structive. There is no clear sign that he wants the existing order to be overthrown, or that he believes it would make very much difference if it *were* overthrown. For in reality his target is not so much society as "human nature." It would be difficult to point anywhere in his books to a passage suggesting that the economic system is wrong *as a system*. Nowhere, for instance, does he make any attack on private enterprise or private property. Even in a book like *Our Mutual Friend,* which turns on the power of corpses to interfere with living people by means of idiotic wills, it does not occur to him to suggest that individuals ought not to have this irresponsible power. Of course one can draw this inference for oneself, and one can draw it again from the remarks about Bounderby's will at the end of *Hard Times,* and indeed from the whole of Dickens's work one can infer the evil of *laissez-faire* capitalism; but Dickens makes no such inference himself. It is said that Macaulay refused to review *Hard Times* because he disapproved of its "sullen Socialism." Obviously Macaulay is here using the word "Socialism" in the same sense in which, twenty years ago, a vegetarian meal or a Cubist picture used to be referred to as "Bolshevism." There is not a line in the book that can properly be called Socialistic; indeed, its tendency if anything is pro-capitalist, because its whole moral is that capitalists ought to be kind, not that workers ought to be rebellious. Bounderby is a bullying windbag and Gradgrind has been morally blinded, but if they were better men, the system would work well enough—that, all through, is the implication. And so far as social criticism goes, one can never extract much more from Dickens than this, unless one deliberately reads meanings into him. His whole "message" is one that at first glance looks like an enormous platitude: If men would behave decently the world would be decent.

Naturally this calls for a few characters who are in positions of authority and who *do* behave decently. Hence that recurrent Dickens figure, the Good Rich Man. This character belongs especially to Dickens's early optimistic period. He is usually a "merchant" (we are not necessarily told what merchandise he deals in), and he is always a superhumanly kind-hearted old gentleman who "trots" to and fro, raising his employees' wages, patting children on the head, getting debtors out of jail and, in general, acting the fairy godmother. Of course he is a pure dream figure, much further from real life than, say, Squeers or Micawber. Even Dickens must have reflected occasionally that anyone who was so anxious to give his money away would never have acquired it in the first place. Mr. Pickwick, for instance, had "been in the city," but it is difficult to imagine him making a fortune there. Nevertheless this character runs like a connecting thread through most of the earlier books. Pickwick, the Cheerybles, old Chuzzlewit, Scrooge—it is the same figure over and over again, the good rich man, handing out guineas. Dickens does however show signs of development here. In the books of the middle period the good rich man fades out to some extent. There is no one who plays this part in *A Tale of Two Cities,* nor in *Great Expectations—Great Expectations* is, in fact, definitely an attack on patronage—and in *Hard Times* it is only very doubtfully played by Gradgrind after his reformation. The character reappears in a rather different form as Meagles in *Little Dorrit* and John Jarndyce in *Bleak House*—one might perhaps add Betsy Trotwood in *David Copperfield.* But in these books the good rich man has dwindled from a "merchant" to a *rentier.* This is significant. A *rentier* is part of the possessing class; he can and, almost without knowing it, does make other people work for him, but he has very little direct power. Unlike Scrooge or the Cheerybles, he cannot put everything right by raising everybody's wages. The seeming inference from the rather despondent books that Dickens wrote in the 'fifties is that by that time he had grasped the helplessness of well-meaning individuals in a corrupt society. Nevertheless, in the last completed novel, *Our Mutual Friend* (published 1864–65), the good rich man comes back in full glory in the person of Boffin. Boffin is a proletarian by origin and only rich by inheritance, but he is the usual *deus ex machina,* solving everybody's problems by showering money in all directions. He even "trots," like the Cheerybles. In several ways *Our Mutual Friend* is a return to the earlier manner, and not an unsuccessful return either. Dickens's thoughts seem to have come full circle. Once again, individual kindliness is the remedy for everything.

One crying evil of his time that Dickens says very little about is child labor. There are plenty of pictures of suffering children in his books, but usually they are suffering in schools rather than in factories. The one detailed account of child labor that he gives is the description in *David Copperfield* of little David washing bottles in Murdstone & Grinby's warehouse. This, of course, is autobiography. Dickens himself, at the age of ten, had worked in Warren's blacking factory in the Strand, very much as he describes it here. It was a terribly bitter memory to him, partly because he felt the whole incident to be discreditable to his parents, and he even concealed it from his wife till long after they were married. Looking back on this period, he says in *David Copperfield*:

> It is a matter of some surprise to me, even now, that I can have been so easily thrown away at such an age. A child of excellent abilities and with strong powers of observation, quick, eager, delicate, and soon hurt bodily or mentally, it seems wonderful to me that nobody should have made any sign in my behalf. But none was made; and I became, at ten years old, a little laboring hind in the service of Murdstone & Grinby.

And again, having described the rough boys among whom he worked:

> No words can express the secret agony of my soul as I sunk into this companionship... and felt my hopes of growing up to be a learned and distinguished man crushed in my bosom.

Obviously it is not David Copperfield who is speaking, it is Dickens himself. He uses almost the same words in the autobiography that he began and abandoned a few months earlier. Of course Dickens is right in saying that a gifted child ought not to work ten hours a day pasting labels on bottles, but what he does not say is that *no* child ought to be condemned to such a fate, and there is no reason for inferring that he thinks it. David escapes from the warehouse, but Mick Walker and Mealy Potatoes and the others are still there, and there is no sign that this troubles Dickens particularly. As usual, he displays no consciousness that the *structure* of society can be changed. He despises politics, does not believe that any good can come out of Parliament—he had been a Parliamentary shorthand writer, which was no doubt a disillusioning experience—and he is slightly hostile to the most hopeful movement of his day, trade unionism. In *Hard Times* trade unionism is represented as something not much better than a racket, something that happens because employers are not sufficiently paternal. Stephen Blackpool's refusal to join the union is rather a virtue in Dickens's eyes. Also, as Mr. Jackson has pointed out, the apprentices' association in *Barnaby Rudge,* to which Sim Tappertit belongs, is probably a hit at the illegal or barely legal unions of Dickens's own day, with their secret assemblies, passwords and so forth. Obviously he wants the workers to be decently treated, but there is no sign that he wants them to take their destiny into their own hands, least of all by open violence.

As it happens, Dickens deals with revolution in the narrower sense in two novels, *Barnaby Rudge* and *A Tale of Two Cities*. In *Barnaby Rudge* it is a case of rioting rather than revolution. The Gordon Riots of 1780, though they had religious bigotry as a pretext, seem to have been little more than a pointless outburst of looting. Dickens's attitude to this kind of thing is sufficiently indicated by the fact that his first idea was to make the ring-leaders of the riots three lunatics escaped from an asylum. He was dissuaded from this, but the principal figure of the book is in fact a village idiot. In the chapters dealing with the riots Dickens shows a most profound horror of mob violence. He delights in describing scenes in which the "dregs" of the population behave with atrocious bestiality. These chapters are of great psychological interest, because they show how deeply he had brooded on this subject. The things he describes can only have come out of his imagination, for no riots on anything like the same scale had happened in his lifetime. Here is one of his descriptions, for instance:

> If Bedlam gates had been flung open wide, there would not have issued forth such maniacs as the frenzy of that night had made. There were men there who danced and trampled on the beds of flowers as though they trod down human enemies, and wrenched them from their stalks, like savages who twisted human necks. There were men who cast their lighted torches in the air, and suffered them to fall upon their heads and faces, blistering the skin with deep unseemly burns. There were men who rushed up to the fire, and paddled in it with their hands as if in water; and others who were restrained by force from plunging in, to gratify their deadly longing. On the skull of one drunken lad—not twenty, by his looks—who lay upon the ground with a bottle to his mouth, the lead from the roof came streaming down in a shower of liquid fire, white hot, melting his head like wax.... But of all the howling throng not one learnt mercy from, or sickened at, these sights; nor was the fierce, besotted, senseless rage of one man glutted.

You might almost think you were reading a description of "Red" Spain by a partisan of General Franco. One ought, of course, to remember that when Dickens was writing, the London "mob" still existed. (Nowadays there is no mob, only a flock.) Low wages and the growth and shift of population had brought into existence a huge, dangerous slum-proletariat, and until the early middle of the nineteenth century there was hardly such a thing as a police force. When the brickbats began to fly there was nothing between shuttering your windows and ordering the troops to open fire. In *A Tale of Two Cities* he is dealing with a revolution which was really *about* something, and Dickens's attitude is different, but not entirely different. As a matter of fact,

A Tale of Two Cities is a book which tends to leave a false impression behind, especially after a lapse of time.

The one thing that everyone who has read *A Tale of Two Cities* remembers is the Reign of Terror. The whole book is dominated by the guillotine—tumbrils thundering to and fro, bloody knives, heads bouncing into the basket, and sinister old women knitting as they watch. Actually these scenes only occupy a few chapters, but they are written with terrible intensity, and the rest of the book is rather slow going. But *A Tale of Two Cities* is not a companion volume to *The Scarlet Pimpernel*. Dickens sees clearly enough that the French Revolution was bound to happen and that many of the people who were executed deserved what they got. If, he says, you behave as the French aristocracy had behaved, vengeance will follow. He repeats this over and over again. We are constantly being reminded that while "my lord" is lolling in bed, with four liveried footmen serving his chocolate and the peasants starving outside, somewhere in the forest a tree is growing which will presently be sawn into planks for the platform of the guillotine, etc. etc. etc. The inevitability of the Terror, given its causes, is insisted upon in the clearest terms:

> It was too much the way ... to talk of this terrible Revolution as if it were the only harvest ever known under the skies that had not been sown—as if nothing had ever been done, or omitted to be done, that had led to it—as if observers of the wretched millions in France, and of the misused and perverted resources that should have made them prosperous, had not seen it inevitably coming, years before, and had not in plain terms recorded what they saw.

And again:

> All the devouring and insatiate monsters imagined since imagination could record itself, are fused in the one realization, Guillotine. And yet there is not in France, with its rich variety of soil and climate, a blade, a leaf, a root, a sprig, a peppercorn, which will grow to maturity under conditions more certain than those that have produced this horror. Crush humanity out of shape once more, under similar hammers, and it will twist itself into the same tortured forms.

In other words, the French aristocracy had dug their own graves. But there is no perception here of what is now called historic necessity. Dickens sees that the results are inevitable, given the causes, but he thinks that the causes might have been avoided. The Revolution is something that happens because centuries of oppression have made the French peasantry sub-human. If the wicked nobleman could somehow have turned over a new leaf, like Scrooge, there would have been no Revolution, no *jacquerie,* no guillotine—and so much the better. This is the opposite of the "revolutionary" attitude. From the "revolutionary" point of view the class-struggle is the main source of progress, and therefore the nobleman who robs the peasant and goads him to revolt is playing a necessary part, just as much as the Jacobin who guillotines the nobleman. Dickens never writes anywhere a line that can be interpreted as meaning this. Revolution as he sees it is merely a monster that is begotten by tyranny and always ends by devouring its own instruments. In Sidney Carton's vision at the foot of the guillotine, he foresees Defarge and the other leading spirits of the Terror all perishing under the same knife—which, in fact, was approximately what happened.

And Dickens is very sure that revolution *is* a monster. That is why everyone remembers the revolutionary scenes in *A Tale of Two Cities;* they have the quality of nightmare, and it is Dickens's own nightmare. Again and again he insists upon the meaningless horrors of revolution—the mass-butcheries, the injustice, the ever-present terror of spies, the frightful blood-lust of the mob. The descriptions of the Paris mob—the description, for instance, of the crowd of murderers struggling round the grindstone to sharpen their weapons before butchering the prisoners in the September massacres—outdo anything in *Barnaby Rudge.* The revolutionaries appear to him simply as degraded savages—in fact, as lunatics. He broods over their frenzies with a curious imaginative intensity. He describes them dancing the "Carmagnole," for instance:

> There could not be fewer than five hundred people and they were dancing like five thousand demons.... They danced to the popular Revolution song, keeping a ferocious time that was like a gnashing of teeth in unison.... They advanced, retreated, struck at one another's hands, clutched at one another's heads, spun round alone, caught one another, and spun round in pairs, until many of them dropped.... Suddenly they stopped again, paused, struck out the time afresh, forming into lines the width of the public way, and, with their heads low down and their hands high up, swooped screaming off. No fight could have been half so terrible as this dance. It was so emphatically a fallen sport—a something, once innocent, delivered over to all devilry.

He even credits some of these wretches with a taste for guillotining children. The passage I have abridged above ought to be read in full. It and others like it show how deep was Dickens's horror of revolutionary hysteria. Notice, for instance, that touch, "with their heads low down and their hands high up," etc., and the evil vision it conveys. Madame Defarge is a truly dreadful figure, certainly Dickens's most successful attempt at a *malignant* character. Defarge and others are simply "the new oppressors who have risen on the destruction of the old," the revolutionary courts are presided over by "the lowest, cruellest and worst populace," and so on and so forth. All the way through Dickens insists upon the nightmare insecurity of a revolutionary period, and in this he shows a great deal of prescience. "A law of the suspected, which struck away all security for liberty or life, and delivered over any good and innocent person to any bad and guilty one; prisons gorged with people who had committed no offense, and could obtain no hearing"—it would apply pretty accurately to several countries today.

The apologists of any revolution generally try to minimize its horrors; Dickens's impulse is to exaggerate them—and from a historical point of view he has certainly exaggerated. Even the Reign of Terror was a much smaller thing than he makes it appear. Though he quotes no figures, he gives the impression of a frenzied massacre lasting for years, whereas in reality the whole of the Terror, so far as the number of deaths goes, was a joke compared with one of Napoleon's battles. But the bloody knives and the tumbrils rolling to and fro create in his mind a special, sinister vision which he has succeeded in passing on to generations of readers. Thanks to Dickens, the very word "tumbril" has a murderous sound; one forgets that a tumbril is only a sort of farm-cart. To this day, to the average Englishman, the French Revolution means no more than a pyramid of severed heads. It is a strange thing that Dickens, much more in sympathy with the ideas of the Revolution than most Englishmen of his time, should have played a part in creating this impression.

If you hate violence and don't believe in politics, the only major remedy remaining is education. Perhaps society is past praying for, but there is always hope for the individual human being, if you can catch him young enough. This belief partly accounts for Dickens's preoccupation with childhood.

No one, at any rate no English writer, has written better about childhood than Dickens. In spite of all the knowledge that has accumulated since, in spite of the fact that children are now comparatively sanely treated, no novelist has shown the same power of entering into the child's point of view. I must have been about nine years old when I first read *David Copperfield*. The mental atmosphere of the opening chapters was so immediately intelligible to me that I vaguely imagined they had been written *by a child*. And yet when one re-reads the book as an adult and sees the Murdstones, for instance, dwindle from gigantic figures of doom into semi-comic monsters, these passages lose nothing. Dickens has been able to stand both inside and outside the child's mind, in such a way that the same scene can be wild burlesque or sinister reality, according to the age at which one reads it. Look, for instance, at the scene in which David Copperfield is unjustly suspected of eating the mutton chops; or the scene in which Pip, in *Great Expectations*, coming back from Miss Havisham's house and finding himself completely unable to describe what he has seen, takes refuge in a series of outrageous lies—which, of course, are eagerly believed. All the isolation of childhood is there. And how accurately he has recorded the mechanisms of the child's mind, its visualizing tendency, its sensitiveness to certain kinds of impression. Pip relates how in his childhood his ideas about his dead parents were derived from their tombstones:

> The shape of the letters on my father's, gave me an odd idea that he was a square, stout, dark man, with curly black hair. From the character and turn of the inscription, 'ALSO GEORGIANA, WIFE OF THE ABOVE,' I drew a childish conclusion that my mother was freckled and sickly. To five little stone lozenges, each about a foot and a half long, which were arranged in a neat row beside their grave, and were sacred to the memory of five little brothers of mine ... I am indebted for a belief I religiously entertained that they had all been born on their backs with their hands in their trouser-pockets, and had never taken them out in this state of existence.

There is a similar passage in *David Copperfield*. After biting Mr. Murdstone's hand, David is sent away to school and obliged to wear on his back a placard saying, "Take care of him. He bites." He looks at the door in the playground where the boys have carved their names and from the appearance of each name he seems to know in just what tone of voice the boy will read out the placard:

> There was one boy—a certain J. Steerforth—who cut his name very deep and very often, who, I conceived, would read it in a rather strong voice, and afterwards pull my hair. There was another boy, one Tommy Traddles, who I dreaded would make game of it, and pretend to be dreadfully frightened of me. There was a third, George Demple, who I fancied would sing it.

When I read this passage as a child, it seemed to me that those were exactly the pictures that those particular names would call up. The reason, of course, is the sound-associations of the words (Demple—"temple"; Traddles—probably "skedaddle"). But how many people, before Dickens, had ever noticed such things? A sympathetic attitude towards children was a much rarer thing in Dickens's day than it is now. The early nineteenth century was not a good time to be a child. In Dickens's youth children were still being "solemnly tried at a criminal bar, where they were held up to be seen," and it was not so long since boys of thirteen had been hanged for petty theft. The doctrine of "breaking the child's spirit" was in full vigor, and *The Fairchild Family* was a standard book for children till late into the century. This evil book is now issued in pretty-pretty expurgated editions, but it is well worth reading in the original version. It gives one some idea of the lengths to which child-discipline was sometimes carried. Mr. Fairchild, for instance, when he catches his children quarreling, first thrashes them, reciting Doctor Watts's "Let dogs delight to bark and bite" between blows of the cane, and then takes them to spend the afternoon beneath a gibbet where the rotting corpse of a murderer is hanging. In the earlier part of the century

scores of thousands of children, aged sometimes as young as six, were literally worked to death in the mines or cotton mills, and even at the fashionable
public schools boys were flogged till they ran with blood for a mistake in
their Latin verses. One thing which Dickens seems to have recognized, and
which most of his contemporaries did not, is the sadistic sexual element in
flogging. I think this can be inferred from *David Copperfield* and *Nicholas
Nickleby*. But mental cruelty to a child infuriates him as much as physical,
and though there is a fair number of exceptions, his schoolmasters are
generally scoundrels.

Except for the universities and the big public schools, every kind of education then existing in England gets a mauling at Dickens's hands. There is
Doctor Blimber's Academy, where little boys are blown up with Greek until
they burst, and the revolting charity schools of the period, which produces
specimens like Noah Claypole and Uriah Heep, and Salem House, and
Dotheboys Hall, and the disgraceful little dame-school kept by Mr. Wopsle's
great-aunt. Some of what Dickens says remains true even today. Salem
House is the ancestor of the modern "prep school," which still has a good
deal of resemblance to it; and as for Mr. Wopsle's great-aunt, some old fraud
of much the same stamp is carrying on at this moment in nearly every small
town in England. But, as usual, Dickens's criticism is neither creative nor
destructive. He sees the idiocy of an educational system founded on the
Greek lexicon and the wax-ended cane; on the other hand, he has no use for
the new kind of school that is coming up in the 'fifties and 'sixties, the
"modern" school, with its gritty insistence on "facts." What, then, *does* he
want? As always, what he appears to want is a moralized version of the
existing thing—the old type of school, but with no caning, no bullying or
underfeeding, and not quite so much Greek. Doctor Strong's school, to
which David Copperfield goes after he escapes from Murdstone & Grinby's,
is simply Salem House with the vices left out and a good deal of "old grey
stones" atmosphere thrown in:

> Doctor Strong's was an excellent school, as different from Mr. Creakle's
> as good is from evil. It was very gravely and decorously ordered, and on a
> sound system; with an appeal, in everything, to the honor and good faith
> of the boys ... which worked wonders. We all felt that we had a part in
> the management of the place, and in sustaining its character and dignity.
> Hence, we soon became warmly attached to it—I am sure I did for one,
> and I never knew, in all my time, of any boy being otherwise—and learnt
> with a good will, desiring to do it credit. We had noble games out of
> hours, and plenty of liberty; but even then, as I remember, we were well
> spoken of in the town, and rarely did any disgrace, by our appearance or
> manner, to the reputation of Doctor Strong and Doctor Strong's boys.

In the woolly vagueness of this passage one can see Dickens's utter lack of
any educational theory. He can imagine the *moral* atmosphere of a good

school, but nothing further. The boys "learnt with a good will," but what did they learn? No doubt it was Doctor Blimber's curriculum, a little watered down. Considering the attitude to society that is everywhere implied in Dickens's novels, it comes as rather a shock to learn that he sent his eldest son to Eton and sent all his children through the ordinary educational mill. Gissing seems to think that he may have done this because he was painfully conscious of being under-educated himself. Here perhaps Gissing is influenced by his own love of classical learning. Dickens had had little or no formal education, but he lost nothing by missing it, and on the whole he seems to have been aware of this. If he was unable to imagine a better school than Doctor Strong's, or, in real life, than Eton, it was probably due to an intellectual deficiency rather different from the one Gissing suggests.

It seems that in every attack Dickens makes upon society he is always pointing to a change of spirit rather than a change of structure. It is hopeless to try and pin him down to any definite remedy, still more to any political doctrine. His approach is always along the moral plane, and his attitude is sufficiently summed up in that remark about Strong's school being as different from Creakle's "as good is from evil." Two things can be very much alike and yet abysmally different. Heaven and Hell are in the same place. Useless to change institutions without a "change of heart"—that, essentially, is what he is always saying.

If that were all, he might be no more than a cheer-up writer, a reactionary humbug. A "change of heart" is in fact *the* alibi of people who do not wish to endanger the *status quo*. But Dickens is not a humbug, except in minor matters, and the strongest single impression one carries away from his books is that of a hatred of tyranny. I said earlier that Dickens is not *in the accepted sense* a revolutionary writer. But it is not at all certain that a merely moral criticism of society may not be just as "revolutionary"—and revolution, after all, means turning things upside down—as the politico-economic criticism which is fashionable at this moment. Blake was not a politician, but there is more understanding of the nature of capitalist society in a poem like "I wander through each charter'd street" than in three-quarters of Socialist literature. Progress is not an illusion, it happens, but it is slow and invariably disappointing. There is always a new tyrant waiting to take over from the old—generally not quite so bad, but still a tyrant. Consequently two viewpoints are always tenable. The one, how can you improve human nature until you have changed the system? The other, what is the use of changing the system before you have improved human nature? They appeal to different individuals, and they probably show a tendency to alternate in point of time. The moralist and the revolutionary are constantly undermining one another. Marx exploded a hundred tons of dynamite beneath the moralist position, and we are still living in the echo of that tremendous crash. But already, somewhere or other, the sappers are at work and fresh dynamite is being tamped in place to blow Marx at the moon. Then Marx, or somebody like him, will come back with yet more dynamite, and so the process continues, to an end we cannot yet foresee. The central problem—how to prevent power from being abused—remains unsolved. Dickens, who had not the vision to see that private property is an obstructive nuisance, had the vision to see that. "If men would behave decently the world would be decent" is not such a platitude as it sounds.

DISCUSSION AND WRITING

1. Trace the origin or history of the following words and show how etymological information helps clarify their meanings and associations: *medievalism, proletariat, bourgeois, subversive, radical, intelligentsia, revolutionary, anomaly, laissez faire, socialism, Cubist, Bolshevism, rentier, deus ex machina, guillotine, Jacobin, burlesque, sinister, alibi, status quo.*

2. Orwell is the author of a famous essay on prose style. After studying his own practice as a writer, what advice would you give a writer trying to imitate the clarity and vigor of Orwell's prose? Use detailed illustrations.

3. Where in the essay does Orwell ask the key question he is trying to answer? Trace the general outline of Orwell's argument. Examine and describe his use of evidence. What sentence in the essay best sums up Orwell's attitude toward Dickens?

4. To judge from the excerpts quoted by Orwell, what are some of the resources, effects, and limitations of fiction in dealing with historical events, social abuses, and similar subjects?

5. In the light of Orwell's discussion, examine one of Dickens's books with which you are familiar. Show in detail to what extent you find Orwell's approach valid, helpful, instructive, or misleading.

6. How familiar is the attitude toward social problems or abuses that Orwell ascribes to Dickens? How effective is it? Limit your illustrations to one area, such as unemployment, segregation, care for the aged, voting rights.

7. Generally, how fruitful or appropriate is it to examine literary classics for their social and political implications? From this point of view, examine a classic that is familiar to you.

8. Compare and contrast George Orwell's and Aldous Huxley's treatment of the relationship between truth and fiction.

9. To judge from your reading about writers and artists, how true is it that a man's literary or artistic personality has "little or nothing to do with his private character"?

10. To what extent have your views on politics or history been influenced by novels, plays, or motion pictures? Discuss detailed examples from one of these media.

FURTHER READING

What work of fiction have you read that has a claim to be considered a "documentary novel," such as Robert Penn Warren, *All the King's Men* (1946); Irwin

Shaw, *The Young Lions* (1948); Norman Mailer, *The Naked and the Dead* (1948); Theodor Plievier, *Moscow* (1953); Graham Greene, *The Quiet American* (1955); or Edwin O'Connor, *The Last Hurrah* (1956)? Discuss the author's "message" and his use of the novel as a medium for conveying it.

ARTHUR MILLER

Arthur Miller was born in New York City in 1915 and attended the University of Michigan in the thirties. He established a reputation as one of America's leading playwrights by a number of important plays: *All My Sons* (1947), *Death of a Salesman* (1949), *The Crucible* (1953). Much of his work shows an awareness of basic social and moral concerns. His plays typically explore man's relation to society—his responsibility toward his fellow man, the causes of injustice. His magazine articles show him as an effective spokesman of serious American drama. The following selection was first published in *Holiday* in January 1955. Miller here uses informal personal reminiscence as a vehicle for his convictions about the collaboration between playwright and actor that results in great theater.

The American Theater

The American theater occupies five side streets, Forty-Fourth to Forty-Ninth, between Eighth Avenue and Broadway, with a few additional theaters to the north and south and across Broadway. In these thirty-two buildings every new play in the United States starts its life and ends it. There will undoubtedly be many objections to this statement—you cannot say anything about our theater without fear of contradiction—and demurrers will come from professors of drama, stock-company directors, and little-theater people in New York, Texas, California and elsewhere who will claim that Broadway is not the United States and that much theatrical production is going on in other places. I agree, and repeat only that with practically no exceptions, the *new* American plays originate on Broadway. I would add that I wish they didn't, but they do. The American theater is five blocks long, by about one and a half blocks wide.

It would seem a simple matter to characterize so limited an area, but I write this with the certainty that whatever I say will appear not only new and strange to many theater people but utterly untrue. And this is because the man or woman whose tapping shoes you hear from the second-story dance studio over the delicatessen on Forty-Sixth Street is in the theater, the ballet girl hurrying to rehearsal in her polo coat with a copy of Rimbaud in her pocket is in the theater, the peasant-faced Irish stagehand sunning himself on the sidewalk with a *Racing Form* in his hand is in the theater, the slow-staring, bald-headed ticket broker blinking out through his agency window is in the theater, the wealthy, Park Avenue–born producer is in the theater and his cigar-smoking colleague from the West Bronx is in the theater.

In the audience itself, though the bulk of it is of the middle class, there is no uniformity either. There will be the businessman in town from Duluth sitting beside Marlene Dietrich whom he will probably not recognize and behind them two esthetes from Harvard. The word theater means different things to different groups. To some its very pinnacle is *South Pacific,* which is despised by the esthetes, who in turn cherish a wispy fantasy whose meaning escapes the Duluth man. There is a vast group of people for whom the theater means nothing but amusement, and amusement means a musical or light comedy; and there are others who reserve their greatest enthusiasm for heavy dramas that they can chew on.

The actors, directors and writers themselves are just as varied. There are playwrights who are as illiterate as high-school boys, and there are playwrights like Maxwell Anderson, who have spent a good deal of their lives studying the Elizabethan drama and attempting to re-create its mood and luxuriance on Broadway. There are fine actors who are universally admired but who have absolutely no theory of acting and there are other actors, equally good or equally bad, who have spent years studying the history of acting, taking voice lessons and learning how to dance in order to walk more gracefully.

The theater, obviously, is an entirely different animal to each of these groups. As for myself, I cannot pretend to any Olympian viewpoint about it either. I believe there is a confusion in many minds between Show Business and the Theater. I belong to the Theater, which happens at the moment to be in a bad way, but since this word, when capitalized, usually implies something uplifting and boring, I must add that the rarely seen but very real theater is the most engrossing theater of all; and when it isn't it is nothing. I make the distinction so that the reader will be warned where my prejudice lies and discount accordingly.

The "glamour of the theater," which is and always will be its most powerful attraction, is a subject of daily reporting by almost every newspaper, gossip columnist, and radio station. Every year, around the first cool days of fall, the illustrated sections of the press and the picture magazines and newsreels run the familiar photographs of the limousines gliding up to the lighted marquees, the taxis and cars pressing into Forty-Fourth Street for the opening of some musical or drama, the inevitable montage of Sardi's restaurant at dinnertime and so on. For anyone who has made the slightest mark in this occupation there is a line of type waiting when he so much as pays his rent on time. Soon after *Death of a Salesman* opened, it was reported that I was a millionaire, which was pleasant news, if not true, and that despite my new affluence I still rode the subways. I keep wondering who was watching me going through the turnstiles. And the importance of this news still escapes me.

In fact, while everybody in the business is worried about its future—and if there is a heart of uncertainty in the country its loudest beat may be heard on these five blocks—to read the columns and the usual sources of theatrical information you would think it was all a continuous carnival of divorce, practical jokes, hilarious wit, elopements and sudden acquisition of enormous wealth.

But there is evidently no way of glamorizing the often inspiring and heart-lifting experiences of the work itself, a kind of labor that began in the Western world about three thousand years ago, and which has provided some of the most powerful insights we possess into the way men think and feel.

The net result of this image of our theater, the carnival image, is that the out-of-towner strolling these streets may quickly sense that he has been bilked. He will discover, especially if he arrives in midday, that the theater buildings themselves are tawdry-looking, and may well be disillusioned when he sees that some of the marquees do not have even the electrically lit signs of his home movie house—only temporary cardboards painted with the title of the show within. When he ventures into the outer lobby he will perhaps be shocked to discover that a seat costs six—or even eight—dollars and, if the show is a hit, that he won't get a ticket for six months or a year unless he pays a scalper twenty-five to a hundred dollars. If it is not a hit, and he buys a ticket legitimately, he may learn that he could have bought two for the price of one; and by the time he gets inside for the performance, some of the glamour of it all may have worn a bit thin.

Once inside, however, our visitor may find certain compensations. He may recognize very important people, from statesmen to movie stars, sitting nearby, whom he would not see in the home-town movie house. He will notice a certain dressed-up air about people, a few even wearing evening clothes. There are ushers to show him to his seat, and there is a program, and possibly a little more surprising is the coat-check man waiting as he passes through the outer door. There is still a vestigial ceremony about playgoing from which one may derive a sense of self-importance if not careful, and it all may lead our visitor to feel that he is, indeed, among ladies and gentlemen.

Then, as the lights go down and the curtain rises, our visitor may feel a certain strange tension, an expectancy, and an intense curiosity that he never knew in a theater before. Instead of the enormity of the movie image before which he could sit back and relax, he is confronted by human beings in life-size, and since their voices do not roar out at him from a single point to which his ear may tune in once and then relax, he must pay more attention, his eyes must rove over a thirty-foot expanse; he must, in other words, *discover*. And if there happens to be something real up there, something human, something true, our visitor may come away with a new feeling in his heart, a sense of having been a part of something quite extraordinary and even beautiful. Unlike the movies, unlike television, he may feel he has been present at an *occasion*. For outside this theater, no one in the world heard what he heard or saw what he saw this night. I know that, for myself, there is nothing so immediate, so actual, as an excellent performance of an excellent play. I have never known the smell of sweat in a movie house. I have known it in the theater—and they are also air-conditioned. Nor have I known in a movie house the kind of audience unity that occasionally is created in the theater, an air of oneness among strangers that is possible in only one other gathering place—a church.

Nevertheless, by every account our theater is a vanishing institution. We have some thirty-two houses going today in New York as against forty or more ten years ago, and between seventy and eighty in the twenties. I could weave you such a tapestry of evil omens as to make it a closed case that we will have no theater in America in two decades. What I should like to do instead, however, is to wonder aloud, as it were, why it is that each year thousands of aspiring actors, directors and playwrights continue to press into these five blocks from every corner of the country when they know, or learn very quickly, that ninety per cent of the professional actors are normally unemployed, that most of the producers are dead broke or within three cigars of being broke, and that to become a director of a Broadway show one must be prepared to gamble five to ten to fifteen years of one's life. And yet, on all the trains they keep coming, aspiring actors and eager audiences both.

As for the aspiring actors, I will not pretend to hunt for an answer, because I know it. It is simply that there are always certain persons who are born without all their marbles. Even so, the fullblown actors are merely the completed types of the secret actors who are called producers, backers, directors, yes, and playwrights. The rest of us would have been actors had we had the talent, or a left and right foot instead of two left ones, or straight teeth, or self-assurance. The actor himself is the lunacy in full profusion—the lunacy which in the others is partially concealed.

All over the country there are nine-year-old girls, for instance, who are walking around the house like my daughter is at this very moment, in high-heeled shoes with the lace tablecloth trailing from their shoulders. If mine doesn't recover before she is sixteen she will wake up one morning and something will click inside her head and she will go and hang around some producer's office, and if he talks to her, or just asks her what time it is, she may well be doomed for life.

The five blocks, therefore, are unlike any other five blocks in the United States, if only because here so many grown people are walking around trailing the old lace tablecloth from their shoulders.

If you know how to look you will find them waiting on you in Schrafft's, or behind the orange-drink counter at Nedick's. As a matter of fact, I have got so attuned to a certain look in their eyes that I can sometimes spot them on Sixth Avenue, which is not in the theater district. I was passing a truck being loaded there one day when I noticed a boy, unshaven, his hair uncombed, wearing paratroop boots; he was pitching boxes into the truck. And he looked at me, just a glance, and I thought to myself that he must be an actor. And about three days later I was sitting in my producer's office interviewing actors for *The Crucible,* when in he walked. Characteristically, he did not remember seeing me before—actors rarely do, since they are not looking at anyone but rather are being looked *at.* When asked the usual questions about his experience he just shrugged, and when asked if he wanted to read for us he shrugged again, quite as though the questions were impertinent when addressed to a great artist, and I knew then why I had tabbed him for an actor. It was the time when all the young actors were being Marlon Brando. He was being Marlon Brando even when loading the truck, for a real truck driver would never show up for work looking so unkempt.

The blessed blindness of actors to everything around them, their intense preoccupation with themselves, is the basic characteristic of all Broadway, and underlies most of its troubles, which, in another industry, would have been solved long ago. But since it is glamour which brings the young to Broadway, as well as the audience, it cannot be so quickly dismissed. The fact is, it exists. But it is not the glamour you are probably thinking of.

The time is gone when the Great Producer kept four or five Great Stars in ten-room apartments on Park Avenue, and they waited in their gilded cages for days and weeks for the Impresario to call for them—for without him they were forbidden to be seen in public lest they lose their "distance," their altitude above the common things of life. The time is gone when the leading lady dared not arrive at the theater in anything but a limousine with chauffeur and lap robe, while a line of stovepipe-hatted men waited in the stage-door alley with flowers in their manicured hands. There are a few hangovers, of course, and I remember a show in Boston a few years ago whose leading lady, an hour before curtain time, phoned the producer to say she was ill and could not play. The poor man was desperate, but there was an old-time doorman in that theater who happened to be near the phone and he said, "Get a limousine and a chauffeur." The producer, a contemporary type who was as familiar with gallantry as any other businessman, mastered his uncertainty and hired a car and chauffeur and sent a mass of roses to the lady's hotel room. Her fever vanished in roughly four minutes and she played better than she ever had, and I must confess I couldn't blame her for wanting the glamour even if she had had to make it herself.

But leading ladies, nowadays, arrive in a taxi, and a lot of them come in by bus or subway.

I have been around only ten years or so and I never knew the kind of glamour that evidently existed. But a few years ago I had occasion to visit John Golden in his office, and I saw then that there was, in fact, a kind of bravado about being in the theater, a declaration of war against all ordinariness that I can find no more.

The average theatrical producer's office today consists mainly of a telephone, a girl to answer it, an outer room for actors to wait in, and an inner room with a window for the producer to stare out of when he has nothing to produce.

John Golden's office is different. It rests on top of the St. James Theater; you rise in a private elevator, and come out in a dark, paper-cluttered reception room where an elderly and very wise lady bars you—with the help of a little gate—from entry. You know at once that behind her is not merely a man, but a Presence.

In his office the walls are painted with smoke. They are very dark and covered with hundreds of photographs, plaques, statuettes, hanging things and jutting things of gold, silver and shiny brass. There is an Oriental rug on the floor, an ornate desk at the distant end of the room, and there sits John Golden. Behind him stands an imposing ascent of bookshelves filled with leather-bound plays he has produced. In a smaller adjoining room is a barber chair where his hair is cut, his beard shaved, and, I presume, his shoes shined. The windows are covered with drapes and obstructing statuary, because when this office was created, the man who worked in it had no time to look out into the street.

It was a time when the railroads were freighting out one after another of his productions, winter and summer, to all sections of the country. It was a time when, unlike now, important performers and even playwrights were kept on long-term contracts, when a producer owned his own theater and used his own money and was therefore not an accountant, nor even a businessman, but an impresario. In short, it was the time before the masses had left the theater for the new movies, and the theater was the main source of American popular entertainment. This office is now a kind of museum. There were once many like it, and many men like John Golden.

Their counterparts, the reflected images of Ziegfeld, Frohman, Belasco and the others, appeared only later in Hollywood, for the masses are needed to create impresarios, or more precisely, a lucrative mass market. In Golden's office I saw the genesis of so much we have come to associate with Hollywood: the stars under long-term contract, the planning of one production after another instead of the present one-shot Broadway practice, the sense of permanence and even security. None of these are part of Broadway now, and they appear in their afterglow above the St. James; for it is not the masses we serve any more, not the "American People," but a fraction of one class—the more or less better-educated people, or the people aspiring to culture.

Golden's eyes blazed with pleasure as he talked of plays long since gone, like *Turn to the Right* and *Lightnin'* and others I remember my father raving about when I was a boy, and finally he sat back and mused about playwriting.

"You fellows have a much harder time," he said, "much harder than in the old days; nowadays every show has to seem new and original. But in the old days, you know, we had what you might call favorite scenes. There was the scene where the mother puts a candle on the window sill while she waits for her long-lost boy to come home. They loved that scene. We put that scene in one play after another. You can't do things like that any more. The audience is too smart now. They're more educated, I suppose, and sophisticated. Of course it was all sentimental, I guess, but they were good shows."

He was right, of course, except you *can* do that now; the movies have been doing it for thirty or forty years and now television is doing it all over again. I remember a friend who had worked in Hollywood writing a picture. The producer called him in with a bright new idea for a scene to be inserted in the script. My friend listened and was amazed. "But just last month you released a picture with that same scene in it," he reminded the producer.

"Sure," said the producer, "and didn't it go great?"

The Golden species of glamour is gone with the masses; it went with the big money to Hollywood, and now it is creating itself all over agin in television. The present-day actors and directors would probably seem tame and dull to their counterparts of thirty and forty years ago. David Belasco, for instance, had even convinced himself that his was a glamorous profession, and took to dressing in black like a priest—the high priest of the theater—and turned his collar around to prove it. He carried on as no contemporary director would dare to do. Toward the last days of rehearsal, when he wanted some wooden but very beautiful leading lady to break down and weep, he would take out a watch, the watch he had been displaying for weeks as the one his mother gave him on her deathbed, and smash it on the stage floor in a high dudgeon, thus frightening the actress to tears and making her putty in his hands. It need hardly be added that he kept a large supply of these watches, each worth one dollar.

The traditional idea of the actor with his haughty stance, his peaked eyebrows, elegant speech, artistic temperament and a necessary disdain for all that was common and plain, has long since disappeared. Now they are all trying to appear as ordinary as your Uncle Max. A group of actors sitting at a bar these days could easily be mistaken for delegates to a convention of white-collar people. They are more likely, upon landing in a hit show, to hurry over to the offices of a tax consultant than to rush out and buy a new Jaguar. For a few years after the war a certain amount of effort was put into aging their dungarees and wearing turtle-neck sweaters and some of them stopped combing their hair, like the boy I noticed loading the truck. But you don't get Marlon Brando's talent by avoiding a bath, and gradually this fad has vanished. There are more "colorful" personalities up here in the tiny Connecticut village where I spend summers than you will find on all Broadway. The only real showman I know of is Joshua Logan, who can throw a party for a hundred people in his Park Avenue apartment and make it appear a normal evening. Logan is the only director I can name who would dare to knock a stage apart and build into it a real swimming pool, as he did for the musical *Wish You Were Here,* and can still talk about the theater with the open, full-blown excitement of one who has no reservations about it. The other directors, at least the half dozen I know—and there are not many more—are more likely to be as deadly serious as any atomic physicist, and equally worried.

There is a special aura about the theater, nevertheless, a glamour, too, but it has little connection with the publicity that seeks to create it. There is undoubtedly as much sexual fooling around as there is in the refrigerator business, but I doubt if there is much more. The notion of theatrical immorality began when actors were socially inferior by common consent; but now a Winnifred Cushing (of the Boston Cushings), the loose woman in *Death of a Salesman,* hurries home to her mother after each show.

Not that it is an ordinary life. There is still nothing quite like it, if only because of the fanaticism with which so many respond to its lure. One cannot sit in a producer's office day after day interviewing actors for a play without being struck by their insistence that they belong in the theater and intend to make their lives in it. In the outer reception rooms of any producer's office at casting time is a cross section of a hundred small towns and big cities, the sons and daughters of the rich families and of the middle-class families and of families from the wrong side of the tracks. One feels, on meeting a youngster from a way-station town or a New Mexico ranch, that the spores of this poor theater must still possess vitality to have flown so far and rooted so deep. It is pathetic, it is saddening, but a thing is only dead when nobody wants it, and they do want it desperately. It is nothing unusual to tell a girl who has come to a casting office that she looks too respectable for the part, and to be greeted by her an hour later dressed in a slinky black dress, spike heels, outlandishly overdone make-up and blond dye in her hair that has hardly had time to dry. One of our best-known actresses had her bowlegs broken in order to appear as she thought she must on the stage, and there is an actor who did the same to his knees in order to play Hamlet in tights.

There is, it must be admitted, an egotism in this that can neither be measured nor sometimes even stomached, but at casting time, when one spends hour after hour in the presence of human beings with so powerful a conviction and so great a desire to be heard and seen and judged as artists, the thing begins to surpass mere egotism and assumes the proportion of a cause, a belief, a mission. And when such sacrifices are made in its name one must begin to wonder at the circumstances that have reduced it to its present chaos. It might be helpful to take a look at how the whole thing is organized—or disorganized.

Everything begins with a script. I must add right off that in the old mass theater that came to an end somewhere in the late twenties, when the movies took over, the script was as often as not a botch of stolen scenes, off-the-cuff inventions of the producer or director, or simply pasted-together situations designed for some leading player. The audience today, however, demands more, and so the script has become the Holy Grail for which a producer dreams, prays, and lives every day of his life. It being so valuable, and so difficult to write, it is leased by the author on a royalty basis and never sold outright.

There are seemingly hundreds of producers, but actually only fifteen or twenty go on year after year. Few are wealthy, and money is usually promoted or lured out of any crack where it can be found. It is a common, although not universal, practice to hold a gathering of potential backers before whom either the playwright or the director reads the script. Established producers regard this as beneath their dignity, but some don't, or can't afford to. These readings usually take place either on Park Avenue or on swank Beekman Place, for some reason, and while I never attended one, I have known many playwrights who have, but never heard of one dollar being raised in that way.

Script in hand, then, and money either raised or on its way—usually in amounts under five hundred dollars per backer—the producer hires a director, also on a percentage with a fee in advance, and a scene designer; the set is sketched, approved, and ordered built. Casting begins. While the author sits home revising his script—for some reason no script can be produced as the author wrote it—agents are apprised of the kinds of parts to be filled, and in the producer's reception room next morning all hell breaks loose.

The basis upon which actors are hired or not hired is sometimes quite sound; for example, they may have been seen recently in a part which leads the director to believe they are right for the new role; but quite as often a horde of applicants is waiting beyond the door of the producer's private office and neither he nor the director nor the author has the slightest knowledge of any of them. It is at this point that things become painful, for the strange actor sits before them, so nervous and frightened that he either starts talking and can't stop, and sometimes *says* he can't stop, or is unable to say anything at all and says *that*. During the casting of one of my plays there entered a middle-aged woman who was so frightened she suddenly started to sing. The play being no musical, this was slightly beside the point, but the producer, the director and myself, feeling so guilty ourselves, sat there and heard her through.

To further complicate matters there is each year the actor or actress who suddenly becomes what they call "hot." A hot performer is one not yet well-known, but who, for some mysterious reason, is generally conceded to be a coming star. It is possible, naturally, that a hot performer really has talent, but it is equally possible, and much more likely, that she or he is not a whit more attractive or more talented than a hundred others. Nevertheless, there comes a morning when every producer in these five blocks—some of them with parts the performer could never play—simply has to have him or her. Next season, of course, nobody hears about the new star and it starts all over again with somebody else.

All that is chancy in life, all that is fortuitous, is magnified to the bursting point at casting time; and that, I suspect, is one of the attractions of this whole affair, for it makes the ultimate winning of a part so much more zesty. It is also, to many actors, a most degrading process and more and more of them refuse to submit to these interviews until after the most delicate advances of friendship and hospitality are made to them. And their use of agents as intermediaries is often an attempt to soften the awkwardness of their applying for work.

The theatrical agents, in keeping with the unpredictable lunacy of the business, may be great corporations like the Music Corporation of America, which has an entire building on Madison Avenue, and will sell you anything from a tap dancer to a movie star, a symphony orchestra, saxophonists, crooners, scene designers, actors and playwrights, to a movie script complete with cast; or they may be like Jane Broder, who works alone and can spread out her arms and touch both walls of her office. They may even be like Carl Cowl, who lives around the corner from me in Brooklyn. Carl is an ex-seaman who still ships out when he has no likely scripts on hand to sell, and when things get too nerve-racking he stays up all night playing Mozart on his flute. MCA has antique desks, English 18th Century prints, old broken antique clocks and inoperative antique barometers hanging on its paneled walls, but Carl Cowl had a hole in his floor that the cat got into and when he finally got the landlord to repair it he was happy and sat down to play his flute again; but he heard meowing, and they had to rip the floor open again to let out the cat. Still, Carl is not incapable of landing a hit play and neither more nor less likely than MCA to get it produced, and that is another handicraft aspect of this much publicized small business, a quality of opportunity which keeps people coming into it. The fact is that theatrical agents do not sell anyone or anything in the way one sells merchandise. Their existence is mainly due to the need theater people have for a home, some semblance of order in their lives, some sense of being wanted during the long periods when they have nothing to do. To have an agent is to have a kind of reassurance that you exist. The actor is hired, however, mainly because he is wanted for the role.

By intuition, then, by rumor, on the recommendation of an agent—usually heartfelt; out of sheer exhaustion, an upsurge of sudden hope or what not, several candidates for each role are selected in the office of the producer, and are called for readings on the stage of a theater.

It is here that the still unsolved mystery begins, the mystery of what makes a stage performer. There are persons who, in an office, seem exciting candidates for a role, but as soon as they step onto a stage the observers out front—if they are experienced—know that the blessing was not given them. For myself, I know it when, regardless of how well the actor is reading, my eyes begin to wander up to the brick wall back of the stage. Conversely, there are many who make little impression in an office, but once on the stage it is impossible to take one's attention from them. It is neither a question of technique nor ability, I think, but some quality of surprise inherent in the person.

For instance, when we were searching for a woman to play Linda, the mother in *Death of a Salesman,* a lady came in whom we all knew but could never imagine in the part. We needed a woman who looked as though she had lived in a house dress all her life, even somewhat coarse and certainly less than brilliant. Mildred Dunnock insisted she was that woman, but she was frail, delicate, not long ago a teacher in a girl's college, and a cultivated citizen who probably would not be out of place in a cabinet post. We told her this, in effect, and she understood, and left.

And the next day the line of women formed again in the wings and suddenly there was Milly again. Now she had padded herself from neck to hemline to look a bit bigger, and for a moment none of us recognized her, and she read again. As soon as she spoke we started to laugh at her ruse; but we saw, too, that she *was* a little more worn now, and seemed less well-maintained, and while she was not quite ordinary she reminded you of women who were. But we all agreed, when she was finished reading, that she was not right, and she left.

Next day she was there again in another getup and the next and the next, and each day she agreed with us that she was wrong; and to make a long story short when it came time to make the final selection it had to be Milly and she turned out to be magnificent. But in this case we had known her work; there was no doubt that she was an excellent actress. The number of talented applicants who are turned down because they are unknown is very large. Such is the crap-shooting chanciness of the business, its chaos, and part of its charm. In a world where one's fate so often seems machined and standardized, and unlikely to suddenly change, these five blocks are like a stockade inside which are people who insist that the unexpected, the sudden chance, must survive. And to experience it they keep coming on all the trains.

But to understand its apparently deathless lure for so many it is necessary, finally, to have participated in the first production of a new play. When a director takes his place at the beaten-up wooden table placed at the edge of the stage, and the cast for the first time sit before him in a semicircle, and he gives the nod to the actor who has the opening lines, the world seems to be filling with a kind of hope, a kind of regeneration that, at the time, anyway, makes all the sacrifices worth while.

The production of a new play, I have often thought, is like another chance in life, a chance to emerge cleansed of one's imperfections. Here, as when one was very young, it seems possible again to attain even greatness, or happiness, or some otherwise unattainable joy. And when production never loses that air of hope through all its three-and-a-half-week rehearsal period, one feels alive as at no other imaginable occasion. At such a time, it seems to all concerned that the very heart of life's mystery is what must be penetrated. They watch the director and each other and they listen with the avid attention of deaf mutes who have suddenly learned to speak and hear. Above their heads there begins to form a tantalizing sort of cloud, a question, a challenge to penetrate the mystery of why men move and speak and act.

It is a kind of glamour that can never be reported in a newspaper column, and yet it is the center of all the lure theater has. It is a kind of soul-testing that ordinary people rarely experience except in the greatest emergencies. The actor who has always regarded himself as a strong spirit discovers now that his vaunted power somehow sounds querulous, and he must look within himself to find his strength. The actress who has made her way on her charm discovers that she appears not charming so much as shallow now, and must evaluate herself all over again, and create anew what she always took for granted. And the great performers are merely those who have been able to face themselves without remorse.

In the production of a good play with a good cast and a knowing director a kind of banding-together occurs; there is formed a fraternity whose members share a mutual sense of destiny. In these five blocks, where the rapping of the tap dancer's feet and the bawling of the phonographs in the record-shop doorways mix with the roar of the Broadway traffic; where the lonely, the perverted, and the lost wander like the souls in Dante's hell and the life of the spirit seems impossible, there are still little circles of actors in the dead silence of empty theaters, with a director in their center, and a new creation of life taking place.

There are always certain moments in such rehearsals, moments of such wonder that the memory of them serves to further entrap all who witness them into this most insecure of all professions. Remembering such moments the resolution to leave and get a "real" job vanishes and they are hooked again.

I think of Lee Cobb, the greatest dramatic actor I ever saw, when he was creating the role of Willy Loman in *Death of a Salesman*. When I hear people scoffing at actors as mere exhibitionists, when I hear them ask why there must be a theater if it cannot support itself as any business must, when I myself grow sick and weary of the endless waste and the many travesties of this most abused of all arts, I think then of Lee Cobb making that role and I know that the theater can yet be one of the chief glories of mankind.

He sat for days on the stage like a great lump, a sick seal, a mourning walrus. When it came his time to speak lines, he whispered meaninglessly. Kazan, the director, pretended certainty, but from where I sat he looked like an ant trying to prod an elephant off his haunches. Ten days went by. The other actors were by now much further advanced: Milly Dunnock, playing Linda, was already creating a role; Arthur Kennedy as Biff had long since begun to reach for his high notes; Cameron Mitchell had many scenes already perfected; but Cobb stared at them, heavy-eyed, morose, even persecuted, it seemed.

And then, one afternoon, there on the stage of the New Amsterdam way up on top of a movie theater on 42nd Street (this roof theater had once been Ziegfeld's private playhouse in the gilded times, and now was barely heated and misty with dust), Lee rose from his chair and looked at Milly Dunnock and there was a silence. And then he said, "I was driving along, you understand, and then all of a sudden I'm going off the road...."

And the theater vanished. The stage vanished. The chill of an age-old recognition shuddered my spine; a voice was sounding in the dimly lit air up front, a created spirit, an incarnation, a Godlike creation was taking place; a new human being was being formed before all our eyes, born for the first time on this earth, made real by an act of will, by an artist's summoning up all his memories and his intelligence; a birth was taking place above the meaningless traffic below; a man was here transcending the limits of his body and his own history. Through the complete concentration of his mind he had even altered the stance of his body, which now was strangely not the body of Lee Cobb (he was 37 then) but of a sixty-year-old salesman; a mere glance of his eye created a window beside him; with the gentle touch of his hand on this empty stage a bed appeared, and when he glanced up at the emptiness above him a ceiling was there, and there was even a crack in it where his stare rested.

I knew then that something astounding was being made here. It would have been almost enough for me without even opening the play. The actors, like myself and Kazan and the producer, were happy, of course, that we might have a hit; but there was a good deal more. There was a new fact of life, there was an alteration of history for all of us that afternoon.

There is a certain immortality involved in theater, not created by monuments and books, but through the knowledge the actor keeps to his dying day that on a certain afternoon, in an empty and dusty theater, he cast a shadow of a being that was not himself but the distillation of all he had ever observed; all the unsingable heartsong the ordinary man may feel but never utter, he gave voice to. And by that he somehow joins the ages.

And that is the glamour that remains, but it will not be found in the gossip columns. And it is enough, once discovered, to make people stay with the theater, and others to come seeking it.

I think also that people keep coming into these five blocks because the theater is still so simple, so old-fashioned. And that is why, however often its obsequies are intoned, it somehow never really dies. Because underneath our shiny fronts of stone, our fascination with gadgets and our new toys that can blow the earth into a million stars, we are still outside the doorway through which the great answers wait. Not all the cameras in Christendom nor all the tricky lights will move us one step closer to a better understanding of ourselves, but only, as it always was, the truly written word, the profoundly felt gesture, the naked and direct contemplation of man which is the enduring glamour of the stage.

DISCUSSION AND WRITING

1. Define or explain: *demurrer, esthete, pinnacle, montage, affluence, tawdry, scalper, tapestry, unkempt, impresario, bravado, ornate, lucrative, genesis, aura, egotism, apprise, fortuitous, ruse, avid, vaunt, querulous, travesty, incarnation, obsequies.* Explain "an *Olympian* viewpoint," "a continuous *carnival* of divorce," "*vestigial* ceremony," "in a high *dudgeon*," "haughty *stance*," "script has become the *Holy Grail*," "a *tantalizing* sort of cloud."

2. Point out examples of a colloquial style. Generally, what is the tone of Miller's essay? Examine his use of humor, anecdote, personal reminiscence.

3. In one paragraph, sum up Miller's account of the "glamour" of the stage.

4. Outline Miller's essay, pointing out the general pattern that underlies his apparently casual discussion.

5. Select someone whom you would call a great actor or actress. Discuss his work.

6. Miller points out that the term "theater" covers many forms, from musical to "heavy drama." What kind of stage offering do you know best? What is its main attraction for its audience?

7. Discuss the appeal of a profession or a way of life that for you has genuine glamor.

8. Is the serious actor or artist an alien in American life? Is the American environment hostile to young people who seek a career in the theater or the arts?

9. Much modern drama—for instance, the plays of Pirandello, Becket, Genêt, Ionesco—radically departs from familiar theatrical conventions. Discuss a modern play you have seen and the special demands it makes on the audience.

10. Study a number of reviews by the theater critic of a newspaper or magazine. What are the critic's standards, expectations, preferences, antipathies?

FURTHER READING

Two well-known discussions of the premises of serious modern drama are Joseph Wood Krutch, "The Tragic Fallacy," *Atlantic,* November 1928 (reprinted in *The Modern Temper*); and Arthur Miller, "Tragedy and the Common Man," *New York Times,* February 27, 1949.

JOHN CIARDI

Critical discussion of poetry often takes the form of highly technical analysis and of controversy among specialists. By contrast, John Ciardi (born 1916) has effectively devoted himself to winning for poetry the wider audience that he thinks it deserves. For many years a professor of English at Rutgers University, he is poetry editor of the *Saturday Review*. Besides his concern with poetry as critic, editor, and teacher, Mr. Ciardi has published several volumes of his own poetry and has been translating Dante's *Divine Comedy*. The following article illustrates well his dogged persistence in trying to make the poet's work and the motives behind it intelligible to the layman.

The Act of Language

At the beginning of *The Divine Comedy,* Dante finds himself in a Dark Wood, lost from the light of God. It was no single, specific evil act that led Dante into that darkness but, rather, the sin of omission. Its name is Acedia, the fourth of the Seven Deadly Sins, and by us generally translated "Sloth."

In American-English, however, Sloth may seem to imply mere physical laziness and untidiness. The torpor of Acedia, it must be understood, is spiritual rather than physical. It is to know the good, but to be lax in its pursuit.

Whether one thinks of it as a sin or as a behavioral failure, Acedia is also the one fault for which no artist can be forgiven. Time, as W. H. Auden wrote in his poem titled *In Memory of W. B. Yeats:*

> *Worships language and forgives*
> *Everyone by whom it lives;*
> *Pardons cowardice, conceit,*
> *Lays its honor at their feet.*

In place of cowardice and conceit, Auden might have cited any catalogue of pride, envy, wrath, avarice, gluttony or carnality, and he could still have said that time forgives. The poet may cheat anything else and still win honor from time, but he may not cheat the poem and live.

For a man is finally defined by what he does with his attention. It was Simone Weil who said, "Absolute attention is absolute prayer." I do not, of course, know what an absolute attention is, except as an absolutely unattainable goal. But certainly to seek that increasing purity and concentration of one's attention that will lead to more and more meaningful perception, is not only possible but is the basic human exercise of any art. It must be added, however, that *in art it does not matter what one pays attention to; the quality of the attention is what counts.*

I have just made a dangerous statement; one that will probably breed protest, that will be difficult to explain, and that will turn out in the end to be only partly true. It is still necessary to make the statement first, and then to go the long way round to explaining why it is necessary, and in what way it is true.

The need to go the long way round brings matters back to another parable of poetry that one may read in Dante's opening situation. The language of parables is always likely to be apt to the discussion of poetry.

As soon as Dante realizes that he is in darkness, he looks up and sees the first light of the dawn shawling the shoulders of a little hill. (In Dante, the Sun is always a symbol of God as Divine Illumination.) The allegory should be clear enough: The very realization that one is lost is the beginning of finding oneself.

What happens next is the heart of the matter. His goal in sight, Dante tries to race straight up the hill—to reach the light, as it were, by direct assault. Note that common sense would certainly be on Dante's side. There is the light and there is the hill: Go to it. Nothing could be simpler. Nor, as Dante discovers, could anything be more false. Almost immediately his way is blocked by three beasts. These beasts—a Leopard, a Lion and a She-wolf—represent all the sins of the world. They represent, therefore, the world's total becloudment of any man's best attention, for all that has ever lured any man away from his own good is contained within them.

The three beasts drive Dante back into the darkness. There Dante comes on the soul of Virgil, who symbolizes Human Reason. In that role Virgil explains that a man may reach the light only by going the long way round. Dante must risk the dangerous descent into Hell—to the recognition of sin. And he must make the arduous ascent of Purgatory—to the renunciation of sin. Only then may he enter, bit by bit, the final presence of the light, which is to say, Heaven.

The point of the parable is that in art as in theology—as in all things that concern a man in his profoundest being—the long way round is the only way home. Short cuts are useful only in mechanics. The man who seeks mortal understanding must go the long, encompassing way of his deepest involvement.

Americans, susceptible as they are to the legend of mechanical know-how and get-it-done, may especially need to be told that there is no easy digest of understanding and no gift package of insight. May they learn, too, that "common sense," useful as it can be in its own sphere, cannot lead a man as deeply into himself as he must be led if he is to enter a meaningful experience of art or of life. Every man who looks long enough at the stars must come to feel their other-reality engulfing his mortal state, and nothing from the world's efficiencies and practicalities is specific to that awareness in him.

Poetry is written of that man under the stars in trouble and in joy, and the truth of poetry cannot be spoken meaningfully in simple common-sense assertions. In poetry, as in all our deepest emotions, many feelings and many thoughts and half-thoughts happen at once. Often these feelings and thoughts are in conflict:

We love and hate the same thing, desire it and dread it, need it and are destroyed by it. Always, too, there are more thoughts and feelings in a profound experience than we can put a finger on. What has common sense to say to such states of man? Common sense tends always to the easier assumption that only one thing is "really" happening in a man at one time, and that a simple, straightforward course of action will take care of it.

Such an assumption can only blind one to poetry. To read a poem with no thought in mind but to paraphrase it into a single, simple, and usually high-minded, prose statement is the destruction of poetry. Nor does it make much difference that one can quote poetry, and good poetry, in defense of such destruction. At the end of *Ode on a Grecian Urn,* John Keats wrote:

> *"Beauty is truth, truth beauty,"—that is all*
> *Ye know on earth, and all ye need to know.*

Heaven knows how many enthusiasts have used these lines as evidence that poetry is somehow an act of inspiration not to be measured by any criteria but an undefined devotion to "beauty," "truth" and "inspiring message."

But if beauty and truth are all that Grecian urns and men need know on earth, Keats makes evident by his own practice that a poet also needs to know a great deal about his trade, and that he must be passionately concerned for its basic elements.

Those basic elements are not beauty and truth but *rhythm, diction, image* and *form*. Certainly Keats cared about beauty and truth. Any sensitive man must care. No matter that one must forever fumble at the definition of such ideas; they are still matters of ultimate concern. But so was Dante's yearning for the light, and he discovered at once that it can be reached only by the long way round.

The poet's way round is by way of rhythm, diction, image and form. It is the right, the duty and the joy of his trade to be passionate about these things. To be passionate about them in the minutest and even the most frivolous detail. To be passionate about them, if need be, to the exclusion of what is generally understood by "sincerity" and "meaning." To be more passionate about them than he is about the cold war, the Gunpowder Plot, the next election, abolition, the H-bomb, the Inquisition, juvenile delinquency, the Spanish Armada, or his own survival.

The good poets have not generally sneered at the world of affairs. Some have, but many others have functioned well within that world. Yet the need and the right of all poets to detach themselves from the things of the world in order to pursue the things of the poetic trade have always been inseparable from their success as poets.

The poet must be passionate about the four elements of his trade for the most fundamental of reasons. He must be so because those passions are both a joy and an addiction within him. Because they are the life of the poem, without which nothing of value can happen either in the poem or to the reader. Because writing a poem is a more sentient way of living than not writing it, because no poem can be written well except as these passions inform it, and because only when the poem is so written can the beauty and truth of that more sentient way of living be brought to mortal consequence.

The act of poetry may seem to have very simple surfaces, but it is always compounded of many things at once. As Robert Frost wrote in *Two Tramps in Mud Time:*

> *Only where love and need are one,*
> *And the work is play for mortal stakes,*
> *Is the deed ever really done*
> *For Heaven and the future's sakes.*

The voice of common sense rises immediately in protest. "Mystification!" it cries. "A poem still has to *mean* something. What does it *mean?*" And the poet must answer, "Never what you think. Not when you ask the question in that way."

But how shall the question be asked? Let the questioner listen first to a kind of statement he has probably passed over without enough attention. He can find one such in Walter Pater's essay on Winckelman. "Let us understand by poetry," wrote Pater, "all literary production which attains the power of giving pleasure by its form as distinct from its matter."

He can find another in a book titled *The Fire and the Fountain* by the English poet and critic John Press. "The essence of the poet," wrote Press, "is to be found less in his opinions than in his idiom." He may even find one in a textbook titled *Reading Poems,* in which Wright Thomas says, "The *subject* is a very poor indication of what the *poem* is"—to which I should add only that it is no indication whatever.

But if the meaning is not in the subject, what then does a poem mean? It means always and above all else the poet's deep involvement in the four basic elements of his trade. It means not the subject but the way the poetic involvement transfigures the subject. It means, that is to say, the very act of language by which it comes into existence. The poem may purport to be about anything from pussy willows to battleships, but the meaning of any good poem is its act of language.

Because it is an act of language, a good poem is deeply connected with everything men are and do. For language is certainly one of the most fundamental activities in which human beings engage. Take away a man's language, and you take most of his ability to think and to·experience. Enrich his language, and you cannot fail to enrich his experience. Any man who has let great language into his head is the richer for it.

He is not made richer by what is being said. It is the language itself that brings his enrichment. Could poetry be meaningful aside from its act of language, it would have no reason for being, and the whole history of poetry could be reduced to a series of simple paraphrases.

Consider as simple a passage as the beginning of Herrick's *Upon Julia's Clothes:*

> *Whenas in silks my Julia goes,*
> *Then, then, methinks, how sweetly flows*
> *The liquefaction of her clothes.*

Who can read those lines without a thrill of pleasure? But now consider the paraphrase: "I like the rustle of Julia's silks when she walks." The poetry and the paraphrase are certainly about equal in subject matter. The difference is that the poetry is a full and rich act of language, whereas the paraphrase, though faultless, lacks, among other things, measure, pause, stress, rhyme and the pleasure of lingering over the word "liquefaction."

"But what is Julia doing there?" cries that voice of common sense. "She must have something to do with the poem or she wouldn't be in it!"

The owner of that voice would do well to ponder the relation between a good portrait and its subject. The subject is there, to be sure—at least in most cases. But the instant the painter puts one brush stroke on the canvas and then another, the two brush strokes take on a relation to each other and to the space around them. The two then take on a relation to the third, and it to them. And so forth. The painting immediately begins to exert its own demands upon the painter, its own way of going. Immediately the subject begins to disappear.

All too soon, for that matter, the subject will have changed with age or will have died. After a while no living person will have any recollection of what the subject looked like. All that will remain then is a portrait head which must be either self-validating or worthless. Because the subject cannot validate the painting, he or she will have become irrelevant. All that can finally validate the portrait is the way in which the painter engaged the act of painting.

And one more thing—the good artist always thinks in long terms. He knows, even at the moment of the painting, that both he and the subject will disappear. Any good painter will be painting for the painting—for the time when the subject will have blown away into time.

So with poetry. The one final and enduring meaning of any poem lies not in what it seems to have set out to say, but in its act of language.

The only test of that act of language is the memory of the race. Bad poetry is by nature forgettable; it is, therefore, soon forgotten. But good poetry, like any good act of language, hooks onto human memory and stays there. Write well, and there will always be someone somewhere who carries in his mind what you have written. It will stay in memory because man is the language animal, and because his need of language is from the roots of his consciousness. That need in him is not a need for meaning. Rather, good language in him takes possession of meaning; it fills him with a resonance that the best of men understand only dimly, but without which no man is entirely alive. Poetry is that presence and that resonance. As Archibald MacLeish put it in his much-discussed *Ars Poetica*:

> *A poem should not mean*
> *But be.*

If the reader truly wishes to engage poetry, let him forget meaning. Let him think rather: "I shall summon great language to mind. I shall summon language so fully, so resonantly and so precisely used that it will bring all my meanings to me." Then let him turn to poetry, and let him listen to the passions of the poet's trade.

Listen to great rhythms. Here is the opening stanza of John Donne's *The Anniversarie*:

> All Kings, and all their favorites,
> All glory of honours, beauties, wits,
> The Sun it selfe, which makes time as they passe,
> Is elder by a yeare, now, than it was
> When thou and I first one another saw:
> All other things, to their destruction draw,
>   Only our love hath no decay;
> This, no to morrow hath, nor yesterday.
> Running, it never runs from us away,
> But truly keeps his first, last, everlasting day.

Worldly things pass away, but true love is constant, says the subject matter. All true enough and tried enough. But listen to the rhythm enforce itself upon the saying, especially in the last four lines. For present purposes, let the voice ignore the lesser accents. Let it stress only those syllables printed in capital letters below, while observing the pauses as indicated by the slash marks. And forget the meaning. Read for the voice emphasis and the voice pauses:

> Only OUR LOVE hath no deCAY ||
> THIS || no to MOrrow hath || nor YESterday ||
> RUNning || it never runs from us aWAY ||
> But truly keeps his FIRST || LAST || EVerlasting DAY.

Not all rhythms are so percussive, so measured out by pauses, and so metrically irregular. Listen to this smoother rhythm from Poe's *Israfel*:

> If I could dwell
> Where Israfel
>   Hath dwelt, and he where I,
> He might not sing so wildly well
>   A mortal melody,
> While a bolder note than his might swell
>   From my lyre within the sky.

Or the rhythm may be percussive, but without substantial pauses, as in the last line of this passage from the end of Gerard Manley Hopkins' *Felix Randal*, an elegy for a blacksmith:

> How far from then forethought of, all thy more boisterous years,
> When thou at the random grim forge, powerful amidst peers,
> Didst fettle for the great gray drayhorse his bright and battering sandal.

Listen to the hammerfall of that last line: "Didst FEttle for the GREAT GRAY DRAYhorse his BRIGHT and BAttering SANdal."

Or listen to the spacing of the "ah" sounds as a rhythmic emphasis in the last line of this final passage from Meredith's *Lucifer in Starlight:*

> *Around the ancient track marched, rank on rank,*
> *The ARmy of unALterable LAW.*

Percussive, smooth, flowing or studded with pauses—there is no end to the variety and delight of great language rhythms. For the poet, his rhythms are forever more than a matter of making a "meaningful" statement; they are a joy in their own right. No poet hates meaning. But the poet's passion is for the triumph of language. No reader can come to real contact with a poem until he comes to it through the joy of that rhythmic act of language.

As for rhythm, so for diction. The poet goes to language—or it comes to him and he receives it—for his joy in the precision of great word choices. Give him such a line as Whitman's "I witness the corpse with the dabbled hair," and he will register the corpse, to be sure, but it will be "dabbled" he seizes upon with the joy of a botanist coming on a rare specimen. So when Keats speaks of Ruth amid "the alien corn" or when Theodore Roethke speaks of sheep "strewn" on a field, the good reader will certainly care about the dramatic situation of the poem, but he cannot fail to answer with a special joy to "alien" and to "strewn."

What, after all, is the subject as compared to his joy in such rich precision? Thousands of English poems have described the passing of winter and the coming of spring. Certainly there is little in that subject as a subject to attract him. But listen to the pure flutefall of the word choices I have italicized in the following passage from Stanley Kunitz's *Deciduous Bough,* and note how the self-delight in language makes everything immediate and new again:

> Winter that *coils* in the thicket now
> Will *glide* from the field, the *swinging* rain
> Be *knotted* with flowers, on every bough
> A bird will *meditate* again.

"Poetry," said Coleridge, "is the best words in the best order." How can anyone reading the Kunitz passage escape a sense that the language is being ultimately and unimprovably selected? The delight one feels in coming on such language is not only in the experience of perfection but also in the fact that perfection has been made to seem not only effortless but inevitable.

And let this much more be added to the idea of poetic meaning: Nothing in a good poem happens by accident; every word, every comma, every variant spelling must enter as an act of the poet's choice. A poem is a machine for making choices. The mark of the good poet is his refusal to make easy or cheap choices. The better the poet, the greater the demands he makes upon himself, and the higher he sets his level of choice. Thus, a good poem is not only an act of mind but an act of devotion to mind. The poet who chooses cheaply or lazily is guilty of aesthetic acedia, and he is lost thereby. The poet who spares himself nothing in his search for the most demanding choices is shaping a human attention that offers itself as a high and joyful example to all men of mind and devotion. Every act of great language, whatever its subject matter, illustrates an idea of order and a resonance of human possibility without which no man's mind can sense its own fullest dimensions.

As for rhythm and diction, so for imagery. To be sure, every word is at root an image, and poetic images must be made of words. Yet certainly there is in a well-constructed image an effect that cannot be said to rise from any one word choice, but from the total phrasing.

So for the sensory shiver of Keats' "The silver snarling trumpets 'gan to chide." So for the wonderfully woozy effect of John Frederick Nims' "The drunk clambering on his undulant floor." So for the grand hyperbole of Howard Nemerov saying that the way a young girl looks at him "sets his knees to splashing like two waves."

We learn both imagination and precision from the poet's eye. And we learn correspondences. Consider the following image from *Aereopagus* by Louis MacNeice, a poem as playful as it is serious, in which MacNeice describes Athens as a cradle of the western mind. Cradles, he makes clear, generally contain children, and all those boy-gods and girl-goddesses had their childish side:

> . . . *you still may glimpse*
> *The child-eyed Fury tossing her shock of snakes,*
> *Careering over the Parthenon's ruined playpen.*

It is a bit shocking to have the Parthenon spoken of as a playpen, but once the shock has passed, what a triumph there is in the figure: everything corresponds! Think how much would have been lost had the Parthenon a surviving roof, or had its general proportions or the placement of the pillars—slats —resisted the comparison. The joy of it is that, despite the first shock, nothing resists the comparison; and we find that the surprise turns out to be a true correspondence.

One of the poet's happiest—and most mortal—games is in seeking such correspondences. But what flows from them is more than a game. Every discovery of a true correspondence is an act of reason and an instruction to the mind. For intelligence does not consist of masses of factual detail. It consists of seeing essential likenesses and essential differences and of relating them, allowing for differences within the likenesses and for likenesses within the differences. Mentality is born of analogy.

Note, too, that the image-idea of "ruined playpen" does not simply happen, but is prepared for in "child-eyed." And note, further, the nice double meaning of "careering" as both "a wild rush" and "to make a career of."

A good extended image, that is to say, is made of various elements and is marked by both sequence and structure. Thus we have already touched upon the essence of the fourth element of the poet's trade: form.

There are many kinds of poetic form, but since all are based on pattern and sequence, let a tightly patterned poem illustrate. Here is Emily Dickinson's *The Soul Selects:*

> *The soul selects her own society,*
> *Then shuts the door;*
> *On her divine majority*
> *Obtrude no more.*
>
> *Unmoved, she notes the chariot's pausing*
> *At her low gate;*
> *Unmoved, an emperor is kneeling*
> *Upon her mat.*
> *I've known her from an ample nation*
> *Choose one;*
> *Then close the valves of her attention*
> *Like stone.*

Whatever the hunters of beauty and truth find for their pleasure in such a poem, the poet's joy will be in its form and management. He responds to the passion of the language for its own sparseness, to the pattern of rhyme and half-rhyme, to the flavor of the images (connotation), and to the way those flavors relate to one another. He responds to the interplay of the four-foot feminine lines (feminine lines end on an unaccented syllable) and the two-foot masculine lines (which end on an accented syllable).

And he responds, above all, to the way those two-foot lines develop in the last stanza into two boldly stroked syllables apiece (monosyllabic feet) so that the emotion held down throughout the poem by the sparseness of the language is hammered into sensation by the beat of those last two words: "Like stone"—thud! thud!

Beauty and truth are no irrelevancies, but they are abstractions that must remain meaningless to poetry until they are brought to being in the management of a specific form. It is that management the poet must love: the joy of sensing the poem fall into inescapable form, and therefore into inescapable experience. For the poet's trade is not to talk about experience, but to make it happen. His act of making is all he knows of beauty and truth. It is, in fact, his way of knowing them. His only way of knowing them.

As I. A. Richards, poet and scholar of the language, put it in a recent poem titled *The Ruins:*

> *Sometimes a word is wiser much than men:*
> *"Faithful" e.g., "responsible" and "true."*
> *And words it is, not poets, make up poems.*
> *Our words, we say, but we are theirs, too,*
> *For words made men and may unmake again.*

And now, at last, it is time to repeat the statement from which this long way round began. "In art," I said, "it does not matter what one pays attention to; the quality of the attention is what counts." It is time to amend that necessary false statement.

For it does matter where the poet fixes his attention. Attention must be to *something.* That something, however, is so casually connected with the subject of the poem that any reader will do well to dismiss the subject as no more than a point of departure. Any impassioning point of departure will do. The poet, being a man, must believe something, but what that something is does not matter so long as he believes it strongly enough to be passionate about it. What he believes, moreover, may be touched off by an image, a rhythm, or the quality of a word *in pursuit of which the subject is invented.*

The poem, in any case, is not in its point of departure, but in its journey to itself. That journey, the act of the poem, is its act of language. That act is the true final subject and meaning of any poem. It is to that act of language the poet shapes his most devoted attention—to the fullness of rhythm, diction, image and form. Only in that devotion can he seize the world and make it evident.

DISCUSSION AND WRITING

1. Define or explain: *torpor, carnality, parable, allegory, encompass, paraphrase, minute* (adj.), *frivolous, sentient, mystification, idiom, transfigure, purport* (vb.), *validate, resonance, percussive, metrical, substantial, hyperbole, stanza.*

2. Examine Ciardi's choice of poets to provide him with examples. Which of them do you recognize? Summarize briefly what you can find out about the identity or significance of each of the poets quoted.

3. Define and illustrate each of the four key terms used by Ciardi in his discussion of poetry: *rhythm, diction, image, form.* What does Ciardi offer for each of these that might help take the reader beyond the obvious?

4. In your own words, restate Ciardi's objections to paraphrase. Explain how he uses the analogy with portrait painting to support his view. How persuasive is the analogy?

5. The author repeatedly uses expressions like "meaningful perception" and "meaningful experience" but rules out simple "common sense" meanings. Can you define and

illustrate the kind of "meaning" that he *does* find in poetry? Can you point to the passages of the essay that are most relevant for this purpose?

6. Limit yourself to *one* of the author's four major categories—rhythm, diction, image, or form. Discuss and illustrate the kind of experience in this area that awaits the reader of a few selected poems by a poet of your choice.

7. What does the author mean when he says that Americans are susceptible to "the legend of mechanical know-how and get-it-done"? How true has this generalization proved in your own experience?

8. Have you encountered any evidence that people often turn to poetry for a "high-minded" statement or an "inspirational message"? Have you found evidence that people turn to other creative arts with similar expectations? Are you prepared to argue in their defense?

9. Do we (should we?) grant the creative artist the right to be more passionate about the details of his craft than about such matters as the H-bomb, juvenile delinquency, racial problems, survival? Limit your discussion to *one* of the creative arts. Use specific references or detailed examples.

10. Compare and contrast Ciardi's view of the art of poetry with Emerson's view of art in general, in his essay on "Art." Are there any basic similarities or differences in their general perspective?

FURTHER READING

Over the years, Mr. Ciardi has published a number of articles designed to explain the language especially of modern poetry to the general reader. Several of these have appeared in the *Saturday Review:* "The Shock Reaction to Poetry" (July 20, 1957); "Robert Frost: The Way to the Poem" (April 12, 1958); "Dialogue with the Audience" (November 22, 1958). Study one of these articles and report on its success in bringing poetry closer to the uninitiated reader.